Dedicated to
Barbara Drew Hoffstot
(1919–1994)

A founding trustee and vice-chairman of
the Pittsburgh History & Landmarks Foundation,
Barbara Hoffstot gave us vision and fortitude to preserve
the historic buildings, neighborhoods, and landscapes
of the Pittsburgh region.

PITTSBURGH'S LANDMARK ARCHITECTURE

THE HISTORIC BUILDINGS OF PITTSBURGH AND ALLEGHENY COUNTY

WALTER C. KIDNEY

PITTSBURGH HISTORY & LANDMARKS FOUNDATION

Published by the
Pittsburgh History & Landmarks Foundation
One Station Square, Suite 450
Pittsburgh, PA 15219-1134

Walter C. Kidney, Author
Louise King Sturgess, Project Director and Editor
Greg Pytlik of Pytlik Design Associates, Designer

Library of Congress Catalog Card Number: 96-72583
ISBN 0-916670-18-X

The printing of this publication was made possible in part by the Revolving
Fund for Education of the Pittsburgh History & Landmarks Foundation,
established in 1984 through a generous grant from the Claude Worthington
Benedum Foundation and later augmented through major grants from The
Mary Hillman Jennings Foundation, the Richard King Mellon Foundation,
and an anonymous donor.

*Pittsburgh's Landmark Architecture: The Historic Buildings of Pittsburgh and
Allegheny County* was typeset in Janson Text and printed on 70 lb. Vintage
Velvet text by Hoechstetter Printing Company, Inc. Beth Buckholtz,
Durinda Blevins, and John Hartley assisted in the design of the book.

ACKNOWLEDGEMENTS

This book builds on the 1985 edition of *Landmark Architecture: Pittsburgh and Allegheny County*, published by the Pittsburgh History & Landmarks Foundation in 1985, but it is to a great extent a new book.

Barbara Drew Hoffstot, a co-founder of Landmarks and its vice-chairman for thirty years, first encouraged our staff to revise and expand the 1985 edition, out of print since 1990. Following her death in 1994, her husband, Henry P. Hoffstot, Jr., and his family requested that all unrestricted contributions donated to Landmarks in memory of his wife be used to support the publication of a new edition of *Landmark Architecture*. We are deeply indebted to Mr. Hoffstot and his family for their genuine interest and enthusiastic support for the production of this book.

Work on *Pittsburgh's Landmark Architecture* began in earnest in the fall of 1995. Walter C. Kidney, Landmarks' architectural historian, began revising his essay, "The Poplar and the Ailanthus," for the first section of the book. Valuable historic photographs were obtained from the Archives of Industrial Society at the University of Pittsburgh, the Pittsburgh Photographic Library at Carnegie Library of Pittsburgh, and the Carnegie Mellon University Architecture Archives.

We thank the following people for reviewing the essay and offering valuable suggestions: Charles Covert Arensberg, Chairman Emeritus, Pittsburgh History & Landmarks Foundation; Martin Aurand, Architecture Librarian and Archivist, Carnegie Mellon University; Laurie Cohen, Reference Librarian, University of Pittsburgh; Michael D. Eversmeyer, A.I.A., Principal Historic Preservation Planner, Department of City Planning, City of Pittsburgh; Henry P. Hoffstot, Jr., Trustee, Pittsburgh History & Landmarks Foundation; and Albert M. Tannler, Historical Collections Director, Pittsburgh History & Landmarks Foundation.

The second section of the book, "A Guide to the Landmark Architecture of Allegheny County," is based on Landmarks' comprehensive historic sites survey of Allegheny County, initiated and first directed by Eliza Smith Brown from 1979 to 1982 and then directed by Lu Donnelly until its completion in 1984.

Beginning in January 1996, Walter Kidney and I toured the city and county, verifying the status of each landmark included in the Guide section of the 1985 edition, identifying new sites, and taking new photographs of many of the 645 sites.

Martin Aurand, Laurie Cohen, and Michael D. Eversmeyer also reviewed the Guide. In addition, the following people reviewed portions of the Guide, and we thank them for their comments and insight: Charles Covert Arensberg; Eliza Smith Brown, President, Brown Carlisle & Associates, Inc.; Elisa J. Cavalier, General Counsel, Pittsburgh History & Landmarks Foundation; Mary Ann Eubanks, Education Coordinator, Pittsburgh History & Landmarks Foundation; Rebecca Flora, Executive Director, South Side Local Development Company, and fellow staff and committee members; Barry Hannegan; Nick Kyriazi; Mary Beth Pastorius; Mary Jane Schmalstieg; Ellis and Christina Schmidlapp; Betty G. Y. Shields; and Lauren Uhl, Special Project Associate, Historical Society of Western Pennsylvania.

Albert M. Tannler wrote the Guide entries on the Frank house ("Shadyside"), Swan Acres ("The Northern Townships"), and Meadow Circles ("Along the Monongahela"), and expanded the entry on Thornburg ("South of Pittsburgh"). He also compiled the bibliography. A constant participant in the project, Al offered encouragement and advice whenever needed.

Clyde Hare, Jim Judkis, and William Rydberg took many new photographs for this edition, and we thank them for their work.

Greg Pytlik, the designer of this book, is to be commended for his work, patience, and professionalism. Beth Buckholtz, typesetter, did an admirable job.

We thank our Board of Trustees and Arthur P. Ziegler, Jr., president of Landmarks, for recognizing the importance of this book and giving our staff the opportunity to publish such a comprehensive work.

And most importantly, we are grateful to the Pittsburgh foundations and businesses and our members and friends who so generously contributed funds to support the publication of *Pittsburgh's Landmark Architecture*. The broad public support we received from so many donors encouraged us in our efforts. We are pleased to acknowledge each contributor on the following page.

Louise King Sturgess
Executive Director
Pittsburgh History & Landmarks Foundation

CONTRIBUTORS

BENEFACTOR

R. K. Mellon Family Foundation

PATRONS

Anne L. and George H. Clapp
    Charitable and Educational Trust
The Roy A. Hunt Foundation
The Mary Hillman Jennings
    Foundation
Katherine Mabis McKenna
    Foundation, Inc.
PNC Bank Foundation
G. Whitney Snyder Charitable Fund
The Walden Trust

DONORS

Mr. & Mrs. Leopold Adler II
Mr. & Mrs. W. James Aiken, Jr.
Charles Covert Arensberg,
    in memory of Gay Hays Arensberg
Andrew Bell Armstrong
Claire Ashkin
Mr. & Mrs. Alfred R. Barbour
Clifford A. Barton
Sanford Baskind
Paul and Nancy Beck
Virginia P. Beckwith
Richard and Jeanne Berdik
Mr. & Mrs. Allen H. Berkman
Mark Stephen Bibro
Sherley T. Blaxter
Mr. & Mrs. William Block, Sr.
Mr. & Mrs. Kenneth S. Boesel
Mr. & Mrs. Mark Bookman
Charles H. Booth, Jr.
Susan E. Brandt
David and Janet Brashear
Mr. & Mrs. Dan Broucek
Carl Wood Brown
Anthony J. A. Bryan
Mr. & Mrs. Donald C. Burnham
Grace J. Burrell
Stuart and Catherine Burstein
Randall L. Campbell
C. Dana Chalfant
Harvey Childs, Jr.
Mrs. James H. Childs, Jr.
Renee Marks Cohen
Ann Connelly—O/P/U/S, Inc.
Mr. & Mrs. John P. Davis, Jr.

Patricia J. Denhart
DeWinter/Ziegler Fund
Mr. & Mrs. Robert Dickey III
George C. Dorman
Thayer Hoffstot Drew
Elizabeth C. Ebbert
Arthur J. Edmunds
Richard Dilworth Edwards
Sarah Evosevich
Mr. & Mrs. James A. Fisher
Alan I W Frank
Mr. & Mrs. John G. Frazer, Jr.
Frank J. Gaffney
Dr. & Mrs. William S. Garrett
Mr. & Mrs. David L. Genter
Mr. & Mrs. G. Donald Gerlach
Gordon and Donna W. Gordon
Ethel Hagler
Charles E. Half
James and Jeanne Hanchett
Mr. & Mrs. Robert W. Hepler
John H. Hill
Mrs. Thomas Hitchcock
Henry P. Hoffstot, Jr.
Mr. & Mrs. Henry Phipps Hoffstot III
Howard Hook
Mr. & Mrs. Glen W. Hopkins
    and family
Thomas O. Hornstein
Mr. & Mrs. William C. Hurtt
Mr. & Mrs. Curtis Jones
Mr. & Mrs. David H. Kain
Monna J. Kidney
Mr. & Mrs. Bayard T. Kiliani
Kimicata Brothers, Inc.
James W. and Valerie Knox
Mr. & Mrs. G. Christian Lantzsch
Mr. & Mrs. Alan G. Lehman
Edward J. Lewis
George D. Lockhart
Bernard Kent Markwell, Ph.D.
Drew and Helen Mathieson
Elizabeth F. McCance
Grant McCargo
Mary A. McDonough
Mr. & Mrs. Walter T. McGough
DeCourcy E. McIntosh
Mr. & Mrs. J. Sherman McLaughlin
Gertrud A. Mellon
The Mendelssohn Choir of Pittsburgh
Bill and Mary Anne Mistick
Thomas D. Mullins
Tom Murphy, Mayor of Pittsburgh
Regis and Evelyn Murrin
Eleanor Howe Nimick

Thomas H. Nimick, Jr.
Mr. & Mrs. David B. Oliver II
Constance H. O'Neil
Edward Parrack
Robert F. Patton
Evelyn B. Pearson
Mr. & Mrs. Nathan W. Pearson
Pittsburgh Steelers Sports, Inc.
Jeanne C. Poremski
Mr. & Mrs. John L. Propst
A. & S. Pyzdrowski
Stanley Pyzdrowski
John and Marirose Radelet
Mrs. Cleveland D. Rea
Mr. & Mrs. William Rea
Stephen G. Robinson
William M. Robinson
Daniel M. Rooney
Wilfred T. and Ruth O. Rouleau
Frances G. Scaife
Richard M. and Ritchie Scaife
Ellis and Christina Schmidlapp
Kelly K. Sinclair
Mrs. Steven J. Smith
Mr. & Mrs. Templeton Smith
Wallace W. and Patricia O. Smith
G. Whitney Snyder
Mr. & Mrs. Furman South III
Robert L. Spear
M. Stahl Plumbing, Heating and
    Air Conditioning
Frank L. Stanley
Frederick J. Stevenson, Jr.
Tom and Teri Streever
William E. Strickland, Jr.
Martin and Louise Sturgess
Professor Franklin Toker
Lyda Jo B. Trower
Albert C. and Margaret Van Dusen
David J. Vater
Douglas Walgren
James and Ellen Walton
Ann Wardrop
Mr. & Mrs. Edward R. Weidlein, Jr.
Mr. & Mrs. Joshua C. Whetzel, Jr.
J. Reid Williamson, Jr.
Mr. & Mrs. James L. Winokur
Mary Wohleber
Dwayne D. Woodruff
World Federalist Association of
    Pittsburgh
Gregory C. Yochum
Ronald C. Yochum, Jr.
Arthur P. and Vinnie D. Ziegler
Arthur P. Ziegler, Jr.

ILLUSTRATION SOURCES

The numbers given below refer to pages on which illustrations from each source are found. All illustrations not given below are from the photographic and library collections of the Pittsburgh History & Landmarks Foundation.

The American Architect and Building News, August 10, 1889, No. 711: 76

American Competitions, T Square Club, Volume 2, 1908, Plate 41–42: 107 (top)

The Architectural Review, Volume 4, No. 3, 1897, Plate XIV: 86 (bottom)

Archives of Industrial Society, University of Pittsburgh Libraries, The Pittsburgh City Photographer Collection: 8 (top), 104, 115 (left), 123 (top), 131, 132, 133 (bottom), 146, 148 (top)

Art Work of Pittsburg, The W. H. Parish Publishing Company, 1893: 30, 60, 61, 62 (bottom), 64 (top left), 66 (left), 70 (right), 77 (bottom), 124 (top)

Art Work of Pittsburg, George E. White Company, 1899: 86 (top), 99 (bottom), 137, 138

Karl A. Backus: 328 (top right), 329 (top left and bottom left); photographs provided through the courtesy of Bohlin Cywinski Jackson

Braddock Carnegie Library: 468 (top left)

Tim Buchman, courtesy of Calvary Episcopal Church: 402 (bottom right)

Carnegie Library of Pittsburgh, Pittsburgh Photographic Library: xviii, 7, 11 (bottom; photo by Clyde Hare), 26, 28, 32 (top), 33, 34 (bottom), 39, 40 (top left and bottom), 42 (top right, bottom left, and bottom right), 44, 45 (top left and top right), 48, 49, 50 (top), 53, 54 (top), 55, 56, 57 (top), 59, 62 (top), 63, 64 (top right and bottom), 65 (photo by Clyde Hare), 66 (right), 67 (top left and top right), 70 (left), 73, 75 (top and bottom left), 77 (top), 78 (top), 80, 82 (left), 83, 85, 87 (bottom), 88, 89 (top), 93, 94 (top left and top right), 96, 97, 99 (top left), 100, 105, 106, 109, 110, 111, 112, 118, 121 (bottom), 125 (bottom), 127 (bottom), 129, 130, 134, 135, 139, 148 (middle and bottom), 152, 158 (top), 360 (bottom left)

Carnegie Mellon University Architecture Archives: 108 (top), 179 (bottom)

The Carnegie Museum of Art, Pittsburgh: 122

The Charette, The Pittsburgh Architectural Club, Volume 4, February 1924, No. 3 (cover): 116

Harry Edelman: 281 (bottom)

Tim Fabian: 572 (bottom)

James J. Ference: 482 (bottom left)

Herb Ferguson, University of Pittsburgh: 287 (bottom right)

Clyde Hare: x, xiv, 4, 6 (top), 10, 13, 14 (right), 15, 18 (top), 19, 68, 144, 170, 182, 184, 186, 193, 194, 198, 199, 204, 206, 209 (bottom), 211 (bottom right), 212 (top left, middle left, and bottom left), 231 (top middle), 234 (top left and bottom right), 238 (top right), 247 (top right), 268 (left), 271 (top left and bottom left), 272 (top left and bottom left), 280 (bottom right), 284 (bottom right), 289 (top left and bottom), 305 (bottom left and bottom right), 323 (bottom left), 326 (bottom left), 327 (bottom), 335 (top right), 338 (bottom left and middle right), 339 (right), 340 (bottom), 341 (bottom), 346 (middle right and bottom right), 356 (top right), 359 (top right), 360 (top right), 364 (bottom left), 385 (bottom left and bottom right), 393 (bottom left pair), 402 (top right and middle right), 403 (bottom left, top right, and bottom right), 413 (bottom left and top right), 416, 427 (bottom left), 436 (bottom left), 456 (bottom), 459 (bottom left, top right, and bottom right), 464 (left), 469 (top right), 470 (top left and bottom left), 477 (top left, bottom left, top right, and bottom right), 479 (right), 480 (bottom left), 481, 485, 521 (top left and bottom right), 535 (bottom right), 542 (bottom right), 543 (bottom left), 555 (bottom left and bottom right), 556 (top right, middle right, and bottom right), 557 (bottom right), 586 (top left and bottom left)

Gerald Hare: 243 (bottom), 250 (top left)

The Heinz Architectural Center: 185 (top right; photo by Joanne Devereaux)

George D. Hetrick Photographic Collection of the Pittsburgh History & Landmarks Foundation: 57 (bottom), 149, 153 (top left and bottom), 226 (bottom), 239 (left), 255, 257 (top left), 717

Hoffstot family: i

The taming of stone: H. H. Richardson at the Allegheny County Buildings.

CONTENTS

INTRODUCTORY NOTE

The Pittsburgh History & Landmarks Foundation was organized in 1964 to help preserve the significant architecture in Pittsburgh and Allegheny County and to educate the public about the historic heritage of this picturesque land we call Penn's Woods West.

Ever mindful of how much the present relies on the past—and knowing the need to educate each generation to the critical importance of its inheritance—the Foundation, through its programs and publications, is helping to create a better future for Western Pennsylvania by assisting the citizens of this area to celebrate and preserve its architectural legacy. Indeed, Landmarks' historic preservation work in Allegheny County has received national acclaim and has served as a model for innovative preservation programs throughout the United States.

The new edition of *Pittsburgh's Landmark Architecture*, by Walter C. Kidney, is considerably more comprehensive in its treatment of the area's architecture than was the 1985 edition, a book itself acclaimed as the preeminent architectural history of the region. This edition is dedicated to Barbara Drew Hoffstot, a co-founder of the Foundation and its vice-chairman for thirty years. An enthusiastic gardener, traveler, and reader, Barbara focused her energy on historic preservation. Through her strength of personality, deep commitment and vision, she became a leader in both Pittsburgh and Palm Beach, as well as nationally. She always was able to arouse constituencies and engage in a good fight.

When our organization began it was Barbara who encouraged us to survey the architecturally significant buildings of the County. She helped raise the funds and took many of the photographs to produce what is now recognized as the first county-wide survey in the United States. A strong supporter of our education and neighborhood programs, Barbara encouraged us to update the 1985 edition of *Landmark Architecture*, a book she considered the "bible" of our organization. Now we have done so, and with deep gratitude for all she did for our Foundation, we dedicate this book in her memory.

The publication of this book as well as the execution of all the programs of Landmarks—including its many architectural surveys, feasibility studies, and educational programs and its work in renewing historic neighborhoods without disenfranchising their residents—is made possible by the generous financial support of many local foundations, corporations, and private individuals.

On behalf of the trustees I thank all who have helped make possible this edition of *Pittsburgh's Landmark Architecture: The Historic Buildings of Pittsburgh and Allegheny County* and supported the myriad other Pittsburgh History & Landmarks Foundation programs.

Albert C. Van Dusen
Chairman of the Board
Pittsburgh History & Landmarks Foundation

Houses and churches: Liverpool Street in Manchester.

PROLOGUE

Why do we want to "save" what we think is interesting in Pittsburgh's architectural heritage? We know that Job said: "Some remove the landmarks . . . they turn the needy out of the way; the poor of the earth hide themselves together." We know that Marcus Aurelius prescribed a law decreeing the loss of a hand for mutilating or destroying a landmark. We are reminded that F. W. J. Schelling described architecture as "music in space, as it were a frozen music *[erstarrte Musik]*." These conceptions have found their modern counterparts in zoning laws, city planning commissions, and organizations such as the National Trust for Historic Preservation and our own Pittsburgh History & Landmarks Foundation. Preservation has come of age in our country.

Age has its beauty too, as we all know who have traveled through Europe and Asia and seen its ancient monuments:

> *The soul's dark cottage battered and decayed*
> *Lets in new light through chinks that*
> *Time hath made.*

But why Pittsburgh? This is not Paris or Salamanca, Venice, or Stockholm. Here we have no Parthenon, Coliseum, or Westminster Abbey. But Pittsburgh is our city, unique in all the world. We were born or transplanted here. We know its hills, its fine rivers and sweeping valleys; many of us are familiar with its Hartford Streets, its Rhine Streets, its Grandview Avenues, its mills, its parks, and yes, its cemeteries, Allegheny and Homewood. And we know its architects too, from Latrobe and Chislett to Richardson and Hornbostel, Scheibler, Janssen, and Stotz, and down to our present day leaders in the field.

We can see its past in the Mexican War Streets and old Manchester, in Shadyside, the South Hills, and Lawrenceville. We can see its future in the ever changing skyline of the Golden Triangle, and in the vitality of Oakland and many of our neighborhoods. We think it has a host of fascinating vistas and quiet streets. We do not apologize that Pittsburgh is our home. We are proud of this city and region.

This book is an attempt to capture some of that unique essence and make a record of it.

Charles Covert Arensberg
Chairman Emeritus
Pittsburgh History & Landmarks Foundation

Edward N. Kaufman writes in Fragments of Chicago's Past: The Collection of Architectural Fragments at The Art Institute of Chicago: *"In Pittsburgh...the young Carnegie Institute—following the example of museums in Boston, New York, and Chicago—embarked on a massive campaign of cast collecting in 1903; its great glass-roofed Hall of Architecture opened to the public five years later and is now the finest such collection to survive in this country."*

THE POPLAR
AND THE AILANTHUS

ARCHITECTURE
IN AN INDUSTRIAL REGION

AUTHOR'S NOTE

Pittsburgh, the seat and principal city of Allegheny County, was founded in 1758. Thus, it is notably newer than Nieuw Amsterdam (1625), Boston (1630), Charleston (1680), and Philadelphia (1682). Yet after the early years of the nineteenth century it was largely in the American architectural mainstream, keeping pace—more or less—with trends elsewhere.

The following essay, "The Poplar and the Ailanthus," is a brief history of Allegheny County architecture, taking into account national trends in architecture as well as our own special circumstances in order to provide a context by which the reader can more fully appreciate the significance of individual buildings and sites.

Our notable early buildings were constructed throughout the county. But from the advent of the Victorian period around 1840, this essay focuses on Pittsburgh. This may seem unfair to the county as a whole, but reflects our history. Money that was made in commerce and industry throughout the county came largely to Pittsburgh, where an ample part of it was converted into office buildings, mansions, and public institutions. Pittsburgh continually expanded, besides, absorbing neighboring cities, towns, suburbs, and farms, and built and rebuilt within its growing boundaries to become the county's economic, social, and architectural heart.

More than 270 photographs in this section illustrate our architectural history. Many of these form a "Lost Allegheny County," a roll call of significant buildings and scenes that have long since passed. We have lost much that was handsome, dramatic, or intimately

familiar, and our architectural history would not be complete without recognition of these notable landmarks. This essay also includes buildings of the last fifty years, buildings under probation now that in time may come to be seen as true landmarks of our region. Finally, buildings are illustrated that are not outstanding in themselves but are so characteristic of this area that without them a local inhabitant would feel that something was being overlooked.

The essay is followed by a Guide to the architecture of Allegheny County preceded by a note describing its preparation and content. The Guide reflects the nature of the Pittsburgh History & Landmarks Foundation, established to serve Allegheny County and whose interest is in the preservation of the designed environment: buildings, districts, engineering works, and landscapes from before, approximately, 1950. It was in this year that the first physical activity of the celebrated Pittsburgh Renaissance began—demolition—and Landmarks' founding in 1964 was a sort of Counter-Renaissance, at least insofar as indiscriminate demolition of historic places was concerned. Since that year Landmarks has saved many notable works of architecture and historic neighborhoods and seen its interests gain popular appeal. Through its Preservation Fund, technical assistance initiatives, and educational and advocacy programs, Landmarks continues to work closely with neighborhood organizations, lending institutions, public officials, and others to encourage the economic, cultural, and social benefits of historic preservation.

The closeness of nature to the heart of the city, the consequence of the deep valleys and steep slopes eroded from the terrain, is remarkable in Pittsburgh.

THE
TERRAIN

We in Allegheny County live in a terrain of hills and ravines, with occasional plateaus and river plains and much rolling country; a place that has been difficult to build on and frustrating to travel, yet one with remarkable natural beauty and grandeur.

The county is very roughly trisected by three rivers: the Allegheny coming in from the northeast, the Monongahela from the south and east, and the Ohio formed by their confluence at the Pittsburgh Point, flowing at first northwest. River elevation at the Point is 710 feet above sea level, and hill elevations in the county can be nearly 700 feet higher. Indeed, the crest of Mount Washington, opposite the Point and only 1,000 feet from the Monongahela shore, is about 400 feet higher. Other bluffs and hills crowd close to the rivers in many places, reducing the areas of river plain to almost nothing.

For nearly two-and-a-half centuries, man has scraped and scratched at this primitive terrain, building roads on its slopes, bridging its voids, tunneling its hills, filling in its shallower depressions. But despite all this activity the nature of the terrain is essentially unchanged. Many hilltop views in the county are dramatic for their vistas along ancient river valleys, up among the hills and over a landscape that is still basically an ancient river delta, eroded by rivers that took nearly their present courses in the Second Ice Age that ended 11,000 years ago.

The engineering presence: approaches of the McKees Rocks Bridge leap over the McKees Rocks industrial flats.

Traffic by the Liberty Bridge.

In such a landscape, engineering naturally is a major presence. The county, and Pittsburgh especially, has been called a museum of bridges. We have had none of the swing and lift bridges needed over navigable rivers in flatter country, but we have had most of the other types, including one or two rarities and several that were very advanced in their times. Some of our bridges, especially those of the late nineteenth century, were grotesques by any aesthetic standard, but much of what we see today is the handsome legacy of a massive bridge-building campaign by the County, begun in the early 1920s and concluded a decade later: bridges of progressive design, clean in their lines, with modest architectural touches in a Classical or Modernistic manner. Most of these bridges, recently repaired, are good for a few years more.

On the other hand, we have lost several striking ones, and three early works by John Augustus Roebling, who later designed the Brooklyn Bridge. A German immigrant living in Saxonburg in Butler County, the

6

Roebling's Sixth Street Bridge of 1859 (gone) over the Allegheny River.

Bygone bridges at the Point: the Manchester Bridge of 1913, crossing the Allegheny River in the background; the Point Bridge of 1927 over the Monongahela, nearer.

A retaining wall along Carson Street, in a view of 1930.

A stonecutter's mark on the Panther Hollow Bridge.

great engineer began manufacture of the first wire cable in America in 1841. This he applied to suspension bridges, first in 1845 in an aqueduct across the Allegheny for the Pennsylvania Canal—an especially tricky problem—then in 1846 to replace the Smithfield Street Bridge which burned in the Great Fire of 1845, and finally in the second Sixth Street Bridge of 1859.

Less frequent than the bridges, less conspicuous in the landscape but striking nonetheless, are the great Victorian retaining walls that appear here and there where the right-of-way for a street or railroad has been cut from a hillside. Until the 1900s, like bridge piers and abutments of the time, these were typically made of massive, rugged-textured, roughly squared stones, which if the stonecutters were on piecework might have their personal symbols scratched on the surfaces. Such walls, which may be fifty feet high and hundreds of feet in length, made of the gray

A railroad tunnel in Shaler Township.

sandstone turned a soft black under the Pittsburgh soot, are impressive in their rugged texture, their perceptible mass. The distinctive Romanesque of Henry Hobson Richardson, once it appeared in downtown Pittsburgh in the Allegheny County Courthouse and Jail (1884–88), was imitated in churches and commercial buildings for a decade, perhaps because it was simply a refinement of the raw engineering masonry that the city had known for years.

Tunnels have, by their very nature, been less conspicuous, and the portals visible from downtown Pittsburgh have been masked with modern boxy structures that reveal nothing of their essential nature as holes drilled into steep hillsides. Of our twenty some inclines of the past, though, two are still to be seen. Half-cable car, half-elevator, the inclines once hoisted passengers, and even wagons and teams, up various of our steep slopes. The two survivors, the Monongahela and the Duquesne Inclines, still carry passengers up Mount Washington on frail-looking structures of girders and bents. The Duquesne Incline uses its original cars of 1877, with their Eastlake interiors. The alternatives to incline travel on such slopes were long heaven-storming roads such as Mount Washington's East Sycamore Street (nicknamed the Burma Road) or flights of public steps, hundreds of them sometimes, of rotting wood or flaking concrete that simply went straight up with the occasional small mercy of a landing or that joggled from side to side to make contact with scattered houses.

The Monongahela Incline, which began operations in 1870.

Above: On the Duquesne
Incline: an Eastlake car interior.
Right: Public steps near the
Bloomfield Bridge, in a view
of 1951.

And of course, the engineering presence in the Pittsburgh area has been felt very strongly in the industrial plants strewn along the river shores and in the inland valleys, wherever the river boat or the railroad could go. The steel plants—huge, complex, mysterious, sullen black and brown, emitting fire, smoke, and steam—are still in many people's eyes the very symbol of the region. Less spectacular installations have come, though, and sometimes gone, in the valleys. We of Allegheny County have built boats, smelted and fabricated iron and steel, manufactured glass and aluminum, made electrical equipment, refined petroleum, canned food, and generated electricity. Here and there on our uplands, too, are the surface structures of coal mines and oil wells.

We are still living down one consequence of this industrial activity: our reputation as a region that has cared exclusively for manufactures and money, and nothing at all for the amenities, public ones especially, that make for a good, well-rounded life. The famous smoke, which until the mid-1940s rose from fires of bituminous coal all over the region, has dwindled to nearly nothing. The rivers, once so polluted, have been

Opposite: A pour of steel from a Bessemer converter. Below: The Isabella Furnaces, by the Allegheny River at Etna, around 1905.

Above: At the Hazelwood Coke Plant along the Monongahela River. Right: The Ohio River and the Aliquippa Works of Jones & Laughlin; this was seven miles long.

greatly cleaned and fish have returned. But for a century and a half we were truly careless of how we were living. Our grimly casual environment had its grand spectacles of fire and clouds, and there were places where nature was left alone and trees and shrubs grew wild, but travelers to Pittsburgh used to greet their first sight with comments—many of them published—of disgust and anguish. Recent observations, those since the 1950s, have been quite different. Even today they retain the pleasant air of discovery with which journalists who first investigated the Pittsburgh Renaissance praised our attainment of civilization at last.

*Blast furnace and stoves at the Duquesne Works, fourteen miles up the Monongahela from Pittsburgh (above left; gone).
Looking toward the Bluff and downtown from the South Side slopes, from a view of 1987 (above right). Remains of the
Jones & Laughlin Cold Strip Mill in 1986 (below), on the site of the present Pittsburgh Technology Center.*

In architecture we have not been a particularly creative, or even tasteful, city. We have had creative architects: to mention two from the past, the native Frederick G. Scheibler, Jr. and the New Yorker Henry Hornbostel, who gradually became one of us. We have also had architects who, if not particularly innovative, have applied existing architectural styles with taste and intelligence: Benno Janssen and Ingham & Boyd did first-rate work in the Eclectic period early in this century. But it has been a long-standing lament of Pittsburgh architects that the really outstanding commissions so often go to out-of-towners who are either in fashion or deemed more competent to handle a specific problem. Thus, H. H. Richardson's Courthouse and Jail are exotics, designed in Brookline, Massachusetts, and faced in Massachusetts granite. Union Station and the Frick, Oliver, and Koppers Buildings were designed in Chicago; the Cathedral of Learning, Heinz Chapel, and First Presbyterian Church, in Philadelphia; the Carnegie Institute of Technology, University of Pittsburgh hillside campus, Mellon Bank, Gulf Building, Alcoa Building, USX Tower, Two Oliver Plaza, One Oxford Centre, One Mellon Bank Center, and PPG Place, in New York; and the East Liberty Presbyterian and Calvary Episcopal Churches, in Boston. The one prestigious building type that has regularly gone to Pittsburgh architects is the mansion—George Orth, Alden & Harlow, and Janssen & Cocken did well in this area—but when the very rich of the past retired to New York, as several did, they left Pittsburgh architects behind. Henry Clay Frick and Henry Phipps, partners of Andrew Carnegie, used well-known New York architects for their New York homes, and Charles Schwab hired a Frenchman.

Perhaps this part of the state has been too busy and distracted to develop a way of life in which good architecture, not exceptionally but as a normal occurrence, is produced. Philadelphia, Boston, and New York have grown as commercial centers, less violent to their environments than the Pittsburgh-area industrial towns, more tightly built up, and with more private and corporate clients who could afford and knew and cared enough to demand good architecture. The Boston and Philadelphia areas, with their gentlemanly mercantile, manufacturing, and professional classes, have been especially creative or at least tasteful with houses, while New York, architecturally a rather dim city until the 1880s, developed a colorful, varied architecture for business and the social life. Such creativity, such taste, have never happened around Pittsburgh in a big way, and most of our architects and builders never developed the

Lobby of the Koppers Building, Pittsburgh's most distinguished Art Deco interior: the design of a Chicago office.

The houses of Pittsburgh's slopes.

sensitive eye for proportion and detailing needed to transform their works, whether simple or elaborate, from collections of features into entities integrated and alive.

Of our buildings generally, the greatest praise we can give is that they do not quarrel with our landscape when seen from afar. The building type most often seen in Allegheny County is the freestanding single-family house, and groupings of these, serrating the skyline of a hill, clinging to a distant slope, or riding the edges of a street that dips and rises with the land, dramatize the contours of the terrain and its great scale. They animate the space, reveal it as inhabited, and articulate the surfaces, otherwise winter-gray or summer-green with trees and shrubs, with their little white, cream, or red cubical forms. On the plateaus and river plains, where brick is more common than frame, they fall in orderly red rows, with the contrast here and there of a church, a school, a store, or an industrial building. So often of no account when seen up close, they become from afar the low-keyed brushstrokes on an Impressionistic canvas.

Above: The South Side slopes in a view of 1995. Beyond the horizon, both quench towers are emitting steam at the Hazelwood Coke Plant. Below: Reaching into the sky on the 400-foot summit of Mount Washington.

The real glory of the region, in fact, is its wonderful spaces, the vivid contours of the land and the sense of distance they create. From Mount Washington you can look out toward the South Side flats, 400 feet down and a mile-and-a-half away, still appearing like an independent town, but a town seen in some peculiar dream perspective hardly credible in a waking state; then look outwards toward the hill that rises behind, crowded with minute houses like white granules and see, behind the hip of land they occupy, a colossal silver cloud of steam rising from a coke plant hidden in the valley beyond. Or walk, again on Mount Washington, down a colorless commercial street toward a void, with the tops of skyscrapers appearing strangely beyond its edge, and distant hill-tops far beyond those; then look up and through a great red-and-white radio tower that rises, a little uncannily, from a lot by the street, and feel that you are inhabiting the sky rather than the ground. Or look out over the city at twilight, when the sun is just down, and see the shapes of buildings and hills begin to fade, tiny lights begin to glow, far away to the horizon, and get a poignant sense of human settlement, how it is spread wide but thin over the huge bulk of the earth.

The city at twilight: looking eastward.

Fort Pitt, as reconstructed by the historian Charles Morse Stotz. A portion of the King's Garden is seen at the bottom of the photo.

SETTLEMENT

The first notable work of architecture in the Pittsburgh region came immediately after the British took firm hold of the Pittsburgh Point in November 1758. This was Fort Pitt, successor to the abortive Fort Prince George, the weak French Fort Duquesne, and the temporary Mercer's Fort. These had been vulnerable affairs of logs and dirt, but Fort Pitt was the most elaborate British fort in North America: a full-blooded Baroque installation with bastions, casemates for munitions and stores, a moat, profiled counterscarps, ravelins, outerworks, and a glacis. The pentagonal fort itself was over two acres within the walls, and had masonry quarters for the officers and good frame barracks for the men. The whole fort occupied seventeen acres. The bastions facing inland and the curtain walls between them were revetted in brick, and the remainder of the work was of dirt carefully profiled and sodded. Harry Gordon, a resident engineer captain, may have been the designer, but the skilled workmen were brought in specially from Eastern Pennsylvania. So was the machinery for a sawmill to cut the timbers; erected on Sawmill Run a mile down the Ohio River, it brought the Machine Age to Pittsburgh almost at its very start.

Begun in 1759 and finished in 1761, the fort had only a moment of perfection. Floods in 1762 and 1763 washed away much of its dirt defensive work, creating a tense situation during the uprising of the Indian tribes under Pontiac in the latter year. To strengthen the riverward defenses so weakened, five redoubts for sharpshooters were built in 1764; Bouquet's Redoubt, the so-called Blockhouse, is all that remains of the fort aside from some of its foundation masonry, and indeed of the eighteenth century in downtown Pittsburgh. Soon after, maintaining the fort seemed pointless to the military, which began to sell its building materials in 1772. Some repairs were made during the Revolution, and a vestigial garrison was kept on until 1792, but the fort gradually faded away, and in a few years even its form and location were locally forgotten.

Shortly after the building of Fort Pitt, Pittsburgh saw its first essays in landscape design and town planning. The ten-acre, trapezoidal King's Garden was basically utilitarian, a place for growing the fruits and vegetables the garrison needed to avoid scurvy, but was intended also as an ornamental layout with promenades. An earlier design with seventy-

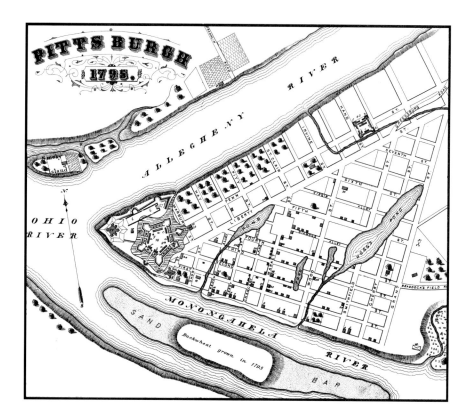

Left: The Woods-Vickroy plan as reproduced in 1869, showing a Fort Duquesne that had wholly ceased to exist in 1795 and a Fort Pitt of which only a few traces remained. In the actual plan, the grids went all the way to the Point.

Opposite: In 1788, David Redick surveyed the land across the Allegheny River from Pittsburgh for the seat of the newly created Allegheny County. Allegheny Town is shown with its surrounding Commons and agricultural "out-lots." The town is the area of tiny lots, a third of a mile on a side. Its center, today, is signaled by the tower of the Carnegie Library. The Commons were converted to park land after 1867. The out-lots north of the western part of the Commons are now the Mexican War Streets. West of the Commons is the Allegheny West area, with Manchester to its north. East of the Commons is Deutschtown.

seven little plots may not have been executed, while it does seem that a later one with radial walks was.

In 1764, Colonel John Campbell took advantage of the destruction of civilian shelters around Fort Pitt in preparation for the Indian siege to lay out the tiny settlement of Pittsburgh in an orderly fashion. He planned a four-block grid, now bounded by Stanwix and Market Streets, Fort Pitt Boulevard, and the Boulevard of the Allies.

In 1784, the Penn family, no longer Proprietors of Pennsylvania but with extensive manors—areas of private property—in Southwestern Pennsylvania, commissioned George Woods and Thomas Vickroy to survey what is now the Golden Triangle so that it could be sold. Woods and Vickroy extended the Campbell grid, though varying the dimensions of the blocks for no apparent reason, so that most of the triangular city plan had streets parallel or perpendicular to the Monongahela River. However, a two-block strip by the Allegheny was laid out with reference to *that* river, its inland edge being Liberty Street, the road to the Northern Liberties on the Allegheny plain just outside town. Liberty Street was thus like a seam joining two pieces of tartan, each with its own

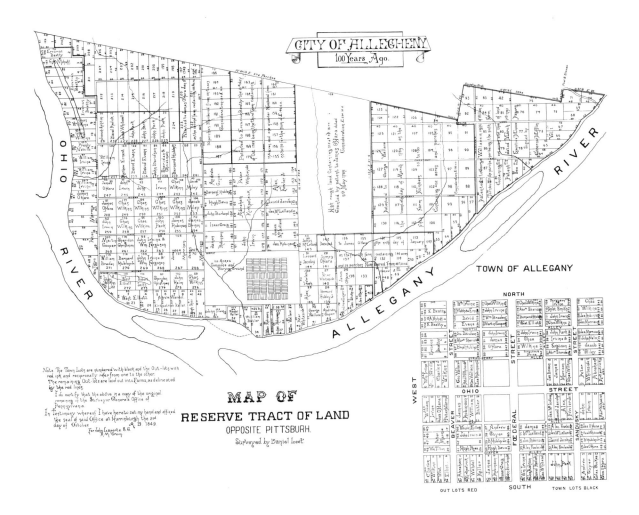

MAP OF
RESERVE TRACT OF LAND
OPPOSITE PITTSBURH.
Surveyed by Daniel Leet

undeviating pattern, and the junction was marked by peculiar triangular and trapezoidal blocks and awkward traffic intersections that remain after two centuries. In the whole plan there was only one public square, the marketplace then called the Diamond—a Scotch-Irish term for such a space—and now called Market Square; this was at an intersection of Market Street and the downtown section of Forbes Avenue, then called Diamond Alley.

The first civilian shelters around Fort Pitt, erected for traders and workmen, shared none of the technical sophistication of the fort itself. They were rough, bark-clad huts and log cabins, none of which survives. From the pioneer days in Allegheny County we have only their successors, the more refined log houses that were built on into the early part of the nineteenth century.

A log cabin was a crib of logs, left round and with only enough notching to lock them together, quite possibly without a chimney and with the only openings the doorway and a smoke hole in the roof. A log house, on the other hand, was as finished a product as an ax, an adze, and a few other rough carpenter's tools could shape. The logs were squared and notched at the corners so that each had a gable-shaped upper edge and a corresponding indentation on the lower edge. The spaces between the logs were chinked with a mixture of clay and stone. Chimneys might be of piled-up logs or sticks with a heavy clay lining, but later on were more likely of massive fieldstone, possibly with jambs and lintels of regularly cut stones. Windows were very likely of oiled paper or merely shuttered openings until after 1800, when locally made window glass was available, and the roof—nails in the eighteenth century were hand-made and expensive—would probably be of planks, clapboards, or shakes held down with horizontal poles.

The Trax house, begun in 1806, in South Park Township.

Typically in demand at first was a log house of one full story with a loft, and later a two-storied house; such a house, with not too much replanning, could serve as a tavern, a store, a school, or even a pioneer courthouse. A church was usually square, but could be built for a fairly large congregation in a blunt cruciform shape. The image of the cross was not important—it was even a drawback in a Protestant culture—but it was useful for structural reasons, and brought the congregation close to the pulpit around which the service centered. This plan was later repeated in masonry churches, and a number of Pittsburgh churches of the end of the nineteenth century recalled pioneer days in their layouts, probably without their congregations being aware of the fact.

These simple log buildings could have been developed into a versatile local architecture of long duration under different conditions. Switzerland, Scandinavia, Finland, and Russia have had log-building traditions equal to the production of large and ornate farmhouses, town houses, storehouses, churches, and even mansions. The log tradition went on into this century, and in Russia there are exposed-log houses with Art Nouveau detailing.

The Fulton house of 1830 in Upper St. Clair Township.

In Southwestern Pennsylvania, such a developed tradition did not occur. Once trees were cleared for farmland, logs had to be fetched from further away, and brick clay and stone were present as rival materials. The population were settlers, busy starting new lives and coming from areas that had passed beyond the bark-hut-and-log-cabin stage long before into one of masonry or frame-and-clapboard, and they had not the cultural background, the time, the tools, or the skills to evolve a folk architecture based on logs. Later generations might look at the log house, with its picturesque unevenness of line, its grays and gray-browns that toned in so well with the browns, greens, and spots of color of the pioneer's garden and the somber green or brown of the hills beyond, and enjoy the picture. And the log house, well maintained, could be quite comfortable. But toward 1785, with conditions in Southwestern Pennsylvania beginning to become stable, log architecture began to be supplanted by the Georgian building tradition from the East and the South.

The Fahnestock house of c. 1830, on Penn Avenue downtown, had a Bostonian-looking recessed doorway (gone).

GEORGIAN
SIMPLICITY

In its simplest form, that used increasingly in Southwestern Pennsylvania between 1785 and 1830, the Georgian manner of designing a building was simple, easy, and obvious: so obvious that even today, if a child draws a house, the house is apt to be Georgian. It was a synthesis of three elements: the natural tendency of humans to make an object symmetrical if it is easy to do and if there is no special reason to do otherwise; the practice in the Italian Renaissance of designing house facades with rather widely and evenly spaced windows, uniform on any one story; and the sliding-sash window, a Dutch invention of the seventeenth century that eliminated the mullions and transoms that subdivided the medieval casement window, thus making a neater contrast between the solid and void areas of a facade. These elements were synthesized in England at the end of the seventeenth century, and from 1710 were present in America as the basis of a tradition that lasted, despite rivalry from styles with different compositional bases, for two-and-a-half centuries.

Essentially, a Georgian building is a combination of rectangles topped by triangles. The perimeter on the ground is a rectangle, easy to lay out, easy to frame with wooden sills or define in masonry, easy to fit into a standard building lot. Walls rise sheer to the eaves, and the roof is usually of the easily framed gabled sort, triangular in section. A house will usually have an ell, a rear wing at right angles to its main body, and may have a front or side porch, but all these are distinct elements, all rectangular in plan and elevation save for the gable areas. The geometry is clear and simple: no buttresses, no bay windows, no turrets, no fancy compositions of roof planes.

On the front, the doorway is normally at the center, though not where this is impractical. The windows, of uniform dimensions on each floor, are symmetrically disposed, and are three or four feet wide and about twice as high: the two-to-one ratio is a good Classical proportion for an opening, and a window so dimensioned allows the sliding sashes to be easily handled. Aside from the simple moldings of the window frames,

"The Meadows," the James Ross house in O'Hara Township, had simple geometry and sparing decoration (gone).

Top: The Federal-period doorway of the Ferree house in O'Hara Township is ill-proportioned but skilled in execution. (Door and fanlight gone.) Above: The same delicate tooling is evident in a mantelpiece of c. 1820 once in the Allegheny Arsenal.

ornament is confined to the doorway, the cornice, and the dormers if any. Basically, this is ornamented construction, relying on good proportion, a nice use of decorative accents, and the attractiveness of local building materials for its effectiveness.

The builder of a Georgian house needs not be a man of any talent or learning; in the overall design he has tradition to guide him, and in decorative detailing he has design manuals, originally from England but after 1800 compiled in America, which show him specimens of doorways, mantelpieces, cornices, and decorative woodwork of all sorts. In Southwestern Pennsylvania the builder is inclined not to keep his library up to date, so that a doorway normal in Philadelphia in the 1780s or 1790s may turn up on a house or church of this region in the 1810s or 1820s.

In one respect the local builder, like others of the Georgian period, is apt to cheat a little. The main front gets the full Georgian treatment, but the other sides of the building may not. The front has regularly disposed openings, but those elsewhere are put wherever expedient; the front has ashlar while the other sides are of rubble, or brick laid in the elegant but expensive Flemish bond while the rest of the building is in the easier but less attractive common bond.

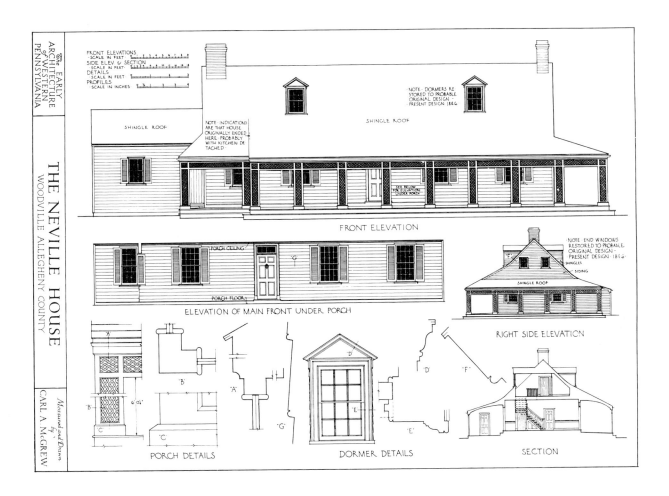

EARLY ARCHITECTURE OF WESTERN PENNSYLVANIA

THE NEVILLE HOUSE
WOODVILLE · ALLEGHENY COUNTY

Measured and Drawn by
CARL A. McGREW

FRONT ELEVATIONS
· SCALE IN FEET·
SIDE ELEV· & SECTION
· SCALE IN FEET·
DETAILS
· SCALE IN FEET·
PROFILES
· SCALE IN INCHES·

SHINGLE ROOF

NOTE· DORMERS RE-
STORED TO PROBABLE
ORIGINAL DESIGN·
PRESENT DESIGN 1846·

SHINGLE ROOF

NOTE· INDICATIONS
ARE THAT HOUSE
ORIGINALLY ENDED
HERE· PROBABLY
WITH KITCHEN DE-
TACHED

SEE BELOW
FOR ELEVATION
UNDER PORCH

FRONT ELEVATION

PORCH CEILING

PORCH FLOOR

ELEVATION OF MAIN FRONT UNDER PORCH

·NOTE·END WINDOWS
RESTORED TO PROBABLE
ORIGINAL DESIGN·
PRESENT DESIGN 1846·
SHINGLES
SIDING

SHINGLE ROOF

RIGHT SIDE ELEVATION

PORCH DETAILS

DORMER DETAILS

SECTION

"Woodville," the Neville house in Collier Township, has had a history of enlargements that is not wholly clear, but its steep roof with high-set dormers suggests Virginian building practice.

Regional traditions had some influence over the specific ways in which the Georgian formula was realized in Southwestern Pennsylvania. Everyone was more or less of a newcomer, and a builder or client brought his own customs and prejudices regarding construction and planning with him. Many of the early settlers south of the Ohio were Virginians—the exact boundary between Pennsylvania and Virginia was not surveyed until 1784, and Virginia had long claimed this whole region—and the original part of "Woodville," the Neville house of c. 1785, for instance, is regarded as a Virginia house in Southwestern Pennsylvania for a former Virginian. Stone was naturally used more often than brick at first, but it was also the preferred material of the Eastern Pennsylvania rural areas from which some settlers had come. Any given design, especially for a house, might indicate the builder's habits, the owner's preference, or a compromise.

The west end of Penn Avenue, where Gateway Center is now, kept its early nineteenth-century look into the 1890s.

Charles Morse Stotz, director of the Western Pennsylvania Architectural Survey of the early 1930s, cited examples of houses in the western third of the state whose diverse forms reflected the places of origin of their owners. As Allegheny and its surrounding counties were officially pronounced part of Pennsylvania just at the time when the Georgian building tradition was coming into use in the region, it may be natural that most of our earliest house architecture in that tradition resembles either the typical Eastern Pennsylvania farmhouse, a roofed cube of masonry with chimneys flush with its end walls but often with a cornice that projects in a way that suggests a pediment, or a city row house that might have been imitated from a builder's guide, with plain side walls. Had the region gone to Virginia, and Virginians been encouraged to go on settling here, we might have had a domestic architecture of prominent and dormered rather than unobtrusive, undormered roofs, of sheltering porches rather than unsheltered doorways, of more frame and brick construction and less stone, and perhaps those big, tapered, exposed end chimneys often found on the gable walls of Colonial Virginia houses.

Behind this new Georgian architecture lay a more advanced technology than Southwestern Pennsylvania had thus far known. To apply the builder's skills there had to be chisels to cut mortises, planes to make true surfaces and moldings, gouges to form delicate reeding and fluting for mantelpieces and doorframes, lathes to turn balusters, lime for mortar and plaster, good brick clay, the right kind of sand for clear window glass and the right kind of heat-resistant clay for the pots that melted the sand, and iron for door hardware and the nails that secured shingles and siding.

Trade and industry had to be organized, therefore, and money and leisure accumulated before thoughts of going beyond log houses and log churches could be entertained. Around 1785 these conditions had begun to be met in Southwestern Pennsylvania, though in 1800 Pittsburgh was still primarily a town of log houses. It was only around 1800 that the region was able to make its own window glass or produce cheap enough nails to shingle a roof economically. By 1816, when Pittsburgh was promoted from its 1794 status of borough to that of city, it had at least one handsome three-story brick house row, and the former King's Garden site, remote from the commercial activity along the Monongahela River, had become a fashionable quarter.

Above: The Diamond and the first Allegheny County Courthouse, painted from memory after its demolition in 1852. Left: The Courthouse belfry dominated early Pittsburgh, as this view of 1817 indicates.

The grandest architectural work of Allegheny County at this time was its first Courthouse, erected on the Pittsburgh Diamond and finished in 1799. This was a square building, hip-roofed and with a central belfry that terminated in a spire. There were two one-story wings. The doorways, the cornice, the belfry, and the interiors had carved decorative woodwork, though which Classical orders were used is uncertain. In front of the Courthouse were two quadrants of brick-pillared open market sheds, and straight sheds eventually flanked the Courthouse itself. Such a building easily dominated the town's early, unambitious skyline, but by the 1830s it was regarded as worn out and a disgrace to the city. In 1841 it was replaced in its role of Courthouse and demolished in 1852.

The first architect to practice in Southwestern Pennsylvania was probably Adam Wilson, an Englishman hired around 1801 by the ironmaster Isaac Meason to build his country mansion "Mount Braddock," which still survives in Fayette County. The first architect to practice in Allegheny County was very probably Benjamin Henry Latrobe (1764–1820), that brilliant, optimistic, often-disappointed Englishman who came to Pittsburgh in 1813 to supervise steamboat construction for Robert Fulton. Fulton, as greedy as he was bold, eased Latrobe out of his interest in the venture as soon as the boat-building operation was well under way, and Latrobe found himself and his family stranded. He had fought the typical package-deal system of the time in Philadelphia, by which a builder supplied the design he then executed, in favor of one in which the architect, a professional designer, supplied the plans and supervised their execution by the builder. In Pittsburgh, Latrobe compromised: as architect-contractor, he produced an indoor circus, several houses, a warehouse, and additions to the First Presbyterian Church. The church, built in 1802 on land donated by the Penns for religious purposes, was to a typical Georgian formula, a brick rectangle with arched windows. Latrobe added two blunt transepts to increase its capacity and two simple but handsome porches of wood at interior angles of the cross-shaped plan. The plan itself was of course like that of the large log churches of the day.

The First Presbyterian Church (gone) as enlarged by Benjamin Latrobe. It faced Wood Street rather than Sixth Avenue, close to the location of the present church.

33

The central building of the Allegheny Arsenal in Lawrenceville as designed by Latrobe (above) and as built (below; gone).

Latrobe's name is also associated with the Allegheny Arsenal, begun in Lawrenceville in 1814, but how far he can be credited with what was actually built is unknown. Certainly, his careful drawings, some of which survive, are different from the executed work in important ways. Of the very little that is left, Latrobe's biographer Talbot Hamlin suggests that the powder magazine in Arsenal Park is the sort of thing Latrobe *might* have designed. Latrobe's role in designing the Arsenal is obscured too by his recommendation to the Army of Thomas Pope, a visionary young engineer who may have done some of the design work.

After Latrobe left Pittsburgh at the end of 1814, Allegheny County appears to have had no professional architects for nearly two decades. Log construction gave way to frame, stone, and brick, and builders continued to erect simple rectangular buildings whose ornamentation might or might not reflect current trends back east. The Georgian tradition was to prove remarkably hardy. The ornamentation of future styles— Greek Revival, Italianate, even Gothic—might cling to the facades of farmhouses and city houses like froth, but the places they clung to were the traditional Georgian places: the doorways, the cornices, and the dormers, and in those later years quite often to the window heads as well. In most buildings the walls remained unadorned, penetrated at regular intervals by sliding-sash windows, just as before. Even in the late nineteenth and early twentieth centuries, when ostentation and a compulsive picturesqueness dominated the fronts of buildings, the less-visible sides might reflect the neat and sober Georgian practice, and the sliding-sash window has never been wholly given up. Around 1930, before air-conditioning, a Modernistic skyscraper still breathed through windows basically identical with those of a Colonial farmhouse, and their limited widths helped determine the spacing of its dynamic verticals.

The Western Penitentiary (gone), in an English print of 1839. It was on the West Common in Allegheny. The penitentiary was the first American building type to draw international interest.

THE
STYLES

The detailing so far applied to the Georgian buildings of Southwestern Pennsylvania had been derived, however remotely, from ancient Rome and a millennium-and-a-half of additions to and variations on Roman forms for artistic and practical reasons. This design practice was only in retrospect a series of styles.

Benjamin Latrobe, however, in his Philadelphia days in the 1790s had applied Gothic detailing to a house and a Grecian Ionic temple front to a bank, breaking with the evolutionary pattern to introduce something consciously different: a style, a distinctive vocabulary of ornamental detail and large-scale composition that could be more or less closely labeled. The use of such a style had obvious temptations: greater artistic freedom; novelty for both the designer and his client; an air of cosmopolitanism; and the opportunity, if the style adopted were to shape the whole building, not its separate decorative features, of creating a showpiece in the community.

A well-chosen style was also the striking of an attitude, a means of saying something about the institution or family housed behind the exotic ornamentation. Latrobe had created designs for the Arsenal buildings in a stripped-down, avant-garde Classical manner without military allusions, but the central building of the Arsenal as built was furnished with symbolic battlements, though these may have been added afterwards. When William Strickland and John Haviland, two Philadelphia architects, successively designed (in 1820) and later remodeled the Western Penitentiary on the West Common of Allegheny, they gave the administration block the air of a castle—though a castle as remodeled by some eighteenth-century gentleman who wanted the feudal look but with big modern windows. Castles were used to keep people in as well as out, and short round towers and battlements seemed like a good expression of a prison.

Trinity Episcopal Church (gone), from John Henry Hopkins' Essay on Gothic Architecture *(1836), which he addressed especially to clergymen who might want to be their own architects.*

When the brilliant and versatile John Henry Hopkins (1792–1868) became rector of Trinity Episcopal Church in 1823, his congregation worshiped in the individualistic but not especially ecclesiastical-looking "Round Church" of 1805, an octagon with a round-headed window in each side. The next year, 1824, Hopkins built a Tudor Gothic church to his own design to replace it, complete with tower, buttresses, battlements, and a ceiling painted—by Hopkins himself—in imitation of fan vaulting. The plan was the old-fashioned meeting-house one, a simple rectangular hall with raised side galleries, but the added medieval elements recalled church tradition. The Catholics, very possibly in a spirit of rivalry, built between 1829 and 1834 their own Gothic church in brick, the first St. Paul's Cathedral at Fifth Avenue and Grant Street.

In the future, speaking very generally, Gothic and other medieval styles were to express tradition in the English-speaking world, while an expanding range of Classical and quasi-Classical styles were to suggest enlightenment, cosmopolitanism, worldly sophistication, and indeed almost any quality expressible in a look of order and elegance. In 1819 the Pittsburgh Academy of 1787 became the Western University of Pennsylvania, and in 1830 built for itself with conscious dignity. Essentially, its new building was a big Georgian structure of the simplest sort, but its ground floor was treated as a rusticated basement whose central three bays broke forward to allow a four-columned, pedimented portico in Grecian Ionic to stand against its plain upper walls; a cupola on a podium rose above the hipped roof. Neither the design formula— a Palladian one quite familiar in England and occasionally used on the Eastern Seaboard—nor the Grecian order may have been used for the first time in the Pittsburgh area, but they do reflect a new desire, not merely to ornament a building but to turn the building itself into an ornament. From a practical viewpoint the applied portico and the broad

The Western University of Pennsylvania of 1830 (gone), in a painting by Russell Smith.

THE POPLAR AND THE AILANTHUS

The Branch Bank of the United States (above left; gone) in a painting of 1832 by Russell Smith. The Coltart house of 1843 (above right; gone), once in Oakland; the main front had a heavily proportioned Ionic porch. The view at bottom shows the Pittsburgh Theater in 1840, with its broad steps and plastered front, on Fifth Avenue between Wood and Smithfield Streets (gone).

podium of the cupola were worse than useless, complicating the roof system, but a dignified gesture took priority. The building had an architect-designed look, but which architect is not known.

Two other city buildings of the 1830s deserve to be mentioned. The Branch Bank of the United States, as it was in 1832, was essentially a big Georgian house, but it had a Grecian Doric portico and a parapet whose raised, bluntly pointed central part hinted at a pediment. Much Greek Revival had this applied character; the big but unpretentious Coltart house that stood in Oakland until the 1970s had a similar front porch of Grecian columns, made of wood but dimensioned for stone, as the Thomas Wilson Shaw house in Shaler Township still does. On the other hand, John Haviland's 1833 design for the Pittsburgh Theater seems not to have been particularly Greek at all; a vague sketch, all we have of its first condition, shows a rusticated, arched ground floor with five rectangular windows, and possibly a pediment, above. This seems a little plain for a 1,200-seat theater, Pittsburgh's most ambitious to date, but by the time the facade was accurately depicted a particularly dreary false front in Italianate had replaced the upper part.

A Federal house (now gone) long survived as the ell of a later building on Chestnut Street above East Ohio Street.

Not long after this public architecture began to appear, individuals began to show the aspirations to grandeur that their counterparts on the Eastern Seaboard had been revealing for quite a while. The latter-day form of the Georgian style that we now call Federal was already loosening up at the time when Greek Revival began to appear. Instead of a narrow front door with a fanlight, a builder might supply a broad doorway with sidelights flanking the door itself and an overdoor light above. As a Federal house on the North Side, once near East Ohio and Chestnut Streets, showed, the rooms might even be lighted by broad three-part windows rather than the standard pairs of narrow eighteenth-century ones. Two extant Federal houses, the Abishai Way house in Edgeworth and the Lightner house in Shaler Township, go further still by extending pedimented porches, like gestures of welcome, to the tops of high entrance steps. Both houses are otherwise rather plain and not especially large, but their raised main floors and the porches themselves give them an air of Palladian elegance.

Be it simple or elaborate in its detailing, a Greek Revival building had a simple, overall rectangularity as a governing compositional principle. The temple formula of the Allegheny Institute and Mission Church (above left) is repeated more elaborately in "Woodlawn" elsewhere in Allegheny (bottom right). The Morning Post Buildings of c. 1840 (above right) show the ultimate in Greek Revival simplicity, while the ballroom of "Picnic House" (bottom left) illustrates its potential for lavishness. (All gone, except for two "Picnic House" interiors.)

*"Homewood" (gone), designed
by Judge William Wilkins,
was demolished around 1925.*

The Greek Revival, as it was being developed back east, suggested even more obvious effects. True, "Picnic House," the best-remembered house of the time, built around 1835 on what is now Stanton Heights for Mary Croghan Schenley, was big but not especially imposing: its grandeur was inside, and the ballroom and vestibule, decorated by Mordecai van Horne of Philadelphia and now preserved with some alterations in the Cathedral of Learning of the University of Pittsburgh, still attest that the grandeur was considerable. But "Woodlawn," the Samuel Church house in Manchester, used the temple-like compositional formula of the time, and Judge William Wilkins' "Homewood," in the East End, had an imposing front with a tall Doric portico and wing pavilions. (Behind the pompous facade of 1835, though, "Homewood's" exterior was utterly bare.) Even a town house built directly on the street and deprived of such a rhetorical device as a portico could make a good appearance. The John Shoenberger house of c. 1847, demolished for

Gateway Center in downtown Pittsburgh but defaced some years before, had an imposing doorway between two Bostonian-looking bow windows, rich grilles in the windows of its frieze, and a parapet in the once-advanced Classical taste—rather old-fashioned in 1847—of Regency England. Inside, like "Picnic House," it had its ballroom, its fine Grecian plasterwork.

The first architect to make a career in the Pittsburgh area may have been John Behan, an architect and civil engineer, in the early 1820s. The first one whose work is known, however, is John Chislett (1800–69), an Englishman who had studied in the elegant city of Bath and who is known to have been practicing in Pittsburgh in 1833. It is just possible that he had designed the Western University of Pennsylvania's building of three years before, and because of the very peculiarly English character of the Shoenberger house parapet, one wonders if that may not have been his as well. There is a possibility too that Chislett designed the Third Presbyterian Church of 1833, though a sketch shows an Ionic entablature handled so clumsily that one is disposed to doubt it. That Chislett knew Grecian Ionic thoroughly is evident in his Bank of Pittsburgh of 1835, formerly downtown on Fourth Avenue. That he was far from a clumsy designer is proven by Burke's Building still on Fourth Avenue, the Butler Street gateway of Allegheny Cemetery, and that cemetery's Romantic layout of

The John Shoenberger house, near the west end of Penn Avenue (gone).

winding roads, at once picturesque and practical for a hillside site. The Regency-looking Shoenberger summer villa in Lawrenceville, absorbed by Allegheny Cemetery in the 1880s, may very well also have been by Chislett.

Chislett's biggest work, though not necessarily his best, was the second Courthouse, built in 1841 on the site of the present one. Its Doric portico and domed cupola gave it the imposing character expected of the courthouse of a thriving county, and beneath the cupola was a rotunda sixty feet in diameter and eighty feet high inside. Sited on a Grant's Hill much higher than it is now, it dominated the city from 1841 to 1882, when it burned.

The Shoenberger villa in Lawrenceville (above left). John Chislett's Bank of Pittsburgh (above right). The second Allegheny County Courthouse is below. (All gone.)

Pittsburgh as shown in a lithograph of 1859 by William Schuchman, with the second Courthouse and the towers of St. Paul's Cathedral dominating the skyline. To the left is Allegheny, and vignettes show the nearby communities of Manchester (bottom left) and Birmingham (bottom right).

THE MID-VICTORIAN PERIOD

Let us pause while we have a quick look around Allegheny County—the year is 1850—and take note of what is there and what—sometimes surprisingly—is not.

Technology had come to the rivers, and the Western River packet, which originated at Pittsburgh in 1811, had matured into a sometimes-beautiful, sometimes-deadly device for moving people and goods west and south. The push towing of barges, which today dominates the rivers, was still in the experimental stage, but coal boats from the mines along the Monongahela drifted down that short and winding river, which a private company was canalizing. The U.S. Army Corps of Engineers had accepted responsibility for the Ohio River in 1824, but its channel-scouring and snag-pulling did little to maintain a navigable amount of water in the river, which might run dry in the summer. Great timber rafts floated down to Pittsburgh from ravaged forests up the Allegheny, and the old-fashioned flatboat, an unpropelled floating box, still was making its slow way down the Ohio on trading voyages as it had been doing for a half-century.

There were no railroads! The first, the Ohio & Pennsylvania, was to come in 1851 with Allegheny as its terminus; through train service to Philadelphia, on the Pennsylvania Railroad, in 1852; and to Chicago, on the Pittsburgh, Fort Wayne & Chicago Railroad (or Railway), in 1859. Travelers from the East arrived either by the Pennsylvania Turnpike, a good macadam road of carefully compacted stone since 1820, or over the "Main Line of Public Works," the State's canal-railroad system, completed in 1834. In Allegheny County, the Pennsylvania Canal element of the Main Line had required two notable engineering works: an aqueduct between Pittsburgh and Allegheny, built as a wooden covered bridge in 1829 then replaced by Roebling's suspension structure in 1845, and a tunnel under Grant's Hill to the Monongahela, where junction with the Chesapeake & Ohio Canal was anticipated but never made.

Until the Indians were subdued permanently in the 1790s, settlement north of the Allegheny was inhibited while that south of the Monongahela, much of it by Virginians, had been going on steadily from the 1760s. By 1850 a network of roads—dirt, plank, and macadam—had developed in both directions. Pittsburgh, between rivers, needed bridges as well for the northern and southern trade. The first Smithfield Street Bridge of 1818, crossing the Monongahela River, was a conventional covered bridge by Lewis Wernwag, whose wooden "Colossus" at Philadelphia had the greatest arch span ever built at that time: 340 feet.

*The Pittsburgh, Fort Wayne &
Chicago Railway Bridge was
probably built in 1857.
A lattice truss of wrought iron,
it replaced the original wooden
bridge over the Allegheny River.*

48

The first Smithfield Street Bridge of 1818 lost several spans in a flood of 1832, as a Russell Smith painting shows, and eventually burned in the Fire of 1845. Its replacement by Roebling (below) is shown in a view of c. 1880, just before its demolition. The view is from the Triangle toward the Pittsburgh & Lake Erie Railroad Station and the Monongahela Incline.

The Union Bridge crossed the Allegheny River between the Point (right) and Allegheny. An old-fashioned wooden covered bridge, it stood between 1874 and 1907. Below is the contemporary and more progressive Point Bridge, crossing the Monongahela River to the foot of Mount Washington. Built from 1875 to 1877 and demolished in 1927, this design by Edward Hemberle had an unusual stiffening and suspension system. In the background is the Duquesne Incline.

After the Great Fire in 1845 this first Smithfield Street Bridge had been replaced by one of Roebling's suspension bridges. The Allegheny River had first been crossed in 1819 at St. Clair (Sixth) Street with a covered bridge by a builder named Lothrop. Other Pittsburgh engineering works were less interesting, albeit useful: the filling-in of four ponds that inconsiderately lay across the Woods-Vickroy street grid; the digging of a reservoir in the late 1820s where the Frick Building is now; and successive lowerings of the miserably steep Grant's Hill Hump, which between the 1830s and 1913 came down sixty feet.

From the 149 people of 1760, Pittsburgh had grown to a population of 47,000 in 1850. Its rival Allegheny now had 21,000. Birmingham and East Birmingham, boroughs now in the South Side flats, were busy iron- and glass-manufacturing centers. Lawrenceville was growing around the Arsenal. Some other river and canal towns were of varying importance. The Pennsylvania Salt Manufacturing Company was building an early company town, Natrona, in Harrison Township. On the other hand, Sewickley and East Liberty were farm villages, the East End and South Hills were very thinly settled, and some manufacturing towns of the future, like Homestead, Wilmerding, and East Pittsburgh, did not exist.

The dense Pittsburgh smoke had already been noted in the 1790s, and by 1850 was quite thick. Iron was processed in and around Pittsburgh, but oddly enough not smelted here; the unfinished product came from stone blast furnaces close to ore deposits and charcoal sources in other Western Pennsylvania counties. Aside from an abortive furnace in Shadyside in the 1790s, the first furnace within the present city limits would come in 1859, shortly after ironmaking technology replaced charcoal with coke, an oven-refined form of coal. Glass, much of it of high quality, was a major industry. Coal was mined within sight of town from the interior of Coal Hill, now called Mount Washington. Boat-building and engine-building were quite important, from Elizabeth up the Monongahela to Shousetown down the Ohio. On the other hand, petroleum—which was to boom a

The 270-foot cabin of the Mississippi River packet Great Republic, *built in 1867. The hull was built at Shousetown and completed at Pittsburgh with joinery by Charles Gearing. The boat contained sixty-four staterooms and could carry 8,200 bales of cotton, but burned after ten years.*

decade later and make Pittsburgh briefly a refining center—was of no importance; electrical equipment, aside from the six-year-old telegraph, was almost without economic significance anywhere; aluminum was a rare product of the laboratory; natural gas went unused. All these were later to become elements of the region's economic base.

In 1850, Greek Revival was being either abandoned or undergoing a mutation. The temple form, which could be cheaply sketched out with pilasters, offered an easy formula for construction of pretense, and Greek Revival at its best was a lucid, balanced, tasteful, but undeniably rather standardized style. After a while, as with Georgian architecture before and Modern architecture in the late 1960s, people began to wish for something different.

The Mid-Victorian architect was typically trained through apprentice-ship, untraveled and unschooled unless he had immigrated from Europe. He was catering to increasingly style-conscious clients, and to help him adapt foreign styles—*never* American styles of the past—to modern requirements and resources, he had to rely on paintings, prints, book illustrations, and perhaps an occasional photograph. He might subscribe to foreign architectural magazines too; there were no American ones.

He might enlarge his income and disseminate the new styles by authoring pattern books, intended for builders and building owners in places deprived of architectural services. These offered plans, elevations, ornamental details, structural drawings, capsulated architectural histories, and advice on interior decoration and sound building practice: any or all of these in a given pattern book.

Mid-Victorian architecture, whatever its style, tended to have a hard look. It was executed in materials to which machinery and craftsmanship gave an unwavering perfection: bright red brick, pale gray sandstone, cast iron, and machine-cut lumber were typical locally, and in the best work all were geometrically regular and carefully surfaced. The architect, and the builder following a pattern book, thought in terms of edges defining surfaces rather than materials with characteristic densities, colors, and textures. While the building might be histrionically decorated in a style that expressed something of the building's purpose, it was still executed in plain Victorian materials, sash with two panes or even one big pane, under a flat roof perhaps, and the architect's fancy was weirdly counter-pointed with the drab common sense of the basic structure.

Mid-Victorian architecture, so recently despised, has not yet had a comprehensive history, and we have much to learn about it. Our historians have gone so far, though, as to label one of its major design idioms the Italianate. Certainly there was a polymorphous design idiom, which made its first mild appearances in the United States in the 1830s and developed around 1850, that owed much to Renaissance Italy, even more to Baroque Italy, and something to Romantic British fantasies about Italy. It had the advantage of being a good all-purpose style, capable of sweet simplicity, capable of the wildest ostentation. A Cubical Tuscan villa's elementary geometry might be gently disrupted by no

The heavily Italianate Exchange National Bank of c. 1870 (gone), flanked by the convex corners of neighboring buildings in a rare attempt at architectural harmony. This stood in mid-block on Fifth Avenue between Wood and Market Streets.

The sparely Italianate Second Presbyterian Church of the 1850s stood at Penn Avenue and Eighth Street (gone).

more than a delicate verandah and a flaring cornice whose widely spaced brackets were sawn in fantastic curves. Yet a bank might present an appearance of sinister luxury, cornices with richly modeled, close-spaced brackets above tall, narrow windows that seemed to stare. A fashionable store building might take on the air of a palace, Renaissance or Baroque window frames jostling one another as if tempting you to speculate on the sumptuous contents, but even a humble store might add wooden brackets to its fascia and frame its display windows to suggest archways. Of the grandest commercial architecture of the time little remains, but the cast-iron fronts at 805 and 927 Liberty Avenue show the open yet ornate character it had.

The arrival of the Italianate in America has been reasonably well documented; we know something about our early Italian villas and our first imitations of Renaissance palazzi. Yet it is tempting, too, to see one strain of the new manner as a sprouting as it were of the Greek Revival. The Shoenberger house for instance was generally Greek Revival, yet it had heavier detail, and more of it, than was standard. To put consoles under a lintel that once simply rested on the wall masonry, to sink narrow panels into a normally flat pilaster and decorate their ends with honeysuckle ornament: such things showed a desire for novelty and lavishness, and this Greek Revival gone to seed blended with the conscious Italianisms.

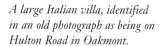

A large Italian villa, identified in an old photograph as being on Hulton Road in Oakmont.

These three pictures of now-gone buildings show Italianate of the simpler sort: Liberty Hall of 1858, once at Ellsworth and Penn Avenues (above left); George Hardy's drugstore in Crafton (above right); and stores in Italianate and other styles on Penn Avenue in East Liberty.

One Mid-Victorian style, which arrived on the heels of the Italianate, was more label than substance. What historians call the Second Empire style in actual practice usually entailed putting a mansard roof on an otherwise Italianate design. The mansard roof, a double-pitched roof with a very steep lower slope, was devised in Paris to increase usable attic-level floor space. It had sophisticated connotations, being from Paris, and was useful in lessening the apparent height of a tall building while giving it a strong terminal feature.

Other styles of the time have never been labeled. There is, for instance, a brick vernacular, a little like the simplest Italian Romanesque and similar to a Central European manner of the 1840s called the Rundbogenstil (Round-arch Style). Of course, round arches were not necessary. Applied to churches it often included Gothic arches, and industrial applications might use segmental arches or flat-headed openings. It was, in fact, used for industrial buildings and churches alike, as shown by St. Michael the Archangel on the South Side slopes and the Westinghouse plant in Wilmerding. In this style the wall was visibly divided into piers and panels. The piers presumably supported the building's principal beams and trusses while the panels, set in from the faces of the piers, excluded the weather. At the top of the wall, corbeling that might be plain or fancy supported the last few courses, which ran in a straight line beneath the roof. Such a style, whose

Second Empire was simply Italianate or some other classicizing manner with a mansard roof. The First National Bank, at Fifth Avenue and Wood Street, had a mansard roof when it was built in 1871 but lost it later to fire (bottom left). The Sommerville house in Crafton, shown below in a view of 1905, has the echelon shape of a typical Italian villa, here stepping back from right to left, though with mansard roofs on all elements.

The Allegheny Market House of 1863 was built in a quasi-Romanesque brick idiom favored for both churches and industrial buildings. Inside, the structure was light and airy, with wrought-iron Phoenix columns supporting timber arches and rafters (gone).

decorative detailing was of standard brick and well within the competence of a Victorian bricklayer, was inexpensive and stately, and allowed for fantasy. In industrial architecture it lasted until after 1900, when the reinforced-concrete frame replaced it.

Toward 1880, another style, again as yet unlabeled, appeared. The French theorist Eugène-Emmanuel Viollet-le-Duc had been arguing for a rational treatment of construction and planning, and had much to say on the technique of building in masonry. Perhaps this is why the elements of masonry construction, exposed, even dramatized, became the basis of a style. At 820 Liberty Avenue for instance, the spanning of wide voids with segmental arches is the main architectural theme. In the Irish Block at Tenth Street and Penn Avenue, red and yellow brick express the function of the arch and the stratified nature of masonry in a facade with an odd harsh beauty.

The Gothic style of this period was a more studied and elaborate affair, at least when budgeting permitted, than heretofore. The Singer house in Wilkinsburg and the much smaller "Heathside Cottage"

Above: St. Philomena's Church stood in the Strip into the 1920s. Above right: St. Peter's Episcopal Church (now gone), after its first half-century, was moved and rebuilt in Oakland with a new porch shown here. The interior is that of St. Peter's, once again in its Oakland years.

overlooking the North Side survive to show the rich decoration sometimes used on secular Gothic. Church congregations, too, had greater ambitions than previously.

As early as 1846, St. Philomena's Roman Catholic Church, built in what is now the Strip district, displayed a novel feature in American church architecture, the clerestory. The raising of the nave windows above the roof level of the adjoining aisles was standard in medieval architecture of course, but at the time perhaps only Trinity Church in New York had such a feature in America. The architect of St. Philomena's may have been Robert Cary Long, well known in Baltimore, or the local Charles Bartberger, or both at different times.

In 1851 the Episcopalians of Pittsburgh had a clerestory to boast of too, and in a more polished work. The Episcopal Church had been under pressure for some time from Ecclesiological Societies in England and New York to build in English Gothic of authentic design, and John Notman of Philadelphia had demonstrated, in St. Mark's in that city, that he had mastered its forms. (Notman, Scottish-born, was a good, stylistically versatile architect. He had used, if not introduced, the Italian Villa idiom in its earliest days, and probably introduced from England the urban, palazzo-like variety of Italianate. He also designed in Romanesque, Baroque, Moorish, and Chinese at various times.) His 1851 design for St. Peter's, on Grant Street at Fifth Avenue in downtown Pittsburgh, was so admired that fifty years later, when the site was to be cleared for the Frick Building, the church was moved stone by stone to Forbes and Craft Avenues in Oakland, where it stood until 1990.

The First Presbyterian Church of 1851 (gone) faced Wood Street. In the background is the present Trinity Episcopal Cathedral.

The year St. Peter's was begun, St. Paul's across Fifth Avenue burned, and the Catholics contemplated a more ambitious cathedral. Thomas Walsh of New York may have supplied the actual design, but the architect who saw to its realization was a local man, Charles Bartberger, who at this time was also serving as architect for the large and handsome First Presbyterian Church on Wood Street. St. Paul's, as built between 1853 and 1870, was an awkward church, too diffused in its elements. Its two high spires joined with the Courthouse dome near by in dominating the city, but did so more effectively than they did the cathedral's own spreading mass. The cathedral lasted until the early 1900s, when it was demolished.

St. Paul's Roman Catholic Cathedral (gone), at Grant Street and Fifth Avenue.

Market Street in 1893, looking north. A market house (left) and the City Hall of 1854 occupied the old Diamond. (Both gone.)

If the church favored Gothic or the brick Romanesque, government held to a Classical range of styles that was notably more subdued than the commercial architecture of the city. Pittsburgh's City Hall of 1854, built in the Diamond along with a quietly Italianate market hall, was an essay in tall archways, quite plain. In 1872 this was replaced as City Hall by a new building at Smithfield Street and Virgin Alley (Oliver Avenue) which was more ornate in its Italianate facades and had a tower with a grandiose mansard roof, yet was still overall a rather sober building. The Post Office and Custom House next to it, begun in 1853 under the direction of the federal architect Ammi Burnham Young, looked almost like a work of eighteenth-century England, stone-fronted and quietly elegant. Allegheny's City Hall of 1864, which replaced the very modest Federal "town house" of 1834, was an austere essay in arches, pediments, and pilasters, probably by the immigrant Charles Antoine Colomb Gengembre.

Apart from a curious Neo-Baroque station in Allegheny, railroads also favored quiet architecture. The 644-foot Duquesne Depot of 1854—actually on the site of Fort Pitt—was a respectable work in the brick industrial vernacular. The second Union Station, completed in

The City Hall of 1872 by Joseph W. Kerr, with the Post Office and Custom House to its left. The City Hall was where Saks Fifth Avenue is now.

The City Hall of Allegheny.

The Duquesne Depot was a freight station near the Point, shown here in 1858 when it served as a festival hall for the Pittsburgh Centennial celebration. The second Union Station (below) was built in 1865 to the design of Collins & Autenreith of Philadelphia, but was burned in the Railroad Strike of 1877. On the hill, behind, stands Central High School. (All gone.)

Central High School of 1871 (above left), by Barr & Moser, and Soho School (above right), built in 1870 (both gone). The South School of 1841 (gone) stood on Ross Street downtown: this view of c. 1910 shows South School (below) with the Allegheny County Mortuary as its neighbor.

1865 on the site of the present one, was fronted with a Renaissance loggia and was crowned by an eagle between two pediments, but otherwise had simple brick fronts with arched windows. Commuter stations along the Pennsylvania main lines were usually simple, cottage-like affairs.

School architecture was also inclined to be plain. A number of Mid-Victorian schools, usually no longer used as such, survive—the former Morse School on the South Side is an example—and others are remembered from the not-too-distant past. The Greek Revival schools, big boxes with pilasters, were replaced by three-story brick edifices which, despite the architectural styles sparingly used in their entrances, had a Georgian gravity about them as a result of the characteristic forward break in their center bays and their tall, regularly spaced windows. Their appearance suggested a specialized and rather genteel industry: here, they seemed to say, educated children are Produced.

The home was less likely than any other building type to be predictable as to style. Perhaps it was too important and too personal a thing to be readily typecast. Its associations for the inhabitants and its appearance to the public were apt to be serious matters, and a good house was, in fact, the symbol of what man in this busy century was

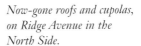

Now-gone roofs and cupolas, on Ridge Avenue in the North Side.

striving for. It was a refuge from the disorderly world and a sign of respectability, or even eminence, attained. The middle class might be content with substantial brick city houses in close-packed rows, still Georgian in form though fashionable in decoration, but roads over the hills, the railroads, horsecar lines, and eventually inclines invited escape from the disorder of the Smoky City, where stray pigs roamed the streets as late as 1860. Some wealthy families might go only as far as Allegheny, where they settled on Ridge Avenue and nearby streets and built with great pomp into the 1900s, but others wanted the open spaces of Oakland, East Liberty, Edgewood, and the Sewickley area, where their Italian villas that suggested civilized leisure, their steep-roofed Gothic cottages and houses that suggested shelter for the essential man, could be seen in the round, set among trees and flowers. Evergreen Hamlet in Ross Township still retains four of the five houses from its beginnings in 1851: two in a very simple Italianate, two in Gothic. Of these, three are clad in the vertical board-and-batten construction that not only gives their walls a fine play of light and shadow but acknowledges that these are simple affairs of wood. "Heathside Cottage" in Fineview, though built of brick and more ornate, has a similar message: Here we take our quiet leisure, content to view the bustling world from a distance.

Left: Irwin Avenue, Allegheny (now Brighton Road) in 1893. The house with the cupola is the house (gone) of B. F. Jones, Sr., of Jones & Laughlins American Iron and Nail Works, also shown above.

66

The G. W. Hailman house of 1864 (above left), which stood at Shady Avenue and Walnut Street, was enlarged around 1890 as the Kenmawr Hotel (gone). The Carrier-Schmertz house (above right) was one of the numerous houses built in Bellefield to designs by the Philadelphian Isaac Hobbs (gone). It stood at Fifth Avenue and Craig Street, with the Duquesne Gardens as its neighbor. Evergreen Hamlet (below): a lithograph of the 1850s by William Schuchman showing the now-gone school.

A new design idiom in Pittsburgh: the stair of "Sunnyledge," built in 1886 in the James H. McClelland house in Shadyside.

NEW

IDEAS

The Philadelphian Frank Furness designed three railroad stations for the Pittsburgh area, as well as this Farmers Deposit National Bank of c. 1885 (gone), once on Fourth Avenue downtown.

After the Civil War the architects of the United States began to have a new sense of themselves as professionals. The American Institute of Architects, founded in 1857, started at last to become an effective national organization, and other professional associations, national, regional, and local, came into being. Furthermore, between the late 1860s and 1890, American architectural schools, journals, exhibitions, traveling fellowships, and a whole apparatus in fact arose to educate the architect, represent him to the public, discipline him, and put him in systematic contact with his colleagues. Not least, architectural publishing continued to develop, and with it forms of graphic reproduction that gave the architect a better idea of architecture he could not see for himself and that allowed him to publish his own designs.

Furthermore, the public became more interested in architecture, more receptive to new ideas, more demanding to some extent. The Centennial Exhibition in Philadelphia exposed visitors to new design trends in England, the art of Japan, and the Colonial arts of America itself, all suggesting something more relaxed and charming than the heavy yet rather stark kinds of architecture and furnishings with which they had been living.

The result was a time of experimentation in the big cities, particularly in Boston and Philadelphia, particularly in domestic architecture. In the office of Henry Hobson Richardson—which had moved to Brookline, a town wholly surrounded by Boston, in 1874—these experiments had been going on even before the Centennial, as they had in a few other offices.

A time was to come when the artistic literacy that the new architects were acquiring would turn all too easily into literalism, the mere imitation of historic styles once vital and evolving, but in the 1870s and 1880s the new sense of what American architecture might be was still fresh: architects were hunting down old forms, inventing new ones, examining the potential for color, texture, and pattern in fieldstone, brick, shingles, contrasting woods, terra cotta, even combinations like stucco inlaid with pebbles and broken glass. Modern attempts have been made to identify styles in this period: Queen Anne, so labeled in its time, which evoked Merrie England indiscriminately over a several-century range with a little of Old Japan thrown in; the Colonial Revival, our home-grown Queen Anne and with no more formal discipline at first than its English counterpart; Eastlake, a hard-looking style of chamfered and incised wood that had begun as a reform in furniture; the Shingle Style, with its sophisticated shaping of roofs and walls; Richardson Romanesque, emphasizing the mass and texture of masonry; and a variety of other manners, blurred at the edges, never labeled and probably never to be labeled.

Before H. H. Richardson presented his revised design—the first was too expensive—for Emmanuel Episcopal Church in Allegheny, there may have been homes reflecting this new architecture in Pittsburgh.

Romanesque was the prevailing style by the end of the 1880s, but other styles gave it some competition. James T. Steen's YMCA of 1883 (above left), at Penn Avenue and Seventh Street, was Queen Anne, more or less. Above right: Government buildings around 1880 or 1890 affected a chateau-like manner with Classical decoration, as shown by the Fourth Avenue Post Office. (Both gone.)

"Lyndhurst," the East End
home of Mrs. William Kendall
Thaw (gone), is shown here in
the mid-1920s after alterations.
The house was built in a
quasi-medieval manner in
brick in the late 1880s, possibly
to designs of a family friend,
Theophilus Parsons Chandler
of Philadelphia.

Emmanuel was begun in 1885, and Eastlake's *Hints on Household Taste*, the book that introduced the American public to some of the new ideas, had been published in Boston twelve years before. Yet this little church, the "Bake Oven" that still stands at Allegheny and West North Avenues, may have been the first completed building in which some of the new thinking appeared locally. It was very much a composition in masses of material, not lines on paper. On paper it looks a little stupid in fact; you have to see the rock-faced stone sills, the patterns in the brickwork bonding, the thickness of the window and entrance arches to get the effect. Yet this claim of priority for Emmanuel may be erroneous. Richardson's Jail, mentioned below, was completed in this same year of 1886. So was "Sunnyledge" in Shadyside, a house by Richardson's recent draftsmen Alexander Wadsworth Longfellow and Frank Ellis Alden that has as pure bloodlines as any building not initially sketched by the master himself can have.

Richardson, a sick man and a busy man, at first ignored the invitation in 1883 to compete for the County Buildings—the new Courthouse to replace John Chislett's on the same Grant Street site, which had burned the year before, and a new Jail. When he agreed he produced a plan of such lucidity that it won against even the well-rendered submission of Elijah Myers, a champion job-getter whose wins included the capitols of Michigan, Texas, and Colorado. The County Commissioners had specified soot-resistant granite for the street fronts, and Richardson claimed that he had detailed these fronts with Pittsburgh's special atmospheric problems in mind. Yet he used his customary rock-faced masonry with passages of the delicate Byzantine carving he enjoyed, and we can take his soot-repelling claim about as seriously as we do his rationalization of his superb tower—the last of a series of lovingly studied towers throughout his career—as the intake for a sort of air-conditioning system. (The specific design, one of a number sketched by Richardson, is said to have been adopted on the advice of the sculptor Augustus Saint-Gaudens.)

The rugged stonework, the delicate carving, the big round arches, and the steep, mountainous roof that rose above the walls had a prompt local impact. Richardson Romanesque, in the 1880s and later, was like lightning: you could only wonder over where it chose to strike. New York and Philadelphia, for instance, were relatively immune. Boston, Chicago, St. Paul, and many others were not, and Richardsonian influence even spread to Nordic Europe and the Netherlands. Pittsburgh

W. W. Boyington's submission for the Allegheny County Courthouse competition of 1883. With four corner pavilions, a tower, high roofs, and Classical ornament, it has basically the same compositional formula as that of the Fourth Avenue Post Office.

The Allegheny County Courthouse and Jail in the 1890s, before enlargement of the Jail. The broach spire of St. Peter's Episcopal Church rises to the left of the Courthouse, and the twin towers of St. Paul's Cathedral are just right of the Courthouse towers. The Supreme Court room in the Courthouse (below) shows an impressive assembly of carved oaken joinery beneath a ceiling of riveted iron box girders, rolled iron joists, and brick vaults.

Richardson Romanesque became virtually the high architectural style of Pittsburgh from the late 1880s into the mid-1890s. Even Theophilus Parsons Chandler, usually individualistic and Gothic, used it in the Third United Presbyterian Church on Shady Avenue (gone).

was very much under the influence of Richardson, not only because of the County Buildings but also because of the commercial buildings, academic buildings, railroad stations, and libraries he had designed for New England. Through the early 1890s little that was conspicuous in our architecture was being designed in a way wholly free from his influence. His successors, Shepley, Rutan & Coolidge, maintained his standards if not his creativity at the Shadyside Presbyterian Church. Longfellow, Alden & Harlow—Frank Alden from Richardson's office had been assigned to supervise construction of the County Buildings— adapted his Romanesque to a more classicizing form in the Duquesne Club downtown and went even further in the Carnegie Institute in Oakland. On the other hand, ordinary builders solemnly vulgarized Richardson Romanesque in the house rows of Shadyside and Allegheny with mock-towers and rugged stonework four inches thick.

And even a sandstone facing a few inches thick was an unnecessarily expensive way of getting a Richardsonian effect. As a store on Jacksonia Street shows, a builder could have his rugged masonry stamped out of sheet metal. Later, when Richardson's Romanesque was completely out of fashion, his characteristic textures were to live on in the rock-faced concrete block that forms many a backyard garage or rural house and underlies many a South Hills porch.

Romanesque designs varied in competence of course. James T. Steen's 1890 building on Perry Hilltop for the Western University of Pennsylvania (above) is rather well proportioned. The Shadyside car barn (below left) of the same year for the Duquesne Traction Company—later, the Duquesne Gardens—is, however, decidedly crude. (Both gone.) The slowly vanishing pressed-metal front at 613 Jacksonia Street on the North Side (below right) is a rarity these days.

Shepley, Rutan & Coolidge used Richardson Romanesque with more polish
than the previous examples reveal in the Freemason's Hall of 1888,
on Fifth Avenue downtown (gone).

*Left: Joseph Stillburg's
Exposition Buildings of 1889,
erected near the Point.
Below: Mechanical Hall
behind the Exposition Buildings
is very different: iron-and-glass
rationalism with fancy touches,
in the spirit of Paris exposition
architecture around the same
time. (Both gone.)*

Houses in Hazelwood dating from around 1890, showing mixtures of Romanesque, Shingle Style, and Colonial Revival forms. Below: Castles with front porches: the fantasy architecture of Alpha Terrace.

In ordinary middle-class house design, under the influence of Romanesque and the picturesque new domestic styles, Georgian simplicity was finally banished, at least from the street front. The basic shape of the house might perforce be a simple box if it were a unit of a close-packed row, but the front was available for picturesque surface treatment; bay windows dressed up to imitate towers, uninhabitably small turrets, false gables masking flat roofs, deep front porches, changes in facing material from level to level, and broad parlor windows with upper panels of stained glass distracted the mind from this essential plainness: witness the remarkable Alpha Terrace in East Liberty. Where there was space around the house the perimeter could be varied with towers, bays, porches, and wings, and the skyline varied with complicated roofs and bristling chimneys. At 5960 Alder Street in Shadyside stands a remarkably successful example from the 1890 period, but less happy examples could be found in many places. Inside such houses were complementary details, ingenious screens of profiled spindles, complexities of paneling, complicated mantelpieces.

Many people lived in the respectable anonymity suggested by these dwellings: little frame houses in McKeesport (above left), with cheap ornamentation and large parlor windows; solid row houses like these in Manchester (below); or after 1900, apartment houses like this one in Bellevue (above right).

Soho Curve, at the western end of Oakland, with cable cars of the Pittsburgh Traction Company; the cable line operated between 1888 and 1895. On the hill is the Ursuline Young Ladies' Academy, by Joseph Stillburg (gone).

There was a demand in this area for the kinds of houses in open settings that had caused the new domestic styles to be devised. The Pennsylvania and other railroads were proving favorable to the development of commuter suburbs, and two cable-car lines to East Liberty opened in 1888 to cut the fair-weather trip from nearly two hours by horsecar to perhaps half that time. Furthermore, with new industrial plants opening in the Monongahela and Turtle Creek Valleys, there was a demand for good executive housing not too far away. The most elegant housing seemed to accompany the steam railroad or flock, at a discreet distance, around heavy industry. Inclines did not have the magic touch, nor did the electric trolley, which was promoted by a fantastic number of local companies in the 1890s. These were the carriers of the classes with enough money to own their homes, but the homes were generally plain.

The picturesque architecture of the 1890 period was unlikely, locally, to be very creative or sensitive. The mannerisms and ornamental trademarks of Queen Anne and the other domestic manners of the day were imported and applied without much sense of how very effective a quite simple composition could be. On the other hand, they usually failed to see the potential of the Shingle Style as it was being developed on the Eastern seaboard, where a tall roof whose planes, folded, cut back, or extended like an origami in shingles, could effectively *be* the architecture of a house. A local and national vice throughout the Victorian period was the assumption that architecture consisted of ornamental features, and that their coordination in the overall composition of a building, a perception of where to put them and how many or few of them to use, was of lesser importance.

This was very conspicuously true in some of the tall buildings that rose in Pittsburgh. The business district of a Victorian city had reason to build tall. Commercial buildings on a downtown street like Liberty Avenue might be only twenty feet wide and one hundred feet deep, obtaining much of their light and all of their ventilation from the windows at the ends. The best space for sales, administration, manufacturing, or rental was that closest to the windows, and the height of many Liberty Avenue fronts shows that such space was in demand. Business offices communicated by face-to-face contact, messengers, telegraph companies whose wires made cat's cradles over the streets, and only eventually by telephone. There was reason, then, to concentrate business space in a small area of town, and thus to pile floor on floor. The Mid-Victorian city, however, held to a maximum level of five stories until the elevator became a practical means of taking people higher; when it did,

The Corliss Engine Shop of the Westinghouse Machine Company at East Pittsburgh: around 1900.

Left: The compositional problem of the tall building: the red-and-white Farmers Deposit National Bank (gone), an Alden & Harlow composition of 1902 with giant wall areas treated with a variety of expedients. Around 1970, the facades at Fifth Avenue and Wood Street of the Farmers Deposit National Bank were "slipcovered" in two-toned sheet metal. To its left is the First National Bank (gone), minus its mansard roof but doubled in height.

Top: The Hussey, or Chronicle-Telegraph, Building of the late 1880s (gone) is fantasy on the street front, drab common sense elsewhere. In a first-floor office, the anarchist Alexander Berkman shot Henry Clay Frick during the Homestead Strike of 1892. To its left is the Exchange National Bank.

the skyline rose with it. The metal skeleton frame, eliminating the need for space-consuming solid masonry, soon after gave the final encouragement. The Times Building of 1892, still on Fourth Avenue, may be the first skeleton-framed business building in the city.

Without much warning, architects who had been thinking of five stories of habitable space at the utmost were being required to design for ten, or fifteen, or twenty, or more. Sometimes a facade on a new building might be a high, narrow slice of the block front. Sometimes it was a square, an acre in extent. All too often, even in Chicago where the skyscraper was largely developed, an architect reacted by applying a little of this and a little of that to various levels of the facade and devising some

The Westinghouse Building of 1889 (gone) was of solid masonry. Later, the upper part was remodeled in a Classical manner. It stood at Ninth Street and Penn Avenue.

picturesque feature for its middle, its ends, or an exposed corner as a distraction from its great expanse and its level skyline.

This futile attempt to make architectural conversation all the way up and across inflated facades was countered in the 1890s by the more Classical conception of the tall building as a column, with a base, a shaft, and a capital. This was actually, despite its fatuous sound, a very sensible approach. The base would ordinarily be shops, banking rooms, restaurants, spaces that the public would visit in large numbers and that were often on two levels. Giving these a special expression was natural enough and would create a distinct composition that passers-by could easily take in. The shaft would contain the majority of the office spaces, manifested in an abstract pattern of windows of no special interest, and could be treated rather plainly. The capital would be a decorated terminal feature, speaking for the building as a whole, announcing it on the skyline, and would include the last few office stories, any service spaces at the top, and a climactic cornice.

As built, George B. Post's Park Building had great elaboration of detailing, much of which has now been removed. The colonnade, kneeling giants, and upper entablature that form the basic "capital" element have survived, but the recessed brick, iron, and terra-cotta panels have gone.

One early skeleton-framed building in Pittsburgh was the Carnegie Building, named in honor of Thomas, brother of Andrew Carnegie, and built between 1893 and 1895. Longfellow, Alden & Harlow approached the new problem calmly, applying the same simple Quattrocento style that they were currently using at the Carnegie Institute in Oakland. If the results were not an expression of steel they at least had visual unity. The same was true in the more florid Park Building of c. 1896, designed by the New York architect George Browne Post and still standing on Smithfield Street. After this there was a retrogression. The Peoples Savings Bank Building, the Farmers Deposit National Bank Building, the Arrott Building, the Standard Life Building, and a number of other downtown highrises of the 1900 period were spread over with decorative detailing, encouraged by the new availability of terra cotta, so that visual coherence was lost. The excesses went on for a few fitful years, but by 1905, simplicity—though not unadorned—had returned and would remain.

Two local offices were prominent toward the end of the nineteenth century. The firm created in 1886 by Alexander Wadsworth Longfellow (1854–1934), Frank Ellis Alden (1859–1908), and Alfred Branch Harlow

Longfellow, Alden & Harlow's Carnegie Building of 1895 (gone). The Frick Building was constructed to its left.

The Carnegie Institute as finished in 1895 shows a primarily Quattrocento style, simple in geometry but still round-arched, as successor to the prevalent Romanesque. The two-pavilioned section, in the right portion of the photograph below, survives in modified form in the present building, but all to the left has either yielded to or been buried in the expansion of 1907.

The Vandergrift Building of 1892 (gone) contained Longfellow, Alden & Harlow's own offices; it stood on Fourth Avenue.

(1857–1927) dominated the local architectural scene briefly but most impressively, with the Carnegie Institute, the Carnegie Libraries, the East Liberty Presbyterian Church that preceded that now extant, several of the Triangle's earliest skyscrapers, the Duquesne Club, and many mansions and near-mansions in the East End and the Sewickley area. Longfellow and Alden had been with Richardson, and brought to Pittsburgh a full-blooded Richardson Romanesque that is manifest at "Sunnyledge." Almost from the start, though, they were looking beyond Romanesque toward a lighter and more Classical manner, and while "Sunnyledge" and the McClure Avenue Presbyterian Church show the dense, succinct red-brick manner of Richardson's contemporary Emmanuel Church, the Conestoga Building and Bank of McKeesport show a sensuous use of the golden-brown, recently invented Roman brick, while the 1891 Carnegie Institute is Florentine Quattrocento (with Venetian campaniles) in pale-gray sandstone. The firm had an equally vigorous practice in Boston at the start, and an amicable split of 1896 left Longfellow in Boston, with Alden & Harlow gathering further momentum in Pittsburgh. The firm was at its peak in 1905, with the addition to the Carnegie Institute under construction and the Carnegie Libraries, skyscrapers, and mansions recently completed. Then, rather suddenly, it all fell away. Henry Hornbostel, the New Yorker who had just won the Carnegie Technical Schools competition, was chosen over Alden & Harlow for the Soldiers' and Sailors' Memorial, and Janssen &

The East Liberty Branch of the Carnegie Library of Pittsburgh (gone) was an Alden & Harlow building of 1903, of white terra cotta and bronze-colored brick.

Abbott, not yet established in 1905, was about to offer an abundance of institutional and residential architecture that had a less heavy effect and was more mellow in its choice of materials and more historically correct in its detailing. Alden & Harlow and the later Alden, Harlow & Jones, carried on quietly through the 1920s.

Their contemporary Frederick John Osterling (1865–1934) was quite as successful, though he seldom approached Longfellow, Alden & Harlow in polish. Artistically he was at his best in Romanesque, though he was uneven in all of the several styles he used. The steel-framed Times Building of 1892 is a handsome stone-faced Romanesque work on Fourth Avenue, yet his Morgue of 1901 is a stale dish of leftovers from the adjacent County Buildings. Called on to expand the Jail he repeated Richardson's detailing meticulously, then disgraced himself by proposing to heighten the Courthouse by two stories. His Bellefield Presbyterian Church of 1887 was Gothic of a very awkward sort, but the Union Arcade building of 1917 downtown is very suave indeed. The Washington County Courthouse and the Arrott Building in downtown Pittsburgh are heavy and rich—but not very coherent—Classicism, impossible to praise if judged with a coolly tasteful eye yet somehow so generous in their ornamentation as to be very likeable buildings. He, like Alden & Harlow, had his East End mansion commissions: "Greenlawn," the home of H. J. Heinz which was demolished in 1924, and the enlargement of "Clayton" for Henry Clay Frick.

Francis T. F. Lovejoy, a former Carnegie partner, commissioned Alden & Harlow to design "Edgehill" in 1903. The house was never finished, because Lovejoy went bankrupt, but its huge garage, completed, stood until 1966.

Two mansions, remodelings of the early 1890s by Osterling: "Greenlawn" (above), the house of Henry J. Heinz (gone), and "Clayton" (below), the house of Henry Clay Frick.

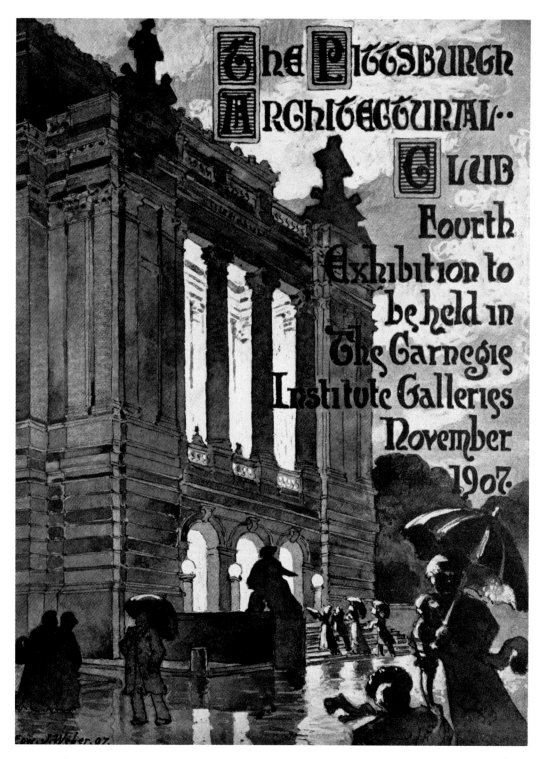

Drawing by Edward J. Weber for the title page of a Pittsburgh Architectural Club yearbook. The 1907 exhibition included many works of advanced architecture in the United States and Europe as well as conventional work by local Eclectics.

ECLECTICISM

The increase of architectural professionalism in the late nineteenth century had local results, as might be expected. The local chapter of the American Institute of Architects was founded in 1891 and the Pittsburgh Architectural Club in 1896, with formal incorporation in 1901. The Carnegie Technical Schools, founded in 1900 and today a component of Carnegie Mellon University, began teaching architecture in 1905, at a time when it had just begun to build for itself. From 1886 to 1919 a good local professional magazine, *The Builder*, was published. Beginning in 1916, the Pittsburgh Builders Exchange published the *Builders' Bulletin*, listing current building projects.

By 1900 the trend among American architects was decidedly away from experimentation in most building types. The knowledge of historic and contemporary architecture acquired through education here and abroad, through travel, through well-illustrated architectural publications, and through well-reproduced photographs encouraged architects to develop a sense of how the architecture they admired had really been composed: how its distinct elements were proportioned to each other; what materials, with what textures and in what colors, were employed; where decorative details were used, and to what extent. Mid-Victorian architecture now seemed mere barbarism, its originality the product of a totally deplorable ignorance.

Aside from a few architects who were consciously searching for a "modern" way of designing, American architects between 1890 and 1930 can be loosely categorized as Eclectics. Though vastly more informed, they retained the Victorian sense of a given architectural style as appropriate to certain institutions of society; indeed, with more styles in their repertoire, they surpassed the Victorians in this way. The old, freewheeling Classical styles, Italianate and Second Empire, were echoed in new all-purpose Classical manners which, like those of the Victorian period, were at the service of business, cultural institutions, and private wealth. This new Classical architecture came in shades of intensity, so to

speak: at one extreme, cool austerity in the Grecian Doric order; in the middle range, that quite often employed around 1900, overall compositional restraint but with passages of florid ornament; and at the opposite extreme, the Beaux-Arts style, a rather overfed version of the Second Empire, mansard roofs and all. A house or a secondary school was likely to be Georgian or Tudor; Georgian was another good multi-purpose style, and both styles had strong associations with Anglo-Saxon culture. A school at the college level, on the other hand, was often Classical. A church would normally be Gothic or Georgian. A non-traditional building—a factory, an automobile dealership, or a skyscraper for instance—might appear in any style, including one made up for the occasion. Theaters were likewise institutions at large among the styles, places where the architect's roaming fancy might inspire that of the audience.

The Pittsburgh & Lake Erie station at Stoops Ferry (gone), on the Ohio River, by Joseph L. Neal, c. 1916. This had Swiss-looking vergeboards but is basically style-less.

92

The Bank of Pittsburgh,
1895, by George B. Post of
New York (gone).

The interior of the Diamond
National Bank, c. 1910,
by MacClure & Spahr
(disappeared). The building,
now 100 Fifth Avenue, remains.

Fancy and plain in financial architecture: The Second National Bank of Allegheny (above left), c. 1900, on Federal Street, and Roy Hoffman's 1930-period remodeling of a printing plant for the Mellon Securities Company (above right). (Both gone.)

The long-disappeared fountain of the Kaufmann & Baer department store, in a view of c. 1927. The store, built c. 1913 to designs of Starrett & Van Vleck of New York, is better remembered by Pittsburghers as Gimbel's.

The Nixon Theatre opened in 1902 on Sixth Avenue, downtown. The design of Benjamin H. Marshall of Chicago, it was considered an exemplary playhouse, and was one of Pittsburgh's rare Beaux-Arts buildings (gone).

A knowing eye can usually place a building of the Eclectic period within its proper decade. There are differences in proportion, in the subordination of the details to the whole composition, in materials, colors, all kinds of subtle things, and it would be wrong to say that in the 1890s the experimentation of two decades was suddenly replaced by a knowing, dedicated imitativeness. Rather, it is as if the profession were self-consciously maturing, acquiring taste, learning to do things right at last, and thus coming closer in visual effect to the "precedents" of the past insofar as modern building programs and the increasingly versatile resources of the building industry permitted.

Thus, Queen Anne's touches of not-too-serious nostalgia disappeared and Tudor's more scholarly quaintness took their place. The Colonial Revival, which began as a cheerfully sloppy style, as loosely organized as the Queen Anne, turned in the 1890s into a style of boxy simplicity—

The Fort Wayne Station in Allegheny was the work of the Philadelphia architects Price & McLanahan. Like the Pittsburghers Kiehnel & Elliott, they could be innovative and imitative on varying occasions, and here the style is Dutch Renaissance (gone).

The Wabash Terminal, head-quarters of the foredoomed Wabash-Pittsburg Terminal Railway, was Pittsburgh's largest Beaux-Arts building. Now gone, it was completed in 1904 and Theodore C. Link of St. Louis was its architect.

though with big front windows of un-Georgian dimensions—under high roofs and with heavy trim imitated from the homes of the Yankee rich of a century before; then the florid detail contracted, the proportions became more carefully studied, and the tasteful and discreet Neo-Georgian emerged. The Shingle Style, at its best as much abstract sculpture as architecture, was tamed into a rustic manner in which the shingled wall surfaces became neutral backgrounds for decorative trim. Richardson Romanesque as a church style was out of date after the mid-

1890s, and a rather dumpy Gothic with bluntly pointed arches replaced it. This in turn was banished from high-style religion, along with pictorial stained glass, by Ralph Adams Cram and others who felt that it was simply not good enough. These architects produced a new, rather synthetic Gothic that was intended as a creative development rather than a mere imitation. Cram testified to his beliefs three times in Pittsburgh— Calvary Episcopal Church in Shadyside, Holy Rosary Roman Catholic Church in Homewood, and the East Liberty Presbyterian Church—and his partner Bertram Grosvenor Goodhue did so as well in the First Baptist Church in Oakland. All of these churches are standing today.

This trend toward a more polished architecture was accompanied locally by a radical change in architectural materials and colors. The Mid-Victorian city had been a place of bright red brick that soot would soon dim and pale-gray sandstone that would become a rich, velvety black—which might prove an improvement over the original color. Richardson's County Buildings, faced in pale pinkish-gray granite, not only towered over the low-built streets around but were startlingly light, and while most of the new Romanesque buildings were faced in sandstone, others too used gray granite; this dignified, soot-resistant stone was to have a certain popularity until 1910. Granite's major rival in downtown architecture from the late 1890s was terra cotta. Shaping granite, carving it especially, was an affair of brute force, while terra cotta, beginning as refined mud, could be modeled to the heart's desire. The 1890s, struggling with the tall-building problem, returning tentatively to Classical architecture after a period when Romantic picturesqueness had prevailed, welcomed such an ornamental resource. Until a little after 1900 the tendency was to use it floridly and in strong reds and ochres. Then, rather suddenly, the color sense changed, and by 1905 terra cotta was apt to be white or cream or some other nearly white hue, and kept on in this way until the end of its popularity in Pittsburgh for major buildings, around 1920. At that time, as part of a general trend toward restrained simplicity, the off-white, fine-grained limestone took its place in prestige architecture though terra cotta remained popular in ordinary commercial architecture into the 1930s. Sandstone declined rapidly in favor; its last great applications in the Pittsburgh area were in the Soldiers' and Sailors' Memorial in Oakland, designed in 1907, and the extension of the Carnegie Institute, finished in 1907; the original section had been designed for sandstone in 1891.

The Logan Armory (above left), by the William G. Wilkins Company, stood at O'Hara and Thackeray Streets in Oakland from 1911 until the 1960s. The Moose Building (above right), downtown on Penn Avenue, was terra-cotta fronted and a little behind the fashion for 1915, with its Beaux-Arts treatment (gone). The architect was Ulysses J. L. Peoples.

The Beaux-Arts style came to the United States early in the 1890s through the New Yorker Ernest Flagg, whose St. Margaret's Hospital stood in Lawrenceville (gone).

The 1905 entrance to Luna Park, at Baum Boulevard and Craig Street, was routinely Classical beneath its fantastic cresting (gone).

This modest shelter on Baum Boulevard, built in 1913, is claimed as the first drive-in gasoline station in the world (gone).

By 1900 brick was no longer necessarily a bright-red material, hard-surfaced and set in thin joints of white mortar. The mortar itself might be dyed red, black, or even purple, and the brick was available or becoming available in buff, golden-brown, warm gray, cream, or white. The standard brick dimension of about eight inches long by about a third as much high was sometimes replaced, from 1890, by brick of the more "Roman" dimensions of twelve by one-and-a-half inches or so, close-laid and typically golden-brown. Toward 1910 "tapestry" brick came on the market, artificially roughened and offered in a large variety of watercolor shades so that a house wall needed no longer appear as a hard, unyielding mass but could become a pictorial element matching the grass and the informal plantings of flowers from which it rose. Around 1910, too, raked mortar joints, outlining the individual bricks, had a vogue; or the mortar itself might be thick, pebbly, slopping out.

"Grandview," the Phipps-Braun house on Warwick Terrace in Squirrel Hill, was begun in 1901 to designs by J. Edward Keirn (gone). Opposite are two of its interiors.

A simple account of what was going on in the composition of polite architecture, in the Pittsburgh area as elsewhere in the United States, between say 1900 and 1940 is apt to be a distortion. The general trend in public and business architecture was toward more interesting massing in large buildings, with carefully designed detailing but less of it and with complete subordination to the whole design. The effect was lighter, more coordinated, more instantly comprehensible. In houses, things were less consistent. The drop-dead mansion with its cornices and porticoes yielded to less formal, more picturesque houses that sometimes had sweet simplicity, sometimes were English or French in a manorial sort of way, and sometimes lost all reason in their displays of convulsive brickwork and irregular roof slates hanging on for dear life. The Depression seems to have put a stop to these excesses, yet in the 1930s large, rambling, quasi-additive houses, suggesting changes over time, were still built around Sewickley.

At the end of the 1920s a way of designing that is sometimes vaguely called Moderne began to appear in the Pittsburgh area. There had been free styles earlier in the century of course, ad hoc combinations of decorative forms invented for specific projects like Highland Towers in Shadyside or the Central Turnverein in Oakland; but Moderne was a less personal, less temporary manner, evolved since the early 1920s by a

"Colonial" houses of c. 1900 on Baum Boulevard, photographed in 1935.

number of architects. Stylistic labels are still uncertain—as is often the case, the styles were named after they passed into history—but it is possible to speak of two varieties of Moderne: Art Deco and Modernistic. Art Deco—the term was invented in the 1960s—is the earlier and more sensuous variety, delicately ornamented, sumptuous in its materials, using color as an expressive means. Modernistic on the other hand is simpler, more geometrical in its form, less detailed or hardly detailed at all, and sober in its color scheme. On this basis of distinction between the two styles, the Koppers Building in downtown Pittsburgh, with its external chateau roof, its interior decorative bronzework and colorful veined marbles, is Art Deco, while the Western State Psychiatric Hospital in Oakland, blocky and full of plain, unrelieved verticals, is Modernistic.

Both styles were additions to the repertoire of the Eclectics rather than radical approaches to twentieth-century architecture such as the Modernists were attempting. Art Deco and Modernistic dressed the steel frame of the skyscraper rather than expressed it, imposing verticals on what was really a cage of columns and girders framing horizontal rectangles, and their appeal was in the feeling of Progress their non-traditional

Two works of D. H. Burnham & Co. (now gone) in Pittsburgh: the Exposition Buildings of 1901 at the Point (above left), and the portion of the First National Bank (above right) built in 1909. In 1912 it was heightened into a twenty-six-story skyscraper.

detailing evoked. For a large philistine part of the public in the Eclectic period, architecture was an affair of manners and dress, and for a business building, a smart shop, or a festive interior like the Joseph Urban Room at the William Penn Hotel in downtown Pittsburgh, Moderne was permissible wear. It was not encouraged for domestic use, and Swan Acres, built in the late 1930s in Ross Township, was quite unusual for the time in its departures from tradition.

Several architectural offices were of great importance locally in the Eclectic period. As it happens, the two that come first chronologically were in other cities.

D. H. Burnham & Co. of Chicago was a very large office for its time, famous and influential. Daniel Hudson Burnham (1846–1912), its principal, was not so much an architect as a master organizer. Given an area of swampy shore by Lake Michigan, he had realized the plans for the World's Columbian Exposition of 1893 in all their enormous detail. He devised master plans for Washington, D.C., Chicago, San Francisco, and Manila. Furthermore, his office specialized in business buildings, and between 1898 and 1910 it provided Pittsburgh with the present Union Station, the Frick Building, McCreery's department store (now 300 Sixth Avenue), the Frick Annex (now the Allegheny Building), the Oliver Building, the Highland Building in East Liberty, and eleven others. This was a large body of work, much of it very conspicuous, and the evolution of Pittsburgh business architecture toward lightness and simplicity was in part the evolution of design in Burnham's own office.

Henry Hornbostel (1867-1961) was a partner in the New York firm
of Palmer & Hornbostel when he won the 1904 competition for the
master plan of the Carnegie Technical Schools. With this excellent start
he proceeded, for the next two decades, to establish almost an architectural domain in an Oakland-Shadyside area a mile across. In 1906 he
began Rodef Shalom Temple on Fifth Avenue, using some of the earliest
polychrome terra cotta. In 1907 he won the Soldiers' and Sailors'
Memorial competition. In 1908 he won the competition for the new
Schenley Farms campus of the Western University of Pennsylvania
(immediately renamed the University of Pittsburgh). In 1915 he designed
the U.S. Bureau of Mines building, in 1922 the Schenley Apartments,
in 1923 the University Club, all in Oakland, and in 1925 the German
Evangelical Protestant Church downtown. He was a collaborator, and
quite possibly the dominant one, on designs for the Webster Hall hotel
in Oakland and the City-County Building and Grant Building downtown. In New York, he was architect for the Manhattan, Williamsburg,
Queensboro, and Hell Gate Bridges, all but the first realized to his plans
and all but the Williamsburg in connection with the engineer Gustav
Lindenthal, who had designed Pittsburgh's third and present Smithfield
Street Bridge, that of 1883.

A successful man, then, and a colorful one in dress and conduct,
Hornbostel was an architect in the Romantic vein even as Frank Lloyd

*The Liberty Theatre of 1915
had a terra-cotta facade by
Henry Hornbostel (gone).*

*Hornbostel's winning design of
1908 for the Oakland campus
of the Western University of
Pennsylvania (above). This was
abortive, but his College of Fine
Arts interior at Carnegie Tech
(right) was realized.*

A rendering of Willo'mound, an unrealized project by Scheibler from 1911 (above). A paired spandrel panel to the left shows much the same toadstool ornament used earlier in Old Heidelberg.

A doorway from Scheibler's Minnetonka Building in Shadyside; the limestone has since been painted.

Wright was to be. His style tended to be very loosely Classical, though in general effect rather than detail, with a freshness of imagination that gives it the cheerful pompousness of Beaux-Arts without the Beaux-Arts vice of overloading the essential fabric of a building. Much remains in the Oakland-Shadyside area to show the genial power of Hornbostel's work, although his Carnegie Tech plan was never wholly realized and one building on the Pitt campus, State Hall built in 1909, has been lost out of the very few erected.

A native architect, Frederick Gustavus Scheibler, Jr. (1872–1958), remains our outstanding Modernist. Yet "Modernist" has to be qualified. He was rather like the better-known San Franciscan Bernard Maybeck, original yet committed to no theory, capable of simple but well-reasoned design yet capable too of being whimsical, even pixyish, at times. Whether he wanted it that way or not, his work consisted almost wholly of modest East End houses and apartment buildings. His grandest works were only medium-sized: the simple but finely crafted Highland Towers on the edge of Shadyside (sixteen units) and the picturesque Old Heidelberg near the eastern border of the city (twelve units as originally built). He was not a complete original: his designs reflect progressive trends in the British Isles and Central Europe, and also work by Frank Lloyd Wright and other Prairie School architects who were concerned with geometry in the composition and decoration of buildings. Yet he was not following in their footsteps; he was walking alongside, perhaps one pace behind.

Two other Pittsburgh architectural offices had something of the same originality. One was that of Titus de Bobula (1878–1961), who around

108

Above: A design for a Greek Catholic church by de Bobula, c. 1905. Above right: The Church of the Holy Ghost (Greek Catholic). Now gone, this stood on Doerr (formerly Sterling) Street, close to the Ohio River, opposite the Western State Penitentiary. In the background are the chimneys of the Standard Sanitary Manufacturing Company.

1905 produced a series of remarkable designs for churches and other buildings, influenced most likely by the Floreale, the rather chunky Italian version of Art Nouveau. The most prominent de Bobula designs executed were St. John's Byzantine Catholic Cathedral and Rectory in Munhall, the First Hungarian Reformed Church in Hazelwood, and the St. Peter and St. Paul Ukrainian Orthodox Greek Catholic Church in Carnegie. In addition, an interesting Greek Catholic church in Woods Run, seen in an old photograph, has very much a de Bobula look. Kiehnel & Elliott, though by no means fully committed Modernists, were broadly Eclectic enough to depart from tradition in at least a little of their work; the Central Turnverein building, at O'Hara and Thackeray Streets, is certainly non-traditional, mildly influenced by the Modernism of Chicago. The handsome Greenfield Elementary School, in the neighborhood of that name, has again a progressive Chicagoan look, more intelligent than any mere imitation.

Benno Janssen (1874–1964) was not basically an original architect, but he was a highly intelligent one: not a creator but a first-rate appreciator. His two partnerships, Janssen & Abbott (1906) and later

Janssen & Cocken (1922), displayed a sensitivity and polish in any style they adopted that no out-of-town office could have surpassed, and in institutional, business, and domestic architecture they did very well from the mid-1900s through the early 1930s. The Janssen offices had a tendency to use either a Classical style, as they did in a series of institutional buildings in Oakland from the Pittsburgh Athletic Association, begun in 1909, through the Mellon Institute, begun in 1931, or a more Romantic range of manners that were modeled, with increasing freedom, on English and French rural architecture. An early house at Schenley Farms, designed around 1907, is not especially better than other houses of the time in its application of half-timbering and other standard domestic motifs, but in the 1920s, at the Longue Vue country club in Penn Hills and "La Tourelle," the Fox Chapel home of Edgar J. Kaufmann, specific styles were sublimated into generalized Old World expressions, and the carefully chosen materials, notably fieldstone, were displayed unhelped and unhindered by large amounts of decorative detailing.

Like most Eclectics, Janssen ventured into other styles from time to time. In 1925 the Shelton Hotel in New York, a red-brick Romanesque mass by Arthur Loomis Harmon that terminated effectively without the use of cornices or pinnacles, seemed to show a new solution to the tall-building problem, and Janssen emulated its redness, its closed character,

Janssen & Cocken's 1930 remodeling of the ground floor (disappeared) of Kaufmann's, with murals by Boardman Robinson.

Left: The Oakland Civic Center in the early 1930s, with the Schenley Farms residential development in the upper middle right portion of the photograph. The land Franklin Nicola sold to the University of Pittsburgh lies between Schenley Farms and the Pitt Stadium. The top of the Cathedral of Learning has yet to assume its final form, the Foster Memorial and Heinz Chapel have not been begun, and the Mellon Institute is still without its columns.

and its slightly joggled skyline in the Keystone Athletic Club—now the dormitory of Point Park College—and the annex to the Duquesne Club, both in downtown Pittsburgh. Called on to remodel the ground-floor sales area of Kaufmann's department store in 1930, he even used Modernistic black glass and silvery metalwork to set off the simple shapes and mild coloration of a mural group by Boardman Robinson.

Franklin Felix Nicola (1859–1938) was not an architect, but his Bellefield and Schenley Farms development companies transformed a large area in Oakland and provided the setting for much of the city's best architecture. In 1897, much of the land close to the newly completed Carnegie Institute was still rural, owned by the Schenley and O'Hara estates. Close to the narrow St. Pierre Ravine, over which the entrance to Schenley Park passed, Nicola purchased a cornfield. In 1899 the Hotel Schenley, glamorous and set in landscaped grounds, was in operation on the site. This was the time of the City Beautiful movement, and Nicola soon developed the vision of a new Civic Center on the Oakland plateau, away from downtown, away from the riverside industry, gathering institutions in an impressive architectural group and with a select residential neighborhood near by. In 1905 he bought 103 acres of land from the Schenley estate and adjacent rising land from the O'Haras and began to

Forbes Field (gone), shortly after its opening in 1909.

sell it with outstanding success. The Western University of Pennsylvania bought the thirty-two-acre hillside site for which Hornbostel was named architect in 1908; the County built the Soldiers' and Sailors' Memorial; and the Pittsburgh Athletic Association, the Masons, the Shriners, the University Club, and several other institutions and businesses built on Nicola land. One of the most important structures was Forbes Field, the now-gone baseball stadium of 1909; the players, like the performers who sang, soloed, and acted at the Shriners' Syria Mosque, stayed at the Hotel Schenley.

The Schenley Farms residential development, tree-planted, without utility poles, and featuring one-of-a-kind houses built to very high standards, was so successful that in 1915 Nicola was able to solicit, and receive, a bookful of letters from the area's very solid residents praising the beauty and the order of their neighborhood.

Syria Mosque, built in 1915 to designs by Huehl, Schmidt & Holmes of Chicago, stood on Bigelow Boulevard north of Fifth Avenue in Oakland. It was demolished in 1991.

In 1922 the Bellefield Company began construction of the 235-suite Schenley Apartments beside the hotel; these opened the next year, and included Nicola's own spacious apartment. A conspicuous void in his holdings was Frick Acres, overlooked by the hotel, but when the University of Pittsburgh gave up on its hillside plan and began the absurd but beautiful Cathedral of Learning, 535 feet high, in the middle of the land, the Civic Center got a focus beyond all anticipation. After the 1920s, trouble came for Nicola. In 1933 he was in litigation with the County over the sale of a Fifth Avenue block, just east of the Masonic Temple, for a new Town Hall; in fact, the lot was not built on until the 1950s. When Nicola died in 1938, he had a little over two thousand dollars.

The firm of Charles T. Ingham and William Boyd, Sr. (1882–1947), like the Janssen firms, was an intelligent office, not creative but tasteful. The Historical Society of Western Pennsylvania building of 1912 in Schenley Farms was delicate Italian Renaissance, the nearby Board of Education building gracious High Renaissance, and the Buhl Planetarium of 1939 on the North Side a work in the compromise Classicism of the time that attempted to combine tradition and modernity. Chatham Village on Mount Washington shows Ingham & Boyd using a quasi-Georgian style, much less radical than the site plan designed by Clarence S. Stein and Henry Wright of New York, but appropriate to its purpose of creating a neighborhood of good homes.

The Arrott house in Shadyside, 1928, by Ingham & Boyd.

Three designs for the Catholic Church by Pittsburghers: St. Agnes' Church (above left), Cleveland, by John T. Comes, c. 1915 (gone); entrance to Synod Hall, St. Paul's Cathedral, Oakland (above right), 1914, by Edward J. Weber; design for a building in Oakland at Mount Mercy Academy (left), c. 1925, by Carlton Strong.

Three Pittsburgh architects who worked primarily for the Catholic Church attained more than local distinction, bringing to its religious and institutional architecture a refinement comparable to that which Ralph Adams Cram and Bertram Grosvenor Goodhue had recently brought to Protestant architecture. John Theodore Comes (1879–1922) was the first in practice, and executed a number of parish churches in this area, as well as elsewhere. Thomas Carlton Strong (1869–1931) moved his practice from New York to Pittsburgh in 1906, and made his early reputation here as designer of the Rittenhouse Hotel in East Liberty and Bellefield Dwellings in Oakland. But soon he turned to Catholic church and educational architecture, and created buildings in both genres that were conspicuously sited. Carlton Strong is best known for Sacred Heart Church in Shadyside, but those who have attended Duquesne University, Carlow College, or St. Vincent's Seminary in Latrobe will have their own memories of Carlton Strong's architecture. Edward Joseph Weber (1877–1968) was perhaps the most fanciful of the three, as the designs of the Synod Hall of St. Paul's Cathedral, Central Catholic High School, and St. Colman's School in Turtle Creek attest. In his book of 1927, *Catholic Ecclesiology*, Weber explored the elements and furnishings of a church, with 122 pictures of his own designs as examples.

Finally, Stanley Lawson Roush (1885–1946) deserves mention. As first City, then from 1924 County, Architect, he was an accompanist more often than a soloist, providing architectural detail for bridge projects and other public works, yet always with a sensitive eye. In the

Mount Washington (P. J. McArdle) Roadway bridge, 1928, by Roush (gone). Lamp post for the Larimer Avenue Bridge (c. 1914) by Roush (gone).

portals of the Armstrong Tunnel, uptown, and the Corliss Street Tunnel in Esplen he designed with power; but when he had the not-very-thankful task of lowering the entrances of the Courthouse he supplied new doorframes in a bland 1920s Romanesque that neither rivaled Richardson's architecture nor showed fear of it. His adjacent County Office Building was never built to the full anticipated height, but what was built is creditable. The exterior expresses masonry, not steel, and the lobby inside is cinematic historical romance, but it is nonetheless a very pleasant building to look at.

The First World War had the usual deadening effect of war on culture, and left the Pittsburgh Architectural Club in a state of torpor. Before the war the P.A.C., like other American architectural clubs, had held exhibitions of current local work and work of interest from elsewhere, and had published well-illustrated, historically valuable exhibition catalogues that were also club yearbooks. These were never resumed after the war, but in 1920 *The Charette* began publication with the explicit purpose of bringing the P.A.C. back to life, and continued as its organ until 1971. It began modestly—for most of 1923 it did not publish at all—but took on new features and ended as a slick publication, well-illustrated, full of professional news, recording from 1956 the region's architectural history through the writings of James D. Van Trump.

A Charette *cover, showing a side entrance of the Allegheny County Courthouse after the lowering of the Hump but before alterations in 1923 filled in the upper part of the archway.*

Old volumes of *Charette* offer a way of taking the pulse of the profession a half-century ago. Members' new work went tactfully unmentioned except for an occasional word of praise, but there were occasional controversies over the work of out-of-towners: the Cathedral of Learning for instance, and a Squirrel Hill house by Goodhue. Movies and even music were reviewed, professional advice given, and an interest in old Western Pennsylvania architecture revealed in both words and sketches. A new club headquarters, opened on Liberty Avenue in 1927, was touted as a lunch place. Toward 1930 the question of "modern" architecture—is there such a thing, should there be such a thing, what form should it take?—broke out from time to time. Then, the Depression. This was the age of the Babbitts, the joiners who knew the occasions for solemnity but otherwise went in for heavy kidding around; and as architects lost work the frequent facetiousness of *Charette's* prose, supplemented by doggerel verse, became more resolute. The journal took on a more social tone, reporting parties and picnics of architects who had not much else to do but spoiling the note of fun in

The Myler house in Squirrel Hill provoked discussion in Charette in 1921. Bertram Grosvenor Goodhue of New York, one of the country's star architects, had the task of building a large double house, and four local critics felt that the contrivedly picturesque result was a not-very-good work of a great designer. Later the house was divided as shown here.

brief passages that urged architects to pay at least part of their dues or that announced meetings of unemployed draftsmen.

Architects of that time have looked back with some nostalgia. From fretting over large commissions that were going out of town, from contemplating an Architects' Building in 1928, they were reduced to consoling each other in misfortune, and in misery they found a new companionship. It was a relief though in 1932, when the Buhl Foundation made a grant for the Western Pennsylvania Architectural Survey that gave some of them jobs and made possible a historical undertaking many architects had long thought important. Under the direction of Charles Morse Stotz, a devoted student of early Western Pennsylvania architecture, the Survey team recorded architecture before 1860 through field notes and the fine draftsmanship of the period. Much of the photography was by Luke Swank, the self-taught Johnstowner who had recently become famous. In the Survey book of 1936, *The Early Architecture of Western Pennsylvania*, Stotz praises Swank's dedication to the work.

With the Depression, Eclecticism ended as a really effective movement in local architecture; the resumption of widespread building activity after fifteen years of depression and war found Modernism triumphant in a community dedicated to self-renewal.

An old house near the Point, sketched by Stotz in the early 1930s. A note says, "Nice chimneys, well detailed shutters."

The Triangle in June 1906, from Union Station, with Liberty Avenue to the right. The city is evolving in a piecemeal way. The skyline is rising, but crudities of the past survive as well. The freight station in the foreground, for instance, will occupy the northern end of Grant Street until 1929.

THE SEARCH
FOR ORDER

We last paused in 1850 for an overview of Allegheny County, just before important industrial and urban development took place. Here is another pause, and the year is 1907. In 1907, among other things:

The Pittsburgh Survey, sponsored by the Charities Publication Committee in New York and concerned local citizens, and largely financed by the Russell Sage Foundation, examined the Pittsburgh way of life. Most of the published findings made very unpleasant reading.

A reluctant city of Allegheny (1900 population 130,000) was annexed by Pittsburgh (322,000), and its old areas became the North Side. The State Legislature had ordained that a majority of the combined vote should determine the annexation issue.

The old Union Bridge between the Point and Allegheny came down, to the relief of steamboat operators. However, the Sixteenth and Forty-third Street Bridges remained as low-built wooden covered bridges crossing the Allegheny River, the latter until 1924.

In 1911, the heart of Allegheny had become the heart of the North Side of Pittsburgh. Ober Park is in the foreground, with the Carnegie Library beyond. Urban renewal has replaced the park these days with a sort of concrete pit, but the exterior of the Library has survived.

*Right: Low bridge clearances
inhibited navigation on the
Allegheny River, as the
confrontation in 1914 of
the towboat* Duquesne *with
the Sixth Street Bridge
of 1892 makes clear.
Below: The Forty-third Street
Bridge of 1870, a wooden
covered bridge, crossed the
Allegheny until 1924.*

The expanded Carnegie Institute was rededicated, and Pittsburgh acquired three sizeable parks: a government donation of land from the Arsenal, long a dead letter, in Lawrenceville, and the two major Allegheny parks, the Commons of 1869 and Riverview Park of 1894.

The Pittsburgh filter beds were about to start operation near Aspinwall. Heretofore, the municipal water had been totally untreated, and every well-equipped house had its own filter. As treated water came to successive parts of the city, the incidence of typhoid, the nation's highest, declined dramatically.

Downtown Pittsburgh and the lower part of Allegheny were flooded. The Chamber of Commerce appointed a Flood Commission to study the problem and make recommendations, but the 1936 flood was to be even worse, six feet high in Wood Street.

The Crowning of Labor *panel from John White Alexander's* Apotheosis of Pittsburgh *murals, in the Carnegie Institute extension opened in 1907.*

Since 1850: What had been a handful of close but separate industrial towns, surrounded by farms, woods, and villages, had changed notably. Homestead, Braddock, Swissvale, and the little boroughs of the Turtle Creek Valley had come into being or been altered out of recognition to serve heavy industry. Iron was smelted in and near Pittsburgh, and steel, a specialty commodity in 1850, was now the principal product. Important, too, were glass, electrical equipment, and increasingly, aluminum, with coal, coke, and natural gas as industrial fuels. Aside from glass and coal, none of these commodities had been industrially significant in the county in 1850. Coal mining had increased as a local industry because of the use of coke in iron smelting and the demands of railroads, steamboats, and powerhouses. Mine structures and "patches," miners' settlements of small uniform houses, could be found in many scattered parts of the county where there had once been only farms. Petroleum had come and gone, but during the Oil Boom of the 1860s and even later, Pittsburgh had been an oil-refining center.

The Baltimore & Ohio Railroad had entered Pittsburgh in 1871, and the Pittsburgh & Lake Erie Railroad in 1879, to break the near-monopoly of the Pennsylvania Railroad and its system of leased trackage; the foredoomed Wabash-Pittsburg Terminal Railway had followed in 1904. All four railroads had impressive passenger stations in or near the Triangle, and the Pennsylvania had built a handsome station at East Liberty in 1906.

The Mission Pumping Station of the Pittsburgh waterworks, built on the South Side slopes in 1912. This raised fourteen million gallons a day to storage tanks on the hilltop. (Chimney gone, buildings much remodeled.)

Pumping engines at the Brilliant Station, by the Allegheny River in Lemington, in a photograph of 1908.

Left: Frank Furness' Baltimore & Ohio Station of 1887 (gone) stood by the downtown approach to the Smithfield Street Bridge. Below: A 1926 view shows the Pittsburgh & Lake Erie Station, at the opposite end of the Smithfield Street Bridge, as intensely built up. The 700-foot trainshed by the Monongahela River, the shelter over the bridge approach, and the cantilever bridge of the Wabash-Pittsburg Terminal Railway to the left have all gone.

Transportation glories now gone. Above: the Pittsburgh & Cincinnati packet Virginia *(1890-c. 1928) turns beneath the Wabash Bridge (1904-48). In the background is Mount Washington, with the Pittsburgh & Lake Erie Station. The* Virginia, *a limber wooden boat, was draped over the contours of a cornfield by a subsiding flood in 1910, but eventually returned to the river. Below: East Liberty Station, shown here around 1915, was the last stop before Pittsburgh for Pennsylvania expresses from the east.*

On the rivers, packet service was dwindling, though it would survive until the early 1930s. Push towing was thriving, and the Monongahela River Consolidated Coal and Coke Company (the "Combine") owned two-thirds of all the tonnage of any kind on the whole Western River system. On land the Pittsburgh Railways Company had restored order after the trolley mania of the 1890s, which had seen the incorporation of over 200 companies in and around Pittsburgh. The South Hills Tunnel, opened in 1904, had allowed the Pittsburgh Railways Company to spread its tracks over the city's hilltop neighborhoods south of the Monongahela and start development of suburbs miles away to the south. The West Penn system, beginning in 1904, was building and buying up interurban trolley lines, and in this year of 1907 two interurban lines from Pittsburgh to Butler and New Castle opened, giving new communications to the rural areas of the North Hills. The trolley gave ordinary people a mobility they had not had before, and entrepreneurs, some of them trolley-company owners, hastened to give them destinations: the Highland Park Zoo was endowed with the trolley-riding public in mind; Kennywood Park and other amusement parks lured them; so did such diverse developments along the right-of-way as camp-meeting grounds and dance halls. Macadam, plank, and dirt roads gave private traffic communications of mixed quality, but the automobile was beginning to be taken seriously enough to create a demand for better routes and surfaces.

Despite its reputation for grim endeavor, Allegheny County had some extremely pleasant quarters. Sewickley, down the Ohio River, had developed from a farm village to a comfortable riverside suburb, with its neighbors Edgeworth, Osborne, and increasingly, Sewickley Heights attaining not only comfort but elegance. Ridge Avenue on the North Side, the old home of wealth, was to receive a few more great houses—the last in 1911—and the other Millionaire's Row, on Fifth Avenue in Shadyside, had good years ahead of it as well. Schenley Farms was building, Shadyside was fairly well built-up already, and the remainder of the sprawling East End was under development. The Pennsylvania Railroad, until the hills of the Monongahela Valley came in sight, passed through one comfortable neighborhood after another on its way to Philadelphia.

The remainder of the Pennsylvania's eastward route in Allegheny County was bleak. Henry L. Mencken, in "The Libido for the Ugly" (1926), wrote, "From East Liberty to Greensburg…there was not one [house] in sight from the train that did not insult and lacerate the eye." Most of the Pittsburgh Survey had to do with conditions of work and life

Above: The Monongahela Wharf, c. 1928, more parking lot than freight-transfer facility at the time. The nearer packet appears to be the Homer Smith, *so called up to 1928, while in the background there is no sign of the first Point Bridge that lasted into 1927. Right: This is the downtown end of the Smithfield Street Bridge in the early 1890s. The bridge has been widened to the right to accommodate streetcars (1891). The Fourth Avenue Post Office up ahead seems externally complete (1891), as are the Courthouse (1888) and the B&O Station in the foreground (1887). But the Coal Exchange remains, with no clearance yet for the House Building (1902).*

in such a setting: "the incredible amount of overwork by everybody, reaching its extreme in the twelve-hour shift for seven days a week in the steel mills and the railway switchyards"; the conclusion that "never before has a great community applied what it had so meagerly to the rational purposes of human life."

There was grandeur in the fires of the steelworks, the organ tone of the river steamboat whistle, the exhaust beat of the laboring locomotive, but there was also billowing smoke from furnaces, steamboats, locomotives, and domestic fires in quantities hard to conceive these days. The coke ovens gave off a powerful rotten-egg stench. The rivers ran with the raw sewage, industrial wastes, and mine runoff that gave water-drinking its air of suicide. Workers, quite often unskilled, inarticulate in English, and generally in a poor or non-existent bargaining position, crowded together in shabby houses and shanties with whatever vermin cared to join them. The laborers found consolation, and a little color in their lives, in churches where their languages were spoken and to which they contributed money, even work, for construction and decoration. Above the gray little houses rose the Catholic spires and the Orthodox onion domes as visual relief from the drabness of the streets and a reminder of something more meaningful than the daily grind.

Above: Trash burning on the Monongahela Wharf, c. 1910. Across the river, where Station Square now is, is the Clinton Iron & Steel Company. To the right of its plumes of smoke and steam is the Clinton Furnace, coke-fired, built in 1859 as the first successful blast furnace in the immediate Pittsburgh area.

Opposite: A view from Union Station over the Strip on the "clear" afternoon of July 20, 1906. The view is northwesterly toward the Shoenberger Works of the American Steel and Wire Company. Faintly visible beyond, over the Allegheny River, is the old, wooden Sixteenth Street Bridge.

VIEW N.W. FROM MIDDLE POINT OF UNION STATION
EAST END. WEATHER CLEAR-VARIABLE WIND
JULY 20, 1906. 2:06 P.M.   Nº 28

The state of things on Sylvan Avenue, in Hazelwood, in 1907.

La Porte Street, in Penn Hills, in 1929.

Duplexes on Forward Avenue,
in Squirrel Hill, in 1929.

Thus it was that Pittsburgh and its county plodded through the first half of the twentieth century without much coherent, over-all improvement. There *were* improvements in detail, many of them: some large and splendid, some minute but welcome. Franklin Nicola's growing Civic Center in Oakland was complemented by the Cathedral of Learning, the Heinz Chapel, and palatial institutional buildings in the adjoining Bellefield area, while the old villas on the Oakland hillside yielded to a widespread Medical Center associated with the University of Pittsburgh. Downtown the skyline continued to rise, and the ziggurat that topped the 582-foot Gulf Building in 1932 was to dominate the Triangle for thirty-eight years. Churches such as Calvary Episcopal and East Liberty Presbyterian, residential constructions such as Chatham Village and the Schenley Apartments, gave some Pittsburghers at least an experience of light and gracious places such as the Victorian city had not known. In Squirrel Hill and the East End neighborhoods, Colonial, Tudor, and houses of a more rustic character filled up the lots into which old farms and woods had been divided, each with its entourage of trees, hedges, flowers, and lawns. The South Hills was now fully open to settlement, its absolute dependency on the trolley lines ended with the opening of the Liberty Tubes in 1924 and the Liberty Bridge in 1928. Here and there a monument was erected, a new and handsome bridge replaced an old, awkward one, or a stately row of Lombardy poplars dignified a property.

A house in Dorseyville, O'Hara Township, built in the late 1920s from a kit supplied by Sears Roebuck.

The south end of the Liberty Tubes in 1932.

133

A North Side scene of the 1930s, photographed by Luke Swank.

Yet the county as a whole was quietly aging in its building stock and casual as ever in its infrastructure. Pittsburgh especially appeared as a casual city, with its scattered bursts of magnificence amid so much that seemed a matter of chance. If a tree were to be its symbol, the elegant poplar was less appropriate than the ungainly but vital ailanthus, which grew wherever a little earth was left undisturbed. Hillside streets might progress from Belgian block to dirt to wild nature in a hundred yards, and off such streets the crazy wooden steps, or their concrete replacements, threaded together precariously sited houses, with their tumbledown sheds and fences. Wooden poles, hung with electric cables like strangling jungle vines, extended steel arms that held lightbulbs over the intersections of streets fantastically named in an effort to give them identities. Often, in a neighborhood, there was an illusion that time had stopped in 1900 or 1920; once completed, the neighborhoods seemed to be immutable. In fact, though, they *were* changing. Masonry was getting dirty. Paint was darkening, cracking, then flaking away. Rotted porch posts were being replaced by brick piers, and drop siding was being covered by Insulbric. Where once there were trimmed hedges, the ailanthus was growing.

The industrial presence was still strong, and to be unaware of it was merely to have succeeded, for a time, in escaping it. The audience of an "Evening in Vienna" concert in Syria Mosque emerged to the faint sulphur smell of coal smoke and the flicker of Bessemer fires reflected off the clouds. The hoarse whistles of steam locomotives and towboats could be heard in the night. The grandeur and the gloom had a compelling effect on artists: John Kane's optimistic primitives; Luke Swank's moody studies of old, dusty neighborhoods in hazy sunlight; Samuel Rosenberg's forlorn houses and heroic perspectives; Harry Scheuch's sad figures in humble streets.

The casual city was a place with the incongruous, possibly ironical, contrasts a social commentator might desire: the superb institutional tower rising beyond shabby-genteel housing, the clip-clop as the huckster's wagon, lantern swinging, passed the aristocratic apartment complex. We can look back, we who knew that city, deplore it even more

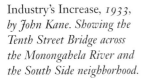

Industry's Increase, *1933, by John Kane. Showing the Tenth Street Bridge across the Monongahela River and the South Side neighborhood.*

because we feel we ought to. But there are features of it that we miss: perhaps most of all the many works of architecture that, with the broader vision that we now have, we might have saved, returned to full life, and now be enjoying.

If Allegheny County was a disorganized place during these times, it was not because nobody cared; it was more that those who did care met an inertia that was insurmountable for years.

The county was a mosaic of towns, boroughs, and townships, each acting by itself and usually not effectively; this is still the case. The Olmsted report of 1910 complained about bad local maps; officials were incompetent even to measure their territories. Since officials, with some exceptions, were also unwilling or unable to do anything effective about the problems—which, apart from working conditions, centered on public health, housing, poverty, recreation, traffic, and visual amenity—business and professional people united unofficially in frustrated attempts to improve things. In vain, there was talk of "Greater Pittsburgh," the whole county united as a municipality. Private attempts were made to supply necessary housing: the greatest success came only in 1932 in Chatham Village on Mount Washington, which demonstrated that capitalism could supply very good middle-class housing but found no emulation. Other groups attempted to unite the charities, to pressure officials to enact or enforce laws promoting public health, with no great success. These private groups contained eminent people; yet in this connection their political influence was wavering, and critics have remarked on a region where industry was organized with supreme efficiency and all else was chaos.

In 1910, Frederick Law Olmsted, Jr., son of the famous landscape architect, submitted a report on the investigation that he and a team of consultants had made for the Pittsburgh Civic Commission. Typically for the time, it concentrated on circulation, public squares, and park and recreation areas, citing European precedents as ways to make them efficient and beautiful. A few of its recommendations were: a Triangle lined with tree-shaded river walks above commercial quays, leading to a landscaped Point; Forbes Street and Penn Avenue as major arteries eastward from town; a grand plaza under the Bluff, with a big new City Hall and access to the new South Hills Bridge the motorists wanted. Outside the Triangle, traffic and recreation were major preoccupations. The South Hills Bridge was to lead to a tunnel that would rise to Warrington Avenue and Haberman Street, from which traffic would be distributed over the hilltops. The Boulevard of the Allies was anticipated from Soho eastward. Formal planning near the Carnegie Institute, close to Nicola's developments, was proposed. In addition the Olmsted report advocated public control of the steep slopes and neighborhood parks. Some of these ideas were to be realized in the future, some not.

The first great triumph in public projects was the Pittsburgh park system. When the completion of the Courthouse and the County centennial were celebrated in 1888, the pale granite tower rose over a city that had no parks aside from very small ones such as the green sliver now occupied by the Boulevard of the Allies ramp up from Grant Street. There were wild slopes for children to scramble on, river banks beyond the railroad tracks for swimmers and boat-watchers, but almost no formal provision of places for what relaxation the industrial life allowed. In 1889, though, the City's new director of the Department of Public Works, Edward Manning Bigelow (1850–1916), helped persuade Mary Croghan Schenley, who had long been living in England, to donate 300 acres of her Oakland farmland for a park. In the same year Bigelow

Outside the Phipps Conservatory in 1899. The stone fore-building and concave cresting of the Conservatory have disappeared; to the right, the Carnegie Institute is still in its first form. Beyond it is the Hotel Schenley, but there is no Civic Center, no Schenley Farms, no University of Pittsburgh yet.

*The main entrance to
Highland Park, at the head
of Highland Avenue, in 1898:
labor-intensive gardening.*

persuaded the City Council to reserve park land around the Herron Hill
and Highland Reservoirs. Over the next few years Bigelow, assisted from
1896 by the landscape architect William Falconer, laid out his new parks.
In 1890 Andrew Carnegie, whose first American library had opened
at Braddock in 1888, repeated his offer of 1881 to the City of library,
natural-history museum, art museum, and concert hall under one roof.
This was now accepted, and in 1892 the Carnegie Institute was begun
at the entrance to Schenley Park. The Carnegie partner Henry Phipps
had donated a conservatory to the Allegheny Commons in 1888 and was
now persuaded to give the new park an even bigger one. The donation of
the Zoo gave Highland Park a similar attraction.

But what Pittsburgh needed was comprehensive planning, and that
came slowly. The City Planning Commission of 1911 was official but,
aside from a veto power over registration of new plans submitted by
developers, it had only advisory powers. The municipal Art Commission
of the same year was almost as ineffective, with a veto power limited to
City art purchases and building designs. The Art Commission did have
two conspicuous successes in the 1920s, though. It backed the city's first
zoning law, passed in 1923. Before this time it was theoretically possible
for incompatible land uses to be packed together in one area, regardless
of property values and amenity, and for a building to rise to infinite

Above: the Panther Hollow Bridge, c. 1900, in Schenley Park. Below: the Casino was a skating rink, across the road from the Carnegie Institute, that burned in 1896. Its burning also injured the first Schenley Bridge that led to the Phipps Conservatory.

height regardless of the effect on natural light and air—this was still a time when, for ventilation, you opened a window. The zoning law regulated these matters. Again in the mid-1920s, the municipal Art Commission exercised its influence by deciding that the new Sixth, Seventh, and Ninth Street Bridges across the Allegheny River should be of the suspension type. The County engineers obligingly used a new German system, imposed by site conditions, that forced them to build the bridges as cantilevers, then convert them to suspension bridges.

These "Three Sisters" were part of a massive series of bridge-building campaigns begun in 1924 by the Allegheny County Department of Public Works and finished in the late 1930s by the Depression-period Allegheny County Authority. American civil engineering has had a reputation for conservatism: yet the Three Sisters had only one predecessor in the world; the hangers of the West End Bridge were among the earliest pre-stressed structural members in the United States; the 460-foot center span of the Westinghouse Bridge was the nation's greatest for a concrete arch; and the Wichert truss of the Homestead High-Level Bridge was a new and clever expedient of the pre-computer period to obviate unknowable stresses in a continuous structural member passing over more than two points of support.

Not only were these bridges progressive: they were handsome, in ways that previous bridges had not been. The Liberty Bridge might appear to the uninitiated as a pair of arches rather than the cantilever bridge it really is, but most of the County's bridges were clean and straightforward expressions of a structural system, modestly decorated perhaps with architectural work by Stanley Roush and in some cases with the sculpture of Frank Vittor. Much of the actual design was by George S. Richardson, who came to the County as draftsman in 1924 and became Chief Bridge Design Engineer in 1932.

The most notable figure in Pittsburgh's complicated planning history was Frederick Bigger (1881–1963). Starting out in private architectural practice, he went on from 1914 to posts in the municipal Art Commission, the Citizens' Committee on City Plan, and the City Planning Commission, whose chairman he was from 1924 to 1954. Meanwhile he worked for other organizations. His work for the Citizens' Committee led in 1920–23 to six reports, well known at the time, on playgrounds, streets, public transportation, parks, railroads, and waterways. He was a steady advocate of comprehensive planning under firm government control. Often frustrated, sometimes resentful of outsiders who were

The George Westinghouse Memorial Bridge across the Turtle Creek Valley, shown here under construction, was one of the most remarkable works in the County bridge-building campaigns of the 1920s and 1930s.

applauded for saying what he had been saying all the time, he still had the consolation of knowing that many people believed him right.

Despite all the inertia, it was becoming clear that fundamental reforms were necessary. It was a matter of finding the right time and the right people to define the reforms, implement them, and get the public to support them. The time came in the mid-1940s with the Renaissance.

Pittsburgh around 1940, with no hint of the Renaissance.

RENAISSANCE

Because the first architectural consequences of the Pittsburgh
Renaissance came only around 1950, people tend to forget that it
began some years earlier.

In 1939 yet another planning study of Pittsburgh took place.
Robert Moses, New York City's famous Commissioner of Parks and
Parkways, was hired by the Regional Planning Association—the Citizens'
Committee on City Plan, of many years' existence, under a new name—
to study traffic conditions. His recommendations were not carried out
in detail, and some Pittsburghers said that he had nothing new to say.
Moses, however, had the benefit of a national reputation, and his report
had at least the advantage of putting all the recommendations, whosever
they may have been, in a single place. The Moses report created an
impetus that survived the War.

Another genuine advance came in 1941, thanks to public agitation
that caused Pittsburgh to pass a smoke-control ordinance that was, at
last, taken seriously. It was a performance specification: whatever fuel
you burn, whatever you burn it in, and for whatever purpose you burn
it—no smoke over a certain low level. There were objections: the law
implied new furnace equipment, new locomotives for the railroads, less
business for the local coal industry. And the War delayed things. But
industry was made to conform in 1946 and homes a year later. In 1947
the State Legislature imposed smoke abatement on the whole county.

For once business and government were united on what needed
to be done. The Republican capitalist Richard King Mellon and the
Democratic political leader David Leo Lawrence, both very powerful,
joined forces for the good of the city. Being who they were, they could
between them make almost anyone listen to their ideas. They were
backed by the Allegheny Conference on Community Development,
an organization of concerned business and community leaders of the
sort that Pittsburgh had had for fifty years, but that under the new
circumstances was unusually effective.

Renaissance as an architectural phenomenon began in 1950. That year, demolition started of everything west of Stanwix and Ferry Streets save for the Blockhouse, the Public Safety Building that later disappeared, and the well-maintained, architecturally inoffensive Pittsburgh Press Building. On the first area cleared, the Equitable Life Assurance Society of New York started the first three units of Gateway Center. In 1949, Mellon Square, a raised public park over an underground garage near the middle of the Triangle, was announced, and shortly thereafter new buildings on the Square were announced for Alcoa—which had been thinking of leaving town—and United States Steel. The architectural Renaissance went on from these beginnings and reached its eventual symbolic climax in August 1974, when the jet of the Point State Park fountain first rose.

The roof of the Blockhouse (behind truck at far right) peeps shyly over elevated ground as its old enemy, the Pennsylvania Railroad freight terminal, comes down and Gateway Center rises in 1951.

The Point in 1916, its tiny amount of parkland hidden by the approaches of the Point and Manchester Bridges. To the right of the roller-coaster are the Music Hall and display space of the fifteen-year-old Exposition Building. The Pennsylvania Railroad freight terminal hides the front. Across the Allegheny River is Exposition Park, the city's baseball grounds before Forbes Field's opening in Oakland in 1909. (All gone.)

The Point was a symbol of Pittsburgh, and had thus been a subject for improvement proposals for years. George Washington himself had noted its suitability as a location for a fort in 1753, and forts had indeed arisen there as the British and French empires clashed. The Ohio River that began there led westward and southward, and from the great early days of flatboat emigration until mid-century when the railroads were built it was *the* way to get to the huge Louisiana Territory and the southern portions of the Northwest Territory. Even later, when the city was a rail and industrial center, nothing within its boundaries had quite the specific symbolic value of the Point: no public square, no railroad station, no industrial plant, no skyscraper, not even the Courthouse. Yet until 1970 the Point was merely a little diamond of land in the shadow of two elevated bridge approaches, a place where a few workers from nearby buildings lunched and napped on nice days, and looked down weedy banks at tied-up boats: a typical piece of the casual city of the past.

145

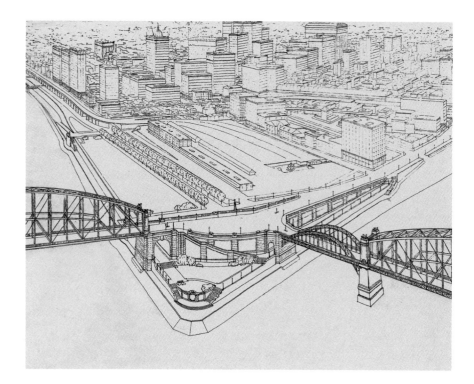

What to do with the Point?
This was Bennett's idea
of 1914.

In 1900 the Pittsburgh Architectural Club published a wishful plan
for a reformed Triangle that showed a park at the Point. In 1914,
Edward H. Bennett, Burnham's partner in the famous 1909 Commercial
Club plan for Chicago, was brought in by the municipal Art Commission
to make landscaping recommendations. In 1930 there was talk of a civic
center and a monumental lighthouse, in the 1930s agitation for a
Washington Memorial National Park, and at various other times other
proposals. Around 1950, Frank Vittor, the monumental sculptor whose
public-works commissions were numerous, displayed a model of his
masterpiece: a hundred-foot stainless-steel statue of Joe Magarac, the
legendary steelworker. Under each hand was to be a Bessemer converter,
pouring water into a third Bessemer at Magarac's feet; no mandate to
erect this came from the people.

Of the Point projects that were never realized, the most famous were
the two of 1945 that Edgar Jonas Kaufmann, the public-spirited depart-
ment-store owner, included among his many commissions to Frank
Lloyd Wright. A detail of the Wright legend is disparaging comments
about Pittsburgh ("it would be cheaper to abandon it"; his advice to
make the Triangle a park-like setting for the County Buildings; his
characterization of the Cathedral of Learning as "the biggest keep-off-

What to do with the Point?
Vittor's Magarac statue
of c. 1950.

the-grass sign in the world"), but he put his fertile imagination enthusias-
tically to work on these two grandiose schemes. The larger contained
a megastructure, based in plan on automobile access to all parts and
in structure on the reinforced-concrete cantilever, that would contain
almost every cultural, entertainment, and commercial facility a city
would need, along with two bridges and a 500-foot tower. To visiting
civic leaders Wright was vague about cost—200 million dollars,
perhaps—and the stunned visitors persuaded Kaufmann not to
release the plans; they were not exhibited for several years.

What to do with the Point? An anonymous design of 1916 for a memorial to William Pitt the Elder, the British statesman for whom Pittsburgh was named in 1758.

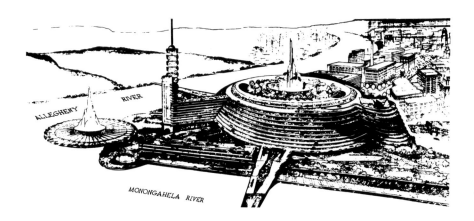

What to do with the Point? Two of Frank Lloyd Wright's ideas, commissioned by Edgar Kaufmann. The upper scheme is the less extravagant, distinguished by two cable-stayed bridges. The lower was to be a fifth of a mile in diameter and 125 feet high, with a sports arena, opera house, convention hall, movies, winter garden, zoo, park, government offices, etc. Cost was no consideration.

What actually was done with the Point. The fountain, hopefully designed to throw a 300-foot jet, draws from the ancient Wisconsin Flow beneath the earth. Replica bastions commemorate Fort Pitt, while a white "tracery" in the grass near the fountain outlines Fort Duquesne. The Blockhouse, of course, simply remains.

The aim of the Renaissance in its physical development was to throw off the dirty rags of the past and put on clean and bright new clothing. Lawrence, reminiscing in the early 1960s, said, "The town has no worship of landmarks. Instead, it takes its pleasure in the swing of the headache ball and the crash of falling brick." This was demonstrably true. While the Blockhouse was saved, and even the ginkgoes the D.A.R. had planted around it were tolerated in the new Point State Park landscaping, the Shoenberger house and all other buildings within the Gateway Center area—the Pittsburgh Press Building alone excepted—were eventually demolished. The first swing of the headache ball, duly celebrated on May 18, 1950, was against a house believed to be 103 years old. Perhaps nothing in the demolition area was in a redeemable state by then, but the next few years saw as well the destruction of the Fourth Avenue Post Office, Burnham's First National Bank, the Nixon Theatre, almost everything on the lower Hill, and almost everything in the original Allegheny Town within the Commons, with more impending at one time or another.

In 1954 it looked as if even the Jail, the county's one building of international fame, might go. Conrad Hilton was considering the site, and the County Commissioners seemed willing to sell it. The Jail had been in intermittent danger for thirty years. Businessmen of the 1920s

Opposite: Familiar things disappeared. The Manchester Bridge came down in 1970, though the portal bronzes by Charles Keck ended up on the North Side at the Old Post Office Museum (now The Pittsburgh Children's Museum).

Many Pittsburghers still remember the Norse Room in the long-gone Fort Pitt Hotel, finished in Rookwood ceramics.

·PUBLIC·BUILDING·GROUP·OF·ALLEGHENY·CO·
·ALTERED·AS·SUGGESTED·BY·THE·
·PITTSBURGH·CHAPTER·AMERICAN·INSTITUTE·OF·ARCHITECTS·

The A.I.A. scheme of 1925,
meant to save the Jail.

saw it as a gloomy entrance feature for the Triangle, and in 1924 the
County Planning Commission had talked of removing it, while the next
year saw publication of a plan for its replacement by a traffic circle and a
small park. Architects and art-loving citizens protested—the Eclectics
saw H. H. Richardson as that rare entity, a *good* Victorian architect—
and the local American Institute of Architects' chapter produced a plan
in 1925 that showed the Jail, with Osterling's additions of the 1900s
removed, converted to a Hall of Records. There was one flaw with
their otherwise-attractive idea: the wall of the jailyard had been extended
by Osterling, though as everywhere else with complete fidelity to
Richardson's detailing, and this was taken as a pretext for removing it
altogether; a rendering shows the Jail building, minus wall, standing
monastically calm in an Old World garden. Yet of all the Jail's features
the wall has been the most greatly admired, and without it Richardson's
work would have been very notably diminished.

As it happened, inertia as well as public protest stopped any attempts
to destroy the Jail. An expansion on adjacent ground helped eventually,
and in 1995 a massive new jail complex by the Monongahela River freed
the old Jail for other use.

The fall of the Fourth Avenue
Post Office, downtown on
Smithfield Street and
Fourth Avenue, in 1966.
The "Ladies of Stone" from
the pediments were saved,
as were some wood carvings.

Demolition has been only a part of the violence done to the older architectural scene since 1950. Building owners in search of a bright new image gave the Jenkins Arcade of 1911—now entirely gone—a sort of cummerbund of gold anodized aluminum and swaddled the Pittsburgh Press Building, a handsome piece of 1920s Romanesque, in patterned brown sheet metal. The Farmers Deposit National Bank, Alden & Harlow's complicated essay in red brick and white terra cotta, was also enveloped in sheet metal. This was quite a sheet-metal period. At the Carnegie Institute, gray sheet aluminum replaced the old bronze cheneau of masks that had invigorated the roofline.

If it was not *quite* true, in the 1950s and 1960s, that New—anything new—equaled Good, it was very nearly true that Old equaled Bad. A fad arose for modernizing old houses. In a masonry neighborhood like Shadyside, the procedure was to take off the porch, patch up the scars more or less, and paint everything else gray or beige or pale green. Or impart a Californian touch, with pebbles instead of grass and dark-stained boards applied to the Victorian walls to convey the effect of an elegant shack. In neighborhoods with simple frame houses, the South Side flats for instance, the old wooden siding was covered with aluminum made to imitate wooden siding, and metal awnings were extended over steps that were covered with indoor-outdoor carpeting when that became available. Faced with large Victorian windows—the early Modernists had ritually deplored the gloom of Victorian interiors—a landlord's response was to fill in their openings around cheap new sash to a half or a quarter of the original area. With energy-conservation policies of the early 1970s, dropped ceilings became popular; houses and institutional buildings alike developed a half-blind look, and generous headroom was treated as a frivolity of the reckless past, now abjured.

To these individual efforts were added urban-renewal projects, some fully realized such as Gateway Center, some aborted partway through, and some merely proposed. "Urban renewal"—rebuilding from scratch, with particular attention to optimum automobile circulation, at least minimum housing standards, commercial and industrial development, and a certain amount of civic display—was of course quite common in the 1950s and 1960s all over the country. Its theories and formulas seemed to offer an obvious way out of all the muddle and squalor of the past. The lower Hill was almost totally cleared for the Civic Arena,

An industrially themed detail from the Bessemer Building, long gone. The 1905-period building, a companion to the Fulton Building on Sixth Street, was by the New Yorker Grosvenor Atterbury.

The Jenkins Arcade, built in 1911 to the designs of O. M. Topp, stood between Liberty and Penn Avenues at Stanwix Street. It was demolished in 1983 for Fifth Avenue Place.

which was built, apartment houses that were only partly built, and a big and showy Center for the Arts, which was never built. East Liberty and Mount Lebanon were cutely street-furnished in their commercial centers, and East Liberty got a new traffic pattern that failed to work. The North Side north of the Commons was replanned in the 1950s as being almost wholly cleared for new housing and a few institutional buildings, and highway engineers working on the road system in the area proposed a viaduct that would cross the West Common fifteen feet from the ground. Manchester and Allegheny West were under similar threats. In the 1960s, Junction Hollow, the unkempt but majestic ravine that separates the Carnegie Institute from Carnegie Mellon University, was planned to be filled to overflowing with a half-dozen or more levels of utilitarian space.

In the mid-1950s the lower Hill was a closely built-up place, as this view northeast along Bedford Avenue indicates. The view on the opposite page, looking in the opposite direction, shows the lower Hill about ten years later, dominated by the Civic Arena.

Left: The west side of the original Allegheny Town appears framed by the North and West Commons. The time appears to be in the 1940s or 1950s.

Below: The whole of the Allegheny Town area, a third of a mile on a side, in 1971. St. Peter's Church, the Allegheny Post Office, the Buhl Planetarium, and the Carnegie Library are four historic structures visible; little else remains from the past.

Opposite: Waiting for the end. A church on Stockton Avenue, replaced by the Allegheny Center mall.

Above: What to do with Junction Hollow? Fill it. Put it to work. The Oakland Corporation plan of 1962. The Corporation, incidentally, preferred the less-accurate name Panther Hollow for this ravine. Further to the utilitarian theme, below: What to do with the Monongahela River? Put a stadium over it. The postcard text publicized this as "a classic structure that will blend with the Renaissance of Pittsburgh. Completely Self-Liquidating. No Tax Loss. No Land Acquisition." 70,000 spectators. 600-room hotel with gourmet restaurants. 4,500 automobile parking stalls. 100 air-conditioned bowling alleys. Consulting architect: M. de Mailly of Paris, France.

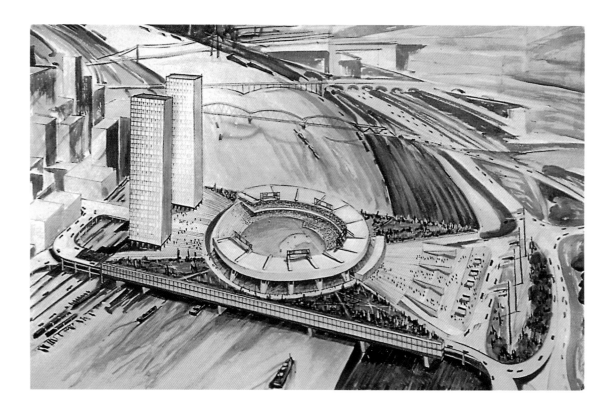

The things done and the things proposed were in part necessary reforms, in part the results of an attitude of revulsion toward the past. Aside from a few colorful recollections and surviving amenities, the past seemed expendable. Most of it was perceived as disgusting; there was no apparent way of or reason for using its buildings for modern purposes; and the new business and professional blood the region wanted to attract would not care about the local past anyway. One official in the 1960s wanted to mask the Jones & Laughlin blast furnaces by the Parkway East as bad for Pittsburgh's new image.

Reaction against this prevailing utilitarian, tidy-minded attitude came already in the 1960s. The Pittsburgh History & Landmarks Foundation, founded in 1964 by Charles Covert Arensberg, Barbara D. Hoffstot, James D. Van Trump, and Arthur P. Ziegler, Jr., set out to demonstrate that a practical approach to historic preservation could save individual old buildings and entire neighborhoods: not merely the architecture of the neighborhoods but the usefulness of their buildings and the well-being of those who used them. Historic preservation, at that time, was emerging from its museum and touristic phase and concerning itself more with the everyday world, and Landmarks was one of the early organizations to think of those who would actually use preserved buildings as homes, stores, places for ordinary purposes: the people who would have to find the buildings convenient, take pride in them, and care for them.

The 1300 block of Liverpool Street in Manchester has a legendary quality, because it was a winter-afternoon walk in 1964 past this house row and hearing that urban renewal had doomed it that led James D. Van Trump and Arthur P. Ziegler, Jr. toward the founding of the Pittsburgh History & Landmarks Foundation.

Landmarks made a policy of conferring with and selling preservation to citizens' groups and individuals who were trying to improve their homes and their neighborhoods, often on very slender means.

For its first fifteen years Landmarks concentrated on physical matters and public advocacy: saving the Post Office of the former city of Allegheny, which became its own headquarters between 1971 and 1984; purchasing and restoring North Side and South Side houses as examples to property owners and signs of better times to neighborhood dwellers; arranging for design-consultation services; establishing a community museum and offering it as a repository for historic artifacts; and rescuing endangered landmark buildings such as "Woodville," the Neville house. At the same time, Landmarks publicized historic preservation; a Van Trump-Ziegler survey of 1965–67 resulted in *Landmark Architecture of*

The Langenheim house on Liverpool Street in Manchester, as it was when the Pittsburgh History & Landmarks Foundation received it for preservation and eventual restoration.

"Woodville," the John and Presley Neville house of c. 1785 in Collier Township, is one of six National Historic Landmarks in Allegheny County. The wood-frame house is the Pittsburgh area's principal physical link with the American Revolutionary War. John and Presley Neville were veterans of that war.

The restored dining room of "Woodville," painted in a bright verdigris green popular in the late eighteenth century.

Allegheny County, the predecessor to the two editions of this book, while the "Stones of Pittsburgh" series of booklets explored individual buildings and building groups.

In the mid-1970s, Landmarks turned its attention to commercial revitalization on a large scale with the main Pittsburgh & Lake Erie Railroad complex. Beginning modestly in a crowded industrial district in 1879, the P&LE had by 1930 taken over almost the whole south shore area on the Monongahela opposite the Triangle, but by the mid-1960s had so dispersed or lessened its services that conventional urban-renewal schemes were being prepared for the land. Landmarks saw in the P&LE site a chance to demonstrate its ideas of historic preservation as an integral feature of urban development and to test the validity of its principles of urban design, its belief in the potential of then-unused waterfronts, and its faith in a quality Pittsburgh consumer market. In 1976, Landmarks reached an agreement with the railroad that resulted in the development of Station Square, a business, retail, and cultural center that is planned to cover fifty acres. The five historic railroad buildings have been saved and adapted for new uses, and new buildings have been constructed.

Station Square, seen across the Monongahela River from the Triangle.

The Grand Concourse restaurant at Station Square. This interior was the main passenger waiting room at the Pittsburgh & Lake Erie Station.

The project, a daring departure from official planning at the time, was initially funded by the Allegheny Foundation, a Scaife family charitable trust. The Pittsburgh History & Landmarks Foundation owned and managed Station Square until 1994, developing a master plan. In 1994 the land was sold to Harrah's-Forest City Associates, joint developers, but Landmarks continues to provide operating services to the owners.

As Landmarks approaches the twenty-first century, it continues to offer a full-range of preservation activities for its members and the public. Through conferences, publications, architectural surveys, Historic Landmark plaques, Awards of Merit, tours, lectures, and educational programs for students and teachers, Landmarks promotes interest in the architectural heritage of this region and the value of historic preservation. Through its revolving loan fund, Landmarks supports neighborhood groups in undertaking preservation projects and works with lending institutions to ensure that opportunities exist in historic neighborhoods for economic development and affordable housing. Many segments of the Pittsburgh community now support historic preservation as a sound method for urban revitalization. Community development organizations, in particular, have been a strong local force in saving the fabrics as well as the community sense in Pittsburgh-area neighborhoods.

A campaign for window box planting in Manchester was an early means of raising the neighborhood's collective spirit.

Historic preservation has been a sort of Counter-Renaissance, not because the dusty city that Luke Swank knew is one that preservationists wish to keep frozen in time but because the progressives of the Renaissance too often ignored what was good about this city's past. They failed to see, certainly, that to break the continuity of a neighborhood's visible history, to sponge away whole streets of buildings, risks diminishing the inhabitants' sense of—their right, even, of sensing—who they are and what they are part of. If they are moved about arbitrarily, old associations are broken up, old friendships, old patterns of living. And how about the old architecture, considered purely as art? Has it perhaps touches of humanity in its detailing, perhaps concessions to human dignity in its deviations from the utilitarian, perhaps more positive visual effect in its color and texture, not to be found in what might replace it? Renaissance brought order, and a prosperity demonstrated in a way that attracted more prosperity, but it was not the most sensitive way of reshaping a city. It had to work fast, and there were penalties inherent in such speed.

Detailing of a saved neighborhood: a Manchester porch.

A panel of the Alcoa Building is bolted into place. The year is 1952.

MODERNISM

Major Eclectic buildings continued to rise during the Depression: the Gulf Building, the Mellon Institute, the East Liberty Presbyterian Church, the Cathedral of Learning, the Heinz Chapel, the Buhl Planetarium, and the Florentine institutions of the Medical Center that were replacing the old villas on the Oakland hillside. These were sensational additions to the architecture of Pittsburgh, yet nothing special was to follow. Eclecticism seemed to have exhausted itself with these last great efforts, and when the Pittsburgh "Renaissance" built, it built in ways that had to be considered Modern.

The decline of Eclecticism was certainly due in part to its demand for expensive materials and workmanship at a time when money was hard to come by, followed by war years when both manpower and the supply of materials were subject to higher priorities. But there was a nationwide feeling, as well, that Eclecticism had simply gone too far. Engineers, contractors, artists, craftsmen, and suppliers had become used to catering to the architect's fantasies, his whims, even. If he ordered the delivery of sixty-two monolithic columns forty-two feet high—the Mellon Institute—a patron might pay the cost. If he and his client dreamed of a 535-foot skyscraper with a richly detailed, tapering silhouette of Gothic masonry—the Cathedral of Learning—their dream could be realized. If he wanted gnarled bricks in a wall, or stucco troweled to a certain quaint texture, or ragged-edged slates on a roof, he got them. The visual effect

The Cecelia and Robert Frank house of 1939–40 in the Woodland Road area by Walter Gropius and Marcel Breuer.

Opposite: The apparition of the Cathedral of Learning, 535 feet of architectural fiction, rising over the roofs of south Oakland.

of a building was too often dependent on historic associations, too often an affair of make-believe; there was too wide a deviation, too often, between the appearance of a building and the realities of the civilization in which it was built, the purpose for which it was built, and the system by which it was built. The architect seemed sometimes like a sportsman who, inept at polo, insisted on playing it by the rules of croquet. Toward 1930 some architects became restless, tried to be "modern" at least when solving specifically modern architectural problems; then broke out into open controversy, with the extremists declaring that *all* building programs should be executed in a style explicitly of the twentieth century. Compromises were attempted, often in a stripped-down Classical manner with sculpture that was greatly simplified though not banished. This short-lived manner gave the impression of an Old Guard retreat rather than the result of positive artistic conviction, and Henry-Russell Hitchcock and Philip Johnson seemed to state a clearer case in *The International Style* of 1932: "The current style sets a high but not impossible standard for decoration: better none at all unless it be good. The principle is aristocratic rather than puritanical."

Now that the Modern-Eclectic controversy of the 1930s and 1940s, a war of religion at the time, has died down, we can look at Eclectic architecture with a less committed eye, smile at the excesses but enjoy and admire the many real accomplishments, the solidity and amplitude and fine taste so often to be found. First-class construction and workmanship were among the best to be found at any period of history—the Cathedral of Learning can stand for 300 years—and the ornament, even when sedulously copied from some "precedent" found in the architect's library, at least conveys the assurance that what you see was built by and for human beings: an assurance that the mute architecture of more recent times has seldom bothered to impart.

If we were to sum up the history of American architecture, we might be tempted to an epigram, sweeping but with some truth in it. In the Georgian period we had an architecture, simple and tasteful; after 1830 we had a hundred years of, not so much architecture as pictures of architecture, appearance and reality increasingly at odds; and since 1930 we have had, not so much architecture as illustrations of theories about architecture.

Certainly, the Modernist polemics of 1930 and later attempted to establish an *a priori* basis for the exclusive use of a "modern" architecture, whatever form it might take, regardless of individual preference. The polemics had a Germanic sternness in asserting the claim that History, in modern times manifested in The Machine, demanded a new architecture. There was a touch of French rationalism, insisting on direct responses to practical requirements. And above all there was a moralistic Anglo-Saxon quality, an insistence on truth: truth to modern civilization, truth to the building program, truth to construction: a building must be honest. Despite Hitchcock and Johnson, there *was* a puritanical quality to the polemics; Modern architecture was being sold like Filboid Studge, the breakfast food in Saki's story that the Edwardian public bought, not because it was delicious—it was not—not because it was nourishing even, but because they had somehow been convinced that it was their duty to eat it.

And yet, in a time when Frank Lloyd Wright, Ludwig Mies van der Rohe, Louis Kahn, Bruce Goff, and Eero Saarinen were all active on the national scene, it was very nearly impossible to characterize Modern architecture with any objectivity; perhaps the only thing they and their less-famous colleagues had in common was the non-use of historically derived decorative forms. This specific abstention may be the one and only hard basis for a definition of Modern architecture, and a very unsatisfactory one it is. Beyond this we wander into a realm of more vague associations with flat roofs, steel frames exposed or suggested, great sheets of glass, no ornament of *any* kind, not much color or texture, and similar features characteristic of most Modernists but not all.

The Richard King Mellon Hall of Science, Duquesne University, 1968, by Ludwig Mies van der Rohe.

Modern architecture has meant different things to various people at various times. Below left: 710 Fifth Avenue is a 1940-ish compromise of old and new, a kind of suppressed Classical manner with lustrous black granite trim for its flat limestone walls and a triple reglet instead of a cornice. Its neighbor, the Central Blood Bank of 1968 (below right), is an elegant essay in welded channel irons, très moderne, that is imitated in trompe-l'oeil on the brickwork to the right. The architects were Curry, Martin & Highberger.

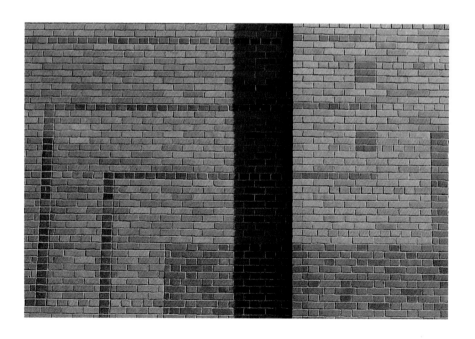

A homegrown, rather naive piece of Modern is Victor G. Tilbrook's Forbes Substation of 1953 for Duquesne Light, on Forbes Avenue near the edge of the Triangle. Tan and bronze-colored brick in different bonds are used skillfully to fashion patterns and textures on a simple shape.

Certainly, the Modern architecture in which the Pittsburgh Renaissance was manifested showed no particular unity of expression, and individual buildings suggested indecision rather than artistic liberation. Some of the works, by Pittsburghers and outsiders both, were boxes covered by unbroken ruled verticals of metal or stone, while others attempted more arbitrary surface modulations. Some architects used no color at all, while others attempted visual hedonism in a smoke-free city with blue panels that eventually faded, or expressed "Golden Triangle" literalistically in sheet metal with a dull golden sheen. Of all the buildings that symbolized the Renaissance, the Alcoa Building by Harrison & Abramovitz was the one positive artistic success; faced with aluminum panels pierced with windows whose gaskets required them to be rounded at the corners, it had the air of a suave work of industrial design.

In 1970, Harrison & Abramovitz followed its Alcoa Building essay in aluminum with another headquarters building displaying the company product. The United States Steel Building was given an exposed frame and curtain walls of weathering steel. But most downtown architecture in the 1960s and 1970s was more standardized, more in the manner of Ludwig Mies van der Rohe, who was actually represented in Pittsburgh by Mellon Hall at Duquesne University, or of that corporate favorite Skidmore, Owings & Merrill, designers of the downtown YWCA, the Equibank Building, and the Research Building at the Heinz plant on the North Side. Meant for business, this colorless architecture suggested, in fact, an oversize business suit: sumptuous in material perhaps but conservative in cut, devoid of individualism, making no damaging personal revelations. At times the business suit was worn, so to speak, with a hand-painted necktie: arbitrary contrasts of material, peculiar roof structures, facings odd in color or texture. These efforts at marginal individualism were so patently uninspired that the public simply ignored them.

Away from the business districts a less rigorous Modernism prevailed, and indeed in house and church design a greatly enfeebled Eclecticism often carried on, powerless to live, powerless to die. Very rarely had these last Eclectic works the sense of proportion that might have given them life, or the air of material solidity that their detailing required to be effective. As to the Modern works, some were plain and rather sullen, while architects of the more ambitious ones tried gesture after gesture, facing after facing, to distinguish them from the others lined up along the highway or the commercial street. Church design of the period revealed a certain anguish, the combined strains of somehow looking like

The Alcoa Building, 1951-53, by Harrison & Abramovitz (New York). Designed to show off every possible decorative and functional use of aluminum, it was company headquarters for about four decades. In the foreground is Mellon Square, and to the left is Hornbostel's German Evangelical Protestant Church of 1925, whose spire is partly of aluminum.

The United States Steel Building of 1970 is once again by Harrison & Abramovitz, and once again displays a corporate product: weathering steel, exposed to the air and with the main structural members fireproofed with a water-antifreeze mixture. The building, 841 feet high, is the tallest habitable structure in this part of Pennsylvania.

a church while abstaining from Federal porticoes and Gothic arches, of being in synch with the dynamic, skeptical present, and of course of building on budget. House design revealed an ambivalence between modernity and homeyness, but typically ended up with lots of plate glass, a certain amount of unpainted wood, a roof with a token amount of pitch, and some sort of chimney, preferably of stone.

Of our local Modernists, Frederick G. Scheibler, Jr. excepted, the outstanding figures are Peter Berndtson (1909–72) and to a lesser degree his wife Cornelia, both students of Frank Lloyd Wright in the 1930s. Their houses are on the Usonian pattern that Wright had developed a few years before, with strong and often unconventional geometrical systems as bases for their plans, an interplay between hovering eaves and emphatic chimneys, and a use of earth materials—brick especially— and unpainted wood. Berndtson is remembered as a man of strong convictions, and one who insisted on the most scrupulous execution of his designs. Certainly, of all the local work under strong or tenuous Wrightian influence, his reveals and imparts the most conviction.

The growing interest in historic preservation doubtless owed something to a growing discontent with Modern architecture. It is surely fair to judge an artistic style or movement by its average productions as well as its outstanding ones, and to do so here was to cast an eye over blank acres of glass, concrete, granite, acoustical tile, and contract carpeting, scaleless and featureless, a Barmecide feast after the old promises of a Radiant City. The reasoning of the polemics often seemed impeccable, and so did the argument, used earlier in the century in connection with every art, that the possibilities of the medium had not been exhausted, that there were further delights to be found. But in Modern architecture, these delights had very largely not appeared. One might wonder if there was to be cold, gray, and very possibly dirty concrete for eternity, and balustrades of planks on steel uprights, and bricks of no positive color, and never a carving, turning, or molding.

Indeed, the ordinary person has probably regarded Modern architecture of the usual sort with passive acceptance rather than pleasure or pride; emerged from his play-it-cool office building to take refuge in the soothing silliness of a theme restaurant; aspired to a house with a vague Colonial air about it; chosen to marry at the Heinz Chapel rather than in a 1960s church attempting relevance. Perhaps Williamsburg, Beacon Hill, and Old Economy, a few miles down the Ohio River, draw tourists not because their orderly streets are quaint but because there the eye is

*Two Usonian houses: the
Abraam Steinberg house in
Squirrel Hill (1951; above) by
Peter and Cornelia Berndtson
and the Douglas house in
Ross Township (1962–65)
by Peter Berndtson.*

nourished with amenities no longer produced: building forms that are simple but eloquent, good proportions, little ornamental touches that lighten the compositions, bricks that are positively red. Historic preservation has doubtless struck such a responsive chord because it values these typical Georgian features and the more lavish ones of later times. A small minority of the buildings preservationists have attempted to save have been masterpieces or historic shrines, but in most there is rather the appeal of some bygone architect's or builder's attempt to please. The results can be ridiculous, but better that, perhaps, than the muteness of what might be built in their place.

The first American attacks on Modern architecture to find any public response came in the late 1950s, and by the mid-1960s deviations from the tidy mainstream of Modernism had begun to be quite wide-ranging. A while later, critics began to use the term Post-Modernism: a term not too satisfactory because the prefix seemed to deny it any central idea of its own. Perhaps there was not one, indeed; perhaps, just as Modernism may boil down to abstention from historic ornament, Post-Modernism may boil down to a rejection of the neat utilitarian package typical of Modernism—any rejection, though *typical* of the new trend is allusion to the architectural past: a few Corinthian columns, perhaps, or the glazed lunette gables of the Crystal Palace. Post-Modernism, indeed, has been like Queen Anne in its raids on history and its witty and unconventional displays of the spoils. It seems almost a point of honor for Post-Modern architects not to use these bygone motifs correctly, perhaps because to do so would make them Eclectics, perhaps because these old forms, combined with new ones, are leading them toward a new sort of Baroque: a free and venturesome architecture, part of whose arsenal of motifs is literate allusion to the older and more codified styles, with all their traditional associations.

For a guess, Post-Modernism is a transitory manner, not to last long, just as Queen Anne was. Its strength lies in an amount of creative intelligence that is not often to be found; it is not easy to imitate, and on that basis may discredit itself as it is imitated. Furthermore, as construction much of it looks frail, and where it deteriorates it also discredits the movement. Finally, like Eclecticism, it deviates so far from a direct response to specifiable architectural programs as to raise the question whether something simpler might not create architecture of at least equal beauty. It may be a Baroque that leads to a Neo-Classical reaction. Yet at the very least it is freeing us of the rectitudes of a half-century, and for that we must be grateful.

Post-Modernism invaded the Woodland Road area around 1980, with neighboring houses by Venturi, Rauch & Scott Brown of Philadelphia (above) and Richard Meier of New York (right).

181

H. H. Richardson's Courthouse tower, simple, delicate, yet strong, among the other towers of the Triangle.

THE LAST
FEW YEARS

One's own times may always lack the color, the vividness of imagery, that we think we perceive in the past. We are seeing the bygone decades in a telephoto lens, its signature images big and jammed close to each other, its drab intervals between the great events compressed to nothingness.

Because of this illusion it may be that our present, here in Pittsburgh in the mid-1990s, seems rather featureless. On the river shores there is little steam and smoke these days, little to suggest mighty forces at work within huge structures: not many forces indeed and quite a lot of blank flat land. In town, proud ex-headquarters buildings seek new tenants. The skyline *has* changed, indeed, since that first Pittsburgh Renaissance of the 1950s and 1960s, with the 841-foot USX Tower (formerly the United States Steel Building) and the 680-foot main tower of PPG Place, the somewhat lower and more peculiar towers of Fifth Avenue Place and CNG. But the Pittsburgh population is growing older on the average, and there is a prevailing vagueness about the future.

Yet some are not ready to give up on the traditional manufacturing economy of the region. The products may be different, formed from different materials, or produced in many plants henceforth with small workforces, but manufacturing seems likely to remain a major element along with the new and potentially glamorous forms of advanced

Above: Sunset on the Triangle. Below: The setting sun lights eight of the 231 pinnacles of PPG Place. The architecture showed off a company product in the design of John Burgee Architect, with Philip Johnson (New York). This six-building group was completed in 1984.

technology and medicine, finance as ever, and the perpetual industry of education.

New construction in the last quarter-century has made its most telling concentrated visual effect in the Triangle. If nothing is quite up to the USX Tower's height, attained in 1970, still we have had some very tall construction downtown; of this, the tower of PPG Place seems most likely to create a strong, lasting impression with its silver-gray reflective glass and its eight great pinnacles that peek over rooflines both downtown and far away. In Oakland the hospitals have continued to build, and the beautiful tapered silhouette of the Cathedral of Learning, as seen from Mount Washington, is now blurred by chunkier medical architecture near by. Carnegie Mellon University is adding greatly to its original Hornbostel campus; three Boston architectural firms have been involved, and of these, two have designed buildings that do not rival Hornbostel's decorative work but do respect it and show, besides, originality and taste. Richardson's Jail has been found primitive and inhumane, and has been replaced in its role with a blocky brick-and-concrete complex along the Monongahela River under Duquesne University. The new terminal of the Pittsburgh International Airport is one of the nation's busiest,

184

Above left: Oakland as seen from the South Side slopes, with the massed hospital architecture to the left. Above right: The main corridor of The Heinz Architectural Center, a research and display facility for architectural history in Carnegie Institute that supplements its older resources. The green window at the top of the picture (partially shown here) is a copper dormer from Andrew Carnegie's New York house. Below is the dormitory/dining facility designed in 1987 for Carnegie Mellon University by Dennis, Clark & Associates (Boston).

over two million square feet under roof on 9,954 acres. These County buildings, both by the local architect Tasso Katselas, are conspicuous places on the Allegheny County scene.

Monroeville, the Patton Township of earlier in the century, is now our first "edge city," mixing capacity and variety of uses in a way dispensing with the presence of an older, more centralized city such as Pittsburgh. The suburbs have continued to develop at the expense of the towns of Allegheny County. South of Mount Lebanon, and elsewhere around the county, there is not much sense of coherence in the new developments, which give the effect in the landscape of inhabited litter.

This scene happens to be on McKnight Road.

The wealthy and those who build for them have abandoned 1960s Modernism for a "traditional" effect, characterized by ill-proportioned dish-ups of gables and Palladian windows.

As ever around Pittsburgh, outsiders have made an occasional good contribution on the domestic as well as the institutional scale, and local architects such as Arthur Lubetz, Leonard Perfido, and a few others have given us striking new buildings.

Yet much that is good in our building art these days is preservation and adaptation of what we have had already. The Pittsburgh History & Landmarks Foundation is best known in this respect, but there are now legal constraints on demolition or remodeling of certain buildings or within certain districts of Pittsburgh, Sewickley, and Sewickley Heights. Pittsburgh's Historic Review Commission, founded in 1979, had a decade and a half later nine districts (with nearly 2,000 buildings), one park, and thirty-nine historic structures under its protection.

The popularity of preservation and the anticipated advantages of adaptive use have led, in some cases, to large-scale makeovers such as the Pennsylvanian or Shadyside Commons apartment buildings, and the eventual conversion of the East Liberty Market House to Motor Square Garden, headquarters for the AAA. But it also has affected mansions, ordinary houses, and churches that have changed function radically—which is nothing new of course—but that recently have been remodeled so as not to lose their architectural character.

Bellefonte Place on Walnut Street, Shadyside, built in 1982 to designs of L. P. Perfido Associates.

Below left: 133 First Avenue, downtown, by L. D. Astorino Associates, 1994. Below right: The office created by Arthur Lubetz Associates in 1982 from an earlier building.

Manchester preserved. Views of West North Avenue (left) and Sheffield Street (below).

The amenities of official historic districts. Above is the 1700 block in Pittsburgh's East Carson Street City Historic District. The fourth front from the left was like those beside it, but was altered before the District was created. Below is a view of Cochran Street in one of Sewickley's three Borough Historic Districts.

Adaptive use: the residential Shadyside Commons on Amberson Avenue (bottom), once the turn-of-the-century Bindley Hardware Company.

Inside Motor Square Garden, the former East Liberty Market House.

Inside the Pennsylvanian apartment house, the former Union Station: this was the passenger waiting room.

The Pittsburgh Technology Center stands on the old Jones & Laughlin site. The University of Pittsburgh's Center for Biotechnology and Bioengineering, by Bohlin Cywinski Jackson (1992), was built where the Strip Mill used to be.

In some areas, most notably East Carson Street on the South Side, concerted efforts have been made not only to give legal protection to commercial facades but also to create new shop fronts in harmony with the prevailing architecture and with one another.

A developing Pittsburgh area cannot make do with its old building stock alone. The river plains, where the steel plants once were, seem to call for wholly new construction and much of it. Again, if the medical institutions of Oakland continue to be marooned on hillside streets once occupied by houses, they may continue to build ponderously there. Concern for the Pittsburgh region generally and for its creative life argue against the future of an aging people doing its aging in aging buildings, neither supplemented by anything fresh. Yet we surely wish that the city and the region will bend rather than break under the pressures and the suctions of our future history, and that a prospering city will still in basic ways be the city we have known.

The South Side: public steps, a church, a former brewery, innumerable little houses, with the towers of the Triangle not far beyond.

Brereton Street in Polish Hill.

The South Side, looking toward St. Josaphat's.

EPILOGUE

Bring to mind some good, long-held memories: Skies, tea-colored or purple in the west. The long, loud rasp of cicadas. The chirp of birds echoing between close-set walls. A house where time seemed to have eased to a halt around 1920. The bite of a winter evening when the streetcar was a long time coming. Lombardy poplars in a row on a hilltop. Quiet front-porch conversations, walks around the block, lamplight through the leaves. The smell of rain on cement, and the lindens turning up their gray-green leaves. Lighted windows seen through heavy rain. Ailanthus trees, and the pungent smell of their bruised leaves. Far away, the shouts of children beneath the white bulb of a streetlight in a dusty, weed-grown alley.

Oddly significant moments of one's life occur in such concrete circumstances, which themselves may sound meaningless. A building, a neighborhood paved in a certain way, lighted in a certain way, built up in a certain way, can be the occasion of such a personal moment in spite of itself, in a way beyond the possible calculations of an architect or planner. Such a professional has to concern himself with the public role of his work: its value as art, its provision of amenity, its performance as a thing to be used. So must the critics and the academics who study and report on it; the purely personal eludes them, and they comment in terms their public will understand.

Yet to a certain extent those familiar with a neighborhood or a city share the same experiences, which nature, geography, history, society, and the constructions of man together provide: the unacknowledged

Across the North Side, toward the Sixteenth Street Bridge.

institutions of a community, which make it unique and whose inertia under forces of change keep it the same place in people's minds even as it is altered in detail.

Historic preservation has been a source of such inertia, keeping widespread destruction from occurring in neighborhoods where good architecture might have been replaced by bad architecture or by mere paved-over vacancy. But there is a sad aspect to the very triumphs of the preservationists: a tacit public confession that we cannot expect much of the building arts today. Handsome, charming, witty, sensitive buildings are being designed—but will we see them erected on our street? We think not, and we cling to what we have. Yet old buildings *will* decay and new ones *will* be built.

In the Georgian period, architecture did not fall below a certain level. The building programs were simple and demanded no extraordinary dimensions. Building materials were limited, and so were constructional techniques. Neither designer nor client felt any compulsion to demonstrate originality. Tradition assured orderly design, and builder's manuals provided ideas for woodwork. Ornamentation and moldings, which imparted graceful touches and articulation to the building, enlivened the work. Our circumstances are much more complicated, and our opportunity to perpetrate aesthetic disasters much, much greater.

Opposite: Murray Hill Avenue in Squirrel Hill.

The same people who have supported historic preservation should find a means of intervening in design in the years to come: create a

The building arts and religion: McClure Avenue Presbyterian Church (above left) and Congregation Poale Zedeck (above right). Below left: St. Michael Archangel, Munhall, and St. Nicholas Greek Orthodox Cathedral (below right).

Bottom left: Good Shepherd Catholic Church, Braddock, and Church of the Epiphany (bottom right).

Above (left to right): Hungarian Reformed Church, Munhall; St. Mary Magdalene, Homestead; and St. Michael Archangel, Munhall.

Above (left to right): Third Presbyterian Church; St. Mary Magdalene, Homestead; and McClure Avenue Presbyterian Church.

public demand, backed by informed ideas from architects and builders, for an architecture suited to the places where we live and the associations they have accumulated. This suggestion does not imply the imposition of a range of historic styles as happens in some preservation districts; unless modern demands are met with modern resources, with only limited artistic modification, the results will be unconvincing, shallow, and painfully artificial. Rather, it is made in the hope that the architecture we have in times to come will be a positive contribution, a thing from our own time that we can be proud of and that will add to, not be a subtraction from, what the past has left us.

Artistry at Carnegie Mellon University: below, terra cotta at Margaret Morrison College; opposite, J. M. Hewlett's ceiling paintings at the College of Fine Arts.

A GUIDE TO THE
LANDMARK ARCHITECTURE
OF ALLEGHENY COUNTY

Richardson in Pittsburgh: the stair in the Allegheny County Courthouse.

AUTHOR'S NOTE

The following Guide is based on a five-year survey of Allegheny County, the county's contribution to the Pennsylvania Historic Resource Survey, conducted by the Pittsburgh History & Landmarks Foundation from 1979 through 1984. Although preceded by Landmarks' 1966 county survey, the 1979–84 survey was an unprecedented effort to record the historic resources of the county fully. With funding support from the Pennsylvania Historical and Museum Commission, Allegheny County Department of Development, Richard King Mellon Foundation, Fisher Charitable Trust, Vira I. Heinz Fund of The Pittsburgh Foundation, and the Pittsburgh History & Landmarks Foundation, our staff canvassed the county, seeking buildings, bridges, monuments—any construction of historical interest with a permanent site—to identify, describe, photograph, research, and evaluate. From Allegheny County's more than two centuries of permanent habitation and 728 square miles, over 6,000 significant historic resources were recorded.

The present edition of this book is a radical revision of that of 1985, with a new design, new illustrations, new typography, and in the main new text. Many subjects have been added to the Guide; only a few have been deleted because of demolition or serious loss of integrity. New photographs were taken at the time of writing and the current states of the subjects were checked on field trips.

The Guide is a carefully considered sampling of our historic architecture, engineering and landscape, discussed and illustrated in 645 entries. They date from the years before 1950, times remote enough from the present to allow for an evaluation of enduring significance. Some of them are old friends, well known to historians and the public. Others are new discoveries, fresh and surprising. Some are the best examples of types found in relative abundance. Others are one-of-a-kind items. All should be preserved as important elements of our heritage.

The Guide is organized in a sequence of geographically based chapters. These correspond to groupings of major neighborhoods and sections of Pittsburgh and regions of the county. Pittsburgh boundaries are generally those established by the Department of City Planning, based on the census tracts of 1990, but with some influence from popular sentiment. The popular name for a neighborhood is usually adopted. Resources with individual entries are identified first by their historic names, then by later or common names. Some areas with high concentrations of

significant resources are acknowledged by introductory paragraphs followed by individual entries for each distinct significant resource. Other areas, where the significance of individual resources is less distinct, are addressed by a single entry.

Some entries conclude with notations indicating historic landmark designation. Several different designation programs are noted:

National Historic Landmark designation acknowledges nationally significant properties, and is the highest possible recognition. National Historic Landmarks are designated by the Secretary of the United States Department of the Interior.

The *National Register of Historic Places* is the official listing of the nation's historic resources worthy of preservation. Nomination of a property or district for inclusion on the National Register requires thorough documentation of its outstanding local, state, or national significance, and final approval by State and federal government agencies. Designation provides nationwide recognition; a measure of protection from harm by State- and federally-supported projects; and in some cases, eligibility for rehabilitation incentives.

The Pittsburgh History & Landmarks Foundation awards *Historic Landmark plaques* to architecturally significant historic resources in Allegheny County. An owner must apply to Landmarks' Historic Landmark Plaque Designation Committee for such a plaque. A plaque does not guarantee protection of a property; it identifies it as a significant element of our local architectural heritage.

In Pittsburgh, there are officially designated *City Historic Districts* and *City Historic Structures*, which cannot legally be demolished or altered in major ways without Certificates of Appropriateness from the City's Historic Review Commission. The Historic Districts of the boroughs of Sewickley and Sewickley Heights are similarly protected.

Designation under any of these programs implies superior worth; but lack of designation does not necessarily imply inferiority. Many eligible properties still await designation. Designations are noted as of 1997.

The architectural resources of Allegheny County are worthy of identification and preservation because their recognition helps us better understand the history, culture, and enduring significance of this region, and furthers our enjoyment of the communities in which we live.

History made visible: the rising skyline of the Triangle as seen from Station Square.

THE ORIGINAL
PITTSBURGH

Pittsburghers speak of their central business district, without any
braggadocio these days, as the Golden Triangle. The apex of the
triangle is the westward-facing Point, the Forks of the Ohio land fought
for by the British, French, and Indians in the eighteenth century.
The sides of the triangle are the Allegheny River to the north
and the Monongahela River to the south. The base of the
triangle to the east is less clearly defined, but can be assumed
to lie a little east of Grant Street and Eleventh Street, the
outer limit of the Pittsburgh that George Woods and
Thomas Vickroy surveyed for the Penn family in 1784.

CITY OF
PITTSBURGH

   The Woods-Vickroy plan, with its two street grids
intersecting awkwardly at Liberty Avenue, was imposed
upon a terrain which included ponds and the Hump, a spur
of the hills that rise east of the Triangle. The ponds were
quickly filled and forgotten, but the abstract street grid
clashed for many years with the reality of the Hump. Bit by
bit, beginning in the 1830s, the Hump was lowered, and existing
buildings rode high above the streets. Between 1911 and 1913, a massive
campaign was launched and the Hump was completely conquered at
last, brought down a total of sixty feet from its primitive state.

   Of eighteenth-century Pittsburgh, aside from the plan, very little
remains. The Blockhouse, Bouquet's Redoubt, stands among the
ginkgoes in Point State Park, and there are a few foundations of
Fort Pitt near by. Of the nineteenth century prior to the Fire of 1845,
there is only one building left for certain, the Greek Revival Burke's
Building of 1836. A few simple buildings erected soon after the Fire
remain in the 100 block of Market Street and in other places.

   To a casual eye, the Triangle's history seems to start in the Mid-
Victorian period. On Fort Pitt Boulevard, the old Water Street that
once overlooked the steep pavement of the Monongahela Wharf, a few
warehouses, stores, and business buildings from the 1850 period and
after remain. Liberty Avenue has a large concentration of Victorian
commercial architecture too, including Mid-Victorian cast-iron fronts

and Late Victorian masonry fronts, much taller, in the fashionable styles of the 1880s and 1890s. Penn Avenue, beyond Liberty, continues in time where Liberty leaves off with an array of turn-of-the-century commercial buildings.

Commercial development was accompanied by financial growth, although regional industrialization provided much of the new capital. Fourth Avenue west of Smithfield Street became a street of banks and financial offices: low-rise banking rooms and early high-rise office towers formed a catalogue of the possible varieties of architectural pretense.

But when Pittsburgh built large, it tended to do so in the Grant Street corridor. The Courthouse tower, which dominated the Triangle in the 1890s, was matched in height by the Frick Building in 1901. The Union Arcade and William Penn Hotel of the 1910s each filled an entire block. And corporate skyscrapers followed.

A view from across the Monongahela River reveals the Triangle's architectural history in the most vivid way. Higher and newer buildings rise above and behind their predecessors, piling up toward the center of the Triangle and Grant Street to the east, raising the skyline from the modest fifty feet or so of the Mid-Victorian pre-elevator buildings to the 841 feet of the USX Tower.

Among the close-built streets are special places, places that invite pause or leave a vivid impression. Mellon Square, opened in 1955 on land given in 1949 by the Mellons, offers not only popular public space but a vantage point for seeing some of the city's best architecture. The Courthouse Park is smaller and more relaxed, with H. H. Richardson's beautiful towers as a permanent display around the landscaped

Mellon Square

courtyard. Market Square, the old Diamond of 1784 that was the only original public space, lives on in pointed contrast with the new square of PPG Place, a half-block away: the first a bit raffish and haphazard; the other consciously elegant, every inch a work of design.

The Triangle once had a boatyard, foundries, and an assortment of rail lines with five stations. Tiny houses still cluster at Strawberry and Montour Ways. But zoning in 1923, Renaissance in 1950, and two centuries of continuous urban growth and change have transformed the Triangle generally into a compact retail and white-collar office district. And the work of building and rebuilding goes on.

Blockhouse (Bouquet's Redoubt)
Point State Park
1764

No shot has ever been fired in military anger at or from this, the sole eighteenth-century building left in downtown Pittsburgh. It was built with four other redoubts to secure the western portions of Fort Pitt after extensive flood damage. In its brick walls are two sill-like members of squared logs, pierced with loopholes for sharpshooters.

If the Blockhouse has escaped war, peacetime has occasionally been dangerous to it. The great fort itself and the other redoubts disappeared as their land and their materials were absorbed by the growing city. The Blockhouse itself was converted into part of a dwelling, which when painted by Russell Smith in 1832 was decidedly slummy; it was here, however, that the newspaper publisher and early Pittsburgh historian Neville B. Craig was born. Later in the century it was a peculiar enclave in a Pennsylvania Railroad freight terminal, vaguely known but not especially cherished as a souvenir of the past and intended for demolition as the terminal expanded. In 1894, Mary Croghan Schenley gave the Blockhouse to the Daughters of the American Revolution, whose Fort Pitt Society restored it and has maintained it ever since. It is open, free to the public, and remains independent of the State's nearby Fort Pitt Museum.

The "Forks of the Ohio" on which the Blockhouse is situated is a National Historic Landmark.

National Register of Historic Places

St. Mary of Mercy Church (Roman Catholic)
Stanwix Street and Third Avenue
William P. Hutchins, architect, 1936

A church in a built-up downtown area presents a challenging design problem. It must hold its own with taller buildings: conventional gables, steep roofs, and spires are apt to be dwarfed and made of little account. At St. Mary's, the architect erected two red brick walls at the property line, cutting deep window openings into them, setting their upper sections back a few inches over a course of limestone, and breaking up the surface lightly with other devices. The tower at the corner is isolated from neighboring buildings and is kept low, with a simple, strong shape. A deep slot in the wall separates the church visibly from its parish house, and the latter has a string-course and an elaborate fretted band of stone to reduce its apparent height. The simplicity and strength of the resulting design maintains the dignity of the church regardless of what may be built around it. Its vivid red looks good, indeed, alongside the steely gray glass of PPG Place. Inside, the church is simple and auditorium-like, with a diagonal axis toward the altar.

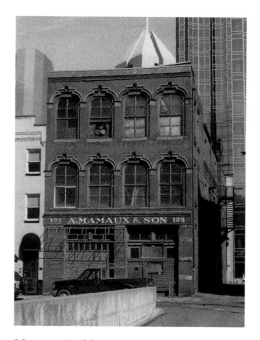

Wabash Bridge piers
Monongahela River, 1,650 feet west of the Smithfield Street
Bridge close to the Triangle near Market Street;
close to Station Square
Boller & Hodge, engineers, 1902–04

These tall twin constructions are the most visible remains
of the Wabash-Pittsburg Terminal Railroad, the foredoomed attempt of George Jay Gould (a son of *the* Jay
Gould) to break the near-monopoly of the Pennsylvania
Railroad in Pittsburgh. The cantilever bridge they supported carried two tracks from a two-track tunnel through
Mount Washington to the short throat of a yard that
consisted of nine tracks, most of them beneath a narrow
balloon trainshed. To accommodate all anticipated arrivals,
departures, and layovers, trains and strings of unoccupied
cars moved back and forth, switching here and there,
above the streets for the full width of the Triangle, about
1,100 feet at this point. Train movement was so inhibited
by this configuration that the railroad, opened in 1904,
was in receivership in 1908. The trainshed collapsed in a
fire in 1946, and the bridge came down in 1948.

The Wabash Bridge was a cantilever structure with a
total length of 1,504 feet and a main span, between the
extant piers, of 812 feet.

Historic Landmark plaque

Mamaux Building
123 First Avenue
C. 1870

This is a double-ended building, the entrance front being
a rather plain 1930-period structure in white brick on
the Boulevard of the Allies. The First Avenue front is the
interesting one, though, a sort of Mid-Victorian Baroque
display piece. The building belonged at one time to
A. Fulton's Sons & Co., bell founders.

National Register District
City Historic Structure

100 block, Market Street

A few simple buildings survive downtown to illustrate
the commercial architecture from immediately after the
Fire of 1845. Several of these still stand on Market Street
just north of First Avenue. To call them Greek Revival
would be straining things a little; they are simple commercial construction, though stone columns and lintels do
impart a slightly Classical feeling.

Jacob Painter & Sons office
226 First Avenue
Andrew Peebles, architect, 1883

This pleasant Queen Anne front is now the rear of
227 Fort Pitt Boulevard, but originally was the facade
of the office and showroom of an iron hoop and band
manufacturer.

National Register District

Commercial buildings
211–47 Fort Pitt Boulevard

This commercial row is in many respects as it was when
Fort Pitt Boulevard was Water Street and these Victorian
fronts overlooked a sloping, roughly paved embankment
at whose edge wharfboats lay and packets and towboats

tied up. This is the city's most tangible reminder of its old days as a diversified river port, with passengers, crates, and barrels coming in and out as well as coal and steel products moving past. A view of the Triangle from across the river begins with these relatively low buildings, then moves inland, finding ever-higher buildings as it moves further away, and thus reveals the history of the Triangle itself over a century and a half.

211 Fort Pitt Boulevard, far left.

227, 231, 235, 237, and 239 Fort Pitt Boulevard.

245 and 247 Fort Pitt Boulevard, and the Conestoga Building.

It is curious too that a look at these waterfront facades from left to right recapitulates the history of our commercial Victorian architecture almost perfectly. The building farthest left, Number 211, is in the very simplest Greek Revival, a reconstruction from shortly after the Fire of 1845. Number 231 is an elegant Italianate front of the 1860s, intact save for the original capitals under its entablature. Numbers 235 and 239 were once twin facades in the Queen Anne style of the 1880s, a style not commonly associated with business architecture. Number 245 seems to match the burly image of a waterfront building more closely: Richardson Romanesque of around 1890, down to the shallow detailing of its sturdy cast-iron piers. Number 247, with its large, slightly bowed windows and its crowning sheet-metal pediment, can simply be called Late Victorian, its date and style not to be clearly established.

National Register District
Historic Landmark plaque

Conestoga Building
Wood Street and Fort Pitt Boulevard
Longfellow, Alden & Harlow, architects, 1890

Of stone, brown terra cotta, and golden-brown Roman brick, this is a sumptuously detailed, carefully studied building by the architectural firm that would soon be designing the first part of the Carnegie Institute. The loss of the cornice is a pity with everything else intact. The exterior is still traditional solid masonry construction, and is visibly divided into solid piers and screen walls of spandrels, mullions, and transoms set slightly back. The admirable care that was taken with details can easily be seen in the ground-floor openings. Not only do little corbels project to give token support to the lintels and help maintain the continuity of the masonry, but the edges of the corbels are carefully rounded in some parts and left sharp in others: an almost-invisible detail that adds a touch of life, a refinement of a refinement.

National Register District

Hartje Building (now West Penn Building)
Wood Street and First Avenue
Charles Bickel, architect, 1906–07

Here the steel frame is decorated yet not disguised; seen in outline, indeed, the building has a rather ladder-like appearance. The lush spandrel and frieze ornament and the heavy cornice are a little old-fashioned for the late 1900s, although the contemporary Machesney (Benedum-Trees) Building has such features too. At the top is a shallow-pitched copper roof.

Loft buildings
109–15 Wood Street
C. 1900

These two buildings were evidently built to be a near-match, yet the corner building seems a little older, with its darker, warmer colors. The detailing is Classical, suggesting a date after 1895, but the cartouche on a rounded corner pier retains a Romanesque massiveness.

Historic Landmark plaque (Number 115, the corner building)

Loft buildings
319–21 First Avenue, 310–14 Boulevard of the Allies
C. 1900

The two masonry-and-timber buildings seem to be nearly but not quite contemporary and to reflect a slightly different design aesthetic. At a guess, 319–21 First Avenue is the earlier front, tawny brick and terra cotta in deference to the smoky air, a little heavy and lavish in its rusticated brick and Ionic capitals. The building to the left is simpler and lighter in tone, with white terra-cotta trim.

Engine Company Number One and Engine Company Number Thirty
344 Boulevard of the Allies
William Y. Brady, architect, 1900; Richard Neff, architect for remodeling, 1926

A broad segmental arch covering the portal for the fire engines is stabilized visually by two blunt semi-obelisks. The rear on First Avenue is simpler but intended equally to please, with its Roman brick upper story and delicate wooden cornice. This is a survivor from a time when a work of governmental architecture was expected to be an ornament to its surroundings and to represent government itself in a dignified manner.

Engine Company Number Two
112 Smithfield Street,
408 Boulevard of the Allies
William Y. Brady, architect,
1900

Built as a firehouse, this is unusual in having a Beaux-Arts style, specifically a kind of Rococo with a little Art Nouveau detailing in the windows: quite a departure from the usual sober municipal architecture, though the heavy cornice with the City arms seems to reprove the mild frivolity below. The plan is L-shaped, and there is a narrower front on the Boulevard of the Allies that once housed a "water tower" truck that carried water to the tops of tall buildings. Number 112 has not been used for fire-fighting purposes for many years; rather, it has been used for commerce, and now houses several businesses.

Pittsburgh has not had much Beaux-Arts architecture, and the Triangle has lost almost all of the little that once existed there; that these pleasant facades have survived almost unchanged is all the more welcome.

Hartley-Rose Building
425 First Avenue
Edward Stotz, architect,
1907

Now remodeled as an office building, this loft structure of masonry and timber was built as a factory and warehouse for the Hartley-Rose Belting Company, manufacturers of the belting that drove pre-electrified industrial machinery. Its cheerful urbanity was wasted for many years on a street that was hardly more than a seldom-visited alley, and it is pleasant to see it appreciated and part of a reviving section of town.

National Register of Historic Places
Historic Landmark plaque

Smithfield Street Bridge
Monongahela River at Smithfield Street
Gustav Lindenthal, engineer, 1881–83; widened, 1891, 1911;
Stanley L. Roush, architect for portals, c. 1915

This, one of the oldest bridges in the county, is also one of the most remarkable. It has two 360-foot main spans of the rare lenticular-truss type, in which the upper chord, an arch thrusting outward, is combined with a lower chord in the form of a catenary, pulling inward. The two forces cancel each other out, and, with the aid of diagonal bracing to counteract moving off-center loads, they have been doing so for more than a century. The product of a time when welded construction was unknown and structural members in bridges had to be fairly light, the Smithfield Street Bridge has a typical Victorian limberness, quivering beneath the loads of crossing traffic.

The downstream part of the bridge is the original, with arches, catenaries, and diagonals of open-hearth steel and other members of wrought iron. The upstream side was added in 1891, then widened to match the first part in 1911, and the City Architect Stanley L. Roush then replaced the ponderous cast-iron portals with light, rather witty, quasi-Gothic ones. In a 1933 reconstruction the original iron and steel floor members were replaced with aluminum, an early structural use of the material that adapted the

bridge for heavier traffic loads by reducing its dead weight. Major floor reconstruction occurred in 1994, replacing the aluminum floor members with steel, removing the trolley lines on the upstream span, and enlarging the southern approach. A second campaign in 1995 restored the Roush portals and returned the main spans to their 1883 colors: deep blue for the trusses and brown for the floor structures; the portals were painted a sort of buttermilk yellow, the principal portal color in 1915. The upper chords of the main-span trusses were outlined in lights, upstream and down. Yet the original eyebars of the catenaries still bear the stamp "Kloman patent process 1881."

The bridge is the third on the site, successor to others also by distinguished engineers. Lewis Wernwag completed the original Smithfield Street Bridge in 1818, the first river bridge in Pittsburgh, and John Augustus Roebling built the second in 1846.

The present bridge has been designated a National Historic Civil Engineering Landmark by the American Society of Civil Engineers.

National Historic Landmark
National Register of Historic Places
City Historic Structure
Historic Landmark plaque

Fourth Avenue

Fourth Avenue, between Market and Smithfield Streets, retains much of its turn-of-the-century image as Pittsburgh's "Wall Street," a street of financial institutions. Banks and trust companies first came to this street in 1835 with the Bank of Pittsburgh and arrived in increasing numbers in the late Victorian period when oil, glass, iron, and steel made Pittsburgh a great industrial city and industrial capital spurred financial growth. The oldest bank building on the narrow street is now the Dollar Savings Bank's 1871 building, but there are numerous others, large and aloof, small and aggressive, which together form an intense historic streetscape.

One curiosity of the street is notable at a distance: a historic skyline of early skyscrapers of almost equal dimensions, evenly spaced along the avenue—the Machesney (now Benedum-Trees), Investment, and Arrott Buildings—and their near-neighbors, the Peoples Savings Bank and Union National Bank Buildings. The architecture that these buildings display at twenty stories is only a hint of that which lines the street below.

National Register District

Burke's Building (now Western Pennsylvania Conservancy)
209 Fourth Avenue
John Chislett, architect, 1836

This is the oldest business building in the Triangle, fortunately spared by the Fire of 1845. It is a small but very polished work by an English-trained architect who had begun practice in Pittsburgh in 1833. Its boxy form is apparent, but both the forward break of the central bay, a sort of token pavilion, and the moldings and rustication that cross the facade show the professional touch, an enlivening of a plain front with contrasting verticals and horizontals. The wreaths on the doorway frieze are unusual in American Greek Revival architecture, probably a borrowing from Napoleonic France. The Grecian Doric doorway, and indeed the whole front, is of stone; this was obviously intended to be a first-class building. Of the interior detailing nothing significant is left, but exterior restoration has reproduced the window sash.

Built by Robert and Andrew Burke, Burke's Building housed a bank at one point in its history.

National Register of Historic Places
City Historic District
Historic Landmark plaque

Machesney Building (now Benedum-Trees Building)
221 Fourth Avenue
Thomas H. Scott, architect, 1905

Here is a skyscraper still evolving out of Victorian elaboration into a more modern simplicity. The base-shaft-capital formula is in effect, with a three-story Corinthian colonnade, piers rising sheer and almost unadorned above a transitional story, and an elaborate conclusion with balcony and cornice jutting boldly. The whole composition is realized in light-colored granite and white brick and terra cotta. The choice of materials is in a contemporary 1905 spirit, but the elaborate ornament of the spandrels and the heaviness of the uppermost part are carry-overs

from the recent past. Inside, the lobby is a remarkable and enjoyable sight; though a mere corridor without the spaciousness of many office-building lobbies of the time, it has decoration in marble, bronze, and plaster in high concentration, little altered since the beginning.

The building was erected for Haynes Allen Machesney but was

bought in 1913 by Michael Late Benedum and his partner Joseph Clifton Trees, oil speculators and principals of the Benedum-Trees Oil Company. It has been a favorite location for stockbrokers.

National Register District
City Historic District
Historic Landmark plaque

**Insurance Exchange Building
(now Investment Building)**
239 Fourth Avenue
John M. Donn (Washington, D.C.), architect, 1927

After the pale granite, terra cotta, and brick of the twentieth century's beginning, Pittsburgh business architecture turned once again to darker colors above lighter base stories. In this case the base was limestone with textured brown brick above, and an elegant limestone "capital." The building's footprint is a fat H, but chamfers filled with obelisks force attention on the top of the front element, which thus reads as an octagon. The contrast with the Machesney Building to the left, two decades older and of very similar dimensions on the street front, shows how progressing Eclecticism attained a light, integrated look in its compositions.

National Register District

Centennial Building
241 Fourth Avenue
1876

The upper stories of this front have a delicacy unusual in Mid-Victorian architecture. Flat surfaces advance from the wall plane but are themselves incised, so that though the whole composition is of sandstone there is a cameo-like effect of layer upon layer of material, cut away to produce the design. The ground floor, remodeled at least twice, is still at odds with the original Victorian work though its present state shows an attempt at harmony. Since the third story is more delicate than the second, the ground floor should probably be the sturdiest-looking of all, stylistically in contrast with the Italianate treatment above but with a reduced amount of decorative detailing and a maintenance of the original rhythm of openings. The front, one of a dwindling number of Mid-Victorian commercial fronts downtown, deserves such thoughtful treatment.

National Register District

Within the entrance arch is a lobby, tall, narrow, a little clumsy in overall design, but rich to the eye and full of character. Ornamental bronze and heavily veined marble inlaid with Cosmati mosaic borders create an effect hard to describe. It is as if someone should descend that rather steep stair, hand trailing along the richly worked balustrade, pause by the newel-post lamp on its four Ionic columns, and say something portentous, possibly reproachful.

National Register District

Arrott Building
Fourth Avenue and Wood Street
Frederick J. Osterling, architect, 1901–02;
Edward B. Lee, architect for remodeling of lower facades, 1928

Osterling's design manner was a heavy one, best suited to Romanesque, and when he did a Classical work the results were likely to be rich and ponderous. Here he tackled the skyscraper problem, using the reasonable base-shaft-capital formula. The base is rather thin in effect, due to the 1928 remodeling and removal of half-columns that originally flanked the entrance, but is given impressive depth by the great recessed archway of the entrance, executed in gray granite. Above this, the shaft shows the common inability

of the turn-of-the-century architect to let any part of a building go unadorned; there is a balcony, and bands of white terra cotta and brown brick stress the horizontals, even though this is a tall and rather narrow building. The capital is the best element of the three, with its tall arcades that some have compared to Venetian palace architecture, its massive cornice, and its crowning cheneau.

Commercial buildings
411, 413, and 417 Wood Street
1876; 1883 (refaced c. 1905); c. 1875, respectively

Three curious buildings of equal height stand side by side, illustrating Victorian fashions in small-scale commercial architecture. Number 411, built in 1876, is Mid-Victorian Gothic executed in cold, white marble. As with many Victorian commercial buildings, its center is accented as if to pull the eye as far as possible away from other buildings.

Its contemporary, Number 417, unusual for the time, attempts Florentine Gothic, with rusticated walls; it used to have Italian-looking split battlements too. Number 413, much newer as refaced, takes advantage of its greater width to display a broadly proportioned North Italian Renaissance front of Roman brick and dark terra cotta, lavish in its decoration.

National Register District

Forbes Avenue front, Colonial Trust Company.

Financial buildings (now the Bank Tower and The Library Center)
317 Forbes Avenue, 414 Wood Street, and 307–17 Fourth Avenue
1893–1926; remodeled, 1976, 1996–97

This building group, a library complex for the Carnegie Library of Pittsburgh and Point Park College, was adapted from a cluster of financial buildings. The nucleus is the T-shaped Colonial Trust Company, much of whose interior is still visible though the space has been filled in, in large part, by new construction. It has similar granite-and-sandstone entrances, pedimented, Corinthian, and with florid Baroque cartouches, on Forbes and Fourth Avenues; for both, the date was 1902 and the architect Frederick J. Osterling. In 1925–26, Osterling added a Greek Ionic entrance on Wood Street.

At the corner of Wood and Fourth is another element, the fifteen-story Peoples Savings Bank Building (now the Bank Tower) of 1901–02 by Alden & Harlow. Here, above a three-story base of pale pink granite, vehemently rusti-

Peoples Savings Bank Building

cated, rises a brick-and-terra-cotta shaft, heavily ornamented and rusticated at its openings, entirely of a deep red. The doorways have tympanum sculptures by John Massey Rhind, who worked with the architects later at the Carnegie Institute. Much of the terra-cotta rustication, badly weathered, had to be chopped out in the early 1960s and replaced with brick, so the tower now has a curious peanut-brittle look. Press C. Dowler extended the rustication of the lower floors along Wood Street in 1926, using composition stone, a colored and textured cement, not granite.

Next to the Peoples Savings Bank Building on Fourth Avenue is the Freehold Realty Building of 1893, unchanged except for its ground-floor window and its parapet, and next to that the Commercial National Bank Building of 1897, whose original big arch, springing from the belt-courses at the sides, is now gone. This is by Alden & Harlow. Remarkable interior features of these buildings include vast stained-glass ceilings, the marble geometrical stair inside the Forbes Avenue entrance of the Colonial Trust Building, and the inlaid marble stair in the Peoples Savings Bank Building.

National Register District

Fourth Avenue fronts

Union National Bank Building
Fourth Avenue and Wood Street
MacClure & Spahr, architects, 1906

The simple design of this formidable bank-plus-skyscraper of gray granite is quite up-to-date in its elimination of detail—if anything, a little ahead of common practice in the mid-1900s—yet it has a corner entrance of the sort common in Mid-Victorian banks, as if an old tradition

were being recalled. The entrance is emphasized, not with a burst of ornament as it would have been thirty years before, but by making the whole corner of the building a quarter-round. The banking room, though much remodeled, is impressive still, with its green Cipollino marble columns and ceilings with silver-dollar motifs.

Two adjoining bank buildings on Fourth Avenue have been annexed. The one next door began as the Commonwealth Trust Company, and its building permit was issued on the same day as that for the Union National Bank, April 30, 1906. There was a race to complete the two buildings, which Union won. The Commonwealth banking room retains some gorgeous cast-bronze railings by Frederick J. Osterling, its architect.

National Register District

Industrial Bank (later Stock Exchange Building)
333 Fourth Avenue
Charles M. Bartberger, architect, 1903

The exaggeratedly large arch and a dwarf colonnade above suggest some Neoclassical work of early in the previous century in Germany or Italy. A banking room with an office floor above provides a rationale for the composition, and doubtless the architect wanted as well to help a small bank building make a big impression on a street that was lined with banks. The contemporary critic Montgomery Schuyler called such places swagger banks.

National Register District

Union Trust Company (now Pittsburgh Engineers' Building)
337 Fourth Avenue
D. H. Burnham & Co. (Chicago), architects, 1898

This was the first Pittsburgh work by the Burnham office. The combination of a cool and correct Grecian Doric temple front with big, florid acroteria on the pediment and the wall behind is typical for the 1900 period. Classicists would produce a simple academic facade or interior, then add bursts of sculptured ornament, intricate metal railings, or great surfaces of heavily veined marble as if some Victorian urge to decorate things would be denied no longer. At the time that this building was going up, Burnham was beginning the design of Union Station.

National Register District
Historic Landmark plaque

Fidelity Trust Company Building
341 Fourth Avenue
James T. Steen, architect, 1888–89

A decidedly thin-looking front of Richardson Romanesque. Its best elements are the low-built doorways, with little red granite nook shafts in contrast to the prevailing gray granite, and the triple windows of the uppermost floors. The bronze grillework of the left doorway is handsome in its own right, though an addition.

National Register District

Times Building (once Magee Building)
346 Fourth Avenue
Frederick J. Osterling, architect, 1892

This is one of Osterling's most successful buildings, a Richardson Romanesque work that is massive in the way that suited his talent best and assured in its detailing. Both the Fourth and Third Avenue fronts are handsome, though different. The building received extensive interior remodeling in the 1980s by The Design Alliance.

It was erected for the *Pittsburgh Times*, a newspaper whose principal owner was the noted local politician Christopher Lyman Magee. It was probably the first skeleton-framed office building in Pittsburgh.

National Register District

Dollar Savings Bank
348 Fourth Avenue
Isaac Hobbs & Sons (Philadelphia), architects, 1868–71;
James T. Steen, architect for additions, 1906

Hobbs designed the sort of "Victorian" architecture the
public had in mind in the middle of this century, when the
word "Victorian" was automatically followed by the word
"monstrosity." But at the time when he was designing this
bank, Hobbs was a favorite of home-builders in the
Bellefield section of Oakland, and certainly not because
he was seen as a creator of monstrous designs. Nor did
the Dollar Savings Bank, a mutual bank run for the benefit
of its thrifty working-class depositors, wish to intimidate
them. The fantastic front of Connecticut brownstone,
with its Baroque display of Composite columns and curved
corners, suggested rather solidity, dignity, wealth to spend.
The recumbent lions by Max Kohler seem to guard the
bank, yet they are not aggressive lions; James D. Van Trump
called them "hearth-rug champions…the Noble Animals so
dear to Victorian sentimentality [with] a gemütlich dignity,
a cozy grandeur that is entirely charming."

National Register of Historic Places
Historic Landmark plaque

**Pittsburgh Bank for Savings (now
Standard Life Building)**
Smithfield Street and Fourth Avenue
Alden & Harlow, architects, 1902–03

The busy rustications and banding, and the strong ochre
terra cotta and red brick of the upper stories are typical of
a transitional phase in skyscraper design. The architects
still hesitated to make their building "a proud and soaring
thing," as Louis Sullivan had been recommending, and
included insistent horizontals to fight its rise and heavy
masonry detailing at the top and bottom to deny the lightness of its construction. Of the original ground floor only
one granite door frame remains; each front originally had a
screen of Doric columns with heavy bands around them
that added still more horizontality and massiveness.

The composition, like that of the Peoples Savings Bank
Building at the other end of the block, was probably
intended not so much to address the compositional
problem of the skyscraper as to state that this particular
bank was the peer of the others on Fourth Avenue, with
capital to spend on solid, dignified display.

National Register District

Marine National Bank (now 301 Smithfield Street)
Smithfield Street and Third Avenue
Frederick J. Osterling, architect, 1890

The broad first-floor arch on Smithfield Street is a reconstruction; there were two arches here originally. Osterling had less wall space to work with than in his almost-contemporary Times Building around the corner, and designed a rather open, airy structure rather than aiming for monumentality. In the Times Building he included sculptured heads and leaf ornament; here, his detailing is more spare, but a dragon gargoyle enlivens the corner.

National Register District

Meyer, Jonasson & Company department store
606 Liberty Avenue
MacClure & Spahr, architects, 1909–10

Built as the Meyer, Jonasson & Co. department store, this building has the large window area and cream-colored terra-cotta facing that was common in department stores in the early twentieth century. Where it differs from Gimbel's or Kaufmann's, which also have these characteristics, is in its style, a mixture of Beaux-Arts and Art Nouveau that was probably intended to impart an air of Parisian smartness. The facades form an obtuse angle because Oliver Avenue, now terminated a block away, used to meet Liberty Avenue at this point. The exterior was restored in the early 1980s, although the original false roof, serving as a cornice, was not reproduced.

Diamond Building (later Dravo Building; now 100 Fifth Avenue)
Fifth and Liberty Avenues
MacClure & Spahr, architects, c. 1905

The former home of the Diamond National Bank, this medium-sized office building fills out an oddly shaped site. Like many buildings of its time it is a gray-and-white essay in the base-shaft-capital formula, here with one slight touch of color in a green copper cheneau on the cornice. Though never one of the star performers on our architectural scene it is a nice solid design, a handsome building of the sort that people enjoy without pausing to study. It punctuates a major intersection quite effectively, with a mass that dominates the immediate area.

City Historic District

Market Square (originally the Diamond)
Forbes Avenue and Market Street

The Woods-Vickroy plan of 1784 left this central square within the Triangle as a public market, though rarely has the space been so open as it is today. From the mid-1790s until 1852 it accommodated not only market stalls but also the first Allegheny County Courthouse. When that came down, construction began on a market house and a City Hall that cut across Diamond Alley (later Diamond Street, now Forbes Avenue), and left no other open space save for that of the remaining streets. These two buildings lasted until 1912, and in 1917 were succeeded by a unified Market House that bridged over a reunited Diamond Street. This market house came down in 1961, and since then the space has been open. Schemes to give it monumental character or to landscape it have come and gone, however, and today it has a rather plain and open character, with grass, trees, and a rostrum built in one corner for rallies.

The architecture around the square and in the immediate area has been varied, in most cases of no distinction, and tending to be small-scaled. Yet it has color and variety, and compares well in this regard with the nearby central piazza of PPG Place, a despotic piece of total design. One wing of PPG Place actually fronts on Market Square, black and silver and of uniform upright elements, like a Prussian regiment formed up to impress the peasants.

Buhl Building
Fifth Avenue and Market Street
Janssen & Abbott, architects, c. 1913

This is a little gem of a building, clad in blue-and-creamy-white terra cotta thickly decorated with Renaissance motifs. The color contrast recalls Italian sgraffito work, in which an outer layer of stucco is cut away while still fresh to reveal, scratchboard-fashion, an inner layer in a contrasting hue. The ground floor has been altered in a Moderne manner.

This was a downtown speculation of Franklin F. Nicola, the developer of the Schenley Farms area of Oakland.

National Register of Historic Places
City Historic District
Historic Landmark plaque

Grand Opera House (later Warner Theatre; now Warner Centre)
336 Fifth Avenue
MacClure & Spahr,
architects, 1906;
reconstructed, 1918,
1983–85

Only the terra-cotta facade and Fifth Avenue lobby remain of a legitimate theater built in 1906, burned in 1917, reconstructed for movies and vaudeville by the movie-house specialist C. Howard Crane (Detroit) in 1918, and gutted in 1983 for a commercial development. After all this, a curious feature is still to be noted: sockets in the upper windows for the light bulbs that once outlined the facade. This device, popular in theaters in the early twentieth century, was also used to outline the arches of the grandiose cab shelter at Union Station.

The upper facade is now restored, including its bulb sockets and the big Warner Theatre sign (which now reads "Warner Centre"); but a large office and retail building now lies behind with part of the original lobby, and presents a Modern glass-box front to Forbes Avenue.

Joseph Horne Company department store (now Penn Avenue Place)
Penn Avenue and Stanwix Street
West Building, 1900, by Peabody & Stearns (Boston);
East Building, 1900, by William S. Fraser;
North Building, 1922–23, by Peabody & Stearns

From 1849 into 1994, the name Joseph Horne was famous in Pittsburgh, appearing in bronze outside a palatial-looking department store. The original building on the present site, by W. S. Fraser, was built in 1892, burned out in 1897, was rebuilt in 1898, burned out again and was rebuilt in 1900, received an annex the same year, and went on in a relatively undisturbed manner thenceforth. The resulting complex is not fully unified and is rather stolid in its individual parts, yet it constitutes an imposing urban mass.

The building complex ceased to be a department store in 1995 and is now used for office and retail space.

Historic Landmark plaque

Penn Theatre (now Heinz Hall)
Sixth Street and Penn Avenue
Rapp & Rapp (Chicago), architects, 1925–26;
remodeled, 1970–71

In the late 1960s the Pittsburgh Symphony was due to move out of its old home at Syria Mosque in Oakland. Yet its promised new concert hall in the showy Center for the Arts, planned for the lower Hill urban-renewal area, had not been started (and never was). To give the Symphony temporary space, the Heinz Endowment bought the old Penn Theatre, which, like many of the silent-movie theaters, had stage space. As the hope of the cultural display case on the Hill was deferred still further, and as interested parties stressed the advantages of a concert hall in the center of the city, the temporary expedient became the permanent plan with a remodeling by the local firm Stotz, Hess, MacLachlan & Fosner. Shop space became a lobby; the old entrance became a huge foyer window; and broad office windows above were

partly filled in, in a rather Viennese Baroque style. The last maker of architectural terra cotta in the United States was commissioned to match the warm off-white of the original facing, and did an almost-perfect job.

Inside, the richly decorated auditorium, originally meant to be dark, was lightened in tones of cream, red, and gold, and Verner S. Purnell of Sewickley painted huge gray-gold trophies in a Neo-Baroque manner. The old spaces outside the auditorium were adapted to intermission crowds, presenting a spectacle of real marble, fake marble, glossy ceramics, and chandeliers.

The popularity of Heinz Hall led to its facilities being over-taxed, and another grand movie house of the 1920s, the Stanley Theatre, was adapted as Benedum Center for the Performing Arts.

Historic Landmark plaque

Fulton Building
Sixth Street and Fort Duquesne Boulevard
Grosvenor Atterbury (New York), architect, 1906

Like some other Pittsburgh industrialists, Henry Phipps, a partner of Andrew Carnegie, became interested in down-town real estate and made his mark on one part of the Triangle with a close-set group of buildings. The architect he chose for the three office buildings he erected was the New Yorker Grosvenor Atterbury, a mildly experimental architect best remembered for the half-Modern, half-quaint station square of Forest Hills Gardens, a Long Island suburb. The Manufacturers Building, gone now, was the location of the once-famous Pittsburgh Natatorium, a health establishment centered around a grandly vaulted swimming bath. The Fulton Building, still extant, and the Bessemer Building, demolished around 1964, were buildings of roughly similar design that once framed the

Sixth Street entrance to the Triangle from Pittsburgh's rival city of Allegheny, the present North Side.

The general design of the Fulton Building follows the common base-shaft-capital formula of skyscraper composition, yet the capital is understated: tile-roofed corner pavilions of somewhat Mediterranean character with arcades between, mostly clad in patinaed bronze. The dramatic feature of the building is in the middle of the shaft, facing north: a tall, cavernous archway opening into an interior light court of the kind that once allowed offices at the center of the building to have air. It is said to have worked very satisfactorily in the days before air conditioning.

The semi-Classical marble lobby, with its grand stair, has been converted to other uses with much permanent impairment, but the main entrance to the building is now through a new and less-spacious passage. An original side entrance off Sixth Street leads to the old Gayety Theatre, now the Byham.

Gayety Theatre (later Fulton Theatre; now Byham Theater)
602 Fort Duquesne Boulevard
Dodge & Morrison (New York), architects, 1903–04

The original entrance, while this was a legitimate theater, appears to have been off Sixth Street though there were also doors on the Duquesne Way front. This front, apparently quite blank from the start, is now covered with a trompe-l'oeil mural by Richard Haas. Like the adjacent Fulton Building and the vanished Bessemer Building, this was a real-estate speculation of Henry Phipps. It has been restored as a stage theater.

Sixth, Seventh, and Ninth Street Bridges
Allegheny River
Vernon R. Covell, T. J. Wilkerson, A. D. Nutter, and
H. E. Dodge of the Allegheny County Department of
Public Works, engineers; Stanley L. Roush, architect; 1925–28

In the early 1920s the County wanted to replace three adjoining Victorian bridges whose appearances ranged from the drab to the grotesque. The municipal Art Commission had a right to decide on the form of bridges within Pittsburgh, and in this case opted for identical suspension bridges.

The catenary of a suspension bridge—the down-curved part from which all else hangs—is usually secured at its ends by anchorages, which are simply heavy weights. Local conditions prevented the six anchorages normally needed for three such bridges, so the engineers looked to Germany and the one self-anchored suspension bridge in existence; instead of weights holding the ends of the catenaries *down*, a rigid girder in the German bridge held them *apart*, with the same result. But to construct such a bridge, it proved expedient to use old-fashioned, clumsy catenaries of eye-bars, bolted together joint by joint, instead of the standard wire cables that could be much more easily built up on single initial strands passed between the shores. Until the catenaries were complete, in fact, the bridges had to be built as cantilever trusses, with struts that were later removed. In brief, a lot of fuss and corresponding expense to build a type of bridge that looked nice but was inappropriate on the site. But the municipal Art Commission was vindicated in the long run; the American Institute of Steel Construction awarded the Sixth Street Bridge, the last to be completed, a beauty prize in 1928.

The Sixth Street Bridge is 884 feet long, the center span being exactly half that length.

National Register of Historic Places
Historic Landmark plaques

Fort Wayne Bridge, Pennsylvania Railroad
Allegheny River east of Eleventh Street
Pennsylvania Railroad engineers, 1901–04; raised, 1918

This is a double-decked railroad bridge with a variation of the Pennsylvania truss, invented for the railroad, in the main span. This truss is a development of the Pratt truss for the purpose of withstanding the heavy, off-center, moving loads of trains. A Pratt truss consists of upper and lower horizontal chords, the upper one in compression, the lower one in tension, with posts supporting the upper chord and diagonals in tension hanging from the heads of the posts and supporting the feet of posts closer to the center of the truss: essentially, a beam with all the non-essential parts left out. The bridge was made three tracks wide, but only two tracks ever existed on each of the decks, and highway construction on the North Side has cut off access to the lower deck.

The bridge was raised in 1918, probably to give clearance for steamboats; the extent of the raising is clearly shown in the concrete tops to the original stone piers.

National Register of Historic Places

Century Building

120 Seventh Street
Rutan & Russell, architects,
1906–07

This is a fairly tall mid-block office building of early in the century, its exterior somewhat modified with a 1940-period Modernistic entrance. Like much commercial architecture of its time, the greater part of the street front is treated as an arcade enclosing window areas treated in a contrasting way. Here, the structure is faced in matte white or near-white materials, while the solids around the windows are in glossy bronze-green terra cotta that creates a miniature architecture within the major architecture of the building frame.

Stanley Theatre (now Benedum Center for the Performing Arts)

Seventh Street and Penn Avenue
Hoffman-Henon Company (Philadelphia), architects, 1926–27;
remodeled and enlarged, 1985–87,
MacLachlan, Cornelius & Filoni, architects

Heinz Hall, opened in 1971, proved such a success as not to be able to handle all the business offered it, and another grand 1920s movie house with stage and orchestral facilities, the Stanley, was adapted for opera, light opera, and ballet. In the process the exterior was preserved as it

had been: suggestions of Georgian England and Napoleonic France in off-white terra cotta and pale tan brick. The foyer and auditorium areas were again left very much as before, but the stagehouse volume was tripled and a new six-story annex on Liberty Avenue was built to house facilities that include two stage-sized rehearsal halls, one of which can serve as a theater.

National Register of Historic Places
City Historic Structure
Historic Landmark plaque

900 block of Liberty Avenue

Penn and Liberty Avenues

Liberty Avenue marks the edge of a narrow street grid of the 1784 Woods-Vickroy plan that was laid out with reference to the Allegheny River. By the end of the nineteenth century, Liberty and its parallel street Penn Avenue were very largely commercial, intensely busy streets where stores and loft buildings were closely ranged with Italianate walkups alongside the much taller Romanesque and Renaissance buildings of the elevator period. Until 1905, a railroad freight line ran down the center of Liberty Avenue, and long after that interurban trolleys continued to mingle with local street railways.

In recent years this area has been a mixture of the forgotten and the unrespectable. But it is now in transition with the rehabilitation of many old buildings. The area between Liberty Avenue and the Allegheny River, east of Seventh Street, is a National Register District and a City Historic District for the most part. Of the buildings that have been restored or may hope to be restored under the

805-07 Liberty Avenue

927-29 Liberty Avenue

new conditions, the oldest are four walkup iron-fronted structures of c. 1870, which have almost a small-town look. Numbers 805–07 and 927–29 Liberty Avenue appear to be made from the same molds; a founder's mark on the former pair names the Anderson & Phillips foundry once on Water Street, the present Fort Pitt Boulevard. The style is Mid-Victorian Italianate, though the ornament in sunken panels in the pilasters is Rococo.

Number 811 Liberty Avenue, an elongated Queen Anne building that begins rather plain but becomes fancier and fancier as it rises until it terminates in a flourish above the sixth story with a pediment and a pair of shell motifs, was built in 1886 except for the sixth story, which was added in 1892. Number 820 from 1881, across the street, is altogether a tougher building, prominent skewbacks resisting the thrust of wide flat and segmental arches beneath a heavy, elaborate parapet. The whole facade seems, with its distribution of forces and its slender supports, to be trying to tear itself apart, yet to be holding together out of some mysterious inner strength. This dramatic exercise serves the practical function, of course, of letting the very maximum of light and air into the building.

The Triangle Building at 926–34 Liberty Avenue, built in 1884, is much calmer in tone despite its floridly Gothic ground floor. (The two top stories are additions.) In fact, it makes rather gracious use of one of the peculiar bits of

land casually created by the Woods-Vickroy plan; with nothing to gain in useable space from acute angles, it squares and rounds them off and appears as a firm, solid shape that is accented by courses of stonework. The architect was Andrew Peebles, who just at this time was entered as a competitor for the Allegheny County Courthouse and Jail. He never submitted designs, and we may wonder what they would have looked like: Gothic again, perhaps?

The Irish Block at 964 Penn Avenue is a red-and-yellow work of c. 1890 by John U. Barr: a study in pattern and color of odd harsh beauty, a celebration of beams and segmental arches that is full of character even though it is almost modest as a structural display.

There are two store buildings by the busy architect Charles Bickel, about twenty years apart. The Ewart Building at 925 Liberty Avenue, built in 1891 for a wholesale grocer, is Richardson Romanesque and once was one of three Romanesque fronts that stood side by side. Having an alley alongside, it was not quite so pressed for light and air as most other Liberty Avenue stores, and the architect made the main facade a little more massive than were some of the others. Still, there is plenty of window space. In 1984–85 the building was cleaned and restored, and the cast-iron mullions of the lower two floors were painted a yellow-gray to match the sandstone above. The Ewart Building was of masonry and timber; around 1910 its architect, at 915 Penn Avenue, produced a counterpart in steel clad in terra cotta. For the most part his building was plain, open, and generally matter-of-fact, almost a frank expression of the structural cage. But he arched his upper-

811 Liberty Avenue

820 Liberty Avenue

Triangle Building

Ewart Building

Second National Bank Building

Irish Block

most windows very slightly, then set off his white surfaces with thin verticals of ultramarine, very strikingly, and concluded in the fashionable manner of the time with a flaring cornice.

Finally, the Second National Bank Building of 1911 deserves mention: an unusually suave addition to this commercial district, this is a work by Alden & Harlow, faced in granite and much quieter in tone than its earlier and more commercial neighbors. Known also as the Victory Building, it stands at Liberty Avenue and Ninth Street.

National Register District (in part)
National Register of Historic Places (Ewart Building)
City Historic District (in part)

915 Penn Avenue

**Keenan Building
(now Midtown Towers)**
*Liberty Avenue and
Seventh Street
Thomas Hannah, architect,
1907*

Col. Thomas J. Keenan,
Jr. was the chief owner of
the *Penny Press*, founded
in 1885, later known as
the *Pittsburgh Press*.
A man with an eye for
publicity, he erected a
skyscraper visible down
Sixth Avenue with an
almost-unique climactic
feature: a reinforced-
concrete dome clad in
shiny copper-finish tiles
that was originally
surmounted by a globe,
which in its turn was
surmounted by an eagle poised for flight. The great dome
was surrounded by four smaller domes, each with a
flagstaff. Now that globe, eagle, and staffs are gone, the
effect suggests a Prussian general with four aides, still a
remarkable terminal feature for a tall building. Originally,
the terra cotta of the lower part of the building contained
ten medallions of Pittsburgh worthies and Pennsylvania
politicians, but several of these have yielded to weathering.

The dome once housed the Baird Studio, the elegantly
furnished workplace of a fashionable photographer.

The building is now used as moderate-income housing.

*National Register District
City Historic District*

German National Bank (later Granite Building)
*Sixth Avenue and Wood Street
Bickel & Brennan, architects, 1889–90; remodelings
c. 1930 and late 1980s*

The old German National Bank has lost its large-scaled
ground-floor arcade, a unifying element that the overall
composition misses greatly; yet its profusion of ornament
has an interest of its own, with the Sixth Avenue doorway
an especially pleasant feature. (Apart from this doorway,
the present ground floor is a pastiche vaguely recalling the
arcaded original.) Together with its much more restrained
neighbor the Duquesne Club, it forms an element of one
of the very handsomest architectural groups in the city.

The bank, founded in 1860, was intended primarily for
the German community and thus, like other banks of
the Victorian period, was created to meet the needs of a
specific class of customers. Presumably a customer could
transact his business in German if need be: a real consideration in a period of massive immigration.

*National Register District
Historic Landmark plaque*

Duquesne Club
325 Sixth Avenue
Longfellow, Alden & Harlow, architects, 1887–89;
Alden & Harlow, architects for addition to main front, 1902;
Janssen & Cocken, architects for tower addition, 1930–31

The Duquesne Club, founded in 1873, is famous as a
wealthy, conservative institution, traditionally the club of
leading industrialists and business people. In choosing
Longfellow, Alden & Harlow to design their new home,
they may have seemed bold, for the firm was quite new.
Yet Frank Alden had been assigned by H. H. Richardson
to supervise construction of the Allegheny County
Courthouse and Jail, and the firm may thus have borrowed
some glamour from the recently dead master, a brilliant
architect who was known also to be a gentleman and who
was a friend of John H. Ricketson, a club founder.

Certainly, the architects for the 1887 design were a new firm, off
to a good start since they won in competition with offices
of growing reputation: Heins & La Farge (New York),
William Halsey Wood (Newark), and Richardson's
successor firm Shepley, Rutan & Coolidge (Boston).

Certainly, the original part of the club has a simple
dignity that rewarded the members' expectations. The
doorway, now a window, is fully Romanesque, but the
remainder is almost Classical in its symmetry, its gently
textured brownstone walls, and its balustrade emphasizing
a level roofline. Furthermore, the bay windows that allow
observation of the passing world from an elevated and

rather private vantage point must have struck the clubmen
as entirely right; their presence suggests clubhouses in both
Boston and the London West End. The office went on
from this good beginning to design the homes of the
wealthy for two decades.

The addition to the club along the street continues
the Romanesque style, and so does the residential tower
to the rear in different terms. In this last, Janssen &
Cocken produced a variation of their Keystone Athletic
Club, built in 1928: a red-brick Romanesque with shallow,
simple detailing that neither celebrates its steel frame nor
explicitly denies it, that neither wastes expensive ornamentation
on a back-alley perspective nor ungraciously denies
the passer-through a little architecture to look at.

National Register District
Historic Landmark plaque

First Presbyterian Church
320 Sixth Avenue
Theophilus Parsons Chandler (Philadelphia), architect, 1903–05

Like the adjoining Trinity Cathedral, this church stands
on former property of the Penn family that was donated in
1787 for religious purposes. The previous church of 1851
was on approximately the same site, but fronted on Wood
Street. The present arrangement is more impressive, with
the two church fronts side by side on their terraced grounds.

Behind a cathedral-like front in thirteenth- and fourteenth-century English Gothic stands a church on the

old-fashioned meeting-house model, a rectangular preaching space with raised side galleries. This is very much the way the earlier church was built, though here the detailing is more elaborate and historically correct. Inside, the walls are made up of small, rock-faced stones, so that the rather exiguous light breaks over them in a rippling texture. Arched trusses cased in heavily molded woodwork run the *length* of the nave to support the roof purlins over the gallery fronts. What seems to be a very shallow apse, paneled in wood, behind the minister's desk sometimes parts, like the doors of an old dirigible hangar, to reveal a chapel-like space with three tiers of Sunday-school rooms on each side of a great "east" window.

The stained glass is notable. The nave windows, all but one, are by the Tiffany Studios and in a technique never used by Tiffany before: paint on grayish glass, backed by a layer of opalescent glass. The "east" window beyond the Sunday-school rooms is a Tree of Jesse—a genealogy of Christ—by Clayton & Bell of London. The most famous window cannot really be seen from the main inner space: the "west" window by William Willett, concealed almost from the beginning by an organ. The pulpit was an early addition, to a design by Charles Bickel.

National Register District
Historic Landmark plaque

Trinity Cathedral (Episcopal)
322 Sixth Avenue
Gordon W. Lloyd (Detroit), architect, 1870–71;
Carpenter & Crocker, architects for parish house, c. 1907

Gordon Lloyd was a successful Detroit architect who designed in a variety of styles. Here he used a long-standing favorite of the Episcopal Church, the Decorated Gothic of early fourteenth-century England.

Despite a fire in 1969 and some rearrangement for liturgical reasons, the interior retains much of its Mid-Victorian character. The ceiling is a ribbed wagon roof, a pointed arch in form, painted pale blue. Accent colors on moldings are a warm gray. Much of the 1871 glass is still in place, along with glass from John Henry Hopkins' church of 1824. The pulpit of 1922 by Bertram Goodhue is one of

those finely wrought decorative designs of which he was a master; its style is generally fifteenth-century but with no specific national character.

Trinity has a historic churchyard, with some of the oldest graves in Pittsburgh set among grass and trees, that was the object of an extensive study and restoration campaign around 1990.

National Register District
Historic Landmark plaque

Henry W. Oliver Building
Smithfield Street and Oliver Avenue
D. H. Burnham & Co. (Chicago), architects, 1908–10

Comparison with the Frick Building of the early 1900s is inevitable. Both have main fronts of about the same size; both have an E-shaped plan, with light courts to the rear; both are Classical in detail and follow the base-shaft-capital elevation scheme of the early twentieth-century skyscraper; both have very high east-facing interior lobbies with rich bronzework against simple white marble; both have memorials to their developers; and both were designed by the same office.

The differences are, primarily, due to the facing materials used. The Frick Building is rather like our image of the man himself, gentlemanly in bearing but made of steel and granite; and granite is best adapted to simple effects. The Oliver Building, above its base, is faced in the much more facile terra cotta, easily molded or modeled

and thus encouraging floridity. And yet the facade is generally restrained, breaking out only in its capital into a pilastered arcade with a broad and delicate cornice, the handsomest that survives in the city, to crown everything.

To contrive a rivalry between the two buildings is futile; there is much to enjoy in each. Frick is a shade heavier in effect, less genial, but it also has more art and more space overhead in its lobbies.

The Oliver Building offers one extra pleasure, though, because of its unique situation: the pleasure of wondering over how good an architectural neighbor it is with the very different Trinity Cathedral. The secret is in the radicalism of the contrast. The cathedral is Gothic, blackened by Pittsburgh soot so that all its rich details are subordinated to a great shape that terminates in the grand gesture of the spire. The spire rises against the Oliver's sheer, glossy, gray-and-cream wall regularly perforated with windows not too much larger than those of a house, creating a broken but not restless pattern. The spire comes nowhere near the level of the office building's cornice; its scale is nonetheless greater than that of the office building facade. It is a big thing against a background of small things whose number no one will bother to count. Neither building disparages the other; they are in contiguous, different, but compatible worlds.

Henry W. Oliver, with interests in railroads, iron specialties, and mining— he is best remembered for early development of the Lake Superior iron mines—was also interested in downtown real estate. He had contemplated this building before his death in 1904, and his estate went on to build it and name it in his memory. After his death the City renamed Virgin Alley, which passes one end of the building, as another memorial in his honor.

National Register District
Historic Landmark plaque

Mellon Bank
Fifth Avenue and Smithfield Street
Trowbridge & Livingston (New York), architects;
E. P. Mellon, associate architect; 1923–24

In a way this is the architectural equivalent of the rich lady's simple but expensive dress. In the gray granite exterior there is no ostentation, just dignity and self-respect. But: in an area of tall buildings, this is only four stories high; this place of money casually throws away the rentals from fifteen to twenty possible stories of upper office space. Inside there is nothing flamboyant about the banking room, sixty-two feet high, lined with beige marble and with marble Ionic columns with gilded capitals.

Thomas Mellon, born to an Irish farming couple, came to the United States at the age of six, and eventually became a lawyer and a judge. Retiring at the age of fifty-six, he founded the private banking house of T. Mellon & Sons in 1869. This became the Mellon National Bank in

1902, and has continued to grow. Mellon Bank Center consists of three buildings adjoining the Mellon Bank itself, and most of their office space is used by the company for administering the huge organization. The Mellon family is famous for its philanthropies, which have had spectacular architectural consequences such as the East Liberty Presbyterian Church, the Mellon Institute, and the National Gallery in Washington.

National Register District
Historic Landmark plaque

Park Building
Fifth Avenue and Smithfield Street
George B. Post (New York), architect, c. 1896

This is the work of a New York architect who had a large commercial practice. The materials are gray-brown brick and terra cotta, with a gray granite rusticated base. Time has been both kind and unkind to the building: the crouching atlantes, figures of Atlas, beneath the cornice remain with not very much damage, but an expediency-oriented remodeling of the 1960s stripped away decorative ironwork that graced every window, altered window proportions, and filled in the spaces within the tall arches in a cheap and flimsy-looking way. Inside, the surfaces of the old elevator lobby were covered or destroyed, though to a knowing eye the odd horseshoe plan of the space still suggests an 1890s office building plan, meant to cram as many one-room offices as possible into the available space.

In 1985 the sad condition was partly reversed, when destroyed exterior stonework at the base of the building was partly restored and discordant shopfronts were replaced with candidly modern ones to a more unified design.

David Edgar Park, for whom the structure was built, was one of the earliest steel manufacturers, a vice-president of the Park Steel Company and a banker. His brother William was a partner in the speculation.

National Register District

Kaufmann's department store
Fifth Avenue and Smithfield Street
Charles Bickel, architect, 1898; Janssen & Abbott,
architects for addition, 1913; later additions and alterations

The first section of 1898, at Forbes Avenue and Smithfield Street, is a rather clumsy design by Charles Bickel, architect of the German National Bank and the Hartje Building. To this, in 1913, Janssen & Abbott added a larger section in the manner typical of the time: cream-colored terra cotta with faint Renaissance relief decoration and plenty of window space. A distinguished ground-floor redecoration of 1930 by Janssen & Cocken, Moderne white metal and black glass, is now gone, but its decorative metal door pulls and heating grilles survive.

The clock at the corner of Fifth Avenue and Smithfield Street is a familiar downtown landmark, a popular meeting place.

Edgar Jonas Kaufmann is still remembered as a public-spirited citizen and as the owner of "Fallingwater" in Fayette County, one of his numerous commissions to Frank Lloyd Wright.

National Register District
Historic Landmark plaque

Kaufmann & Baer (later Gimbel's department store)
Sixth Avenue and Smithfield Street
Starrett & Van Vleck (New York), architects, 1914

This building is wholly faced in cream glazed terra cotta, including a delicate-looking cornice that has survived. The overall effect looks a little lacking in substance, yet the building is a good visual neighbor to the Oliver Building across Sixth Avenue. It was constructed as the Kaufmann & Baer department store, but spent a much longer time as Gimbel's Pittsburgh store. Today it has multiple tenants.

National Register District
Historic Landmark plaque

**German Evangelical Protestant Church
(later Smithfield Congregational Church;
now Smithfield United Church)**
620 Smithfield Street
Henry Hornbostel, architect, 1925–26

Here, Hornbostel was designing a new church for a
congregation of long existence, one of the recipients of
land from the Penn family in 1787. He chose to design in
Gothic, even though he was a Classicist by inclination;
perhaps he felt that only Gothic expressed the Christian
religion properly, or perhaps he wanted the challenge of
using the style effectively among tall downtown buildings.

In its massing the church is broad and bulky, not too
different in its proportions from his Beaux-Arts designs of

the past. And the Gothic
exterior, examined in
detail, is literally super-
ficial, a perceptible application of a stone veneer
and panels of composi-
tion-stone ornament to a
steel frame. The style is
quite eclectic, with a small
"e": a Tudor arch at the
entrance and plaster fan
vaults inside suggest
England, but the square
tower with one belfry
arch per side between

solid corners
looks Italian,
while the intri-
cate traceries
of the decora-
tive panels and
the openwork
spire have
a fifteenth-
century
German feeling. The spire represents a very early architectural use of aluminum; City officials refused permission to
build the whole spire of the material as planned, but the
panels are cast aluminum supported by a steel frame.

Inside, the church has an eighteen-foot rose window
from an earlier church of 1875 and stained-glass windows
that depict historical scenes in the life of the church
and Pittsburgh.

National Register District
Historic Landmark plaque

Houses
Strawberry and Montour Ways
C. 1850

A fragment of Old Pittsburgh has somehow remained
between Sixth and Seventh Avenues and Grant and
Smithfield Streets. Jostled by such proud neighbors as
Bell Telephone, Alcoa, the First Lutheran Church, and
the Smithfield United Church, three tiny old houses
have managed to survive in company with their not-too-
different neighbor the Harvard, Yale, Princeton Club.

Except as survivors they are not remarkable, but there is drama in the contrast of scale and elaboration they provide with so much that is bigger and newer. Looking uphill along Strawberry Way, the visitor sees the USX Tower of 1970 in a particularly dramatic perspective.

National Register District

Harvard, Yale, Princeton Club group
William Penn Place and Strawberry Way
After 1889; Edward B. Lee, architect for remodeling, 1930

Development in 1930 converted what had begun as workers' row housing in a little residential court into the Harvard, Yale, Princeton Club on one side and into offices on the other. Two Romanesque columns from a demolished building at Princeton terminate the view into the courtyard. The rose window of the Smithfield United Church makes an impressive backdrop ornament to this picturesque, retiring little scene in the middle of the city.

National Register District

Bell Telephone Company
Seventh Avenue and William Penn Place
Frederick J. Osterling, architect, c. 1890;
Alden & Harlow, architects for addition, 1905;
James T. Windrim (Philadelphia), architect for additions, 1915, 1923, 1931

There are two distinct parts to this building, Osterling's red-brick Romanesque and Windrim's multi-phase annex. Of the whole complex, what appears to be the last part is the best. A one-story covered walk on Strawberry Way, with shallow vaults in green and cream Guastavino tile and limestone piers, is not only an elegant space in itself but frames the view of the old and tiny houses opposite and creates an appreciable relationship between the tall building above and the little street. The crowning

feature of the post-Osterling construction is a limestone Ionic colonnade with a frieze of strigil ornament into which octagonal panels of grillework are set: little noticed, but one of the handsomest Classical compositions in Pittsburgh.

National Register District

Chamber of Commerce Building

Seventh Avenue and Smithfield Street
Edward B. Lee and James P. Piper, architects, 1916–17

One of the interesting aspects of Eclecticism is the sense of the stylistically appropriate that seems to have guided its architects. Here is a Chamber of Commerce building, and a rather tall building as well. It was quite common for a tall business-oriented building to be in a Classical or Gothic style, yet by 1915 it was not absolutely necessary; a free, *ad hoc* manner was acceptable too, even a decade before Art Deco was imported to give the occasional experiments some sort of orientation. On the other hand, a Chamber of Commerce had an institutional character, which usually implied a Classical treatment.

Our architects chose innovation, and the greater part of their building is a matter-of-fact fabric executed in red brick—strong color was beginning to return to fashion in city architecture—with a decorative terra-cotta top that included false gables to enliven the skyline. The lowermost floors, however, include a very stylized Ionic colonnade, so that there is at least a touch of Classicism in the composition. The attractive lobby is a free reproduction of the original, by L. D. Astorino Associates, executed after a period of cheap "modernization."

National Register District

Union Station (now the Pennsylvanian)

Grant Street and Liberty Avenue
D. H. Burnham & Co. (Chicago), architects, 1898–1903

Theoretically, the Pennsylvania Railroad went no further west than Pittsburgh; yet that did not stop it from leasing other railroads that did do so, such as the Pittsburgh, Fort Wayne & Chicago Railway and the Pittsburgh, Cincinnati & St. Louis Railway, and running its own trains over their tracks. Hence, at Pittsburgh, it had a "union station," where these and other "Pennsylvania Lines" converged. The present station is the fourth of these.

The initial design was relatively modest, both in the office block with its ground-floor passenger and baggage spaces and in the shelter for the cabs' turning circle; but the office block rose on the drawing board while the cab shelter evolved into a 1900 architectural student's dream, the fantastic Beaux-Arts "rotunda" that we see today. The scheme was executed in buff terra cotta with matching brick in the office tower; the color was suited to both the taste of the 1890s and the station's exposure to billows of locomotive smoke. The ornamentation was French in flavor, like the rotunda itself: urns, heads, leaf ornament, in florid episodes here and there. Inside the rotunda, on pendentives beneath the skylit central dome, four women's heads smiled over tablets naming four destinations of the Pennsylvania Railroad. The arches of the rotunda were outlined in light bulbs. The waiting room was lined with green marble and white terra cotta, and skylit from an internal courtyard. To the rear was a "balloon" trainshed, a barrel vault of steel 556 feet long and 258 feet wide.

The trainshed was demolished in the 1940s, and passenger service diminished. The railroad merged with the New York Central, tried to diversify, then went bankrupt.

Long-distance buses used the rotunda as a Pittsburgh station—and were able to drive under its *little* arches, so large is its scale. Railroad personnel left, and the office tower stood empty. Amtrak ran a passenger service, but camped out in a minor space behind the station building. Terra cotta deteriorated; snow fencing kept the public at a safe distance from the high walls. The rotunda's round skylight wore a shabby nightcap of tarpaulin to keep the weather out. In 1988, though, a rehabilitated Union Station reopened as the Pennsylvanian apartment house, the terra cotta cleaned and repaired, the rotunda skylight open again, and the arches once again outlined in softly glowing bulbs mimicking the carbon-filament lamps of 1902.

National Register of Historic Places

Grant Street

Close to the eastern edge of the Golden Triangle, the original Pittsburgh that Woods and Vickroy carved from the manor of the Penn family, is Grant Street, which over two centuries has made an unsteady march toward grandeur. A spur of Grant's Hill, the notorious Hump that was finally tamed in 1913, originally raised it near its center to an inconvenient gradient. In the late nineteenth century it was terminated at Seventh Avenue so that the Pennsylvania Railroad could build a freight terminal near Union Station. A street, then, which passed Richardson's Courthouse, the City-County Building, the Frick Building, the Union Arcade, the William Penn Hotel, the Grant

Building, and ultimately the Koppers Building dead-ended in a shed full of boxcars.

But the erection of these buildings and later ones, and restoration of the street's full length in 1929 marked progress toward fulfillment of Grant Street's potential. Now, with its concentration of major historic buildings and modern skyscrapers, Grant Street is downtown Pittsburgh's showplace thoroughfare. In 1990 an end-to-end scheme of paving, planting, and lighting was completed.

Federal Reserve Bank of Cleveland
717 Grant Street
Walker & Weeks (Cleveland), architects; Henry Hornbostel and Eric Fisher Wood, associate architects; 1930–31; additions

Walker & Weeks had a rather heavy repertoire of Classical and Art Deco forms, with which they designed many of the prominent buildings of Cleveland; the most familiar of their works there to Pittsburghers is probably Severance Hall, home of the Cleveland Symphony.

Here, white Georgia marble and decorative aluminum form a dignified Art Deco exterior with the aid of the sculptor Henry Hering. Situated between the prominent Gulf Building and the big and banal Moorhead Federal Building, the Federal Reserve Bank is little noticed, yet it is a very agreeable work.

National Register District

Gulf Building (now Gulf Tower)
Seventh Avenue and Grant Street
Trowbridge & Livingston (New York), architects;
E. P. Mellon, associate architect; 1930–32

After Grant Street was extended northward in the late 1920s, valuable building land became available. On one parcel of this, opposite the new Koppers Building, the Gulf Oil Company built a forty-four-story 582-foot tower that would be the tallest building in Pittsburgh until 1970.

The architects were Trowbridge & Livingston, who had designed the main Mellon Bank. They went down ninety feet to find a proper footing for their great tower— Allegheny River water lay under the site—then raised it in a sober Modernistic manner that began and ended with allusions to Classical architecture: a colossal doorway with a fifty-ton granite entablature on Seventh Avenue and a limestone ziggurat top that recalled the Mausoleum at Halicarnassus. The treatment in between followed a skyscraper formula quite common at the time, the verticals of the steel skeleton emphasized, the horizontals suppressed. Such verticality said Steel to the public in 1930, yet the architects somehow made the building exterior an expression of stone, giving the facing of the tower and its base a high relief and softened outline proper to massive construction.

The interior, with its dark marble, is more simple and serious than that of the Koppers Building across the street; the two buildings, contemporaries, are indeed conceived in two different spirits.

The top was long covered with neon tubes in the Gulf corporate colors of orange and blue that predicted the weather: steady blue, precipitation and rising temperatures; flashing blue, precipitation and falling temperatures; steady orange, clear and rising temperatures; flashing orange, clear and falling temperatures.

As a result of the Gulf/Chevron merger initiated in 1984, the Gulf Building was sold to New York developers, and has become rental office space.

National Register District
Historic Landmark plaque

Koppers Building
Seventh Avenue and Grant Street
Graham, Anderson, Probst & White (Chicago),
architects, 1927–29

Here, the successor firm of D. H. Burnham & Co., which had designed so many business buildings for the Triangle, created an Art Deco skyscraper, the sort that imparted a progressive image. Such an image went well enough with the client's business. Heinrich Koppers, in 1908, had invented a by-product coke oven, one that captured wastes so that they could be utilized rather than releasing them to the air, where they were worse than useless. He had moved his business to Pittsburgh in 1915 and entered into the production of coke, coking equipment, illuminating gas, and chemicals.

The limestone facing of the building, like the tall lobby spaces inside with their colored marbles and ornamented bronzework, suggests a cool urbanity remote from industrial toil; business took itself very seriously in the 1920s and was very much on its dignity. Yet a little quiet humor crept into the design, with or without management's approval. The crowning chateau roof, being made of copper, can be taken as a pun, while the downstairs mailbox is a doll's-house version of the whole building, roof included.

The lobby spaces are among the very best Art Deco works in Pittsburgh, restrained in overall design but rich in detail and full of quiet color.

National Register District
Historic Landmark plaque

First English Evangelical Lutheran Church
615 Grant Street
Andrew Peebles, architect, 1887–88

When this church was built, Grant Street still had the air of a small-town Main Street, with the new Courthouse and St. Paul's Cathedral by far its most imposing objects. A picturesque cluster of steep-roofed Gothic elements and a 170-foot spired tower had still, for a brief while, a chance to dominate the immediate area. But the fairly tall buildings made possible by the elevator were already rising, and now of course the church is overlooked on all sides. Inside are several attractive objects: an altarpiece in the fifteenth-century Italian Renaissance style with mosaics,

a Tiffany *Good Shepherd* window, and a font in the form of a kneeling angel with a basin, a copy of one at Copenhagen by Bertel Thorvaldsen.

National Register District
Historic Landmark plaque

William Penn Hotel
Grant Street and Sixth Avenue
Janssen & Abbott, architects, 1914–16;
Janssen & Cocken, architects for enlargement, 1928–29

The hotel stands just north of the Union Arcade, and its older part, overlooking Mellon Square, is one of Henry Clay Frick's ventures in real estate. By the time it was designed, the big-city hotel had attained the form exemplified here, an adaptation of the base-shaft-capital formula. The base is clad in warm off-white terra cotta and designed in a generalized eighteenth-century Classical manner. The shaft is plain and of warm red brick, with broader areas of wall surface than would

A detail from the 1916 section of the William Penn Hotel.

have been convenient in an office building. The capital reintroduces the terra cotta against a background of the brick, and terminates with a cornice and a parapet. Deep light courts allow the maximum number of guest rooms to have natural ventilation and some sort of outdoor view. The choice of red brick for the greater part of the building—becoming typical of hotel design at the time—may have been intended to impart a domestic feeling, a warmth not found in the impersonal surfaces of business structures. Soon, business buildings like the Chamber of Commerce Building, under design around 1915, were to revert to color for their upper walls as well, as if they too had come to seem too cold and monotonous with their perpetual grays and whites.

The 1928 addition carried on in the spirit of the original, with highly decorated public interiors that were mansion-like, but genially so, on the lower floors and on the seventeenth floor as well. On the latter is a remarkable exception to the Classical spirit that prevails: the Urban Room of 1929, the ultimate in smartness at the time, designed by the New York architect Joseph Urban who was best known for the Ziegfeld Theater. This Art Deco interior of black and gold is now to some extent restored, although Urban's bowl-shaped bronze chandelier was removed in the 1950s. The public rooms have been redecorated several times, and many of the guest suites have been enlarged to keep the hotel competitive with newer ones.

National Register of Historic Places
Historic Landmark plaque

Detail from the Urban Room

Union Arcade (later Union Trust Building)
Grant Street and Fifth Avenue
Frederick J. Osterling, architect, 1915–17

All of Henry Clay Frick's building speculations in the Triangle were first-class, but here he was persuaded to build something not only solid but lyrical. Though he was just moving into his New York mansion, a very polished work by New York architects, he chose the Pittsburgher who had remodeled his East End house "Clayton" two decades before to construct this new work. Osterling, in his turn, consulted Pierre A. Liesch, a native of Luxembourg, on the general design. Liesch suggested the building substantially as it is, but Osterling carried the scheme to Frick with the roof eliminated. Frick, in turn, went to his interior decorator Charles Allom and his art consultant Joseph Duveen, both eminent men, who said that the building would be even better with a prominent roof. Liesch was no longer working for the office, but Osterling supervised the working-out of the details of the design with a lightness of touch quite unusual for his firm.

The style is Flemish Gothic of the period around 1500, its ornament executed primarily in stone-colored and white terra cotta. There was probably inspiration from the similar Gothic of the Woolworth Building in New York, then the tallest building in the world. The relatively low skyline and the delicate lines disguise the fact that this is a spacious building, and a tough one. Inside was space for 240 shops, facing two four-story open arcade spaces, and about 700 offices. The office floors were built with a

strength remarkable today, intended for loads of at least 150 pounds per square foot since tenants were apt to bring in massive iron safes and locate them as they pleased.

The tall arcade spaces were floored in in 1923, when the Union Trust Company remodeled the building, and some of the openings into the great central well, ten stories high, were blocked. Otherwise, though, the building has been treated with great respect. Four street entrances, now as originally, meet at this dramatic central space beneath a stained-glass dome. Semi-gloss white terra-cotta walls line the public spaces instead of Pittsburgh's habitual white marble, but gorgeous bronze fixtures still play off against their more neutral surfaces.

Above the entrances are windows of leaded glass with colored inserts, and the vestibules are covered with vaults of colored mosaic.

The building had a partial restoration in the late 1980s. The arcade spaces were not reopened, and four interior courts were filled with floor and mechanical space, but old decorative work, inside and out, was put back. The Union Arcade now has much of its old brightness and freshness of effect and is handsomely illuminated at night.

National Register of Historic Places
Historic Landmark plaque

Frick Building
Grant Street and Fifth Avenue
D. H. Burnham & Co. (Chicago), architects, 1901–02

Henry Clay Frick made a number of major real-estate investments that resulted in construction of a close-set group of buildings in the Grant Street area: the Frick Building, Frick Annex, Union Arcade, and first part of the William Penn Hotel. In the Frick Building, the earliest of these, he created a personal monument and the location of his own office.

The tall new building that was finished in 1902 put an end to the fourteen-year dominance of the Pittsburgh skyline by the Courthouse directly across the street. It also occasioned the removal of St. Peter's Episcopal Church, stone by stone, to a new site in Oakland. The steelwork and sturdy granite facing, hauled to the site by horse and wagon, rose with remarkable speed to reveal a simplicity of skyscraper design quite unusual in Pittsburgh. Inside, its corridors of simple white marble with ornate bronze fittings were once again a little severe for the early 1900s, though certainly no one could call them meager, and two lions by Alexander Phimister Proctor and John La Farge's window *Fortune on Her Wheel*—Dame Fortune as a unicyclist—gave these spaces a special distinction. To these was added a memorial bust by Malvina Hoffman after

Frick's death. When the Grant's Hill Hump was lowered between 1911 and 1913 the already spacious ground-floor lobby and corridor system was made even more so by lowering it to give an entire story of extra height.

When built, the Frick Building had several peculiarities that are now gone: hydraulic elevator machinery and a generating plant in the basement, washrooms for the whole building on the tenth floor, and the very spacious rooms of the Union Club on the twenty-first floor. One reminder of the past survives in the main corridor in four bronze telephone booths with an operator's space between each pair; in this corridor there were once three telegraph offices as well.

National Register of Historic Places
Historic Landmark plaque

Allegheny County Courthouse and Jail (the County Buildings)
Courthouse, Grant Street and Fifth Avenue;
Jail, Ross Street and Fifth Avenue
Henry Hobson Richardson (Brookline, Mass.),
architect, 1884–88;
Frederick J. Osterling, architect for Jail alterations, 1904;
Stanley L. Roush, architect for Courthouse entry alterations, 1928

The "County Buildings" that H. H. Richardson started in 1884 but never lived to see completed are the county's only architectural works of international fame. The Jail especially will have a place in any comprehensive history of Modern architecture. Richardson's designs were chosen over those of his competitors because of the lucidity of his planning, but architects and architecture-lovers have found much else to admire according to their personal preferences. The Modernists admire the undecorated arches of the Jail and the Courthouse courtyard and the apparently simple but actually subtle walls of the Jail, with their tapered surfaces and their use of smaller stones over larger ones to convey a sense of mass. The Eclectics admired these things too, but also the masonry textures, the carving, the mountainous roofs, and the towers, dominated by the great tower—slender yet strong, solid when seen from some angles, diaphanous when seen from others—that was once the most prominent object in the city.

Richardson might have been indifferent, amused, or mildly annoyed at attempts to conscript him as a Modernist.

His schooling at the Parisian Ecole des Beaux-Arts had trained him to think clearly about an architectural problem, and he was certainly concerned to eliminate inefficiencies of plan and fussy detailing. Yet he was no tidy-minded utilitarian, opposed to ornament. The Courthouse tower is one big ornament, despite its rationalization as an air-conditioning intake; Richardson had been designing towers for a decade and a half, and this was the biggest and most refined of all, one of the world's great towers. The Italian Romanesque lions by the Grant Street doorways are attributed to no sculptor but are splendid pieces, and the guiding spirit in their carving may well have been Richardson's. The carved leaf ornament of the Courthouse, inside and out, has a crispness yet a lushness that is in harmony with both the rugged granite of the exterior and the interior's fine-grained limestone. The Courthouse main stair is a set of variations on the theme of the arch, with arches in massive repose, arches leaping, and arches lightly skipping from one slender shaft to another. The "Bridge of Sighs"

over Ross Street between the Courthouse and Jail is itself a very dramatic use of the arch.

At times both the Courthouse and the Jail have been threatened, but their most visible features have always been ardently defended and alterations have been mild. The lowering of the Hump in 1913 and the widening of Grant Street in 1927 forced the lengthening-downward of the Courthouse entrances; in the case of the Grant Street entrances the County Architect Stanley L. Roush designed inoffensive new doorways with ironwork by Samuel Yellin, leading to a basement vestibule-and-stair system covered by Guastavino tile vaulting. In 1904, Frederick J. Osterling was commissioned to expand the Jail and between 1904 and 1908 copied Richardson's wall system meticulously while adding a round tower at Fifth and Ross in something of the original spirit.

In the Courthouse courtyard, long a parking lot, there is now a park with trees, shrubs, and benches, very

The restored Small Orphans' Court

popular in the summer. This came into being as a joint project of the County and the Pittsburgh History & Landmarks Foundation, with the aid of a grant from the Sarah Scaife Foundation.

The Jail was vacated in 1995, its future use uncertain.

National Historic Landmark
National Register of Historic Places
City Historic Structure
Historic Landmark plaques

County Office Building
Forbes Avenue and Ross Street
Stanley L. Roush, architect, 1929–31

Roush, the County Architect who had recently acquitted himself well in altering the Courthouse entrances, had here the problem of adding a new neighbor to the Courthouse and Jail, directly across the street from the City-County Building. What we see is the first phase of a building campaign for a structure nine stories taller. Outside, a Romanesque arcade with polished granite columns on the two more conspicuous fronts opens up the limestone wall; above, the same heavy and conservative Modernistic found on the contemporary Gulf Building takes over. Inside, in the public corridor off Forbes Avenue, antiquity as seen through the lens of 1920s Hollywood prevails: the dark stone walls, the groin vaults, and the ironwork call for a parade of halberdiers or adventurers crossing swords, not engineers going to their offices or property owners on their way to dispute assessments.

City-County Building
Grant Street and Forbes Avenue
Edward B. Lee, with Palmer, Hornbostel & Jones,
architects, 1915–17

There was a trend, early in the twentieth century, toward making public administrative buildings look somewhat like ordinary business buildings. The sheer growth of public services may have imposed an architecture of little windows, and perhaps there was as well an official desire to hint that public affairs were being handled in a business-like manner. Yet a certain monumentality had to survive when the towers, pavilions, and mountainous roofs of the

older public architecture were swept away. At the City-County Building, too, the greatly respected Courthouse was to be a neighbor. The architects here designed a big Classical box, recalling neither the massing nor the style of the Courthouse. Yet they repeated its Grant and Ross Street portal scheme, three at one end, one at the other, on a colossal scale, and used gray granite again, albeit in a smooth not a rugged form.

Inside, as at the Courthouse, was a light court, but through it the architects put an airy Classical corridor of great windows and bronze columns, a composition more light and charming than the frowning exterior allows you to guess.

The Grant Street archways under the allegorical sculptures of Charles Keck open from a vast vaulted porch, whose space, surprisingly, is exhilarating, not oppressive. The building's glum exterior, in fact, is totally misleading. The whole place shows an attempt to reconcile a modern no-nonsense attitude with Classical dignity, to play off episodes of lavish ornament like the sculptured elevator doors and subtleties such as contrasts of matte and polished granite against a prevailing rational simplicity. This is a sort of Modernism, but one, you might say, that has conversation, not the mute thing we have had to get used to in the last few decades.

Historic Landmark plaque

Later, pinnacles that rose above the stepped-back parapets were cut off short. In the early 1980s, the old sash was replaced with single panes of reflective glass, so that the void-solid relationship was changed. Once, under the setting sun, the brickwork had a bronzy glow when seen from afar; now it is the windows that gleam. The most flamboyant feature of the early days survives, however: a neon-covered beacon tower that spells out P-I-T-T-S-B-U-R-G-H in Morse. Like the Empire State Building's dirigible mast, this had pretensions to usefulness in the developing technology of aviation; and it may be that, in the days before radio navigation, it really did help aviators to tell where they were.

The original lobby is gone, but a Post-Modern renovation of the mid-1980s has created an honorable substitute in an interior of pink and cream marble, set in panels in a way that has a Classical feeling.

Grant Building
Grant Street and Fourth Avenue
Henry Hornbostel and Eric Fisher Wood, architects, 1927–30

The Grant Building, as we see it today, has undergone several modifications. Hornbostel's initial Beaux-Arts treatment was first simplified into a trendy but quiet Modernistic, executed in bronze-colored brick and buff-colored cast stone over a base of dark Swedish granite.

Allegheny County Mortuary (the Morgue)
604 Fourth Avenue
Frederick J. Osterling, architect, 1901–03; moved, 1928

Here are H. H. Richardson's County Buildings in lugubriously amusing caricature, by the architect who on the one hand enlarged the Jail with faithful adherence to Richardson's detailing and materials and on the other proposed to heighten the Courthouse, very awkwardly, by two stories. The dormers imitate those of the Courthouse. The rear towers imitate that over the Jail end of the Bridge of Sighs. And the entrance portal is copied from the rear entrance of the Courthouse, the impost blocks included. The little monsters carved on these last are at least quite

appropriate in this place; they seem to say, with Poe, "That the play is the tragedy, 'Man,' And its hero, the conqueror Worm."

This building was moved downhill, on rails, one block in 1928. It originally stood across Diamond Street (i.e., the present Forbes Avenue) from the Jail.

Jones & Laughlin Building (now John Robin Civic Building)
200 Ross Street
MacClure & Spahr, architects, 1907

This Tudor Gothic office building was built as the head-quarters of a steel company. It seems almost penitential of J&L to have raised a building faced in sandstone and highly textured brick that the smoke from its plant, two miles away, would help quickly to darken. Now cleaned, the rich medium red of the brick makes a beautiful appearance in its contrast with the pale-brown sandstone trim.

The Jones & Laughlin Steel Corporation traces its origins back to 1851 and the Jones & Lauth ironworks, and in the year of this building's construction had a plant that extended down the Monongahela River on both sides.

On the north side of the river, it went from the Soho Iron Works a mile and a half away to the coke ovens at Hazelwood two miles beyond. Ann furnace, one of the Eliza group, was the last blast furnace to operate in Pittsburgh. When it shut down in 1979, it ended 120 years of iron smelting in the city.

Memorial columns, Boulevard of the Allies
Boulevard of the Allies and Grant Street
Frank Vittor, sculptor, 1921–22

The downtown conversion of Second Avenue into the Boulevard of the Allies did not create a grand avenue; the street was merely widened northward, and the results even today suggest the aftermath of a street widening: one side old and haphazard, the other side of a single later period but otherwise with nothing much in common among its components. At Grant Street, though, where the Boulevard rises to go along the side of the Bluff, a statement of its memorial function was inserted in the exiguous spaces at the edges of the ramp. Twin Doric columns of granite rise from pedestals carved with Liberty heads, patriotic symbols, and dedicatory inscriptions. Above, American eagles clutch globes. A row of iron bollards leads away from each column. The columns, hardly noticed from speeding cars, are scrutable to pedestrians only with a certain amount of mortal danger.

Until Schenley Park was created in 1889, the land now covered by this ramp may have been the City of Pittsburgh's only official park. Earlier, it was a public marketplace.

Panhandle Division Bridge, Pennsylvania Railroad
Monongahela River west of Liberty Bridge
1903

Two camelback Pratt trusses and one Pennsylvania truss of 351-foot span once served to bring Pennsylvania Railroad trains from the south shore of the Monongahela into town. The trains went underground at Forbes Avenue, following the approximate route of the old Pennsylvania Canal, and saw daylight again just before reaching Union Station. The bridge is now used by the Light Rail transit line from the South Hills.

The bridge marks the approximate location of the mouth of Suke's Run in Pipetown, the area where some of the earliest Western River steamers were built and where the Pennsylvania Canal emerged from its tunnel under Grant's Hill.

Liberty Bridge
Monongahela River between the Boulevard of the Allies
and the Liberty Tunnels
George S. Richardson of the Allegheny County Department of
Public Works, engineer, 1926–28

The Liberty Bridge, a direct automobile link between town and the new Liberty Tubes, was as useful in opening parts of the South Hills to development as the trolley tunnel to South Hills Junction had been two decades before. The bridge had been sought by motorists for two decades, and opening day was celebrated with a mile-long procession of cars.

The 450-foot main spans suggest arches, but this is a deception. This is in fact a rather complicated cantilever bridge. Its main portion rests on three piers, and in the pre-computer days when it was designed, calculation of the possible forces acting on a continuous bridge truss with more than two supports was practically impossible. The continuity therefore was deliberately broken up into two cantilever structures, each calculable, and a "suspended span," an ordinary truss, was hinged to cantilever arms extending into the northern main span from both structures. In 1982 the deck and ornamental parts of the bridge were so altered that it has lost its original beauty of detail.

National Register of Historic Places

The North Side from Perrysville Avenue.

OLD ALLEGHENY

Directly across the Allegheny River from the Triangle lies Pittsburgh's
North Side, which until annexation in 1907 was the independent city of
Allegheny. The original Allegheny Town had been surveyed by David
Redick in 1788 as a square of blocks and streets a third of a mile on a
side, surrounded by grazing commons that were themselves surrounded
by "out-lots" for agriculture. Allegheny Town was to be the seat of the
new Allegheny County, created in 1788, but since the town existed for
many years only as a plan, Pittsburgh became at first the
temporary, then the permanent, County seat. Thus began
more than a century of inter-city rivalry.

It was only around 1810, when the Indian menace
was long past, that industry and a sizeable residential
population moved north of the Triangle. After this,
development was rapid. The first bridge to Allegheny
opened in 1819. The Pennsylvania Canal made Allegheny
a terminus in 1829, as did the Ohio & Pennsylvania Railroad
in 1851. After 1867 the Commons, muddy and unused,
were laid out as a handsome Victorian park. In 1889,
H. J. Heinz moved his plant down the river from Sharpsburg to Allegheny, strengthening an economic base that was
already well founded.

CITY OF
PITTSBURGH

The original town soon became too small, and the out-lots were
developed, parcel by parcel, with houses. Neighborhoods, each with
its own distinct character, ringed the perimeter of the Commons and
gradually climbed the steep hillsides to the north. The Anglo-Saxons
tended to stay in the old Allegheny Town within the Commons, but the
Germans settled to the east in Deutschtown on the plain and on Troy
Hill further east still, and the Irish and Scotch-Irish settled west of the
Commons. Allegheny's citizens lived in homes that ranged from back-
alley houses in Deutschtown to grandiose mansions on Ridge Avenue.
It is apparent that many of them lived quite comfortably because their
neighborhoods became rich displays of Victorian residential architecture. Deutschtown and the Mexican War Streets were developed with
collections of large houses facing the Commons and interesting but
more modest, close-set housing behind. The streets of Allegheny West

were lined with substantial houses to the north of the Ridge Avenue mansions. Manchester, laid out in 1832, merged with Allegheny in 1867 and developed as a solid bourgeois neighborhood with stately, tall houses in red brick. Perry Hilltop and Fineview, high above the river plain, acquired Romantic villas with expansive views.

More modest houses clustered on other hilltops and hillsides, reached by inclines and public stairs, or were strung along narrow valleys. Annexations of new neighborhoods quadrupled the area of Redick's original survey, out-lots included, prior to 1873, and Allegheny's population passed 100,000 by the turn of the century.

The new century, however, saw Allegheny's own annexation in 1907 and subsequent decline. There was still a distinct sense of the newly named North Side as a separate place; its crossroads of Ohio and Federal Streets retained very much

the look of a town center with a towered Carnegie Library, a City Hall that was eventually replaced by the Buhl Planetarium, a Post Office, a market hall, a park, and the respected Boggs & Buhl department store. Yet the North Side, as the years passed, took on the air of a respectable lady alone with memories in a dusty parlor, or latterly, even, of an old pensioner sitting exhausted on an unkempt front porch. In the 1930s, Luke Swank photographed the North Side and revealed poetry in century-old houses and streets on hazy mornings, but a North Side survey of 1951 found no romance in housing that was forty-one percent slum and six-tenths of a percent fully satisfactory.

Conventional urban renewal was the planners' obvious answer, sweeping and theoretically humane. Almost everything north of the Commons was to go, to be replaced by garden apartments of uniform design. The original Allegheny Town was to be stripped of all existing housing, as well as the Post Office and market house, and a shopping mall and new housing were to be built. Much of Manchester and most of the river shore area were to be cleared; so was the East Street Valley, which was to contain an expressway.

Some of these plans have been realized, some not. The old crossroads is now merely an intersection of walkways. The market hall and Boggs & Buhl are gone. The shopping mall and apartment and business slabs dominate the former Allegheny Town. The shore area is partially redeveloped with more to come, and the East Street houses are gone, replaced by I-279. Yet the canal, the railroads and the road projects have left battered, odd, isolated stretches of construction such as the houses along General Robinson and Progress Streets, on the North Shore.

On the other hand, the Post Office has been a museum since 1971, and for thirteen years was the home of the Pittsburgh History & Landmarks Foundation,

In Manchester

which saved it. Landmarks, the City, neighborhood organizations, and private citizens have worked to rehabilitate large portions of the Mexican War Streets, Manchester, Allegheny West, the Central North Side, and Deutschtown or East Allegheny. Other neighborhoods are displaying renewed pride and revitalization. Today, the big, heterogeneous North Side is in transition, with some emptiness, decay, and impersonal architecture. But it is also a place of charm and warmth with Victorian streets returned or returning to their old well-being.

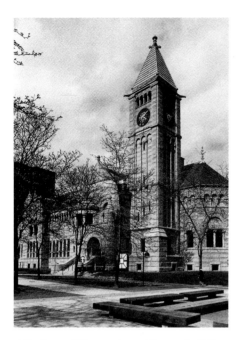

Allegheny Library (now Carnegie Library of Pittsburgh, Allegheny Regional Branch)
Allegheny Square, Central North Side
Smithmeyer & Pelz (Washington, D. C.),
architects, 1888–90

This was the first Carnegie Library commissioned, though opened later than the one at Braddock. It was designed by the architects who had created the controversial plan for the Library of Congress shortly before. The Library interior is generally modernized now, and the adjacent Carnegie Hall, the auditorium where the evangelist Kathryn Kuhlman held services for many years, is now a theater. In general, despite rock-faced granite exteriors, the building has a rather thin effect. There are some excellent finials though: an urn on the Library tower, a lyre on the Carnegie Hall gable, and a splendid flourishing plant in copper on the Library's hip roof.

National Register of Historic Places
City Historic Structure
Historic Landmark plaque

Colonel James Anderson Monument
Buhl Planetarium opposite Allegheny Library,
Central North Side
Daniel Chester French, sculptor; Henry Bacon, architect, 1904

Colonel Anderson is remembered both at Anderson Manor, his 1830-period house in Manchester, and in this monument that originally stood with its back to the Library. The Colonel had been the first to encourage Andrew Carnegie, immigrant working boy, to acquire an education, and Carnegie returned the favor a half-century later in this tribute in the form of an exedra. The same collaborators who later produced the Lincoln Memorial in Washington, D.C., were sculptor and architect here.

**Buhl Planetarium and Institute of Popular Science
(later Buhl Science Center)**
Allegheny Square, Central North Side
Ingham & Boyd, architects, 1939

One of the most polished architectural firms in the city,
especially good at Classical design, had here the task of
creating a window-less building with institutional dignity
at what was at the time a busy, noisy intersection. Science
was the theme and the climactic feature was the round
auditorium, where the ant-like Zeiss planetarium machine
projected the stars on the dome above.

Outside, a
sparing use of
rustication and
six pieces of
sculpture by
Sidney Waugh
in the simplified,
high-relief style
favored in the
1930s mitigate
the utter plainness
of the basic shell.
Around back, the taller, copper-domed octagon of the
Planetarium varies the perimeter and skyline. Inside, a
gorgeous application of various marbles to the walls creates
a resonant public gallery once dominated by the silvery
Foucault pendulum whose serene passes over a compass
rose illustrated the rotation of the earth. The building was
in use until 1994.

Henry Buhl, Jr. was an Allegheny merchant who
entered a partnership with Russell Boggs in 1869. The
Boggs & Buhl department store, which survived the conversion of Allegheny into the North Side and remained a
Pittsburgh institution, indeed faced the Planetarium until
its closure in 1958. The Buhl Foundation, founded at the

time of Henry Buhl's death in 1928, advanced money for
Chatham Village, funded the Western Pennsylvania
Architectural Survey in the early 1930s, and gave the
Planetarium to the City.

**Allegheny Post Office (later the Old Post Office
Museum; now The Pittsburgh Children's Museum)**
10 Children's Way, Central North Side
*William Martin Aiken of the U.S. Treasury Department
(Washington, D.C.), architect, 1894–97*

This was once the central Post Office of an independent
city, one of the buildings that gave a monumental character
to its major crossroads. Yet unlike many later buildings of
government, its formality of character was kept within the
human scale. Its arched windows are ample but not yawn-
ing voids, and its Early Italian Renaissance wall treatment
is delicate and crisply cut in pale-gray granite, evincing
not the slightest intention of overwhelming the public for
whose use it was intended. It was designed, obviously, to
maintain the dignity of government but without presenting
government as a superhuman, alien power. The central
domed space inside is surprisingly tall, mosque-like, a little
overawing perhaps, but in Post Office days the public
caught only glimpses of it through wickets in the wooden
screen that restricted them to outer corridors.

It is curious to know that the plan was a standard
one that could be clothed in other styles. At Clarksville,
Tennessee, for instance, it is interpreted in French
Renaissance, with a big chateau roof in place of the
dome that looks so right in Pittsburgh.

In the late 1960s the Post Office was destined to
disappear in the Allegheny Center urban-renewal clearance,
but the Pittsburgh History & Landmarks Foundation,

then only a half-decade old, was able to acquire it intact after a year-long struggle. The remodeling at the time included opening the central space to the public, installing a new stair and office mezzanine, and making other alterations in which artifacts saved from the nearby Henry W. Oliver mansion and other demolished Allegheny County structures were built into the construction. The remodeled building was returned to use in 1971 as a community museum and as offices for Landmarks itself.

In 1974 a garden court, designed by the Foundation, was opened. It has artifacts from demolished Pittsburgh buildings built into and set within its paving-block walls. Its proudest display is Charles Keck's portal sculptures of 1915 from the Manchester Bridge.

In 1983, the Pittsburgh History & Landmarks Foundation began its relocation to Station Square, and eventually gave the building to The Pittsburgh Children's Museum, the present owner and occupant.

National Register of Historic Places
City Historic Structure
Historic Landmark plaque

St. Peter's Church (Roman Catholic)
West Ohio and Arch Streets, Central North Side
Andrew Peebles, architect, 1872–74

With its large, intricately traceried windows, St. Peter's presents an impressive front to a major avenue of the former city of Allegheny. This was even more the case when a tall spire rose above the gables of the tower. For the 1870s, and for Catholic churches especially, this was in fact a very polished design. The side walls,

high because there is no clerestory, suggest a Protestant meeting-house plan, however, rather than that of a Catholic church. Following a fire, some reconstruction work occurred in 1886–88. Behind the chancel is a picturesque rectory of 1876, unfortunately with some of its ornamental work cut away.

Historic Landmark plaque

Allegheny High School (now Allegheny Middle School)
810 Arch Street, Central North Side
Frederick J. Osterling, architect, 1904;
Marion M. Steen, architect, 1937

The red brick-and-sandstone portion of this building, that of 1904 facing the West Commons part of the ring road around Allegheny Center, is almost like a branch library grown gigantic: sober, solid, a little fancy at the entrance, and with long banks of windows in a time when light and ventilation depended on them. This was annexed to an 1889 school in the Richardson Romanesque style, rather compulsively picturesque, which yielded in 1937 to a more block-like yellow-and-white building in mild Art Deco.

National Register of Historic Places
Historic Landmark plaque

Garden Theatre
12 West North Avenue, Central North Side
Thomas H. Scott, architect, 1914

Here is an early movie house, with a lobby open to the weather, a full terra-cotta facing, and a Classical facade not calculated to overawe the visitor, as facades of a decade later were intended to do.

Engine Company Number Three
Arch and Jacksonia Streets, Central North Side
Bailey & Anglin, architects, 1877

The style of this red brick and sandstone firehouse is indeterminate though the banding of the arches has a medieval Italian air that is doubtless due indirectly to the propagandizing of John Ruskin, the British critic and social reformer of this same period who advocated Italian Gothic as a style for the architecture of his own time. The overall composition, though, suggests the Italian Villa style, the tower—which once had an open cupola—being placed at the exact center of the front. This placement is unusual; most old firehouses, whose towers were used for hanging hoses to dry, had them to one side.

The original Orphan Asylum building

Orphan Asylum of Pittsburgh and Allegheny (later Allegheny Widows' Home)

306–22 North Taylor Avenue and
1319–27 Sherman Avenue, Mexican War Streets
John Chislett, architect, 1838; additions, c. 1873

The principal element of this institutional complex, three stories high, was built in 1838 to house the Orphan Asylum of Pittsburgh and Allegheny. The design, a very simple one in the Grecian Doric order, was donated to the charity by John Chislett, the English-born architect who had begun practice in Pittsburgh about five years before. The Asylum and Burke's Building in the Triangle are, as far as we know, the only extant works in the Greek Revival by Chislett, and this is one of his five known extant works of any description.

The Sherman Avenue houses for the Widows' Home.

Built for thirty orphans, the Asylum became overcrowded and was vacated in 1866, at which time the Allegheny Widows' Home Association moved in. In 1872, the City of Allegheny decided to extend Taylor Avenue through the Widows' Home property, a measure that obliged removal of part of the Asylum building. The City's compensation and the loss of floor space stimulated the Widows' Home to build simple row houses, of a Greek Revival character, along the adjacent streets and in the yard area behind.

In the early 1980s, the entire complex was rehabilitated and externally restored, and the row-house plans were revised to make the courtyard, not the street, the principal means of access.

National Register District
City Historic District

Monterey Street

Mexican War Streets

Just north of the West Commons is a twenty-seven-acre area whose street names allude to places and people of the Mexican War. The war had just ended when the district, part of Allegheny's original out-lots, was laid out in 1848 by General William Robinson as the Buena Vista Extension.

In the next fifty years the land was very largely built up, houses and a few commercial establishments side by side with no front or side yards, and only occasionally with porches, in the streets behind the more spaciously sited houses that faced West North Avenue and the Commons. For the most part the houses were about twenty feet wide and set together, simple Italianate being quite typical as a style, though Gothic, Romanesque, and turn-of-the-century Classical were to be found as well.

1245–47 Monterey Street

1215–21 Buena Vista Street

Numbers 1245–47 Monterey Street, a residential block with a corner shop, is unusually large for a building in the Mexican War Streets. Its handsome but unassuming Italianate detailing of c. 1870 is shared by adjacent row houses. The contemporary Gothic treatment of 1213 Resaca Place, on the other hand, is unique. The front, which is

1213 Resaca Place

now somewhat remodeled, has angular detailing and added decorative features that distinguish it from the houses to either side, and of course the little dormer-plus-turret is a real bravura touch; yet like its neighbors, Number 1213 has regularly spaced sash windows and thus attests to the continuing strength of the Georgian building tradition as much as to a growing individualism in city house design.

With 1215–29 Buena Vista Street we see attempts to impart more tone, a higher style, to a pair of builder's house rows. These houses of c. 1890 are in the fashionable Richardson Romanesque, their brick fronts veneered in rock-faced stone. Decorative parapets and carved porch capitals contribute to the air of sophistication the builders wished to give, while the porches themselves give a gracious appearance to the aloof stone fronts. Number 1201, just down the street from these houses, is their contemporary but assumes the air of a mansion, albeit a very thin mansion: indeed, it is a small-scaled counterpart of the

1201 Buena Vista Street

long, narrow Darlington house on Brighton Road, four blocks away. Of the houses in the blocks north of West North Avenue this is the most pretentious.

In the late 1960s, the Pittsburgh History & Landmarks Foundation defined and named the area the "Mexican War Streets," and launched a neighborhood restoration program that became the first in the nation to benefit a mixed-income, integrated neighborhood. The Mexican War Streets Society and the Central Northside Neighborhood Council, independent neighborhood organizations, now continue the restoration program.

National Register District
City Historic District
Historic Landmark plaque

Russell H. Boggs house
604 West North Avenue, Mexican War Streets
Longfellow, Alden & Harlow, architects, 1888

The massive, understated style of the architects' Pontefract and McClelland houses soon yielded to decorative applications of varying success. The oval window above the doorway of the house, and the decorative gable above that, demonstrate no compelling reason to exist, and it may be that the stable is the real compositional success on the property. The porch, originally, was only one bay wide.

The owner was a partner in Allegheny's Boggs & Buhl department store.

National Register District
City Historic District

A view from West North Avenue.

Allegheny Commons parks
Between Brighton Road and Cedar Avenue,
North Avenue and Ridge Avenue-Canal Street

In David Redick's plan of 1788, Allegheny Town, a third of a mile square, was surrounded by a 102-acre quadrangle intended for use as a grazing common. In practice, the West Common at least became subject to intrusions: the Western Penitentiary from 1820 until 1886, the Western University of Pennsylvania in 1828, a Presbyterian theological seminary in 1827, and various private parties at various times. The Pittsburgh, Fort Wayne & Chicago Railroad—the Pennsylvania, in effect—sliced into the West Common in 1850, on its way to bedevil the streets of Allegheny and Manchester with a right-of-way skewed to the grid and grade crossings throughout.

By 1867 the Commons as grazing ground were out of use, and in most parts amounted to no more than a squalid vacant lot. The City engaged a New York engineering firm, Mitchell, Grant & Co., to create a park that was completed in 1876. This was "passive," an ensemble of partly straight, partly winding, mainly symmetrical paths for quiet strolling and sitting, punctuated by fountains and, eventually, statues and monuments. West Common (or West Park) was the broadest and most favored space, having in the 1920s a conservatory donated in

The Soldiers' Monument

1887 by the former Alleghenian Henry Phipps; a bandstand; a memorial of 1914 to the U.S.S. *Maine*, with sculpture by Charles Keck and architecture by Stanley L. Roush; Lake Elizabeth, a pond of often-changed configuration; a monument to the naturalist Alexander von Humboldt; and one of the Commons' numerous fountains. By this time the Pennsylvania

main line had been lowered into a cutting, within West Common and beyond. In 1931 the Soldiers' Monument that had stood south of Ridge Avenue since 1871, conspicuous from the rivers, was moved beside Lake Elizabeth without its original tall base. It still stands beside a lake of 1968 that is rather Modern in form, with boomerang-like angled embankments. The architect was Louis Morganroth, the sculptor Peter C. Reniers, though the well-known Pittsburgh architect Robert W. Schmertz was involved in the 1931 truncation.

The Commons have lost all their fountains, some of their sculpture, and with these anything threatening to be labor-intensive. The National Aviary, despite the addition of a glass dome, is a rather plain building, but a positive addition to these subtractions, a major institution as its name implies.

City Historic District

Beech Avenue

Allegheny West

Immediately north of Ridge Avenue is a small area called Allegheny West or Lincoln-Beech, a portion of the original Allegheny Town's western out-lots beyond the Commons. Western Avenue, which passes through the district, has long been the main street, containing today a mixture of domestic architecture from the latter half of the nineteenth century and commercial buildings from the twentieth. Lincoln and Beech Avenues, running parallel to Western, are much quieter streets, lacking its visual disorder and its pressure of traffic. Demolition as well as commercial development have impaired the integrity of the area—here a cornice gone or windows badly remodeled, there a vacant lot where a large house stood—but there is still character and plenty of good architecture in Allegheny West. This serves as a reminder that early in this century, if its houses

The Maine *memorial*

934 Western Avenue

827 North Lincoln Avenue

948–50 Beech Avenue

848 Beech Avenue

930 North Lincoln Avenue

954 Beech Avenue

were not so grand as those of Ridge Avenue, this was still a very substantial place to live.

Number 934 Western Avenue illustrates the oldest type of house found in the neighborhood: a house of about 1850 in which the new Italianate manner is treated, not in the usual rich and heavy way but with an attenuated lightness that still suggests the spareness and precision of Greek Revival design. The cottage at the rear of 827 North Lincoln Avenue dates from 1878, and shows a matured Romanticism in its Gothic windows and its exterior

woodwork, which the Victorians would have regarded as Swiss. Numbers 948–50 Beech Avenue were built in 1876 as a speculation or as a boarding house for employees by two partners in a paving company; each unit of the double house is individualized by a curved, Dutch-looking gable with a Gothic finial, and bright inset tiles add a little extra sparkle to the usual mixture of brick and sandstone. The 1890-period Romanesque front of 848 Beech Avenue, a refacing of a somewhat older house, is very individual in its false gable and especially in its great front arch, half-concealing a trio of windows and a doorway, set in a delicate wooden frame beyond a very shallow porch. Number 930 North Lincoln Avenue, surviving in a block otherwise almost vacant, belonged to a member of the Thaw family, whose wealth came mainly from railroading. The house, now divided into business and residential quarters, was built in the last part of the nineteenth century, apparently in three separate campaigns.

Harry Darlington house
721 Brighton Road, Allegheny West
C. 1890

This is a tall, long, very narrow Romanesque house, grand in its brownstone and red brick, impressive in its wall area, but a mansion in filet form: what in some parts of the country would be called a flounder house. There is just a possibility that it is a work of Longfellow, Alden & Harlow, but no positive evidence of an architect has appeared. Frank Alden's daughter, however, later married into the Darlington family.

National Register District
City Historic District
Historic Landmark plaque

850 Beech Avenue   *841 North Lincoln Avenue*

At 954 Beech Avenue is a plain, turn-of-the-century Classical house with literary associations; here the author Mary Roberts Rinehart lived between 1907 and 1911. Another house of literary interest in Allegheny West is the Mid-Victorian Italianate one at 850 Beech Avenue; here, Gertrude Stein—a figure never associated in the public mind with Pittsburgh—was born in 1874. Her family left the area almost at once.

Number 841 North Lincoln Avenue was bought by the Pittsburgh History & Landmarks Foundation in 1977, and the Junior League of Pittsburgh rehabilitated the house as apartments, as an example of what could be done in the Allegheny West area. Landmarks went on to provide loans for other restorations in the neighborhood.

National Register District
City Historic District
Historic Landmark plaque

Holmes house
719 Brighton Road,
Allegheny West
C. 1871

This was the house of Letitia Holmes, widow of a pork packer, and has subsequently been among other things a boys' home and a funeral home. The limestone facing is very unusual for a Mid-Victorian house in this area. Inside, original woodwork and decorative painting have been carefully restored and preserved.

National Register District
City Historic District

Ridge Avenue
Allegheny West

Ridge Avenue was once a street of mansions. The process began at least as long ago as the 1850s; a Greek Revival house of that period survived here until the late 1960s. Italianate, Second Empire, Queen Anne, and Romanesque houses followed in the course of the nineteenth century, some packed close together, some freestanding though in rather restricted grounds. As the twentieth century began, the confidence in Ridge Avenue and its future seemed only to increase. The mining millionaire Henry W. Oliver, the iron-pipe manufacturer Alexander M. Byers, the steelmaker Benjamin F. Jones, Jr., and the ironmaker William P. Snyder built within a block of each other between 1891 and 1911.

The Snyder house of 1911 was the last one of any consequence. Soon, noted residents left Ridge Avenue's urbane but urban environment for country estates. Many of the houses they left behind were converted to business uses or began to deteriorate. In the late 1960s the south block front between Brighton Road and Galveston Avenue was razed for the building of the Community College of Allegheny County over the objections of the Pittsburgh History & Landmarks Foundation. The college did agree to take over the Jones and the Byers-Lyon houses as well as the Western Theological Seminary's Memorial Hall. The remaining Ridge Avenue mansions recall the days when wealth and prestige were at home in Old Allegheny.

B. F. Jones, Jr. house (now Jones Hall, Community College of Allegheny County, Allegheny Campus)
Ridge Avenue and Brighton Road, Allegheny West
Rutan & Russell, architects, c. 1908

This, one of the last of the great houses built by the industrial millionaires of Ridge Avenue, was also one of its biggest. It has forty-two rooms within and an Elizabethan exterior composed of red brick and ochre terra cotta. The sheer bigness of the place is impressive, though the architects were obviously a little concerned about it. The outline of the main body of the house is softened by buttresses, and the upper windows of the central part are crowned by a heavily modeled frieze; both devices give horizontal emphases that mitigate the height of the construction. The wing is monotonous in its fenestration, but the parapet is bowed upward in three places to give variety.

The owner was a son of Benjamin Franklin Jones, partner and co-founder of the Jones & Laughlin Steel Company, who lived close by in a smaller but still ample Second Empire house.

B. F. Jones, Jr., like many residents of this wealthy area, had a summer estate in Sewickley Heights, about twelve miles away; "Fair Acres" lasted until 1964.

National Register District
City Historic Structure
Historic Landmark plaque

**Memorial Hall, Western Theological Seminary
(now West Hall, Community College of Allegheny
County, Allegheny Campus)**
809 Ridge Avenue, Allegheny West
Thomas Hannah, architect, 1911–12

Terra cotta makes a splashy display in this red-and-cream
academic building, ending in a burst of glory on the
entrance tower. It is amusing to see how the architect
manipulated blocks in several standard sizes to give an
effect of randomness to his quoins and window jambs,
then absent-mindedly repeated his "random" combinations
in adjoining windows. Inside is a peculiar essay in early
concrete construction, a circular well surrounded by
balconies: a forerunner in miniature of the one at the
center of the Union Arcade downtown. The building
was to be the central element of a new complex for the
Western Theological Seminary, an institution that had
been in the neighborhood since 1827. Only a little more
than this one building was ever erected.

A fine Tudor-style library and free-standing Tudor
tower were demolished in the late 1960s.

National Register District
City Historic District
Historic Landmark plaque

William Penn Snyder house (now Babb, Incorporated)
Ridge and Galveston Avenues, Allegheny West
George S. Orth & Brothers, architects, 1911; addition, 1948

An office with an extensive practice in homes for the
wealthy was called upon to design what proved to be the
last of the great Ridge Avenue houses. The exterior, with
its Ionic order, was built in brownstone. Inside, the style
was primarily Elizabethan though not completely so.
The house had some curiosities of plan. In place of the
old-fashioned porte-cochere that projected to shelter the
ordinary mansion entrance, there was a motor entrance
off Galveston Avenue that admitted cars into the house,
then to a six-car garage or to an exit onto the alley behind.
From this motor entrance guests could walk to a mezzanine overlooking a basement ballroom. There was also a
central vacuum-cleaning system, with outlets at convenient
placcs in every room; this was a popular device early in
the century until fears of explosive mixtures of air and lint
caused its abandonment. The annex of 1948 was faced in
the original stone and is not readily noticed.

William Penn Snyder was in the iron brokerage
business and was a partner with Henry W. Oliver in the
development of iron mining in the Lake Superior area.
He was also proprietor of the Shenango Furnace Company,
makers of pig iron.

The Snyders lived in the house until 1920; then the
family began to use "Wilpen Hall," their summer home
in Sewickley Heights, the year around.

National Register of Historic Places
City Historic Structure
Historic Landmark plaque

Byers-Lyon houses (now Byers Hall, Community College of Allegheny County, Allegheny Campus)
901 Ridge Avenue, Allegheny West
Alden & Harlow, architects, 1898

This is in fact a double house, built for the wrought-iron and pipe manufacturer Alexander M. Byers, with a smaller adjoining unit for his daughter and her husband, who was the banker J. Denniston Lyon. The style is Flemish Renaissance. The houses are arranged in an L, with cloister-like arcades on a small garden court, bordered with an iron fence and a very elaborate wrought-iron gateway. A partial restoration in the late 1980s brought the major rooms back to their original state.

National Register of Historic Places
City Historic District
Historic Landmark plaque

Chalfant house (now Chalfant Hall, Community College of Allegheny County, Allegheny Campus)
915 Ridge Avenue, Allegheny West
C. 1900

Many well-to-do or rich Pittsburghers around 1900 built new houses such as this. The human parallel might be a serious, preoccupied man who dresses correctly for a social occasion without feeling social. The golden-brown Roman brick is a fine material, the porch in an unfluted Grecian Ionic order is very handsome, and the Federal-style iron-work above it is quite delicate. These and other individual features could have been elements of a forthcoming and even witty design. And yet this house is grave in effect as so many large Pittsburgh houses are; the local genius could make Georgian feel like Romanesque. But this is not to disparage the Chalfant house, which has character and invites the passer-by to speculate on the lives that were spent within its slightly brooding depths.

National Register District
City Historic District
Historic Landmark plaque

James G. Pontefract house
1014 North Lincoln Avenue, Allegheny West
Longfellow & Harlow, architects, 1886–88

This is a very early house by this distinguished Boston-
Pittsburgh firm, designed before Frank Alden was officially
a partner. Like its contemporary the McClelland house in
Shadyside it has a corner tower and dispenses with a front
porch, but it has variegated golden Roman brick with a
simple diaper pattern in the upper floor rather than the
uniform and bold red of the McClelland walls. Such
simplicity was short-lived in Pittsburgh, coming between
two periods of ostentation.

    Pontefract, a partner of Henry Clay Frick and manager
of the Overholt Distillery, also commissioned "Bagatelle,"
in Edgeworth, from the architects.

**Joseph O. and Elizabeth
Horne house**
*838 North Lincoln Avenue,
Allegheny West
Longfellow, Alden &
Harlow, architects, 1889*

The very controlled
stonework textures and
the delicate outlining
of the openings with
moldings reveal the slow
mutation of the architects'
style from Romantic to
Classical. The delicate
metalwork and glazing

celebrate neither the natures nor working of the materials
in a Romantic way, nor are they the details of a bold and
simple Classical composition, scaled to contribute to its
initial effect. Rather, they require close-up study as
compositions in themselves.

*National Register District
City Historic District
Historic Landmark plaque*

Henry Buhl house
*1241 Western Avenue, Allegheny West
1885*

This is a remarkable
Queen Anne survivor, one
of the prouder and among
the most picturesque of
the houses in this area in
1900. Its surroundings
now are utilitarian and
colorless and obliterated
by roadways, but houses
of its time nearer the river
were notably more hum-
ble, and such neighbors as
the Union Salt Works, the
Excelsior Coffin and
Casket Works, and the
LaBelle Steel Works were
within a quarter-mile in
those pre-zoning days.

West End Bridge
Ohio River, between Western Avenue and
West Carson Street at Saw Mill Run Boulevard
George S. Richardson of the Allegheny County Department
of Public Works, engineer, 1931

One of the handsomest bridges in a county that has
perhaps two thousand, and an innovative design for its
time. Technically, this is a tied-arch bridge, the 780-foot
arch from which the deck is suspended being anchored by
ties that run beneath the deck. The trusswork in the arch
itself is to keep it from distortion under off-center loads.
The cable hangers from the arch were put under tension
before the deck was built: one of the first uses of prestress-
ing in the United States. It is best seen from Point State
Park, or from the western end of Mount Washington,
where the great rise of its arch appears most dramatically.

National Register of Historic Places

Calvary Methodist Episcopal Church
(now Calvary United Methodist Church)
Allegheny and Beech Avenues, Allegheny West
Vrydaugh & Shepherd (Kansas City), with T. B. Wolfe,
architects, 1893–95

For a Pittsburgh Protestant church of the early 1890s,
this is unusual both in the elaborateness of its architecture
and in being designed in Gothic, not the fashionable
Romanesque. It had a wealthy congregation however, and

one that desired to build
grandly. Therefore, the
congregation paid for two
sandstone spires, much
carving that includes
gargoyles, windows by
Louis Comfort Tiffany
and woodwork, brasswork,
and mosaics befitting
the impressive interior.
New glazing, new refur-
nishing of the altar area
and covering-over of the
original stencil work have
weakened the original
effect. The church,
whose spire is conspicuous in distant views of this part of
the North Side, makes a dramatic termination to a quiet
domestic block of Beech Avenue.

Tiffany's St. John on the Isle of Patmos.

Calvary Methodist's congregation had just come to Allegheny in 1891, after their old church in the Triangle, Christ Methodist, had burned. Another part of the congregation went to the East End, where they built a new Christ Methodist—now First United Methodist—Church at Baum Boulevard and Aiken Avenue.

The centennial of the building's opening was marked by a cleaning, and what North Siders long had known as a dark and sooty church became one of ash gray.

National Register District
City Historic Structure
Historic Landmark plaque

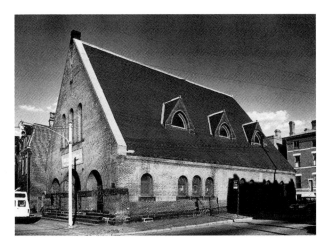

Emmanuel Episcopal Church
West North and Allegheny Avenues, Allegheny West
Henry Hobson Richardson (Brookline, Mass.), architect,
1885–86

Richardson was commissioned to design Emmanuel Church in 1883 or 1884 but it was only in 1885, after rejection of a more expensive design intended for stone and with a central tower, that his plans were approved and put into execution. Such ornamentation as the building has comes mainly from the treatment of the brickwork. The entrance arches are laid in five rings, with a narrower outer ring: a very conventional way of building an arch in brick.

The apse and the parish house.

Above these, to the sill level of the upper windows, the bricks are laid in a basket-weave pattern. Other levels in the wall are marked by soldier courses, laid with the bricks on end, and the gable coping is formed by tumbled work, with bricks perpendicular to the gable slope and making tooth-like indentations into the main gable area. At the top is a rounded capstone. And that is all. (Unimpressed by its simplicity, neighbors called Emmanuel the Bake Oven Church.) On the sides, the lower walls slope inward toward sill level, and the sills themselves are connected by a soldier course. The bonding of the brickwork, along with a very small amount of rock-faced stone trim, is what really carries the architectural message without. It is the materials and their perceptible solidity that count. The outward flare of the side and apse walls above window-sill level is not, however, a subtlety of design, as one might expect; Richardson simply underestimated the thrust of the laminated wooden arches that support the roof.

The interior is rather dark beneath the low-set,

West North Avenue at Fulton Street

varnished wooden roof, and was quite simple as built. There is however a marble and mosaic reredos of 1898, designed by Leake & Greene. This has its own beauty but seems a little luxurious for such a primitive interior. The three front gable windows are by Tiffany.

The parish house of 1888 is a work of Frank Alden of Longfellow, Alden & Harlow. Not only do its arches and brickwork, and the rounding of a corner carry on the architectural spirit of the church; the mass of the building helps buttress the east wall of the church against the spread, acting in concert with a clever undermining of the wall to put weight on the haunches of the arches above.

National Register of Historic Places
City Historic Structure
Historic Landmark plaque

Manchester

After its 1867 annexation by Allegheny, Manchester developed in most of its area as a solid, comfortable residential neighborhood of red brick houses with stone trim and wooden porches, set on an orderly grid of streets laid over an old flood plain, with industry near the Ohio River shore. Some houses, along West North and Pennsylvania Avenues especially, were detached and villa-like, but many were double houses, uniform row houses, or houses set directly side by side: configurations made possible by the unusual flatness of the land.

1131 West North Avenue is an aspiring piece of Richardson Romanesque, attempting a castle effect on a narrow city lot: a work of fantasy not different in mood from East Liberty's Alpha Terrace.

Of the detached houses the Isaac Wertheimer house at 1220 West North Avenue is a pleasant late example, probably from 1892: a work in what is usually called the Shingle Style, though brick is as much in evidence here as shingles. The very high roof and prominent chimneys

1131 West North Avenue

1220 West North Avenue

1414 Pennsylvania Avenue

1203–05 West North Avenue

1220–22 Sheffield Street

1324–26 Sheffield Street

1315 Liverpool Street

symbolize shelter, while the polygonal dormer and tower-like bay window next to it dramatize the view outward from the shelter and add strong sculptural elements. In the round bay window, even the stone transoms and the window panes are curved so as to be in harmony with the basic cylindrical form. Some twenty years earlier is 1414 Pennsylvania Avenue, a typical Italian villa with front, tower, and side wing set in an echelon pattern and an ample verandah facing the street.

1203–05 West North Avenue and 1220–22 Sheffield Street illustrate the double houses. Both are from about 1880, and reveal the Late Victorian tendency to give each house individuality in spite of a uniform design, in one case with sharp gabled dormers against a false mansard roof, in the other with miniature hipped roofs rising above the roofline. The Sheffield Street houses are quite unusual in their window canopies, a carryover from the Italian Villa mode that was then obsolete. 1324–26 Sheffield Street are not so much double houses as the first two elements of a house row that was never completed; the stonework of the

right-hand house awaits the stonework of an adjoining entrance. The projecting window bays and the false half-timbering in the gables have a British look; houses of very similar appearance were going up in English cities for respectable tradesmen around this same time, the 1880s and 1890s.

The Langenheim house at 1315 Liverpool Street is large, showy, and freestanding though closely surrounded by other buildings: a small city mansion, in fact. The Pittsburgh History & Landmarks Foundation acquired the house in 1967 at the request of the area residents, when it was in a miserable state of disrepair, and held it for over a decade until a buyer was found who would restore its exterior and adapt its interior for apartments. The original owner was a wholesale grocer, Gustav Langenheim, who may have entrusted its design to his son-in-law Alfred Schwerd, an architect, builder, and manufacturer of architectural woodwork.

Beginning in 1966, Landmarks worked with neighborhood residents to create the first historic preservation district in the nation primarily for African-Americans; the first federally funded historic district program administered by community residents; the first preservation program using Title I urban-renewal funds for the restoration of houses for low- to moderate-income residents; and a series of incentive programs designed to combat displacement and encourage long-time residents to stay and become part of the revitalized community. The Manchester Citizens Corporation now continues the neighborhood restoration effort.

National Register District
City Historic District
Historic Landmark plaque

Double house
1222–24 Liverpool Street, Manchester
C. 1870

This genial double front is now about one room deep, a portion of the modern and much-larger Manchester Youth Development Center next door. The double-width, double-height porch is very unusual for Manchester, and seems a little more relaxed in expression than is the typical solemn, dignified three-story Manchester house.

National Register District
City Historic District

Houses
1300 block of Liverpool Street, Manchester
C. 1880 and after

The impressive but forlorn spectacle that this block presented in the early 1960s led to the idea of a preservation organization for Allegheny County, and it is largely because of the efforts of the Pittsburgh History & Landmarks Foundation that the block is generally in good condition today, an outstanding element in a historic neighborhood. The north side of the block is occupied by nine identical double houses in the Second Empire style, all with delicately detailed wooden entrance porches. These, which form the most impressive house row in Pittsburgh, were built in successive campaigns that began some time before 1882.

Across the street the west end begins with a solid five-unit row whose masonry detailing is similar though not identical to that of the houses opposite. Two pairs of houses share very showy wooden porches with arched motifs, spindles, Romanesque capitals, and intricate cast-iron crestings, the dry Mid-Victorian manner of the porches on the north side of the street abandoned. Further east, sobriety sets in; a tame and rather thin Classicism appears in all subsequent porches of the development.

After this comes greater variety: the Romanesque Stifel house of 1885 by Charles M. Bartberger, outwardly picturesque and housing elaborate decorative glass and woodwork; the Langenheim house in a bold if indeterminate style; a little more Second Empire; and a Romanesque house row, stone-fronted, boldly gabled, and with continuous front porches. Together both sides of the 1300 block of Liverpool Street form a picture of Victorian middle-class respectability and comfort.

National Register District
City Historic District
Historic Landmark plaque

James Anderson house (now Anderson Manor)
1423 Liverpool Street, Manchester
C. 1830; additions and remodelings, 1905, 1983

This was the home of Colonel James Anderson, an industrialist and philanthropist who encouraged bright working boys to read the books in his library. His best-known beneficiary was the teen-age Andrew Carnegie, who memorialized him in the semicircular exedra by Daniel Chester French and Henry Bacon that faces the entrance to the Allegheny Regional Branch of the Carnegie Library of Pittsburgh.

The house has undergone many changes, but the Federal-period porch and some internal woodwork have survived, while pressed-metal ceilings and other decorative work of later times are good in their own ways.

National Register District
City Historic District
Historic Landmark plaque

Union Methodist Church (now New Zion Baptist Church)
Manhattan Street and Pennsylvania Avenue, Manchester
Barr & Moser, architects, 1866–67

Brick is used in a very simple way to create a church of formal dignity. The result could be a clubhouse or a public hall at least as readily as a place of worship but the design is a very handsome one. Only the three curved false gables represent a step too far, impairing the clarity of the design. Inside, the church space is decorated in pressed tin as a result of a remodeling early in the century.

National Register District
City Historic District
Historic Landmark plaque

Warehouse
Sandusky and Isabella Streets, North Shore
C. 1900, 1920; Hunting-Davis Co., engineers for 1920 part

This warehouse, now adapted for use as an office and retail building, is actually the product of two building campaigns and two technologies. One side is heavy masonry and timber; the other, steel frame of a later date. The in-and-out surface of rock-faced rusticated stonework on the ground floor is uncommon and quite effective. The bold corbeled cornice suggests machicolations, which allowed defenders of medieval fortifications to drop rocks and other deadly objects on besiegers. The general appearance is one of impressive strength, suitable to a warehouse.

Frick & Lindsay Building (now The Andy Warhol Museum)
Sandusky and General Robinson Streets, North Shore
William G. Wilkins Co. (?), architect, c. 1913

Faced for its entire height in cream-colored terra cotta, the Warhol displays a cheerful, charming style that is partly Beaux-Arts, partly one of those improvised Modern manners that architects used on commercial and industrial work around 1910. Insofar as there is a philosophy in such a way of designing, it recalls the attitude of the Queen Anne period: anything is all right if it looks good. Here the architect accepted the discipline of a steel frame and the need for big, broad windows, and applied his decoration to good effect. The present cornice is an approximate replica of the original, lost one.

Volkwein's, a well-known Pittsburgh music store, long occupied the building. Previously it belonged to

the Frick & Lindsay Company, dealers in machinery. Despite the rather delicate exterior, this is a very strong structure. The 1993 interior remodeling by Richard Gluckman (New York) has left the inner construction largely revealed.

Osterling studio and office
228 Isabella Street, North Shore
Frederick J. Osterling, architect for facade, 1917

Osterling's father had owned the original Victorian build-ing on this site and an adjacent area on which he had a lumber yard. Osterling's reconstruction of 1917 for his own offices included this facade, whose light Gothic detailing recalled his recent triumph, the Union Arcade downtown.

In the main, the facade has a strength and decisiveness, together with a lightness, not usually associated with Osterling's work. The great window, which includes a doorway, is divided into three compartments, defined by mullions that rise sheer to the molding that frames the whole opening. The first impression is Venetian but the tracery itself is more French, with its ogee curves for the door head and the heads of the main window compart-ments. The parapet, with its battlemented silhouette, is a fairly common feature of the early twentieth century, a device for masking an uninteresting flat roof and giving an interesting skyline. The original doors, too, must have been decorative.

Architects of this time usually rented their personal working space, or incorporated space for themselves into larger commissions. An independent building housing an architect's studio and office and built to his design is a rarity.

National Register of Historic Places

Allegheny General Hospital
East North and Cedar Avenues, Central North Side
York & Sawyer (New York), architects, 1928–30

York & Sawyer were well known in the 1920s as bank and hospital specialists, and specialized as well in two styles, fifteenth-century Italian Renaissance and Italian Romanesque. The latter is used here in a sauve composi-tion typical of the architects. The facing is white brick, set off with granite colonettes that are red and gray alternately and terra-cotta cornices and capitals that are yellow, blue, and green. The gentle colors against the prevailing cold white are very effective.

The seventeen-story tower is the most conspicuous element of the North Side as seen from a distance, more so even than the vast but dark-hued Heinz plant. It termi-nates the northern end of Cedar Avenue and marks the northeast corner of the Commons in a way that makes it seem especially to belong.

Major hospital functions have been assumed by the modern building seen in the background, but the original structure remains in use housing clinics, offices, and a visitors' center.

Cedar Avenue

404 Cedar Avenue

Deutschtown

East of the Commons lies Deutschtown, the area where the German-speaking peoples settled as newcomers arrived in Allegheny early in the nineteenth century and over-flowed the original little Allegheny Town.

East Ohio Street, the Butler Turnpike of 1830, developed as the main commercial street of Deutschtown, with

413 East Ohio Street

impressively decorated Victorian facades rising above the shopfronts two or three stories. Many of these remain, seldom cared for, a reproach to the visual chaos below. The lively perspective of these fronts is interrupted, though, by demolitions and especially by the clearances of the years around 1970 for the East Street Valley Expressway that was completed only twenty years later. The Hollander Building of 1888 at Number 413 is one of the most impressive of these commercial buildings, with a front in the Queen Anne style. The bricklayer has been hard at work here, showing his skill at paneling and corbeling, and using terra-cotta panels of leaf ornament here and there to offset the geometry of his own inventions. The building was purchased in 1985 by the East Allegheny Community Council for restoration, with the aid of a loan from the Pittsburgh History & Landmarks Foundation.

The residential showplace of Deutschtown is Cedar Avenue, facing the East Common, especially the part north of East Ohio Street. As was the case with North Avenue, the view of a handsome park stimulated good residential construction in the Mid- and Late Victorian periods. Number 404 is distinguished by its good proportions and by the period of construction—the middle of the nineteenth century—revealed in its spare Italianate style. Numbers 814 and 816, shown here after the masonry had been painted, stand out, partly because of their pointed roofs, terra-cotta decorative panels, and leaded glass, partly because they look a little alien to the Pittsburgh area. The shallow projecting bays with chamfers are more characteristic of Washington, D.C.; might a Washington builder have supplied the design? Number 910 is odd too in another way, with its emphatic lintels and lumps of carving that give it a big-boned look; these contrast with extremely thin moldings that pursue their own independent courses on the facade, while a split round arch and two wavy metal star medallions further the effect of brash individualism. A commercial building of about 1890 on Fifth Avenue in the Uptown area, now gone, showed these same traits, suggesting that an interesting Pittsburgh architect is waiting to be discovered or to be better known: the extravagant Joseph Stillburg, perhaps.

Avery, Lockhart, and Pressley Streets, narrow passages lined with good Late Victorian houses, comprise a rather quaint quarter of Deutschtown that has experienced rehabilitation activity, including new, visually compatible infill houses. These streets, along with Cedar Avenue, are now in a City Historic District.

National Register District

814–16 Cedar Avenue

910 Cedar Avenue

Avery Street

Lockhart Street

Pressley Street

Latimer School (now the School House)
Tripoli and James Streets, Deutschtown
Frederick C. Sauer, architect, 1898

This many-windowed school is built of yellow-gray brick and sandstone trim that has darkened in the Pittsburgh air. Its Tripoli Street entrance, with a tower above, is impressive, but more impressive still is the chimney that rises on the side: a square, solid tapering stack rising toward a deep ornamental termination, contrasting its solid mass against an open facade that by comparison looks delicate. There is a sort of barbaric energy about the chimney as it breaks the symmetry of the composition that is oddly pleasing to see.

The school has been converted into apartments.

National Register of Historic Places

St. Mary's Priory (now The Priory—A City Inn)
616 Pressley Street, Deutschtown
Henry Moeser, architect, 1888

Set alongside the former St. Mary's Church, The Priory shares a narrow, deep, tranquil courtyard, one of the most agreeable enclosed outdoor spaces in the city. The Priory's conversion into a bed-and-breakfast inn has done little to disturb its main-floor plan of parlors, dining hall, and kitchen. A loan from the Pittsburgh History & Landmarks Foundation helped in the acquisition and restoration of the building.

Historic Landmark plaque
National Register District
City Historic District

St. Mary's Church (Roman Catholic; now Pittsburgh's Grand Hall at The Priory)
Pressley and Nash Streets, Deutschtown
Father John Stibiel, designer, 1853–54;
Sidney F. Heckert, architect of vestibule, 1906

The plain though harmonious exterior of this large church, which looks Neoclassical because of its semicircular windows, disguises the elaboration within. There, barrel vaults meet at a crossing dome thirty feet in diameter. The vaults themselves are supported on Corinthian columns crowned by entablatures of an unorthodox and so to speak homemade appearance. To these original details were added a mural in 1882 by M. Lambart of New York, twelve Austrian stained-glass windows in 1912, and a three-manual Gottfried organ. An entrance vestibule was added c. 1900.

The towers were once topped by flamboyant onion domes that differed radically in mood from the placid masonry below to add a touch of Central European Baroque, and only the lunettes of the side windows were originally glazed, allegedly to prevent vandalism by anti-Catholic "Know-Nothings." St. Mary's was one of three churches, named after the Holy Family, that

were planned for Deutschtown, Troy Hill, and Manchester in the mid-nineteenth century.

In 1995 the long-empty church reopened as a banquet and conference facility. It had been saved from demolition by the present proprietors, neighbors, and the Pittsburgh History & Landmarks Foundation.

National Register District
City Historic District

H. J. Heinz Company
Progress Street east of Chestnut Street, East Deutschtown
1896 and after

A bird's-eye view of 1909 shows the buildings of the Heinz plant, already big after twenty years of growth and with more to come, ranged along a Progress Street that had the air of a grand avenue. Three of these buildings, including the Bottling Building of 1896 which is the oldest now extant, had corner spires and elevated central panels that said HEINZ over and over to the passer-by. Opposite the Administration Building, white terra-cotta and brick Ionic in a complex of brown-brick Romanesque, was a little park with a cubical guardhouse, topped by a cupola with a dome in its turn topped by a smaller cupola, topped finally by an eagle about to take off.

Much of this glory is now gone: the spires, the park, the guardhouse, even the Ionic capitals of the Administration Building. On the other hand the plant has grown since 1909, and we can still see the less fancy but still ornate additions of the 1910s and 1920s, when architects struggled to harmonize with the sadly unfashionable Richardsonian piles already there. Three buildings in all were by Albert Kahn, architect of Detroit's industrial plants and mansions both. Later, a clean break was made with Kahn's Office Annex of 1937, light buff brick and devoid of round arches.

In 1952 came an even greater departure: Skidmore, Owings & Merrill's glass-walled Warehouse and Vinegar Plant, followed by their green-glass box of a Research Building. The oldest structure once on the site is gone but extant: the house where Henry J. Heinz had started in business was floated down from Sharpsburg to the new plant in 1904 as a memento, and was later shipped out to the Greenfield Village Museum at Dearborn, Michigan.

Henry J. Heinz is well known as one of the early producers of canned and bottled foods. His business began in Sharpsburg, up the Allegheny River, in 1869, then moved to Allegheny in 1889.

Teutonia Männerchor
857 Phineas Street, East Deutschtown
George Ott, architect, 1888

There is just a little genuine half-timber construction in the United States, with real, massive framing timbers and gaps filled with brick or some other substance. Most of it is of German origin, and Teutonia at first appears to be an outstanding example, but a closer look denies this; it is just a convincing effect. The front is not quite as built, after careless remodelings of the past. Inside are a rathskeller on the ground floor and a handsomely decorated singing hall above.

Sarah Heinz House
East Ohio and Heinz Streets, East Deutschtown
Robert Maurice Trimble, architect, 1915

This is a worker's resource not unlike those that Andrew Carnegie built at Braddock, Munhall, and Duquesne, save that here there was only a small library facility. The style is Jacobean, a little like that of the Oliver Baths of the same period on the South Side: gracious, stately, home-like, not monumental. It nearly fell for highway interchange construction in the 1970s, but the Pittsburgh History & Landmarks Foundation and the neighbors together were able to save it.

Schiller School
Peralta and Wettach Streets, East Deutschtown
Marion M. Steen, architect, 1939

Here is a fine essay in the use of deep-red textured brick-work, laid to produce zigzag Modernistic ornament. Steen was architect for the Board of Education during the 1930s, and designed a number of school buildings in varieties of the Moderne, all different, all handsomely decorated. The "precedent" for this design seems to have been a German crematorium of the 1920s.

The very interesting facades have been attributed to Edward Joseph Weber, best known for his religious work of a decade before.

National Register of Historic Places

Eberhardt & Ober Brewing Company (now Penn Brewery and The Brewery Innovation Center)
Troy Hill Road and Vinial Street, East Deutschtown
C. 1880 and after; Joseph Stillburg, architect of stock house;
E. M. Butz, architect of stable

Three buildings remain from a prosperous brewery, established at the foot of Troy Hill by two of its prominent residents. The office building of 1897 is quite simple and unassumingly pleasant, with a round corner bay for an entrance. The central building, the stock house, dates in its present form from 1894. The northwest wing adjoining is tall, warehouse-like, and minimally ornamented. Across the street from these three stands the two-story, Romanesque, Bottling Department.

Brewing began on this site in 1848. The Eberhardt & Ober Brewery began in 1870, when John Ober and William Eberhardt, both brewers as well as brothers-in-law, went into partnership. The firm remained independent until 1899, when it was absorbed into the Pittsburgh Brewing Company. Eventually, both partners were buried, side by side, in similar mausoleums in Allegheny Cemetery.

A public-private partnership combined in 1986 to transform the buildings into a business center where the focal tenant is a "craft" brewery and restaurant, making beer in authentic German style on the premises. A loan from the Pittsburgh History & Landmarks Foundation helped initiate this successful renovation project.

National Register of Historic Places

Ober-Guehl house
Troy Hill Road and Lowrie Street, Troy Hill
1877; additions

This conspicuous Troy Hill house combines the typical Italian Villa formula of gable wall, tower, and side wall in echelon arrangement with the board-framed wall panels of the so-called Stick Style. Extensive one-story additions obscure the original form. At some point some of the surfaces were covered with shingles whose exposed edges are cut in bands of fancy patterns: a treatment commoner to the Shingle Style, with its concern with surfaces, than to the older Stick Style, with its interest in lines.

The house was built for James Dewhurst, who in 1884 sold it to John Ober, a partner in the Eberhardt & Ober Brewery at the foot of Troy Hill. The new owner built a brick stable near by, still standing, with a stone carving of a horse's head above its heavy round arch.

John Ober is remembered for his philanthropies. The Ober Foundation transformed the old Haymarket Square at Federal and Ohio Streets into Ober Park, a green area that in its later days stood between the Boggs & Buhl department store and the Buhl Planetarium.

Historic Landmark plaque

Rectory, Church of the Most Holy Name of Jesus
1700 Harpster Street, Troy Hill
C. 1875

The window sash is not the original but otherwise this is a perfect example of American Second Empire domestic architecture. Yet in one respect it looks curiously European: where is the front porch? After all, there is a front yard. But this is a neighborhood with a European tradition, and Father Mollinger, for whom it was built, seems simply not to have wanted one. A ceremonious doorway—which may actually be later than the house—is the more reticent way chosen of greeting the world outside.

Historic Landmark plaque

St. Anthony's Chapel
1700 Harpster Street, Troy Hill
1880; towers, 1890–91

This is the most interesting building on Troy Hill: a brick Romanesque church fronted in rock-faced sandstone. Although the building campaign went through the years when Richardson Romanesque was in fashion, the style here is used in an attenuated Mid-Victorian way.

The interior is even more remarkable. The Chapel was built by Father Suibertus Gottfried Mollinger, who placed in it his collection of 5,000 holy relics, housed in ornate reliquaries, as well as saints' images and ex-votos. The collection of relics is said to be the largest in the Western Hemisphere. Father Mollinger's parish, that of the Most Holy Name of Jesus, now owns the Chapel and

offers public tours. Through the efforts of the parishioners, the Chapel was thoroughly restored in the 1970s.

City Historic Structure
Historic Landmark plaque

Henderson-Metz house
Warren and Henderson Streets, Fineview
C. 1860

In detail this imposing, dark sandstone house is Gothic, with some Italianate allusions in its bay window, the window hood above, and the quoins and window surrounds. Seen from the side, where the entrance is, it looks quite Georgian though in its plain, regular fenestration. It has not the fantastic elaboration of the only other large surviving Gothic house in the county, the Singer house in Wilkinsburg, but it is a fortunate survival all the same. It is not far from "Heathside Cottage."

In 1975 the Pittsburgh History & Landmarks Foundation purchased the Henderson-Metz house through its revolving fund, and sold it in 1984 to a development company that has restored its exterior and converted its interior, much altered already, and that of the adjoining carriage house into apartments.

National Register of Historic Places
Historic Landmark plaque

Cottage
434 Lee Street, Fineview
C. 1860 (?)

Nothing is known of this board-and-batten house, originally a double, though it appears Mid-Victorian and was moved from another site, to judge from old atlases. Board-and-batten houses are rare in the Pittsburgh area, and this is a simple but pretty one that now has, in "Heathside Cottage" and the Henderson-Metz house, two Gothic neighbors.

"Heathside Cottage"
Catoma and Myler Streets, Fineview
C. 1860

This kind of outright Gothic Revival is rare in Allegheny County today, and it is quite rare to find it with its verge-board and other sawn-out wooden trim still present and diamond-paned sash still in the windows. This is an Early

Victorian design in spirit rather than a Mid-Victorian one, emphasizing delicacy rather than dignified massiveness, and is very much a borrowing from English Romanticism. The very word "heath"—an open area with wild shrubbery—is English, not American. It suggests the Romantic seclusion this house originally had, looking southward over the growing city of Allegheny from a vantage point 400 feet up.

The photograph shows the house when it was painted to give accent to the details.

National Register of Historic Places

House
1801 Clayton Avenue, Perry Hilltop
C. 1885

This is a house built to see from and to be seen, with its porches and bay windows and its steep tower roof. The siding is quite rare in the Pittsburgh area: wood grooved to imitate rusticated ashlar. The house commands a view of the Allegheny and Ohio Rivers.

House
2001 Perrysville Avenue, Perry Hilltop
C. 1870

This is a rather delicate and well-proportioned Italianate house, evidently placed to enjoy a remarkable hilltop view and eventually surrounded by later housing. The interiors were luxuriously fitted, and much of the marblework and woodwork has remained.

St. Boniface Church (Roman Catholic)
I-279 at Royal Street, East Street Valley
Albert F. Link, architect, 1925–26

St. Boniface is in a free style, part-Romanesque, part-Byzantine, executed in limestone. Its location at a slight bend in East Street helps make it a specially prominent landmark, although it has always been the grandest construction on this unassuming residential road. Inside is a lavishly decorated space beneath Guastavino tile vaulting. Behind it is a school of 1884, a large but very basic building of brick whose wooden cupola, a paraphrase of the Courthouse tower, is its only notable feature.

For decades this was a neighborhood church, well attended. But a long, bitterly controversial clearing of land for a major expressway displaced many of the parishioners in the 1960s. Now, however, St. Boniface is more secure. The State sold it back to the Diocese of Pittsburgh, and the parish itself is strong once again.

National Register of Historic Places
Historic Landmark plaque

East Street (or E. H. Swindell, or Essen Street) Bridge
Over I-279 between North Charles and Essen Streets,
East Street Valley
City of Pittsburgh Department of Public Works,
engineers, 1930

Well known to northbound drivers, the East Street Bridge is a cantilever span with a lower chord in the form of an arch with half-arches at each end. Unlike most trusses, a cantilever truss has an upper chord in tension and a lower chord in compression; this makes possible the two arms that form the ends of the structure. The bridge is 160 feet above the valley and nearly a quarter-mile long.

Allegheny Observatory
159 Riverview Drive, Observatory Hill
Thorsten E. Billquist, architect; John Alfred Brashear and
James E. Keeler, consultants; 1900

Built in light tan brick and terra cotta, this observatory is clad in a mixed Classical style that includes Greek Ionic columns and distinctively Roman balustrades. Such mixtures could be found in Greece itself in these years, since well-intentioned architects there were attempting to establish the national identity through revival of the

ancient architecture; yet they had a nineteenth-century
urge to embellish basically Greek designs with features
from the Latin world. In Pittsburgh, a sort of return of the
Greek Revival took place around 1900; executed in grayish
brick and terra cotta, it appeared in several schools and
libraries as well as here. Quiet, serious, just a trifle florid
at times, it may have been regarded as a specifically
intellectual style.

The three domes were built to house two of the old-
fashioned refracting telescopes, giant spyglasses of 1860
and 1912 using lenses only, and a reflecting telescope of
1905. The support of this last is a columbarium, housing
the ashes of John Brashear and his wife, and of James E.
Keeler, a former director, and his son. Brashear, a well-
known local figure who died in 1920, was an astronomer
and maker of scientific instruments who did all the construction and repair work for the Observatory's equipment.
His reputation as an astronomer and teacher was such
that in 1915 he was officially named "the state's most
distinguished man."

National Register of Historic Places
Historic Landmark plaque

John Morrow Elementary School
1611 Davis Avenue, Brighton Heights
Samuel T. McClarren, architect, 1895;
additions, 1904, 1922, 1957

McClarren's portion of the building is reposeful in its
mass and fenestration, vivid in its quoin-like and random
touches of brown against Roman brick and diapering at the
second-floor window level. The architect is also known for
design of the Woolslair School in Bloomfield and of a
number of houses in his own borough of Thornburg.

National Register of Historic Places

McClure Avenue Presbyterian Church
3128 McClure Avenue, Woods Run
Longfellow, Alden & Harlow, architects, 1887

Situated almost underneath a bridge of Ohio River
Boulevard, this handsome, sparingly detailed church goes
all but unnoticed. It has lost the short tower above one
porch that was its only fancy external touch, and presents
itself to you as a taciturn red mass. Inside, a variety of the
Akron plan, popular once for Protestant churches, allows
a partition to be drawn aside to connect the church itself
with a Sunday school-auditorium space that is covered by
a roof of impressive carpentry. The church has three wheel
windows with glass in strong Late Victorian colors.

The last worship service for the original congregation
was held on Palm Sunday, 1996.

Western State Penitentiary (now State Correctional Institution)
Doerr Street at the Ohio River, Woods Run
E. M. Butz, architect, 1876–82

A glance at the main cell blocks suggests a local imitation
of the architecture of H. H. Richardson, and at one time
the suggestion was all the stronger, for until the 1970s
the roofline was varied at points with steep hip roofs that
had dormers with round-arched windows and little spiky
turrets. Richardson, however, was not an influential architect locally when the Penitentiary was under design, and
what we see here in fact is a work of Mid-Victorian
engineering masonry, faced with stone and ornamented
on its publicly visible fronts to do credit to the State.
The Warden's house facing the river is in that elaborately
picturesque but angular manner of the early 1870s that
was to become more supple and integrated as the decade
progressed and evolved into the Shingle Style and its
masonry equivalent.

The notorious escape of 1997 brought the future of the
building into serious doubt.

Looking upward from South Nineteenth Street, on the South Side.

PITTSBURGH SOUTH
OF THE RIVERS

Across the Monongahela River from the Triangle rises a 400-foot
bluff, now called Mount Washington but originally known
as Coal Hill. Pittsburgh owes much to the eight-foot coal
seam in this hill, which was first mined in the 1760s, since
its development from an 1800-period flatboat town
depended on the furnaces and engines that this coal
served to fire. The shore at the foot of Coal Hill and the
other bluffs along the river began its rapid evolution from
farmland to industrial land in 1797 when the glassworks of
James O'Hara and Isaac Craig began production opposite
the Point. In the next seventy years, four miles of ironworks,
glassworks, railroad lines, and tiny boroughs replaced the
farms along the river.

CITY OF
PITTSBURGH

Among the Monongahela-shore boroughs were three early nineteenth-century developments of Nathaniel Bedford and his relatives by
marriage, the Ormsbys, which are together now known as the South
Side flats. Birmingham, with Bedford Square and its market place at the
center, was laid out between South Sixth and South Seventeenth Streets
in 1811; East Birmingham lay between South Seventeenth and South
Twenty-seventh Streets; and Ormsby extended for a mile-and-a-half
further eastward. Their riverside ironworking plants are now nearly
imperceptible as such; even the huge Jones & Laughlin plant has disappeared, and the local producers of fine glassware that was once famous
have all shut down. What remains is a most interesting, intimately
scaled neighborhood of Victorian houses, many meticulously kept with
flower-planted yards, and churches reflecting a multitude of national
origins. And down the neighborhood's center runs East Carson Street
with an extraordinary display of Victorian commercial architecture.

On Sarah Street in the South Side flats.

South Side residents are proud of their houses and they like the settled quality of life; businesses like the local work ethic and ease of access. The South Side, in fact, arouses a sentiment in Pittsburgh to which the street scenes certainly contribute but which also comes from a good feeling about those who live and work there.

Above the flats are the South Side slopes, with more churches among little houses that cling to the hillside, tenuously connected with the neighborhoods above and below by narrow, giddy streets.

Ascending the hills was an early problem that found no easy solution until the advent of the incline. The South Side area eventually acquired twelve inclines, over half of those known to have been in the immediate area of Pittsburgh. Some carried coal from the hillside mine tunnels; others carried pedestrians and vehicles. Only two survive. Of those that are gone, only a vague trace on a hillside or occasional foundations for trestlework survive to recall the impressive structures which opened the hilltops to development.

The edge of Mount Washington has some commerce along Grandview Avenue, especially restaurants which exploit the dramatic view of the rivers and the Triangle. Here and there are fairly tall apartment houses, but the coal seam, mined out save for pillars of coal, makes for tricky constructional problems in many places, and much of Grandview Avenue has buildings no more than three stories high; in fact from below, the skyline suggests a row of house models ranged on a mantelshelf.

Station Square, so far beneath this lofty skyline as to have its own skyline against a background of trees, is the former site of the Pittsburgh & Lake Erie Railroad. In 1976, the Pittsburgh History & Landmarks Foundation began renovating the historic railroad buildings to create a lively urban environment along the river bank.

The trolley, beginning in 1888, supplemented the inclines, allowing settlement far beyond the brows of the hills, and the back slopes and the adjacent hills of Mount Washington were eventually built up almost completely with detached houses of unassuming design scattered over ridges and hollows. When the South Hills Tunnel opened in 1904, the way was clear for development miles away from the rivers, and Pittsburgh, which had annexed the shore areas in 1872, began annexations of the newly developed adjacent neighborhoods. Only Mount Oliver, a borough now totally surrounded by Pittsburgh, escaped. These neighborhoods, so quickly built up, still retain a look of 1900 or 1910: blocky houses of buff, cream-colored, or red brick or white siding, picturesquely disposed over the varied contours of the land.

Fallowfield Avenue, Beechview

**Pittsburgh & Lake Erie Railroad Station
(now Station Square)**
*Smithfield Street Bridge and West Carson Street
1897–1918; remodeled, 1976 and after*

In 1879 the Pittsburgh & Lake Erie Railroad began operations, breaking a near-monopoly of the Pennsylvania
Railroad in the Pittsburgh area. Its first installation on the
Monongahela shore, in the industrial settlement beneath
Mount Washington known as Sligo, was quite modest,
but by 1930 it had taken over almost all the shore land
facing the Triangle. While coal hauling was its specialty,
it also carried other types of freight and had an extensive
passenger operation, and erected buildings large and small
alongside its vast yard.

By the late 1960s, though, much of this activity had
declined; one proposal was made for conventional redevel-
opment of this property that would have removed most,
if not all, of the buildings. Nothing was done, though,
until 1975 when the Pittsburgh History & Landmarks
Foundation proposed an adaptive-use project that would
save all the historic buildings. Against expert advice and
public disbelief, Landmarks proceeded with sub-developers
to convert the Freight House of 1897 into a commercial
and retail arcade; the Passenger Station of 1901 into
The Landmarks Building which houses offices and the
Grand Concourse restaurant; the Express House of the
early twentieth century into an office building of the same
name; the Terminal Annex of 1916, an office building,
into the Gatehouse, with modern offices; and the Shovel
Transfer Warehouse of 1918 into Commerce Court,
with shops, restaurants, and offices.

More recent constructions have included a Sheraton
Hotel, the docking facilities and headquarters of the
Gateway Clipper excursion fleet, a new parking garage,
parking lots, and public open areas with benches,

landscaping, and historic artifacts that include railway
rolling stock and, as symbols of the region's past, a
Bessemer converter and numerous other industrial
artifacts along a riverside walk.

An important aspect of the project for Landmarks
was to demonstrate its basic urban planning principles as
opposed to those used in Allegheny Center, East Liberty,
and the lower Hill: to reuse historic buildings, make
vehicular access easy, create humanely scaled open squares
and spaces, treat familiar artifacts as sculpture, and utilize
undeveloped riverfront land as an amenity for people.
In addition, the project was based on Landmarks' belief
in tapping existing markets in the city and mixing uses
in a clean, varied, urban environment. The Allegheny
Foundation launched the project with a five-million-dollar
equity grant in 1976. The fifty-acre Station Square has
become popular and successful.

*National Register District
Historic Landmark plaques*

**Pittsburgh & Lake Erie Railroad Passenger Station
(now The Landmarks Building)**
*One Station Square, south end of Smithfield Street Bridge
William George Burns, architect, 1901; remodeled, 1978–83*

At the turn of the century, the P&LE replaced its first
small wooden passenger terminal with the present
grandiose structure, planned also as company headquarters.
Crossman & Sturdy, Chicago decorators, gave the main
waiting room a Classical appearance, with imitation-marble
columns, carved and varnished woodwork, and a huge
fanlight and vault of stained glass, all in the browns, ambers,
and greens that appealed to the turn-of-the-century color

sense. More modest yet very handsome interiors opened off this great space. Upstairs a small but decorative two-story lobby led to offices with ebonized woodwork and brass hardware that bore the intricate P&LE monogram. Outside was a balloon trainshed whose ultimate length was 700 feet.

In 1978 the first great triumph of the Station Square project came with the opening of the Grand Concourse restaurant, a sympathetic conversion of the old passenger rooms and the adjoining baggage room. In 1983 the office space, which was thoroughly modernized in functioning yet retained the old ornamental detailing, was reopened. Substantially, the building is in its old form today, with two exceptions: the trainshed was demolished in the 1930s and the view from Station Square is now open to the river, and a trolley shelter across Smithfield Street, added in 1912, came down in the 1960s.

The Landmarks Building now houses the offices of the Pittsburgh History & Landmarks Foundation together with commercial tenants.

National Register of Historic Places
City Historic Structure
Historic Landmark plaque

Monongahela Incline
West Carson Street near Smithfield Street to Grandview Avenue at Wyoming Street. John Endres and Samuel Diescher, engineers, 1869–70; rebuilt 1882, 1982–83

Apart from coal-hauling roads elsewhere on Mount Washington, this was the first of Pittsburgh's score of inclines and, with the Duquesne Incline a mile away, it is one of the two survivors. A reconstruction of 1882 gave it a trestle-like structure of wrought iron that was replaced with steel a century later. In 1884 a parallel incline was built immediately to the east to carry wagons and teams; this lasted until 1935. In the latter year, too, the power was converted from steam to electricity.

The West Carson Street station is a reconstruction of c. 1900 by MacClure & Spahr in a cheerful Neo-Georgian style (but with a Jacobean lantern on the roof). In 1983 it was restored inside to approximately its original condition. The Grandview Avenue station has been remodeled many times but the exterior recalls its Mid-Victorian original design, apart from a 1994 annex to the west. The cars are entirely new. The tracks are 635 feet long and rise 367 feet at a 35-degree angle.

The incline is very popular with tourists, and the view from Grandview Avenue, almost 400 feet up, is the most famous one in Pittsburgh. The old bull wheel of the upper station, which held the safety cable and was controlled by the brakes, is now a display outside the Gatehouse office building at Station Square.

National Register of Historic Places
City Historic Structure
Historic Landmark plaque

W. W. Lawrence Company (Lawrence Paint Building), Station Square
1124 West Carson Street
1902

This massive, long-neglected industrial building, once a paint factory, is a reminder of the industry that once crowded the south shore of the Monongahela River opposite the Triangle. It stands in a conspicuous place, across West Carson Street from the Duquesne Incline and almost opposite the Point. For years people have looked at it, admired it, and deplored its deteriorating condition. It is a colossal brick-and-timber construction, with over 100,000 square feet of floor space, ceilings up to twenty-four feet tall, and six stories, including two below street level.

Duquesne Incline

1197 West Carson Street
to 1220 Grandview
Avenue
Samuel Diescher,
engineer, 1877;
rebuilt 1888

The younger of the two inclines still operating in Pittsburgh, this nonetheless has far the oldest rolling stock of any transit system in the county. The original cars of 1877 are still running, their bodies similar to those built for horsecars, with Eastlake interiors of contrasting cherry and birdseye maple with simple incised ornament.

The original track structure of wood and wrought iron was rebuilt wholly in iron in 1888. It is 793 feet long on a 30.5-degree slope, with a 400-foot rise.

The West Carson Street station appears, with its Ionic pilasters, its big round arches, its heavy turned newel posts, its elaborate wrought-iron stair balustrades, and its ochre brick, to be a product of the 1890s. Here, indeed, you step into the past: the flavor of the old industrial city remains untamed, unprettified.

The Grandview Avenue station has been partially restored. Its hauling machinery, partly exposed, still uses the old wooden-toothed gear wheels that promote silent running, though the original steam plant was electrified in 1932. The station's waiting room is a pictorial museum of Pittsburghiana and of inclines, aerial tramways, and trolleys around the world. There is a viewing terrace.

The incline is operated by a non-profit community group, the Society for the Preservation of the Duquesne Heights Incline.

National Register of Historic Places
Historic Landmark plaque

Corliss Street Tunnel

Corliss and West Carson Streets, Esplen
Stanley L. Roush, architect; D. N. Sprague, chief engineer;
1913–14

Taking Corliss Street under the tracks of the old Pennsylvania Railroad Panhandle Route, this work of the City of Pittsburgh was carried out with a Baroque flourish: the concrete portal imitates a rusticated archway, and above it an overscaled stone tablet gives name and date to the speeding traffic. Beneath this is the City escutcheon, decorated with festoons.

400 block, South Main Street.

Corner of South Main and Wabash Streets.

West End business district

Less than a mile down the Ohio River from the Point, the hillsides part to release Sawmill Run—which must have been a much larger stream in the past. Within the valley, beyond a treacherous road system for commuters, is a small, narrow street grid, framed by the steep, wooded slopes. This grid was laid out in 1839 as Temperance Village, and until annexation by Pittsburgh in 1872, alcohol was indeed forbidden. The neighborhood is a place of shifting levels, largely constructed of red brick and with a general air of 1890 about it. The simple compositions of brick and contrasting stone are handsome and crisp, and the buildings and their spatial enclosure make it a distinctive and interesting place.

Former Presbyterian Church, 500 block, South Main Street.

400 block, South Main Street.

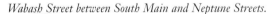

Wabash Street between South Main and Neptune Streets.

West End United Methodist Church (now West End A.M.E. Zion Church)
623 South Main Street, Elliott
Longfellow, Alden & Harlow, architects, 1887

Like its Woods Run contemporary the McClure Avenue Presbyterian Church, this is a distinguished church in a hard-to-find place. Here, too, is a pragmatic Akron plan, where church and Sunday school hall can be turned into a single space. The massing hints at the principal divisions within the walls, and plays off against the slopes, on the street and inwards, of the site. The stonework is carefully textured and the ironwork is well suited to the openings.

Historic Landmark plaque

Old Stone Tavern
434 Greentree Road, West End
C. 1800

Despite a date stone giving 1752 as the building year, this, a work in masonry not logs, is most likely to be of the early years of the nineteenth century. At that, it is one of the oldest buildings in the city and the oldest in steady use for commerce. The two-over-two window sash is typical of the mid-nineteenth century.

John Frew house
105 Poplar Street, Oakwood
Before 1800; c. 1840

The original stone farmhouse was two-storied, with rubble walls secured at the corners by tall, shallow quoins. A plan of 1936, made for the Western Pennsylvania Architectural Survey, shows only one room on the ground floor with a

stair along an end wall. To this, around 1840, a one-and-a-half-story addition of brick was built, five bays wide and with a porch on each side. Perhaps the roof of the stone part was remodeled at the time; in any event the two parts share the same roof, which extends downwards over the broader brick section and its porches. East of the house is a two-story springhouse, sympathetically incorporated into a modern garage and greenhouse structure. Its stonework consists of tall, shallow slabs tied into backup masonry by alternate thin, deep courses: the very facing methods that can be seen on the walls of the Courthouse.

Small and simple though it is, this is one of our handsomest survivors of the Georgian period.

Historic Landmark plaque

Railroad arch
Sawmill Run Boulevard north of and opposite Woodruff Street
C. 1902

This was one element in the ponderous system that brought the Wabash-Pittsburg Terminal Railway into the Golden Triangle via tunnel and cantilever bridge. The line of the archway is skewed, and within the rock-faced stone exterior a series of shallow cylindrical brick vaults are overlapped.

Lowen house
311 Lowenhill Street, Beechview
C. 1860

Board-and-batten siding was apparently introduced in 1834 by the New York architect Alexander Jackson Davis, and was popular for several decades thereafter. Those who have seen it will understand why. Like a row of Lombardy poplars in the front yard, it seems able to turn any construction, however aesthetically empty, into architecture. Its insistent verticals blur the effect of bad proportions, organize haphazard fenestration schemes, create a striking pattern under direct sunlight, and glorify a frame structure as a thing made of wood, making the material tangible through visual means. In this house, Gothic trim romps under the roof, a little ineffectually against the strong rhythm of the battens. Window surrounds in carpenter's Greek Revival fare better, with their broad and large surfaces. Traces of a porch remain on the center of the house; should a compatible new porch be added this would be a very balanced house front, a piece of dignified architecture unique in this neighborhood. It is badly deteriorated, and may have no future, but at the time of printing a prospective buyer and the Pittsburgh History & Landmarks Foundation were attempting to find a way to save it.

City Historic Structure

The view toward town

Numbers 105 and 111, The Boulevard

The Boulevard and Amanda Street

Houses

105–12 The Boulevard, 1500 Amanda Street, and
1425 Brownsville Road, Carrick
C. 1910

Though not perfectly kept and not designed to a unified
scheme, this cluster of turn-of-the-century Colonial
Revival houses makes a solid, coherent impression.
They give an East End impression, though, and doubtless
the Brownsville Road trolley line brought them into
being as the streetcar did the houses of Highland Park
and Shadyside. At the junction with Brownsville Road is
a remarkable Queen Anne house of wood.

1425 Brownsville Road

Number 122

Concord Elementary School
Brownsville Road at Biscayne Drive, Carrick
Marion M. Steen, architect, 1939

Although Steen is best known for Art Deco schools, he
provided Carrick with a Georgian Revival building with
rich red brick, fine bricklaying, and excellent proportioning
of the banked windows that were the schoolhouse's special
challenge to an architect.

A side view of Concord Elementary School.

**Stewart Avenue
Lutheran Church**
*2810 Brownsville Road,
Carrick*
O. M. Topp, architect, 1927

This is really a lively and
well-proportioned design
by an architect remem-
bered for a little conspicuous work—especially
the Jenkins Arcade—
rather than for a steady

output of consistently appealing work. The bold limestone
striping of the Stewart Avenue front and the big church
windows overlooking Brownsville Road are vigorous pieces
of design. The principal material is a rich, deep red brick.

House
231 Grandview Avenue, Mount Washington
C. 1870

Mid-Victorian house architecture tended toward the
picturesque, asymmetrical, and ornate, yet here is a
well-proportioned Second Empire house of great lucidity:
a simple, well-phrased statement.

Chatham Village
Virginia Avenue and Bigham Street, Mount Washington
Ingham & Boyd, architects; Clarence S. Stein and
Henry Wright (New York), planners; Ralph E. Griswold of
Griswold & Kohankie, landscape architect; 1932, 1935

In 1929 the Buhl Foundation, located in Pittsburgh, decided to sponsor an experimental for-profit large-scale housing project for limited-income families. For planning they went to Clarence Stein and Henry Wright of New York, already known for their innovative plans for Radburn, New Jersey, and Sunnyside Gardens, Long Island. Over two years of study resulted in 197 units in an idyllic setting of trees, lawns, and flowers. The gentle Eclectic architecture, realized in medium-red brick with slate roofs, is perhaps more English Georgian than anything else, but a little bit rural French as well. The automobile is kept firmly in its place, relegated to three garage courts on the perimeter. A recreational area

lies alongside to the northwest and the original Bigham house of 1844, at the far end of the development, serves as a community center.

Radburn, being started earlier, has had most of the publicity as an example of American "garden city" planning, but Chatham Village has had notice from such well-known students of urban life as Lewis Mumford ("… one of the high points in site planning and architectural layout … its failure to excite even local imitation remains inexplicable …") and Jane Jacobs, who found it socially insular, matriarchal, and boring. (Neither has actually lived there.)

Historic Landmark plaque

Thomas J. Bigham house
655 Pennridge Road, Mount Washington
C. 1844; revisions by Ingham & Boyd, 1935,
Ingham, Boyd & Pratt, 1950

Now used as a clubhouse for the Chatham Village dwellers, the simple Greek Revival house has received some alterations that fit its style to that of the whole development

without violence to the simple original. Thus, the rather wispy ironwork that may have replaced Greek Revival woodwork alludes to the nearby house porches, echoes in height the shallow, narrow break-forward of the central bay, and is not out of keeping with the little Italianate brackets of the cornice.

Thomas Bigham was an attorney, newspaper publisher, Congressman, and abolitionist whose home was on the Underground Railroad.

Historic Landmark plaque

Prospect School
Prospect near Southern Avenues, Mount Washington
James T. Steen, architect, 1931;
1936 addition by Marion M. Steen

It is believed that Marion M. Steen, the busy staff architect of the Board of Public Education, was the actual designer for both portions of this, the first fully Art Deco school in the city. The school as it evolved was both an elementary and a junior high school, with two auditoriums, handsomely decorated, and one gymnasium. Externally

the building is almost monochrome, with white limestone and terra-cotta sculpture and decoration, and light-brown brick.

National Register of Historic Places

South Hills High School
Ruth and Eureka Streets, Mount Washington
Alden & Harlow, architects, 1916–24

On the sort of broad hilltop that in Istanbul would support an imperial mosque, Pittsburgh has put several of its public schools. So it is here: this massive brown-brick, slightly Gothic high school rises with easy dominance among little houses and looks out over South Hills Junction and the surrounding valley. Its nearby neighbor is another powerful structure, the ventilator building for the Liberty Tunnels.

Liberty Tunnels ventilating plant
201 Secane Avenue, Mount Washington
Stanley L. Roush, architect, 1928

The Liberty Tunnels, or Liberty Tubes as they are usually called, fulfilled a long-felt desire of motorists to get to the South Hills directly rather than by going over or around Mount Washington. Ventilation proved more of a problem than the engineers had calculated, and while the first of the two Tubes was finished in 1922 the opening had to be put off until 1924 while a solution was worked out. In 1928 a mechanical plant with four tall stacks was built over the center of the Tubes. The material is a bright-red brick with limestone detailing, and the style is a bland quasi-Gothic manner. The four great stacks could not have been more fortunately placed from a scenic point of view; their powerful forms thrust upward from the shelf-like spur of the hillside on which the plant stands, in dramatic contrast with the broad valley spaces around them, framing views of distant hillsides, contrasting their simple surfaces with the tiny-looking houses and trees beyond and their vivid redness with the more neutral colors of the landscape.

Beltzhoover Elementary School
Cedarhurst and Estella Streets, Beltzhoover
W. J. Shaw, architect, 1905; addition by Thomas Lloyd, 1909

This hard-edged school of brown brick dominates the skyline of a neighborhood of houses in a forceful manner. The tower of the 1909 portion (built to house an old-fashioned school bell) adds drama to the rather plain composition. Later Pittsburgh schools sometimes shared this honorific placement on a hilltop: we have already noted Prospect School and South Hills High School.

National Register of Historic Places

St. George's Roman Catholic Church
Allen and Climax Streets, Allentown
Herman Lang, architect, 1910

This church, with its adjacent buildings, makes a great architectural show in its neighborhood. It is sited halfway uphill in an area of small-scaled buildings, and it has much fancy decoration and surrounds in real, imitation, or painted stone to contrast brightly with its blood-red brick. The brick, in a very 1910 way, is Flemish bond with broad, deeply raked mortar joints. The whole effect is genial and aggressive.

St. Paul of the Cross Monastery
143 Monastery Street, South Side slopes
Charles Bartberger, architect, 1854, 1858–59;
additions and alterations

The monastery stands directly uphill from the St. Michael's Church complex, and is in the hands of the Congregation of Passionist Missionaries as St. Michael's long was. Formerly, a hillside garden connected the two institutions, with Stations of the Cross along its winding path. The exterior of the monastery church of 1858–59 is in the Italian-type Romanesque of the mid-nineteenth century, but an overdone facade remodeling was reworked at some point early in this century to soften the effect and add picturesqueness to the silhouette. The interior is light and cheerful, early Italian Renaissance in cream and gold, with color in the form of medallions painted on the vaults and good Mid-Victorian and early twentieth-century glass. The other parts of the monastery have been added to and altered a number of times with varying artistic success.

The view toward the Triangle and Oakland from in front of the church is one of the best in Pittsburgh.

Historic Landmark plaque

**St. Michael the Archangel Church
(Roman Catholic) building group**
South Fifteenth and Pius Streets, South Side slopes
Charles Bartberger, architect for church, 1857–61

Halfway up the South Side slopes, an impressive spired church stands with its entourage of buildings, all of red brick against a hillside of trees and frame houses.

The church itself was built for the Passionist Fathers in a simple pre-Richardson Romanesque, derived from medieval Italy but fashionable in the 1850s: an economical, adaptable style that could dignify an industrial building and not be unworthy of a church. Here, a tall, solid tower and tall proportions in the church itself suggest that money was not too restraining an influence. A few concave curves give a touch of Baroque styling that fits in well. Inside are the original German windows and a white marble altar.

The Rectory

The Rectory of 1889 carries on the Romanesque-plus-Baroque idea in a more vivid and worldly way, mixing several styles quite cheerfully and successfully, responding to the heaven-seeking spire of the church with two bulbous domes, with their sheet metal roofs laid in swirls.

On the opposite side of Pius Street are three buildings. Our Lady of Charity Center and Eudes Institute occupy an impressive, little-ornamented brick building that presents eighteen bays of segmental and round arches, is three stories high, and ends in a dormered mansard roof.

Next to this are the East and West Buildings of South Side Catholic High School. The former, built in 1887, is a mixture in brick of Queen Anne and Romanesque, picturesquely shaped and now obscured in design by wooden decks in front of the windows. The latter, once St. Michael's Mädchen Schule, has taller lines and mixes Romanesque and Classical in a way old-fashioned for 1900 when it was built.

The Casino of 1897 does not conform to the swaggering Monte Carlo image suggested by its name; aside from a little religious symbolism at the doorway, it looks like an ordinary plain apartment house of its time. It has been used for various parish activities.

Historic Landmark plaque

Institutions across Pius Street

Our Lady of Charity Center and Eudes Institute.

The former East Building, South Side Catholic High School.

The West Building

Mission Pumping Station
340 Mission Street, South Side slopes
Thomas H. Scott, architect, 1912

Isolated partway up the South Side slopes, big and simple
in its design, this is a conspicuous object in the hilly landscape. The main building contained two vertical triple-
expansion steam engines with a capacity of seven million
gallons a day apiece; the small building housed the boilers.
The style, a very quiet Beaux-Arts manner realized in red
brick and white terra cotta, has a distant ancestry in French
country architecture of the seventeenth and eighteenth
centuries. On the main building the original cornice has
been removed, and a tile roof has been replaced by corru-
gated sheet metal. The giant windows that once let out the
heat are now blocked up, and a very tall chimney that once
stood beyond the west end of the boiler house has long
been gone. The same architect designed the similar
Aspinwall Pumping Station a few years later.

The station was an element in the newly reformed
water system, which drew water from the Allegheny River
at Aspinwall, filtered it, and pumped it to reservoirs in
Highland Park for distribution to most of the city. The
Mission Pumping Station raised the water to storage tanks
on the hill above, in the neighborhood of Allentown.

St. Josaphat Church (Roman Catholic)
2304 Mission Street, South Side slopes
John T. Comes, architect, 1909–16

The need for economy seems to have driven the architect
to a terseness of detailing unusual for the earliest part of
the twentieth century. The suave porch of composition
stone is massive in form and delicate in detailing, and the
Baroque tower top of copper is robust in shape; but the
body of the church depends on pale-yellow brick forms
inlaid in plain red brick for effectiveness, and the sandstone
masonry of the basement is of the simplest sort, the kind
that might be found in any house. The architect, who could
handle elaborate decorative schemes well at St. Agnes' in
Oakland or St. Anthony's in Millvale, did equally well
with this simpler church. The tower especially is a very
handsome feature of the South Side townscape.

Hot metal bridge, Monongahela Connecting Railroad
Monongahela River at Mile 3, at the former Pittsburgh Works,
Jones & Laughlin Steel Corporation
1900

The present bridge is a successor to the original of 1887.
They were built to carry freshly smelted iron—"hot
metal"—from the Eliza blast furnaces of Jones &
Laughlin, on the north shore of the Monongahela River,
to the puddling furnaces, Bessemer converters, open-
hearth furnaces, and electric furnaces, successively, of the
South Side Plant. Before this time, the cooled iron was
ferried across, then remelted.

The Works that lay on both sides of the Monongahela
had solidified from three distinct entities: the American
Iron Works of Jones & Lauth, formed in 1851 to puddle
and roll iron; the Eliza Furnaces of Laughlin & Co. blown
in in 1859; and the Soho Works of Moorhead, McCleane
& Co., with a furnace blown in in 1859 as well. Of all
that the Jones & Laughlin Pittsburgh Works eventually
became, extending two miles along the river's north shore,
very little remains but this bridge and the nearby
Hazelwood Coke Plant.

Morse School (now Morse Gardens)
Sarah and South Twenty-fifth Streets, South Side flats
T. D. Evans, architect, 1874; additions and alterations, 1984

A big Italianate school, whose tall windows, useful for light
and air, give its facade an air of challenge that the forward
break of the center augments. The entrance arches are
"Florentine": the intradoses, the inner edges, are round,
while the extradoses are bluntly pointed. The same design
was used for a school in the Strip.

The Housing Authority of the City has made the school
the focal element of a seventy-unit apartment group.
While not restored, the school has been integrated into
the complex in a sympathetic manner.

National Register of Historic Places

**Methodist Episcopal Church of East Birmingham
(later Walton Methodist Church)**
*Sarah and South Twenty-fourth Streets, South Side flats
1882*

A slight bend in Sarah Street gives this rather tall red brick
church a little extra focus, and the front gable and the
hipped roofs on quasi-towers are a little self-assertive too.
The proportions are agreeable, and the delicate corbel
tables under the gable and the eaves are exceptionally vivid.

City Historic District

East Carson Street

East Carson Street, the main street of the South Side flats,
has a mile-long low-rise commercial district stretching
from South Ninth to South Twenty-fourth Streets,
which is remarkable for its abundant and vivid Victorian
commercial architecture. The street is flanked by nearly

continuous building walls of two- to four-story structures.
Street-level shops are a flourishing mixture of establishments for residents—food and clothing stores, bars,
services of all kinds—and new restaurants, antique shops,
and artists' studios. The storefronts have often been
altered, and altered again. But upper stories generally
remain unchanged and striking in their Victorian ornamentation. In some cases, builders repeated basic building
designs with slight variations in proportion and ornamentation. Other facades display widely divergent Victorian
stylistic variations. Occasional cast-iron facades and
Classical bank buildings add even greater contrasts.

2104–06 East Carson Street

Humble, but quite
interesting, are the twin
shop fronts at Number
2104–06, the oldest in
the district and very rare
survivors in Pittsburgh
from the Greek Revival
period. Carefully
restored, they now form
the front of Le Pommier,
one of the restaurants in
the area. At 1736 East
Carson Street is a build-
ing in complete contrast:
a Beaux-Arts structure
of 1902 that was later
lengthened. Here,
yellow-gray sandstone appears in contrast with bright-red
brick to create rich color. The few touches of Rococo
ornament are very mild accents in the composition, whose
true strength, apart from its color, lies in the rhythmic
procession of tall arched windows. Facing this bank, at
1739 East Carson Street, is a grandiose cast-iron building
in the Second Empire style, probably from the 1870s.

1736 East Carson Street

1739 East Carson Street

We reproduce an old photograph of it here in order to show its design clearly; partly blocked windows and dark-brown paint have since obscured its lines, though not irreversibly. With its mansard roofs and fancy dormers, the building has the most panache of those in the district. At South Fourteenth Street, the old German Savings Deposit Bank, now a branch of Mellon Bank, has the rather ponderous Classicism that prevailed in 1896, when it was constructed; yet its light-gray granite is treated with the crispness and cleanness that suits the material best, with plain surfaces and delicate details in contrast. At 1201–05 East Carson Street, Bedford Square is grandly introduced by a three-story triple Italianate building with a cast-iron arcade on its shop fronts; the strong effect of the repeated round arches makes this one of the most effective designs on the street.

Beginning in 1968, the Pittsburgh History & Landmarks Foundation helped develop an education program to show merchants how business could be increased by restoring commercial shop fronts to their original architectural character. Landmarks also acquired

1401 East Carson Street

1201–05 East Carson Street

several historic structures and restored them as model properties. Neighborhood restoration efforts continue today through the leadership of several local organizations.

National Register District
City Historic District

Independent Brewery (later Duquesne Brewery)
South Twenty-first and Jane Streets, South Side flats
1899 and after

No longer a brewery, this big complex whose buildings range from 1890s Romanesque to 1940s Modernistic survives underused. Its clock, 60 feet across and clearly readable from a half-mile away, is a prominent South Side feature. The tall cooker building which carries the clock is now used by artists and craftsmen, and other buildings in the complex are used for offices, commerce, and light industry. Architecturally, the most interesting building is the original one, built as the Brew House and Stock House as stone plaques indicate. The architecture is all one expects of a brewery: Germanic in a decidedly pre-Bauhaus way, heavy and elaborate. It has been added to in the original spirit and also has received some unfortunate modifications, so that its original symmetry is gone.

Maul Building
1704 East Carson Street, South Side flats
William G. Wilkins Co., architect, 1910

The Maul Building marks a change of direction and breadth in Carson Street, and attracts attention too with the delicately modeled facades, in white terra cotta, that front on the streets. The cornice, as so often with terra-cotta facades, has yielded to weathering and has gone. The Pittsburgh History & Landmarks Foundation holds a facade easement for this building.

National Register District
City Historic District

Christian Moerlein Company beer warehouse (now B. M. Kramer & Company, Inc.)
South Twentieth and Sidney Streets, South Side flats
C. 1915

A handsome commercial building, taking a full block. The urbanity is typical of the Eclectic period, and the bright-red brick with raked-out mortar joints suggests a date around 1915. Such a surface indeed is often found in houses of the time. The brickwork is laid up in Flemish bond, which is unusually labor-intensive since each successive brick is laid in a direction different from its predecessor. Someone took care over this building, plain as it may seem at first. The ground-floor windows have the so-called Florentine tracery, Early Renaissance in origin, popular in the 1850s, rare in the early twentieth century.

Birmingham Public School (now St. Adalbert's Middle School)
118 South Fifteenth Street, South Side flats
1871

One of the last acts of Birmingham as an independent borough was the construction of this simple Italianate schoolhouse, the oldest in the city still to function as such. The Italianate style is simple but the proportions are handsome, and the bulk of the building rises impressively in a narrow street of small houses.

National Register of Historic Places
City Historic District

St. Adalbert's Church (Roman Catholic)
162 South Fifteenth Street, South Side flats
1889

A massive work in Richardson Romanesque built for a Polish congregation, St. Adalbert's dominates and forms the climactic feature of a narrow, gently sloping street. The most impressive way to see it, however, is from several blocks eastward on Mary Street; from this viewpoint the

facade and towers rise above an intervening block of small houses, concluding the vista of a broad but unassuming street with a piece of architectural drama. Next to the church is the rectory, round-arched and in a free style as much Classical as Romanesque.

Historic Landmark plaque

Number Seven Police Station
93 South Thirteenth Street, South Side flats
Charles Bickel, architect, c. 1900

This former police station has three fronts. Two of these are of warm-gray brick with a matching, richly patterned banding of terra cotta under sheet-metal cornices. The treatment is one that Stanford White used in several New York buildings early in the 1890s, notably the Judson Memorial Church. Architects in this period often enjoyed such intensely detailed surfaces; the Carnegie Library in Lawrenceville is another such example, using very similar terra cotta. The third front, on Uxor Way, is a stable wing of ordinary brick, quite plain except for a frieze of recessed panels. At the time of writing, this building is deserted and boarded up. Some use needs to be found for it, though the economics have been daunting. Police station or not, this has a festive exterior, and one can imagine it full of life again, its masonry clean, its metal ornamentation repaired and freshly painted. When such buildings are rehabilitated, it is hard to imagine how they could ever have been neglected.

**First Associated Reformed Church
(later Ninth United Presbyterian Church;
now Birmingham Gallery)**
South Fourteenth and Bingham Streets, South Side flats
1854

This is the oldest datable church building on the South
Side flats, and one of the oldest in Pittsburgh. In general
a sober Greek Revival work, sparing in ornament, it has a
simple but impressive front with later Gothic openings.
The thick piers, framing the panels in which the windows
are actually set, establish a strong compositional rhythm.

National Register District
City Historic District
Historic Landmark plaque

**Birmingham Methodist Episcopal Church
(later Bingham Street Methodist Church;
now City Theater)**
1300 Bingham Street, South Side flats
1859

Even without its original wooden belfry this is a handsome
and well-proportioned building in the Romanesque of
the 1850s: red brick nicely laid and a little stone trim.
The present adaptation as a theater has caused many
internal changes, including blocking of the upper windows
that lit the church space. Accompanying the main building
are a much-altered former church of 1835 and a mansard-
roofed house on Thirteenth Street.

City Historic District

South Side Market House (now South Side Recreation Center)
Bedford Square, South Side flats
Charles Bickel, architect, 1893; remodeled, 1915, 1950, 1978

As built, this was a Richardson Romanesque work, with four peaked towers in the compulsively picturesque spirit of Late Victorian public architecture. When it was rebuilt in 1915 after a fire, the towers came off, the gable roof was brought down to the eaves on both fronts, and a well-scaled stone cartouche was set into the south front memorializing the new work. This cartouche is the

Bedford Square

building's one decoration today, set off by swags and surmounted by a bull's head. The Romanesque walls, though painted, otherwise survive largely as built, industrial rather than civic architecture.

When the building was threatened with demolition in the 1970s, South Side residents and the Pittsburgh History & Landmarks Foundation campaigned to save it. Now one of Pittsburgh's two remaining market houses, it gains extra distinction from being situated at the center of a public square. The buildings that surround it are generally smaller, so that the market has a monumental quality by contrast.

National Register of Historic Places
City Historic Structure
Historic Landmark plaque

Tenth Street Bridge
Monongahela River between South Tenth Street, South Side, and Armstrong Tunnel, the Bluff
Sydney A. Shubin, engineer, 1931

Apart from the near-unique, self-anchored "Three Sisters" bridges across the Allegheny River, Pittsburgh has only one extant suspension bridge: this one. Its cables are conventionally anchored by weights at their ends, the main span is an unremarkable 750 feet, and the styling is Modernistic.

Birmingham Number One (later Bedford School)
910 Bingham Street, South Side flats
1850

A big Greek Revival schoolhouse, the oldest surviving in Pittsburgh. The window arrangement is purely utilitarian with no attempt at architectural effect, at mitigating the impression of a big box, but the gables have nicely executed brick dentils. Originally, each upper floor had eight uniform windows and there were Doric entrance porches. There was also a two-stage belfry and clock tower at one end.

Like a number of other large Victorian schoolhouses in Pittsburgh, this has ceased to be a school. But in its time it was a sign of progress. The apparatus for free, though as yet not compulsory, education had been created by the State Legislature in 1836, in the confident hope that this would create better, as well as more competent, citizens. As is true in this case, the new schoolhouses were usually large and rather factory-like. They constituted fire hazards, with their wooden stairs and floor structure, and were eventually replaced by larger and modern schools.

National Register of Historic Places
City Historic District

Mackintosh-Hemphill Company
Bingham and South Ninth Streets, South Side flats
Alden & Harlow (?), architects; 1890s

The two elements of the foundry on Bingham Street consist of a corner administration building and a pattern shop with a linking entrance element. Both the diapering at the arch level of the administration building and the connection of the architects' acquaintance John H. Ricketson with the foundry support the Alden & Harlow attribution. The other building, more industrial in character, uses rough-surfaced sandstone lintels and sills for textural contrast. The treatment of its arches is very peculiar: they seem unsupported, with the curtain wall falling back at their spring line. The idea was probably to sketch out a Palladian window in minimal terms.

The Pittsburgh Foundry dates back to 1803, progressing from early casting of iron utensils to the making of ordnance in this century. It became the Mackintosh-Hemphill Company around 1860.

National Register District
City Historic District

South Side Public Baths (Oliver Bath House)
South Tenth and Bingham Streets, South Side flats
MacClure & Spahr, architects, 1915

As was the case with the contemporary Sarah Heinz House, a Tudoresque manner was used to clothe a philanthropic gift to the workers. It was a little pompous, a little genteel perhaps, but it was also home-like. Its mellow, textured red brick with raked joints were in marked contrast with the prevalent hard industrial surfaces, and plunging dolphins on the buttress tops hinted at the bodies of water within.

South Side High School (now South Vo-Tech High School)
900 East Carson Street, South Side flats
Edward Stotz, architect, 1897 and 1923

The original building is a picturesque affair of red terra cotta and red brick, more or less Renaissance in design and with delicately detailed stair railings. Stotz, who had an extensive public-school practice, returned twenty-six years after to build a large Classical annex in a mellower red brick with accents in white terra cotta, so in contrast to the original part as to suggest artistic repentance in the meantime.

National Register of Historic Places
City Historic District
Historic Landmark plaque

Ripley & Company (now Salvation Army Adult Rehabilitation Center)
South Ninth and Bingham Streets, South Side flats
1891

In a more fashion-conscious city, this would be assumed to be a building of the mid-1870s, and even in Pittsburgh it

must have seemed old-fashioned. It has a one-fronted design. On South Ninth Street, it is a highly articulated structural skeleton of red brick with sandstone lintels and sills, decorated with bands of richly molded red terra cotta and with a doorway of polished gray granite. The doorway, a low basement entrance, is given an uncertain dignity by a rudimentary pediment at the level of the first-floor window heads, and still more by the raised portion of the corbeled cornice above. At the corner is round corbeling for an oriel window, now gone. On the Bingham Street side, all this homely but lavish display falls away, and plain industrial construction prevails.

Here, once again, is a work in that unlabeled style based on masonry construction that can be seen at 820 Liberty Avenue in the Triangle. Somehow this spare and hard building is very handsome.

The rare surviving presence of a glassworks structure is fortunate. Into the early twentieth century, the South Side was a famous glassmaking area, especially for tableware. Ripley & Co. was one of the largest, with a diversified production. At the top of the line were engraved-glass and imitation cut and flashed-glass tableware.

National Register District
City Historic District

St. John the Baptist Ukrainian Catholic Church
East Carson and South Seventh Streets, South Side flats
1895; enlarged, 1917

This church is a major landmark of the South Side flats, conspicuous from far away, not only because of its size but also because of its eight lofty onion domes with their bronze finish. The Eastern European presence in

Pittsburgh and the industrial areas of the county is manifest in such domes, often to be seen, but this is an extraordinary group, conspicuous in their number and their placement at the entrance to the South Side. The present Seventh Street entrance leads to the original church under a brown-painted Ionic portico in whose pediment is a mosaic of St. John the Baptist.

National Register of Historic Places
Historic Landmark plaque

Dilworth, Porter & Company, Ltd.
Bingham and South Fourth Streets, South Side flats
C. 1910

This is the handsome office block of a railroad-spike factory, executed in sandstone and hard-finished red brick. A Tudor-arched entrance is flanked by windows with medieval-looking transoms that are capped with Colonial Revival flat arches while the central gable has the mildly experimental look often found in commercial and industrial buildings around 1910. All in all, a striking building if not stylistically pure.

Terminal Buildings
East Carson Street and Terminal Way, South Side flats
Charles Bickel, architect, c. 1900

This is an impressive commercial development, reaching from the 300 block of East Carson Street to the Monongahela River and itself reached from the two levels of East Carson and McKean Streets. It contains offices, light industry, shops, and most importantly, warehousing. In all there are five buildings, executed in a coppery-brown brick. The architect and the bricklayer worked out a scheme of ornamentation—enough to demonstrate that they cared—but it is obvious that efficiency was the real object. Some of the architectural efforts have been undone in recent years: parapets have had to be reconstructed, and the craftsmanly practice of thinking of how to place each individual brick is long out of date.

McKean Street looking westward from the Terminal Buildings, with the Liberty Bridge in the foreground.

Bedford Avenue on the Hill, looking toward the Triangle.

EAST OF THE TRIANGLE

Just beyond the Triangle two hills present steep slopes to the rivers, meet in a rising valley, and eventually merge. The northern hill, by far the larger, is Herron Hill. The smaller, overlooking the Monongahela River, is the Bluff. The strong contours of the terrain have created a number of separate neighborhoods, each with its own history and character.

For more than a century the Bluff has been the home of two institutions, Duquesne University and Mercy Hospital, and of a dwindling neighborhood of Victorian houses. Institutional expansion has unsettled the place visually, as large buildings both graceful and awkward, as well as parking lots, have replaced the houses and increased the building scale.

The rising valley, which gradually approaches the upper level of the Bluff, is known vaguely as Uptown: an early extension of the original Pittsburgh, full of close-set red brick houses, mostly Italianate, with occasional churches. Into this matrix, along Fifth and Forbes Avenues, commercial buildings and warehouses were inserted between 1870 and 1910, so that the original domestic architecture was upstaged by high, ornate facades, and relegated more and more to the side streets. In recent years developers have been restoring and adapting the commercial buildings, even the houses, for offices. Naturally, this renovation activity is most intense closest to town; further east, along Fifth and Forbes Avenues, Uptown blends, along with the eastern part of the Bluff, into Soho, a neighborhood of houses, apartments, and shops where respectability and ruin stand side by side.

Herron Hill's vast, tilted surface is simply known almost everywhere as the Hill. Early in the nineteenth century the Hill was country, with small scattered settlements of varying purpose. It had country estates, working farms, coal mines, and a village of black freedmen. From the middle of the nineteenth century until its end, the city expanded into this area, building over the enormous surface. The Hill became a place

CITY OF
PITTSBURGH

of many cultures and many levels of prosperity, where solid middle-class houses and atrocious slums could both be found on close-built streets. In the twentieth century, the older ethnic and Jewish population moved away, and the Hill became largely black, the Harlem of Pittsburgh, the place where the best jazz could be heard but a place also with most of the problems of Harlem. Urban renewal in the 1950s removed virtually all of the lower Hill, closest to town, in anticipation of a great municipal showpiece of amphitheater, Center for the Arts, and apartment slabs. The grand plan was never fully realized, and the Civic Arena and apartment houses that were built seem lost in a desert of paving and bare ground.

The steep northern face of Herron Hill, looking out over the Allegheny River Valley, contains a little and rather isolated neighborhood called Polish Hill. Its angular and close-built streets are not conspicuous in themselves, but in the church of the Immaculate Heart of Mary, with its Baroque domes, Polish Hill has one of the conspicuous landmarks of the city, visible for miles.

Shopping in the Strip, Penn Avenue and Twentieth Street.

Below Herron Hill is a long, narrow area of the river plain known as the Strip. There is little to recall the intensely active, extremely smoky industrial quarter of a century ago, the promiscuous blend of furnaces, industrial sheds, railroad buildings, houses, and churches that arose under the stimulus of the Allegheny River timber rafts, the Pennsylvania Canal, the Pennsylvania Railroad, and the oil barges drifting down from the north: the Strip where the devastating riots of the Railroad Strike of 1877 took place, where George Westinghouse began his manufacturing operations, and where the aluminum industry as we know it began in 1888. Today this is a pleasingly haphazard and vital district of warehouses and wholesalers, best known for its food markets. Its busiest time is the dead of night when the food is sold in bulk; but by day, the domestic shoppers come in search of the best salami, fruit, vegetables, and fish in the city. Other merchants have come to Penn Avenue and Smallman Street as well, as have restaurants and night spots. In addition, the Senator John Heinz Pittsburgh Regional History Center opened in 1996, giving a strong institutional presence to the western end of the busy district.

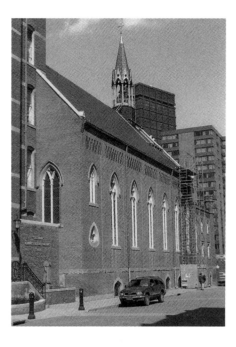

Administration Building and Chapel, Duquesne University

Bluff and Colbert Streets, the Bluff
T. D. Evans, architect(?), 1883–84; c. 1900

Duquesne University was founded in 1878 as the Pittsburgh Catholic College of the Holy Ghost, and its five-story Administration Building, sited at the western end of the Bluff, has been a prominent skyline object for a century. The style is that nameless one in which basic masonry construction is used decoratively, to the extent that decoration exists at all. Stone beltcourses at the levels of the window sills and arch springings offer contrast to

the verticals of the window openings and the buildings as a whole. The somewhat later Chapel is in the Victorian brick vernacular used equally for ecclesiastical and industrial buildings, though Gothic arches make clear its function as a church.

Armstrong Tunnel

Between the Tenth Street Bridge and Forbes Avenue, the Bluff
Stanley L. Roush, architect; Vernon R. Covell of the Allegheny County Department of Public Works, chief engineer; 1926–27

The tunnel portals are constructed in the heaviest and simplest Italian Renaissance style, with cut-stone arches and cornices of an urbane, even bland, character that tempers somewhat the heavy, rock-faced engineering stonework of the rest. This is the end of a long tradition of such stonework; the Liberty Tubes, opened earlier, already had portals of concrete.

The tunnel is 1,300 feet long, and makes a forty-degree change of direction just inside the Forbes Avenue portals to lead properly to the bridge.

National Register of Historic Places

Kaufmann Warehouse and Reymer Brothers Building (now Forbes-Stevenson and Forbes-Pride Buildings)
1401 and 1421 Forbes Avenue, the Bluff
Kaufmann Warehouse, 1901; Reymer Building, c. 1912,
Charles Bickel, architect

These are separate buildings in origin but nearly contemporary to judge from their rather light red brick, their use of corbelling to produce a small-scaled repetitive pattern, and their use of old-fashioned sash windows. The Reymer Building has a steel frame and is the later one.

Reymer Brothers Building

Fifth Avenue High School
Fifth Avenue and Miltenberger Street, the Bluff
Edward Stotz, architect, 1894

Abandoned, then half-cleaned, this has been a sad sight: the more so because its broad proportions, its generous ornamentation, and its warm, orangeish brick create a genial building. Unlike the Mid-Victorian schoolhouse, which tends to stare you down as you approach, this one seems to invite you to come in and be educated. This, by the way, was the first fireproof school in Pittsburgh.

National Register of Historic Places

Church of the Epiphany (Roman Catholic)
Washington Place and Centre Avenue, the Hill
Edward Stotz, architect, 1902

A red Italian Romanesque church, which with three parochial buildings survived the lower Hill clearance of the late 1950s. Beside it is Epiphany School of 1910, behind the school is the St. Regis Residence of 1914, and attached to the church at the rear is the Parish House of c. 1900.

The church is handsome, and is the more valuable as evidence that this barren hillside was once the location of a neighborhood.

It served as the Roman Catholic cathedral in the 1900s, between the time when the second St. Paul's in the Triangle was sold and 1906, when the new St. Paul's in Oakland was consecrated.

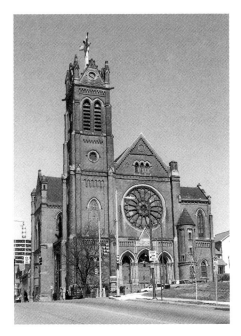

Holy Trinity Roman Catholic Church (later St. Brigid's Church; now Church of St. Benedict the Moor)
89 Crawford Street, the Hill
Moeser & Bippus, architects, 1894

Now primarily for a black congregation, this church was built originally for Irish and German immigrants. The presence of a statue on top of the tower, placed there in 1969, is quite rare locally though not unique; there is a statue, also, on the tower of St. Michael Archangel in Munhall.

Clifford B. Connelly Trade School (now Connelly Technical Institute and Adult Education Center)
1501 Bedford Avenue, the Hill
Edward B. Lee, architect, 1931

This is an impressive Classical mass, rising from a site some 200 feet above Union Station. The Central High School of 1871 survived for some years to its immediate west.

National Register of Historic Places

Letsche Elementary School (now Letsche Education Center)
1530 Cliff Street, the Hill
1905; Marion M. Steen, architect for addition, 1941

It is Steen's floral Art Deco terra cotta, set between rising warm gray stone panels in an outer fabric of rich red brick, that distinguishes this school.

National Register of Historic Places

Kaufmann Auditorium
1835 Centre Avenue, the Hill
Edward Stotz, architect, 1928

This is a prominent feature of Hill House, formerly the
Irene Kaufmann Settlement and Community House,
and called The Columbian School when founded in 1895.
The building has a Classical air of grandeur unusual on
the Hill, to be compared only with its near-contemporary
Connelly Center. There is sculpture by Frank Vittor from
the building period, and a bronze relief of 1975, *Together*,
by Selma Burke.

**Carnegie Library of Pittsburgh, Wylie Avenue Branch
(now First Mosque of Pittsburgh)**
1911 Wylie Avenue, the Hill
Alden & Harlow, architects, 1899

The architects' familiar devices for the Pittsburgh Carnegie
Library branches are present here: a symmetrical front
with a strong central entrance element and high banks of
windows to either side, on the main-floor and basement
levels: economical, strong, a monument but neighborly.

Pythian Temple (later New Granada Theater)
2000–13 Centre Avenue, the Hill
Louis A. S. Bellinger, architect, 1927

This has been a noted entertainment center, with a movie
house and a ballroom. The style is a simple version of
Art Deco. Billy Eckstine, Cab Calloway, and other musi-
cians performed here for decades. Long a focal point
of cultural and social life in the Hill, the New Granada
was purchased in 1995 for eventual restoration as a cultural
center and movie house. A loan from the Pittsburgh
History & Landmarks Foundation to the Hill Community
Development Corporation helped make the building
purchase possible.

Minersville Public School (now Madison Elementary School)
Milwaukee and Orion Streets, the Hill
Ulysses J. L. Peoples, architect, 1902

The dominant feature of this gray-gold brick school is an extravagantly modeled entrance with monkeys, snakes, and cherubs in terra cotta. The rusticated quoins are probably due to Stanford White influence; the New York architect had been quite fond of such things a decade before. It looks as if an original cornice has been removed.

Goodyear Tire and Rubber Company (now Geyer Printing)
3700 Bigelow Boulevard, the Hill
1919

This is a conspicuous building on Bigelow Boulevard as it turns southward toward Schenley Farms. Off-white brick and terra cotta ornament create a quiet, graceful composition. Terra-cotta inserts under the parapet are multicolored. Eclectic architects seem to have chosen innovative styling for buildings associated with that innovation the automobile; other such buildings can be found along that early automobile paradise Baum Boulevard. The handsome corner entrance is not original to the building; it came with a renovation by Charles L. Desmone & Associates.

Immaculate Heart of Mary Church (Roman Catholic)
3058 Brereton Street, Polish Hill
William P. Ginther (Akron), architect, 1904

Centered on a domed
space ninety-eight feet
high inside, this church
has the most Baroque
silhouette of any in the
county, signaling the
otherwise-inconspicuous
Polish Hill neighborhood
for miles. There is spare
carving in sandstone.
The facade pilasters
have Composite capitals.
The color contrast
between light-gray and
medium-brown brick
enlivens the masonry. Inside, the church is lavishly
furnished in a heavy Classical way characteristic of the
1900s. The same architect designed St. Philip's in Crafton
and St. Mary's Help of Christians in McKees Rocks.

Historic Landmark plaque

Armstrong Cork Company
Twenty-third and Railroad Streets, the Strip
Frederick J. Osterling, architect, 1901, 1902; addition, 1913

A trio of massive buff-brick buildings, long unused.
The two long blocks perpendicular to the Allegheny River
are by Frederick J. Osterling, one of the busiest Pittsburgh
architects of the 1900 period. Such buildings appear in
every city: idled where they were once busy, they challenge
those who hate to see them deteriorate or disappear.

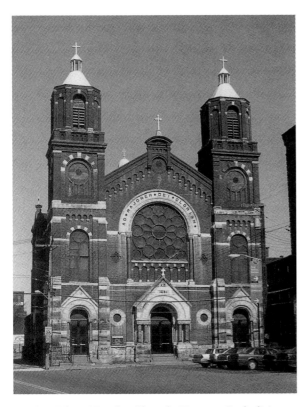

St. Patrick's Roman Catholic Church
Liberty Avenue and Seventeenth Street, the Strip
Father James R. Cox, designer, 1936

After an older Greek Revival St. Patrick's burned in the mid-1930s, the parish priest designed a new church, which eventually acquired a grotto to one side and a marble stair to the sanctuary inside. The stair was salvage from the Pittsburgh Natatorium, a bath house and pool designed around 1905 by Grosvenor Atterbury for Henry Phipps. The central stair is to be ascended on one's knees only.

St. Stanislaus Kostka Church (Roman Catholic)
Twenty-first and Smallman Streets, the Strip
Frederick C. Sauer, architect, 1891–92

In the middle of the produce district stands this Romanesque church of darkened red brick with trim in stone that is now painted. The towers were once taller, but the upper parts were removed after weakening by an explosion. The inscription on the central arch, *Ad Majorem Dei Gloriam*, means "To the greater glory of God." Inside, art depicts the religious and secular history of Poland, since this is a Polish Catholic parish, the earliest in Pittsburgh. The church is a prominent sight among the warehouses of the Strip, its decorative architecture in welcome contrast with the plain and time-worn buildings around.

National Register of Historic Places
Historic Landmark plaque

Sixteenth Street Bridge
Allegheny River between Sixteenth Street, the Strip,
and Chestnut Street, East Deutschtown
H. G. Balcom (New York), engineer; Warren & Wetmore
(New York), architects; 1923

Seahorses by Leo Lentelli (New York), leaping off in all
directions from beneath armillary spheres, dramatize the
crossing of the Allegheny, which at this point is about
700 feet wide. The bridge undertakes this passage in
three trussed-arch spans, the longest being 437 feet.
Four masonry piers by the architects who completed
Grand Central Station bear the Lentelli sculptures and
other, very handsome, ornament. The municipal Art
Commission, which had a say in any river bridge design
within Pittsburgh, determined both the design and the
ornamentation.

National Register of Historic Places

Chautauqua Lake Ice Company (later Adelman
Lumber Company; now the Senator John Heinz
Pittsburgh Regional History Center, the home of
the Historical Society of Western Pennsylvania)
1212 Smallman Street, the Strip
Frederick J. Osterling (?), architect, 1898; remodeled 1993–96

Big, red, and utilitarian, this building designed to hold ice
harvested from frozen lakes has still some touches of
detailing artistry. The construction is massive, as its
original purpose required: steel on the ground floor,
massive timber above. The remodeling for the Historical
Society, by Bohlin Cywinski Jackson, has removed some of
the inner cagework to create an atrium. The former
Historical Society building in Oakland is a highly finished,

A view of the Senator John Heinz Pittsburgh Regional History Center from Smallman Street.

small-scaled institutional structure, a decorous accommodation for documents, pictures, and artifacts. Here the displays may be much larger, and adaptable: unpretentious construction meets the new requirements.

The William Collins King Atrium

Gloekler Building
1127 Penn Avenue, the Strip
1892

Applied to commerce, the Richardson Romanesque style attained a remarkable degree of attenuation. In the typical store or loft building, only the front and the rear offered window space, and the need for the maximum area of sash conflicted with the demands of an architectural scheme that offered prestige. In the fashionable Romanesque, the usual solution was one or more giant arcades framing light window and spandrel construction, with a smaller-scaled upper story and a fancy parapet. Such is the case here.

National Register of Historic Places
Historic Landmark plaque

Looking up Fisk Street in Lawrenceville.

LAWRENCEVILLE

Lawrenceville is a dense but sprawling neighborhood, full of incident and discovery as the South Side flats are, with a northerly view from its sloping streets toward wooded hills across the Allegheny River that better-known neighborhoods on flat terrain cannot match. Butler Street at its base is busy and commercial; but a block or two away the somewhat narrow residential streets are calm and solid and thoroughly Victorian. Red brick houses are interrupted only by an occasional church or school, or the local branch of the Carnegie Library: institutions seem to prefer the homey obscurity of Lawrenceville's side streets. A visitor gets the impression of a community that keeps itself to itself, is not too interested in publicity, but knows its worth.

CITY OF
PITTSBURGH

Lawrenceville was a development of William Barclay Foster, father of the songwriter Stephen Collins Foster, who was born there. A broad strip of Foster land was purchased in 1814 by the U.S. Army for the Allegheny Arsenal, the neighborhood's greatest employer and—in an

A surviving Arsenal building

explosion of 1862—the cause of its worst disaster. The Arsenal, long vanished as an institution, survives in a few taken-for-granted buildings, fragments of the whole, and a few other Lawrenceville buildings which may have been influenced by the Arsenal's design. But it is the ascending strip of land of the upper Arsenal site, now including a high school, park, and County health facility from bottom to top, that is the great reminder of the past.

The neighborhood has an attractive small urban space in Doughboy Square, a wedge of land with a statue at Butler Street and Penn Avenue. But Lawrenceville's great open space is found further east on Butler Street, where a slight bend reveals the Gothic gateway and Romantic landscape of Allegheny Cemetery, where trees and tombs seem to stretch into infinity.

4100 block of Butler Street near Main Street.

Section 28, Allegheny Cemetery

Pittsburgh Brewing Company
Liberty and Herron Avenues
1888 and after

This large old brewery, producer of the locally popular Iron City Beer, still functions in Lawrenceville. Its most interesting building is the original office block, built of red brick and stone with buff terra-cotta detailing in the uncertain Classical manner of the 1890 period. Other brewery buildings repeat its round arches and its brick corbeling in various ways, but without the same intensity of detail.

Historic Landmark plaque

Engine Company Number Twenty-five
3343 Penn Avenue
William Y. Brady, architect, 1896

Here is a powerful and apparently incomplete building, a slightly startling incident as one passes along Penn Avenue in Lawrenceville. The right-hand tower is just *half* a tower!

Somebody split it down the middle. And it has the windows of a winding stair that rises blindly into a coping. The turrets over the center archway have skillfully corbeled bottoms, but no tops. Something was but is no more, or should have been but never was. The power of what is, is considerable, although the great arch over the two fire-engine doors has a crutch-like pier of stone to offset the uncertainty of its abutment.

Pennsylvania National Bank
Penn Avenue and Butler Street
Beezer Brothers, architects, c. 1900

At Doughboy Square, Allen Newman's *Doughboy* of 1921 stands alertly before a small bank building of brownish Roman brick and terra cotta. The bank's style is a simply detailed Beaux-Arts that enlivens and does not overburden the facades. Both the style and color remind one at once of Union Station.

The building was rehabilitated in 1994 by Charles L. Desmone & Associates, and now houses several businesses.

333

McKee house
3600 Penn Avenue
C. 1870

**St. John the Baptist Roman Catholic Church
(now The Church Brew Works)**
3501 Liberty Avenue
Beezer Brothers, architects; John T. Comes, designer; 1903

Like St. Augustine's near by, this was a work of Comes
for others, shortly before he set up independent practice.
The bold stripeyness of the church front was originally
echoed in a campanile, of which only the lowermost
part remains.

This house has very
tenuous associations
with the family of
Stephen Collins Foster,
but only because of
some cellar masonry
surviving from his
birthplace. In fact,
it is a very pleasant
medium-sized Second
Empire house, whose
exterior has been care-
fully restored.

A small urn on the
front lawn commemorates
Foster's birth.

The former convent

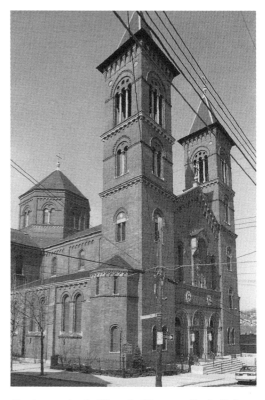

St. Augustine's Church (Roman Catholic)
Thirty-seventh and Bandera Streets
Rutan & Russell, architects; John T. Comes, designer; 1899

St. Augustine's, the second church of the parish, is a
notable landmark in Lawrenceville, rising above the house-
tops. The church is designed in Italian Romanesque, with
that style's distinctive jutting hood over a facade sculpture

of St. Augustine. Yet it was
built for a German parish,
which had the right to
receive instruction in
German. The interior,
fifty-eight feet high, has
an octagonal lantern at
the crossing that rises to
seventy-two feet, and is
decorated with stained glass,
murals, and marblework.
Five altars, including the
main altar, are from the
original church of 1863.

John T. Comes, the designer, was soon to begin
independent practice and become the best-known local
architect of Catholic churches and institutional buildings.

Washington Crossing Bridge
Allegheny River at Fortieth Street
Charles Davis, County Engineer; Janssen & Cocken,
architects; 1923

In November 1753, Major George Washington, returning
from an unsuccessful debate with the French in Northwest
Pennsylvania, attempted to cross the Allegheny River in
the Lawrenceville area. He nearly drowned, nearly froze
to death, but reached Shannopin's Town, the nearest
approach to civilization in the Pittsburgh area. The plate-
arch bridge shown here, similar to the Thirty-first Street
Bridge downstream in its general design, commemorates
this event. The bridge has a Classical dignity that under-
states its size: the central span is 360 feet and gives seventy-
two feet of clearance above the water. Dimensions on the

Thirty-first Street Bridge are similar. The balustrade has metal plates bearing coats-of-arms of historic significance.

National Register of Historic Places

Arsenal Junior High School (now Arsenal Middle School)
Butler and Fortieth Streets
Schwab, Palmgreen & Merrick, architects, 1931;
west wing by Marion M. Steen, 1939

This coolly elegant, limestone-faced school occupies the entire breadth of the old U.S. Arsenal property, about 525 feet. Inside, decorative work is concentrated on the auditorium, which has an elaborate proscenium with Classical motifs. Uphill is Arsenal Park, but the building looks out to Butler Street and the very little that remains of the Arsenal toward the Allegheny River.

National Register of Historic Places

The powder magazine in its present form.

Allegheny Arsenal area
North of Penn Avenue between Thirty-ninth and
Fortieth Streets
1814 and after

Allegheny Arsenal once dominated Lawrenceville, an apron of land running downhill from Penn Avenue to the Allegheny River. Two famous names were associated with its early buildings: Benjamin Henry Latrobe, an outstanding early architect, while he was in Pittsburgh setting up a steamboat yard for Robert Fulton, and Thomas Pope, a brilliant engineer. Some of the early buildings may have been built after Latrobe's designs, and Pope may also have had some designs executed. Today only fragments exist. An explosion in 1862 destroyed at least one building, and after the Civil War the Arsenal became less and less important; in 1907 part was given to the City for a park, and in 1926 the rest was sold. In Arsenal Park is an adapted version of the original powder magazine, a massive, low-built stone structure that carries a handsome cast-iron symbolic plaque.

United States Marine Hospital (now Allegheny County Health Department)
Penn Avenue and Fortieth Street
C. 1900

To obtain some conception of this building's style, one must look at the split curved pediment of the doorway, the window arches with their keystones, and the window sash with their many panes. The conclusion is: English, somewhere around 1700, though the flaring eaves with exposed rafter ends have more of a Latin flavor. Indeed, if you try to label the building's style you are frustrated; this is a genial piece of Eclecticism in the most literal sense. Once a hospital, it was obviously intended to be reassuring: a nice big house rather than a mere institution. The rather broad proportions themselves suggest a relaxed attitude, as does the bright red of the brickwork. The landscaped setting with enormous sycamore trees enhances the effect.

Carnegie Library of Pittsburgh, Lawrenceville Branch
279 Fisk Street
Alden & Harlow, architects, 1898

Three years after their Quattrocento Carnegie Library in Oakland was finished, the architects built this neighborhood library on a sloping street of homes in Lawrenceville. The banded arches over the windows have a Low Countries quality about them, especially over such big windows separated by narrow piers. The doorway element of brick and richly figured white terra cotta suggests, however, the free variations on Italian Renaissance architecture that Stanford White was making earlier in the decade. This library, it is believed, was the first in the United States to have a separate children's room. The building is well suited to its setting: monumental as is appropriate, yet rather modest too, and like the neighborhood generally, of red brick.

Historic Landmark plaque

St. Mary's Church (Roman Catholic) building group
300 Forty-sixth Street
James Sylvester Devlin, designer for church, 1873–74;
John T. Comes, architect for Chapel of St. Anne, 1921;
Carlton Strong, architect for Lyceum, 1913

At the top of a hillside street, ending at a back gate of
St. Mary's Cemetery, is a group of buildings that seem
set off from the rest of Pittsburgh. St. Mary's Church,
designed by the civil engineer who laid out the Cemetery,
is plain in form but with a front heavily buttressed and
ornamented with elaborate brickwork. The Chapel of
St. Anne and a Lyceum are both by architects who were
prominent in Catholic church work in the Pittsburgh area.
The rectory of c. 1900 is one of those loose, amiable,
generally Colonial Revival houses that abound around
Pittsburgh, remarkable though for its great depth.
St. Mary's School of 1881 is a stern Victorian schoolhouse,
three stories high and still with its belfry; the Victorian
school, like some other Victorian factories, summoned you

St. Mary's School

for the day with a bell.

The Academy of c. 1850
is Greek Revival of the
simplest sort with the
exception of a very fancy,
delicate cast-iron porch,
the sort usually associated
with New Orleans or
Mobile although once
common too in the
industrial North.

Historic Landmark plaque

Cast iron, St. Mary's Academy

St. Mary's Lyceum, 1913, by Carlton Strong.

St. Mary's Academy

Grand Army of the Republic Plot.

St. Francis General Hospital
Penn Avenue and Forty-fifth Street
1871 and after; Schmidt, Garden & Erikson (Chicago),
architects for Mary Immaculate Hall (now Mental Health
Center), 1932

Along with older parts in massive 1890s Gothic and 1900s Beaux-Arts, which in themselves are striking, this hospital complex has a remarkable and very large building, visible on its hillside site for miles. The 1930ish Mental Health Center was once a nurses' residence. The detailing is Art Deco, the general effect is Romanesque, and the fantastic bricklaying suggests the sort that avant-garde architects in Amsterdam were calling for around 1920. Here is a building from a moment in architectural history when incongruous forces might contribute to a single design: craftsmen clothing a steel frame brick by carefully laid brick, ornament affectedly modern on a tall building with a medieval silhouette.

It is not possible now to see the general view shown here because of new construction.

Allegheny Cemetery

Allegheny Cemetery was the sixth "rural" public cemetery established in the United States when it was incorporated in 1844. John Chislett, superintendent of the cemetery and architect of its Butler Street gateway, designed a Romantic landscape plan of lawns, plantings, and winding roads on the hillside site. The cemetery's original 100 acres have since been trebled to extend to the Penn Avenue Entrance.

Victorian Pittsburgh used the cemetery as its primary burial ground, and enjoyed its planned open space as a rare pleasure. A tour of Allegheny Cemetery is still one of the great visual adventures of Pittsburgh, full of the beauty and curiosity that a major Victorian cemetery has to offer. The verdant landscape, the massed obelisks and other monuments of every kind, and the famous Pittsburgh names to be seen throughout—B. F. Jones, Henry W. Oliver, Stephen Foster, Lillian Russell—make for a unique experience. The cemetery administration knows this, and issues a map, guide, and educational programs for those who want to learn more about the cemetery. The Pittsburgh History & Landmarks Foundation published a book on the cemetery in 1990.

Allegheny Cemetery's funerary monuments are extremely varied, yet present a more unified effect than they once did. The earliest tombs were of sandstone,

Moorhead mausoleum

Wilkins monument

Ford mausoleum

marble, even zinc, and it was quite usual for family plots to be surrounded by iron fences. Tightened regulations around the beginning of this century eliminated the fences and other visually distracting auxiliary features and demanded that new tombs be made of materials that would be proof against deterioration. As a result, this is largely a cemetery of granite and bronze, though plenty of weathered sandstone and marble tombs remain.

The very grandest of the sandstone tombs is the Moorhead mausoleum of 1862, in a remote hollow of Section 26: a Gothic tomb, eroded by time but full of barbaric splendor. The Wilkins monument of 1888 in Section 14 is a tree stump in granite, each missing limb being a family member, memorialized by a bronze plaque on an individual stump. Granite too is the tall mausoleum in Section 1, dating from 1893, of J. B. Ford, founder of the Pittsburgh Plate Glass Company: a hard, challenging edifice accompanied by brooding statuary but with a blaze of warm color inside from stained glass in the rooftop lantern. The Eberhardt and Ober mausoleums, side by side in Section 14 and similar in design, recall the famous brewery at the foot of Troy Hill. These two are of granite, with designs worked out in contrasting matte and glossy finishes; William Eberhardt's, the larger and more elaborate—he was the dominant partner even in death—dates from 1893.

Many of the cemetery's own structures have been restored by the Allegheny Cemetery Historical Association.

National Register District
Historic Landmark plaque

Eberhardt and Ober mausoleums

Wrought iron, Penn Avenue Entrance

340

Butler Street Entrance, Allegheny Cemetery
4734 Butler Street
John Chislett, architect for gateway, 1847; Barr & Moser,
architects for Office Building, 1868–70; A. & S. Wilson Co.,
architects for Office Building annex, 1926; John Chislett,
architect for Lodge, 1861

As well as planning the Cemetery, Chislett was architect of the Butler Street Entrance, probably of the adjacent Lodge, and of the original Receiving Vault, now gone, within the grounds. The very handsome Tudor gateway is a carefully proportioned composition, in warm gray sandstone like the other elements of the entrance. Only the Early Victorian softness and lushness of the leaf ornament in the spandrels has a period look—as if the carver had copied a lithograph—while the rest is timeless good Gothic. The Office Building has a less reposeful look but is fully worthy of the gateway, and in fact the two together form the great Victorian architectural masterpiece of Pittsburgh prior to the County Buildings. The one-story portion of the Office Building was added in 1926, at a time

when Victorian architecture was habitually detested; yet it copies the adjacent 1870 detailing faithfully. The little Lodge across the road from the Office Building tends to go overlooked; its mansard roof looks odd above Gothic walls, and its delicate little porch no longer exists.

National Register of Historic Places
Historic Landmark plaque

Penn Avenue Entrance, Allegheny Cemetery
4715 Penn Avenue
Dull & Macomb (Philadelphia), architects, 1887

This red-roofed tower stands out in a general view of Bloomfield, at whose border it is situated. This is naive Richardson Romanesque, designed when the form of the Allegheny County Courthouse tower was known but before it was completed, and imitating it in a very general way. The openings have wrought ironwork with all the wayward fancy of which the 1880s were capable. Wrought iron had made a return at the beginning of the decade, replacing the more facile cast iron that had dominated architectural ornament since 1840, and architects were eagerly exploiting its distinctive limitations and possibilities, the artistry attainable by the smith rather than the pattern-maker.

The caretaker's house, despite the Victorian granite walls and steep tile roof, is in commonsensical contrast, almost a Georgian design realized a hundred years later.

National Register District

The multiple nature of Oakland.

OAKLAND

At the eastern end of Soho, Fifth Avenue winds upward and eastward in an S-curve, while Herron Hill retreats to form the backdrop of a plateau that extends southward to overlook the Monongahela River. On this plateau about 200 feet above the river, and on the Herron Hill slope behind, a few wealthy Pittsburghers began to build villas early in the nineteenth century. Fifth Avenue, then a country road, was a major route eastward, and the setting was airy, offered good views, and lay well beyond the city and the factories and house rows that were developing on its outskirts. Members of the Third Presbyterian Church downtown so favored this western part of Oakland that it was sometimes called the Third Church Colony.

Horsecar service in 1860, followed by cable traction in 1888 and electric trolley service in 1896, changed the character of the neighborhood. Houses, close-set but very solid and respectable nonetheless, arose along Fifth Avenue and the parallel Forbes Street in the area of the villas, while housing and commerce extended eastward and southward into what had once been farmland.

At the eastern end of Oakland, a narrow tract called Bellefield had been platted in 1850 next to the vast acreage of farmland owned by Pittsburgh's most famous expatriate, Mary Croghan Schenley. South of Fifth Avenue, Bellefield developed as an unpretentious section of homes on little streets; to the north it was notably more pretentious, with Italianate and Second Empire villas and houses, many by the Philadelphian Isaac Hobbs.

The donation of 300 acres of Schenley land for a major urban park and the consequent donation of the Carnegie Institute suggested that the central part of Oakland was destined for great things, and beginning in 1897, Franklin F. Nicola bought more Schenley acreage for development. One consequence of the land he put on the market was the transfer of the University of Pittsburgh, after 1908, from its Perry Hilltop campus. The Oakland hillside campus of Henry Hornbostel's grand plan was hardly realized at all, but the University made its mark on Oakland with the Cathedral of Learning, begun in 1926 and built into the 1930s, and in its further constructions of the 1950s and 1960s. In its takeover of existing buildings, it continues to make its mark. Carnegie Mellon University, whose largely Hornbostel campus lies to the east across Junction Hollow, made its mark in a more orderly fashion, beginning in 1904.

The villas, meanwhile, yielded to early twentieth-century development. Magee Hospital was built on the plateau land below Forbes Avenue, and in the late 1920s other hospitals began to build on the hillside close to the Pitt Medical School. The first Georgian and Florentine constructions seemed sufficiently gigantic at the time but construction has gone on and on, swallowing up blocks of houses, engulfing the original buildings in annexes, until today the Medical Center, once reasonably gracious, suggests an industrial district with some aesthetic pretensions.

In Bellefield, apartment buildings rose. Beginning with the Bellefield Dwellings of 1902–04, this became Pittsburgh's premier district for apartment living—apartment living, that is, with comfort, in prestigious buildings with careful architectural treatment. Near by, in Schenley Farms, Nicola developed a tightly controlled City Beautiful development of fine houses. Today Schenley Farms' residential streets retain a studied early twentieth-century graciousness in an Oakland subject to an ever-increasing level of activity and spatial demand.

Consequently, the present nature of Oakland is that of a neighborhood assembled from incongruous pieces rather than one that has evolved. Nicola's Civic Center of institutional palaces, his Schenley

Parkman Avenue in Schenley Farms

Looking up Junction Hollow from North Parkview Avenue.

Farms housing district, the factory-like hospitals, and Pitt's large buildings of varying age and quality are insertions, though sometimes beautiful ones, into a smaller-scaled neighborhood of houses and shops. Along the avenues a few houses survive, though their ground floors are mostly given over to the commercial froth of cheap restaurants and shops that large institutions generate.

But south of Forbes Avenue, the general effect is different. Here are Victorian houses in various states of repair, seedily respectable apartment buildings, little stores, close-built streets that meet at odd angles, and an occasional grand effect such as the open green of Oakland Square or the proscenium-box view up Junction Hollow from North Parkview Avenue. The institutions seem remote, although the hillside hospitals are quite visible to the north and the tapering silhouette of the Cathedral of Learning dominates the horizon.

The history of Schenley Park is intimately connected with that of Oakland, but here the land has escaped the developer's hand. Although it is intensively used for recreational purposes, it extends an arm into the heart of the Civic Center, and has its own incidents of formality—in particular a fine collection of public sculpture—as well as wooded valleys and grassy slopes, seemingly remote from institutions and close-built streets.

Houses
2701–07 Fifth Avenue and 1–7 Robinson Street
C. 1875

Despite losses from a fire, one retains some sense here of a notable row of eight houses, similar though not absolutely uniform in design, whose basic simplicity, a survival of the Georgian tradition, is varied with bay windows, large dormers, and modest Italianate ornament. At this point, Fifth Avenue curves eastward out of Soho, and the lower four houses originally were set into an echelon formation to follow it. The unified composition was a very pleasant one, well-proportioned and dignified, and even now makes a good emphatic introduction to Oakland.

St. Agnes' Roman Catholic Church
Fifth Avenue and Robinson Street
John T. Comes, architect, 1917

This is a church in brown, textured brick and lavishly modeled terra cotta, acknowledging no one historic style—Byzantine and Romanesque are both suggested—and original in its rose window and Crucifixion. This, and St. Peter's Episcopal Church formerly across the street, once constituted the western gateway to Oakland.

Houses
368–82 McKee Place
C. 1915

This is a very unusual house row, white-stuccoed and climbing the gentle slope of the street. One-story front walls, two-story roofs, and highly visible chimneys create an Old World effect that the sight of the original casements, opened in the summertime, would have enhanced. There has been much remodeling since the houses were built, but the row remains impressive.

House
315 Oakland Avenue
C. 1860

Forlorn at the end of a parking lot stands one of Oakland's best houses. Its porch has lost the brackets it must once have had, but the vergeboards of the front gable and dormer have held on. The style is a mixed one, half-Italianate, half-Gothic. The mixture is typical of the mid-nineteenth century; so is the formula of one building

mass with a gable toward the street and an adjacent mass presenting its side. This house, well preserved outside in spite of everything, should be restored and put to distinguished use.

Iroquois Apartments
Forbes Avenue and Atwood Street
Frederick J. Osterling, architect, 1901

A block-wide expanse of apartments with three light courts on the front, designed in an indeterminate Classical style. A brown brick and lighter gray terra-cotta trim show the preference of the time for rather dark colors as do the Iroquois' contemporaries the Hotel Schenley and Union Station. Three elaborate entrance halls once led to the interior, while open galleries to the rear connected the service rooms. Built at a time of considerable apartment-house construction, the Iroquois was grander than usual: no homely porches stacked three high, but slightly swelling window bays over-looking Forbes Avenue to create a bold effect from down the street. It shows the same sort of heavy elegance that Osterling put into the Arrott Building downtown. The Iroquois Apartments building has been remodeled for offices, with a very large annex to the rear.

Medical Arts Building
Fifth Avenue and Atwood Street
Maximilian Nirdlinger, architect, 1931–32

The Medical Arts Building introduced Oakland to "modern" architecture in the first significant way. Very little of the original Modernistic detailing on the ground floor outside has survived cheap remodeling, though the lobby inside is still of some interest. The upper stories, outside, are as built.

Forbes National Bank (now Mellon Bank)
Fifth Avenue and Oakland Avenue
E. P. Mellon, architect, 1930

Here is a very pleasant Italian Renaissance neighborhood bank, whose banking room once had a polychromed beamed ceiling vividly contrasting but stylistically in keeping with the monochrome limestone exterior.

The style is that found in several of the medical institutions built near by in the 1930s; Mellon was involved as an architect with some of these. Such a simple and well-studied building is a treat to see. It uses only enough detailing, and most details are of exactly the right size and form. Such buildings are not "exciting," and they can be merely bland, but when they are good they are very good indeed.

Western State Psychiatric Hospital (now Western Psychiatric Institute and Clinic)
O'Hara and De Soto Streets
Raymond M. Marlier, architect, 1939–40; addition

Built in a hard-featured Modernistic style of orangeish brick, this mental hospital arose in a neighborhood of academic and medical buildings. The other medical buildings were urbanely Georgian or Italian Renaissance. Perhaps, whatever the style, the architecture was meant as a message to the entering patient: entering a Florentine hospital you will be treated graciously; entering a Modernistic hospital you will be briskly and efficiently repaired.

Pitt Stadium
DeSoto and Terrace Streets
W. S. Hindman, engineer, 1925

A large stadium, with its ramps, sloping tiers of seats, and supporting frame, is apt to display an untidy anatomy to the outer world, and this attempt to suppress the elements with a grand-scaled arcaded effect is not untypical of early twentieth-century design. The walls are of concrete in a rather warm color, cast in forms of rough boarding that imparts quiet life to its texture.

The Soldiers' and Sailors' Memorial and the carefully scaled buildings that frame its lawn.

Civic Center

The crown of Oakland is the Civic Center that Franklin F. Nicola dreamed of from the time he purchased his first cornfield in 1897, and that others soon helped him realize. Many American cities have planned such splendid places, begun them, and sometimes even largely finished them, though usually with public funds. Around 1900 the City Beautiful was a common ideal, a place of palaces and avenues, trees and lawns, elegant costumes and carriages.

The Pittsburgh Athletic Association and Masonic Temple along Fifth Avenue.

Beggars, ramshackle wagons, gangling wooden poles strung with wires had no place there. In such visions they ceased to exist, or existed elsewhere.

Eventually, splendid architecture did surround, almost entirely, that great fourteen-acre lawn where the Cathedral of Learning rose. The homely, sooty buildings of Victorian Oakland were only a few steps away, but there were points of view from which the spectacle was *almost* perfect.

Nor did it involve the cold perfection of a grand avenue. Bigelow Boulevard, the fast road from town that terminated at the entrance to Schenley Park, approached the Civic Center by way of a curve and two right angles and reached Schenley Plaza off-axis. This was eccentric, literally, in a City Beautiful boulevard, but this and other irregularities of the street layout encouraged architects to

Detail of the Pittsburgh Athletic Association.

treat each building individually while giving the ensemble their best efforts.

City Historic District
National Register District

Henry Clay Frick Training School for Teachers (now Frick International Studies Academy)
107 Thackeray Street
Ingham & Boyd, architects, 1927

The long limestone front toward Fifth Avenue is of no special interest, and was in fact partly concealed by the Mid-Victorian Bellefield School  when built. The wing on Thackeray Street is a much more showy affair, mingling Grecian Ionic piers with carefully controlled rustication of an Italian Renaissance sort: Eclectic indeed but in the restrained, almost bland visual taste that so often characterized the American 1920s.

National Register of Historic Places

First United Presbyterian Church (now Bellefield Presbyterian Church)
Fifth Avenue and Thackeray Street
Thomas Boyd, architect, 1896

A Richardson Romanesque church of sandstone with a low sixteen-sided central lantern that serves, like the arcaded bow window of the front, to emphasize that this is basically an auditorium. It is a "lantern" church, similar in conception to the Shadyside Presbyterian Church of 1889. To the rear is a semicircle of Sunday-school rooms around a space once lighted by a stained-glass dome.

City Historic District

Central Turnverein (later, various institutions of the University of Pittsburgh)
O'Hara and Thackeray Streets
Kiehnel & Elliott, architects, 1911

Built by a German-American gymnastic association, this building passed into the hands of the University of Pittsburgh in less than a decade and has served a variety of purposes ever since. The basic organization is Classical, but the detailing is avant-garde by 1911 standards, with stone doorways and terra-cotta frieze ornamentation of a new sort. The ornament has not the authority of that by Frank Lloyd Wright or Louis Sullivan—it wants to be new but is not quite sure how—yet it does suggest progressive Chicago trends. Treating the second-floor window zone as a broad band gives the whole composition a unity and a horizontal emphasis that it needs.

City Historic District

Concordia Club
University Place and O'Hara Street
C. 1914

This building tops the gentle rise of University Place, standing opposite Thaw Hall of the University of Pittsburgh and the Soldiers' and Sailors' Memorial. It is less grand than these Hornbostel neighbors with its false roof and simple detailing, but its forty-foot height and gray-yellow brick vary yet complement the heights and materials of the fronts that adjoin it.

City Historic District

National Union Fire Insurance Company (now Thackeray Hall, University of Pittsburgh)
University Place
Abram Garfield (Cleveland), architect, 1923

This is Classicism almost to the minimum, with a few moldings only to articulate the plain limestone surfaces. The lessening in size of the windows from the main floor up may or may not have suited light and ventilation requirements. This building and its left-hand neighbor, the University Club, both have towers to the rear while presenting fronts about fifty feet high to University Place. The Concordia Club has an overall height similar to the others on University Place, so that the three present a harmonious group, a portion of an architectural frame for the Soldiers' and Sailors' Memorial that dominates the great lawn across the street.

City Historic District

University Club
123 University Place
Henry Hornbostel, architect, 1923; addition, 1963

The clubhouse, built of warm-gray brick with limestone detailing, has externally a very generalized Renaissance character that could be English as readily as Italian. Inside, spaces are Tudor, Italian Renaissance and, in the case of the great dining room overlooking the street, Adam. Above the dining room is a dining terrace, an excellent place to view the architecture of the Civic Center. The building is quite dignified yet is modest too, and has a warm, home-like feeling inside.

City Historic District

Thaw Hall

Schenley Farms campus, University of Pittsburgh
Bigelow Boulevard and Parkman Street
Palmer & Hornbostel (New York), planners and original architects; planned 1908

In 1908 the Western University of Pennsylvania, then on Perry Hilltop on the North Side, purchased a hillside cow pasture in Oakland from Franklin F. Nicola and instituted a competition for its development as a new campus. Palmer & Hornbostel's winning master plan was most ambitious, with a great Classical temple at the top and a multitude of lesser buildings flanking a broad descending lawn criss-crossed by a zigzag road and stairs.

Of the great plan that Henry Hornbostel designed, only fragments were built. Thaw Hall of 1908–09, on O'Hara Street opposite the Soldiers' and Sailors' Memorial, is the most easily seen and the most interesting. Its uncompleted terraced front, ending in a single temple-like pavilion, makes an interesting composition while its richly modeled terra cotta attests to Hornbostel's brilliance with ornament. The cream-colored brick and rough gray granite are good complementary materials; Hornbostel was to use the same materials superbly at the Fine Arts Building at Carnegie Technical Schools (now Carnegie Mellon University) a few years later. The brick and the terra cotta were used again in the other buildings erected: the now-gone School of Mines,

The original Dental School

Part of the original Medical School.

later State Hall, built in 1908–09 and notable for its elaborate doorway; the Dental School of 1912, plain save for a frothy terra-cotta doorway; an even plainer gymnasium of 1912; and the Medical School of 1910 at the top of the hill, now Pennsylvania Hall. On the gable of this last is Charles Keck's *Aesculapius* in white terra cotta, modeled with the ancient Egyptian technique of sinking the outline

Aesculapius

of the figure into the wall surface, then modeling the figure itself in very shallow relief. At the time of publication, it appeared that the former Medical and Dental Schools might be demolished, although there was hope

Allen Hall, the original Mellon Institute.

that the figure of *Aesculapius* and the doorway of the Dental School would be preserved for reconstruction.

Lacking Hornbostel's fancy decoration but in harmony with his materials and overall composition is J. H. Giesey's 1915

building for the Mellon Institute of Industrial Research, on O'Hara Street facing down Thackeray.

To these buildings was added Benno Janssen's severely Grecian Alumni Hall in 1920, and there have been several more recent buildings and annexes.

Historic Landmark plaque (Allen Hall)

Allegheny County Soldiers' and Sailors' Memorial
Fifth Avenue and Bigelow Boulevard
Henry Hornbostel of Palmer & Hornbostel (New York), architect, 1907–11

In a competition of 1907 for a County war memorial hall, Hornbostel's design won out over the submissions of such nationally known architects as Ernest Flagg, Cass Gilbert, and Peabody & Stearns, as well as those of prominent local offices. It was built nearly in the form submitted, but the original orientation toward "Grant Boulevard," as Bigelow was then, was sensibly changed on Hornbostel's initiative to take advantage of the long lawn sloping gently to Fifth Avenue. The central mass of light-colored sandstone and terra cotta holds an auditorium for 2,500, with a clerestoried banquet hall above, beneath the pyramidal tiled roof. The spreading base holds two meeting rooms and an ambulatory with cases of military memorabilia, primarily from the Civil War. The auditorium had four artificial lighting systems above a glazed ceiling—the rather soft incandescent lamps of the time, mercury-vapor lamps, nitrogen-vapor lamps, and "flaming" arcs—that allowed thirty-two light combinations simulating daylight.

Charles Keck's *America* sits enthroned over the central doorway, grasping a sheathed sword; on the terrace to the right and left stand a soldier and a sailor of the Civil War by Frederick Cleveland Hubbard, added in 1923.

Except for the landscaping, which is rather plain and

353

fragmentary and has been hoisted by an underground parking garage, the Soldiers' and Sailors' Memorial illustrates Beaux-Arts design in its grandest mode: symmetrical, impressive in massing, rich in detail, Classical in its lines—the Mausoleum at Halicarnassus was a general model. The great public halls rise above a spreading base of insistent horizontals, outcurved in a welcoming gesture on the Fifth Avenue front in a way that dignifies the small meeting rooms while allowing the ambulatory to pass around the auditorium uninterrupted. Behind this building, Hornbostel's grand hillside campus for the University of Pittsburgh was to have risen.

National Register of Historic Places
City Historic District
Historic Landmark plaque

Schenley Apartments (now Schenley Quadrangle, University of Pittsburgh)
Fifth Avenue opposite Thackeray Street
Henry Hornbostel, with Rutan & Russell, architects, 1922

This was Franklin F. Nicola's final speculation, and his home. The Bellefield Company, the developer, printed up a fancy booklet to describe the Apartments: 235 suites, from two to nine rooms in seven units of ten to twelve floors, the ground floors on Fifth and Forbes Avenues being for stores, and colonnaded and landscaped courts over an

underground garage. Meals could be sent up from the Hotel Schenley, and servants could be hired by the hour. The renderings show very nice planting indeed, by the French-looking gateways from Fifth Avenue, along the Doric colonnades of the courtyards, and above the villa-like steps down to Forbes. The materials are brown brick above lower stories of limestone. These are more heedless and utilitarian days for the complex, now used for dormitories, yet the gateways and colonnades remain with their old suave charm.

National Register District
City Historic District
Historic Landmark plaque

Hotel Schenley (now William Pitt Student Union, University of Pittsburgh)
Bigelow Boulevard and Fifth Avenue
Rutan & Russell, architects, 1898

Before its closing in the 1950s this was arguably the most elegant hotel in Pittsburgh: not least because it stood in its own landscaped grounds. Here visiting artists performing at the Syria Mosque a half-block away would stay—Eleanora Duse, in fact, died here—as well as baseball teams playing at Forbes Field, a couple of hundred yards to the south. The design is in the still-tentative Classical manner of the 1890s, executed in brick and terra cotta of a strong tawny shade that suited the taste of Pittsburghers at the time. The grounds originally had an Olmsted Brothers plan. Inside, the public rooms were spacious and elegant, with a considerable use of marble in the lobby. Conversions in the hotel days were minor: an open portico toward the Boulevard was rebuilt and glazed in as a lounge, and a colonnaded bridge was added to give a connection to the

Schenley Apartments when these were opened in the 1920s. In the 1960s, less fortunately, the cornice had to come down. In 1983 the upper floors were gutted and completely reworked inside, while the ground-floor rooms were generally restored and refurnished. The basement was fitted up in a wholly new Post-Modern way and a Corinthian basement colonnade was added on the Forbes Avenue front.

National Register District
City Historic District
Historic Landmark plaque

Cathedral of Learning campus, University of Pittsburgh

Bigelow Boulevard and Fifth Avenue
Charles Zeller Klauder (Philadelphia), architect;
Cathedral of Learning, 1926–37; Heinz Chapel, 1934–38;
Stephen Collins Foster Memorial, 1935–37

When John Gabbert Bowman accepted the chancellorship of the University of Pittsburgh in 1921, he found that his university consisted primarily of Hornbostel's few achieved buildings, Benno Janssen's new Alumni Hall, and a great many badly deteriorated wooden barricks from the recent

war; and further, that the institution was spectacularly in debt and its creditors out of patience. To say the very least, he took a bold line with the rich and powerful of Pittsburgh. To believe his own account, he must have been one of the most impudent and persuasive diplomats of all time, with a personality and a vision that some very unimpressionable businessmen failed to resist. Having decided to vacate the original hillside site, he persuaded Andrew W. and Richard B. Mellon to give him the fourteen-acre Frick property near by, around which the Civic Center was growing, and began to push his vision of a great university tower.

Common Room gateway by Samuel Yellin.

When the fifteenth-century Cathedral of Seville was being planned, one of the cathedral chapter urged the construction of a church "so great and of such a kind that those who see it finished shall think that we were mad." Some such Gothic fervor was in Bowman's mind, but his struggle, on the contrary, was to convince everyone that he was sane. A university skyscraper was unheard-of, and the thought of class changes by elevator appalled everyone—reasonably enough, as time would show. Bowman realized that he had to have a plan to display; people had to taste the idea, not merely hear it. He went to Charles Z. Klauder, a sensitive Eclectic architect and a specialist in college design. Klauder reacted coolly, but he and his staff started designing. They tried and tried, and Bowman kept saying that the inspiration was not there; his students must be *inspired* by the building. Temperaments flashed. One evening—this is all Bowman's account—Bowman and Klauder happened to be hearing the Magic Fire Music from *Die Walküre*, and Bowman said that that was what he wanted: climax building on climax, leaping ever higher. Klauder and his draftsmen achieved a breakthrough shortly thereafter, an absurd but beautiful tower that Bowman sold to the trustees, the rich donors, the ordinary laboring people, and even the schoolchildren, who were caught up in the growing enthusiasm and gave their dimes to the building campaign.

Seen from a distance, the Cathedral of Learning—so

called by a draftsman—rises like solid rock, an irregularly tapering mass 535 feet high. Closer-up, it mingles English Perpendicular and French Flamboyant of the fifteenth century, powerful, ascending lines and delicate detailing. The corners, as they rise, break up again and again as solid stone grows into a multitude of pinnacles; between the corner masses are great traceried arches. Under the textured limestone, though, is a massive steel frame cased in concrete; the tower, it is predicted, will last 300 years. Inside, a ring of eighteen first-floor classrooms, each designed in a different national style as a symbol of Pittsburgh's multinational heritage, surround a great vaulted common room sixty feet high; there are six other Nationality Rooms on the third floor. In the building too are the Greek Revival ballroom, slightly lessened in height, from "Picnic House," the old Croghan-Schenley villa, and an eighteenth-century library from a house in Damascus, Syria.

If the Cathedral of Learning was the result of a reverie, the Heinz Chapel, donated by the Heinz family, may have been the product of a dream. Bowman wanted a splendid chapel for his students, and Klauder is rumored to have dreamed of the unique form the chapel took, with an apse at each end and a higher portion, like a pair of transepts, at the center beneath a tall spire. The style is fifteenth-century French Flamboyant again, with windows by Charles J. Connick of Boston that wash the interior in a gentle purple light. Opinions differ on the chapel. It has

Pier detail, Heinz Chapel

been called a frog in a lace nightgown, and its ornamentation has been said to lack the vitality of that in the Cathedral of Learning. Most people, however, would probably react to the chapel with enthusiasm: form, detailing, and all. It is surely much more than a typical product of a slickly professional period of architecture. Inter-denominational, it is a favorite wedding church.

The Foster Memorial, with a museum like a polygonal chapter house from a medieval monastery and a small theater, probably has a little less vitality than the other two, yet its detailing is crisp, delicate, and never mechanical. Lithographed sheet music from minstrel shows certainly looks odd inside this vision of fifteenth-century France, but an evocation of Foster's native Lawrenceville or of the Victorian period anywhere was out of the question in the 1930s.

National Register District
City Historic District
Historic Landmark plaques

Heinz Chapel

Foster Memorial

Pittsburgh Athletic Association
Fifth Avenue and Bigelow Boulevard
Janssen & Abbott, architects, 1909–11

One of the best buildings in the Civic Center is this clubhouse, built in limestone and a closely matching terra cotta. The style is Venetian Renaissance, with some details traceable to two works of Jacopo Sansovino: the Palazzo Grimiani and the Library of St. Mark in Venice, Italy. A hipped tile roof finishes off the composition in an appropriate way. Critics have gently reproached the architects for having a strong entablature halfway up, on the grounds that it divides the composition in two; the more so since one Corinthian order stands on another. Yet the facade is strong in its general lines, and its decorative details are good in themselves and well designed for harmony with the whole composition. Under the circumstances, a theoretical fault seems not all that important.

National Register of Historic Places
City Historic District
Historic Landmark plaque

Masonic Temple
Fifth and Lytton Avenues
Janssen & Abbott, architects, 1914

A fanciful paraphrase of ancient temple architecture, of limestone with detail work in matching terra cotta. The very tall basement conveys a suitable impression of remoteness from the outside world, and the great doorways are of awesome impressiveness. The Corinthian capitals have an intricate Hellenistic quality. This is very obviously an arcane building, in marked contrast to the openness, almost jollity, of the Pittsburgh Athletic Association next door.

National Register District
City Historic District

357

Twentieth-Century Club
Bigelow Boulevard and southern end of Parkman Avenue
Janssen & Cocken, architects, 1929–30

An earlier building of 1910 was swallowed up in this Italian Renaissance remodeling of a women's club. The building itself is delicate and rather prim; the wall enclosing the motor entrance is more robust in general, but the urns have their own delicate detailing. Inside, some interiors are Art Deco.

National Register District
City Historic District

Historical Society of Western Pennsylvania (former building)
4338 Bigelow Boulevard
Ingham & Boyd, architects, 1912

Although the front of this building long carried the three flags that have flown over Western Pennsylvania, its style is fifteenth-century Italian Renaissance of the most delicate sort. The materials are white brick and matching terra cotta. Inside, the details are American of the eighteenth and early nineteenth centuries.

The first Pittsburgh attempt at a Historical Society came early, in 1834, but the present society, founded in 1879 and assuming its present name in 1883, was the first such organization to last. It has moved to the former Chautauqua Lake Ice Company building in the Strip.

National Register District
City Historic District

Western Pennsylvania School for Blind Children
Bayard Street and North Bellefield Avenue
George S. Orth, architect, 1893–94; enlargements, 1980s

The derivation of this unusual facade treatment, a yellow-ish brick striped with red brick, can only be guessed at. Certainly, the City Hospital at Copenhagen, Denmark, built thirty years before, had had a very similar treatment that may have occurred to an architect who was trying to achieve a striking appearance with institutional economy. The more recent impact of "Ruskin Gothic," which also made quite a feature of striped walls, may have been the inspiration. Or Byzantine architecture for that matter.

When the school moved into its new quarters, it was only a few years old, having been founded with a bequest of 1885. The land, adjoining Schenley Farms, was a gift of Mary Croghan Schenley.

National Register District
City Historic District

First Baptist Church
North Bellefield Avenue and Bayard Street
Bertram Grosvenor Goodhue of Cram, Goodhue & Ferguson
(New York Office), architect, 1909–12

Goodhue's treatment of the Modern Gothic his firm so successfully promoted is well shown here. At first glance it is terse, a piece of summarized Gothic that feels modern in its abstention from pinnacles outside and capitals inside,

its refusal to be in any way quaint. Its corner masses, gradually falling away as they rise, even anticipate the forms that Moderne skyscrapers were to take some fifteen years in the future. But a second look shows gentle ornament, carving in wood and stone with a half-Gothic, half-Arts-and-Crafts flavor about it, contained in the severe overall composition, and outside a delicately detailed copper flèche rises from the crossing. A third look, for instance at the exterior masonry, shows the subtlety that Goodhue, stimulated by a lavish budget, was prepared to put into a work: verticals that are slightly inclined, stones whose jointing is varied to give a subliminal feeling of life to an otherwise textureless surface.

Inside, limestone arches rise from piers without capitals, and Guastavino tile vaults close the spaces. The nave has very narrow aisles and terminates in a preacher's desk and a

wooden screen concealing the baptismal tank. Above, in a loft, is an organ with a stained-glass window behind it, giving a climactic feature. Grisaille glass is used in the nave windows.

National Register District
City Historic District
Historic Landmark plaque

Carving on the screen

**Rectory, Bellefield Presbyterian Church
(now Music Building, University of Pittsburgh)**
Fifth and North Bellefield Avenues
Frederick J. Osterling, architect (?), 1891

The tentative attribution to Osterling is based on his having been the architect for the now-gone Bellefield Presbyterian Church across Bellefield Avenue, for whose pastor this was built. Yet this is a very polished Romanesque design and the church was a very gawky Gothic one: can the swan and the ostrich hatch in the same nest? A long arcaded side porch was later enclosed for a ballroom.

National Register District
City Historic District

Webster Hall
Fifth Avenue and North Dithridge Street
Henry Hornbostel and Eric Fisher Wood, architects, 1925–26

Built as a men's residence club, Webster Hall soon became a regular hotel, and now is a condominium. The exterior style is Italian Romanesque, though the entrance was originally Baroque. Inside, public rooms were French, Spanish, Tudor, Empire, Victorian, and Georgian; little of this Eclectic decoration now remains. The hotel has lost its uppermost cornice and wall treatment as well, but retains some of its exterior distinction all the same, thanks to its location at a turn of the street and its boldly striped wall.

National Register District
City Historic District

St. Paul's Cathedral (Roman Catholic)
Fifth Avenue and North Craig Street
Egan & Prindeville (Chicago), architects, 1903–06;
Edward J. Weber, architect for Synod Hall and Chancery, 1914;
Carlton Strong, architect for rectory, 1926

The twin spires of St. Paul's Cathedral are prominent, familiar objects on the Oakland skyline, establishing the eastern part of the neighborhood. The two previous cathedrals had been downtown on the site of the Union Arcade, and the move to Oakland was one from an area almost without a remaining resident population to one that was soon to become surrounded by homes. When the decision to build in Oakland was made there was no Civic Center, of course: only houses, hillside pastures, and the vague

The Synod Hall by Weber

The rectory by Strong

obviously supporting lighter weights than the vaulted forms suggest. The trend in the future would be toward greater mass inside a church, a feeling of abundant stone or brick supporting the upper walls and the vaults or trusses that covered the space.

Two prominent Pittsburgh Catholic architects have contributed to the cathedral complex: Edward J. Weber in the Synod Hall and Chancery of 1914, which has for the most part a fifteenth-century English look, and Carlton Strong in the uncompleted rectory of 1926, in a sophisticatedly simplified Tudor manner.

National Register District
City Historic District
Historic Landmark plaque

Mellon Institute for Industrial Research, Carnegie Mellon University
Fifth and South Bellefield Avenues
Janssen & Cocken, architects, 1931–37

While the interiors are in a somewhat-Classical somewhat-Modernistic style, the exterior is resolutely Classical. Perhaps the cornice projects less in proportion to the building height than it would have at one time, but against this we must set sixty-two unfluted Grecian Ionic columns with monolithic shafts, forty-two feet high, in colonnades on all four sides. A nine-story building—half underground—for scientific research is thus screened by a pure piece of architectural rhetoric, sober in its design, wild in its expense. Stylistically independent of both the exterior and the greater part of the interior is the library, Carolean English of the late seventeenth century, with wood carvings in the manner of Grinling Gibbons.

The Mellon Stuart Company, the contractor, relates that a detailed full-scale mockup of a corner and the nearest two columns was erected for study, and that to

promise of a fine neighborhood that was to be read in the presence of the Carnegie Institute, Schenley Park, and the Hotel Schenley.

The new cathedral was faced in limestone, which suggested a new spirit in its design, a turning-away from the strong and somber colors of the Victorian past. Yet the actual design was still Victorian in important ways. The new Eclectic architects, who in church architecture were led by Ralph Adams Cram and Bertram Goodhue, tended to think in terms of an overall composition from which the decorative details would grow. The Victorians were more apt to think of the details first, then try to bring them together: this at least is what their actual designs imply. So it is here: the details have a detached quality.

There is no true masonry vaulting, and the outer walls lack the flying buttresses one might expect in a five-aisled masonry church, while the piers inside are slender, erect the columns safely and in their precise positions they were lowered onto carefully placed blocks of ice and allowed to settle.

The Institute was founded in 1913 by Andrew W. and Richard B. Mellon, who were impressed by the proposal of Robert Kennedy Duncan, a chemistry professor, for industrial research fellowships. Duncan became the first director of the new Institute. Its first permanent building of 1915 survives at Thackeray and O'Hara Streets.

National Register District
City Historic District

Board of Education
341 South Bellefield Avenue
Ingham & Boyd, architects, 1926–27

The architects were among the most tasteful this area has seen. The former building of the Historical Society of Western Pennsylvania, Chatham Village, and the Buhl Planetarium are witnesses to the quality of their work. Here they executed a suave official building in limestone, Italian Renaissance with a few discreet Baroque touches. Inside is a landscaped courtyard of the same quality as the facades.

National Register District
City Historic District

Young Men and Women's Hebrew Association (now Bellefield Hall, University of Pittsburgh)
315 South Bellefield Avenue
Benno Janssen of Janssen & Cocken, architect, 1924

Of the three buildings presently on this block, the YMWHA has a compelling warmth that neither the Board of Education nor the Mellon Institute, with their limestone fronts, can match. The great rusticated arch is of limestone and so are some other details, but this is primarily an essay in brick. A rough-surfaced mulberry-red brick, laid in a "garden-wall" bond that emphasizes horizontals, creates a beautiful textured surface against which the smooth white stone plays. In the uppermost story, special settings of brick in different hues make a quietly colorful frieze. Above is a tiled hip roof. The general effect is Italian Renaissance, but only in a very loose way. Inside, the effect is more Hispanic, with an auditorium ceiling that imitates *artesonado*, the intricate ceiling woodwork of Spain around 1500, in plaster.

National Register District
City Historic District
Historic Landmark plaque

The Schenley Plaza front, with the original building in the foreground.

First Congregational Church (now St. Nicholas Greek Orthodox Cathedral)
419 South Dithridge Street
Thomas Hannah, architect, 1904

A Grecian Ionic portico, executed in sandstone, is the grand and appropriate introduction to a church that has belonged to the Greek Orthodox Church since 1923. The exterior, with its big round-arched windows, is not otherwise specifically symbolic, but the interior is rich with paintings and mosaics. Notable inside are the painting in the dome of Christ the Pantocrator (Ruler of All), with its background of gold leaf, and the iconostasis of metal and mosaic, with peacocks finely depicted on the Royal Doors. Further art is to be found within the sanctuary, including a painting of the Mother and Child and a fresco of the Last Supper.

City Historic District Historic Landmark plaque

Carnegie Institute and Carnegie Library of Pittsburgh
4400 Forbes Avenue
Longfellow, Alden & Harlow (Boston and Pittsburgh), architects for original building, 1892–95; Alden & Harlow, architects for Forbes Avenue section, 1903–07

Mary Croghan Schenley's 1889 gift of the land for Schenley Park prompted Andrew Carnegie to offer the City a cultural institution to stand at the park's main entrance. The present Carnegie Library section that now faces Schenley Plaza was the first built, outwardly an unfancy Italian Renaissance building, dignified but simple, richly carved in only a few places. Only toward Forbes Avenue was it fancy: there the Music Hall bowed forward in a hemicycle flanked by two Venetian campaniles, and the entrance and foyer group in front of it were surmounted by a carved balustrade, two domes, and four lampposts so elevated from the street that they must have been intended to be seen rather than to see by.

Inside are calm vaulted corridors, decorated with medallions and leaf ornament by the Bostonian Elmer Ellsworth

The Forbes Avenue front

The Stephen Collins Foster monument

Garnsey and originally more decorated than now, and a great skylit reading room. The effect of this earlier portion, aside from its indecisive and now-removed Forbes Avenue features, is exactly right for such a public institution: a beauty that comes partly from decorative stonework and bronzework, partly from the simple, placid geometry of the vaulted spaces; a refreshing sense of solidity in the stone walls, oaken bookcases, and heavy, varnished doors with brass hinges; and a home-like feeling too: the rooms are big but make no attempt to overawe the public, and you are comfortable in them.

The Forbes Avenue enlargements begun in 1903 were conceived in a different spirit, one of ostentation, with two complicated entrance pavilions that include Corinthian columns and numerous bronzes by John Massey Rhind (New York). The showiness is typical of the time, and most people see in it the Beaux-Arts style; yet there is a stiffness, a lack of curves anywhere, that suggests rather Imperial

The Music Hall foyer

Germany. One of the entrance pavilions leads to a new foyer for the Music Hall, an interior that must be seen to be believed, sumptuous in the truest sense with many kinds of marbles, richly molded bronzework, and heavy plaster; there is a story that Carnegie demanded that it cost more than any throne room as a tribute to the sovereign people.

The other entrance leads to the marble stair hall of the 1907 home of the Museum of Art, locus of the famous Carnegie International art exhibitions; around the walls are the *Apotheosis of Pittsburgh* murals of John White Alexander, which have drawn the sneers of several generations but that sin mostly in being out of fashion. At the center, between the entrances, is a great hall of architectural casts, doorways, windows, pulpits, columns, capitals, and fragments of every sort from the historic architecture of Europe, reproduced in plaster.

The Scaife Gallery addition of 1974, by Edward Larabee Barnes, added vastly to the spaces of the Museum of Art.

Humbler, set apart, but very big all the same is the Bellefield Boiler Plant in Junction Hollow below the Institute, an industrial building of 1903–07 by Alden & Harlow added to in 1943. Brick, not ashlar, it is a self-respecting construction despite its almost-total lack of decoration. When it was built, the public was invited to inspect the dynamos and engines in the Institute

The Bellefield Boiler Plant

basement, driven by the steam from this boiler house. This was often the case at the time: The Machine was not yet an idol of culture in any important way, yet modern society was proud of it. Even a boiler house had to be decent if not elegant in a first-class architectural group such as this.

National Register of Historic Places
City Historic District
Historic Landmark plaques

Parkman Avenue

Hamerschlag house, Bigelow Boulevard and Parkman Avenue.

Schenley Farms

The northern end of Franklin F. Nicola's massive purchases from the Schenley and O'Hara estates was for houses, and from 1907 on was offered to home buyers on a leasing basis with strict obligations on both sides. Nicola was determined that his residential development would be of high quality from the start, with all utilities buried, a special police force, and the best equipment in the houses he himself built on Lytton Avenue. Most of the gently rising streets were planted with sycamores, and along these streets very substantial houses rose from the late 1900s through the 1920s. Grant Boulevard, soon to be named Bigelow Boulevard, passed through the area on its way from town to the Civic Center; here, trees by the curb yielded to a more open effect of lawns and flowers. The early houses, respectable as they were, were not as well designed as those of the 1920s, but all suggested—and continue to suggest—a very comfortable way of living. Both Schenley Farms proper and its uphill fringe, Schenley Farms Terrace, retain the air of domestic happiness as conceived early in this century.

Something of the same ruggedness found in the Parkman Avenue retaining wall (described next) is present in the house that Henry Hornbostel designed at Bigelow Boulevard and Parkman Avenue. Built around 1910 for Arthur Hamerschlag, president of the Carnegie Technical Schools that Hornbostel was designing and erecting, it has rubble walls up to the second-floor window sills, and rough red brick in stack bond—brick literally just stacked—from there to the eaves. This design has the same slightly mannered down-to-earth quality that Hornbostel was putting into the Carnegie Tech dormitories. A similar

Stengel house, 4136 Bigelow Boulevard.

quality is to be found in Kiehnel & Elliott's Stengel house of 1913 at 4136 Bigelow Boulevard. There is more explicit ornament here, and a little allusion to both Prairie School and Classical design practice, yet inside and out, in brick and wood, the house expresses the ideals of the Arts and Crafts movement of the twentieth century's first two decades; things are simple and sincere, as if an honest workman with a trained eye had formed and arranged stone, brick, wood, and wrought iron in a harmonious way so that the results were at once humble and sophisticated.

In such a development as Schenley Farms, though, reconsidered old ideas are more commonly found than new ones. Number 4123 Bigelow Boulevard, which appears to be from the 1920s, suggests a small English manor or a prosperous farmhouse of the seventeenth century, fitted with new window sash in the eighteenth; its roof is extended in the front to cover a normal American front porch in the way that its historic model might have had an extended roof to shelter a hay wagon. Number 4309 Parkman Avenue, by Louis S. Stevens, is more manorial with its delicate stone balustrade edging a terrace, yet it has a homely as well as a gentlemanly quality. Number 4405 Bigelow Boulevard, also by Louis S. Stevens, has a grander air, with its limestone facing, its loggia with a polychrome terra-cotta medallion, its rusticated doorway, and its *altana* that rises above the main roof: an Italian villa looking coolly across at Goodhue's mixture of zeal and cunning in the First Baptist Church.

National Register District
City Historic District
Historic Landmark plaque

4123 Bigelow Boulevard

4309 Parkman Avenue

Retaining wall
Western bend of Parkman Avenue
C. 1905

Site preparation in the Schenley Farms residential neighborhood required cutting into an outlying part of Herron Hill, so that the house blocks are well below the adjacent hillside campus of the University of Pittsburgh. To retain the earth this handsome wall of typical engineering masonry, a kind of dam, was built. Roughly textured, darkened by the Pittsburgh air, romantically overgrown by plants, following the directional change of Parkman Street with a broad curve, the wall is a poetic feature as well as a necessary one. A stair built into the wall gives access to Centre Avenue properties above the street.

National Register District
City Historic District

4405 Bigelow Boulevard

Schenley High School

Bigelow Boulevard and Centre Avenue
Edward Stotz, architect, 1915–16

In the two decades since Stotz had designed the Fifth
Avenue High School both school plans and school facades
had changed. The older school was warm in color and
picturesque in detailing; here, the limestone fronts are
monochrome and monotonous, relying on good proportions, a few architectural motifs, and the dramatic rounded
corners useful in a large building whose perimeter is a
scalene triangle. The many windows, though, are expressive in themselves; this was a very large and well-equipped
school for its time, and the open utilitarian fronts hint at
the complex technology of modern education.

National Register of Historic Places
City Historic District

Bellefield Dwellings

Bellefield area

Directly east of Franklin F. Nicola's Schenley Farms development, including his Civic Center, is Bellefield, whose
western boundary is marked by Bellefield Avenue. The
name of this narrow district was given by Neville B. Craig,
the first recorder of Pittsburgh history, who sold a portion
of his farm—"Bellefield"—to developers around 1850.

   The remarkable aspect of Bellefield is the number of its
apartment houses. The oldest is Bellefield Dwellings,
Centre and North Bellefield Avenues, built in 1902–04 by
Carlton Strong, who had just arrived from New York and
was to become one of the best-known architects with
Catholic connections. Bellefield Dwellings has a bold red-
and-white effect, and a rising effect, that suggests that a
mildly avant-garde apartment house from the Morningside
Heights area of Manhattan had migrated to a still-pastoral
part of Pittsburgh. In the next seven decades other apartment houses followed near by, some pretentious, some dull
but adequate. There were those 1915 apartment houses
where everything seemed to be white in color and relaxed
in mood, and then there were meaner places, mainly much
more recent. The King Edward Apartments of 1930, at
North Craig and Bayard Streets, illustrates one solution to
the problem of the older apartment house, that of packag-
ing its inhabitants graciously. The window sash is commonsensical Georgian, but the exterior otherwise is early
English Renaissance in the easily modeled and not-too-
expensive terra cotta in favor at the time.

   Another well-known apartment house stands near by,
close to Schenley Farms Terrace. This is the Royal York

King Edward Apartments

Royal York Apartments

Apartments, 3955 Bigelow Boulevard, designed in 1937 by Frederick Stanton of Chicago: a work of off-white terra cotta and light warm-gray brick in a mild Art Deco style. It is big and urbane, and gets some notice from these facts, but its great feature is a porte-cochere supported on columns of wrought iron and milk glass, lit from within.

Central Catholic High School
4720 Fifth Avenue
Edward J. Weber of Link, Weber & Bowers, architect, 1926–27

A very impressive composition in both size and detailing. The material is warm bright-red brick laid with calculated irregularity; into this are set, here and there, bold diaper patterns in a darker brick. This is remarkable: at the time when Victorian architecture was most despised, here is decoration that William Butterfield, one of the boldest and baddest Mid-Victorians, might have designed. The central portion of the High School is exalted in its verticality. The towered faculty house behind is much more home-like; it could be a monastic dormitory in Flanders.

Weber was a respected architect of the 1920s who designed other Catholic structures. Notable for a similar boldness of pattern is St. Colman's School in Turtle Creek.

Historic Landmark plaque

369

United States Bureau of Mines (now Hamburg Hall, Carnegie Mellon University)
4800 Forbes Avenue
Henry Hornbostel, architect, 1915

Here, as in the contemporary City-County Building, Modern succinctness and Classical pomp are combined. The base and the great portal are in poured gray concrete with a very slight texture that may be due to weathering rather than design. An eagle with upraised wings used to rise above the escutcheon over the doorway. The walls are in Hornbostel's favorite cream-colored brick. Inside is a grand corridor vaulted in Guastavino tile. Such a building reveals a nice balance between the utilitarianism needed in a structure of laboratories and offices, and the monumentality appropriate to an institution of public significance.

Between rear-extending wings stands the two-storied Smith Hall, presumably of c. 1915 and by Hornbostel: a simple but very well-proportioned building.

National Register of Historic Places

The center of the Hornbostel campus.

Carnegie Technical Schools (later Carnegie Institute of Technology; now Carnegie Mellon University)
Tech and Frew Streets
Henry Hornbostel of Palmer & Hornbostel (New York, then Pittsburgh), planner and architect; planned 1904

In 1900 the Carnegie Technical Schools were founded, and by 1904 they were ready to think of a big, coordinated campus, and held a competition. Having won the competition, Hornbostel was often in Pittsburgh to supervise the execution of his plans and to be the institution's first professor of architecture. Over the years his plan was greatly modified, by him as well as by others, and was never fully realized, but one basic idea remained: a double range of buildings on a lawn sloping gently down toward the edge of Junction Hollow, with a building terminating the axis at each end and other buildings close by. The style was a personal kind of Beaux-Arts, quite Classical in some details, quite free in others, with an overall clarity of organization and a simplicity of general form that allowed, nevertheless, for infinite variations of detail. The materials were cream-colored brick, brick of a slightly darker, light-caramel tone, white semi-matte terra cotta, pale-gray granite, and exposed concrete, varied with bands of polychrome terra cotta, and a bronze sheathing for window spandrels and mullions and for cornice brackets. The roofs were covered in a lustrous raven-black tile. An almost-white campus with occasional touches of strong color, theatrically presented.

Hamerschlag Hall (formerly Machinery Hall) of 1913 stands at the edge of Junction Hollow, with its great arches front and back, and its thick chimney surrounded by an arcade. Such a feature is most unusual, and Hornbostel's explanation of it as a temple of Venus gives the chimney, adequate symbol of her consort Vulcan, a peculiarly erotic

Hamerschlag Hall

Hamerschlag Hall entrance

quality. The contrasts of richly modeled white terra cotta
and raw Guastavino vaulting tile that line the entrance
niche are bold Hornbostelian composition too. One subtlety of detailing is in a band of sunken squares within
squares, in very faintly contrasting tints of white. For
eighty years the tower of Hamerschlag dominated the half-
wild, half-casually built-in void of Junction Hollow, which
at this point is 300 feet wide and 75-feet deep. The contrast
of this elegant building and the wild slopes is now gone.
In 1995 the University began construction of a major
building, Roberts Hall, directly before the Junction Hollow
front of Hamerschlag to the loss of much of the latter's
architectural power. This required removal of a notable
feature of the campus: the large, fancily scrolled bow
ornament of the armored cruiser *Pennsylvania* (1905; later,
Pittsburgh), no longer required when the Great White
Fleet was painted gray and borrowed somehow by
Hornbostel as an outrider to his great quadrangle.

The northern and southern ranges consist of Porter
Hall (formerly Industries Hall) of 1905 and Doherty Hall
(formerly Engineering Hall) of 1908, whose wings project
into the central lawn like stage flats with touches of polychrome terra cotta. The corridors in the southern range
have archways strapped in iron like kiln doors, railings
of pipe, and lamp brackets also of pipe striking the
technological note.

Baker Hall (formerly Administration Hall) of 1914 has
vaults of raw Guastavino tile and an open-newel stair,
gravity-defying, in the same material.

The College of Fine Arts of 1912 and 1915 is distinguished by outer niches illustrating five styles of architecture; its corridor floors of marble are inlaid with the
plans of five great buildings; its dean's-office doorway is a
cast from Pierre Puget's portal for the Hôtel de Ville of

Porter Hall

Doherty Hall

Baker Hall

College of Fine Arts

Guastavino tile stair, Baker Hall

Margaret Morrison College

Henderson Hall

Welch Hall

Gymnasium

Welch Hall

rural Italian construction. McGill and Boss Halls have basements of much the same rubble to be found on the Hamerschlag house. Above this is dead red brick in running bond, willfully uninteresting, up to a third-story frieze in a basket-weave pattern of red brick. These materials are much exaggerated in Henderson Hall, invisible from the street, where the rugged stonework looks fanged, up to a frieze-like band of red brick that begins at second-floor sill level. Scobell and Welch Halls are subtler, in their cream and pale gray-brown brick patterns above rubble basements.

Extensive recent additions by Dennis, Clark & Associates and Kallmann, McKinnell & Wood, both of Boston, have complemented Hornbostel's buildings very well.

Toulon, and its vault paintings by J. M. Hewlett are a random survey of the arts.

Margaret Morrison College of 1906 stands beside the main campus; it has a circular Doric colonnade and a gorgeous polychromed entablature. The colonnade is modeled on a courtyard at the stables of the Chateau of Chantilly, a Baroque construction that is probably the world's most distinguished accommodation for the horse.

The Gymnasium of 1923 behind the main campus is Hornbostel's last work here.

Five dormitories of 1915 and 1918 stand east of Margaret Morrison on elevated ground. Their rather capricious style seems vaguely ethnic, maybe alluding to

Schenley Park

Edward Manning Bigelow, the new Director of the City's
Department of Public Works, determined in the late 1880s
that Pittsburgh should have real parks, not just whatever
tiny greens that it may have acquired from time to time.
He had his eye on the large Oakland property of Mary
Croghan Schenley, the rich runaway bride of the 1830s
whom "Picnic House" had failed to keep at home and who
had been living in England for about forty years. The
southern part of her land was an area of knolls and ravines,
a place with the potential for a Romantic park but seemingly not too useful otherwise. And yet, in 1889, a land-
development company seemed ready to make her an offer.
There is a story of a friend of Bigelow's being roused in the
small hours, hustled to New York and on board the same
liner that carried the development company's agent, a race
through the streets of London, an impassioned plea for
the people of Pittsburgh over the Schenley breakfast table,
a pledge of 300 acres, and a polite greeting as Bigelow's
friend walked out the door and the agent walked in.
The story is more or less true.

The land *was* developed as a Romantic park, with landscape design in part by the Scotsman William Falconer.
Additional land was added (to a current size of 456 acres),
and a casino (primarily a skating rink), band shell, zoo,
merry-go-round, auto race track, and horse-racing oval all
made temporary appearances. More permanent features are
a set of handsome bridges, the Phipps Conservatory, a
collection of monuments, and two log houses which were
caught up in the net of park land. In the 1930s, through
the Works Progress Administration, the park was laced
with stone steps and walls.

The park now shows evidence of years of neglect,
despite areas of restoration. In the mid-1990s the need for
wider restoration was quite apparent.

National Register District
Historic Landmark plaque

Phipps Conservatory
Schenley Drive between Schenley and Panther Hollow Bridges,
Schenley Park
Lord & Burnham (Irvington, N.Y.), designers and builders,
1893; entrance rebuilt, 1960s

Henry Phipps, a partner of Andrew Carnegie, had given a
conservatory to Allegheny City and in 1891 he offered one
as well to Pittsburgh. The builders were Lord & Burnham,
specialists in greenhouse design and construction, who
erected the first nine display houses. To these in 1896 were
added three more, and in 1900 the City added nine growing houses to the rear. In its final form the public areas
centered on a great palm house, at whose very center was a
fountain with a copy of Giovanni di Bologna's *Mercury*.
From this, three wings led to the sides and the rear, where
crosswings branched off from octagonal domed spaces.
The entrance to the palm house was originally a stone
Romanesque structure, but has been replaced by an

expedient modern construction. The Palm Court, the
Fern Room, the original Economic Room, and the Cactus
Room remain substantially from the early days, the Fern
Room of the late 1890s being closest to its original condition. In time, pools, flower terraces, statues, and trees came
to surround the Conservatory. These surroundings are not
quite what they once were due to considerations of economy and security, but the greenhouses themselves underwent a thorough restoration and modernization in the late
1970s and early 1980s under the joint supervision of the
Pittsburgh History & Landmarks Foundation and the City
of Pittsburgh. A volunteer committee was established and
its members raised close to one million dollars for the
restoration of the Conservatory; the City and Federal
government added approximately five million dollars.

National Register of Historic Places
City Historic Structure
Historic Landmark plaque

Magee Memorial

Schenley Park monuments

Monuments gravitate to, or are precipitated in, parks,
their formal spaces and their sylvan glades. Here are
three of the outstanding ones in Schenley Park. The
Christopher Lyman Magee Memorial stands on axis with
the entrance to the Carnegie Library that is the central
element of the original Carnegie Institute building. It takes
the form of a gray granite stela designed by Henry Bacon
(New York)—later, the architect of the Lincoln Memorial
in Washington, D.C.—and a bronze bas-relief by Augustus
Saint-Gaudens (Cornish, N.H.), one of the great American
sculptors. The figure with the cornucopia has sometimes
been called Abundance and sometimes Charity. Magee, a
political leader, loved to gain abundance but also wanted to
be liked, and the ambiguity of naming seems fitting.

The Schenley Memorial Fountain of 1918 terminates
the axis of Schenley Plaza and stands on the buried bridge
that once crossed St. Pierre Ravine. The bronze sculpture

Schenley Memorial Fountain

by Victor David Brenner, *A Song to Nature*, demonstrates that "Pan the Earth God answers to the harmony and magic tones sung to the lyre by sweet Harmony." The granite basin itself is the design of H. Van Buren Magonigle, an architect who specialized in monumental work and is best remembered for the Liberty Memorial in Kansas City, Missouri. Both artists were New Yorkers.

Finally, the George Westinghouse Memorial rests in the depths of the park at West Circuit and Schenley Drives. This is very dignified Art Deco work of 1930 by Henry Hornbostel and his partner of later years Eric Fisher Wood, with sculpture by Daniel Chester French (Stockbridge, Mass.) and Paul Fjelde (New York). Fjelde

Westinghouse Memorial

executed bas-reliefs on six panels to illustrate the great industrialist's accomplishments while French did all the rest, including a bas-relief bust of Westinghouse and a statue of a knickered schoolboy of a half-century ago, books in hand, contemplating his role model. Beneath Westinghouse is a diagram of his first air brake, possibly the only mechanical drawing to be so immortalized. The whole memorial has a kind of solemn verve to it, creativity and dignity intimately mixed.

Panther Hollow Bridge

Panther Hollow and Schenley Bridges
Schenley Park
H. B. Rust, engineer, 1896–97

Technically the Panther Hollow Bridge is a three-hinged parabolic steel-arch bridge, 360-foot span and 45-foot rise: an arch, then, whose vertical dimension is one-eighth that of its horizontal. Four ribs carry the roadway across the

Panther by Giuseppe Moretti

ravine and Panther Hollow Lake. The stone abutments are remarkable for two features: Giuseppe Moretti's bronze sculptures of panthers on pedestals above the pavement and the mason's marks scratched into the rock-faced abutment stones so that stonecutters could be paid for the number of stones cut.

At the same time, Rust built the Schenley Bridge, a few hundred yards away, to the same basic design. Crossing Junction Hollow between Carnegie Institute and Carnegie Mellon University, the Schenley Bridge used to offer a beautiful, dramatic view of the latter. In the early 1960s it was confidently expected that Junction Hollow would be filled with utilitarian space to serve nearby institutions, but this was not carried through.

The early 1990s witnessed citizen effort to keep both bridges from the defacements imposed upon public works under repair by the muse of Liability. In the case of the Schenley Bridge the cause was lost. A wire fence rises above each sidewalk to confine the pedestrians and put them on notice that they are under suspicion.

Schenley Bridge: the architecture of suspicion.

Neill Log House
East Circuit Road, Schenley Park
C. 1790

Writers on American log architecture distinguish between a log cabin, where the logs are laid still rounded to make what was usually a temporary shelter, and the log house, where the logs were squared and carefully fitted together for durability. Here is a pioneer log house, one of the very few surviving eighteenth-century structures in Pittsburgh. A big chimney offered warmth, and a plank door and small, shuttered windows offered protection in a time when Indians were still a threat to frontier families. The roof is made of overlapping planks. This building was restored by the Pittsburgh History & Landmarks Foundation in 1968 and pioneer furnishings were provided by the Junior League of Pittsburgh.

City Historic Structure
Historic Landmark plaque

Westminster Place, Shadyside

SHADYSIDE

Shadyside stretches eastward from Oakland on land bordered by the former Pennsylvania Railroad line to the north and more or less bounded by Fifth Avenue to the south. It came into being as a city neighborhood rather slowly despite the stimulus of the railroad after 1852, but the extension of horsecar service from Oakland to East Liberty in 1874 was a help. Shadyside's existing architecture suggests that development began in earnest about 1880 and continued through the 1920s.

The Aikens were early landowners here, and in the 1850s Thomas Aiken erected a country house known as "Shadyside." The name was adopted for the local railroad station and eventually for the whole district. But the name *could* as readily have been devised to promote streetcar-suburb real estate, or been given from simple observation of the area's sylvan streets, so appropriate is it for the neighborhood that developed.

CITY OF
PITTSBURGH

Shadyside acquired associations with gracious living. A rich variety of fine houses on ample lots is found throughout the district, and there are still a few Fifth Avenue mansions from the Millionaire's Row days of the early twentieth century.

The Shadyside area's gradual change from farmland to suburban estates to a neighborhood with a surprising variety of occupation densities led to the subdivision of large old properties, and these to the penetration of the older blocks with culs-de-sac, not through streets. These culs-de-sac are not a purely Shadyside phenomenon, but there are more of them in Shadyside than in any other Pittsburgh neighborhood. The Pennsylvania Railroad, serpentining its way westward toward Skunk Hollow and Union Station, did its part by cutting off ready communications north to Bloomfield, but so did a habitual lack of accord between owners—new owners, probably, with development in mind—of properties back-to-back along Ellsworth Avenue, Fifth Avenue, and the parallel streets in-between.

Alder Street, Shadyside

The culs-de-sac vary in architectural character, in apparent luxury, but implicit in their presence is the desirability of the location they occupy, within or adjacent to the western part of Shadyside. Typically, though not always, their names end in "Place," and they contain nothing but houses: row houses, almost-suburban houses, city houses with their own fair-sized lawns. Coordinated architectural ensembles, groups with casual harmony. Materials and workmanship from the fine to the acceptable. Each of the "Places" is individual, offering its separate experience.

Fashionable shops and restaurants line a quarter-mile stretch of Walnut Street at the neighborhood's very center. But this street scene is actually no more elegant than in any other neighborhood where the shopkeepers have been struck with a mania for remodeling over several decades. In the eastern part of Shadyside, the remodeling mania has also lain heavy on houses, manifest particularly in a grudge against porches and a feeling that bricks ought to be painted: not red as they might be in less-cultured districts, but elephant gray, pale green, beige, or something of the sort. The removal of porches gives the house facades a curious noseless look, and the paint makes them look as if their pores are clogged.

A portion of Shadyside is situated on rising ground south of Fifth Avenue, notably the still-private Woodland Road district, hilly and full of trees with mansions and ample houses along winding roads, with Chatham College as a sort of acropolis to the west.

Fortunately, Shadyside has retained many magnificent architectural gestures: picturesque Victorian villas, handsome houses of worship, and early Modern apartment buildings. Pleasant streets abound, and Shadyside remains a green and gracious area.

The chapel of Chatham College seen from Woodland Road.

Church of the Ascension
Ellsworth Avenue and North Neville Street
William Halsey Wood (Newark, N.J.), architect,
1896–98

Wood, always interesting though not always right,
designed this Episcopal church a few years after a fantastic
submission in the Cathedral of St. John the Divine competition in New York that historians still remember. His
Gothic is infinitely tamer here although forcefully introduced by a massive black stone tower modeled after that
of a church at Wrexham in Wales. Inside, the walls are
brick, once buff, now painted, bearing a heavy wooden
roof. The Late Victorian glass is strong and warm in color.
A side chapel has a splendid, sinuously carved screen. The
blunt Gothic arches throughout the church are typical of
the 1900 period as are the rather broad, squared-off wall
masses; this may be because Richardsonian massiveness
was still appreciated even as Richardson Romanesque was
going out of fashion, or perhaps in order to dissociate
this most recent Gothic, in a Classically inclined period,
from the gaunt, sharp Mid-Victorian variety.

Historic Landmark plaque

Ellsworth Terrace
4800 block, Ellsworth Avenue
William M. Justice (?), designer, 1912

Behind two large modern works in a gaudy Victorian-
pastiche manner stand more modest housing groups
from the past, built in warm gray brick with fully glazed
ground-floor fronts and pedimented doorways.
Unpretentious taste is the result.

Historic Landmark plaque

House
4841 Ellsworth Avenue
C. 1870

Set back on a raised lawn, this is one of the most distinguished houses in Shadyside. The arcaded verandah contrasts finely with the rich red brick, and though the property is crowded by Ellsworth Terrace to the west the effect is nearly that of a Victorian Hudson River villa. In fact, it faced a country road.

First Church of Christ Scientist (now Child Development Center, University of Pittsburgh)
623 Clyde Street
Solon Spencer Beman (Chicago), architect, 1904–05

As Christian Science spread at the end of the nineteenth century, it cultivated an image of sober good taste that resulted in a collection of Classical churches, undemonstrative but appealing through the high quality of their design and execution. This medium-sized work in Greek Ionic on a residential side street has the respectability the controversial sect wanted, the dignity and large scale appropriate to a public building, and yet the tact not to overwhelm the houses near by.

Historic Landmark plaque

Ferguson house
705 Devonshire Street
C. 1890

This is a rather energetic piece of Richardson Romanesque, notable especially for the porte-cochere and its upper chamber with a stylistically impure Palladian window. The high-and-low coursing of the stonework shows that it is bonded to a humbler backup material.

W. L. Jones house
803 Devonshire Street
Brandon Smith, architect, c. 1925

Harvey Childs house
718 Devonshire Street
Peabody & Stearns (Boston), architects, 1896

This is Colonial Revival work from a time when increasing formality was setting in. Yet this is an 1890s house, not a Georgian imitation. The detailing is rather heavy as the period liked it, the warm gray Roman brick was a modern material, the window sash is a Late Victorian compromise of modernity and quaintness, multi-pane over single-pane. The gambrel roof is New England, but the doorway seems to recall Mount Pleasant in Philadelphia. It was too soon to take Pittsburghers' porches away, but the dignity of the front was preserved by setting the porch at the south

A pleasant, carefully detailed English Gothic house of limestone and tawny brick. The breadth of the house and its slight recession from the street give the approach area the air of a forecourt more than a front yard; the house quietly dominates its particular setting on the street rather than being merely isolated in a yard as are most Shadyside houses.

end of the house, balancing a porte-cochere to the north.

The house is best known as the residence of the Chancellor of the University of Pittsburgh.

Historic Landmark plaque

Rodef Shalom Congregation
Fifth and Morewood Avenues
Henry Hornbostel of Palmer & Hornbostel (New York),
architect, 1906–07

Hornbostel designed two synagogues for Pittsburgh of
which this Reform temple is the earlier and the better
known. There is no specifically Hebraic architectural
tradition, and most architects of the early twentieth
century faced with the problem of a synagogue would
have either adapted Islamic motifs or have treated it as a
Classical public hall. Hornbostel was more original. Using
his favorite materials, cream-colored brick and terra cotta,

he created a compact,
massive structure that
appears as a simple enclosure of the inner spaces.
To dramatize the skyline
of the building, yet
emphasize the space
within, he covered the
temple itself with a great
Louvre dome of cream-
colored terra-cotta ribs
and green roof tiles.
To enliven the brick wall
surfaces, he inserted bands
of terra cotta that serve
as well to tie together
details that might other-
wise have seemed to drift
in such large plain areas.
At the entrance he made
early use of polychrome
terra cotta—the glazing
technique had recently
been developed—in frames with mingled geometrical
and leaf ornament, and over the central doorway he put a
pediment with a menorah against a stained-glass window
of leaping flames.

Inside, beneath a Guastavino tile vault with a large
central skylight, Hornbostel designed a quietly sumptuous
interior of mahogany and gilt, focused on an ark in the
Ionic order. Lit from above by the skylight, which is
framed by lightbulbs, the
temple is also lit by six
stained-glass windows and
blue-and-gold chandeliers.

Rodef Shalom has
served two purposes well:
as a dignified place
of worship and as an
ornament to an elegant
neighborhood.

Temple skylight

National Register of
Historic Places
Historic Landmark plaque

Hillman house
5045 Fifth Avenue
E. P. Mellon, architect, 1924–26

A skeptical look at this house, its proportions especially, suggests its origins. For all practical purposes this is a house of the 1920s, but the Second Empire style of a half-century before haunts the design, with reason. It began in the late 1870s as a mansion, stiff and symmetrical and made of red brick, for a James Rees: probably the prominent boat- and engine-builder whose works were on the Allegheny River near the Point. In 1919, John Hartwell Hillman, Jr. bought the property and commissioned Benno Janssen to design a wholly new house. Janssen produced a number of sketches, but eventually Hillman decided to remodel the house already on the site. E. P. Mellon, architect for such Renaissance buildings as the Forbes National Bank and the Falk Clinic, cased the old house in limestone, covered the mansard roofs in extravagantly irregular slates that speak of the peasant rather than the aristocrat, and added a matching wing. The new style was one of those fusions that a good Eclectic architect could attain, coolly French in the overall impression, British in specific details, eighteenth-century in any case.

Inside, trim and ornament of the Victorian interiors were retained, even copied in new spaces; this was heresy in the Eclectic period, but such heresies do crop up now and then.

The house is now a condominium.

Moreland-Hoffstot house
5057 Fifth Avenue
Paul Irwin, architect, 1914

The three fronts of this house that are visible from Fifth Avenue are executed in white terra cotta in a Louis XIV style: a reduced version of McKim, Mead & White's "Rosecliff" at Newport, Rhode Island, and more remotely a mixture of themes from the Palace of Versailles and the Grand Trianon in the Palace grounds. The driveway entrance has a metal-and-glass domed marquee, however—an amenity decidedly of the early part of this century. The Hoffstots purchased the house in 1929, and the rooms remain much as they were in the 1930s.

National Register of
Historic Places
City Historic Structure
Historic Landmark plaque

Gwinner-Harter house
Fifth and Amberson Avenues
C. 1870; Frederick J. Osterling, architect for remodeling, 1911;
restored 1986, 1996

This is one of the oldest survivors of the old Millionaire's
Row in this area; only "Willow Cottage" at Chatham
College is older. It was probably built for William B. Negley,
whose presence at this location is noted in an 1871–72 city
directory. The 1911 expansion and enlargement for the
contractor Edward W. Gwinner brought the grand first-
floor interiors of marble, varnished wood, and richly
figured bronze into being. The big Second Empire house

is surrounded by well-
tended grounds. An early
twentieth-century porch,
characteristically double-
columned in a way that
removes some of the air
of flimsiness single
columns so widely spaced
would have had, opposes
a strong horizontal to the
nervous verticality of the
original front. Second
Empire, at the height of
its fashion in the 1870s,
was much despised four
decades after, and the "new" porch at least mitigated the
annoyance of its continuing presence.

The house lost its roof to fire in 1986, just as it was
approaching a full restoration. The house remained vacant
for almost ten years, but fortunately was then purchased
and restored. The present front porch and the roof date
from this restoration of 1996.

McCook house
Fifth and Amberson Avenues
Carpenter & Crocker, architects, 1906

A typical Rich Man's House in the Elizabethan style
popular at the turn of the century. It has the besetting
vice of domestic architecture of this period, a compulsion
to make every few feet along a facade different from all
the rest as if repetition were evidence of artistic laxity.
Yet it has some good points too: the use of plain, smooth
lintels and transoms that maintain the integrity of the
wall despite such a variety of openings; the framing of
the right-hand bay window with paired Tuscan columns,
which creates a pleasing puzzle as to where the wall is
supposed to have gone; and the frisky stringcourse above
the second-floor windows that jumps over a third-floor
opening and down again.

Shadyside Presbyterian Church
Amberson Avenue and Westminster Place
Shepley, Rutan & Coolidge (Boston), architects,
1889; additions, 1892 and after; Wilson Eyre & McIlvaine
(Philadelphia), architects for alterations to interior, 1938

H. H. Richardson's successor firm designed this church, and its form and detailing reveal the level of competence to which the master, then three years dead, had brought his office. This is a "lantern" church, probably the first in Pittsburgh. It was modeled after Richardson's own Trinity Church in Boston of some fifteen years before, and itself inspired a number of local imitations. The interior is basically a preaching space, yet the architects wanted to avoid the old-fashioned, box-like meeting-house plan. The solution was to provide broad and very short nave and transept arms beneath a huge central lantern. The transepts, rather than accommodating altars as they might have in the Middle Ages, thus became part of the principal space and their gabled fronts varied the outline of the building and gave visual support to the lantern with its great pyramidal roof. Whether anyone realized it or not, the blunt cruciform plan recalled that of some of the early Western Pennsylvania log churches, where transepts added space while giving structural stability.

The interior was entirely remodeled in

1938, in a blander Romanesque than that of the exterior. The sanctuary terminates in a niche-like apse, with a figure of Christ in gold and colored mosaic by Rudolf Scheffler.

National Register of Historic Places
Historic Landmark plaque

Double house
5023–25 Castleman Street
1890s

A double house is given a triangular facade composition by two spreading Ionic porches and twin central pediments. The style is very approximately Queen Anne, executed in a deep-red brick, and the porches may be substitutions from a later period for more ornate originals. Whether this is so or not the results are very pleasant: a quiet building in a quiet street. The fact that the porches have no railings—are porticoes, in fact—allows them to assume the role of intermediary spaces between the private spaces of the interiors and the public spaces of the street, making the houses seem accessible and welcoming.

imitating the effect of thatch. The inhabitants got their porch despite its un-Englishness, tucked in under the end roof and looking toward Amberson Avenue. The house walls are of reinforced poured concrete.

Amberson Place
700 block, Amberson Avenue
1910

Amberson Place is a little over 400 feet long, with fourteen lots, and of these the Brown, Hunt, and Chandler houses and "The Homestead" are worthy of individual attention. Like Pitcairn Place, Amberson Place has a variety of architectural styles.

Hunt house
5050 Amberson Place
Maximilian Nirdlinger, architect, 1913

While this house has Classical symmetry and even Classical columns, it experiments with varied window proportions, sunken panels, and an unconventional entrance porch. It is an exact contemporary of Frederick G. Scheibler, Jr.'s Highland Towers elsewhere in Shadyside, and like that apartment house suggests a period of experimentation (that was not to last).

L. E. Brown house
704 Amberson Avenue
Edward J. Weber, architect, 1913

Weber, known best as an architect for the Catholic Church, here turned his fancy to a domestic program, which was expressed as an English farmhouse, more or less. The shingled roof, it will be noted, has rounded edges

"The Homestead"
5020 Amberson Place
C. 1864

The Italianate villa of David Aiken, Jr., manufacturer and member of a family with extensive land holdings in Shadyside, survives among buildings sixty or seventy years newer.

Chandler house
5016 Amberson Place
Janssen & Cocken, architects, 1924

This not-very-large house is obviously intended as a terminal feature for Amberson Place, and its rusticated Florentine entrance arch—very like that of the contemporary YMWHA in Oakland—is a conspicuous terminal feature, a little showy for a house but appropriate for ending a short vista.

Macbeth house
717 Amberson Avenue
Bartberger & Dietrich, architects, 1884

In its interaction of verticals and horizontals, its folding and extension of planes in a roof that a chimney seems to skewer down, this house seems to reveal some of the sophistication developing on the East Coast, especially in using the Shingle Style.

Spencer house
719 Amberson Avenue
George S. Orth, architect, 1886

Here is an early work by an architect who later was to have a distinguished practice. Colonial Place in Shadyside and "Wilpen Hall" in Sewickley Heights have a refinement not yet to be seen here, yet the house has strong associative value. Ethel Spencer, in *The Spencers of Amberson Avenue*, tells the story of her family: herself, her father who was in Henry Clay Frick's middle management, and all the others who managed to crowd into the house: a family plus nine servants.

Acheson house
5131 Pembroke Place
MacClure & Spahr, architects, 1903

This is a pleasant Tudor design in white terra cotta and warm-red brick: unpretentious, orderly, without the would-be picturesque features that obscured the designs of many Tudor houses of the 1910 period. The famous critic Montgomery Schuyler, in a series of articles on Pittsburgh in 1911, chose this house as a good example of East End architecture. At the time it was owned by M. W. Acheson, Jr., a member of a family group that had settled in the immediate area.

Hasson house
5211 Pembroke Place
1906

A curious variant on the Tudor theme, hard and crisp in its window bays of red brick and bold in its cantilevering of the timber porch roof from two entrance piers.

Von Lent Place
5200 block, Pembroke Place
1905

The intention here, as with other "Places" in Shadyside, was to sell spare land to the best advantage. An 1899 atlas shows a north-south Pitcairn Street on paper that never materialized and a sketched-in westward extension of Elmer Street that never happened either; each might have obviated the need for Von Lent Place: which would have been too bad, for it is a very pleasant little inlet with a half-dozen large red-brick houses.

Abbett and Marshall houses
918 and 920 St. James Street
C. 1860

These are two of the best-looking houses in Shadyside, both clad in boards and battens. The left-hand house is more Romantic in tone with its steep roof and high-set dormers—a little like the eighteenth-century Neville house, "Woodville," that survives in Collier Township. The other house is Italianate. Both compose well together.

Spinelli house
5302 Westminster Place
C. 1865 and later

Mid-Victorian board-and-batten and Late Victorian shingles, diamond window panes, gables, dormers, and window bays in a not-very-big house do not make for architectural repose, but they do suggest an eventful history of habitation.

Minnetonka Building (Wefing apartment house)
Walnut and Copeland Streets
Frederick G. Scheibler, Jr., architect, 1908

This is a Scheibler commercial and apartment building from three years after the very different Old Heidelberg. Two stories of cream-colored brick with clean-cut window openings rise above tapered square columns of limestone.

Few architects anywhere in the world were willingly designing city architecture with such extreme simplicity, and a considerable amount of art glass—in the doorways outside and in, and in the stair skylights—supports the cut stonework in giving the impression that parsimony was not the cause of this general plainness. The curved

corner windows, too, imply an experiment in new, pure forms. Calling attention to a rounded corner, and even putting windows in it, suggests Viennese Secession architecture of this time.

The eight apartments are largely in the original condition, with marble-and-brass gas fireplaces with inset ceramic designs.

Third Presbyterian Church
Fifth and South Negley Avenues
Theophilus Parsons Chandler (Philadelphia),
architect, 1901–03

Chandler, who also designed the present First Presbyterian Church, was one of those architects of wayward imagination that Philadelphia produces every now and then. The supreme effect in this case is inside, where the arches and struts of a cross-gabled double-hammer-beam roof leap about in all directions. The walls are lined with the same rockfaced indoor-outdoor masonry, so to speak, that is to be found in First Presbyterian, and double thicknesses of glazing create spatial ambiguity in places. The major windows are Tiffany. But the exterior, with its sinuous Flamboyant tracery, its pinnacles and gables, and its

red-and-white stonework, suggests too the work of a lively mind. Behind the church is a stately medieval hall more reposeful in design, a grandiose presence in the domestic streets of Shadyside.

Historic Landmark plaque

St. Regis doorway

Apartment house group
Maryland Avenue and Howe Street
C. 1910

Three corners of a Shadyside intersection are occupied by apartment houses, all in place by 1910. On the southeast corner is the St. Regis, with Art Nouveau detailing very similar to that of the Emerson on Alder Street. On the

The St. Regis, with the Chesapeake in the foreground.

The Chesapeake, with the Howe across Howe Street.

The Kent

southwest corner are the twinned Chesapeake and Chamberlin buildings with big bracketed cornices, a little fancy brickwork, and mildly experimental detailing in terra cotta. Across Howe Street from these are the Kent and the Howe, traditional in an unfocused way with Richardson Romanesque entrance arches and Colonial Revival flat window arches.

The Chamberlin

Kohn house
328 Morewood Avenue
1892

This is a house of truly refined simplicity, a basic gabled shape, well proportioned, with arching of certain windows, jutting shingle courses functioning as string courses, and some special patterning of shingles to enliven the composition. That is all it takes. The integration of the porch into the bulk of the house is unusual, but a good idea if ground-floor space requirements and second-floor insulation offer no problems. Some considerable time ago the whole house was painted gray, and the original entrance was altered to serve a basement garage. The original colors were probably red for the brick and the corduroy brown of creosote for the shingles.

Bindley Hardware Company (later J. A. Williams Company; now Shadyside Commons)
401 Amberson Avenue
Albion Bindley, designer, 1903

John Bindley commissioned this gravely handsome, well-proportioned warehouse from his brother, a builder. It is now residences.

National Register of Historic Places

Pitcairn Place
5100 block, Ellsworth Avenue
C. 1926

Second to Colonial Place and Amberson Place, this is the grandest of Shadyside "Places," carved out of the Robert Pitcairn property "Cairncarque." A rigid Queen Anne house yielded to fourteen lots, one of which was built on by 1928. Styles are vaguely Old World without imitating the manners of particular places and times, and the prevailing material is red brick.

Colonial Place
5141 and 5205 Ellsworth Avenue and Colonial Place
George S. Orth, architect, 1898

Edward B. Alsop, a developer, laid out Colonial Place in twelve lots. The two houses facing on Ellsworth Avenue are blocky three-storied buildings of light-brown brick with sandstone Ionic colonnades that were meant not as entrances, not even probably as porches, but rather as twin fanfares to announce the project. The remainder of the houses were designed to be lower, gable-roofed, much more informal, but spacious and gracious all the same. The integrity of the inner houses has been badly compromised, but the original intention is still apparent.

St. James Place

St. James Place and Terrace
5200 block, Ellsworth Avenue
1915

One can admit that St. James Place is not as grand, as imposing, as Colonial Place down the street, yet still find its open character very pleasant. And go further to find the pedestrian St. James Terrace, with its porches and its lawns rising from the walk, a most comfortable outdoor area, sociable yet private in a desirable proportion.

St. James Terrace

Roslyn Place
5400 block, Ellsworth Avenue
1916

Thomas Rodd, an engineer, developed a little over an acre of his Shadyside home into a development of eighteen units, single, double, and in a row of four. The results are so pleasant that inquiries about vacancies are frequent. A former resident, Allan Jacobs, has presented this as one of the "great streets" worldwide, in his book of the same name. Its wood-block pavement of 1914 has received a Historic Landmark plaque.

Historic Landmark plaque

The Everett
5420 Ellsworth Avenue
1907

We do not know the architect of this building, which derives its ornament from Modernism in Central Europe, but it is interesting to see something so unconventional so early. In this same year of 1907, Frederick G. Scheibler, Jr. was also using non-traditional detailing, and the annual exhibition of the Pittsburgh Architectural Club included numerous avant-garde designs from Europe. It was apparently a rather venturesome time, and that still rather novel building type the apartment house appeared to some developers a suitable place to apply new forms. Actually, the first-floor windows are quite tritely American, and the presence of porches suggests habits of living not readily broken.

The William Pitt and the Negley (right).

The William Pitt (now Jean Manor) and
Negley apartment houses
South Negley Avenue and Elmer Street

These two apartment houses are interesting for the ways in which they use brick. The William Pitt, built in 1912, is faced in a "tapestry" brick, heavily textured, varied in tone from a rich deep red to a blackish red, and with thick mortar joints, warm-toned and full of tiny pebbles. The doorways are surrounded by brick inlays with an outer molding of sandstone. In all, an Arts and Crafts essay. The Negley of c. 1909 across the street, is the victim of cheap remodeling, and one must imagine wooden balustrades in the archways, 8/1 window sash, and a Chinese Chippendale balustrade over the cornice. On paper, then, this was a Neo-Georgian apartment house. But the brick contradicts this orderliness. It is a rather hot cranberry red, and furthermore is frequently warped, so that each brick stands out as a distinct if occasionally grotesque entity.

Brickwork, the William Pitt

Brickwork, the Negley

The Ontario: Ellsworth Avenue front.

The Ontario and the Panama
Maryland and Ellsworth Avenues
C. 1910

The similar though not identical apartment-house blocks frame the opening of Maryland Avenue with rounded

The Ontario: Maryland Avenue front.

The Panama

corners. The corners not only flatter the side street by suggesting by their special shapes that they frame something special: they offer a pretext for creating corner windows, a feature that the architect or architects may have copied from Frederick G. Scheibler, Jr.'s Minnetonka Building on Walnut Street near by and that would have been a mildly daring, eye-catching detail at the time. The concrete entrance of the apartment house on the left includes Tuscan columns with a little quasi-Baroque trim behind them: the sort of unorthodox but not-totally-radical decorative detail that architects from Glasgow to Budapest were producing—and getting published in architectural journals—in the 1900s.

House
5960 Alder Street
C. 1890

There are many such houses in and near Pittsburgh: picturesque massing, a little craftsmanship expended on the chimneys, plain brick construction elsewhere. Usually the overall effect is a little pinched and rather unbalanced, but this double house is quite an effective composition. The porch posts must originally have had curved braces at their tops.

Highland Towers
340 South Highland Avenue
Frederick G. Scheibler, Jr., architect, 1913

Scheibler was generally inclined toward quaintness when the budget permitted, but here he produced one of the earliest, and still one of the best, works of Modern architecture in Pittsburgh. In overall massing and to some extent in its geometrical ornament it owes something to Frank Lloyd Wright, but it is far from thoughtless imitation. This is a sensitive Modernism, its strong, simple forms realized in a textured golden-brown brick, its windows glazed with small, leaded panes, its spandrels filled with geometrical designs of blue tile on cream-colored stucco. The craftsman, not The Machine, is the presence felt here, notwithstanding the clean lines and the visible concrete work in the courtyard. Once-large apartments are now subdivided.

National Register of Historic Places
Historic Landmark plaque

Emerson Apartments
6111 Alder Street
1906
Samuel N. Crowen (Chicago) (?), architect

An apartment house
that reflects avant-garde
trends in Central
Europe, though in a
stolid Pittsburgh way.
The pilasters are
crowned with sculptured
Art Nouveau impressions
of ancient theatrical
masks, and the stair
windows above the
sinuously pedimented
entrances have delicate
near-Rococo tracery.
A big cove cornice, a
hollow quarter-round
in the tradition of
ancient Egypt, makes
an emphatic conclusion
to the entire building
mass. Similar detailing is
to be found not far away,
in the St. Regis apart-
ment house at Maryland
Avenue and Howe Street.

Alder Court
6112 Alder Street
Henry M. Kropff, architect, 1913

A large Jacobean apartment house, U-shaped in plan, of
light-brown brick with terra-cotta detailing. The detailing
is not original at all, yet there is a pleasant home-like
quality about the building, formed as it is around a garden
court. The scale is domestic; the tenants are domiciled, not
merely stacked as they are in so many apartment houses.

Historic Landmark plaque

Captain Alfred E. Hunt Armory
324 Emerson Street
William G. Wilkins Co. (?), architect, 1911; 1916; 1921

Repeated Doric pilasters lend a magnificence, and yet
delicacy as well, to a Pennsylvania National Guard artillery
armory that has as its neighbors the Alder Court apartment

house and Sacred Heart Church. The great length of the building is broken up by many closely spaced verticals, and the scale is so ambiguous that one is pleasantly unclear whether this is a big building trying to look small or a small building trying to look big. Either way it is a dramatic feature of a quiet neighborhood street.

National Register of Historic Places

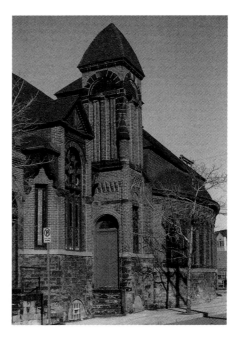

Shady Avenue Presbyterian Church (now Shady Avenue Christian Assembly)
Shady Avenue and Aurelia Streets, Shadyside
C. 1890; annex, 1911

This bright-red church mixes Queen Anne and Romanesque, so that a pediment with a fan-motif tympanum rides over a Dutch neck gable, and that above rock-faced round arches. There is an element of the fantastic about the results, to say the least, and in that way it is very effective. The boxy 1911 annex on Shady Avenue contributes to the mix with battlements and a metal-and-glass marquee.

Calvary Episcopal Church
Shady Avenue and Walnut Street
Ralph Adams Cram of Cram, Goodhue & Ferguson
(Boston Office), architect, 1906–07

Cram was justly proud of the crossing tower of this church, which bears the most successful spire in the city. The general style is Early English, English Gothic of the early thirteenth century, but as creatively reworked by an architect who perceived Gothic as a living style and a natural expression of the Christian religion. It should be compared with the nearly contemporary First Baptist Church, in

Oakland, by Cram's partner Goodhue. The personalities of the two men, eventually to go their separate ways, are evident in their buildings: Cram the idealist, seldom brilliant but always good and certainly getting his convictions across; Goodhue the artist, using the challenge of a church commission to exercise his compositional wizardry.

The interior has a rather plain nave leading to a crossing with a lantern that has squinches to support the diagonal faces of the spire. Beyond is a splendid chancel with an internal arcade a few feet within the clerestory windows, so that there is a rich play of color and space above the handsome, finely carved oak of the choir stalls. The effect is welcoming.

Historic Landmark plaque

Detail of font

Sacred Heart Church (Roman Catholic)
Shady Avenue and Walnut Street
Carlton Strong, architect; completed by Kaiser,
Neal & Reid, architects; 1924–53

In its squared-off corner buttresses, its segmental pointed
arches, and its segmental-arched doorways caught between
flanking masses, this church shows the influence of
Bertram Goodhue, architect of the First Baptist Church
in Oakland. Inside, an unusual and powerful timber roof
leads to an east wall painted in muted patterns. There is

Chapel of the Blessed Virgin

much grisaille glass, and an unusual font that is more or
less Art Deco. All in all, this is a very effective interior.
A chapel to one side, in fourteenth-century English
Gothic, has vaulting bosses in the form of brightly
painted escutcheons.

Historic Landmark plaque

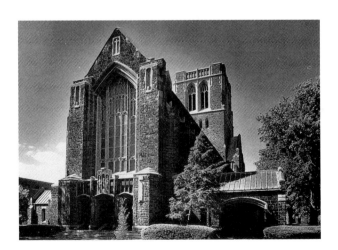

Sellers-Carnahan house (later rectory, Calvary Episcopal Church)
Shady Avenue and Walnut Street
1858 ?

This red-brick house, although now painted, gives a good idea of an early East End mansion. It shows the casual attitude to stylistic purity that the Victorians had; the composition is informal to a degree that seems to call for Gothic detailing—and indeed all the gables once had vergeboards and pinnacles. Yet much of the detailing is Italianate, with characteristic traceried window sash in round-headed windows.

The interior is very spacious, with signs of 1880-period remodeling: parquet floors with polychrome tile borders, new newel posts, and stained glass in the Anglo-Japanese taste.

Built by Francis Sellers, this was one of the first mansions in the area, whose settlement was encouraged by the opening of rail service from the Triangle in 1852. It originally stood on a ten-acre estate.

National Register of Historic Places
City Historic Structure
Historic Landmark plaque

Montgomery house
424 Shady Avenue
1877

This late the Italianate persisted, easy style that it was. The rather narrow windows and porch bays are typical, while the central pediment and forward break represent the first stage of elaboration beyond the simplest form.

House
424 Denniston Street
C. 1892

Traces on the front porch, the tower, and the chimney indicate a large wrap-around porch now removed. For the rest, the house is a blithe mixture of Queen Anne, Shingle Style, and Colonial Revival, not uncommon in the early 1890s when fashions were changing.

McClelland house ("Sunnyledge"; now Sunnyledge Inn)
Fifth and Wilkins Avenues
Longfellow & Harlow, architects, 1886

This is as nearly a Richardson house as is possible without origin in a sketch by the master himself. Its principal designer was Alexander Wadsworth Longfellow, who until earlier in 1886 was in Richardson's office with considerable design responsibility. The house is a remarkably economical, succinct work externally, with only a little special brickwork bonding and a quarter-round edging of the main doorway arch as detailing. The simple, strong shape in brick is full-blooded Richardsonian designing, visible in the last works of the master, such as Emmanuel Church in Allegheny or the railroad station in New London, Connecticut: datable by an expert no doubt, but "beyond fashion" as James Van Trump has said of Emmanuel.

   The house was built for James H. McClelland, a homeopathic doctor whose office was in the corner tower beside the patients' entrance. The interior is fully paneled in most of the ground-floor spaces, but a lavish carved and spindled stair dominates the scene with detailing that recalls stairs in Richardson's Glessner house in Chicago (1885–87) and, more remarkably, the balusters in the Colonial Vassall-Craigie-Longfellow house in Cambridge, Massachusetts.

   "Longfellow & Harlow" was a short-lived name for the firm, used while Frank Ellis Alden fulfilled his obligations to Richardson's successor firm Shepley, Rutan & Coolidge.

City Historic Structure
Historic Landmark plaque

Berger house (now Shadyside Bed & Breakfast)
5516 Maple Heights Road
1904

Polygonal gray stonework with a little cut-stone trim give this house its special effect. There is no particular attempt at symmetry or formal organization, and no claim to a stylistic label. "Arts and Crafts" is as near as one can come.

Woodland Road

Between Fifth Avenue and Wilkins Avenue is a hilly, wooded area, privately owned including its roads, that has escaped intensive development. Some of the land is owned by Chatham College (originally, Pennsylvania Female College; later, Pennsylvania College for Women), which began in a mansion (now gone), built an academic complex on a high knoll, and then absorbed other mansions that had gathered in the area. Mansions, near-mansions, and comfortable homes from the Eclectic period, the time of real wealth, appear along the winding roads almost casually, and there are important modern houses here as well. But the true glory of Woodland Road is its verdant landscape, which envelopes and creates a setting for its architecture.

Historic Landmark plaque

Darsie house
5850 Fifth Avenue
C. 1910

This house is distinguished for the quality of its stonework: the way in which excellently scaled rubble plays off against flat lintels, belt courses, and jambstones. As tended to happen in houses of some pretense at this time, the porch is not abandoned but rather put to one side. The front toward Woodland Road is a little lacking in repose, but the porchless Fifth Avenue front shows the stonework to the full.

"Willow Cottage" (also Howe-Childs Gatehouse, later Gateway House, Chatham College)
Fifth Avenue and Woodland Road
C. 1860

This, the oldest surviving element of Fifth Avenue's "Millionaire's Row," was the gatehouse of the estate of Thomas Howe, whose main house was replaced by "Greystone." "Willow Cottage" is not the typical gatehouse; it is large, and well-enough outfitted that members of the Childs family, relatives of the Howes, lived here at the turn of the century. The style may have been considered Gothic, or possibly Swiss, in Mid-Victorian times. In any case, it remains a charming feature of a street that has lost too much of its old character, and a promising introduction to the park-like area of academic buildings and mansions beyond.

The house has been privately owned since 1988.

City Historic Structure

Howe Springs
Fifth Avenue opposite South Highland Avenue
C. 1910

This little reinforced-concrete temple, now unused, once gave access to water from springs that ran through the Howe estate on the hillside behind. The triple outlet, long dry, was a welcome stop for cyclists and passersby on summer days, who could enjoy not only a long drink of water but some shade.

"Greystone" (later Benedum Hall, Chatham College; now Benedum Mansions)
East Woodland Road near Fifth Avenue
W. H. Vantine, architect, 1911–12

This was the mansion of Michael Late Benedum, a famous entrepreneur in the oil business who had bought the old Howe estate and razed its Gothic main house. While the inside, now converted into apartments, contains ornate interiors in the styles of seventeenth- and eighteenth-century England, the exterior is rather homely, an expanded version of a middle-class house. A five-bay porch

with doubled Tuscan columns precedes a front with two bay windows beneath a dormered tiled roof. The principal block is symmetrical, but at the rear, where the main entrance is, symmetry is completely given up and windows are pierced through the stone walls wherever is handiest. The masonry imitates that of the demolished Howe house: small, squared, not perfectly regular stones laid in courses of varying heights. The cornice shows a peculiarity of the time, a return to the Victorian Italianate practice of using paired brackets of fancy outline.

The house has been divided into six dwelling units. The former lawn that plunged toward Fifth Avenue is now largely taken up with new housing.

Laughlin house (later Andrew W. Mellon house; now Andrew W. Mellon Hall, Chatham College)
Woodland Road
MacClure & Spahr, architects, 1897; enlarged after 1917

This house was built for the Laughlin family of Jones & Laughlin Steel in 1897. It was bought by Andrew Mellon in 1917 and enlarged with tennis courts, bowling alleys, and a large underground pool. Olmsted Brothers planned the grounds in 1919, elaborately. Little of this landscaping survives. It remained in the Mellon family until 1940, when it was given to Chatham College. The style is Early Tudor. An adjoining carriage house, whose roofs are much more prominent than those of the main house and whose style is less correct historically, has much more of a Late Victorian appearance today.

A view into the Frank house

Cecelia and Robert Frank house
96 East Woodland Road
Walter Gropius and Marcel Breuer (Cambridge, Mass.),
architects, 1939–40

The silhouette is International Style but the stonework of
the exterior walls and the dramatic glass-block entry of this
innovative house, designed for one of Pittsburgh's oldest
glass and steel manufacturing families, bespeak a more
detailed and richly textured building than the norm. Inside,
graceful curves soften rectilinear spaces; walls are paneled
with warm pearwood, English sycamore, and redwood,
or are travertine or stone. Breuer designed wood, fabric,
and leather furniture to express the individual character of
each room. Carpets, curtains, and other furnishings were
designed or chosen by the architects. With four levels of
living space, an indoor swimming pool, and a rooftop
dance floor, the Frank house was the largest residence
designed by the Gropius and Breuer partnership.

The study

Darcy's and Kimberly's pool

The house has long served as a gallery for local artists' associations, and has become a popular institution of the city. Its location beside Mellon Park, the site of the former Richard Beatty Mellon estate, gives it an especially agreeable setting. The photograph shows the house before remodeling of the site for the Pittsburgh Center for the Arts.

Historic Landmark plaque

Bissell house
108 Woodland Road
C. 1890

In 1890 there was no Woodland Road, but one Colonial Revival house along it has been dated to 1893. Such a date seems right, too, for this accomplished work in the Shingle Style.

Marshall house (later Arts and Crafts Center; now Pittsburgh Center for the Arts)
Fifth and Shady Avenues
Charles Barton Keen (Philadelphia), architect, 1911–12; remodeling and additions, late 1980s.

Despite its hard, white stucco finish, which is not seventeenth-century, the general design suggests an English house of the Carolean period. This is so especially because of the columned doorway with its curved pediment, the tall, simple chimneys, and the hip roof with simple hip-roofed dormers. Yet it is a suggestion, not an imitation: proportions, finish, and the design of the short porte-cochere block deviate from precedent.

Highland Avenue near Jackson Street, Highland Park.

EAST LIBERTY
AND VICINITY

The tower of East Liberty Presbyterian Church marks the
traditional crossroads of a neighborhood which still has
some of the character of an independent town. Five successive churches have stood on this site since 1819 while a
farming hamlet, home of the enterprising Negley
family, first developed into a village; then, with the
completion of the Pennsylvania Railroad main line in 1852,
became a commuter suburb; and in time developed still
further, with the successive arrivals of horsecar, cable-car,
and trolley lines from the Triangle. By 1910, East Liberty,
though part of Pittsburgh since 1868, was like a city itself.
Expresses stopped at its handsome train station. Penn
Avenue was a retail street equal to those of the Triangle, in the
process of acquiring a wealth of terra cotta and tile-faced commercial
buildings and theaters. On Highland Avenue stood the new thirteen-
story Highland Building, built by Henry Clay Frick to the designs of
D. H. Burnham & Company of Chicago. Around this center were
streets of houses, apartment buildings, churches, and public institutions.

CITY OF
PITTSBURGH

West of East Liberty was the Friendship neighborhood, mainly
residential, solidly middle-class, largely Late Victorian. The two, and
Bloomfield still further west, were connected by Baum Boulevard which
already, in 1910, was becoming a gathering place for those who dealt
with automobiles: dealers, body builders, filling station proprietors.

Highland Park, on land acquired piecemeal and painstakingly by
Edward Manning Bigelow, opened to the public in 1893 and had as
notable features two large reservoirs and a zoo; the zoo was intentionally
sited here to serve as a trolley destination.

South Atlantic Avenue in Bloomfield

At Sheridan and Wellesley Avenues in Highland Park.

By 1960, the business center of East Liberty had declined, and much of the local civic energy had vanished. With local approval at the start, planners ruthlessly applied urban renewal in the late 1960s: a circular road around the business center, pedestrian malls, new street furniture, the conventional devices of the time. The Pittsburgh History & Landmarks Foundation opposed these remedies, which attempted to suburbanize what was really a "downtown" area and broke up familiar patterns of human activity. The new plan was, in fact, not a success: demolitions for the circular road exposed the plain, grimy backs of buildings and left vacant spaces; drivers were confused by the parking and traffic layouts; and the street furniture was visually ineffective. Some of the urban renewal measures were undone in the next two decades, but not before long-established businesses had failed. Today a more conservative approach is being tried, which seeks to preserve existing buildings and rebuild local morale while attracting new businesses.

memoirs, Cram insists on
the structural integrity of
the church—like many
Gothicists, he demanded
that what seemed to be
masonry construction *be*
masonry construction—
but in truth the great
tower is framed in steel
and concrete. No matter:
it is a big, glorious tower,
300 feet high, a reminder
that the often-mishan-
dled neighborhood of
East Liberty still lives.

Historic Landmark plaque

East Liberty Presbyterian Church
South Highland and Penn Avenues, East Liberty
Cram & Ferguson (Boston), architects, 1931–35

In the center of East Liberty stands this church of
cathedral dimensions, one of those colossal architectural
gifts that the Mellon family has given; this was donated
by Richard Beatty and Jennie King Mellon in memory
of their mothers.

Cram, recently delighted and inspired by Spanish
Gothic, put much of what he had learned into the church
itself, and he and his partners designed the elaborate and
adjoining church "plant" in a plain fifteenth-century style
that would not look out of place anywhere in a large part
of Western Europe. The effect, on a large Pittsburgh city
block, is of a medieval
town clustered around
its Great Church.
Though building with
Presbyterian money,
Cram had his mind on
older sects—he himself
was Anglo-Catholic—and
so designed the chancel
that at a half-hour's notice
it could be set up for a
Catholic or Anglican
High Mass, beneath John
Angel's sculptured reredos
of the Last Supper. In his

Regent Theatre
5941 Penn Avenue, East Liberty
Harry S. Bair, architect, 1914

East Liberty's character as almost an independent entity,
a commercial center with an identifiable focus and a
growing economy, lasted well into the twentieth century.
Commercial construction in East Liberty went on through
the great terra-cotta period from 1900 to 1930. At the
Regent Theatre, Harry S. Bair was not commissioned,

in 1914, to design the sort of extravagant picture palace that was common a decade later. Nevertheless, he was already designing in a genre that had matured, and he sought to attract the public with a white facade that had a polychrome frieze and, in the deep entrance, colored tiles depicting European villa scenes. Above the doors were art-glass windows.

The 1995 re-opening of the Regent as a stage theater, after many years of darkness, was celebrated as an important event in the economic and social revival of East Liberty.

This front is in glazed off-white terra cotta and has a strong vertical emphasis, but on the northern front, which originally was less visible, the treatment is much plainer though, typically of the time, there is a small amount of decorative treatment. Here, the design changes direction; horizontal bands of white terra cotta define the heads and sills of the windows in the buff-brick wall. At the top of this side wall the greater part of the cheneau survives.

National Register of Historic Places

East Liberty Market House (later Motor Square Garden)
Baum Boulevard and South Beatty Street, East Liberty
Peabody & Stearns (Boston), architects, 1898–1900

A single-story hall of about 40,000 square feet, this served as a public market until 1915 and has been used, fitfully, for spectator sports, exhibition, sales, and business purposes since. The brick is deep yellow and the dome is glazed and quite handsome in its transparency. The interior's present open character is due in part to a remodeling of the 1980s by Landmarks Design Associates Architects.

National Register of Historic Places
Historic Landmark plaque

Highland Building
121 South Highland Avenue, East Liberty
D. H. Burnham & Co. (Chicago), architects, 1910

Henry Clay Frick, besides building extensively in the Triangle, erected this building at the center of East Liberty. The Highland Avenue front shows a new evolution of the base-shaft-capital formula, though modernization has marred both the base and the upper part of the cornice. Instead of giving the uppermost stories of the building a distinctive treatment, Burnham's designers put a decorated band across the level of the uppermost story, then flared the columns outward into a coved form, almost like a vault seen in longitudinal section. The original molding in which this cove terminated is gone, as is the cheneau that once rested on it to give a scalloped skyline.

Stevenson Building
South Highland Avenue and Penn Circle South, East Liberty
W. Ross Proctor, architect, 1896

Built for the George K. Stevenson Co., a grocery that remained here until 1977, this building of sandstone and golden-brown Roman brick shows in its simplified Italian Renaissance style the influence of McKim, Mead & White, New York architects who were famous in the 1890s. Little ornamented, the design is strong, simple, and refined. Its dignified corner entrance gives it the air of a small Victorian bank, not a grocery store.

Historic Landmark plaque

Nabisco Brands Bakery
6425 Penn Avenue, East Liberty
1917

The earliest factories in the United States looked like slightly overgrown schoolhouses, complete with belfrys for summoning the employees. Mill buildings soon grew to colossal size though, and many owners sought ways of giving them polite architectural treatment. Here is such

an effort, adapted to a frame of reinforced concrete. The skeleton is clothed in red and buff brick, and strips of white terra cotta are used for accent. A rudimentary entablature, broken forward at each column, crowns the building beneath a brick parapet. The building is a familiar East End sight.

Sixth United Presbyterian Congregation of Pittsburgh (now Eastminster United Presbyterian Church)
North Highland Avenue and Penn Circle North, East Liberty
William S. Fraser, architect, 1893

With its rock-faced stone, numerous round arches, and broad proportions, this is a very convincing work of Richardson Romanesque. Unlike many other such churches for denominations that emphasize preaching, there is no big central lantern. Instead there is a spired corner tower, its upper story an octagon with four square turrets. This compositional scheme is probably derived from the towers of Coutances Cathedral in France.

Congregation B'Nai Israel (former building)
327 North Negley Avenue, East Liberty
Henry Hornbostel, with William S. Fraser, Philip Friedman,
and Alexander Sharove, architects, 1923

This very unusual design has all the massive repose usually
to be found in synagogue architecture of the early twentieth
century, yet its various elements have a mutual independence quite uncommon. A great drum of dark random
ashlar, austere and massive as if in response to the steep
hillside close behind, terminates in a blind arcade of
contrasting lightness. Above, immediately beneath the
dome, is a very original band of blue and orange asbestos
tiles in a diamond pattern, a weightless feature above the
weighty stonework. A porch of buff brick and limestone,
paraphrasing Brunelleschi's porch to the Pazzi Chapel in
Florence, shows the way into the drum. Here again is
contrast; the porch, though substantial, lacks the sense of
sheer mass found in the stone in which it is set. It has
delicate metal tie rods, and a remarkable mosaic, mainly
golden, representing the Ten Commandments.

Here is a design
executed a decade and
a half after Hornbostel
built Rodef Shalom and a
few years before Friedman
and Sharove built Poale
Zedeck in Squirrel Hill.
These two synagogues,
twenty-one years apart,
have much more in
common with each other
than with B'Nai Israel;
both are set in undramatic
residential neighborhoods,
and are light in hue and
open in character. The inference is that here the architects
wanted a simple and powerful shape that would not be
overwhelmed by the hill behind, yet wanted the building
to have a cheerful, welcoming quality too.

The interior has been much remodeled, with new
stained glass by Jean-Jacques Duval replacing the original
clear glass.

In 1996, the congregation moved to a new location in
the suburbs, and the future of this building was unclear.

Historic Landmark plaque

East side of street

Alpha Terrace
716–740 and 721–743 North Beatty Street, East Liberty
C. 1889; 1894

Rationalism is sometimes a burden in looking at architecture, and occasionally one owes it to oneself to entertain a willing suspension of disbelief. Here are twenty-five deep, narrow row houses ranged on both sides of a street, with fronts that are contrived to make them look like little castles and Queen Anne villas. Nothing could be more absurd than to take two building types that are in their nature free-standing and assemble them tightly together in seemingly casual order. Yet there is a relaxed and slightly melancholy charm about Alpha Terrace that overrides rational objections. Somehow the results are evocative; the slight elevation of the house rows above street level, the separation from the street by shallow areas of lawn and terrace, and even the slightly unkempt appearance of

West side of street

the whole place work with the facades themselves to give it a special feeling.

National Register of Historic Places
City Historic District
Historic Landmark plaque

House
6021 St. Marie Street, East Liberty
C. 1890

The remarkable feature of this otherwise-commonplace house is its heavily detailed porch, with short urn-like posts supporting tall, heavily scalloped brackets. The balustrades are made of short, thick chamfered pieces, much less delicate in effect than the typical Victorian porch balustrade. The braces in the porch frieze suggest, and possibly impart, structural strength. The style is more Eastlake than anything else, though Charles Locke Eastlake would have disowned it. An English designer, he had been agitating since the late 1860s for simple craftsman-like furniture rather than the pseudo-Rococo and vaguely Louis XIV or XVI pieces fashionable in his day. His reform designs included chamfers, turnings, and visible construction, and once his ideas became fashionable the architectural consequences were often as seen here.

Dilworth School
Collins Street and Stanton Avenue, East Liberty
Vrydaugh & Wolfe, architects, 1915

Here is a mildly "advanced" work by a conservative firm, influenced perhaps by the untraditional styling of contemporary schools in Chicago. Cream-colored terra cotta creates accents, but the bonding of the deep red brick keeps the whole surface lively. The multiple windows are explicable enough—they light and ventilate classrooms—but the relations of the smaller windows in between to auxiliary spaces is less clear.

National Register of Historic Places
Historic Landmark plaque

House
812 North Highland Avenue, Highland Park
C. 1890

Here, Richardson Romanesque and Queen Anne are mixed in a singular but effective way. The partial blocking of windows impairs the full effect of the arches, unfortunately. The bell-bottomed look of the porch piers may or may not have been a felicitous design decision.

House
830 North Highland Avenue, Highland Park
Frederick C. Sauer, architect, 1891

Although not a very well-composed house, this upper-middle-class residence is attractive both as an expression of stone and because of its carved detailing. The porch columns are of stone quite as vigorously textured as the walls and in fact appear as gangling stacks of slightly bulging drums, while the walls are of a random ashlar that creates a pleasantly diversified pattern of large and small rectangles. The carved ornament contrasts with this ruggedness: delicately cut capitals on the porch columns and a rinceau, a sort of continuous vine motif, above the bay window in front. The kneelers at the bottoms of the front gable copings are lions, in repose yet watchful.

Coleman apartment house
136 Mellon Street, Highland Park
Frederick G. Scheibler, Jr., architect, 1907

Time has not been kind to this little apartment house, which among other things has been painted blue, but it reveals Scheibler taking an intelligent look at the work of the Scot Charles Rennie Mackintosh and creating a succinct composition of his own.

Elliot house
935 North Highland Avenue, Highland Park
1891

When terra cotta became a popular decorative material in the early 1890s it freed architects who wanted to experiment with unfamiliar, ornate styles. It was simply clay, modeled rather than chipped away as stone was, and was therefore much less time-consuming to shape than stone. Here, the architect has applied terra-cotta ornament to a large house in the Flemish Renaissance style. The main body of the house is symmetrical, but the arcaded porch wrapped around one corner gives it the effect of looking out toward the two streets that intersect at the property line. The original all-red look of the house is gone, thanks to the application of paint.

At the time when the house was built, its owner Robert Elliot was the City's Director of Charities.

J. Horace Rudy house
920 Sheridan Avenue, Highland Park
1901

This eleven-room, two-and-a-half story red brick and half-timbered stucco Tudor Revival house was built in 1901 by East Liberty contractor Samuel Feltyberger for J. Horace Rudy.

From the outside, the house suggests unremarkable yet comfortable solidity common to houses of its era.

However, the house is noteworthy for its superb art glass: a glass mosaic fireplace composed of some 3,200 individual pieces and twenty-nine leaded- and stained-glass windows (the inner front door window is composed of approximately 1,000 individual pieces of transparent glass) designed predominately in an Arts & Crafts or Art Nouveau manner between 1901 and 1905.

John Horace Rudy and his three brothers opened Rudy Brothers Art Glass studio in East Liberty in 1894 after they and their parents came to Pittsburgh from the Philadelphia area at the behest of H. J. Heinz. The firm achieved success with high-quality glass designs for houses, schools, churches, etc.; architect Frederick G. Scheibler, Jr. usually had Rudy Brothers fabricate his art glass designs. J. Horace Rudy, chief designer of the firm, was also influential as a teacher and mentor to stained glass artists such as Lawrence Saint and Charles J. Connick, Jr.

whole is very characteristic of the 1900 period: blocky and with a tile hipped roof. The Gothic arches themselves have the broad, low proportions favored at the time.

The house was built for Bill Woodside, a vice-president of the H. J. Heinz Company, and the transom lights over the ground-floor windows are by J. Horace Rudy.

Johnston house
6349 Jackson Street, Highland Park
Frederick G. Scheibler, Jr., architect, 1921

This is one of Scheibler's later works, a composition that balances his Modernist tendencies with his Romantic ones. The sheer white walls, stucco on hollow tile, are crisply pierced with large openings, including that at one corner for an upstairs porch. On the other hand, roofs are prominent, even a little overemphasized perhaps, as expressions of the idea of shelter. The entranceway is splayed outward to exaggerate its prominence. And the leaded glass of the windows includes delicate, random-looking plant motifs in stained glass, as if Nature had invaded spaces designed for plain clear glass.

Woodside house
930 Sheridan Avenue, Highland Park
1902

It is unusual to see a Gothic house at just this period on less than a mansion scale. This one has Mid-Victorian characteristics: a false gable to accent a porch entrance arch that itself suggests certain Gothic villa designs of the 1840s; a dormer with a heavy vergeboard; an indifference to authenticity of composition and detail. Yet the house as a

Tim house
1317 Sheridan Avenue, Highland Park
1861

This is a handsome, spacious early Italianate villa of the
form once called Cubical Tuscan. The fenestration,
especially the trio of windows of the second floor center,
gives the house a rather thin effect in general, yet the
cornice brackets are rich and vigorous. Apart from these
brackets the detailing is light, as if the restraint common
in the previous Greek Revival style were still an inhibiting
influence. Indeed, most of the windows have cambered
lintels with little brackets under them: a late Greek Revival
treatment more than an Italianate one.

This was the home of J. W. Tim, whip, cane, and
umbrella maker whose office was on Wood Street.
This was one of the new commuter villas, a mile and a
quarter from East Liberty Station.

Highland Park gate piers
Highland Avenue and Stanton Avenue entrances,
Highland Park
Giuseppe Moretti, sculptor, 1896, 1900

Though there were no monumental buildings at the main
entrance to Highland Park, the Parks Department of 1900
left you in no doubt whatever that you had arrived at a
very special place. Two great piers of clustered Ionic
columns terminated Highland Avenue in a very monu-

mental fashion. From
their tops, laurel-wreathed
women with babies waved
at you; closer to ground
level, half-dressed women
raised torches in salute;
and on the nearby balus-
trades eagles gestured with
their wings. Beyond the
gate piers were decorative
beds of flowers and grass,
centered on an ornamental
pool with a fountain, and
the embankment of the

reservoir beyond was planted in floral designs that might show stars or portrait heads.

Of this stunning display the gate piers—women, babies, eagles, and all—survive to amuse and delight the eye.

At the Stanton Avenue entrance, two sculptures of horses being tamed represent Man subduing the forces of Nature. Moretti modeled them after sculptures made for a palace at Marly, France, by the early eighteenth-century sculptor Guillaume Coustou, but the theme of the horse tamer goes back to ancient Rome.

These photographs were taken before restoration began in 1996.

Director of Public Works, a reservoir put in service in 1879, but it was through his mixture of open and stealthy land acquisition—110 transactions—and creative departmental bookkeeping that the park quietly grew. In 1895, Christopher Lyman Magee of the Fort Pitt Traction Company offered the City the Zoo that remains, much altered, and that opened in 1897. Around 1900 the park was elaborately planted, with the reservoir embankment especially planted to show the year, a portrait head, or other such images, but all that has disappeared. The elevated walks around the reservoirs, once a favored promenade, were in the early 1990s destined to look over an expanse of material intended to protect the water from skyborne pollutants.

Historic Landmark plaque

House
5906 Callowhill Street, Highland Park
Frederick C. Sauer, architect, 1893

This was a speculative house for Emil Winter, the barber's son who eventually bought the Thaw mansion "Lyndhurst" and whose sphinx-guarded mausoleum is one of the sights of Allegheny Cemetery. Sauer, best known for Catholic churches, did not have a light touch, and the overall composition is not graceful. Yet the house intrigues one by its peculiar expression of stone. The porch columns are little cylinders of black granite, and the wall surface makes absolutely no bones about being a facing. The low courses, which bond the high ones to the hidden backup masonry, are rock-faced. The high courses are smooth slabs, so that the house has a peculiarly stripey effect.

Highland Park
Between Bunkerhill Street and the Allegheny River,
Highland Park
Begun 1889

This 366-acre expanse of hill land is the result of Edward Manning Bigelow's determination that there should *be* a park. The first element pre-existed Bigelow's naming as

Park View Flats is in the foreground; 5713 is to the left.

Park View Flats and 5713 Callowhill Street
Callowhill and St. Clair Streets, Highland Park
C. 1910

This pair of apartment houses illustrates different ways of being striking. Park View Flats treats its inset porches as giant archways that give power to an otherwise unremarkable building. Number 5713 is in many ways a standard apartment house of its time, unusual only in having a stone front and a crowning split pediment that peeps over the porch roof. What distinguishes it is the builder's Baroque intricacy in handling the second-floor porch, a violation of the staid geometry that otherwise prevails.

"Baywood"
1251 North Negley Avenue, Highland Park
C. 1880; additions and alterations, 1890s

Alexander King, owner of this house, was a glass manufacturer and the father-in-law of Richard Beatty Mellon. After Alexander King's death in 1890 his widow remodeled

the rather stiff Second Empire house, adding a new wing and a broad front porch and apparently altering the windows in the tower.

Behind the house, in 1898, King's son Robert Burns King added a feature more notable than the house itself: the "English Parapet" at the edge of the ravine, a mock castle with four small stone towers and a brick keep that served as a storage space. This landscape feature, now largely disappeared, was a folly in the old English sense—an elaborate, showy construction with little or no practical purpose—and, as such, a great rarity in the Pittsburgh area.

Robert Burns King lived on at "Baywood," but promised the City in 1949 that on his death the estate would be available as a public park. He died in 1954, and the house became a teaching center for the arts and an office for the City's Department of Parks and Recreation for some four decades. It is now, once again, a private home.

City Historic Structure

Henius house
1315 Cordova Road, Highland Park
Kiehnel & Elliott, architects, c. 1918

The photograph given here shows the present condition of the house, after a fire that required extensive restoration. As built, there was considerably more decorative half-timber. Like their more eminent colleague Scheibler, this pair of architects was both venturesome in design and yet given to quaint whimsy on occasion.

Bendet house
1321 Cordova Road, Highland Park
Theodore Eicholz, architect (?), c. 1927

Eclecticism in the late 1920s used the formidable resources that had developed in the building industry to produce architecture, houses especially, of remarkably contrived quaintness. Here for instance, is a basically simple composition: a gable roof with a chimney and a projecting

entrance on one side. Yet the roof is made to curve toward the eaves and sag wearily elsewhere, and is pierced by hairpin-shaped dormers of a most unusual sort, while the little entrance tourelle bears a candle-snuffer roof as tall as the main roof. The house is executed in rubble, randomly laid brick, clapboards, and slating that is ragged on its exposed edges. The neatness of the clapboard and banded pier on the end wall seems almost a betrayal of the architect's intention to produce an image of a picturesque, time-worn cottage.

Goeddel house
1157 North Negley Avenue, Highland Park
1906

North Negley Avenue has many a hip-roofed house, but this is a peculiarly extravagant example. The style was probably considered to be Colonial—there are showy flat arches over most windows and a swan's-neck pediment over the central upstairs window—but the porch piers and the big central dormer are not to be labeled, and the dormer especially is a spirited essay in excess. The lampposts are probably additions but are in the mood of the house itself.

Alan M. Klages house
5525 Beverly Place, Highland Park
Frederick G. Scheibler, Jr., architect, 1923

This is a consciously quaint design, contemporary with the better-known Parkstone Dwellings but set in a minor domestic street among trees. The material is Wissahickon schist from the Philadelphia area, a silvery-gray laminated stone that Scheibler also used in the Harter house. The front is symmetrical, with French doors of leaded glass giving onto a terrace, but the house entrance is off to one side in a turret-like appendage where a doorway roof and a second-floor balconette encounter in a strange clash. Inside is more leaded glass, especially in doors, and a living-room fireplace with a mantel of rough colored tiles and an overmantel of stained glass fabricated, like all the glass in the house, by Rudy Brothers.

Historic Landmark plaque

House group
1123–45 King Avenue, Highland Park
1914

Despite conjecture that this trio of quadruple row houses is by Frederick G. Scheibler, Jr., there is no proof. The two stories of dormers in a rather steep roof show an original mind at work, surely, and the roof composition is in a German tradition.

Frosch house
1200 Chislett Street, Morningside
Edward B. Lee, architect, c. 1915

This was the property of the landscape architect Berthold Frosch, who had laid out Highland Park in the early 1890s. The house is set well back to the street so that its pergolaed rear terrace overlooks the valley west of Highland Park from a height of fifty feet. The length of the straight front walk and the thick piers of the entrance porch give the street front almost a ceremonial character, but the rear is asymmetrical and homely. Frosch had intended an accompanying group of houses closer to the front, but the ensemble never came to be.

Vilsack Row
1659–93 Jancey Street, Morningside
Frederick G. Scheibler, Jr., architect, 1912

Eighteen housing units stand in three groups on an embankment above the street. Wide, glazed openings alternate with solid brick walls that contain arched doorways. The crisp contrast of voids and solids, remarkable in 1912, is still fresh and enjoyable. Some unfortunate remodeling has taken place, visible primarily on the porches.

The design for Vilsack Row was used also for a row at 7124–34 Churchland Street in the Lincoln-Lemington neighborhood.

Automobile dealership
Baum Boulevard and Roup Avenue, Friendship
Albert Kahn, Inc. (Detroit), architects, 1933

A plain piece of Modernistic, but conspicuous in the crowded Baum Boulevard scene because of its corner tower: a simple but bold touch like this sometimes enlivens an otherwise-drab area. A pulsating light originally appeared in the tower after dark. Baum Boulevard and Beatty Street, which crosses it, have been home to automobile dealers, and in earlier days to parking garages and automobile body builders. This was a Chrysler sales and service building.

Friendship School
Friendship Avenue and Graham Street, Friendship
Charles M. Bartberger, architect, 1899

Here is a school in the gently sad Classical style found elsewhere in Pittsburgh institutional architecture, the Allegheny Observatory for instance. The materials are a light-brown brick and a warm pale-gray terra cotta, the latter used to execute a Composite order as well as surrounds to all the windows. There is a slight lavishness to the treatment, and yet an air of dignity, that is found for instance in the contemporary work of the New Yorkers McKim, Mead & White. There is a quiet charm about the building, to which its open setting contributes. The broad front windows are the result of an early remodeling.

National Register of Historic Places

the North Side is a sister church in a way; both congregations worshiped in the original Christ Methodist Church until it burned in 1891.

Historic Landmark plaque

Christ Methodist Church (now First United Methodist Church)
Aiken Avenue between Centre Avenue and Baum Boulevard, Bloomfield
Weary & Kramer, architects, 1891–93

This is a very large and conspicuous Richardson Romanesque "lantern" church, whose principal massing is a broadened and simplified version of Richardson's own Trinity Church in Boston. The geometrical power of the basic church, however, is complicated by the entrances and the little arcades at ground level; these are added onto, rather than integrated with, the main body of the building and in themselves are over-assertive. Yet the overall boldness of the design and the siting make this a landmark of the most literal sort.

Calvary United Methodist Church in the Allegheny West area of

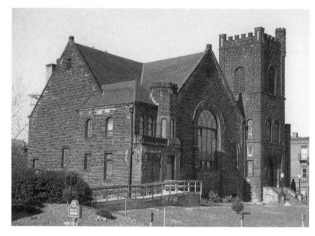

First Evangelical Church (now Albright United Methodist Church)
Centre Avenue and Graham Street, Bloomfield
After 1890

In Christ Methodist Church, one branch of the denomination built grandly under a conspicuous roof. Chance eventually led other Methodists to a humbler church within the same block. The soot-blackened Romanesque church is a common Pittsburgh sight, and there are more sophisticated ones around, but this does have a certain presence, set back and slightly elevated as it is.

House
5510 Centre Avenue, Bloomfield
C. 1870; remodeled c. 1930 (?)

On a 1923 atlas appears a cruciform house separated from Centre Avenue by a shallow lawn. Somewhat later the house, a Second Empire villa of perhaps the 1860s, underwent strange mutations. Two shop blocks were built in front of it, one quoined, one crenelated. Then or at a later time, the villa became more villa-like despite its restricted view, with an arcade, a horseshoe stair, shrubs, and Classical decoration as elements of a bouillon-cube version of a gracious landscape.

Fourth United Presbyterian Church (now Greater Pittsburgh Christian Temple)
South Pacific and Friendship Avenues, Bloomfield
C. 1895

Here is Richardson Romanesque, often found in Pittsburgh churches, but of a special sort. The arcaded entrance front with a flanking turret is derived, not from Richardson's churches but from the libraries that he designed for various small New England communities. The big apse-like feature is an Akron-plan Sunday-school arrangement, with classrooms around a central space. The alternation of high and low stonework courses indicates that the stone is a facing: the low courses go into back-up brickwork to anchor the higher courses, which are only a few inches thick. The same treatment is visible on the exterior of the Courthouse. The forms have a telling effect, and the big rounded wall, although so simple in treatment, is the most effective feature of all.

Henry Lynch house

Ursuline Academy (now Victoria Hall)
201 South Winebiddle Street, Bloomfield
1867 (?); Carlton Strong, architect for chapel, gymnasium,
and sisters' residence, 1913; additions, 1926

Here is an attractive little academic group centered on a
mansion of the 1860s, used as a convent and school after
1893 and now a neighborhood center. Winebiddle Street
is one of the pleasantest in Pittsburgh, and this is its most
interesting feature. The Second Empire house, originally
built for Henry Lynch, is the nucleus of the group. It has
a rather bristling effect alongside the quieter medieval
forms of the other units, but the contrast is certainly
not discordant.

At the south end of the property stands a plain but
handsome Stick Style house, and at the center a small
chapel of 1913 by Carlton Strong: one of the earliest works
of Catholic architecture in the city to show the simplicity

Chapel

and refinement that Ralph Adams Cram and Bertram
Goodhue had introduced to American church design.

The old mansion now is occupied by Ursuline Center,
Inc., a social service agency, and Victoria Hall, an entertainment and conference center.

City Historic District
Historic Landmark plaque

Woolslair Elementary School
Fortieth Street and Liberty Avenue, Bloomfield
Samuel T. McClarren, architect, 1897

This orange-brick hip-roofed building suggests a relaxation from the rather compulsive picturesqueness of some
slightly earlier Pittsburgh schools that are all now gone.
The Romanesque has segued here into a mildly Classical
manner—including Palladian windows and balconies on
Renaissance consoles—and instead of a tower there are
two-storied bays with semi-independent roofs. In the
coming century the roofs, apart from a token gable or
pediment here and there, would be kept out of sight.

National Register of Historic Places

McPherson Boulevard near Linden Avenue, Point Breeze.

THE EASTERNMOST NEIGHBORHOODS

Neighborhoods of differing character lie at the eastern border of Pittsburgh. The neighborhoods north of the old Pennsylvania Railroad main line are densely developed and modest, but not without episodes of architectural distinction. Two impressive displays of bridge architecture cross Washington Boulevard in the ravine between Larimer and Lincoln-Lemington; and the latter neighborhood has two of the city's lesser-known architectural gems—Engine Company Number Thirty-eight and Lemington School—along Lemington Avenue. Homewood has the large and handsome Holy Rosary Church of Ralph Adams Cram, but it is basically a neighborhood of simple row houses.

CITY OF
PITTSBURGH

In Point Breeze, south of the railroad, spacious planning and architectural elegance prevail. McPherson Boulevard and Thomas Street were part of the Boulevard Park Plan as laid out in 1885: boulevard streets with grassy islands, lined with very substantial houses. Near by were some of Pittsburgh's greatest mansions such as George Westinghouse's "Solitude" and H. J. Heinz's "Greenlawn." These two are now gone, although the Westinghouse property remains whole as a public park and "Greenlawn" is survived by its carriage house and an elegant metalwork fence along the 7000 block of Penn Avenue. Of the great houses, only Henry Clay Frick's "Clayton" remains, very much as it was, inside and out. "Clayton" remains a large property, but 151 acres of the "back yard" became Frick Park in 1919, and an additional parcel became the site of the Frick Art Museum in 1970. Now, the Frick Art &

Historical Center includes the Art Museum and "Clayton," open to the public as a house museum.

Nor far south of Penn Avenue, Frick Park and The Homewood Cemetery break up the street pattern with a total of over 600 acres of open space. The main entrance to Frick Park is close to "Clayton" in Point Breeze, and Homewood Cemetery is considered by the City also to be within Point Breeze. To the east of this open ground, at the edge of the city, we talk of Park Place to the north and Regent Square to the south.

These neighborhoods are the particular territory of Frederick G. Scheibler, Jr., building economically in Homewood, and more luxuriously in Park Place.

Richland Street, in the Briarcliff Road area, in Point Breeze.

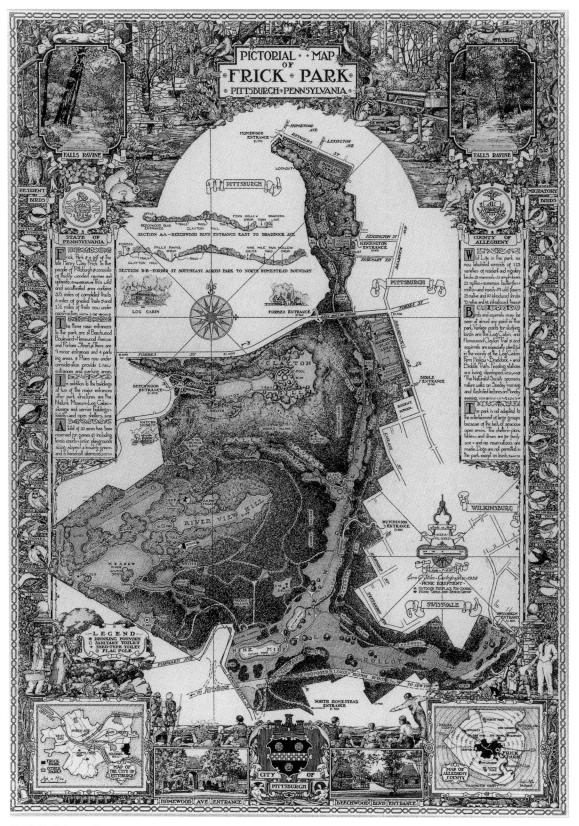

Frick Park in 1938

Larimer School
Larimer Avenue and Winslow Street, Larimer
Ulysses J. L. Peoples, architect, 1896; additions

The outstanding feature of this school was a clock tower like an Italian Romanesque campanile, added in 1904, removed again in the 1950s. Its prominence in the Larimer scene is evident in the primitive painting of Larimer Avenue Bridge (1932) by John Kane. The school was built in stages and is a mixture of design approaches from the most matter-of-fact brick construction of the 1890s, vestigially Romanesque, through Italian Romanesque, Palladian, and very simplified 1930s Classical. A richly detailed recessed entryway, which served as the base of the tower, is the most intriguing element.

National Register of Historic Places

Larimer Avenue Bridge
Larimer Avenue over Washington Boulevard, Larimer
T. J. Wilkerson of the City of Pittsburgh Department of
Public Works, engineer, 1911–12

Early in the century, interest in concrete increased sharply as its properties became understood and reinforcing systems were devised. The Larimer Avenue Bridge was an early triumph: the second-longest concrete arch in the world at the time with a span of 300 feet, four inches. Slender piers rise from the main arch to end in an arcade beneath the deck; the arches and capitals are probably both merely decorative, a concession to a public used to the masonry tradition. Such bridges continued to be built in the Pittsburgh area into the 1930s. The inherent vice they share, a readiness to decay progressively as concrete falls away to expose reinforcement, which rusts and swells, stripping away more concrete, has led to either demolition or drastic alteration in most cases.

Stanley L. Roush, then City Architect, gave the bridge handsome decorative lampposts, now gone.

Engine Company Number Thirty-eight
Lemington Avenue and Missouri Street, Lincoln-Lemington
Kiehnel & Elliott, architects, 1909

An architectural firm that sometimes did experimental
work early in the century here produced a firehouse in an
advanced manner that owes something to Continental
Europe. There seems to be no specific precedent, but the
bands of upper-floor windows and the stepped gables of
the tower suggest the Netherlands. The materials are
yellow-orange glazed brick—unusual itself—stone, and on
the tower, stucco. The doorways are not as originally built.

Lemington School
7060 Lemington Avenue, Lincoln-Lemington
Marion M. Steen, architect, 1937

A buff-brick school with Mayan-influenced terra-cotta
decorations on the projecting auditorium and gymnasium
wings and over the central classroom block. The colors
are purple, green, red, and blue on an amber background,

and the effect is out-
standing and unusual,
a testimonial to the
potential of terra cotta
as a decorative material.
This vivid exterior
has been attributed to
Edward Joseph Weber,
better known for his
religious architecture
but an occasional ghost
for other architects.

*National Register of
Historic Places*

Pennsylvania Railroad and Lincoln Avenue viaducts
East of Washington Boulevard, Larimer
*William H. Brown, chief engineer for Pennsylvania Railroad
viaduct, 1902–03; Lincoln Avenue viaduct, 1906*

Around 1900 the Pennsylvania Railroad built its bridges
of masonry rather than steel trusswork whenever possible,
thus acquiring structures that needed little maintenance
and were equal to any future loads. This viaduct was part
of a new freight line, the Brilliant Cutoff, running from
the main line to a junction at Aspinwall. The exterior is
typical engineering masonry of the time: heavy, rugged
ashlar filled with concrete. Track level was seventy-eight
feet above the now-vanished Silver Lake; five arches have
an eighty-foot span and one other arch a hundred-foot
span. Through this viaduct another has been threaded to
carry Lincoln Avenue across Washington Boulevard; this
includes two elliptical stone arches. Both make a very
impressive sight, among the last stone viaducts to be
created. A few years later, concrete would have been used,
as in the Larimer Avenue Bridge near by.

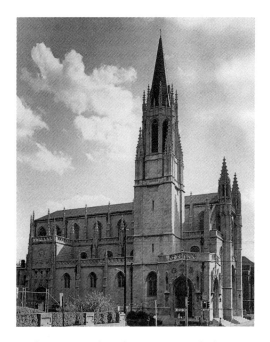

Holy Rosary Church (Roman Catholic)
North Lang Avenue and Kelly Street, Homewood
Ralph Adams Cram of Cram & Ferguson (Boston),
architect, 1928

Of Cram's three churches in Pittsburgh, this is the least known. Yet it is a large and handsome building in a kind of synthetic fifteenth-century Continental Gothic that includes a grandiose French Flamboyant rose window and broad wall areas, under a low pitched roof, that have a Spanish quality. The interior was specifically inspired by the Gothic churches of Barcelona, Spain, with tall, slender piers and high aisles beneath a relatively low clerestory.

The corner porch, with crocketed French accolades over the arches, has slightly cambered parapets to hint at gables, but the whole church has the sort of high-shouldered look that Cram always favored in parts of the city where land was exiguous: a boxy office building or apartment house next door could make steep roofs and tall gables look silly, but not such predominantly rectangular forms as these.

Historic Landmark plaque

Carnegie Library of Pittsburgh, Homewood Branch
7101 Hamilton Avenue, Homewood
Alden & Harlow, architects, 1910

The actual designer of this library was Howard K. Jones, a partner in the firm in its latter years. The detailing is of white terra cotta and the brick is red, laid up in English bond. The effect is not so vigorous as that of the earlier Classical libraries of the firm, and the Gothic suggests the style of the large new high schools then going up. The firm's South Hills High School, most likely by Jones and begun in 1916, suggests a break from this rather imitative Gothic.

Syria, Kismet, and Nelda apartment houses
7530–40 Bennett Street, Homewood
Frederick G. Scheibler, Jr., architect, 1904

Scheibler was on the verge of the Europe-inspired Modernism that gained him his local reputation. Syria and Nelda differ in treatment from Kismet between them. The ground-floor porch openings have "gunstock" stiles that allude to seventeenth-century carpentry as well as to recent Arts and Crafts practice.

Meado'cots
425–47 Rosedale Street and 7817–23 Madeira Street, Homewood
Frederick G. Scheibler, Jr., architect, 1912

Commissioned to design twenty residential units around a courtyard, Scheibler produced a design in buff brick with exposed steel beams to carry the masonry over the openings. The economy is apparent in such materials, as it is in the simplest plank vergeboards to mask the junction between the roofing and the gables, and the absence of ornament, even capitals for the porch columns. Yet gables,

chimneys, and porches individualize the units and break up the skyline and perimeter of the construction, and visible roofs with broad eaves state the theme of shelter. "Cot" is an Anglo-Saxon word for a simple home, and in itself states such a theme.

Meado'cots (only sixteen units of which were built) is not in good condition today, and it is to be hoped that the necessary repairs and maintenance will restore it to its former self.

Linwood Apartments
McPherson Boulevard and North Linden Avenue, Point Breeze
Frederick G. Scheibler, Jr., architect, 1907

The Linwood was built two years after the central part of the Old Heidelberg apartments and is similar in a number of details: the porches with tapering wooden posts above a masonry ground floor, the touches of non-historical ornament, and the openings of varying size cut neatly into the cemented wall. Here was a typical six-unit East End apartment house with its characteristic compositional problem of unifying something that in its nature is a duality, and Scheibler forced a measure of unity on the front with a pergola between the porches and a central chimney.

Historic Landmark plaque

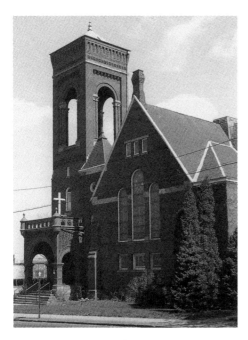

Point Breeze United Presbyterian Church
Penn and Fifth Avenues, Point Breeze
1887; alterations and additions
Lawrence B. Valk (New York), architect

Built of red brick with matching terra-cotta ornament, complex in its form, this church has something of a small-town or even rural air, with a dramatic tower to mark the crossroads where it stands. Its design has not been greatly admired, at least since the disappearance of the spire that once forced a certain unity on the numerous details through its dominance. And yet the gable fronts are well-proportioned, the ornate arcaded porch contrasts well with the plain brickwork behind, the siting is excellent, and the appearance of the sky through the tall tower arches is a beautiful sight.

Parkstone Dwellings
6937 Penn Avenue, Point Breeze
Frederick G. Scheibler, Jr., architect, 1922

After the Modernism of Highland Towers and the Minnetonka in Shadyside, Scheibler did not go on Towards a New Architecture. Like his San Francisco contemporary Bernard Maybeck, his Modernism was of an undogmatic sort, and he could on the other hand be quite pixyish at times. Here he is very much in a pixyish mood: four little doorways, separated by concrete toadstools, lead to the four housing units. Persian rugs imitated in Moravian tile seem to hang from upper porch parapets. Steep roofs of irregular slate cover everything. Inside over the fireplaces are dinosaurs, again in Moravian tile.

THE EASTERNMOST NEIGHBORHOODS

Le Roi Road

This is a pleasant little
cul-de-sac off the 2100 block
of Reynolds Street in Point
Breeze, developed apparently
in the mid-1920s and planted
with trees on a median strip.
Its climactic feature is the
Church of the New Jerusalem
(now the New Church)
from 1929 by Harold Thorp
Carswell of Philadelphia.

"Clayton"
Penn and Homewood Avenues, Point Breeze
C. 1870; Frederick J. Osterling, architect for remodeling,
1891–92; additions

In 1882, Henry Clay Frick bought a Mid-Victorian house
and a few years after entrusted Osterling with a general
remodeling. Osterling gave the Penn Avenue and a portion
of the Homewood Avenue fronts a chateau-like appearance, with steep roofs and gables, yet saved the airy original porte-cochere and left
the less visible portions of
the house alone. In these
remaining areas, simple
additions appear to have
been made later. "Clayton"
is thus not a thoroughly
conceived work of art, as
Frick's New York mansion
of twenty years later, by
Carrere & Hastings, was to
be; in the way of many
Pittsburgh mansions it
impresses the viewer with
size and sobriety, an air of
massive dignity, rather than by compositional elegance.

Other buildings were erected on the long property,
which ran 1,100 feet back to Reynolds Street; these
included a conservatory and, eventually, the Frick Art
Museum. After Frick's death in 1919, his daughter Helen
Clay Frick inherited the house and maintained it as it was
in her father's lifetime; though she lived in New York, she
visited occasionally, especially to vote. She died in 1984,
willing the house to a private family foundation as a
museum; this opened in 1990.

Beechwood Boulevard and Forbes Avenue

Frick Park
*Since 1919; Lowell & Vinal (New York) and
Innocenti & Webel (Roslyn, N.Y.), landscape architects;
John Russell Pope (New York), architect*

The park began in 1919 with the donation by Henry Clay
Frick, in this year of his death, of "Frick's Woods,"
151 acres south of the back yard of "Clayton." Acquisition

At the Homewood Avenue entrance

At the Beechwood Boulevard entrance

of further property eventually brought the total acreage
to 456. In 1931 and 1935, shelters, gatehouses, and walls
of granite-like Neshaminy stone in a rural French style
appeared at the south end of Homewood Avenue, along
Forbes Avenue, and along Beechwood Boulevard to designs
of John Russell Pope. Pope was the architect who converted Frick's New York house, a design of 1914 by Carrere
& Hastings, into The Frick Collection. In 1934, further
landscaping was added to the original, the designers being
Umberto Innocenti and Richard K. Webel. A handsome
map of 1938 shows the park in full glory, with a bowling
green (very rare in the United States), a Nature Museum,
nature-study areas, 20 acres for sports, etc. The park was
claimed to house 123 species of birds, 28 of mammals,
21 of amphibians, 22 of reptiles, butterflies and the like
unclassified, 191 of wild flowers, 25 of native shrubs, 147
of introduced shrubs, 93 of native trees, and 42 of introduced ones. This, we repeat, in 1938. In that year, a future
parking lot is shown beside two future parks in Nine Mile
Run Hollow. As with other City parks, though, maintenance has varied, and the Nine Mile Run area especially
has been long in need of cleaning up.

Frank Ellis Alden house (I)
617 South Linden Avenue, Point Breeze
Longfellow, Alden & Harlow, architects, 1890

Frank Alden designed and lived in a total of six houses in Allegheny, Pittsburgh, Edgeworth, and Sewickley, houses built between 1887 and 1904. The first, now gone, was a double; this one was the first done solely for his family. The exterior, with its imitation half-timber, looks medieval, and in fact two corbels by the doorway may be heads of Alden's wife Jessie, in youth and old age. The interior is more delicate, rather Classical, with a stair of spindles that form a screen of quasi-Japanese effect but with Colonial profiles.

In 1892 the house was moved along the street a short distance; shortly thereafter, the Alden family was living in Sewickley.

Historic Landmark plaque

Linden Avenue School
731 South Linden Avenue, Point Breeze
Ellsworth Dean, architect, 1903

This grayish-brown building is prominent in its area, a sad and gentle design that, however, violates a basic Classical principle. The recessed central wall area is divided in two by a column, in defiance of correct practice, though the open archway of the ground floor is strong enough to keep the central pavilion visually unified.

National Register of Historic Places

Section 14

The Homewood Cemetery
Dallas and Aylesboro Avenues
Incorporated 1878

The outstanding cemetery of the East End is some
200 acres in area, with some 150 of these developed thus
far. Famous names include Michael Late Benedum,
Edward Manning Bigelow, Henry Clay Frick, Erroll
Garner, George and Perle Mesta, William Wilkins, and
members of the Mellon, Heinz, Brown, Worthington,
Baum, and McCallister families. Its founding date, so long
after the 1844 of Allegheny Cemetery, deprives it of most
of the latter's extravagance of style, but it has its own
outstanding places.

The building group at the Cemetery's main entrance on
Dallas Avenue includes a gate lodge and a building that
contains a chapel, a crematory, a columbarium, and offices.
The year of construction was 1923, and the architects were
MacClure & Spahr. These have 1920s bland good taste, its
control of massing, surface, and detail, its ability not to
offend if also not to thrill. The ironwork is by the most
famous American master at the anvil, Samuel Yellin, whose
craftsmanship is also to be found in the Cathedral of
Learning in Oakland.

Elsewhere stands another notable building: a
carriage house of 1909, known as the Stable or Barn,
by Billquist & Lee.

Historic Landmark plaque

Administration Building

Gatehouse

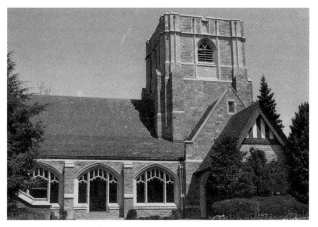

Chapel

Stable

*Worthington (Louis S. Stevens, 1919),
Section 11*

*Heinz (Vrydaugh & Wolfe, 1897),
Section 14*

*Walker (Max Bachmann, sculptor,
1913), Section 17*

Section 14, with the Brown pyramid (Alden & Harlow, c. 1907)

Schoonmaker (1910), Section 14

The Whitehall
East End Avenue and Tuscarora Street, Park Place
Frederick G. Scheibler, Jr., architect, 1906

A six-unit apartment house, with the customary Pittsburgh porches but without the usual Ionic columns. Relying on proportion for effect, the front has only one fancy touch: the entrance, with its wavering arch that may have had its source in the avant-garde architecture of Finland.

Historic Landmark plaque

Park Place School
427 South Braddock Avenue, Park Place
Ellsworth Dean, architect, 1902

This is very similar to the Linden Avenue School, with the same curious duality of composition at the center.

National Register of Historic Places

Old Heidelberg
South Braddock Avenue and Waverly Street, Park Place
Frederick G. Scheibler, Jr., architect, 1905; additions, 1908

This is one of Scheibler's best-known and largest works, and one that illustrates both his rationalism and his love of fantasy. He had a commission typical of the 1900s, to add to the rapidly growing stock of three-story apartment buildings in the East End, giving each apartment its own porch. The original structure was to have twelve units, double the usual amount.

Instead of providing the usual box with Classical ornament, Scheibler looked to the advanced pre-Bauhaus architecture of Central Europe, which often experimented with decorative detailing while retaining a Germanic partiality to high roofs. His design, mainly influenced by the Austrian Joseph Maria Olbrich, emerged as a big gabled structure, simple in its overall form and with windows cut crisply through its cemented walls. The roof plane in front descended in three places to cover projecting porch structures, the one at the center being treated as an entrance pavilion. An inset decorative tile panel and an eyebrow dormer on the center line helped the mass of this pavilion in unifying a building that otherwise would appear as two distinct elements butted together without any real cohesion. The windows, varying as they did in dimensions and placement, were prevented from setting up visual rhythms that would break up the integrity of the wall. To the basic composition Scheibler added mildly innovative ornament, including the famous toadstool relief that gives a fairy-tale effect to what is not in actuality a very fanciful design.

The cottage wings projecting toward the street, also by Scheibler, are much plainer, but their simple masses add strength to the whole composition.

Adjoining Old Heidelberg at its right end is Scheibler's house of 1909 for William C. Hoffman, so similar in treatment as often to be taken for another cottage unit.

National Register of Historic Places
City Historic Structure
Historic Landmark plaque

"Rockledge"
579 Briarcliff Road, Park Place
Frederick G. Scheibler, Jr., architect, 1910

The Briarcliff Road was a speculation of William G. Hamnett, whose own house this was. Scheibler designed a very simple house, almost archaic at first glance with its sheer walls and projecting end chimneys. Yet the exposed steel beams—used in other masonry houses by Scheibler, of course—are here particularly long and prominent, and dispel any Early American illusions.

Shady Avenue, Squirrel Hill

SQUIRREL HILL,
HAZELWOOD,
AND ENVIRONS

Most of Squirrel Hill developed late. It was close to the heart of the
enormous area annexed by Pittsburgh in 1868, but its central road,
the present Forbes Avenue, was not an important communication
route. It had no commuter rail line and no major industry,
and the passengers of the Fifth Avenue streetcar line that
passed along its northern edge had the easier alternative of a
level walk to homes in Shadyside and East Liberty, where
building land was readily available until after 1900. And
yet the steep Murray Hill Avenue, leading down to Fifth,
was popular from the time it was laid out, around 1890.
Today, for sheer picturesqueness, it is one of the most
enjoyable streets in Pittsburgh.

CITY OF
PITTSBURGH

    A population map of 1910 shows Squirrel Hill very
sparsely settled in most parts, yet at this same time conditions were beginning to change. This was due partly to new electric
trolley lines, which were built in anticipation of traffic their presence
would generate, and partly to the 1922 opening of the Boulevard
of the Allies, offering fuss-free communication with town by way of
Schenley Park. As a result, the neighborhood generally is a product of
the 1910-to-1930 period with a number of architectural and scenic
variations. Murdoch Farms, north of Forbes Avenue near Schenley Park,
is a small 1920s area of conscious elegance, with well-studied English-
looking houses among tall trees. Beechwood Boulevard, toward the
eastern edge of the neighborhood, is a broad residential street of loop-
ing turns, a showplace of the 1910s and 1920s with trees, lawns, and
flowers as a setting for comfortable houses.

    Shingle Style, Colonial Revival, and Craftsman houses appear in
many parts of Squirrel Hill. Yet if there is a typical Squirrel Hill house,
it is probably a detached house of about 1925, veneered in artificially
roughened brick and given an Old World flavor through gables, a porch

Murray Hill Avenue, Squirrel Hill.

Murray Hill Avenue near
Fifth Avenue, Squirrel Hill.

with tiny arches, and perhaps an entrance through a miniature tower. Toward Schenley Park, apartment houses also vary the scene, but quaintness at moderate expense is the common theme on most streets.

Most of Murray Avenue and the length of Forbes Avenue that crosses it are active commercial streets, places where one can go for specialty items not found even downtown as well as for the ordinary requirements of a middle-class neighborhood. The rows of shops on Forbes have broad walks with the worldly character of an esplanade, but Murray is close-built and almost East European, the prevailing Jewish heritage evident in many of the small shops.

South of Squirrel Hill and beyond Greenfield is Hazelwood, looking south and west over a great bend in the Monongahela River. Until shortly before 1900 Hazelwood was an exurb, enjoyed by villa-dwellers for its scenic views, its peace, and its pure air. In 1871, however, the Pittsburgh & Connellsville Railroad which ran along the shore became the final link to Pittsburgh for the Baltimore & Ohio, and a yard and repair shops were established. Around 1900 the Jones & Laughlin Steel Company extended its plant from the foot of Oakland to Hazelwood, installing there a large battery of coke ovens. This was before any attempts were made to control pollutants, and the air was so fouled in a short time that the nearby hillsides were stripped of plant life. The sylvan retreat, the pleasant suburb, became an industrial town. But even now it retains a few old villas and other architectural reminders of its remote past.

Forbes Avenue near Murray Avenue, Squirrel Hill.

Pergola, Heinz house
Dorset and Holyrood Roads, Squirrel Hill
1924

The Heinz house itself, visible from Warwick Terrace, is large but not especially interesting on the outside. But this pergola, built of dark red brick with raked joints, is an impressive object at the meeting of two tiny private roads.

Charles W. Baird house
1090 Devon Road, Squirrel Hill
Frederick G. Scheibler, Jr., architect, 1909

This house is a transitional work, somewhere between the early Germanic Modernism of Old Heidelberg four years before, and the geometrical yet craftsman-like Modernism of Highland Towers, four years thence. Some window heads have small visible I-beams as lintels; such a feature was often used by Scheibler, but quietly, not as a Machine Age bit of muscle flexing. Early photographs suggest simple, spacious interiors with almost nothing in the way of built-in ornament save for some art glass.

House
5427 Wilkins Avenue, Squirrel Hill
C. 1900

This is a very curious composition. From the front it looks as if the main roof is attempting levitation, while a tower nudges it from below and a polygonal dormer rides uneasily on its back. There is crude energy about the whole thing, and character.

C. K. Binns garage
1205 Murray Hill Avenue, Squirrel Hill
Kiehnel & Elliott, architects, 1915

This is not one of the firm's really progressive designs, having as it does a rather Jacobean effect with its jamb-stones and cupola. But it is interesting in having such large second-floor windows. The chauffeur would usually sleep in such an upper space, but the windows imply something for C. K. Binns himself or his family: a studio or something of the sort.

McClung house
1180 Murray Hill Avenue, Squirrel Hill
C. 1900

This is not a unique Colonial Revival house; much the same design appears elsewhere in Pittsburgh. It has associative value, though, for it was in the home of Judge Samuel A. McClung that Willa Cather lived from 1901 to 1906.

House
1175 Murray Hill Avenue, Squirrel Hill
C. 1895

The date given above is a matter of guesswork, since the house reveals a transition from Shingle Style to Colonial Revival: symmetrical on the front, a return cornice making the admittedly steep gable a pediment, the oval windows,

Palladian window, and other trim laid upon the shingled surfaces rather than being contained by them. As built, the house had a wooden porch across the entire front.

House
1171 Murray Hill Avenue, Squirrel Hill
C. 1890

This very handsome Shingle Style house must have been among the first on "Murray Hill Place," whose lots are shown unoccupied on an atlas of about 1890. The roof geometry is ample and crisp, with simple elements harmoniously assembled.

Robin Road

Murdoch Farms

Some time in the 1910s the property of James Murdoch, a raised area above Forbes and Beeler Streets, was laid out for development that was carried out through the 1920s. It was rather like a new Schenley Farms: tree-planted, pole-less, attractive for both the wealthy and the architects who ministered to them: Janssen & Cocken, Lamont Button, Ingham & Boyd, Henry Hornbostel, Alden & Harlow. A development within the development came in the late 1920s: Robin Road, with five Old World cottages, three of them stone veneer on frame, by Janssen & Cocken.

One Robin Road

House
1424 Bennington Avenue, Murdoch Farms
Lamont H. Button, architect, c. 1925

Button, assisted perhaps by Sydney Brown, designed a handsome house in a quasi-seventeenth century English manner that Sir Edwin Lutyens had previously used in Hampstead Garden Suburb. The rather high-waisted look that comes from a string course just below the second-floor windows *could* be an allusion to Prairie School design, but this seems far-fetched. The mellow red brick—Button had an excellent feeling for brick—overlies a structure of hollow tile.

5644–62 Forbes Avenue

John Worthington house (now part of Temple Sinai)
5505 Forbes Avenue, Squirrel Hill
Louis S. Stevens, architect, 1910 and 1915

Louis Stevens was an architect who handled the subtleties
of period style with great skill if not much originality.
The Worthington house is a persuasive piece of
Elizabethan design, set on a balustrade terrace a few feet
above street level with excellent stonework and ironwork.

Historic Landmark plaque

5703–39 Forbes Avenue

House groups
5644–62 and 5703–39 Forbes Avenue, Squirrel Hill
C. 1910

Two housing groups facing central courts were built a
block apart around the same time and in the same style,
the manner now called Arts and Crafts or sometimes
Craftsman. Their construction is plain, they are undecorated, there are no visible subtleties of detail, yet enough
effort has been made to create variety and picturesqueness.
The designer of the 5600-block houses, some of which are
known to have existed in 1911, is unknown, but Thomas A.
and I. K. Watkins both designed and built those in the
5700 block.

House
5605 Aylesboro Avenue, Squirrel Hill
C. 1910

Here is a house in a style not to be identified but quite common in the 1900s. It suggests the simplest kind of Victorian Italianate but is broader and more solid, and the wide span of the porch especially varies from the Victorian model, if model it was. The effect is usually solemn, yet there are the fancy touches such as the trails of husks that hang from the capitals. Such houses are not Pittsburgh's alone—they have a Midwestern feeling about them—yet an architect around 1910 said, "If a Pittsburgh man were let alone, that is the kind of house he would have."

Thomas McLaughlin house
5844 Marlborough Avenue, Squirrel Hill
Frederick G. Scheibler, Jr., architect, 1915

This white-brick house seems to allude to work of the English architect Charles Francis Annesley Voysey, particularly in the tapered buttress-like terminations of the front and rear walls.

1715 and 1717 Denniston Street
Squirrel Hill
Frederick G. Scheibler, Jr., architect, c. 1927

Scheibler is no longer the Modernist of Highland Towers in 1927, and there is no doubt that he has turned to the quaintness that had become a major trait of 1920s architecture in general. Yet his detailing in brick in these two mirror-image houses is more than merely cute. It has not the virtuosity of the contemporary Amsterdam School, but it is still brick craftsmanship to be enjoyed as something in itself.

John apartment house
2200 Wightman Street, Squirrel Hill
1922

The 1920s was a time of vigorous apartment-house construction in the part of Squirrel Hill near Schenley Park, but this is perhaps the most unusual one built. The general appearance suggests progressive villa design in Italy around this time.

Hamilton Cottages (now Beacon Gardens)
5629–79 Beacon Street, Squirrel Hill
Frederick G. Scheibler, Jr., architect, 1911

This is an extensive, conspicuous development close to Schenley Park, a composition of five ranges veneered in red brick: well proportioned, handsomely set among trees and in places with the blind cross-gables better known from Meado'cots, a contemporary development in Homewood. A little art glass is the sole ornamentation.

Congregation Poale Zedeck
Shady and Phillips Avenues, Squirrel Hill
Philip Friedman and Alexander Sharove, architects, 1928

At a time when many synagogues were in a more or less
Near Eastern style, alluding to the origins of Judaism,
Poale Zedeck held to the turn-of-the-century tendency to
create a massive Classical exterior. The architects had
worked with Hornbostel a few years before at B'Nai Israel,
and there is a certain Hornbostelian air to this building,
specifically suggesting Rodef Shalom. Here once again
are cream-colored brick, gently polychromed terra cotta,
and a big arch with a triple entrance beneath. One of the
pleasantest features is the skeletal inner archway, a
Palladian motif executed in terra cotta of Della Robbia
blue with off-white edging. Situated among trees and
houses at a slight bend of Shady Avenue, the synagogue
has a very attractive site.

Frank and Eva R. Harter house
2557 Beechwood Boulevard, Squirrel Hill
Frederick G. Scheibler, Jr., architect, 1923

Here, Scheibler adopted a practice sometimes found early
in this century: that of imitating thatch, with its rounded
verges and eaves, in another material. In this case he used
blue-green shingles laid with extreme irregularity. The
imitation thatch roof has been replaced.

Kinsman Road gate piers
At Wilkins Avenue and South Dallas Avenue entrances,
Squirrel Hill
Early twentieth century

Although a public thoroughfare, Kinsman Road, itself a
pleasant little street one block long, is distinguished by
these vivid red-brick and stuccoed piers.

House
6661 Aylesboro Avenue, Squirrel Hill
1886; remodeled 1920s (?)

Number 6661 Aylesboro Avenue is quite exceptional,
a quasi-medieval house with a sandstone bay window
that looks Mid-Victorian, though the house is in fact
from 1886. Four bands of random stonework enliven its
walls with a sort of barbaric energy, yet this is tamed by
a broad dormer and a segmental-arched porch, both
very likely added when the house was moved in 1920.
Originally it was the office and sexton's house for
The Homewood Cemetery.

though the brick masses are rather heavy and the central doorway surround seems to billow almost menacingly outward before retiring beneath the entablature.

National Register of Historic Places

St. Rosalia's Church
Greenfield Avenue and Lydia Street, Greenfield
Albert F. Link, architect, 1923

A Romanesque church in orangeish brick, by the architect best known for St. Boniface's Church on the North Side alongside I-279. At the top of the front, a miniature arcade runs beneath a slightly recessed gable: a borrowing it seems from Bertram Goodhue's recent St. Bartholomew's Church in New York.

Woods house
4604 Monongahela Street, Hazelwood
C. 1790

A forlorn-looking house in an industrial neighborhood, the Woods house is holding fast because of its simple, solid construction and the absence of any use for the land that it occupies. This is one of perhaps five or six eighteenth-century buildings left in Pittsburgh, and with proper grading around it, it would be seen as well-proportioned. Stone voussoirs over the door and lower story windows are the only ornaments.

National Register of Historic Places
City Historic Structure

Greenfield Elementary School
Alger Street near Greenfield Avenue, Greenfield
Kiehnel & Elliott, architects; design c. 1916, built 1922–23

The often-progressive architects show here much of the Prairie School influence that appears too in the Central Turnverein building of 1912. A spacious, well-proportioned main facade wears its terra-cotta ornamentation lightly,

Carnegie Library of Pittsburgh, Hazelwood Branch
4748 Monongahela Street, Hazelwood
Alden & Harlow, architects, 1900

There is no mistaking a Carnegie Library branch in
Pittsburgh, at least as designed by Alden & Harlow:
brick with a little decorative detail in stone or terra cotta,
a massive look, crisp geometry, and banded windows.
As built, the Hazelwood Branch had a Roman dome on
an octagonal drum: the only branch in Pittsburgh to have
such a feature.

Episcopal Church of the Good Shepherd
Second Avenue and Johnston Street, Hazelwood
William Halsey Wood (Newark, N. J.), architect, 1891

The smallest of Halsey Wood's three buildings in the
county, Good Shepherd has an artfully rustic expression.
An industrial town has grown around it, yet with its low
walls of rubble and dark-red brick, its prominent roof, and
its much-louvered, shingled little tower it announces itself
as a simple country church. Such a quality of sophisticated

humility, a practice of rejecting pompous gestures and
ornamental displays in favor of plain materials and
vernacular forms—yet composing these with a very
knowing eye—had begun early in the Romantic period
and would persist far into the twentieth century.

Historic Landmark plaque

once, into something almost beautiful. The buttresses of the tower rise in a long, steady slope, an Art Nouveau or Beaux-Arts treatment unlike the Gothic practice of setting them back in stages. Finally, and most remarkably, the windows beside the tower are rampant arches, as if the sheer mass of the tower had exerted a gravitational pull on their crowns.

Historic Landmark plaque

First Hungarian Reformed Church
221 Johnston Street, Hazelwood
Titus de Bobula, architect, 1903–04

A small de Bobula church, at first glance well-proportioned but no more, reveals some interesting details on closer examination. The texture of the doorway arch, crisp and emphatic, turns the ordinary sandstone of this area, for

Princess Suzannah Lorantffy, benefactor of the Hungarian people.

Rampant arches flank the entrance.

Quench from south of the plant

Hazelwood Coke Plant
Second Avenue, Hazelwood
Established late nineteenth century

Though no attempt at visual artistry is apt to be found in the producing part of an industrial plant, the power and mystery of such a place compel notice and have an effect that little polite building design can ever hope to achieve.

The refining of bituminous coal into coke, a hot-burning blast-furnace fuel, was introduced to Pittsburgh in 1859, and in 1884 Laughlin & Co., owners of the Eliza blast furnaces in south Oakland, began building their own coke ovens along the Monongahela River shore in such hundreds that by 1900 they had reached the once-desirable community of Hazelwood. These were the infamous bee-hive ovens, where coal smoldered in a meager ration of air until its tars precipitated and its volatiles either burned or released sulphurous fumes into the air.

In 1919, with the introduction of by-product ovens that trapped off and reclaimed these wastes, environmental conditions began to improve. The coke now baked in airless ovens at 2,200° F for eighteen or twenty-four hours, then was quickly pushed into the open air and quenched. In the mid-1960s, when the Pittsburgh Works of the Jones & Laughlin Steel Corporation was at peak production, the Hazelwood Coke Plant was operating 315 by-product ovens and producing, not only coke but tar, ammonium sulphate, light oil, gas (to fuel the ovens), and tar acids. Hazelwood's hillsides, once defoliated, were planted again, and a peach tree was rumored to be growing inside the plant.

Prominent in the complicated landscape of the plant are the two quench towers, where the burning coke is given a shower and from which rise great plumes of steam; the elevated coal bins from which coal pours into the larry cars that charge the ovens; and the flare that burns off waste gases and dramatically terminates some Hazelwood street scenes.

The Eliza furnaces have been gone since 1983, but the plant goes on, its coke shipped out of the region.

Quench from Monongahela Street

Looking toward Homestead, from the Homestead High Level Bridge.

ALONG THE
MONONGAHELA

Upriver from the South Side, the Monongahela River turns generally eastward, then turns southward in a series of zigzag bends toward its source at Fairmont, West Virginia, 128 miles from the Pittsburgh Point. The hills advance toward the water's edge, then retreat. In the narrowest parts, with room only for a road and a rail line, the slopes are wild, trees and shrubs interrupted only by pipelines or electric pylons. The "Pittsburgh" as the world has conceived it has largely in fact consisted of these shores and their industrial plants, with towns behind them on the river plains and the slopes beyond.

In spite of massive steel plant closings and demolitions there are still parts of the Monongahela Valley that seem to be engineer's, not architect's, country. Blast furnaces and hot-air stoves, giant industrial sheds, machinery of all sizes, billows of steam, bridges, and dams establish a heroic scale, while by contrast the towns behind seem like semi-permanent encampments, hastily called into being a century ago to serve the industrial plants and never fully put in order. Yet a closer look shows architectural works like the Carnegie Libraries of Braddock and Munhall or the cluster of churches in Homestead and Munhall, built to last and indicative of stable, prosperous communities with more on their minds than the making of steel and money.

Before 1870 the industrial valley to be seen today hardly existed. Elizabeth, founded in 1787, West Elizabeth, and a few other places were boat-building centers. Drifting flatboats, coalboats, and even ocean-going vessels whose true careers began at New Orleans were launched from their yards earlier in the nineteenth century, and later steamers and diesel towboats were built here as well. Toward the middle of the century, both mining and navigation were stimulated by a steady and increasing demand for coal: steam coal for domestic hearths, for boilers to drive machinery, and for the locomotives that replaced the earlier

COUNTY OF
ALLEGHENY

463

On Tenth Avenue in Homestead

On Eleventh Avenue in Munhall

wood-burners; metallurgical coal, suitable for coking, to feed the new river's-edge blast furnaces that were replacing the old, remote charcoal furnaces. Beginning in 1841 a private company canalized the Monongahela, partly for the packet trade, mostly for the coalboats that first drifted, then were driven by sternwheelers, to their markets.

The mines, the boatyards, the navigation, and the occasional small factories in riverside settlements here and there introduced a modest industrial presence to the river above Pittsburgh before 1870. So did the Pittsburgh & Connellsville Railroad on the north shore; when the Pittsburgh & Connellsville came to McKeesport in 1857, that small community of 1795 began to grow, and in 1870 became the home of the large National Tube Works. In 1873, Andrew Carnegie, who already had manufactured steel, began construction on a large Bessemer plant, with a specialty in rail, on a site next to Turtle Creek where the British General Edward Braddock had met his celebrated defeat in 1755. Named the Edgar Thomson Works after the president of the Pennsylvania Railroad, the shipper and best customer for the product, the plant attracted a work force that turned the adjacent village of Braddock's Field into the industrial town of Braddock. In 1873, the Homestead Bank & Insurance Company laid out a little town on the south shore of the river, which it named after itself. In 1879, Andrew Kloman bought land next to Homestead for the Pittsburgh Bessemer Steel Company, whose plant was sold in 1883 to the Carnegie Phipps Company. In 1884, the Carrie Furnaces—blast furnaces are often named after women—were built at Rankin on the north shore to supply smelted iron to customers; eventually they supplied hot metal—molten iron straight from the furnace—to the Homestead plant across the river. In the mid-1880s, George Westinghouse relocated the Union Switch & Signal Company to the semi-rural commuter area of Swissvale, and toward the end of the decade began the move of his other plants to the Turtle Creek Valley, near Braddock and along the Pennsylvania Railroad main line. In 1900, Henry Clay Frick established the St. Clair Furnace Company and the St. Clair Steel Company nearly opposite Elizabeth; from these grew the town of Clairton, which also became the location of a still-functioning coke plant.

Thirty years, then, sufficed to turn this portion of the Monongahela from a shore and hillside area where one settled to farm, mine coal, do a little manufacturing, or merely enjoy the scenery from one's porch into a place of infernal if heroic sights, noises, and smells. Yet areas remained where this industrial intensity never came, or came only in limited ways. West Mifflin Borough, which touches the river at three places, does have large plants on its uplands but is also part-rural, part-suburban, and has accommodated as well the old Curtis-Bettis Airfield of 1925, the Allegheny County Airport, and Kennywood, one of the nation's great amusement parks. Other areas with river frontage, Elizabeth and Forward Townships and Jefferson Borough, have always been rural. Here large untamed spaces and farmhouses from the early nineteenth century still abound.

On Sunny Side Hollow Road in Forward Township.

Union Switch & Signal Company (now Towne Centre Office Building)
Braddock Avenue at Swissvale and Edgewood Avenues, Swissvale
Janssen & Cocken, architects, 1927

The most interesting element of a large industrial group remains: the former administration building, faced in red brick. In its overall simplicity, with just a few decorative touches such as the crenelated skyline, it suggests the mildly progressive commercial and industrial architecture of Germany in the 1920s. A covered arched bridge, faced with brick as well, once made a slightly jarring connection with the exposed concrete skeleton of a factory building by the architects Hunting & Davis.

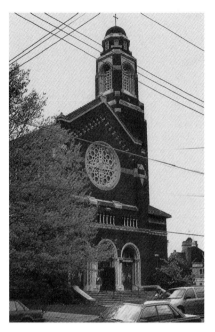

St. Anselm's Roman Catholic Church (now St. Anselm's Worship Site, Word of God Parish)
7446 McClure Avenue, Swissvale
Albert F. Link, architect, 1924

A historical essay on Catholic architecture in this area sees influence in this design from the more famous John Theodore Comes, and this seems true if we consider the latter's St. Agnes' Church in Oakland: Romanesque up to a point, original, though with respect for tradition, from there on. The tower, notably, is an original design. The color of the brickwork is rather dark, but the sides of the front terminate in friezes of brilliantly colored tile inlay.

466

Houses
7506, 7508, and 7510 Trevanion Avenue, Swissvale
Frederick G. Scheibler, Jr., architect

Three houses by Pittsburgh's creative, ambivalently Modern architect. Number 7510, the Hellmund house, was built in 1915–16 and seems to show a mixture of Germanic rigidity—windows on two stories, originally with an intervening balcony to emphasize the vertical alignment—and Anglo-Saxon informality, derived perhaps from English architecture of the time, in the horizontals of the porte-cochere and the porch.

7510 Trevanion Avenue

   Its interior is as built, an Arts and Crafts environment of abundant woodwork, tile, and stained glass. It includes a fireplace with openings into both the living and dining rooms: a feature that appears to be derived from Prairie School planning.
   Number 7508, built c. 1917, is a small, simple, and pleasant gambrel-roofed house. Number 7506, from 1905,

7506 Trevanion Avenue

is the most complex, less obviously organized; it was restored externally in 1981, and the interior is much as it was originally.

Historic Landmark plaque (7510)

Carrie Furnaces, Homestead Works, United States Steel Corporation
Swissvale, at Mile 8.5 on the Monongahela River
Operations begun 1884

Of the Carrie Furnaces that supplied hot metal to the Homestead Works of U.S. Steel, only Furnaces 6 and 7 remain, possible elements in a National Park some day. These are furnaces of 1907, last remodeled apparently in the 1940s, with attendant stoves to heat the blast and in one instance still with the cast house that sheltered the tapping of smelted iron and slag and its pouring, respectively, into hot-metal cars for transport to the steel-making furnaces of Homestead and into "thimbles" for conveyance while still molten to a slag pile. The furnaces are small by later standards, but there is a mute presence about them that would make a superb display. The mass, force, and heat of actual smelting and transportation could be inferred or perhaps even simulated.

Historic Landmark plaque

Braddock Carnegie Library and Carnegie Hall
Library Street and Parker Avenue, Braddock
William Halsey Wood (Newark, N. J.), architect for
Carnegie Library, 1888; Longfellow, Alden & Harlow,
architects for Carnegie Hall, 1893

This was the first of the American Carnegie libraries to be dedicated, a few hundred yards from the Edgar Thomson Works, Andrew Carnegie's first major venture in steel-making. With the 1893 annex, the institution became a community center of a diversified nature; besides the 20,000-volume library it had an 1100-seat theater, meeting rooms, swimming pool, baths, bowling alley, billiard room, and gymnasium.

The floral carving of the 1888 section.

William Halsey Wood was a short-lived architect of fantastic ideas that went unrealized and more realizable designs that were executed. Here, he supplied a simple Richardson Romanesque design, symmetrical on the front, with bow windows framing a narrow pavilion with a gable. These carry the most interesting details: cast-iron mullions in the broad first-floor windows and crude, vigorous leaf carvings beneath the cornice. Carnegie Hall is less hearty Romanesque, the product of a firm that was seeing its Renaissance design for the Carnegie Institute to completion; in order to harmonize with the library, Longfellow, Alden & Harlow revived a style they had more or less abandoned. Frank Vittor's World War I Memorial, a figure of Victory from 1922, is a third element of the group, a light Classical sculpture set against the heavy Romanesque masonry.

The second-floor arcade and dormer of the 1893 section.

In 1983 the Braddock's Field Historical Society acquired the building and, in collaboration with several other groups including the Pittsburgh History & Landmarks Foundation, began a campaign to re-open and find new uses for it. Volunteers had been keeping it open to some extent, in a depressed community with a population only a quarter the size it had been fifty years before. At the time of writing, the campaign of restoration and return to useful life is proceeding with success.

National Register of Historic Places
Historic Landmark plaque

The entrance arcade of the 1893 section.

United States Post Office

Parker Avenue and Orchard Street, Braddock
Louis A. Simon, designer; James Knox Taylor or
Oscar Wenderoth of the U. S. Treasury Department
(Washington, D. C.), supervising architect; 1913

The federal presence in a community—manifested usually
in a post office—often contrasts markedly with its ordinary
buildings. If the government has built for itself rather than
renting space, it is almost bound to have done a creditable
architectural job, and in the Eclectic past it tended to
create palatial pavilions, on a level with banks and passenger stations, that might seem deliberately to one-up the
homely buildings around them. Yet citizens were proud
of such post offices, not annoyed about them, as public
interest in federally sponsored mural projects of the 1930s
was to show.

   In Braddock, the federal presence *was* in contrast to the
surrounding houses. The very delicate detailing is curious,
given that the material is limestone. The panels in the
piers, the ornament in the spandrels, and the small scale of
the balustrade suggest modeling in terra cotta rather than
carving in stone, to an extent that raises the question
whether some quirky governmental decision substituted
the more dignified material after the design was approved.

Church of St. Michael the Archangel (Roman Catholic; now Good Shepherd Catholic Church)

Braddock Avenue and Fraser Street, Braddock
Carlton Strong, architect, 1930

This was one of the architect's last works, a church of
masonry with a generalized Romanesque feeling and a
masonry expression, but also a response to the malaise of
architects in the 1930 period about going on with stylistic
imitation. The rather tall exterior that culminates in a low-
set octagonal lantern has little that can be called decorative,
although there is a small bellcote tucked into an alley side.
Inside, the color and texture of brickwork and the simple
and powerful curves of the arches and the squinches that
bear the lantern are the most telling elements.

   The chancel is shown here in its original state, having

The chancel in its original state.

since been remodeled into extreme plainness. The walls had vine and diaper patterns, and the bracketed ciborium was supported by stone piers representing attenuated, highly stylized angels. These were sculptured in an innovative way associated with the New York architect Bertram Goodhue and his favorite sculptor Lee Lawrie: a very simple mass of stone, from bottom to top, was increasingly broken up into elements that resolved themselves into a conventionalized living being. In this case, the rising and receding masses continued behind the upraised wings of the angels in skyscraper-like forms. Perhaps these, with the very simple arches and the elaborate patterns of the chancel walls, implied that the Church is rooted in tradition yet as modern as today.

Schwab house
541 Jones Avenue, North Braddock
Frederick J. Osterling, architect, 1890–93

A Richardsonian Romanesque example of company housing at the upper end of the range, this was the house provided for Charles Schwab, the famous superintendent of Carnegie's Edgar Thomson Works from 1889 to 1892. The house stands on a slope, now rather desolate, looking down toward the Monongahela River and the mills. It has simple, powerful forms: one of those dark, brooding places of which a few still survive, inviting one to imagine the life that goes on inside. Year by year, they yield to bland new buildings, or to nothing at all, to vacancy.

Historic Landmark plaque

House
817 Kirkpatrick Street, North Braddock
C. 1885

An example of upper-rank company housing, rented to
U.S. Steel foremen who also received options to purchase.
The symmetry of the main building block suggests that all
else is additions, including the projecting cubical element,
with its stained-glass window, over the porch.

St. Michael's School (now Unsmoke Systems, Inc.)
1135 Braddock Avenue, Braddock
Titus de Bobula, architect, c. 1905

This is a stripped-down remnant of a building by Pittsburgh's
one Art Nouveau architect. The fenestration, especially on
the front, keeps it interesting even with much gone.

Edgar Thomson Works
Braddock Avenue and Thirteenth Street, North Braddock
Operations begun 1875

Although this was not Andrew Carnegie's first attempt
at making steel by the quick, cheap Bessemer process,
it was the first to succeed in the Pittsburgh area. Low-
phosphorous iron ore was the secret, and Carnegie was
shrewd enough to place his plant, with rail its only finished
product, alongside the Pennsylvania Railroad and to
name it after that line's president. Bessemer steel was made
simply by blowing air through hot metal, newly smelted
iron, at about 3,000° F, so as to burn away impurities
and to leave a critical amount of carbon. The steel was
not of outstanding quality, not up to that made by the slow,
craftsman-like crucible process, but tons of it could be
made in about twenty minutes, and it was better for rail
than the easily deformed wrought iron previously in use.

In 1882, after a half-dozen years in operation, "ET" had
five blast furnaces producing hot metal for three ten-ton
converters, producing 750 tons of steel ingots and 650 tons
of rail and billets daily. In the mid-1960s before the great
decline, seven blast furnaces were supplying sixteen open-
hearth furnaces—Bessemers were almost out of existence
by then—each producing 205 tons per heat. Now the
open-hearth process is a thing of the past, but the basic-
oxygen process promises a future for the Works.

Historic Landmark plaque

McKeesport and Versailles Cemetery
1608 Fifth Avenue, McKeesport
1856 and after

This is a picturesque "rural" cemetery on a hillside, similar in kind to Allegheny Cemetery if less interesting. It suffers in part from being overlooked by a huge and mindlessly designed hospital building. The gateway, though it bears the dedication date of 1856, has decorative carving that suggests the 1880s. The Queen Anne house alongside, though of different materials, is probably a near contemporary. There was at first a similar building on the other side of the arch, used for offices.

Bank of McKeesport (later McKeesport National Bank; now Three Rivers Bank)
Fifth Avenue and Sinclair Street, McKeesport
Longfellow, Alden & Harlow, architects, 1889–91

Longfellow, Alden & Harlow, who at this same time were designing the Conestoga Building in the Triangle, were recommended for this job by the president of the bank. Some features of both designs are similar: the use of mullion-and-transom windows slightly recessed between structural piers, the presence of arched windows in the uppermost floor (which was a late addition to the design), and the feeling that a moment of transition between styles of different character has been reflected in a building design. The Romanesque tendency to glorify masonry as a constructional means is present in the very hard-looking granite corner column, the rock-faced stone of the basement quoins, and the mullions and transoms that bind the solids together despite the width of

the voids. Yet the level roofline, the regular rhythm of the longer front and the long, thin, Roman brick that minimizes texture are characteristics of the Classical future that was arriving.

In the 1970s the exterior was restored under the guidance of the Pittsburgh History & Landmarks Foundation. Since, however, upper window compartments have been filled in and give the fronts a sad, blind look.

National Register of Historic Places
Historic Landmark plaque

St. Peter's Roman Catholic Church rectory
(now St. Martin de Porres Parish Center)
704 Market Street, McKeesport
C. 1900?

Located in a desolate area of the city, this would be just another Late Victorian institutional building were it not for the bold verticals of the front pavilion.

Lysle Boulevard Bridge
Youghiogheny River at Lysle Boulevard, McKeesport
Allegheny County Authority; George S. Richardson and
Eugene Hunting, engineers; 1937–39

The Allegheny County Authority was organized in the mid-1930s as a recipient of federal PWA money. Among other things, the Authority built this two-hinged crescent-arch bridge whose span is about 320 feet. Since only two hinges, at the springing of the arch, were necessary, the parabolic crescent form was exactly right for supporting evenly distributed dead loads and reinforcing the arch against off-center and moving loads. Aside from its ornamental railings, the bridge is undecorated, relying on the inherent grace of the arch for visual effect.

National Register of Historic Places

McKeesport Water Filtration Plant
Railroad Street at the Fifteenth Street Bridge, McKeesport
Alexander Potter, engineer, 1907–08; 1925

At the same time that Pittsburgh began filtering its water, McKeesport built a plant for filtering and softening water from the Youghiogheny River. Water was taken from the river beneath the small octagonal Active Intake System

Building and piped to the large circular Chemical Treatment Building. After treatment there, it was filtered underground, then sent to the adjacent Pump House, and thence to a reservoir. A fourth building on the site was a chemical-storage plant and power station.

Of the four buildings, the Chemical Treatment Building, whose circular plan reflects the radial flow of the water after its arrival from the river, survives.

Historic Landmark plaque

Muse house
4222 Third Street, McKeesport
1820; additions, c. 1824 and 1910

To the two-bay original stone house, a three-bay section was added about four years later, giving a typical Georgian house plan with a center hall. The stone is in a lively pattern of random ashlar, roughly axed. Drafts of roughly parallel grooves have been cut around some of the openings and used to outline the adjacent stones. The lintel over the main door has an oval raised medallion, neatly cut with the initials of Fauntley and Catherine Muse, the first owners. Near by is the temple-like springhouse, at 4232 Walnut Street, now used as a home.

Walker house
1026 Third Avenue, Elizabeth Borough
1844

Occasionally in Western Pennsylvania a one-and-a-half-story Greek Revival house survives. Here is a simple but elegant example, built as a summer home for an in-law of the Walker family, which still owns it.

Scott house
Round Hill Park Exhibit Farm, Round Hill Regional Park,
Elizabeth Township
1838

At the center of a farm, maintained as an exhibit and containing three barns, the simple but solid Scott house illustrates the most basic sort of Greek Revival. The brick-layer has used the elegant Flemish bond on the front and the cheaper common bond on the other fronts. The practice of making a fine facade toward the road, regardless of the treatment of other fronts, came to Western Pennsylvania as an element of Georgian building practice.

Hutchinson farm
Round Hill Road near Pennsylvania Route 51,
Elizabeth Township
House, 1865

The Georgian building tradition persisted through most of the nineteenth century in ordinary house construction even while the fashions in applied ornament changed. Here is the old formula, still vital: rectangular perimeter, gable roof, symmetrical front, sash windows twice as high as wide, disposed—as was often the case in the eighteenth century—so as to be paired on each side of the central element. To the simple brick shell are added an Italianate porch and brackets, delicate enough to be decorations of the basic geometry, not distractions.

National Register of Historic Places

Van Kirk farm
Round Hill Road and Scenery Drive, Elizabeth Township
House, c. 1845

This is the main house of a farm, yet its front gives the appearance of an elegant Greek Revival villa. But it is amusing: should you move around the house, the "architecture" disappears and ordinary vernacular construction swiftly comes into view, with pitched roofs and plain walls. The Georgian way of dressing up a road front and being more casual about everything else has obviously persisted here.

National Register of Historic Places

Mesta house
540 Doyle Avenue, West Homestead
C. 1900

This was the Colonial Revival mansion of George Mesta, founder in 1887 of the Mesta Machine Company. The company's gigantic plant (now much altered) is the most conspicuous sight in West Homestead. It manufactured heavy machinery for steel mills until 1983.

The house is big, decorated, and symmetrical on the front, but still rather artless externally as so many homes

of the local rich were. The second floor of the conspicuous side wall has three types of window, for instance, used randomly. The dormers are unusual in being shaped as Palladian windows.

Marrying in late middle age, Mesta was building a home on Beechwood Boulevard (now demolished) for his wife Perle—later a famous Washington hostess—when he died in 1925.

National Register District

Homestead High Level Bridge
Monongahela River at Mile 7.25, between Pittsburgh and Homestead
Allegheny County Authority; George S. Richardson, design engineer; J. E. Greiner Company (Baltimore), consulting engineers; 1934-37

In the days before computers the appeal of the so-called continuous truss, passing over more than two points of support and functioning as a single structural member throughout its length, was greatly tempered by the practical impossibility of finding out exactly what was happening under given conditions. The Swiss-born Pittsburgh engineer Ernest M. Wichert devised a simple solution. Instead of having a post rise from each pier, the Wichert truss had a Y-shaped member to which the lower chord of each span was hinged. This slight break in structural continuity permitted easy stress calculation and allowed a measure of control over the forces acting on the structure under any condition of loading or settlement. Wichert is reported by

George S. Richardson, who designed the main trusses, to have received a royalty of $25,000 for this first application of his truss. It received limited use thereafter.

National Register of Historic Places

St. Mary Magdalene Church (Roman Catholic)
East Tenth Avenue and Amity Street, Homestead
Frederick C. Sauer, architect, 1895; Button & MacLean, 1936

This large work by the favorite turn-of-the-century Catholic architect, facing Homestead's Frick Park, was a

prominent feature of a Homestead street that soon filled with churches. In 1936, though, occurred the fire that opened the way to true distinction. Saving much of Sauer's yellow brickwork, and even some of his trite wooden tracery, Lamont H. Button introduced rich red terra cotta, molded red brick, and red brick tracery outside, and delicately carved limestone

The red terra cotta of the rose window.

St. Anthony's Church (Roman Catholic)
East Tenth Avenue and Ann Street, Homestead
Lamont H. Button, architect, 1943

Expansion of the Homestead Works of U.S. Steel as a measure of wartime preparedness forced the moving of St. Anthony's Parish, and brought into being this handsome composition of mellow red brick and pantiles: a simple church designed with a sure eye, though perhaps a little suburban in expression for a steel town.

National Register District

The altar, with its wooden baldachino.

and woodwork inside. A restrained but lavish taste thus enriched what had begun as a big but rather plain church.

National Register District

477

St. Nicholas Orthodox C. R. Church
903 Ann Street, Homestead
Lamont H. Button (?), architect, 1937–50

The mellow red brickwork and the use of molded, patterned brickwork are excellent, and recall two known

works of Button close by: St. Anthony's and the Button rebuilding of St. Mary Magdalene. The light yellow walls, in fact, look like allusions to Sauer's masonry in the latter church though the patterning here is more jaunty.

National Register District
Historic Landmark plaque

St. Gregory the Theologian R. G. C. Church
East Fifteenth and Maple Avenues, Homestead
Basil Verkoskow (New York), architect, 1950

Here is a rather interestingly massed church, among the last to use traditional forms with conviction.

Remains of the pit furnaces

Homestead Works, United States Steel Corporation
Munhall, at Mile 8 on the Monongahela River
Operations begun before 1880

The Munhall section of the Homestead Works of U.S. Steel was the scene of a famous conflict of labor and management: the so-called Homestead Strike of 1892, which resulted not only in fourteen deaths but also in a forty-five year break in the power of organized labor in the steel industry. The plant's history goes back to some time in the 1870s, when Andrew Carnegie's rival Andrew Kloman built a rolling mill, and 1881, when the Pittsburgh Bessemer Steel Company opened next door to supply Kloman with his steel. Both plants were in direct rivalry to Carnegie's Edgar Thomson Works three miles away, but not for long: Carnegie got both plants in 1883. "Homestead" subsequently became one of the most famous place names in steel worldwide, best known for its production of structural members but also a producer of naval armor. World War II, imminent but not yet declared as regarded the United States, led to the annexation of more than a ward of the neighboring borough of Homestead and a huge expansion of the Works, but now all production has ceased and the land is very largely cleared. As in the case of the Carrie Furnaces across the river in Swissvale, there is hope of a National Park, centered on the place where the Pinkerton mercenary troops attempted a landing to overpower the labor forces in 1892.

Historic Landmark plaque

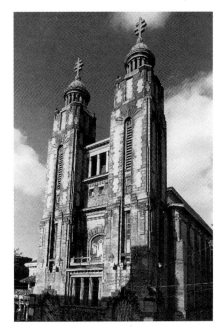

St. John's Cathedral (Byzantine Catholic; now St. John's Eastern European Cultural and Information Center)
Tenth Avenue and Dickson Street, Munhall
Titus de Bobula, architect, 1903

This is the masterpiece of the little-known but interesting de Bobula, probably the largest and most complex product of his curious art. The style is a sort of Art Nouveau, not the sinuous French or Belgian variety but the blockier sort associated with Italy and Central Europe. With de Bobula's use of the style, as in some Italian Art Nouveau designs, Classical detailing is associated.

The central front has a compressed look, with its upper part seemingly squeezed upward from the pressure of the close-set towers. From bottom to top, it has a rusticated arch, surmounted by a colonnade; then, set back a little, another rusticated arch, a cornice, a plain, neutral story, another cornice, and a crowning colonnade. Despite the open colonnade at the top there is no sense of an upward progression toward a climactic feature. Rather, there is layer upon layer of horizontals. The towers, on the other hand, are resolutely vertical, their corners stepping back, breaking up into sub-corners, then chamfers, and finally terminating in domed tempietti. The vertical thrust is strengthened by tall, narrow archways within which the real openings of the towers are set; their surfaces are complicated, yet visually strengthened, by mixture of stone and brick; and flat, raised crosses rising from stepped elements add to the three-dimensional effect.

The body of the church is plainer, yet is visually tied to the front by diagonally set corner buttresses above which the cornice itself runs toward the towers on a diagonal.

The adjoining rectory is more commonplacely American of its time save for the porch, where open panels above the Classical columns and the architrave are a very unusual feature with Italian precedents from the 1900 period.

The church was built for a Carpatho-Ruthenian parish founded in 1896. It has found a new purpose as a place for displays and demonstrations of East European culture.

National Register District
Historic Landmark plaque

Carnegie Library of Homestead
510 Tenth Avenue, Munhall
Alden & Harlow, architects, 1896–98

Much more than a library, this golden-brown building also houses a concert hall and social and athletic rooms. It stands at the top of a small hillside park, a fine setting for its serene architecture in which Renaissance symmetry is combined with mild Romantic variations of perimeter and roof planes. The library had been promised by Andrew Carnegie in 1889 at the dedication of the Carnegie Library at Braddock; the calm scene today offers

no reminder that, before Carnegie fulfilled his promise, the violent Homestead Strike had occurred within sight.

National Register District
Historic Landmark plaque

Houses
502 and 516 Eleventh Avenue, Munhall
C. 1895

These houses have not been attributed to the architects of the Carnegie Library across the street, yet the possibility must be admitted, since these too are of golden-brown brick and have Carnegie associations. They were for division managers of the Homestead Works, and until the 1960s the chateau-like Superintendent's House stood as another element of the building group.

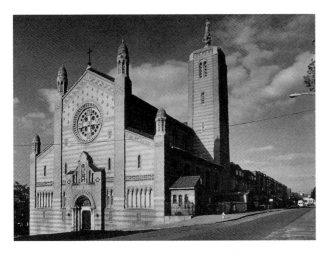

St. Michael Archangel Church (Roman Catholic)
Ninth Avenue and Library Place, Munhall
Comes, Perry & McMullen, architects, 1927

This is one of the largest
churches in the Home-
stead-Munhall area, a
work in a free version of
Italian Romanesque, in
two shades of tan brick,
by Pittsburgh's best-
known office for Catholic
churches. The congrega-
tion that commissioned it
was Slovak. On top of the
tower, which apparently
was designed for a more
conventional termination,
is Frank Vittor's *St. Joseph
the Worker* of 1966.

Behind the church are a
convent and a rectory,
conventional turn-of-the-
century buildings that
frame the vista of the
curious domed belfry of
a school within the block.

National Register District

The Casino

The floral clock

Kennywood Park
4800 Kennywood Boulevard, West Mifflin
1898 and after

There were thirteen parks intended as trolley or railroad destinations in Southwestern Pennsylvania in the early part of the century. Kennywood is the outstanding survivor, an orderly, family-type amusement park that today is like a house that several generations have helped to furnish. The gardening, which includes a floral clock, still has a Late Victorian quality regardless of the innovations and changes of nearly ten decades. Even the plants look Victorian. The pavilions are in 1940 Modernistic or styles from before or since. It appears that amusement-park design has an inertia of its own. The Carousel, a big four-row merry-go-round, was built for the Philadelphia Sesquicentennial of 1926 but is in the Baroque tradition, and though the pavilion that shelters it was built when the merry-go-round came here, it has the look of an open-air Shingle Style park shelter of the 1890s; the Casino, the original dining pavilion, looks no older. The Thunderbolt

The Racer has a restored 1927 facade that seems to parody the Union Station rotunda.

of 1968, judged by connoisseurs to be one of the world's greatest roller-coasters, is still constructed in the primitive bolted-together-white-painted boards manner though it flings you over the edge of a bluff. As you hurtle downwards, the Edgar Thomson Works across the river raises austere dark shapes to remind you of the hard work days that made Kennywood a great pleasure for so many through the years.

National Historic Landmark
National Register of Historic Places
Historic Landmark plaques

The Carousel

Allegheny County Airport Terminal
Lebanon Church Road, West Mifflin
Stanley L. Roush, architect, 1931; Henry Hornbostel,
architect for additions, 1936

Like other Eclectics, Roush and Hornbostel had occasion to turn their hands to non-historic styles. Here, in something so progressive as an airport, Modernistic seemed appropriate, so Roush created a work in white brick with touches of black, green, and silver, which Hornbostel enlarged using similar detailing. Above the stainless steel canopy—which may be an early addition—is a semi-hexagonal doorhead, edged with green, black, and silver mosaic, with lavish green tracery: a feature that is Art Deco of a very Parisian sort rather than Modernistic. To each side is an Art Deco urn with medallions bearing images of flight, human and animal.

James D. Van Trump has pointed out that, despite the aggressive newness of the surface style, the ensemble suggests a small Baroque country palace, symmetrical and building up from low side wings to a climactic feature at the center.

The airport was used for commercial flights until 1952, when the Greater Pittsburgh Airport took over this function. It can still accommodate airplanes up to the size of a DC–9, but today handles only private and corporate traffic.

Historic Landmark plaque

125 Lutz Lane, Hulda and Louise Notz house.

Meadow Circles
Lutz Lane, West Mifflin

Even before the Taliesin Fellows Peter Berndtson (1909–72) and Cornelia Brierly Berndtson (b. 1913) established their joint practice in Pittsburgh in 1947, Cornelia had designed the region's first Usonian house in 1939 for her aunts, Hulda and Louise, in West Mifflin. The Notz house and a sizeable tract of land were subsequently sold, and the Berndtsons were asked to design two more houses in what was known as Meadow Circles. The Katz and Bear houses

120 Lutz Lane, Fay T. Bear house.

were completed in 1950; the Notz house was enlarged in 1959 to a design of Peter Berndtson. The geometric shapes, open floorplans, cypress and plywood siding, fieldstone and brick walls and fireplaces, gravity floor heating systems, and built-in furniture of the one-story buildings

111 Lutz Lane, Joseph Katz house.

are heirs of the domestic house type developed by Frank Lloyd Wright around 1936 and are early characteristic examples of the essentially residential work of these talented local architects.

Historic Landmark plaques (Katz and Bear houses)

Superintendents' Office, Duquesne Works, United States Steel Corporation
South Braddock Avenue and Library Place, Duquesne
C. 1900

Operations at this plant began for the Duquesne Steel Company in 1886, but in 1890 it was in the hands of Carnegie Brothers and Company. It quickly became famous as a place of advanced technology, with automated blast-furnace charging in place of the noxious "top filling" by hand that had been accepted practice theretofore, and the direct-rolling process for ingots that avoided extravagant cooling and re-heating. The 297-foot-high Dorothy Six blast furnace of 1961 was a skyscraper in the genre,

toppled in 1988. The Superintendents' Office, surviving though the Works as a whole has disappeared, is a piece of Colonial Revival which, as is the case of much Colonial Revival around Pittsburgh, has a dark and heavy Romanesque feel to it. Uphill, into the 1960s, was one of Carnegie's so-called libraries, which ministered to the ears and the muscles of the population as well as their eyes.

United States Post Office
Grant Avenue and Second Street, Duquesne
1900

In the broad proportions of its openings and its Classical ornamentation, this is a good example of turn-of-the-century business architecture, a cheerful feature of the street scene.

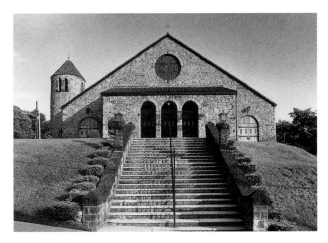

St. Paulinus' Roman Catholic Church
622 Delaware Avenue, Clairton
Rev. Joseph L. Lonergan, designer, 1938

The rector was the architect. The same had been true at St. Patrick's on the Strip two years before, and was to be true again at Mount St. Peter in New Kensington in the early 1940s. Artistic success resulted in all three instances.

A view of Wilmerding from the Triboro Expressway.

THE TURTLE CREEK VALLEY

Just upstream from the Edgar Thomson Works in North Braddock, the Monongahela River is joined by a westward-flowing creek whose outlet is nearly concealed by a railroad bridge. This is Turtle Creek, a stream of no great size but one that has worn a deep valley through the hills. Along this valley the Pennsylvania Railroad main line was laid in the early 1850s, determining the role of the valley in the last hundred years as an industrial place.

As so often in the Pittsburgh area, it is the landscape that catches the eye rather than the constructions set against it. The valley floor and the hillsides are occupied by plain wooden houses and commonplace commercial buildings. Yet the large industrial plants that George Westinghouse built along the valley in the late 1880s and early 1890s, the George Westinghouse Memorial Bridge near the mouth of the valley, and a few smaller constructions here and there distinguish the Turtle Creek Valley as a landscape apart.

The first non-Indian settler of the valley is believed to have been John Frazer, a trader who built a cabin near the mouth of the creek in 1748. During the eighteenth century there was a small amount of settlement, mainly agricultural, both in the valley and on the uplands. A military road made during the French and Indian War developed in time into a main road from the East. As elsewhere in the Monongahela Valley area, the early nineteenth-century discovery of coal and the large and increasing demand for coal by local industry effected change. Mines in the hillsides sent coal down by incline to the valley floor for loading into coalboats, which then drifted down the creek into the Monongahela and so to their destinations. Mining, however, did not spoil the scenery to any great extent; in fact, the valley became a resort area around 1850—with at least one large hotel—served by a plank road from Pittsburgh.

COUNTY OF
ALLEGHENY

The beginning of Pennsylvania Railroad through service in 1852 along the Turtle Creek Valley and of local operations on the Pittsburgh & Connellsville Railroad along the Monongahela shore in 1857 gave the valley a new character and changed the mode of coal shipment from water to rail. But no trace remains today of Port Perry, a once-busy railroad transit center for coal that flourished in the later nineteenth century on the east side of the mouth of Turtle Creek; its site lies beneath crisscrossing railroad lines.

The decision of George Westinghouse to unite the scattered operations of the Westinghouse Electric & Manufacturing Company in a new plant a mile up the valley was the major element of a series of events that transformed its lower end from a thinly settled wooded area to a heavily populated series of industrial boroughs. Opened in 1894, the plant occupied 170 acres by 1905, demanding a large labor force. In 1894 too, the Union Railroad, which serves local industry, built a line through the area and eventually made East Pittsburgh, one of the boroughs in which the Westinghouse Electric plant was built, its headquarters. Finally, trolley service at the beginning of this century made the lower Turtle Creek Valley attractive to workers in various industrial installations who were seeking homes.

Wilmerding: the industrial valley and residential slopes.

The upper Turtle Creek Valley developed rapidly as well. In 1889 construction began on the new plant of the Westinghouse Air-Brake Company, and at the same time Westinghouse began construction of a large section of company housing in the newly incorporated borough of Wilmerding. Further up the valley, the railroad workers' towns of Wall and Pitcairn grew in the 1900s around a large rail yard and freight terminal. This facility has since declined, but its broad wedge of land and the memory of its former activity still dominate the surrounding communities.

Today, the observer in the valley is still impressed by the industrial presence. The keen observer may even notice Turtle Creek itself, channeled between factory and rail.

George Westinghouse Memorial Bridge

U.S. Route 30 over Turtle Creek between East Pittsburgh and North Versailles Township
George S. Richardson and A. D. Nutter of the Allegheny County Department of Public Works, engineers, 1930

Not only does this bridge carry a major highway, it also has served as a triumphal entrance to the Pittsburgh area for rail passengers from the east for over half a century. When it was built, its five concrete arches were regarded as a little conservative by European standards, yet the central span of 460 feet was the broadest in this material in the United States. The form is parabolic, the natural form for an evenly loaded arch. The total length is 1,596 feet. By the late 1970s, it was all too apparent that the deck had to be reconstructed, yet the bridge as repaired is very much as before. The entrances have four tall concrete pylons with granite reliefs by Frank Vittor, honoring Westinghouse's development of the Turtle Creek Valley.

National Register of Historic Places
Historic Landmark plaque

United States Post Office

701 Linden Avenue, East Pittsburgh
James A. Wetmore (Washington, D.C.), architect, 1915

This is a refined composition, an unusually meritorious work of public architecture for a small industrial town. The textured brick and bold rusticated stone arch were later to be used advantageously by Benno Janssen.

Union Railroad General Offices

666 Linden Avenue, East Pittsburgh
1914

A major architectural problem early in this century was giving a civilized appearance to the large skeleton-framed industrial building, with its big horizontal windows, that had just emerged. A doorway could be given a special surround of stone or terra cotta; spandrels beneath the windows could be faced with brick in fancy bonding; but in general, architecture fled to the parapet, with its uninterrupted wall space and possibilities on the skyline.

So it is here: modeled terra cotta that includes lion's masks and friezes of colored tile assist a doorway of Classical character in the decoration of this headquarters for a small industrial railroad.

St. Colman Catholic School
Hunter and Thompson Streets, Turtle Creek
Link, Weber & Bowers, architects, 1928

Contemporary with Central Catholic High School in Oakland and by the same architects, this school's jaunty diapering in raised brick is even more pronounced than the diapered brickwork of the larger institution. Twin bow

The diapering in raised brick

windows at either end add to the lively effect. The head of the doorway has a typically Renaissance scallop-shell motif, distorted to fit within a rather tall Gothic arch. The whole composition has an unexpected gorgeousness.

Edward Joseph Weber was the actual designer.

Historic Landmark plaque

Main entrance, St. Colman's

Machine Shop

Westinghouse Air-Brake Company
Airbrake Avenue and Bridge Street, Wilmerding
Frederick J. Osterling (?), architect, 1890 and after

At one end of the long Westinghouse industrial complex in Turtle Creek Valley is this thirty-five-acre plant, which contains several impressive works of Richardson-influenced Late Victorian industrial architecture. The most interesting is the Machine Shop, with its three long monitor roofs side by side. The outer two roofs have gable ends, now lopsided from the addition of upper space, while the inner one is masked by a kind of false front bearing a tablet. Round and segmental arches, very large as one might expect, pierce the walls to the utmost in a variety that seems capricious until one remembers the problems of arch abutment in a solid-masonry structure. Sloping buttresses flank the side, probably to help sustain the loads of traveling cranes. In the gables, trios of little arches beneath deep corbel tables mark a transition from engineering to architecture in the designer's mind. The engineering would look better without them. A hip-roofed office building next to the Machine Shop continues the round-arched theme. The Foundry, not readily seen from outside the plant, has a more closed character, with smaller round arches.

Westinghouse Air-Brake Company General Office Building (formerly Library Hall; now George Westinghouse Museum)
Herman Drive and Commerce Street, Wilmerding
Frederick J. Osterling (?), architect, 1890; rebuilt 1896;
Janssen & Cocken, architects for addition, 1927

The Westinghouse Company built the original building, possibly to designs by Frederick J. Osterling, as a public library and community center. This was a philanthropy in the Carnegie manner—immediately after construction of the Braddock Carnegie Library—with a restaurant, library, baths, bowling alleys, and swimming pool. Library Hall burned in 1896, though, and was rebuilt to designs of Frederick J. Osterling as a Westinghouse Air-Brake Company office building, with the reconstructed parts in brick instead of the original random ashlar. Janssen & Cocken's annex is in the chateau spirit of the original, but uses the basic manner in a more sober and orthodox way. The building, halfway up a hillside, is a striking feature, lordly and melancholy, among the trees and commonplace houses.

National Register of Historic Places
Historic Landmark plaque

First National Bank of Pitcairn
Second Street and Center Avenue, Pitcairn
Kiehnel & Elliott, architects, c. 1910

Primarily an apartment house, this off-white building housed a banking room behind stately arcades. The effect is Classical, the detailing is not. As with other works by these architects at this time, capitals and other decorative members are without historical references, and have something of a contemporary Prairie School look.

Potomac Avenue, Dormont

SOUTH OF
PITTSBURGH

Beginning at Pittsburgh's southwestern edge, a chain of communities runs southward along Chartiers Creek. These have had varied characters: industry and workers' housing in Carnegie and Heidelberg; middle-class houses in Ingram and Crafton; and upper-middle-class houses in Thornburg. At Thornburg, members of the Thornburg family, which had owned land along Chartiers Creek since 1791, decided in 1900 to subdivide part of it to create a suburb similar to Tuxedo Park, New York, with informal-looking houses in a wooded setting and good rail access from Pittsburgh. The idea was a success, and today the borough is most visibly a place of rustic houses, Shingle Style or Craftsman, dispersed over the hillside setting.

COUNTY OF
ALLEGHENY

The South Hills area, however, which extends directly south from Pittsburgh, consists of more uniform suburban development. Before 1904 the terrain of hills and valleys was there but few buildings. The inclines had made the areas overlooking the Monongahela River accessible, and trolley cars had begun climbing the South Side slopes in 1888 for a trip to Mount Oliver a mile and a half inland, but the area beyond was primarily farmland and woods. Only in Castle Shannon, five miles south of the Monongahela, had a serious attempt been made at a South Hills suburb. Around 1870, real-estate promoters went to seemingly fantastic lengths to persuade Pittsburghers to settle on this unpromising land. To render their suburb accessible, they built the Pittsburgh & Castle Shannon Railroad. Travel by this involved a trip to the Carson Street terminal, east of the Smithfield Street Bridge; being hauled in a train coach up a shallow-grade incline; and being pulled by steam locomotive the remainder of the journey, which began with a passage through a 1,700-foot tunnel.

The promoters might have been spared trouble and expense had the electric streetcar been in existence, and the 1904 opening of the South

Art glass and Old World tiling: Longuevue Drive, Mount Lebanon.

Hills trolley tunnel, running five-eighths of a mile from the Smithfield
Street Bridge to the far side of Mount Washington, was a much more
effective way of opening up the South Hills. From its elevated southern
end at South Hills Junction, trolleys could disperse throughout the hills,
running over bridges and along ridges and meeting occasional feeder
lines, and builders took quick advantage of the opportunity to build
boxy houses, apartment houses, and commercial buildings within an
easy walk of the rights-of-way. Their architecture was not sophisticated.
There seemed to be no special sense of proportion, no system of design.
They built in cream-colored or buff brick, made the porch columns
Classical, perhaps threw in a suggestion of half-timbering in an occasional unnecessary gable; and somewhere, on the stair or beside the
mantelpiece, put windows with art glass. The trolley suburbs of the
South Hills are a veritable realm of art glass, in smeary, opalescent
colors, intricately geometrical or evoking flowers in May. A design
purist can fret over a street scene in the older suburbs like Dormont
or Brentwood, want to tidy up its architecture, make it worthy of the
well-kept lawns, the flowers, the trees, and the whole rolling, inhabited
landscape. Yet there is a relaxed charm to these places, a feeling of
well-being attained in material terms, a pride evident in those well-kept
lawns, that makes good architecture no more than the final perfecting
touch.

The suburbs have spread greatly since 1928, when the Liberty
Bridge was opened to lead from town to the slightly older Liberty
Tubes through the hills. The newer suburbs naturally have a character
different from that of the older ones. Carried to their very doors, the
automobile commuters were able to disperse in a way that was impractical for trolley riders, get well away from main streets, build on larger
properties. And while the other architecture of the trolley suburbs
tended to be essentially style-less, the newer houses of the 1920s and
somewhat later in a community like Mount Lebanon were more subtle,
more carefully studied for the most part, full of quaint effects and
allusions to Colonial, Cotswold, or Tudor, while the official and commercial buildings of the main street might be discreetly Modernistic.
After World War II the expansive trend, long interrupted, resumed,
and new tracts of houses, now without much style or character at all,
spread over what had been areas of farms and forests.

South Park was a product of the late 1920s and early 1930s, an old
farming area given over to serve an increasing population with recreational facilities and the Allegheny County Fairgrounds. The Allegheny
County Fair was a popular attraction for many years, but ended in
the 1970s, while suburbanization absorbed farmland and expanded
the limits of the South Hills and other rapidly developing areas of
Allegheny County.

Rocklynn Place, Mount Lebanon

First Presbyterian Church (now Ingram Masonic Hall)
West Prospect and Mackin Avenues, Ingram
1899

A prominent building is
sometimes imitated in
unexpected ways or
places. Here is a round,
apse-like termination to
a church—unusual for
the Presbyterians, but
possibly accommodating
an Akron-plan Sunday-
school arrangement.
To one side of this is a
tower, and to the other
what may have been the
base of another tower,
never built. The very
same disposition could be
seen in the contemporary
Carnegie Institute, where
two campanili originally
flanked the visible semi-

circle of the Carnegie Music Hall. In materials—here,
a slightly variegated, light-colored brick—details, and
proportions, the two buildings are very different, as they
are in purpose. Yet the Carnegie Institute's compositional
formula gave the unknown architect of the church a hook
from which to hang the rather loose features of his design.

House
80 Berry Street, Ingram
C. 1870; alterations and additions, 1968–73

Challenged to give this house a stylistic label its architect
would probably have said, "Swiss." It has the far-flung
eaves and the solid brackets of a chalet, and a general
woodiness of expression. Modern authorities would be
more inclined to apply the more recent label Stick Style
for the same reason, especially since wall areas are characteristically marked off into panels by the application of
slats. A modern enclosure of a porch and extension of the
rear were done with great care and respect.

Creighton house
51 Noble Avenue, Crafton
Eli Crum, architect, 1871

There are two curious things about this house. First, its stone was salvaged from a railroad tunnel. Second, the pungent, intricate detailing of the pediment, so brashly Mid-Victorian in look, is actually a creation of the 1960s. An interesting and sophisticated detail is the extension of the vertical lines of the posts through the entablature with lengths of board and molding. The design in the pediment carries the verticals still further.

Creighton Avenue, Crafton
1895 and after

This is a pleasant and well-kept street only a block long, brick-paved, and with twenty houses dating mainly from the 1900s. Remodeling and new fashions have passed the street by to a remarkable extent.

Historic Landmark plaque

St. Philip Church (Roman Catholic)
West Crafton and Broadhead Avenues, Crafton
William P. Ginther (Akron), architect, 1906

This stone church is effectively sited on a hillside and has a single tall tower on one side. The location of the tower is unusual, yet it has important Central European precedents in the Cathedrals of Vienna and Prague. Such a position gives an emphatic central feature to the church but eliminates the structural problems of building it over a crossing.

The complex also includes a large school built in three

campaigns, a rectory, and a much plainer convent. The most conspicuous part of the school dates from 1927, and has a lavishness of treatment due to the hand of Edward J. Weber. The stonework is rock-faced sandstone random ashlar with strong contrasts between stone and stone, and above is rich red brickwork with artful randomness of brick length and course

height. Limestone overdoor sculptures show children at their studies. Facing the street is a crenelated turret, whose merlons are fashioned in a stepped way that takes the triteness from a typical Tudor motif. Around the same time Central Catholic High School in Oakland and St. Colman's School in Turtle Creek were being constructed to Weber's designs, and the same rich imagination was at work here.

Historic Landmark plaque

Dartmouth Road

Thornburg

Thornburg's wooded, hilly terrain, careful planning, and advertising rhetoric—"Pittsburgh's Most Attractive Suburb"—attracted home builders from the start. While the earliest houses date from 1900 and houses of the 1920s and later can be found here, one comes away with the impression of a rather elegant but rustic settlement of the 1905 period, a country place of stone and wood and calculated informality.

The first buildings were a half-dozen Queen Anne houses erected at the bottom of the bluff on Princeton Avenue around 1900. During the next few years they were joined across the street by a block of Shingle Style houses, some exhibiting Colonial Revival and others Craftsman detailing. Typical of the 1903–05 houses is the "Cobble-stone House" at 1137 Cornell Avenue, probably from around 1905 but carrying on the Shingle Style's use of rugged materials and interest in roof planes, with a small amount of Colonial Revival detailing here and there. The cobbles that face the chimney and porch piers are quite unusual. (In its general massing, the house bears a striking resemblance to Gustav Stickley's first Craftsman house of 1903, designed by E. G. W. Dietrich.)

In 1905, developer Frank Thornburg returned to Thornburg from Los Angeles with some sixty photographs of Southern California houses—described by the press as "mission type" and "artistic"—to serve as models for future construction. Some of these California images were turned into Western Pennsylvania reality by the developer's cousin, architect Samuel Thornburg McClarren. It is not known if McClarren designed 1124 Cornell Avenue in the Spanish Mission style or 1109 Cornell Avenue, which shows

Above: The "Cobblestone House" at 1137 Cornell Avenue in a photo of 1967 and, below, after it was painted in 1996.

1124 Cornell Avenue

1109 Cornell Avenue

529 and 533 Hamilton Road

1080 Stanford Road

1132 Lehigh Road

the influence of Myron Hunt; he did design several houses that show an awareness of the Prairie School and two decidedly craftsman houses at 529 and 533 Hamilton Road, c. 1906, one of which was the architect's own house.

Other architects and other styles were welcome in Thornburg. One example is the house at 1080 Stanford Road, built in or around 1906 to designs by C. E. Willoughby. White, formal, detached, this house is said to have been modeled after the eighteenth-century Morris-Jumel house in New York City, though it differs from the model in several ways; especially in having an Ionic instead of a Tuscan order.

Close to the top of the rise is Frank Thornburg's third and last house in the community, at 1132 Lehigh Road, an open V of coursed rubble and shingles with ample porch areas set in the basic building mass. The focal point is a brick chimney, which functions as an outlet for a fireplace with a large brick hood in the central two-storied hall. It was built around 1907 to McClarren's design.

National Register District
Historic Landmark plaque (1132 Lehigh Road)

St. Peter and St. Paul Ukrainian Orthodox Greek Catholic Church
Mansfield Boulevard near Walnut Street, Carnegie
Titus de Bobula, architect, 1906

A church by the interesting but obscure de Bobula. The style of the front is novel, sparing in detail, in a blocky sort of Art Nouveau that may have some derivation from contemporary Italian design. The stonework at the base of the central tower builds up very effectively, with the transition from a square element to an octagon handled in a very original paraphrase of eighteenth-century English practice. As usual with Orthodox churches in America the distinctive onion domes are on the front, not distributed around the center as they would be in Russia. The interior was redecorated in 1966.

Historic Landmark plaque

First Presbyterian Church
East Main Street and Washington Avenue, Carnegie
1894

This is a pleasant feature of Carnegie's principal street, executed in the once-fashionable Richardson Romanesque style though the narrow tower with the tall spire has rather Mid-Victorian proportions. The high-and-low sandstone coursing can also be found in the street fronts of the Courthouse, and implies bonding to concealed brickwork.

Andrew Carnegie Free Library
300 Beechwood Avenue, Carnegie
Struthers & Hannah, architects, 1899

Of all the Carnegie Libraries, this is the only one permitted to use the donor's given name. The architects have contrasted the projection of the entrance with the recession of the section above. The windows have the same "Florentine" tracery that Longfellow, Alden & Harlow had used at the Carnegie Institute earlier in the decade. The interior also contains a music hall and Civil War memorial room.

National Register of Historic Places
Historic Landmark plaque

Tunnel
Washington Road near Chartiers Creek, Scott Township
C. 1900

This is a tunnel through the great embankment that brought the economically suicidal Wabash-Pittsburg Terminal Railway to Pittsburgh. The Railway began operations in 1904.

St. Luke's Episcopal Church (now Old St. Luke's)
Washington Pike and Church Street, Woodville, Scott Township
1852

This is a primitive church from a time when, to Episco-palians especially, Gothic was apt to be *the* style for a church. Even at the height of the Renaissance, Gothic had never quite died out in northern Europe for ecclesiastical and academic architecture, and in the early nineteenth century American country builders had sometimes combined Greek pilasters with pointed arches in churches. This building was the best a country congregation could do in Southwestern Pennsylvania, while in Pittsburgh the exactly contemporary St. Peter's Church, much more

elaborate, expressed the
same aspirations with
greater means. John
Notman, architect of
St. Peter's, may have
suggested the general
design. The porch is a
modern reconstruction
of one seen in old photo-
graphs. The organ, built
in 1822 by the English
builder Joseph Harvey,
was probably the earliest
church organ west of the
Alleghenies.

The church and its graveyard fell into disuse at one
time, but both have been restored by the Committee to
Save St. Luke's, which now, through the Episcopal Diocese
of Pittsburgh, holds ecumenical services and opens the
church to the public.

Historic Landmark plaque

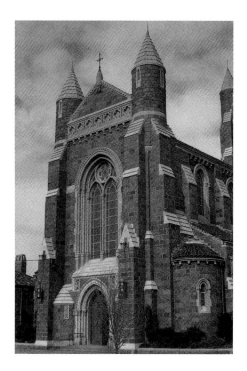

St. Bernard's Church (Roman Catholic)
311 Washington Road, Mount Lebanon
Leo A. McMullen, architect, 1933–47

This large church, conspicuous on the Mount Lebanon
skyline, was actually begun in 1933, but its superstructure
waited until 1942 for construction that took until 1947 to
complete. The massive early French Gothic style, the
richly textured rubble with limestone trim, and the overall
air of conviction show it to be a full-blooded design of the
Eclectic period that survived to be built well after its time.
Churches *were* designed in traditional styles in the 1940s,
to be sure, but such an air of confidence about the results

had become quite rare. A curious and charming contrast
with the rugged stonework comes from the tile roofs,
fairy-tale surfaces glazed in random colors, red, green,
blue, and others. The apse, inside, is also bright with color.

Historic Landmark plaque

701 Washington Road

Gatehouse, Mount Lebanon Cemetery
509 Washington Road, Mount Lebanon
C. 1876

This is a well-preserved frame house, retaining its decorative trim.

1929, with its Gothic detailing in white terra cotta and its iron-and-glass marquee. It is said to have been built as a movie house. The corner building is Art Deco, probably from the early 1930s, with panels of elaborate ornament, with a caduceus as the central element, that owe nothing to history. Patriotic eagles with upraised wings add boldness to the design.

695 Washington Road

Commercial buildings
695–701 Washington Road, Mount Lebanon

Two agreeable commercial fronts mark one side of what used to be a trolley junction. Number 695, designed by Geisler & Smithiman, is obviously the older, dating from

Mount Lebanon Municipal Building
710 Washington Road, Mount Lebanon
William H. King, Jr., architect, 1930

Municipal buildings in the 1920s tended to be Classical: Renaissance in its full limestone or marble pomp in the cities, white-and-red Georgian in the suburbs. But now and then a Moderne example appeared as well toward the end of the decade: the image of Progressive Government as opposed to that of the City Fathers, quite possibly. Mount Lebanon chose Modernistic. The doorway, with its diamond-faced stone surround and its bronze relief of *Wisdom in Government*, is mildly allusive to the Renaissance, and the little ziggurat above is monumental

Entrance detail, Mount Lebanon Municipal Building.

in intention. So is the main front, with its steady rhythm of piers. This municipal Modernistic, in short, has much of the traditional solemnity though the specific forms are new. Inside the entrance is a tall reception space, monumental in expression again though scaled to the activities of a borough, with decorative paintings in its upper area.

350 and 344 Jefferson Drive, Mission Hills

Mount Lebanon developments

Although the cedars of Lebanon that gave this community its name were planted in 1850, this community five miles southwest of Pittsburgh is a child of the trolley, which got here from Pittsburgh in 1901, and of the automobile, after the Liberty Tubes opened in 1924. The latter circumstance especially stimulated developers to buy land remote from the trolley line, and lay out streets and house lots with greater or lesser attention to the contours of the land, the picturesque potentials of street patterns, and the ensurance of amenity through architectural controls. Of the eighteen developments that appear on a recent map of Mount

Lebanon, Mission Hills, Virginia Manor, and Hoodridge are those best known for their architecture.

410 Jefferson Drive, Mission Hills

391 Jefferson Drive, Mission Hills

The old real estate office of Virginia Manor.

626 Osage Road, Virginia Manor

83 and 87 Hoodridge Drive

82 Hoodridge Drive

93 Hoodridge Drive

The houses of such developments vary between extremes in a way that reveals some of the peculiar architectural dynamics of the mid- and late 1920s. On the one hand, there is a relaxed and even phlegmatic sort of house that often is faced in white brick and hip-roofed in green tile, and is unashamed to have an ample front porch. But much more common are the marvels of contrivance that, taking the Gothic, the Renaissance, the rustic vernaculars of European countries real or imagined as points of flight, mingle gables, chimneys, turrets, bay windows, dormers, balconies to the limit of affordability, realizing these forms in brick and stone in ingenious mixtures of color, texture, and pattern. In just a few years these Old World evocations were in place, awaiting the slower maturation of the trees and shrubs that would complete the picture.

Clark house
776 Valleyview Road, Mount Lebanon
Joseph Cooper, architect, 1936

This, one of the early houses in Virginia Manor, was built for Harold Clark, son of the founder of the Clark Candy Company. The house abounds in stained glass with an Arthurian theme and with other fanciful subjects, including vignettes fired onto otherwise clear glass; the artists were Edwin Bright and William F. Oxenriter of the Aurora Glass Company.

Garman house
631 Osage Road, Mount Lebanon
Thomas B. Garman, architect, 1931

Garman was staff architect for the Virginia Manor development in Mount Lebanon, and there he placed his own house. He is said to have reproduced a grandparent's home in the Cotswolds.

"Sunnyhill"
(now Unitarian
Universalist Church)
1240 Washington Road,
Mount Lebanon
Stanley L. Roush, architect,
1919

Roush, Pittsburgh's tasteful public-works architect, designed this handsome, rambling house for Joseph Roush, a nephew. The general effect is English, with rounded roof eaves

1240 Washington Road

to give the effect of thatch. The actual original material was probably wood shingles. The dormers' original cladding was probably clapboard.

Arlington Park
Arlington Park Road, Mount Lebanon
1883 and after

This is a cul-de-sac group of houses, most of them originally built in a Gothic or Italianate style, for members of the Arlington Camp Meeting Association of the Methodist Protestant Church of Pittsburgh. The houses have undergone remodelings that have damaged their character, but in some of them original canopies, balconies, brackets, and vergeboards have so far survived. The setting originally was sparsely settled, and a suburb of the trolley and automobile period has grown around it.

Holleman house
3200 Brownsville Road, Brentwood
1920

The compositional secret to this attractive house lies in the broad, well-proportioned, and crisply detailed front gable that imposes calm on restless stonework and massing.

Historic Landmark plaque

Davis house
3423 Brownsville Road,
Brentwood
C. 1880

An elaborate porch, decorative brackets, simulated quoins, and decorated window and door heads give an otherwise-simple house touches of elegance. Though not set on a high basement, this house, in its Italianate way, has a similarity to the Federal-style house of Abishai Way in Edgeworth, another one-and-a-half-story house with a pedimented porch and the air of a villa.

Historic Landmark plaque

Stevens house
4344 Brownsville Road, Brentwood
Louis S. Stevens, architect, 1925

Louis Stevens was a most accomplished Eclectic, as some very smooth and literate house designs in Schenley Farms and Squirrel Hill attest. He had a certain prominence in his own time as president of the Pittsburgh Architectural Club with his own column in *Charette*, "Louis XVI" (pronounced, Looie Says). Yet he has not retained the fame of Benno Janssen or even Brandon Smith.

His own house in Brentwood has a remarkable early nineteenth-century touch, and one would be easily tempted to assume that it was a hundred years older than it is. Yet an advertisement in an architectural magazine points out that no special molding profiles were used. The proportions, the slightly awkward shapes, imparted the genuine effect. The weathered stones are re-used and come mainly from an old church.

Historic Landmark plaque

Thomas Jefferson Garden Mausoleum
Jefferson Memorial Park, Pleasant Hills
George B. Post & Sons (New York; 1895) and
Edward F. Griffith (c. 1960), architects

When the Bank of Pittsburgh building on Fourth Avenue was to come down in 1944, Edward Griffith, an admirer, prevailed on the owner of the property to let the temple front stand. Proposals came and went for re-use of the facade elements, but now it is recast as a hypaethral tholos, with the old main door as gateway to the outer enclosure.

John Work house
Curry Hollow Road, Jefferson Memorial Park, Pleasant Hills
1800

This is an early house of mixed construction, two bays of stone, three bays of squared logs, both parts built apparently at the same time. The relation between the two elements suggests that the house was begun in stone, then completed in logs. The big quoins at the lower part of the front outer corner, diminishing greatly after the sixth course, seem further evidence of an ambitious beginning followed by decreasingly energetic building activity. The projecting chimney in the stone gable wall suggests Virginia practice.

corbeled arch, so that the walls seem to be parting like curtains. Panels between the windows have wampum-like figures of golfers, the background being in a rather hot contrasting red. All together, sort of proto-Post-Modernism.

Golf clubhouse, South Park
Off Brownsville Road, South Park
Henry Hornbostel, architect, 1938

This is among the last of Hornbostel's designs, and certainly is one of the most fantastic. The deep-red mass of the long, narrow building is nearly split by a concave

Allegheny County Fairgrounds
Brownsville Road between Corrigan and McCorkle Roads,
South Park, South Park Township
Opened 1933

South Park, begun in 1927, was one of the large new County parks, remote from urban areas and planned for automobile access. There was still a considerable number

of working farms in the county, and the establishment of
a fairgrounds that could also be used for equine sports
seemed natural enough. The largest area began as a polo
field with grandstands, then was converted to an oval for
harness racing with a half-mile track. At one end of this is
a barn-like transportation museum of yellow brick. At the
other are a circular stable and octagonal blacksmith shop,
now privately operated. Near by are stables and exhibit
pavilions, some of frame, some of yellow brick.

South Park calls up associations with Henry
Hornbostel. In the Depression years, the aging architect
had little to design and interested himself in the County
Fair. From 1935 to 1939 he was director of Allegheny
County Parks, and performed this unaccustomed role
with the flamboyance and charm he had brought to the
pursuit of his architectural career.

James (or Oliver) Miller house ("Stone Manse")
Stone Manse Drive east of Corrigan Drive,
South Park Township
1808; 1830

The Millers, of North Irish origin, were among the earliest
settlers in this area. Having sided with the rebels in the
Whiskey Rebellion of 1794, the family was reduced, yet

James Miller was able to live on in a log house that the
family had built on its arrival in 1772. In 1808 the lower
portion of the present stone house was added by James
Miller, and in 1830 his son Oliver replaced the log house
with the larger stone section. In 1927 the County bought
the property from the Millers of the time.

Now a museum, the Miller house is restored inside and
out. It not only illustrates in concrete terms the life of a
farming family just after the pioneer period but shows the
Georgian architecture of this region in its simplest form:
undecorated but orderly and well proportioned, and with
surfaces made interesting by the random patterning and
contrasting sizes of the stonework.

National Register of Historic Places
Historic Landmark plaque

Boyer house
5679 Library Road, Bethel Park
C. 1840

Peter Boyer built this Greek Revival frame house that
stands in basically unaltered condition. The two-story
porch is original, as are the window sash and their glass.
Even the kitchen, though modernized, contains its original
fireplace and crane.

Historic Landmark plaque

View from Hilltop Road, Collier Township.

THE WESTERN
TOWNSHIPS

Settlement of the western end of Allegheny County south of the Ohio River began in the 1760s, but Indians raided the farms that were established by pioneer families into the 1780s. Even after this menace ended, much of the land remained rather thinly settled. While some construction from the eighteenth century can be found, and an occasional handsome farmhouse or barn from the nineteenth century, man's presence in this area is most evident in other constructions.

Coal mining, which began in the late nineteenth century and continued into the twentieth, has left both worked-out and working mines and "patches" of small uniform miners' houses. The Montour Railroad was built in 1878 specifically to haul coal over an 11.5 mile route between the mines of the Imperial Coal Company at Imperial in North Fayette Township to connecting rail lines along the Ohio River in Robinson Township. (It was later extended and absorbed by the Pittsburgh & Lake Erie Railroad.) Oil production was also a major local industry. Oil wells with metalwork derricks are strewn across the landscape; some still operate as do a number of small oil transfer facilities.

Suburbanization since World War II has absorbed farms and erected houses, commercial strips, and office buildings in the western townships. Upper St. Clair Township experienced residential growth early in the century along an interurban trolley line from Pittsburgh to Washington in Washington County. It has since been highly developed in many areas and is now one of Pittsburgh's modern suburbs of choice for the wealthy. But most of the suburbanization in these townships has

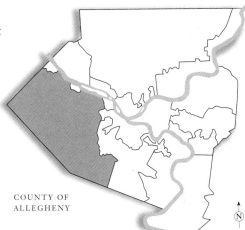

COUNTY OF
ALLEGHENY

been stimulated by the Pittsburgh International Airport. This facility has evolved from a few World War II-era U.S. Army airstrips into an international airport which occupies sizeable acreage in both Moon and Findlay Townships. Development spawned by the airport and its access roads has resulted in a rash of suburban office parks.

One of the area's earliest and most significant houses was an early casualty: General John Neville's "Bower Hill," the center of a thousand-acre estate, was burned during the Whiskey Rebellion in 1794. But "Woodville," the predecessor and companion house of "Bower Hill" begun by Neville in c. 1785, survives in Collier Township. Its site is now limited, but the house remains remarkably unscathed by the 200 years of rebellion, extraction industry, and modern development which have swirled around it.

Farm, Oakdale Road, North Fayette Township.

conventional suburban development has come to much of the one-time farmland.

National Register of Historic Places

Gilfillan farm
1950 Washington Road south of Orr Road,
Upper St. Clair Township
House, 1857

The Gilfillans have been in Upper St. Clair since the 1760s, and this property, though no longer a farm, is still in family hands. The house shows the break away from the Greek Revival that had been taking place for about a decade and a half. The ground-floor window heads have Greek-looking ornaments over their centers, and the doorway has the typical

sidelight and overdoor-light framework of an ambitious Greek Revival building. But the front windows are doubled, and the proportions of the house are spread horizontally in an abandonment of the old Georgian verticality. Vivid paired brackets are positively Italianate, and their use directly under the peaks of the gables, along with the projection of the cornices, suggests an attempt to make the design expressive through ornamental features. This is a late work of a time that was moving from Classical harmony, which had few elements that might challenge the eye, toward fantasy. Around back the windows however are still placidly Georgian of the simplest sort. A big, plain Pennsylvania barn of 1868 and ten other buildings remain as an example of a large Victorian farm group, though

Barn
2333 Lesnett Road, Upper St. Clair Township
1897

Octagonal barns are a rarity anywhere, though for activities like distributing hay to cows they have practical advantages. Allegheny County may have had more of the type at one time, but this is the only one now in existence.

Joseph Wright house
653 Bank Street, Bridgeville
Frederick G. Scheibler, Jr., architect, 1907

The clean-cut simplicity of this house distinguishes it among the other buildings of this town. The lower part is of dark red brick and the upper part is a pale gray stucco. Some windows contain art glass.

bought what was left of the estate, which had been reduced and the house itself threatened, for restoration. Neville House Associates, established with the support of Landmarks in 1976, continues to raise funds for and sponsor events to support the restoration of this historic house.

National Historic Landmark
National Register of Historic Places
Historic Landmark plaque

John (or Presley) Neville house ("Woodville"; now the Neville House)
1375 Washington Pike, Collier Township
1785; many additions and alterations

The large steep roof with dormers indicates the preferences of the original owner, General John Neville, for the customs of his native Virginia. The placement of end chimneys directly within the clapboarded walls is also frequently to be found there. The exterior was originally quite plain and simple in its geometry, but there have been numerous additions. Victorian alterations included the trellised porches and Gothic windows in the front dormers and one of the gable walls; the front dormers have gables of a scalloped, almost Jacobean, appearance. Inside is a good Federal mantelpiece with the delicate woodcarving of the style. As in some other old houses of the United States, the window glass was used as a register of family members and guests, who scratched their names in it with diamonds.

The house passed from John Neville to his son Presley, and thence to other members of the family down to 1973. In 1976 the Pittsburgh History & Landmarks Foundation

Walker-Ewing house
Noblestown Road east of Pinkerton Run Road, Collier Township
C. 1790

Though somewhat modernized inside and out, this two-and-a-half-story log house retains a generally authentic appearance and suggests how such a building can be adapted to present-day needs in a way that respects its antiquity. The house was in the Ewing family until 1973, when the latest owner gave it to the Pittsburgh History & Landmarks Foundation.

National Register of Historic Places
Historic Landmark plaque

Barn
Head of Old North Branch Road, North Fayette Township
C. 1850

This is the only surviving brick barn in Allegheny County: an architecturally rather ambitious one, with its arches and its diamond- and hourglass-pattern ventilator holes. Such barns with brick patterns are almost all confined to South Central Pennsylvania. The photograph dates from about 1980, and shows the barn in better condition than it was at the time of this publication.

Wilson house
Seabright Road north of North Branch Road, North Fayette Township
1810–12 (?)

Unkempt but charming in its proportions and detailing, this Federal-style house on an English basement has a kinship in its design to the Way house in Edgeworth and the Lightner house in Shaler Township, and it is quite possible that, though supposedly older, it dates from the 1830s as they do. The porch may be much newer than the

house; certainly the roof, cutting off the old cornice moldings on the front, must be a replacement. Yet the porch is very well proportioned to the house, the result of careful consideration whenever it was built.

Hyeholde
Coraopolis Heights Road near Beaver Grade Road,
Moon Township
William Kryskill, designer, 1931–38; additions, 1952

This is among the county's most audacious essays in the quaint, built in part from the weathered stones and materials of an old barn and having all the contrived rusticity of which the Eclectic period was capable. It was built by the owners themselves, half as a restaurant, half as a residence, and still functions as a restaurant.

Looking upriver toward Neville Island

DOWN THE OHIO

The Ohio River is one of the most historic rivers of the United States. It was a 981-mile link in the 2,500-mile route, almost wholly by water, that the French of the early eighteenth century contemplated between Quebec and Louisiana. The British victory in the French and Indian War, the formal opening of the North-west Territory, the defeat of the Indians of the Northeast in 1794, and the Louisiana Purchase of 1803 made the Ohio a grand highway to the West and South, the route of flatboats, keelboats, and from 1811 on, of steamboats. Packet and towboat traffic throve on the Ohio, and even as late as 1980, before the crisis in the steel industry, there was agitation for river locks big enough to accommodate barge tows whose length exceeded that of the largest ocean liners.

COUNTY OF ALLEGHENY

And yet the Allegheny County towns along the Ohio have generally been towns by the river rather than river ports. McKees Rocks on the south shore, though strategists *almost* chose it as the site for Fort Pitt in the early 1750s, and though its location was to some extent settled in the eighteenth century, is really a creation of the Pittsburgh & Lake Erie Railroad, which began operations through the town in 1879 and located its shops there the next year. Other industry soon gathered as well, and the town attracted the immigrant workers who were coming from Continental Europe in large numbers. The churches of the Industrial Bottoms, next to the river, attest to the variety of cultures represented. Coraopolis, further down the river, was another railroad town, though more residential than McKees Rocks, that was further developed in 1894 by a trolley line that crossed Neville Island.

The conversion of the north shore of the river into a series of suburbs, again beside but not greatly related to the water, came in two principal phases. The Sewickley area—which developed its own special character, to be treated in the next chapter—lay close to river level, and the opening of the Ohio & Pennsylvania Railroad in 1851 offered such easy access from Allegheny that its conversion from farm area into suburbs happened in a few decades. Closer to Allegheny, the land by the water rose to a hundred-foot elevation, making a daunting climb for rail commuters alighting on the river shore. Here a trolley route, opened around 1900, made the difference; running along the brow of the bluff, the trolley was obviously much more convenient than the railroad. Where villas and small houses had once stood in isolation, middle-class houses much like those of the South Hills were soon being built in abundance in communities such as Bellevue, Avalon, and Ben Avon.

Industry on Neville Island

Between the shores are three islands. Brunot's Island, closest to the Pittsburgh Point, once had a racetrack, but since the turn of the century it has been the location of a series of power stations. Davis Island, small and now deserted, was the location of the first dam on the Ohio, completed in 1885: the first step in a great undertaking that had all but the very end of the river canalized by 1929. Neville Island, just below Davis and five miles long, was covered by gardens in the nineteenth century, producing fruit and vegetables for the Pittsburgh market; then, beginning around 1900, it was industrialized so fully and diversely that today, with the exception of a very small residential area, it looks like a showcase of industrial specimens. The great Dravo boatyard, now closed, and a towboat fleeting area were among the exhibits. There had been a few other boatyards along the Ohio, notably those at Shousetown (now Glenwillard) on the south shore, where the hull of the *Great Republic*, one of the largest Mississippi River sidewheelers, was built in 1867. But the Dravo yard operated on a grand scale, producing towboats and barges on almost an assembly line basis, giving Neville Island an exceptionally intimate contact with the river itself.

On the McKees Rocks Bridge

Industrial Bottoms, McKees Rocks

Close to the Ohio River and almost isolated from the rest of McKees Rocks is an area called the Industrial Bottoms. A traveler crossing the McKees Rocks Bridge may be intrigued by a row of church towers as he passes above, and frustrated when he tries to double back and approach them. Rising above nearby industry, railroad yards, and streets of close-set housing, they are symbols and expressions of the varied ethnic heritage of the industrial workers of the Bottoms.

The nearest of these churches to the bridge is St. Mark's Church (Roman Catholic; now part of St. John of God Parish), built for a Slovak congregation in 1916 to designs by E. B. Lang. The style is Gothic, with a spired tower.

St. Mark's Convent

St. Mark's School

Doorway, St. Mark's School

St. Mark's Roman Catholic Church

St. Nicholas Russian Orthodox Church

Detail, St. Nicholas

Next to it are a convent and school of 1928 that were designed by the fanciful Edward J. Weber. The convent looks like other work of his, particularly St. Scholastica's convent in Aspinwall, and the strangely formed school, in brown brick, has a rusticated Gothic doorway of peculiar panache. Close by is St. Nicholas Russian Orthodox Church of 1914, whose front has three onion domes (there are three others elsewhere on the church); inside, beneath a large and elaborate crystal chandelier, is a colorful iconostasis. Both of these churches are on Munson Street. Nearby, on Ella Street, are two other churches of note: St. Mary's Ukrainian Orthodox Church of 1922, a simplified Byzantine building by Carlton Strong, and Holy Ghost Byzantine Catholic Church of 1917, by John H. Phillips: a curious church with a single domed tower flanked by domed buttresses; its detailing includes a small starburst window, a unique Mexican Baroque touch.

Above and below: Holy Ghost Byzantine Catholic Church.

St. Mary's Ukrainian Orthodox Church

McKees Rocks Bridge
Ohio River at Mile 3.25, between McKees Rocks and Pittsburgh
Vernon R. Covell of the Allegheny County Department of Public
Works, chief engineer, 1929–31

Writing around 1960, Carl Condit, a historian of American
civil engineering, approved of much that Allegheny County
was doing in bridge construction in the 1920s and 1930s,
but he could not find it in his heart to like the McKees
Rocks Bridge. Expediencies of clearing a river, its banks, a
railroad yard, and streets dictated such a variety of bridge
structural types in the various spans that he called the
whole visual effect "most dissatisfactory." There are indeed
seventeen spans formed in five different ways. The most
notable is the undoubtedly handsome 750-foot river span,
a two-hinged steel arch with an enveloping truss that
resists off-center loads. The clearance above the river is
100 feet, and the whole bridge length, the greatest in the
county, is a little over 4,500 feet. Art Deco pylons bear
sculpture by Frank Vittor.

Disunified the total structure may be, yet the overall
impression *is* satisfactory. The arch above the river, a
graceful shape, is what is really noticed.

Mann's Hotel
Chartier and Singer Avenues, McKees Rocks
1803(?) and after

This is an old tavern that, like many others along old post
roads, has been a halt for travelers, a post office, a lockup
for prisoners on their way to court, and in addition, toward
the end of the last century, a dormitory for workers during
a brief boom in petroleum. The bar, heated by a coal stove,
is still about the way it was in 1900, and by the standards of
that time was on the plain side. Like the lower station of
the Duquesne Incline, the starkness of the bar interior
takes you back.

St. Francis de Sales Church (Roman Catholic)
Chartiers Avenue and Margaret Street, McKees Rocks
Marius Rousseau, architect, 1899

A church of variegated, warm-colored random ashlar, plain
except for the triumphal-arch entrance, the four statues
above that have a false attic as background, and a red-tiled

entrance towers, complete with spires, there is a stubby flèche over the crossing.

Additional buildings on the large church property include a rectory of the same period with a corner tower and a masonry Gothic porch; a handsome convent of Ligonier paving block from 1930, designed by Edward J. Weber in a Romantic manner with Gothic arches; and a buff-brick school.

dome that bears a statue of St. Francis. The design may be modeled after that of Heins & La Farge for St. Matthew's Cathedral in Washington, D. C., its exact contemporary. The white-and-blue interior centers on the inner pendentive dome, supported by paired Corinthian columns.

Above and below: The former St. Mary's Convent.

St. Mary's Help of Christians Church (Roman Catholic)
St. John Street and Church Avenue, McKees Rocks
William P. Ginther (Akron), architect, 1901

This very large church has in its form, size, and setting the air of a cathedral. The very dark, almost black, peculiarly rough brick of the walls is in sharp contrast with trim and ornament of painted composition stone. Besides two

Taylor-Wilson Manufacturing Company
Thompson Avenue south of Kennedy Street, McKees Rocks
Robert A. Cummings, engineer, 1905

This is an early reinforced-concrete industrial building, from the period just after the pioneering phase of this structural medium. What reinforcement system was used is not known, but the double lower edge of the beams over each side opening may have a structural basis. Given the starkness of the building, its air of indifference to visual amenity, the same may be true of the big round-arched window at the northern end; it is built as if it were one span of the poured-concrete bridges that were beginning to be constructed around the country.

Presston
Ohio and Orchard Streets, Stowe Township
C. 1900

This settlement of about one hundred frame double houses was begun as a company town for the Pressed-Steel Car Company, complete with its own police force and jail. It is surrounded by railroad and industrial property, but Pressed-Steel sold the houses in 1949, and Stowe

Township now administers the neighborhood. Many individual houses have been modernized, but the steady repetition of facades, characteristic of a company town, remains.

Shenango Furnace Company
Grand Avenue, Neville Township
Operations begun c. 1915

A furnace company smelts iron and makes castings and pig from it; it makes no wrought iron and no steel. When Shenango ceased to make iron in its remaining operative Neville Island furnace around 1990, an element of Southwestern Pennsylvania history going back to 1790 became extinct. The blast furnaces have gone, but the Shenango plant still makes coke for sale to others, marking its presence with a huge gas holder and clouds of steam from the quenches. The entrance to the office building has decorative figures by Robert Qualters.

Repair facility, Locks and Dams Number Two
River Road and Cottage Avenue, Neville Township
C. 1905

Locks and Dams Number Two were built between 1896 and 1906 as part of the system that by 1929 was to have the Ohio River canalized—divided into level pools of water—for almost its entire 981-mile length. The main- and back-channel dams were located at Glenfield, close to the point where I–79 now crosses the river. Locks and Dams Number

Two were in use until August 1922, when the Emsworth Locks and Dams upstream took over the greater part of

its function. This repair facility on Neville Island is a large, sober work of governmental architecture, dignified if not especially graceful. A cantilevered window allowed the state of the dam and its repairs to be observed. This is a rare survivor of the county's river-related architecture.

Duquesne Light Company substation
1335 Fourth Avenue, Coraopolis
C. 1925

This is a pleasant little architectural incident, a utilitarian monument intended to contribute to the street scene.

Pittsburgh & Lake Erie Railroad Station
Neville Avenue and Mill Street, Coraopolis
Shepley, Rutan & Coolidge (Boston), architects, 1895

This station is by H. H. Richardson's successor firm. Its style is Richardson Romanesque, and its brownstone and buff brick are consistent with the style. Richardson himself would have been bolder in form and scale, as his numerous stations around the Boston suburbs show, but this is a valuable work of architecture all the same. Like the much later railroad station at Wilkinsburg, it reveals the hand of an accomplished designer applied to one of the most conspicuous of small-town building types.

National Register of Historic Places

Shouse house
Main and Bridge Streets, Glenwillard, Crescent Township
C. 1840; additions

In March of 1997, when this book was at the printer's, the Pittsburgh History & Landmarks Foundation learned that the Shouse house was to be demolished. This promised a

sad end to a building of historical significance in a small community near the county line.

Glenwillard was originally Shousetown, and this was the house of its founder Peter Shouse, a boat builder who came here in 1822. The original house was a three-bay construction with a chimney at one end; at a later date, a five-bay addition with a chimney at each end was added, reproducing the original details, and the porch that gave the street front a nearly symmetrical appearance must have been added later still.

Shousetown was a boat-building area through most of the nineteenth century, but its grandest moment was probably in 1867, with the launching of the hull of the *Great Republic*, designed by Nathan Porter, a relative of Peter Shouse. This, one of the grandest packets in the Lower Mississippi River service, was fitted with machinery and cabins at Pittsburgh.

Historic Landmark plaque

Emsworth Locks and Dams
Mile 6.2, Ohio River, at Neville Island
1922; 1938

The Emsworth Dam maintains river level at the Point at 710 feet above sea level. Its completion in 1922 eliminated two earlier Ohio River dams: the Davis Island Dam of 1885, the very first on the river, and Locks and Dams Number Two, on either side of Neville Island at Glenfield. The original Pittsburgh Pool level maintained by Emsworth

Dam was 703 feet above sea level, but the reconstruction of 1938 raised the crest to 710, making possible the elimination of the two lowermost dams on the Allegheny and Monongahela Rivers. The main-channel dam is 967 feet long. The "lift" is now 18 feet, from 692 feet below the dam. Lock chambers are 600 by 110 feet and 360 by 56 feet. Planned at a time when river navigation seemed in decline, these dimensions require the largest tows, which can be about 1,150 feet long, to lock through in two sections.

Balph house (now Andrew Bayne Memorial Library)
34 North Balph Avenue, Bellevue
James Madison Balph, architect, 1875

This Italianate mansion was the home of its designer who had an architectural practice in Allegheny. Since 1914 it has been a library and its grounds a park.

Historic Landmark plaque

House
735 Ohio River Boulevard, Avalon
C. 1870

Although not all it once was, this is an interesting feature of this part of Route 65, antedating almost everything in the trolley suburb around it. Walls and quoins suggest stucco and stone, but in fact the house is built of wood.

Grotto
Oak Street and Bellevue Road, off Starr Avenue, Avalon
C. 1928–32

Here is an "eye catcher" in the grand tradition of European
landscape gardening, overlooking an unfrequented suburban street. The Slovak Franciscans moved to this area in
the mid-1920s, and the annual pilgrimages that soon began
resulted in this massive grotto, built by the congregation
itself, with walls of vigorously textured rubble, urns of
cobbles in cement, and steps faced in marble. The grotto
chamber contains an altar faced in marble and three niches,
once containing religious images. The grotto now belongs
to General Suburban Hospital.

Frederick Avenue in Sewickley

THE SEWICKLEY AREA

Sewickley, twelve miles down the Ohio River from the Pittsburgh
Point, is the focus for an exceptional group of residential boroughs.
In this area the hills retreat from the water's edge to leave a fairly
broad river plain. The land is easy to build on and in contact
with the routes of communication along the river that are
closely associated with the area's history.

At first there was an Indian path by the river, which late
in the eighteenth century was widened into a road between the
towns of Pittsburgh and Beaver. Until the late 1790s, however,
there was no settlement on the plain or in the hills, though the
Pennsylvania Legislature had surveyed them in 1785 as part of
the Depreciation Lands, purchasable with the "depreciation
certificates" issued to Revolutionary War veterans as part of
their pay. Virginia's claim to Southwestern Pennsylvania, maintained
until 1779, and the menace by the Indians, locally ended only in 1792,
had discouraged settlement, while land south of the Ohio River was
more accessible to settlers from the South and was easier to farm.
Settlement began in 1797, and as the Beaver Road gained more traffic
and as farmers moved into the land along it, what was to become
Sewickley took on the character of a village, while the Edgeworth
district a mile further down, halfway along the twenty-six-mile distance
between Pittsburgh and Beaver, became a location for small taverns
catering to the teamsters.

The opening of service on the Ohio & Pennsylvania (later, the
Pennsylvania) Railroad in 1851 started an evolution from a thinly settled
place of farms, taverns, and a little commerce into a highly desirable
suburban area. Sewickley was incorporated as a borough in 1853, and,
while it was a very small borough at first, it was developing rapidly by
the mid-1870s as a town of large, comfortable commuter homes with
sizeable yards. Immediately to the west was a part of Leet Township

COUNTY OF
ALLEGHENY

531

generally known as Edgeworth after the Edgeworth Female Seminary of the 1830s, itself named for the once-famous Irish novelist Maria Edgeworth. Here were some of the oldest houses of the area, and here came newer houses in the late nineteenth century that were generally even more elegant than those of Sewickley. Edgeworth, like Edgewood east of Pittsburgh, developed a self-awareness and a determination to keep its special character. This led it to free itself in 1904 from Leet Township (which had become industrialized), bury all utility lines, and forbid the interurban trolley line then under construction along the river to pass through.

Above these communities on the river plain, the hills were for a long time thinly settled; they made poor farmland. In the 1890s, though, a number of wealthy citizens of the still-independent city of Allegheny perceived that the hills would make a good location for summer estates. Families who wintered in the mansions of Ridge Avenue began to change the character of the place, building estate houses with myriad auxiliary buildings, formal gateways, and curving drives. The move to Sewickley Heights of the Allegheny Country Club in 1902 confirmed the trend which grew in force through the 1920s. The automobile, which offered independence from the train and the horse-drawn carriage that once met the train at the station, encouraged building in the hills even for year-round occupation, and the gradual decline of the North Side promoted the estate dwellers to make Sewickley Heights their permanent home.

Outside this handsome residential trio of Sewickley, Edgeworth, and Sewickley Heights are other riverside boroughs. East of Sewickley lie Haysville, now signaled by a little street of wooden houses by the river but the location of a large mineral-springs resort hotel in the 1870s, and Osborne, which has its own little houses by the water and larger uphill houses too. West of Edgeworth is the industrial borough Leetsdale, which is actually of a piece with Ambridge and the other industrial communities of Beaver County that lie beyond.

In these communities some of the best architecture of the county is to be found. The variety is great: sturdy Georgian houses from the early nineteenth century; mansions and villas that have survived in the hills; churches from the Mid-Victorian period on. But the image that pre-dominates is of a substantial house in Sewickley, or a collection of many

Beaver Street west of Grant Street, Sewickley.

such houses: not mansions, just nice big upper-middle-class houses of about a century ago or thereabouts, Second Empire, Colonial Revival, or vaguely chateau-like, standing in ample yards, contemplating the world through big windows and the pillars of their porches. These places represent the norm of Victorian living: full of respectability and well-being, counting on good service by the cook, the local merchants, and the Pennsylvania Railroad, free from the dirt and turmoil of places where money is made, but not ostentatious by the standards of the day.

Beaver Street in central Sewickley

House
1207 Beaver Road, Osborne
1872

This is for the most part a classic Second Empire house as executed in wood, with corner boards framing conspicuous areas of siding. The porch, however, appears to be from the early part of this century.

A rare hooded side door

McKnight house
1107 Beaver Road, Osborne
Longfellow, Alden & Harlow, architects, 1894

This was among the earliest Pittsburgh-area houses to use decorative half-timbering. It was designed for a picturesque ten-acre site. The interior was lavishly furnished with stencil work and leaded glass, with the Delft tiling around the mantelpiece in the dining room as the most striking feature.

McKown/McDonald house
1008 Beaver Road, Osborne
C. 1860; Rutan & Russell, architects for remodeling, 1898; various additions and alterations

The grand temple-front porch, facing the Ohio River, imposes some unity on a rather disunified composition.

Beaver Road entrance

700 block of Beaver Street

Sewickley

Sewickley has not quite the spaciousness of private properties and the antiquity of individual buildings found in Edgeworth just down the river, but it is a place nonetheless with big old houses in big yards as well as smaller houses with little yards. Although it is located along the Ohio River, it is less a river town than a Victorian railroad suburb beside a river. The second half of the nineteenth century was the time when it flourished, and from that period many excellent houses remain.

Above and top right: front toward the river.

The main building block juts prominently toward Beaver Road as a simple, symmetrical mass, and a little semi-circular porch suffices on this side.

Davis-McKnight-Ramsey house
963 Beaver Street, Sewickley
Alden & Harlow, architects, 1904

Here is a speculative construction, built close to homes for the architects themselves. The principal material is yellow brick, but the upper porch, quite possibly open to the weather at first, suggests a similar motif in the Samuel Black house of 1892 in Edgeworth.

Sewickley Borough Historic District

Harlow house
943 Beaver Street, Sewickley
Alden & Harlow, architects, 1906

This was the house of the architect Alfred Branch Harlow.
The style is very nearly Neo-Georgian, purged of the
picturesque waywardness of the old Colonial Revival. And
yet the dormers are hip-roofed in a rather medieval way,
and the strong axial statement made by the ground-floor
colonnade and the arcaded entrance is quietly impaired by
little unbalanced windows in the second floor and attic.

Sewickley Borough Historic District

Samuel Adams house
940 Beaver Street, Sewickley
Alden & Harlow, architects, 1904

A double-width lot allows passers-by to take in the two-
fold nature of the composition of this house: simple and
broad on the front, picturesque on the side with massing
and fenestration accommodating a variety of functions.
At the time of construction, this house appeared in several
local and national publications.

Sewickley Borough Historic District

Double house
922–24 Beaver Street, Sewickley
C. 1910

The Shingle Style of the 1880s was a supple manner, its shingled wall and roof surfaces extended, folded, faired into one another, with masonry piers, foundations, and chimneys to some extent in evidence. By 1910 the real virtuosity was over. The shingles here are attached to flat, clearly bounded areas, and window trim that would have been much less in evidence some twenty years ago now overlies the shingled surfaces. This is a good-looking building, though.

Sewickley Borough Historic District

Spahr house
527 Cochran Street, Sewickley
MacClure & Spahr, architects, 1904

This house, pretty much Arts and Crafts though with slight allusions to half-timber, was the home of the architect Albert H. Spahr. His firm was a favorite, in the Sewickley area and in Pittsburgh, for houses and business buildings. MacClure & Spahr's work was rarely innovative, rarely imitative, rarely tasteless.

Sewickley Borough Historic District

House
904 Centennial Avenue, Sewickley
MacClure & Spahr, architects, c. 1907

House
900 Centennial Avenue, Sewickley
1874

A well-proportioned house, faced in orange Roman brick and with an unusual arcaded porch let into the building mass.

Sewickley Borough Historic District

This is the oldest house in the immediate area, a pleasant Italianate inclusion in a turn-of-the-century district. Only a shed dormer, added to the front slope of the roof, is a little discordant.

Sewickley Borough Historic District

The arcaded porch requires stout corner buttresses.

House
807 Beaver Street, Sewickley
C. 1900

Several Sewickley houses have little bay windows or quasi-turrets caught up under their eaves, and in this case there are two such, in a house of bold and airy design.

View from the east

Porter house
406 Peebles Street, Sewickley
C. 1870

Second Empire is rare in Sewickley, and this is its only outstanding example.

Smith houses
304–20 Peebles Street, Sewickley
1872

Jehu P. Smith built four houses, side by side, for his children. Their overall composition was originally the

Number 320

Number 316

539

Number 310

Number 304

same, but their pleasant Italianate detailing differs on each, and later porches emphasize the differences still further.

Sewickley Borough Municipal Building
Chestnut and Thorn Streets, Sewickley
Charles W. Bier, architect, 1911; addition, 1984

Occasionally an architect early in this century attempted a hybrid Beaux-Arts-Georgian style, as here. The facade is symmetrical and has its windows disposed in a Georgian manner, but each window is rather broad for its height and the sash design compromises between quaintness and utility by having twelve panes above and one below. The entrance and the window above it are not Georgian at all; the division of the window suggests a Greek Revival doorway. The bracketed cornice harks back to Mid-Victorian Italianate: brackets were somewhat in fashion again in the 1910s. The tower, which doubles as a monumental feature and a hose-drying space for the firehouse, has a plausibly Georgian cupola over a very Beaux-Arts cornice. Except on the main front the pattern of openings is very irregular. A curious rear wing, topped by its own little cupola, seems to have been a stable before the fire department was motorized. The plainer modern addition is in clear contrast to the original work though also faced in red brick.

Sewickley Public Library
Thorn and Broad Streets, Sewickley
Henry D. Gilchrist, architect, 1923

A dark building of
coursed rubble with
stone trim, the Sewickley
Library is a quiet,
reserved, rectangular
mass with four corner
pavilions. The detailing,
on inspection, turns out
to be Mannerist, flouting
accepted Classical practice
in a conscious, sophisti-
cated way. The flat arch
over the doorway bulges
uneasily downward,
the volutes of the Ionic
pilaster capitals creep into

The Mannerist doorway

the pediment area, and the round windows by the doorway
have keystones at their bottoms, not their tops.

Sewickley Borough Historic District

Flatiron Building
Beaver and Division Streets, Sewickley
C. 1875

A local architectural curiosity, and surprisingly the only
well-preserved Victorian commercial building in Sewickley.
The odd perimeter is caused by the angle of Division
Street, laid down on the border between two early land
surveys. The Pittsburgh History & Landmarks Foundation
acquired and restored the building with community
support in the 1970s.

Historic Landmark plaque

of an accumulation of features. Yet there is a drama in the starkness of it all; it is by no means a boring ensemble. You have to inspect it bit by bit, that is all, as you might look at successive illustrations in a dictionary. The church clock, which functions by its position almost as a town clock, was restored to its Victorian Gothic form in 1996.

Sewickley Borough Historic District

**Sewickley Methodist Episcopal Church
(now Sewickley United Methodist Church)**
Broad and Thorn Streets, Sewickley
1884

This is not a graceful church. The proportions are not especially good, the openings trimmed in light sandstone jump out from the red brick, and the general effect is that

St. Stephen's Episcopal Church
Broad Street and Frederick Avenue, Sewickley
Bartberger & East, architects, 1894; parish hall by Alden & Harlow, 1911–14; Jennings Memorial Chapel, 1937, by Ingham & Boyd; further additions

This is a large, sprawling complex in stone, occupying the same large block as the Sewickley Methodist Episcopal

The raw-boned masonry

Parish hall

Jennings Memorial Chapel

Church. The general effect is Gothic, yet the church itself has some Richardson Romanesque features.

Sewickley Borough Historic District

House
210 Broad Street, Sewickley
Henry D. Gilchrist, architect, 1923

A work of the architect for the Mannerist Sewickley Public Library, this house is extremely rare in having slate-hung walls. Shingling a wall, so to speak, with slates is very occasionally found in Eastern Pennsylvania but all but never at this end of the state.

Sewickley Borough Historic District

House
422 Frederick Avenue, Sewickley
C. 1850

Here is a board-and-batten, bracketed cottage whose roof has a low Italianate pitch but whose delicate porch—original or not—alludes more to Gothic intricacy. The bay window at one end has leaded glass in rectangular panes, a modification it must be of early in this century. The house is of a kind that Andrew Jackson Downing, 1850-period arbiter of taste, recommended for people of modest means.

Sewickley Borough Historic District

Atwell-Christy house
403 Frederick Avenue, Sewickley
1862

Sided with flush vertical boarding, this follows the classic cottage formula developed around 1840 by Andrew Jackson Downing, the Hudson Valley landscape architect and arbiter of taste, and the Romantic architect Alexander Jackson Davis. The front is symmetrical, with a jutting gabled element at the center framing an entrance portal, and wing-like, more open porches standing almost as far from the front wall.

Sewickley Borough Historic District
Historic Landmark plaque

Duquesne Light Company substation
Chadwick Street, Sewickley
C. 1935

A Modernistic twelve-foot wall of white brick and tile, displaying a colored-tile panel with a cloud-and-flame motif. Set against this is a wrought-iron grille with the figure of a torch-bearer. The mixture of media is very unusual, but a success.

**Pittsburgh, Fort Wayne & Chicago Railway Station
(now American Legion Post 450)**
Chadwick Street, Sewickley
1887

Research has not yet turned up the name of the designer of
this essay in decorative half-timber. Wilson Brothers, who
were more or less the house architects of the Philadelphia-
based Pennsylvania Railroad, are possible. The building is
now on a new site, the railroad itself in 1928 having shifted
to make way for Ohio River Boulevard, and has long been
an American Legion post.

Historic Landmark plaque

Sewickley Presbyterian Church
Beaver and Grant Streets, Sewickley
*Joseph W. Kerr, architect, 1859–61; Rutan & Russell, architects
for parish hall, 1914; additions*

Six years after Sewickley's
incorporation, the Presbyterians could afford to
hire a Pittsburgh architect
to build a picturesque
stone church. The con-
gregation, in fact, was
already twenty years old,
and had outgrown its first
building in 1840. Barr &
Moser soon added to the
present church with a
chapel, designed in 1864
and finished in 1872;

Rutan & Russell added the Tudor parish hall in 1914,
replacing this chapel; and J. Phillip Davis added the new
Gothic Chapel of the Resurrection in 1953. In the church
hall is a mural of the Faërie Queen by Hanley Menoch,
executed on canvas in a tapestry-like style.

Historic Landmark plaque

House
36 Beaver Street, Sewickley
C. 1880

This is an extraordinary piece of Queen Anne, a High Baroque extreme of that picturesque manner.

McKnight house
Beaver Street and Pine Road, Sewickley
C. 1870

This was the home of Charles McKnight, a brick manufacturer who nevertheless chose to build in wood. The house is a simple but pretty Mid-Victorian essay in Gothic. Diamond-paned upper window sash and rippling vergeboards allude to the Middle Ages, at least.

Lowrie house
520 Pine Road, Sewickley
Alden & Harlow, architects, 1905

This is a curious but
attractive house exterior,
a game played with sym-
metrical and picturesque
elements together. It is
not a particularly unified
composition as a result,
but crisp overall geometry
rescues it, if in spite of
itself, from disorder.

*Sewickley Borough Historic
District*

House
625 Pine Road, Sewickley
Charles Barton Keen (Philadelphia), architect, 1918

Here is another of Keen's Pittsburgh-area works, akin to
the Lord and Clapp houses near by in Edgeworth. The
undetailed stuccoed columns are something of a trademark.
The house has a "saltbox" form, its eaves lower at the rear
than on the front. This is really a New England form;

A surprising triple tier of porches.

547

so is the jettying of the second-floor front over the ground floor, though the little bracketed pediment above the central doorway is generically Colonial. The service wing goes off at a marked angle from the main body of the house—an expression of its different function, perhaps—and terminates in a "catslide" that may suggest a humble place, having no proud gable.

Sewickley Borough Historic District

Fleming house
53 Woodland Road, Sewickley
C. 1875

Here is a house in the so-called Stick Style. In this, wooden surfaces are marked off into panels by applied slats that suggest a building frame, though in fact the real frame is concealed beneath the siding. The presence of a ribbed, stepped chimney at one end, an oriel window jutting from a gable,

a mild imitation of half-timbering in the gable peaks, and the use of shingles for siding suggest an architect who was aware of the latest trends of 1875. The shingles are an American substitute for the flat tiles used in smart English design as siding, and the other motifs are fashionably English and only recently in American use. Though the design as a whole still has a Mid-Victorian rigidity of effect, these features were soon to be identified with the Queen Anne style.

Sewickley Borough Historic District

306 Meadow Lane

Edgeworth

Just down the Ohio River from Sewickley lies Edgeworth, a spacious residential community with a special character that is emphasized by its situation between Sewickley's main-street commerce and Leetsdale's commerce and industry. Edgeworth has always been concerned to control

312 Meadow Lane

its development and to maintain its natural and social amenities; in 1906, it resisted even the building of a trolley line with success. Edgeworth has some of the most agreeable houses in Allegheny County, including a few that were

318 Meadow Lane

322 Meadow Lane

418 Maple Lane

426 Maple Lane

Edgeworth Club
511 East Drive, Edgeworth
Brandon Smith, architect, c. 1930; additions

The feeling of this building is institutional and domestic at once, particularly the former. The masonry has a rather hard quality, with some diapering in the brickwork it is true, but with not much in the way of carving or texture to soften its effect.

built not long after settlers first felt safe from the Indians of the area. Maple and Meadow Lanes, especially, are to be inspected end to end.

Abishai Way house
108 Beaver Road, Edgeworth
1838

This is a rare type of Federal-style house in Allegheny County, with its deep pedimented porch leading to a single story over an English basement. The doorway has engaged columns beneath an overdoor light. The front is substantially in the original condition; not so, the back. A similar composition is to be seen in the Lightner house in Shaler Township. Such houses represent an early departure from the local Georgian manner of decorating basic construction in favor of treating the whole building—on its front at least—as a decorative object. The ample porch of temple-like form is not merely a place to sit; it implies that this is the house of a well-to-do, cultured family.

National Register of Historic Places

Walker-Way house
Beaver Road near Quaker Road, Edgeworth
1810–20; rebuilt, 1841; additions and alterations

The original building is the tall three-bay central element, built in 1810: the first brick house between Pittsburgh and Beaver and the second-oldest house in the Sewickley area. To this was added a five-bay section with a long front porch in 1820. The house burned in 1841 and was rebuilt. A two-story porch was added to the original house around 1910, and a rear wing with another two-story porch in 1912. The house thus shows traces of a long, eventful history, during which it has been an inn and a school as well as a family home.

Historic Landmark plaque

Chaplin house
212 Creek Drive, Edgeworth
R. Clipston Sturgis and Allan Sturgis (Boston), architects, 1929

This is a large but rather simple Tudor house of brick and stone, with window-and-wall proportions that look authentic.

Shuck house
535 Irwin Drive, Edgeworth
Henry D. Gilchrist, architect, 1913

A house of rubble, symmetrical on the front. Unusually, hip roofs on corner porches carry the main roof surfaces closer to the ground, and the entrance is sheltered by a semi-dome.

Clapp house
425 Woodland Road, Edgeworth
Charles Barton Keen (Philadelphia), architect, 1920

It is not unusual for a large house to present a formal face to the public and be less formal elsewhere: and so it is here. The house is basically a "saltbox," with two stories on a symmetrical street front that has an ornamented, axial

Pergola and porch, northwest end

Garden front

doorway and one story on the garden front. On the latter, the second floor appears as a very long shingled shed dormer, an architectural fiction common around 1920 to impart a cottage look. Another architectural maneuver of the period replaces the Victorian front porch with end porches—here, indeed, with one open porch and a sun-porch-and-pergola combination—so that the elegant frontal composition stands unobscured.

Higgins house
Woodland Road, Edgeworth
Janssen & Cocken, architects, 1928–29

Here is a mansion of a rural French cast, similar to some found in the Chestnut Hill area of Philadelphia but using brick instead of the rubble common there. Windows are kept small to allow the walls to display their color and texture to the maximum. The roofs have exaggerated pitches—a trait common enough in Renaissance chateau architecture—but the extravagant textural roughness of the slating is an excess typical of the Eclectic period.

Lord house
208 Chestnut Road, Edgeworth
Charles Barton Keen
(Philadelphia), architect, 1902

Keen, a popular architect in Philadelphia, also had clients around Pittsburgh; his best-known work in this area is the Marshall house in Shadyside, the nucleus of the Pittsburgh Center for the Arts. Here is

more typical work: stone, shingles, the whitewashed columns of a porch and a pergola.

House
311 Pine Road, Edgeworth
1870

This is a remarkable Second Empire house, still in very good condition.

The garden portico

building continued as a house, and after its acquisition in 1903 by J. Wilkinson Elliott received a five-bay two-story Tuscan portico to the rear.

Former Edgeworth Female Seminary
420 Oliver Road, Edgeworth
1836; J. Wilkinson Elliott, architect for enlargement
c. 1905; numerous alterations

The five-bay stuccoed stone nucleus of this house was at first the Edgeworth Female Seminary, a girl's school named after the Irish novelist Maria Edgeworth. In 1865 a fire burned out this element of the building and destroyed two frame wings, terminating the school. The repaired

Samuel Black house
433 Maple Lane, Edgeworth
Longfellow, Alden &
Harlow, architects, 1892

This, a pioneering Colonial Revival house in the Pittsburgh area, is a somewhat-reduced version of a design by the architects executed in Cambridge, Massachusetts in 1886. The rectangular Adamesque porch, however, is original to the Edgeworth design.

The picturesque composition seen from Maple Lane.

Inside, the main feature is a Colonial-style stair with a central straight run terminating in a landing with short return flights.

Umbstaetter house
451 Maple Lane, Edgeworth
Longfellow, Alden & Harlow, architects (?), c. 1895

It is not certain that this is a work of the famous Boston-Pittsburgh firm, but the swan's-neck pediments over the front windows are consistent with detailing that the

partners used elsewhere. The house is not strictly symmetrical on any front, even that with the pediments, and a porch two uneven bays deep shelters what must be seen as the main entrance. This is still a rather loose Colonial Revival design, then, allowed liberties the Neo-Georgian could not take.

Leake and Greene house
206 Church Lane, Edgeworth
Longfellow, Alden & Harlow, architects(?), 1893

It is very likely that the architects of "Red Gables" and the Samuel Black house, near by on Maple Lane, were architects too of this simple and sophisticated brick house. Theodore H. Leake and George Greene, the owners, were decorators; their work is visible at Emmanuel Episcopal Church, in the altarpiece.

House
205 Church Lane, Edgeworth
1866

Now stuccoed, this is
a frame house loosely
derived from a design
in Andrew Jackson
Downing's *The Architecture
of Country Houses* (1850).
The fancy brackets
beneath the jutting gable
are especially distinctive.

Very Downingesque

"Red Gables"
517 Maple Lane, Edgeworth
Longfellow, Alden & Harlow, architects, 1891–94

The carriage house
and main house of
"Red Gables" were
respectively the sec-
ond and third houses
of Frank Alden's
family. The shingle-
hung carriage house,
with a gambrel main
roof and cross-gables,

has a very domestic look. The main house, gambrel-roofed
again, has gables hung with clay shingle tile, a siding not
uncommon in England but quite rare in the United States.
The interior is eclectic and informal in taste, Arts and
Crafts in general effect, with carved wood, stained glass,
and a notable chimneypiece sheathed in Delft tiling.

Other Maple Lane houses from the early 1890s *may*
be by Longfellow, Alden & Harlow.

Historic Landmark plaque

The vernacular rear of the house.

The carriage house

Shields Mausoleum
Church Lane, Edgeworth
John U. Barr, architect, 1893

Adjacent to the Shields Presbyterian Church, this Gothic mausoleum is unusual in both location and size. It is almost another church in fact, with an impressive bluntly pointed brick barrel vault over a broad central space; the dead are entombed in niches, early Italian Renaissance in style, in the walls. The exterior masonry, narrow and wide courses of a quartz-like material, suggest a facing of the basic brick construction.

The mausoleum was constructed at the urging of John K. Wilson, related to the Shields family, who deplored the Shields' burial in a neglected cemetery near by.

Shields Presbyterian Church (now Shields Sanctuary of Sewickley Presbyterian Church)
Church Lane and Oliver Road, Edgeworth
Joseph W. Kerr, architect (?), 1868–69

This is a stone church of refined simplicity, none the worse inside for Late Victorian additions. The style is Early English, as the triple lancet windows indicate. Inside, minister, choir, and congregation are united in an almost-intimate space of unpretentious dignity, lighted with Mid-Victorian and 1900-period glass.

The Shields family had been in Western Pennsylvania since about 1800, and lived at "Newington" near by. The congregation, which separated from Sewickley Presbyterian Church in 1864, named the church after Eliza Leet Shields, who rented the land to the congregation at a very nominal rate.

Historic Landmark plaque

Thomas Leet Shields house
436 Beaver Road, Edgeworth
Joseph W. Kerr, architect, 1854

Simple though it is, this is one of the Sewickley area's earliest architect-designed houses. Kerr was the designer of the Sewickley Presbyterian Church.

"Newington"
Shields Lane, Edgeworth
1816; 1823; additions and alterations

"Newington" is a handsome estate that has passed by inheritance from generation to generation since its beginning. It was created by Major Daniel Leet for his married daughter and her husband, Eliza and David Shields. The house has a smaller southern part from 1816 and a northern part from 1823. To the northern part were added two ornate cast-iron porches around 1857 (one removed c. 1900), two mid-Victorian cupolas, and a gable fanlight, c. 1900, replacing an oriel window that was probably an addition itself. The house is surrounded by fine, well-maintained landscaping, apparently to designs of Samuel Parsons in the 1870s with a formal garden of 1910 by Bryan Fleming. On the estate as well are a barn of the

The porch of 1857

1890s, a smokehouse, a springhouse, a miller's house, a blacksmith's house, and a schoolhouse.

National Register of Historic Places
Historic Landmark plaque

Lark Inn
Beaver and Winding Roads, Leetsdale
1798

Originally this was the Halfway House, a tavern halfway between Pittsburgh and Beaver. The corners are built up in an ashlar form with large stones, and the remaining masonry is laid for the most part in partial courses. This is one of the very oldest houses in the Sewickley area, and it is fortunate that it has survived so well.

Historic Landmark plaque

"Pulpit Rock"
Little Sewickley Creek Road, Edgeworth
Rutan & Russell, architects, 1901

A house built out of stones, timbers, and tiles, the stones especially maintaining their individuality. Indian chiefs are alleged to have addressed their tribes from a rock on the property.

Below: an interesting column, bracket, and beam detail.

"Bagatelle"
Little Sewickley Creek Road, Edgeworth
Longfellow, Alden & Harlow, architects, 1894

Externally, this long, narrow house on a hillside road is a simple expression of stonework and carpentry. The long, thin plan is unusual for the 1890s, though it became popular later in country houses and is suited to steeply sloping land. It was designed for James G. Pontefract, whose house in Allegheny the architects had designed a few years earlier.

Historic Landmark plaque

The picturesque entrance

"Muottas"
Little Sewickley Creek Road, Edgeworth
Alden & Harlow, architects, 1903

The original owner of this handsome Colonial Revival house was William Walker, son of the founder of Harbison-Walker Refractories, producers of ceramics for industrial use. Because of this circumstance, no doubt, the gray stone walls are topped startingly by a roof of red shingle tile, and tile and tapestry brick appear here and there inside. The house does not have a multitude of rooms, but they are quite ample and the house as a whole is big. Its hilltop site is one of the highest in the county, about 500 feet above the Ohio River.

Historic Landmark plaque

The formal lawn front

560

Bridge
Over Sewickley Creek between Little Sewickley Creek and Woodland Roads, Edgeworth
Charles Davis, engineer, 1889

This is a carefully thought-out work of architecture as well as an expedient for getting a minor road over a creek. An iron truss would have been a possible alternative at the time, as a wooden covered bridge might have been a few decades earlier. The choice of a masonry arch, then, may have been aesthetic.

Singer water tower and stable
Chestnut Road, Edgeworth
W. Ross Proctor, architect, 1900

William H. Singer, Sr., a partner of Andrew Carnegie, bought land in the northwestern part of Edgeworth late in the nineteenth century, although his own "Edgehill Manor," by Alden & Harlow and now gone, was built only in 1905. In the meantime his son-in-law W. Ross Proctor designed houses, still surviving, as well as the two service buildings seen here. The water tower is Beaux-Arts in

wood, handsome in its clear contrasts of white cupola and trim with dark-brown weatherboarding. One side of the tower has a water-level gauge. The stable, which was enlarged by Alden & Harlow, is simple Georgian in effect.

Singer water tower

Estate off Blackburn Road

Sewickley Heights

Through most of the nineteenth century, the hilly land above Sewickley was merely unprofitable farmland and woods, a place where log houses might linger on for lack of any means or incentive to replace them. Then, city dwellers began to rent summer quarters in the town; the practice was established by the mid-1880s, and soon led to the wealthier families—many from Allegheny—building for themselves in the hilly, wooded upland areas. For about half a century, Sewickley Heights was a place of fine estates reached by country roads, but by 1940 the greatest period was over.

Many of the estates were subsequently subdivided, and many of the houses disappeared. The remaining historic landscape is less a matter of estates than of estate fragments: walls, gates, gatehouses, carriage house/garages, stables, barns, cottages. But even these have a certain pomp, like servants in livery.

"Newberry Hill"
Way Hollow Road at Backbone Road, Sewickley Heights
Janssen & Cocken, architects, 1927

The consciously medieval look of this house—including pointed windows, some of them traceried—is unusually stagey for Janssen. The artful chaos of the roof slating is curiously beautiful.

Sewickley Heights Borough Historic District

Clause house
Persimmon Road at Backbone Road, Sewickley Heights
Carl A. Ziegler (Philadelphia), architect, 1928

A rambling house of rubble, extended to give the maximum effect from the road.

Sewickley Heights Borough Historic District

Entrance front

"Treetops"
Lane's End off Quaker Hollow Road, Sewickley Heights
James P. Piper, architect, 1929

Vigorous use of stone

This picturesque house, whose most prominent feature is a two-storied Tudor window bay, was intended to house the vast art collection of George Hann, an early entrepreneur in commercial aviation. A Spanish decorative theme appears in heads of Ferdinand and Isabella alongside the bay window, and the story of Don Quixote in tile inside.

Sewickley Heights Borough Historic District

Northeast end of the entrance front.

House
Country Club Road, Sewickley Heights
MacClure & Spahr (?), architects, c. 1910

This is supposed to have been the dairy farm manager's house on the estate of Edith Oliver Rea. In any case it is a good-looking piece of domestic architecture, strong in form and well proportioned.

Sewickley Heights Borough Historic District

Houses
Darlington Lane off Blackburn Road, Sewickley Heights
1920s(?)

The crisp geometry, large chimneys, and wayward randomness of the roof slating suggest minor works of Janssen & Cocken, but this has not been documented.

Sewickley Heights Borough Historic District

West front

"Wilpen Hall"
Blackburn Road, Sewickley Heights
George S. Orth & Brothers, architects, 1897–1900

Here is a big, informal stone-and-shingle house, built as the country residence of William Penn Snyder, whose Classical and dignified city house at Ridge and Galveston

North front

East front

Service building

Avenues still stands. The two houses seem to express different ways of living, appropriate to different occasions. The city house is precise and polished, a setting for formality of conduct. Here a measured relaxation is the

Garage

theme. The arched windows flank the Classical porch symmetrically. Above, cross-gables impose a rough symmetry on the long front, but on an axis slightly different from that of the entrance. The big roof and the chimneys speak of shelter and comfort, the necessities of life well accommodated.

The interior is spacious, home-like but well-suited to entertaining large numbers. At one end is a huge living room with a stairwell overlooking a billiard area: a Late

Barn

Victorian combination of functions that is used to create a dramatic space on various levels.

The main house is accompanied by simple but handsome service buildings and smaller houses in the Shingle Style.

William Penn Snyder's barn, built around 1900, is a simple but emphatically architectural work, with its symmetry, its arched doorway that has a token keystone, its pediment-like gables, and its beltcourse connecting the heads of the first-floor windows.

Sewickley Heights Borough Historic District

"Woodmont"
Scaife Road, Sewickley Heights
Vrydaugh & Wolfe, architects, 1902

Time has not been kind to this house, built for Charles C. Scaife. Three large porches have disappeared from the garden front and the ends; the original wooden siding with corner pilasters has been replaced by aluminum; and the original dentiled cornice and dwarf roof balustrade have also departed. The basic structure remains, a great box beneath a complicated gambrel roof.

Porte-cochere

Sewickley Heights Borough Historic District

"Cherry Hill"
Scaife Road, Sewickley Heights
Janssen & Cocken, architects, c. 1925

Janssen was lavish in his colors and textures but reticent, usually, in his detailing when the designs were intended for rural settings. The carved stone door surround and tablet are thus unusual, and for Janssen a little florid.

Sewickley Heights Borough Historic District

Wardrop house
Scaife Road, Sewickley Heights
Janssen & Cocken, architects, 1934

An outstanding example, in brick, of the English rural vernacular at which Benno Janssen excelled. The brick is now painted gray.

Sewickley Heights Borough Historic District

"Sunnymede"
Scaife Road, Sewickley Heights
William Boyd, Sr., architect, 1921

Big roofs, big chimneys, no obvious scheme of fenestration. In many of these country places of the Eclectic period a cultivated air of ample informality became the thing to aim for, a relaxation from the would-be palatial air that had lasted, say, until 1910. There is little ornament, though the front door has a delicate François I frame.

Sewickley Heights Borough Historic District

Carriage house

House
Scaife Road, Sewickley Heights
Janssen & Cocken, architects, c. 1925

This design depends for its success on brick of strong red, a very little fancy bricklaying, and good proportions.

Sewickley Heights Borough Historic District

"Hillside"
Blackburn Road west of Scaife Road, Sewickley Heights
William Boyd, Sr., architect, 1927

There seems to be a willful effort here to suggest a mixture of periods, and it does in fact work rather well. The long, low building range that contains the main entrance is very nicely proportioned. The fenestration was greatly altered around 1990; the large bay windows and round window of the entrance front, and the floor-length windows of the garden front date from that time.

Rear of house

Sewickley Heights Borough Historic District

Garden front

Former stable, "Robinwood"
Scaife Road, Sewickley Heights
Early 20th century

This is a nicely composed building, smaller than the main house near by and showing to better advantage its rather dark selection of colors.

"Oak Knoll Farm"
Blackburn Road, Sewickley Heights
Janssen & Abbott, architects, 1915

As first designed, this house would have presented a slightly Italian look, with arcades on slender columns as prominent design features. As built, the effect was more Hispanic, with broad, plain wall surfaces into which openings were let, faced in stucco now painted blue. Around 1960 the house was divided in two, leaving a fifty-foot gap between the parts.

Sewickley Heights Borough Historic District

House
Audubon and Hunt Roads, Sewickley Heights
C. 1800

Here is a log house that illustrates the earliest architecture
of the county. Both side elevations are the same: symmetrical or very nearly so, with the windows carefully aligned
and a door in the center. The chimney is faced in limestone ashlar, and there is a large outside fireplace. Its
simple, clean geometry, functionally unnecessary, indicates
a builder who was taking care to produce a good-looking
house. Restoration of log houses is popular these days, and
this is a worthy beneficiary.

902 and 900 Glenshaw Avenue, Glenshaw.

THE NORTHERN
TOWNSHIPS

Although the greater part of the land in Allegheny County north of
the Ohio and Allegheny Rivers was included in the Depreciation Lands,
it was no more eagerly settled before 1795 than Allegheny or the
Sewickley area. When the Indian threat ended, however, settlers
arrived and agriculture spread over the rolling land. In many parts
there are still early log houses and simple masonry farmhouses
from the early days.

The settlement that occurred in those first years did not
stop at the county line. In 1803 Allegheny's northern neighbor Butler County was organized, and the adjacent Armstrong
County was organized in 1805. Butler, Zelienople, and Kittan-
ning were all surveyed in 1803, and beyond these communities
lay Franklin and Erie, centers of further settlement.

This northern development meant roads, laid out along
the valleys and heading generally northward. Such a road was
the old Venango Path, an Indian trail that was converted into a plank
road in 1865 and paved for automobiles in 1911; this road, beginning in
the central North Side, is today the Perry Highway, U.S. Route 19, ending near Meadville. Another branch of the Venango Path became the
Butler Pike which opened in 1822 and passed through Shaler Township.
This route survives as Mount Royal Boulevard, a road with a century's
worth of interesting houses dating from the early nineteenth to the early
twentieth century. Close by and approximately parallel runs the old
Butler Plank Road of 1852, now Pennsylvania Route 8 in most places,
originating in Etna. This passes through Glenshaw, the settlement
where the Shaw family ground grain, made sickles, and mined coal;
the road itself was partly a Shaw enterprise.

Railroads have had a lesser influence in these northern townships.
The mines of Indiana and West Deer Townships sold coal to the
Pittsburgh, Bessemer & Lake Erie Railroad that passed near by.

COUNTY OF
ALLEGHENY

57I

1005 Charles Street, Glenshaw

1486 and 1484 Butler Plank Road, Glenshaw

The Pittsburgh & Western Railway (later belonging to the Baltimore
& Ohio) stimulated Glenshaw's development as a railroad commuter
suburb, with Late Victorian houses joining the early Shaw family
homesteads. Products as diverse as ice and cut flowers have been
produced locally and shipped by rail. But more influential were two
interurban trolley lines of 1907: the Butler Short Line that turned inland
and northward at Etna and passed near Glenshaw, and the Harmony
Short Line that went northwesterly through Ross, McCandless, and
Marshall Townships, giving rise in the last of these to Bradford Woods,
a sylvan trolley suburb of 1915. The trolleys stimulated commuter
settlement and gave the farmers fortunate enough to live near by ready
access to town.

120 Nelson Run Road, Ross Township

Roads and rail lines originating in or near Pittsburgh were not
the only means by which the city influenced this part of the county.
Reserve Township, adjacent to the Troy Hill section of Allegheny,
became a place of summer villas and of cemeteries for Pittsburgh and
Allegheny congregations. Evergreen Hamlet and Swan Acres were
suburban developments of architecturally distinct character, the one
1850s Romantic, the other 1930s Modern. Estates appeared here and
there as well. There was, for instance, the spectacular "Hartwood
Farms," the Mary Flinn Lawrence estate. And into the early 1990s
there was "Vosemary Farm," the Pine Township home of Edward Vose
Babcock, lumberman and politician, to whom the county owes, among
other things, North Park. The park, which lies mainly in McCandless
Township, opened in 1927 when that area was still sparsely settled.

Nelson Run Road, Ross Township

It was much improved during the 1930s through the Public Works Administration, and now serves as vital open space for a burgeoning suburban population.

Finally, the mineral resources, gas, oil, and especially coal, have left their mark on the area: in Indiana and West Deer Townships in the form of 1900-period company towns near deep-mine portals, in the adjacent Fawn Township in the form of strip mines.

The county townships north of the river are thus an old farming area that has been civilized in some places and violated in others. But there are still areas where the rural character has been only slightly frazzled by suburbanization, and the shape of the land creates beautiful spaces and distant views.

On Route 8 in Glenshaw

Glenshaw Valley Presbyterian Church

Glenshaw Valley
Shaler Township

Although first developed for small-scale industry, the Glenshaw Valley—apart from the now-busy Route 8—has an almost rustic character. The flood plain along Pine Creek has the aura of an earlier era with a number of Shaw family houses and the picturesque bell tower of the Glenshaw Valley Presbyterian Church along the largest remaining independent section of the Butler Plank Road. A small grid of streets which backs up to the wooded hillside has a rich collection of late nineteenth- and early twentieth-century houses, particularly along part of Butler Plank Road and the tree-lined Glenshaw Avenue.

metrical front and a central doorway porch. The front portion, built a half-dozen years later, is of equal size, but here the porch is a three-bayed Grecian Doric composition of square channeled columns with an elegant Greek Revival doorway behind. As in 1824, the bricklayer put up a simple building block; the pomp of the new entrance was the carpenter's work.

Historic Landmark plaque

The addition of 1832 (left) and the ell (right).

Thomas Wilson Shaw house
1526 Butler Plank Road, Glenshaw Valley, Shaler Township
1824; addition, 1830–32

The ell of this house, built by Thomas Wilson Shaw, an eminent doctor and the son of founding settler John Shaw, was a house in itself and still appears as such, with a sym-

House
Glenshaw Avenue and Wilson Street, Glenshaw Valley,
Shaler Township
C. 1890; addition, 1995

At first glance this seems to be a bungalow, but it has an upper space that erupts through the roof in the form of two gables and, in its remodeled form, three turrets. Quite

88888

a plain little house thus takes on the air of a concentrated mansion. The angled chimney suggests diagonally set fireplaces in room corners.

Despite modernization in 1929 the house exterior, very fortunately, remains substantially as built.

National Register of Historic Places
Historic Landmark plaque

DeHaven-Leet house
Mount Royal Boulevard and Eade Street, Shaler Township
1831 or 1836

Here is a handsome brick farmhouse that gains unusual stateliness from the matching lower wings at its ends. In vernacular guise, this is a Palladian composition: a primary central block with flanking dependencies.

The later doorway shelter, unfortunately, is quite plain; a Greek Revival entrance feature such as may have been present when the house was built would complete the composition. The front of the house is in Flemish bond, with common bond elsewhere. To the rear of one wing is a spacious back porch, and a frame carriage house stands to one side.

Isaac Lightner house
2407 Mount Royal Boulevard, Shaler Township
1833

Similar in general appearance to the Abishai Way house in Edgeworth, the Lightner house also has a Federal-style porch of four Roman Doric columns bearing a windowed pediment; in this case the window has a raised surround with its own little pediment. The front dormers have windows of a segmental-arch form; these are characteristically Federal, whether or not they are part of the original design. There is a detached summer kitchen as well.

Mount Assisi

934 Forest Avenue, Ross Township
Link, Weber & Bowers, architects, 1927

A history of local Catholic
architecture attributes this
work to Edward Joseph
Weber, and its brilliant
use of stone and deep red
brick makes the attribu-
tion likely. The turreted
main entrance makes a
great display of rugged
stonework and the bricks'
quasi-Flemish bond—two
stretchers to a header.
The blind arcade around
the apse of the original
chapel has shaft sections
of rather random length
banded in brick. And,
most sensational of all,
the chapel entrance has a
fizzy pattern of brick
quatrefoils surrounding a
statue in a niche. The
results are a sort of Italian
Romanesque, but tran-
scend any mere imitation.

Hill-McCallam-Davies house, 164 Rockridge Road.

Evergreen Hamlet

Rockridge Road, Ross Township
Hastings & Preiser, surveying and planning, 1851 and after

William Shinn, a lawyer, founded this tiny suburb, originally with five homes on eighty-five acres, to give middle-
class families some of the advantages of country living
while allowing reasonable access to places of business. The
charter of the Evergreen Association bound the members
to certain obligations such as the joint upkeep of a school,
yet the houses and their lots were privately owned. The
Association lasted only fifteen years, but settlement still has
some of the qualities of a Romantic village with which it
began. Especially good are the four surviving original
houses: the Gothic Hill-McCallam-Davies house (Joseph
W. Kerr, architect, 1852); the Shinn-Beall house, Gothic
again but of a simpler design; and the very simple and
rather Italianate Sellers and Hampton houses: all possibly
by Kerr. Unlike the others, which are board-and-batten,
the Sellers house has a close-fitting shiplap siding on the
front, clapboard elsewhere.

Shinn-Beall house, 168 Rockridge Road.

Sellers house, 161 Rockridge Road

111 Circle Drive

As an early cooperative, Evergreen Hamlet shows a certain socio-economic adventurousness, and its role as a refuge from urban and industrial environment preceded slightly the growth of railroad suburbs, such as East Liberty, Hazelwood, and Sewickley for the same purpose. In fact, Evergreen Hamlet's 1851 founding perhaps gives it the distinction of being, modest though it is, the first planned Romantic suburb in the United States: a distinction that some have given to Llewellyn Park, New Jersey, planned in 1853.

Hampton house

National Register of Historic Places
Historic Landmark plaques

Hampton house, 102 Rockridge Road

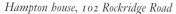

Swan Acres
Swan, Circle, and Wick Drives and Candle Way, Ross Township
Harry C. Clepper with Quentin S. Beck (?), architects; 1937–38

Here are a dozen houses, none outstanding but offering several interpretations in one place of the concept of Modern architecture as understood here in the late 1930s. Blueprints of the earliest houses bear the name of the developer, Beck, Pople & Beck—"Pioneers in Modern Fire Safe Home Construction"—although some and perhaps most of the designs were by their employee, architect Harry C. Clepper. To use innovative styles at all was a bold decision at the time.

114 Swan Drive

Candle Way

Golf clubhouse
Kummer Road, North Park
Henry Hornbostel, architect, 1937

Anyone who has compared Hornbostel's two golf clubhouses for the County parks will agree that the one for South Park is the more frankly fantastic. Yet here, reinforced-concrete beams lie on Doric columns of clanking sheet metal, and red brick and humble concrete block line doorways vivid in color contrast. The sheet-metal columns began to rust, and their bottoms are now clad in brick.

The whole composition, not very large, rides grandly on a ridge and looks across to gorgeous masses of trees.

Sisters of Divine Providence Mother House and La Roche College
9000 Babcock Boulevard, McCandless Township
John E. Kauzor, architect for Mother House, 1927

This large complex, conspicuous in the North Hills, contains a large number of religious and academic buildings clustered around the large, tall Mother House with its chapel. The style of the Mother House is North Italian Romanesque, though the tower with its conical spire may imitate none of the numerous examples in Italy. The other buildings are generally without character.

Historic Landmark plaque

Covenanter Presbyterian Church (now Depreciation Lands Museum)
4743 South Pioneer Road, Hampton Township
C. 1835

Calvert house
2538 Middle Road, Hampton Township
Janssen & Abbott, architects, 1910; addition

Now a museum of late eighteenth- and early nineteenth-century life, this was built as a church of the simplest type with only a Greek Revival cornice for exterior decoration. The windows have the original glass. The restored James Armstrong Log House of 1803, moved to the site, is also used for museum purposes.

Another display is the McClarren-McCully Schoolhouse.

Termed a bungalow by the architects, this house in fact had a fully finished bedroom story in the roof. The house was originally laid out as three sides of an octagon, with the living room at the center facing northwest so as to take in the summer sunset. Pergolas on cylindrical piers still shade the greater part of the ground story and there is an outside fireplace. Planned with five family bedrooms—one on the ground floor—and two large servant's rooms, this was a spacious house but an unassuming one. The plans were widely published.

"Hartwood Farms" (now Hartwood Acres)
Saxonburg Boulevard, Indiana Township
Alfred W. Hopkins (New York), architect; house, 1929;
stable group, 1926

Here is the largest of the country estates—639 acres—developed in the Pittsburgh area in the 1920s. It was the property of Mary Flinn Lawrence, daughter of the well-known contractor William Flinn. The main house is typical 1920s Cotswold, an English rural Tudor style expressed in limestone and slate. Learned taste, not original inspiration, is what most rich clients of the time wanted in their homes, and that is what Alfred Hopkins offered. Random-coursed ashlar, slightly irregular roof slating, and

leaded windows, some square-paned, some diamond-paned, give a certain variety to a design almost irreproachable as a faithful reproduction of the English original. The big stable, garage, and barn group in a nearby hollow is of a humbler material, concrete block, but is quite as picturesquely composed as the house itself. Today, Hartwood Acres is County property, and is used as a cultural and recreational center.

Historic Landmark plaque

The concrete-block service buildings.

"Olive Grange"
Mingo Road south of Valley Road, Marshall Township
C. 1850

The vergeboard, a border
of planking that in
medieval times hung from
the outer edge of a gable
roof to shelter the joint
between the roof and the
wall, was an obvious
feature for decorative
treatment. Romanticism,
rediscovering the Gothic
style, took up the verge-
board with enthusiasm. In
Swiss chalet architecture,
the Romantics found still
further expressions of
wood, quite notably in the
use of sawn-out boards for balustrades and applied ornament. From such sources come the lavish, remarkably
intact ornamentation of this house. Most of the ornament
is sawn out, but the vergeboards themselves have been
carved with chamfers that give an extra richness of effect.

Barn
Clendenning Road between McMorran and Shepard Roads,
West Deer Township
C. 1870

Barn builders indulged their modest fancies in the nineteenth century just as architects did, though their means
were more limited. Here, from bottom to top, the carpenter was able to include three types of pointed window
heads, though admittedly the lowermost ones, typical
carpenter's Greek Revival, are pointed very bluntly.

Bridge
Over Bull Creek, west of Bull Creek Road, Fawn Township
"Reno," engineer; Morse Bridge Company (Youngstown),
builder; 1878

Victorian bridge engineering tends to be light and rather
limber, since human or animal power was usually needed at
some point in getting the parts from the fabricating plant
to the site. Once there, parts were bolted together or,
where rigidity was needed, riveted. This bridge, built the
year the Morse Bridge Company was founded, is a Pratt
truss of wrought iron. It is probably the oldest extant metal
bridge in the county.

The Allegheny River, upstream from the Longue Vue Club.

UP THE ALLEGHENY

The history of the Allegheny River has been markedly different from that of the Monongahela. Though industry has grown up along its banks here and there, especially near Pittsburgh, it has a rather open, rural quality. Pleasure boats are common, and such towboat activity as exists is on a much smaller scale than on the Monongahela. Industrial plants have generally taken the form of storage tanks, sheds, and small factories rather than the unique, powerful forms of the steel plants. Yet this has been a very busy river, carrying the flatboats of the early nineteenth century on the swollen waters of the spring thaws from remote points of origin, the upstate timber rafts of the mid-nineteenth century, the oil barges of the great boom of the 1860s, and the coalboat bottoms, loaded with simple wood products, that through most of the century went down to Pittsburgh for completion. Where the Monongahela traffic has largely been driven by steam and diesel, the traffic of the Allegheny's great days drifted on water that, before the upstream dams and reservoirs, could run high and fast.

COUNTY OF
ALLEGHENY

The Pennsylvania Canal, completed in the Pittsburgh area in 1829, ran along the western shore of the Allegheny and contributed to settlement and industrial development in a way that this drifting traffic, largely independent of the shore, did not. Sharpsburg began as a canal port, and Tarentum as a canal port and industrial town. The development of the Western Pennsylvania Railroad in the 1860s and of interurban trolley lines around 1900 further stimulated settlement, with Millvale, Etna, Blawnox, Brackenridge, and Natrona attracting industry and Aspinwall and Cheswick becoming residential towns.

Several Allegheny Valley communities stand out. Millvale is notable not only for St. Anthony's Church, with its Baroque front, but also for St. Nicholas Church, containing a remarkable set of murals and decorations by Maximilian Vanka portraying the Croatian experience in

The atrium of the Fox Chapel Golf Club, designed by Brandon Smith.

America. Etna, at one time, was like a Monongahela River town with the Isabella blast furnace in operation until 1954 and Spang, Chalfant & Company, which had evolved from a rolling mill of 1817, manufacturing pipe until 1969. Fox Chapel began early in this century as an area favored for golf clubs and summer homes, acquired a number of estates and a fox hunt in the 1920s, and gradually became a year-round home for many wealthy Pittsburghers. Springdale Borough has the birthplace of biologist and author Rachel Carson, architecturally undistinguished but preserved and operated as a nature study center. Natrona, in Harrison Township, is a riverfront industrial town of narrow close-built streets which has changed little since early in the century owing to its isolated site with industrial plants to either side and a bluff behind. Much of the town is company housing built by the Pennsylvania Salt Manufacturing Company between 1850 and 1900.

The Rachel Carson Homestead in Springdale.

Two significant towns lie on the east shore of the Allegheny River: Verona and Oakmont. In the 1860s, Verona was the location of an engine house and machine shops for the Allegheny Valley Railroad. Later it was built up with a mixture of industrial plants near the railroad and the river and suburban houses on the hillside beyond. Oakmont, adjoining Verona to the north, has had the same mixed character. The railroad, which the Pennsylvania absorbed, runs at grade along the main street, faced by stores and churches. Here, too, have been light industrial plants near the river and commuter houses on hillside streets inland.

Plum Borough, touching the Allegheny River north of Oakmont, is an area of rolling land that is still partly rural though the part near Monroeville has been suburbanized and strip mining has marred the land in some areas. Plum still has examples of early nineteenth-century architecture in primitive country, less because they have been seen as historic treasures than because neither mining nor suburbanization has been extensive.

As elsewhere in the county, the landscape demands attention in this valley. But here the landscape has clearly been altered by man, and the path of Pennsylvania Route 28 on the western shore of the Allegheny River is the result of blasting operations. Nevertheless, the high bluffs, now of naked stone in many places, dominate the surrounding settlement and activity.

Millvale and the Washington Crossing Bridge.

St. Nicholas Church (Roman Catholic)
24 Maryland Avenue, Millvale
Frederick C. Sauer, architect, 1900

Although the design of this yellow-brick church is pleasant
and compact, and though its siting affords a little drama,
the true value of this church is within. Here, two
painters—Maximilian "Maxo" Vanka, beginning in 1937,
and Jocko Knezevich, beginning in 1970, covered the
interior with images of the Croatian experience (seen
through Socialist eyes) as well as those more common to
Catholicism. A Madonna and Child on plaster rise thirty-
six feet above the main altar, with praying peasants and
miners to the sides. These are by Vanka. Beneath them, at

Immigrant Mother Raises Her Sons for American Industry.

altar level, is the *Farewell* mural by Knezevich: thirty-two
life-size figures representing a departure for America.
But the other paintings, by Vanka, are those best known:
Immigrant Mother Raises Her Sons for American Industry;
Mothers in the Old Country; the rich man at lunch rejecting
the beggar, and being rejected by the angel.

The church is alleged to be haunted.

National Register of Historic Places
Historic Landmark plaque

St. Anthony's Church (Roman Catholic)
Howard Street and North Avenue, Millvale
John T. Comes, architect, 1914

Set high to compensate for a sloping street, St. Anthony's displays an impressive front of brown brick and beige terra cotta with bands of colored tile, designed in a free version of Mexican Baroque. The window over the entrance and the tower-tops, with their patterned tile domes, have a full-blooded Mexican look, but the style is not consistent; behind the facade only scalloped gables carry the theme through.

St. Mary's Church (Roman Catholic)
Garnier and Altmayer Streets, Sharpsburg
Peter Dedrichs, architect, 1916

The dominant building of Sharpsburg, St. Mary's is sited in a way that suggests the great church of a small Old World town. Its style is very generally Renaissance, but of no one nation, and its three rose windows are of course less Renaissance than medieval. A triumphal-arch portal with Corinthian columns faces the street. At one point the small domes were imperiled but a plea from the Pittsburgh History & Landmarks Foundation to save them was successful.

Sharpsburg and Etna Savings Bank (now Amgard, Inc.)
Main and Sixth Streets, Sharpsburg
C. 1868

This is a simple but well-proportioned piece of vintage bank architecture, prominently sited.

Ferree house
403 Dorseyville Road, O'Hara Township
C. 1810; remodeled c. 1840 (?)

A curious little Greek Revival house with an inset porch, supported by wooden Doric columns. The original effect may have been one of severely simple elegance, but probably this was always a primitive-looking building that relied on the columns to make a good impression. Inside the porch is a Georgian doorway, raising the possibility that part of the house is older by twenty or thirty years than the present exterior suggests.

Doorway detail

227 First Street

103 Eastern Avenue

Aspinwall

Although only two Aspinwall places are treated individually here, the town as a whole offers a most pleasant experience. Many trees, some of them very tall; brick-paved streets; and well-kept and tastefully designed houses are characteristic of the place. Here are some of the buildings to be seen.

233 Third Street

The former Evangelical Lutheran Church (1891), now residential, Center Avenue and Fifth Street.

Sauer Buildings
607–717 Center Avenue, Aspinwall
Frederick C. Sauer, architect, 1894–1942

Sauer, an architect, builder, and real-estate developer, spent several decades as a producer of colorless buildings before turning his attention to this hillside property, on which he

"Heidelberg"

Benjamin Franklin in "Heidelberg"

had already built in a conventional way. He proceeded to remodel and build anew in a primitively fantastic manner, salvaging used materials and ornament, imparting a flimsy quaintness to all but the original house. He was building in a time when quaintness was a selling point in residential construction, yet the impression these buildings gives is not one of commercial calculation; rather, Sauer really seems to have made one of those odd essays in personal expression in building that turn up now and then in some otherwise-staid part of the world. The pride of the place is "Heidelberg," a three-story conversion of a chicken coop into an apartment house.

National Register District

Sauer's own house

Ross Pumping Station

St. Scholastica Convent
309 Brilliant Avenue, Aspinwall
Edward J. Weber, architect, 1925

A few subtle touches turn what is basically just another four-square yellow-brick house from early in the century into an institutional building. Several not-too-extravagant devices that impart distinction to the building are: the way in which the common-bond wall *swells* into the corner tower; the polygonally ended chapel, which looks as if it had been whittled from a rectangular wing; and the good color and patterning of the slates. The roof the slates cover is more vivid than the usual dumpy hipped roof of our suburbs.

City of Pittsburgh Department of Water
226 Delafield Road, Pittsburgh
C. 1907 and after

Into the beginning years of the twentieth century, Pittsburgh drinking water, incredibly, was not treated at all, and the city, drawing its water from the very polluted rivers, was not a healthy place. Filtered water, distributed from this large new intake plant on the Allegheny River beginning in 1908, lowered the incidence of typhoid fever spectacularly, and chemical treatment since has helped still further in preventing contagion.

The Ross Pumping Station of 1907, Rutan & Russell, architects, is the actual intake station. Of golden-brown Roman brick and gray-brown sandstone, it is grandly Beaux-Arts. Such a building was a shelter for tall steam reciprocating engines, compound or triple-expansion, that might rise twenty-five or thirty feet from the main floor: impressive mechanical constructions whose slow, unvaried beat was a fine thing to witness. They had to be readily accessible and auxiliary equipment had to be accommodated, and since such engines gave off heat the space they occupied had to be airy. Furthermore, when they were in a government facility, the mood of the time demanded that they be housed with a certain elegance. Hence this grandiose pavilion and other imposing pumping stations of the 1900 period around town.

Details from the Ross Pumping Station: before and after water filtration?

Old Administration Building, and its doorway (below).

Aspinwall Pumping Station

Also from 1907, and by the same architects, is the old Administration Building, a handsome Italian villa, now closed up, among the forlorn remains of the old filtration beds it once administered.

The Aspinwall Pumping Station, not far from the Ross, was built in 1913 to designs by Thomas H. Scott, who also designed the Mission Pumping Station on the South Side slopes. It is built of gray brick, stone, and terra cotta, and distributes the treated water to the Lampher Reservoir, from which it is relayed elsewhere.

143 North Drive

Fox Chapel

This borough is an entity of 1935, and its present role as a wealthy residential suburb is not much older. Although some farming was done here into the 1920s, the place as we think of it dates from the early part of that decade, with the relocation of Shady Side Academy, the establishment of the Pittsburgh Field Club and the Fox Chapel Golf Club, and the growing use of the automobile as a means of commutation. Within the wooded terrain of hills and valleys stand the houses to be expected in prosperous communities of the 1930 period: much Neo-Georgian, much Tudor, a certain contrived air of centuries of change, sometimes, though in truth a rambling house was built in one campaign. Here are some of the houses to be seen.

Above: 130 South Drive. Below: 632 West Waldheim Road.

"La Tourelle"
8 La Tourelle Drive, Fox Chapel
Janssen & Cocken, architects, 1924

The home of the merchant and philanthropist Edgar J. Kaufmann, who a decade later commissioned Frank Lloyd Wright to design "Fallingwater" in Fayette County. Here as in that more famous house, Kaufmann lived amid rugged materials: brick laid in English bond, artfully irregular roofing slates, fieldstone walls, and flagged and cobbled pavements. The tourelle itself is the cylindrical entrance, with its gratuitously steep roof.

Associate Reformed Church (now Harmarville United Presbyterian Church)
Church Road, Harmar Township
1851

This is a very simple Greek Revival country church, with Doric pilasters all around. The cornices and capitals are of wood, the architrave of brick like the pilaster shafts. No water table or bases for the pilasters appear above ground. The interior seems to have its original pews.

Central Presbyterian Church
Third Avenue and Allegheny Street, Tarentum
1913

There is a naive subtlety, or a subtle naïveté, about this front. The pedimented order and the paired pilasters attempt to impose axial symmetry on the whole entry, *but* the main window of the church space is off to one side—and is Gothic, by the way—so that the pediment favors one of its symmetrically disposed doors. The square upper windows have their own rhythmic pattern, single at the ends, doubled over the right door and in the bay to the immediate right, so that the church and ancillary spaces

seem to interlock. The traceries in the church windows have almost an Art Nouveau look, far from the geometrical purity of typical Gothic.

Brackenridge Plant, Allegheny Ludlum Steel Corporation
River Avenue and Mile Lock Lane, Harrison Township
Operations begun c. 1900

This plant, still a successful producer of specialty steel, was built for the Allegheny Steel and Iron Company. The area is about 3,000 feet along the Allegheny River and 1,500 feet inland. Most of the buildings are steel industrial sheds, but various periods have added brick buildings in Romanesque, Neo-Georgian, and vernacular styles.

Pennsalt housing
*Blue Ridge, Greenwich, Wood, Center, Penn, and Federal
Streets, Natrona, Harrison Township*
1850 and after

The Pennsalt housing district is a prime example of a
Western Pennsylvania company town of the mid- and late-
nineteenth century. The Pennsylvania Salt Manufacturing
Company, a chemical works whose principal product was
caustic soda, assumed the role of paternalistic landlord and
erected about 150 houses and a company store next to its
riverfront manufactory. The sixteen earliest houses along
Federal Street were tiny—fourteen by thirty feet with two
rooms on each of two floors—but their picturesque steeply
pitched roofs and board-and-batten siding gave them once
the look of "model cottages," intended to attract workers,
ameliorate the harshness of industrial conditions, and
promote good behavior among workers and their families.
Later came board-and-batten houses, drop-sided houses,
brick row houses, and an assortment of other housing
types. Two of the brick row houses were restored by the
Pittsburgh History & Landmarks Foundation in 1981.

National Register District

House
2503 Buchanan Street, Harrison Township
C. 1850

If this house is of the mid-1830s, as may be the case, it was
refaced later, some time around 1850. Aside from the
paired eaves brackets, the decorative effect depends on
ways of using two thicknesses of boarding. The decorative
window surrounds are flush with the battens of the walls;
the immediate surrounds of the openings are flush with the
boards of the siding. The difference in layers is emphasized
by the "printer's brace" ogee form on the first-floor
window heads.

Pittsburgh and Tarentum Camp Meeting Association
East of Main and Fifth Streets, Harrison Township
C. 1905

Thirty-two cottages stand in a rough oval around an open
wooded tabernacle in a rare surviving local instance of a
permanent religious revival center. The Methodist group
was already established on the land when the original
buildings were virtually eliminated by a fire; those seen
today are on a new site, and date from 1905 and later.

Above and below: cottages of the Pittsburgh and Tarentum Camp Meeting Association.

The tabernacle, which has the appearance of a large open picnic shelter, was built to replace the tent originally used; it contains stained glass from a Methodist church formerly on Bingham Street on the South Side. The small, narrow cottages have been remodeled to the extent that no two are now alike. It is interesting to see that some of them, despite being from 1905 or later, are board-and-batten or have Gothic Revival vergeboards on their gables: features more characteristic of fifty years before.

Burtner house
*Burtner Road east of Pennsylvania Route 28,
Harrison Township
Philip Burtner, builder, 1818–21*

Currently undergoing restoration, the Burtner house will return to its original appearance as the home of a substantial rural citizen of early in the last century. This is a simple, solid house, with little pretense. If the porch, a restoration, has very slightly arched fascias there is almost nothing else to be called ornamental. The rather deep-set windows attest to the thickness of the walls—thirty inches thick in the basement, eighteen inches thick at the eaves—whose surfaces have an attractive but practical random pattern of large and small stones.

In 1969 it appeared that the house would be demolished for an access road to an expressway: a plan that aroused public interest in saving it, ill-kept though it was at the time. Important local events had taken place in the house, and it had been the home of an important local citizen, and in 1970 a petition with 2,000 names was submitted to

the Governor. He intervened, hours before demolition was to occur, with a reprieve. The access road was realigned, coming near the house but sparing it, and in 1971 a preservation group, Burtner House Restoration, Inc., acquired the house and began its restoration. The Pittsburgh History & Landmarks Foundation was involved in negotia-

tions for both the saving of the Burtner house and the transfer of its title, and now provides its services in the restoration itself.

National Register of Historic Places
Historic Landmark plaque

Rubble and slating

Entrance

Gateway

Longue Vue Club
Oakwood Road, Penn Hills Township
Janssen & Cocken, architects, 1924–25; additions

There is a nice ambiguity about the style of the original club building. The big chimneys, flush with the gable walls, could be Georgian, yet the overall feeling is that of French rural architecture, a

feeling heightened by the use of casement windows. This is the suave rusticity often found in Philadelphia-area architecture of the 1920s, but much less often in Southwestern Pennsylvania; long, slender pieces of rubble in thick mortar, the masonry equivalent of a good hand-woven tweed, and above, thick, rough-edged roofing slates. A building as unornamented as any Modern work, it still conveys a lush impression through its picturesque exaggerations of form and texture.

Historic Landmark plaque

First Presbyterian Church (now Riverside Congregation)
Allegheny River Boulevard and Washington Avenue, Oakmont
1895

This church is prominently sited, and the front it presents to Oakmont's main street is a very creditable exercise in Richardson Romanesque, but the long side wall is remarkable in the variety of its openings, a piece of eloquent awkwardness one might say, expressed in rock-faced stone and bright red brick.

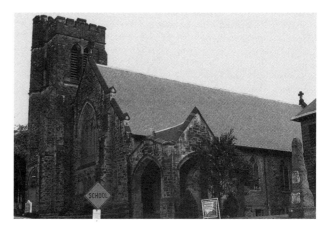

St. Thomas Episcopal Church
Delaware Avenue and Fourth Street, Oakmont
1906

This is a strong example of the sort of Gothic that briefly succeeded Richardson Romanesque in local fashion: itself massive in bulk and rugged in masonry, with pointed arches tending to be broad. However, the lighter and more delicate Gothic of Cram and Goodhue—exemplified in Pittsburgh by Calvary Episcopal and First Baptist Churches, built only slightly later—was to prevail.

Carnegie Library of Oakmont
Allegheny River Boulevard, Oakmont
Alden & Harlow, architects, 1901

This is a relatively small library, but a generous budget allowed the use of carved sandstone rather than the molded terra cotta standard in the branch libraries of the Pittsburgh system.

Historic Landmark plaque

598

Oakmont Country Club
Hulton Road, Plum Borough
*Edward Stotz, architect for clubhouse, 1904; additions and
alterations*

Country clubs tend to be sprawling affairs, with a variety
of social rooms on the first floor handy to terraces,
verandahs, and kitchens and other necessary service areas.
Surrounded by golf courses, tennis courts, and other
facilities that create large areas of open ground, they are
usually low-built and rural in character. Here is an early
golf club, noncommittal as to style, shed-dormered on the
ends, half-timbered on the entrance front, and with a big
American front porch. As with many architect-designed
buildings of its period, it strikes an attitude, it presents
itself in a certain character. The front as originally
designed is symmetrical and perhaps a little prim; yet
the decorative half-timbering and the big porch are
symbols of informality, relaxation. Perhaps these features
hint at a specific degree of relaxation from social formality
permissible on these premises.

Service wing

The eighteen-hole course, of championship calibre, is
regarded by golf historians as a monument in its own right.
As designed by Henry C. Fownes in 1903, its hazards
penalized careless or incompetent play to an extent
unknown on modern courses, and though there have been
many modifications, much of the old "penal" quality
remains.

National Historic Landmark
National Register District
Historic Landmark plaque

Church
Coxcomb Hill and Logan's Ferry Roads, Plum Borough
C. 1900

This former church is a mystery, though it may be a
Presbyterian church for a Logan's Ferry congregation
founded in 1842. A small cemetery, adjoining, has graves of
a Stewart family and dates back at least to 1862. The style
is primitive and mixed, with a Tuscan portico and angle-
topped windows suggesting Gothic arches. In this last
detail the church is ahead of its time, since PPG Place in
Pittsburgh has the same form.

Looking south toward the Monongahela Valley, from Braddock Catholic Cemetery.

EAST OF PITTSBURGH

Between Pittsburgh and the Westmoreland County line lies a mixture
of communities that together summarize the ways in which the land of
Allegheny County has developed.

Should one follow the old Pennsylvania Railroad out of Pittsburgh
on its easterly course the first town reached will be Wilkinsburg,
once called the Holy City because of its abundance of churches
and absence of taverns. It received its distinctive character
early in its history thanks to James Kelly, a real-estate
dealer who himself was a teetotaler and a man of great local
influence in the mid-nineteenth century. It was under his
paternalistic hand that the taverns were banned—even though
the first building within the present boundaries had been a log
tavern—and that the borough was returned to independence
after being swept into Pittsburgh's great annexation of 1868.
Wilkinsburg has always been a town of modest sufficiency
rather than elegance, but has a great house in the Singer mansion
of the 1860s.

COUNTY OF
ALLEGHENY

The railroad then turns south and passes through Edgewood, a
borough with its own determined character. Like so many other places
on the Pennsylvania Railroad, this made an early transition from a
farming area to exurb, a place where persons in search of fresh air and
a quiet life could make a nightly escape from Pittsburgh. Commuter
service began in 1864 and incorporation took place in 1888. In drawing
up their boundaries, the people of Edgewood prudently included
the greater part of the Union Switch & Signal Company plant that
George Westinghouse had established in the area two years before,
and thus got an excellent contribution to their tax base; the workers'
entrance, however, they left in the less-fortunate and then-unincorpo-
rated Swissvale to the south. They banned other industries and many
types of business however, and consolidated their town as a middle-class
community of pleasant streets and respectable ways. Early in this
century there was talk of the "Edgewood Idea": low taxes, model

312–06 Hutchinson Avenue, Edgewood

government, community institutions that offered sociability under
the eye of the community. Edgewood had its own church and school,
its Civic Club, its Edgewood Club for social purposes, and through
these institutions developed a self-sufficiency that promoted the
Edgewood Idea.

    Of quite a different character is Monroeville, a borough associated
with spectacular successes in real-estate development—though not
architecture—since the early 1950s. This is the automobile suburb
in all its triumph: strip development, shopping centers, office buildings,
research facilities, and housing developments, with a population rise
from 8,000 in 1950 to 29,500 in 1995. Yet away from all this,
Monroeville retains traces of the Patton Township it once was, with a
farming, coal mining, and railroading past.

Between Wilkinsburg and Monroeville lie suburbs in rolling, often wooded country, a mosaic of little boroughs. Churchill, today a prosperous residential suburb, has eighteenth-century roots. One part of it was Bullock Pens, a supply base for the British army and later a veteran's settlement. Forest Hills is associated with Westinghouse Electric and its history. Here KDKA, the country's first commercial radio station, was located in the 1920s, and here too stands the early "atom smasher" of 1938 in the modern Westinghouse Research and Development Center.

In general, the area east of Pittsburgh shows the stimulus that a railroad main line could give in the nineteenth century, and road construction in our own time. Where the Pennsylvania main line and the Allegheny Valley Railroad went, commuter and industrial towns grew as the terrain permitted; elsewhere, development awaited the automobile. When this became common, a Monroeville could grow on cheap rural land.

The Westinghouse atom smasher, when new.

Pennsylvania Railroad Station, Wilkinsburg
Hay Street at Ross Avenue, Wilkinsburg
Walter H. Cookson, architect, 1916

To eliminate grade cross-
ings in the populous sub-
urb of Wilkinsburg, the
Pennsylvania Railroad
track level was raised
around 1915, necessitating
a new station. The new
building, limestone with
pale-buff brick, is a pleasant gesture to the town,
terminating Ross Avenue.
The Ionic order between
paneled piers and the
clock that rises partway
above the parapet still
have a little of the Beaux-
Arts showiness about them, but there would have been
much more ten or even five years before: architectural
practice, more and more, was favoring well-schooled good
taste, and less and less expressiveness. The basement to one
side has its own marqueed entrance, probably a loading
dock for Railway Express trucks.

The suburban service to Pittsburgh, and indeed train
service of any kind out of Wilkinsburg, has long been
ended. Yet the station remains as a reminder of the railroad
to which Wilkinsburg owed its nineteenth-century development and of the Golden Age of American railroads,
which attained their greatest track mileage in the year of
this building's erection, 1916.

National Register of Historic Places
Historic Landmark plaque

Wetherall apartment house
501 Hill Street, Wilkinsburg
Frederick G. Scheibler, Jr., architect, 1911

This is a three-unit building with a mountainously tall
roof, looking back in this respect toward Old Heidelberg.
It has a quasi-domestic air, and its rough red brick not only
reinforces this impression but relates the building to other
small apartment houses near by. Each floor has a porch,
though that of the uppermost apartment is toward the rear.

Singer house
1318 Singer Place, Wilkinsburg
1869

The architect of this lushly Romantic Gothic house is not
known, though James D. Van Trump sees Joseph W. Kerr
as a possibility. As with most Victorian architecture, stylistic
purity was not a consideration. The walls of coursed rubble
have rusticated quoins, very Renaissance, the vergeboards
have little turned pendants—Italianate—on their cusps,
and the lambrequins and window hoods are of an
elaboration beyond anything that an ordinary Gothic
Revivalist, let alone any medieval architect, would have
used. There is twice the usual amount of everything, except
on the relatively restrained porches. Victorian, too, was the

private chapel—Singer was an Episcopalian—with a
carriage house thriftily installed in its basement. This,
unfortunately, was burned in 1976.

This is the handsomest building in Wilkinsburg, and
one of the most accomplished works of Victorian Gothic
in the county. The
present grounds are a
small surviving portion
of a large estate.

John F. Singer was a
steel manufacturer and a
partner with Alexander
Nimick in Singer,
Nimick & Company
on the South Side.

*National Register of
Historic Places*

Houses
1328–66 Singer Place, Wilkinsburg
Frederick G. Scheibler, Jr., architect, c. 1909 and 1914

The floridly Romantic, vertical Singer house has as a
neighbor a plain, very horizontal, hillside house row by
Scheibler. The two are not in strident opposition, but
Scheibler's row opposes middle-class bland common
sense —and the typical anonymity of builder's housing—to
Singer's individualism. This is Scheibler at his most ration-
alistic, neatly presenting the fundamentals of a row-house
design without fancy touches. As in some other of his
designs, Scheibler uses casement sash, slightly Old World
in effect and allowing more ventilation than sliding sash.

1328 Singer Place

The Sheltering Arms Home for Aged Protestants
(now Jane Holmes Residence)
441 Swissvale Avenue, Wilkinsburg
1869; additions

In its time one element of this building has been a home
for "wayward girls" and another has been a home for aged
couples. The Italianate architecture, sadly calm, is designed
with economy in mind. The great porch faces southeast
toward the adjoining neighborhood. The two round bays
are additions that add a feeling of mass and inner space to
the hard, brittle Mid-Victorian exterior.

Beech Street

Edgewood

The Borough of Edgewood came formally into existence in 1888, but Pennsylvania Railroad trains had been stopping there since 1864. An early image of the place as a desirable location for homes was cultivated with increasing deliberation toward the end of the nineteenth century. Industry was not exactly excluded—indeed, the Union Switch & Signal Company, with the notable exception of the workers' entrance, was within Borough limits—but this was seen as a place for the decorous spending of wealth, not its acquisition.

Maple Avenue near Hawthorn Street

Western Pennsylvania School for the Deaf
Swissvale Avenue and Walnut Street, Edgewood
After 1892; Alden & Harlow, architects for administration building, 1903

An administration building of 1903 with a tall portico of eight Grecian Ionic columns graciously dominates a sizeable campus. The remainder of the campus conforms to no one style, though a loose sort of Neo-Georgian is often to be found. The chapel attached to the administration building has windows with so-called Florentine tracery, two round-headed lights with a rondel above.

607

House
326 Maple Avenue, Edgewood
C. 1890

This is really a bold and admirable design, all red, simple in its forms, large in its scale. The arches of the porch are a little too small for the remainder of the house, but otherwise this has a special quality.

C. C. Mellor Library and Edgewood Club
Pennwood and West Swissvale Avenues, Edgewood
Edward B. Lee, architect, 1914

This calm, low-set, simple but refined work is unusual for Pittsburgh but echoes contemporary trends elsewhere. The stucco, the hipped tile roofs, and the pergola suggest the simplest sort of country-house architecture then being built in California. On the other hand, pergolas were popular throughout the United States as alternatives to the old-fashioned front porch, offering shade with vines without greatly darkening the rooms behind. Such thick piers were to be found supporting both pergolas and porches in the Philadelphia area, for example.

The Edgewood Club of 1903 expressed the "Edgewood Idea" of amenity and decency in concrete terms. It was founded to enable the young to socialize under the supervision of their elders. The library was begun with Carnegie Foundation money and a gift of books by a citizen at the time of the Club's decision to build the present clubhouse.

Gardner-Bailey house
124 West Swissvale Avenue, Edgewood
1864; additions

This Italianate house, almost a bungalow in its basic form, is one of the oldest houses in Edgewood and the most imaginative. The house is plain in its essential construction, with a doorway and window trim that are still Greek Revival; it is likely that the cupola, the monitor-like construction on the rear wing, the porch, and the ornamentation that put it out of the ordinary were added to the original structure. The simple house thus took on the air of an elegant villa, using Victorian Italianate features just as the Abishai Way house in Edgeworth, basically similar, had made use of a temple-fronted porch to attain the same purpose in Federal-style terms.

National Register of Historic Places
Historic Landmark plaque

Tunnel
Race Street, Edgewood, under former Pennsylvania Railroad main line
C. 1915 (?)

Around 1915 the Pennsylvania Railroad raised its main-line trackage in the Wilkinsburg-Edgewood area in order to eliminate awkward and dangerous grade crossings. This tunnel, close to Edgewood Station, may be a product of the campaign, though the concrete above the stonework and the outlying steelwork suggest a heightening of the track level *after* the tunnel was built.

La Crosse Street houses

Pennsylvania Railroad Station
Edgewood Street and Swissvale and Maple Avenues, Edgewood
Furness, Evans & Co., architects, 1903

The powerful, quirky hand of Frank Furness is now to be seen in the Pittsburgh area only in this brick-and-shingle commuter station whose exterior has been casually but not severely remodeled over the years.

Houses
115–121 and 129 La Crosse Street and 143 Gordon Street,
Edgewood
Frederick G. Scheibler, Jr., architect, 1909 and 1910

Here are picturesque, low-cost houses, revealing Scheibler's knack for adding distinction with relatively inexpensive touches such as art glass.

143 Gordon Street

Bullock Pens Church (now Beulah Chapel)
Beulah and McCready Roads, Churchill
Williams McCrea, builder, 1837

Although the interior is much changed, the exterior of this simple church is substantially as built. Aside from a few very elementary moldings and a semicircular window in the front gable, the only effort at architecture comes from the Flemish bond of the entrance-front brickwork as opposed to common bond elsewhere.

The cemetery is one of the oldest in Allegheny County. The oldest marked grave dates from 1793. The church and cemetery anchor this twentieth-century suburb in history, so to speak, and Churchill can account itself lucky to have them. So many of our suburbs are all too evidently devoid of a past.

National Register of Historic Places
Historic Landmark plaque

Linhart homestead
221 Farnsworth Avenue, Wilkins Township
Christin Linhart, builder, c. 1782; addition, 1794

Linhart, one of the earliest settlers in this area and proprietor of a sawmill, built himself a simple log house, later doubled in size for a married daughter. The two-story form seems rather advanced for 1782, raising the possibility of an addition above the original walls. There is a rough symmetry to the completed house, emphasized by the massive stone and brick chimneys at the ends, yet no special attempt has been made to place the windows

regularly. Among other things, those of the older section are set higher, and the exposed joist ends on the long walls show that the ground-floor ceiling was higher too; indeed, the upper story is more of a loft, with windows almost at floor level.

The house is probably the oldest continuously occupied house in Allegheny County. The window casements and the frame ell to the rear are later work, and so probably is the front porch; yet the house has a pleasant air of great antiquity about it as well as being handsome in itself.

Crossroads Presbyterian Church (now Old Stone Church)
Northern Pike and Stroschein Road, Monroeville
1896; bell tower, 1976

Built of a golden-brown coursed rubble, this is a very simply detailed church but one of sophisticated design nonetheless. Gabled plainly at one end and gabled with a lower slope at the other, the building expands on both sides

into broad, hip-roofed polygonal bays. The result is an interplay of roof planes such as the Shingle Style architects of the previous decade had reveled in; with them, the roof might be the archi- tecture, and so it is here. The modern bell tower is well placed to add to the play of form; it is a memorial to George Westinghouse and Nikola Tesla, the brilliant

inventor who worked for Westinghouse and helped develop the alternating-current system that is standard in modern power transmission.

Historic Landmark plaque

House
1397 Abers Creek Road, Monroeville
Henry Hornbostel, architect, 1939

This may be Hornbostel's last work, and would make a strong conclusion to his career. The warm, variegated tannish color and the texture of the stonework are quite appealing. The ornamentation lavished upon Carnegie Tech thirty-five years ago is now wholly relinquished.

MAPS

CITY OF PITTSBURGH
COUNTY OF ALLEGHENY

CONTENTS

The following section of maps is based on the United States Department of the Interior Geological Survey of 1993. Counties adjacent to Allegheny are frequently shown because of the quadrangle system used in these maps. The contents follow the sequence of chapters and sites in "A Guide to the Landmark Architecture of Allegheny County."

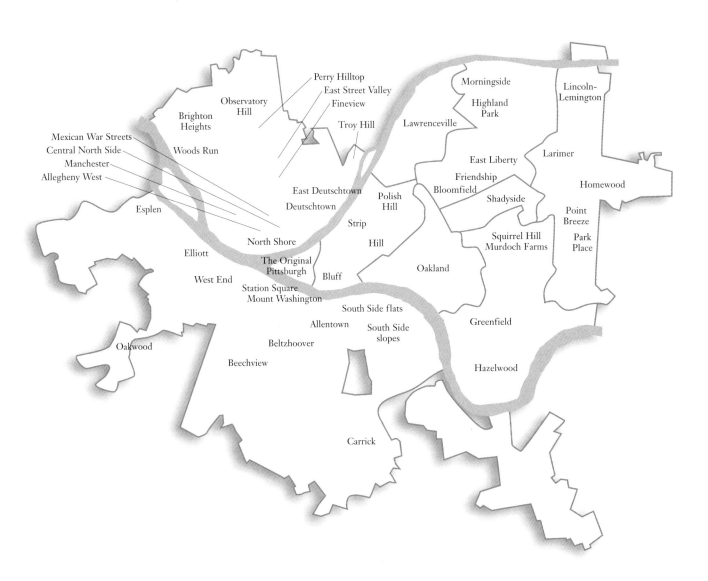

Perry Hilltop
East Street Valley
Fineview
Observatory
Hill
Troy Hill
Brighton
Heights
Morningside
Lincoln-
Lemington
Highland
Park
Lawrenceville
Mexican War Streets
Central North Side
Manchester
Allegheny West
Woods Run
East Liberty
Larimer
Friendship
Bloomfield
Homewood
Esplen
East Deutschtown
Deutschtown
Polish
Hill
Shadyside
Strip
North Shore
Elliott
Hill
Squirrel Hill
Murdoch Farms
Point
Breeze
Park
Place
The Original
Pittsburgh
Oakland
West End
Bluff
Station Square
Mount Washington
South Side flats
Greenfield
Allentown
South Side
slopes
Beltzhoover
Oakwood
Hazelwood
Beechview

Carrick

CITY OF PITTSBURGH

The neighborhood names given are those used in "A Guide to the Landmark Architecture of Allegheny County."

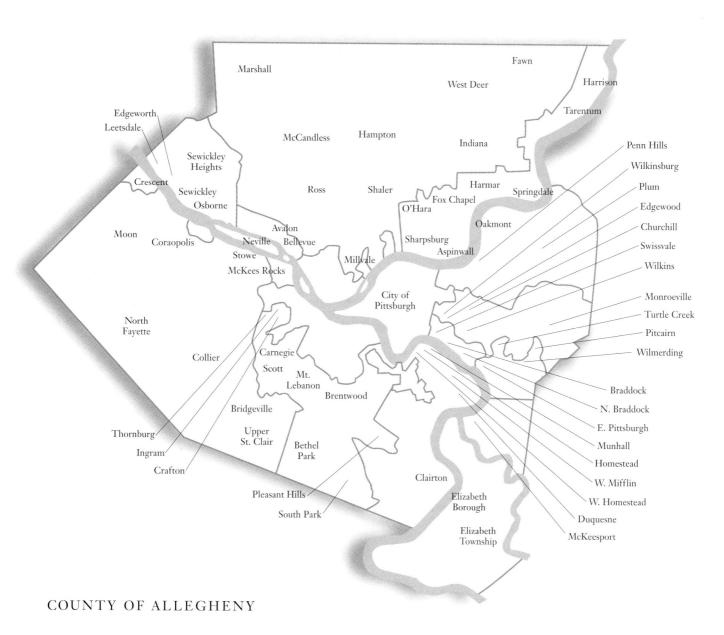

COUNTY OF ALLEGHENY

The community names given are those used in "A Guide to the Landmark Architecture of Allegheny County."

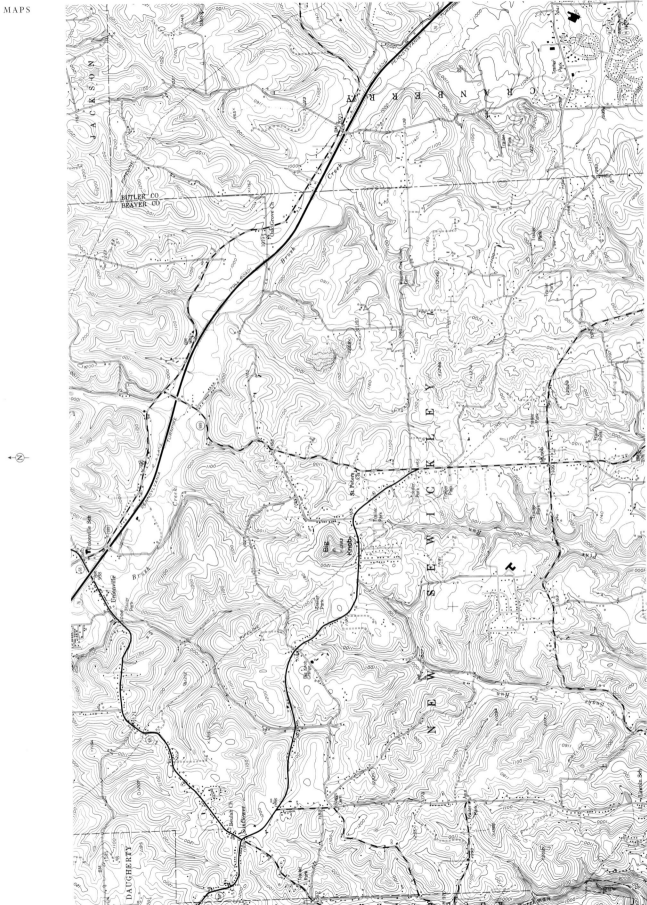

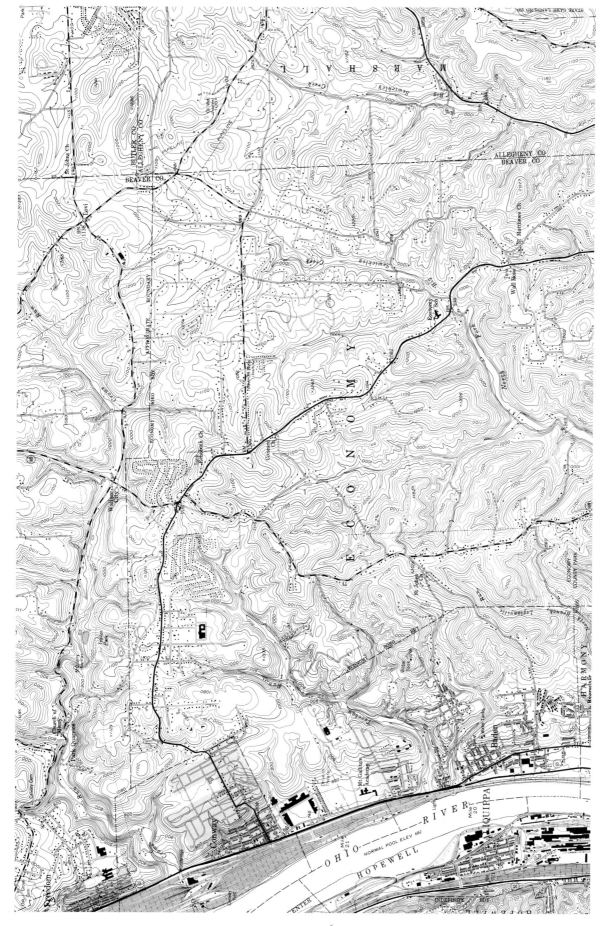

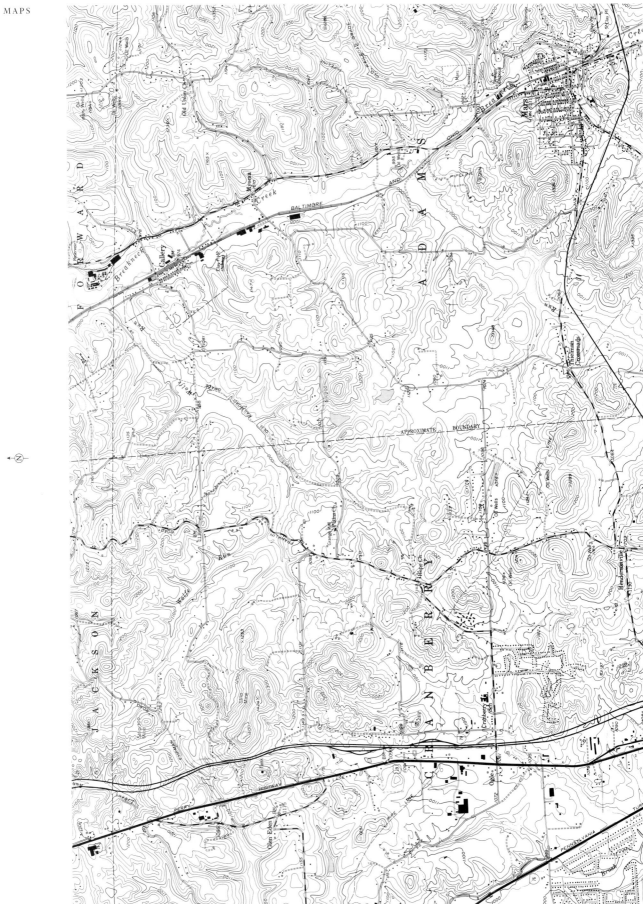

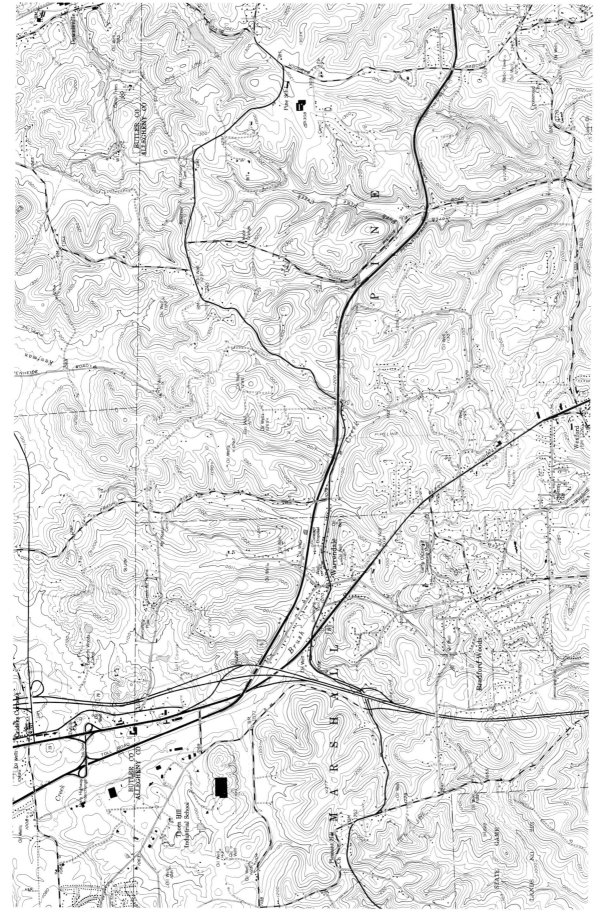

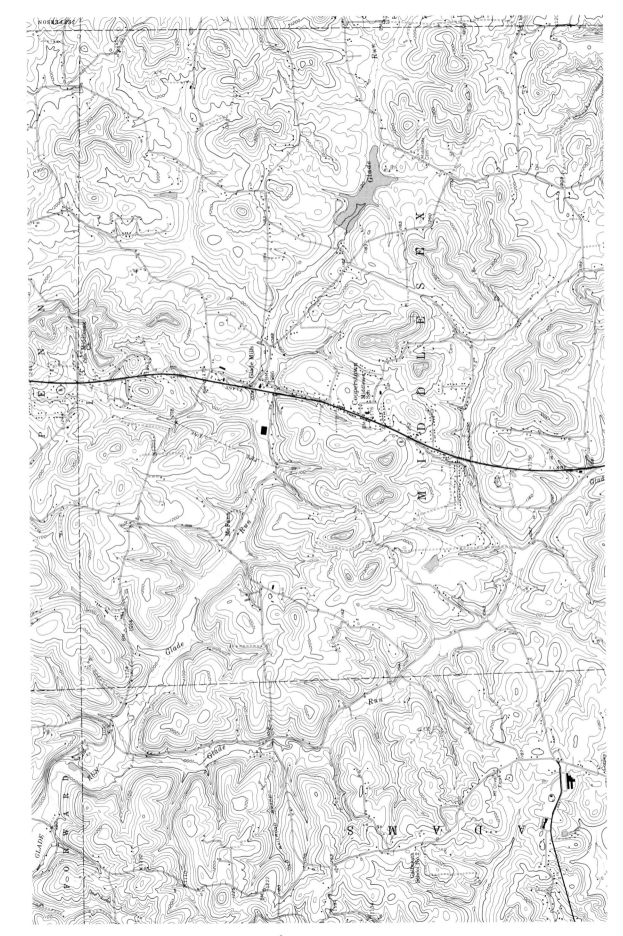

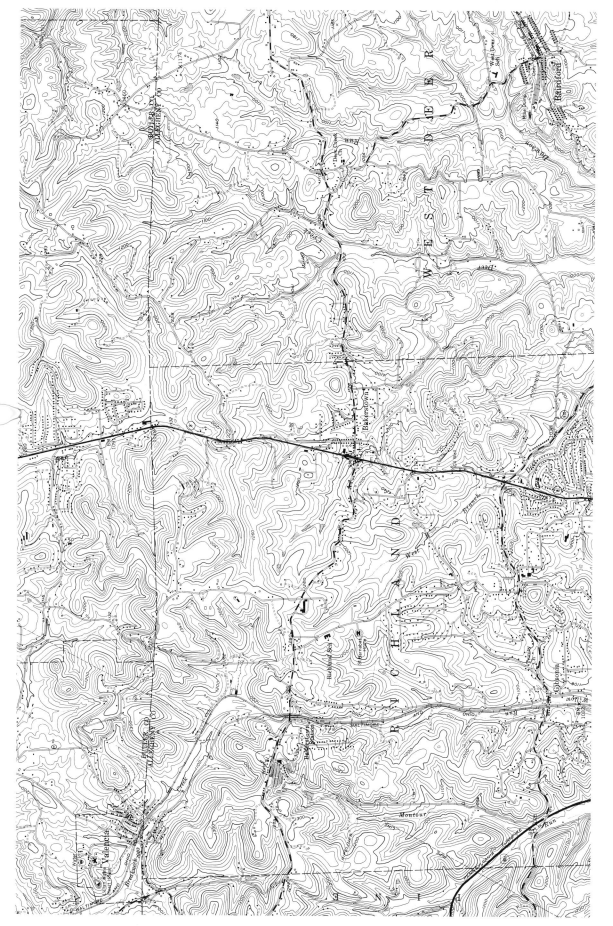

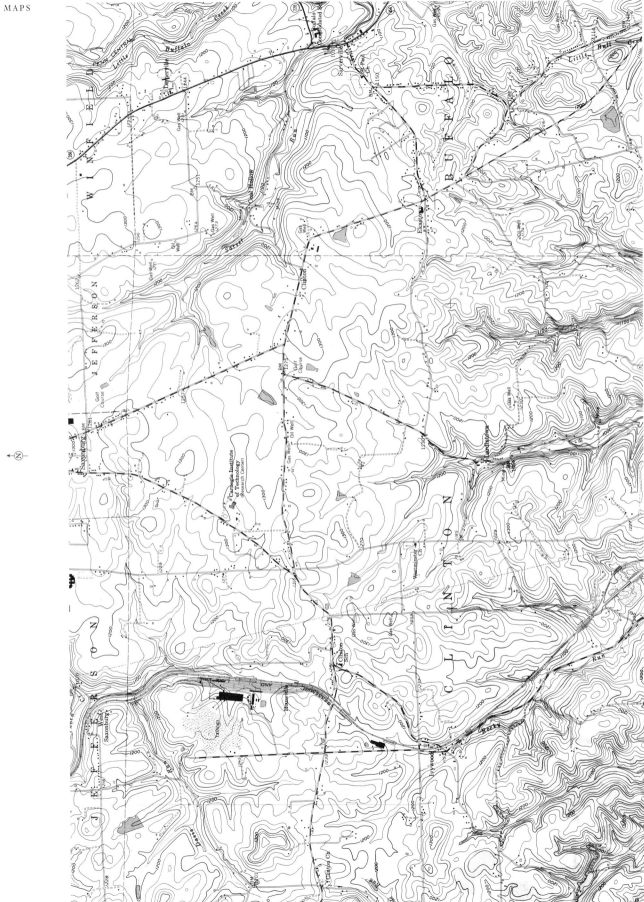

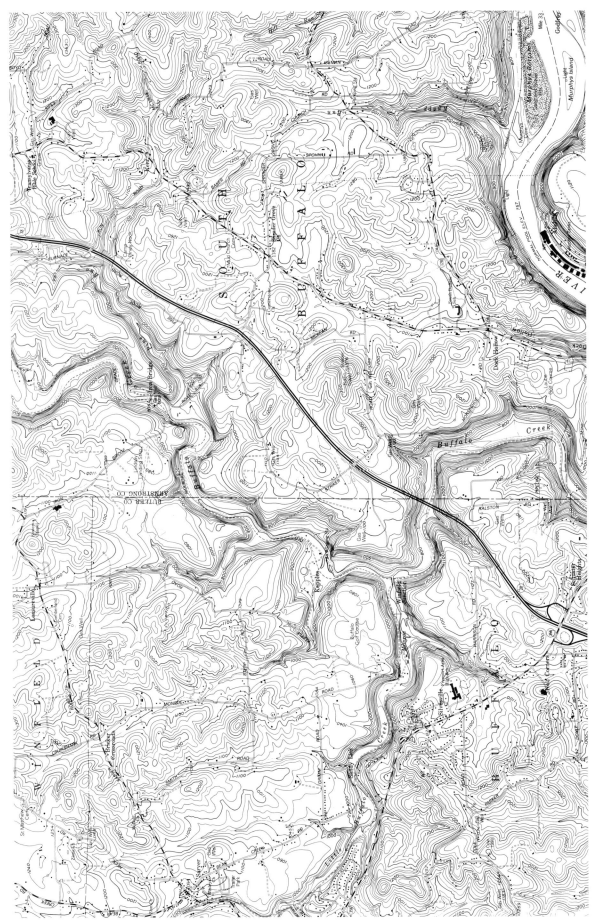

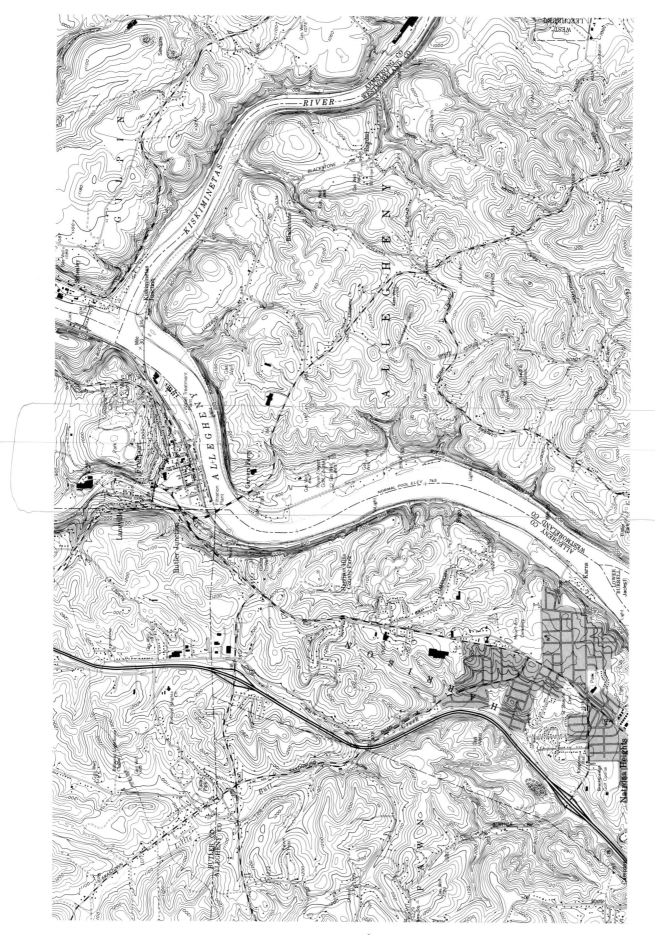

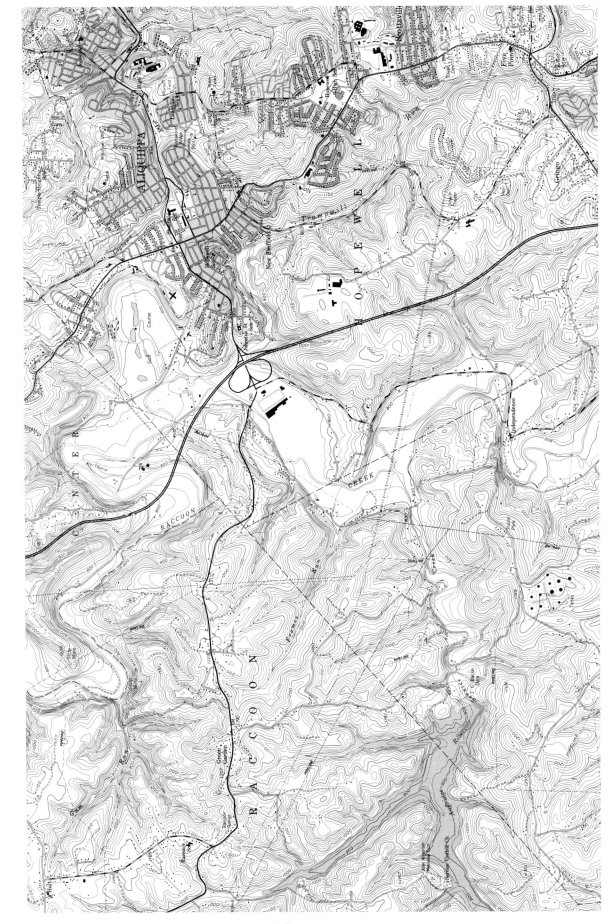

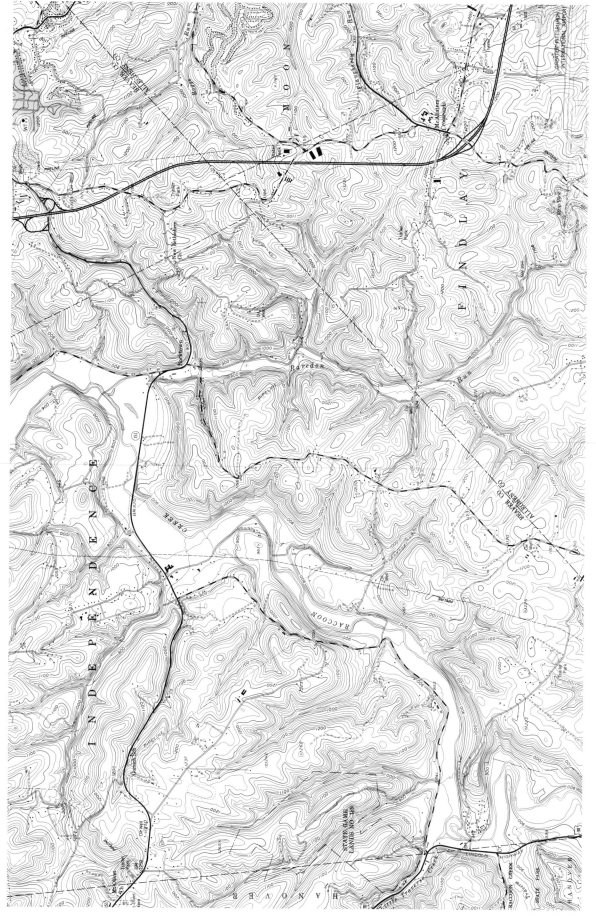

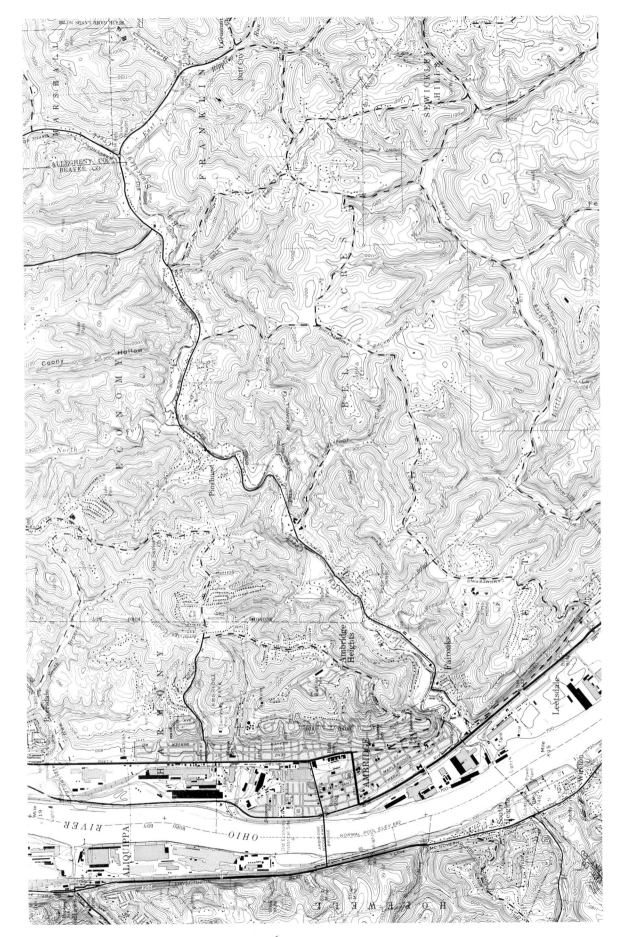

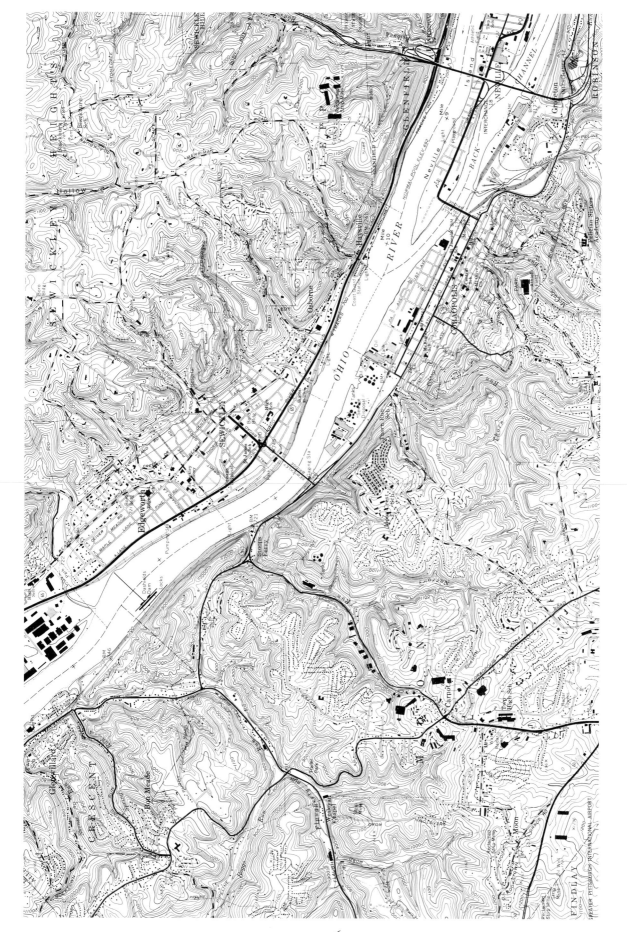

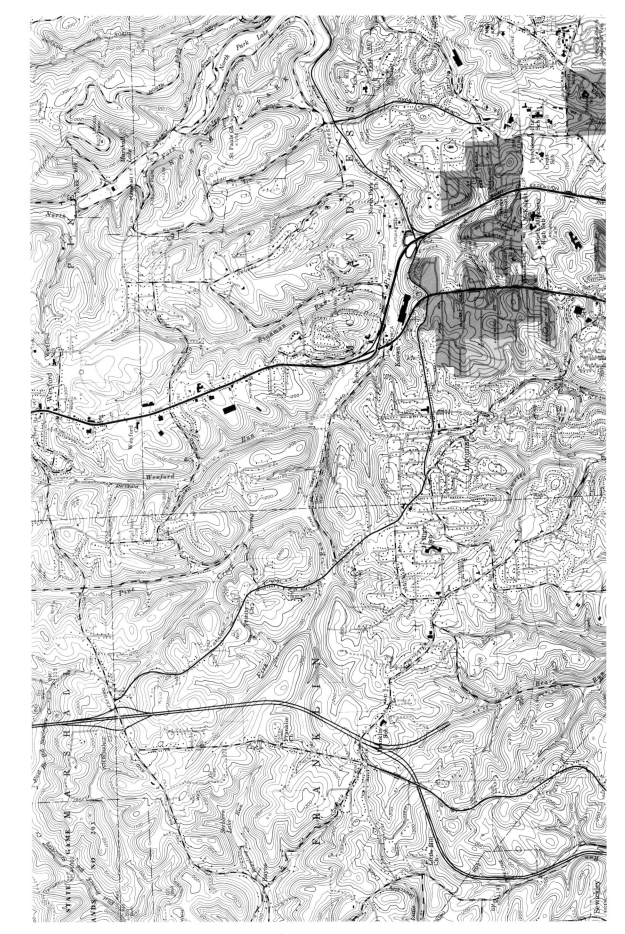

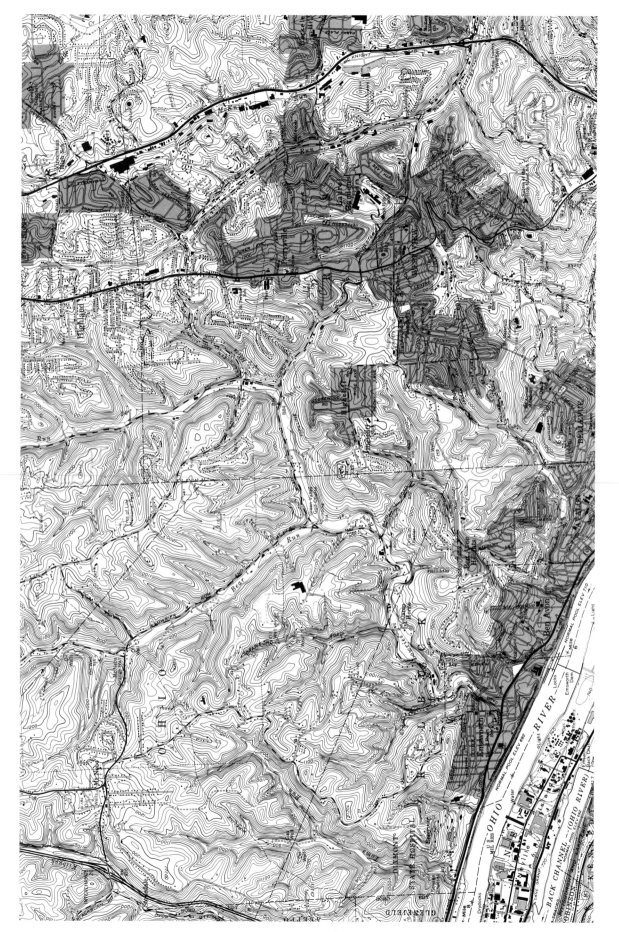

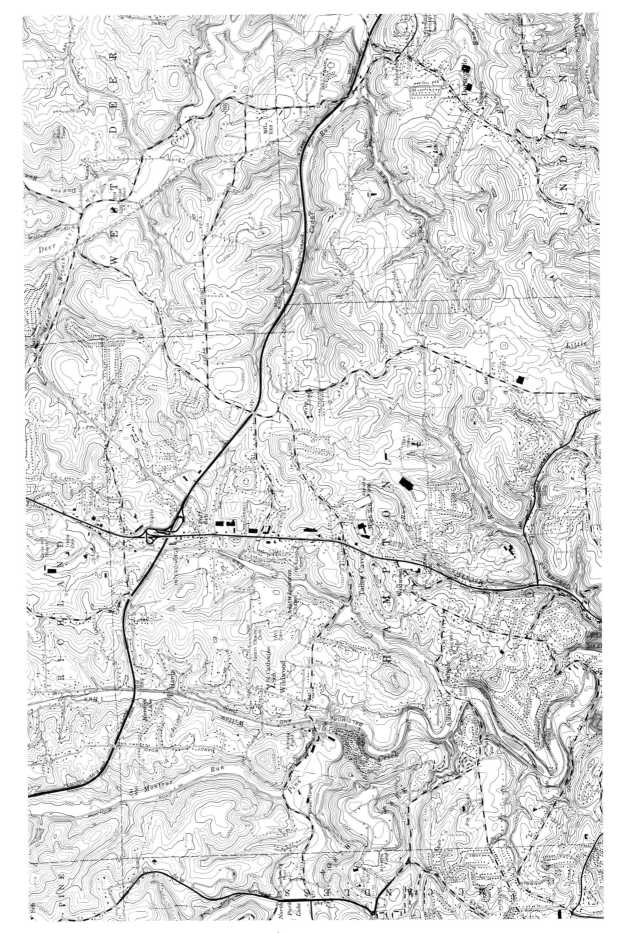

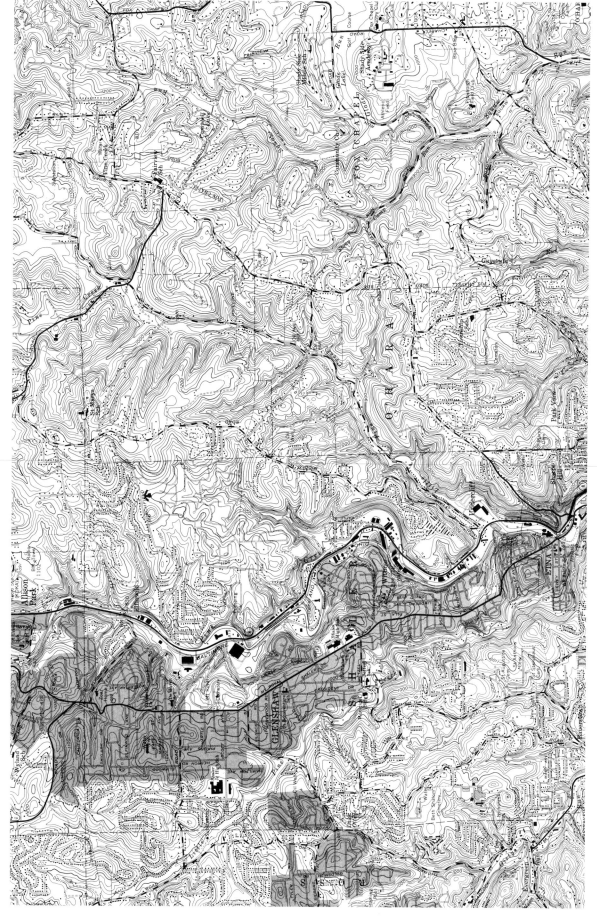

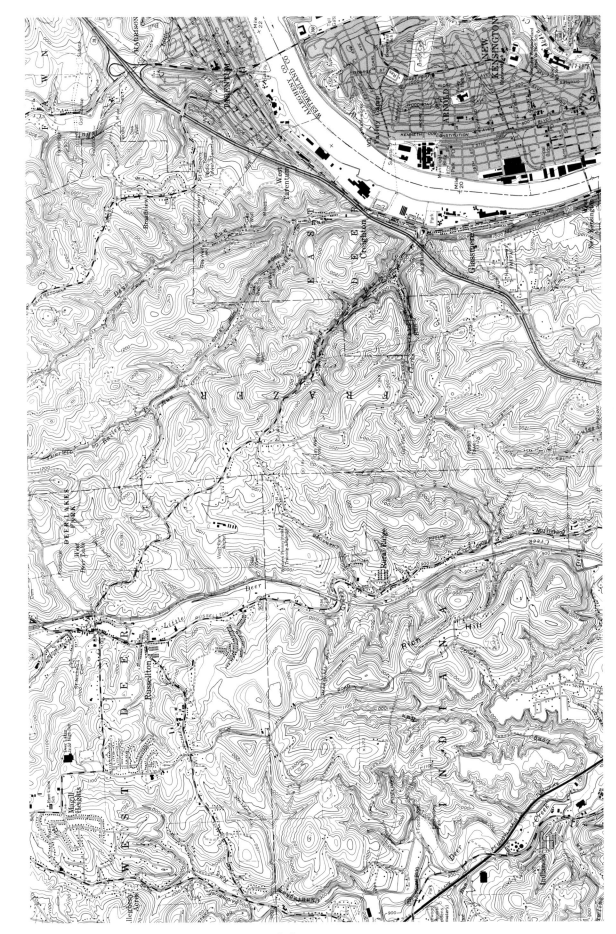

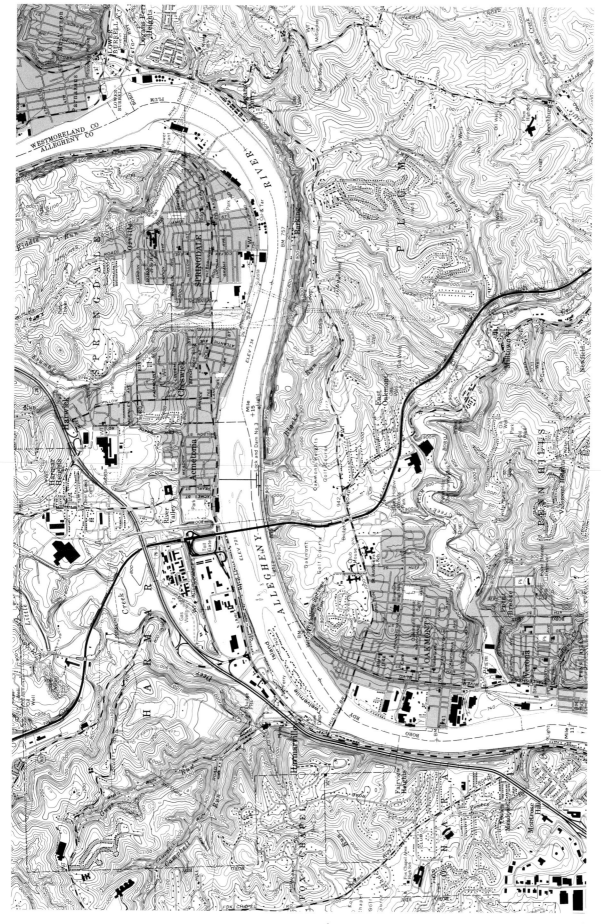

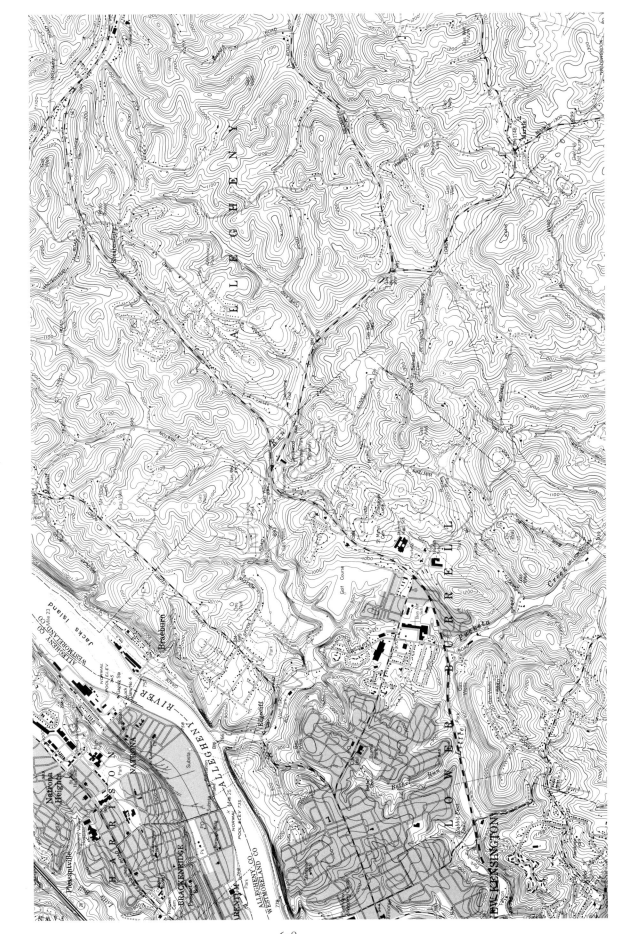

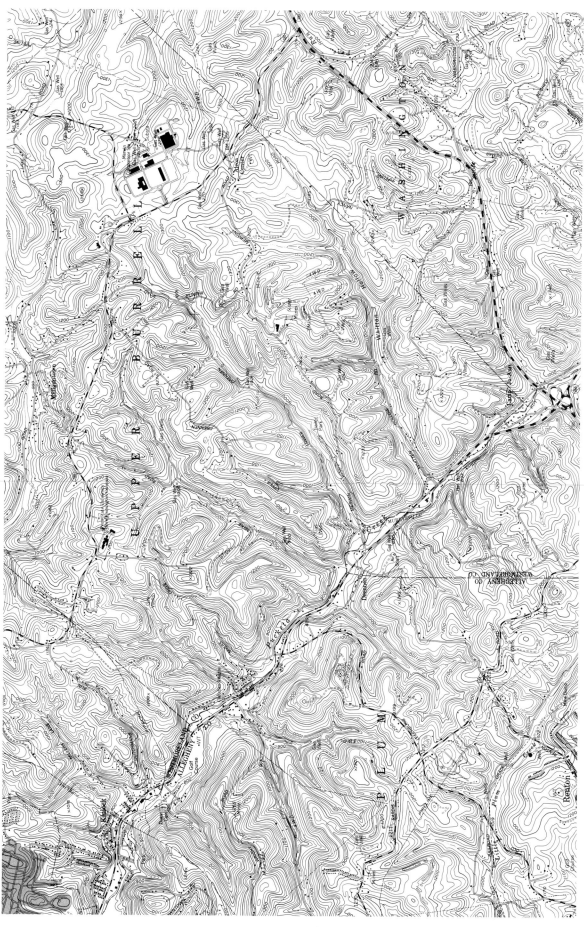

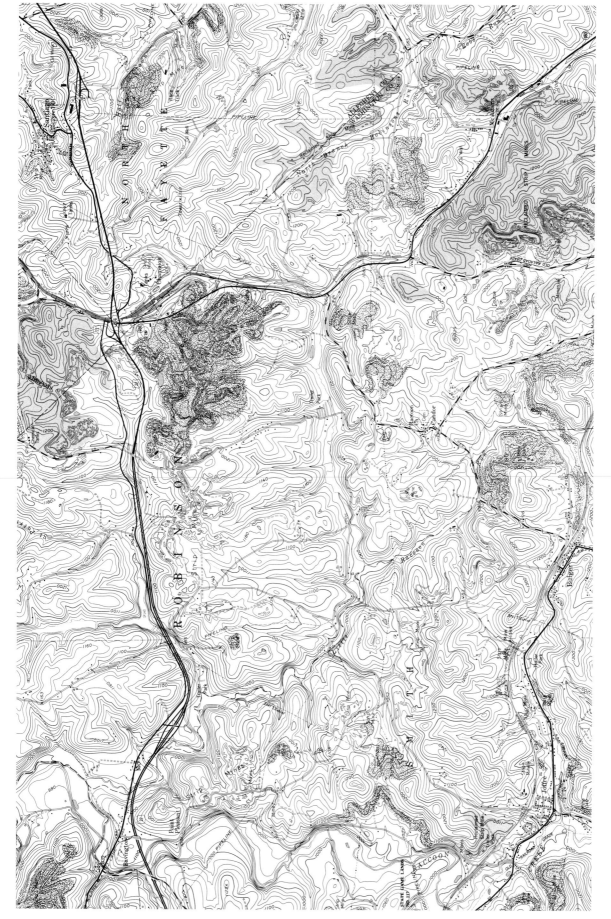

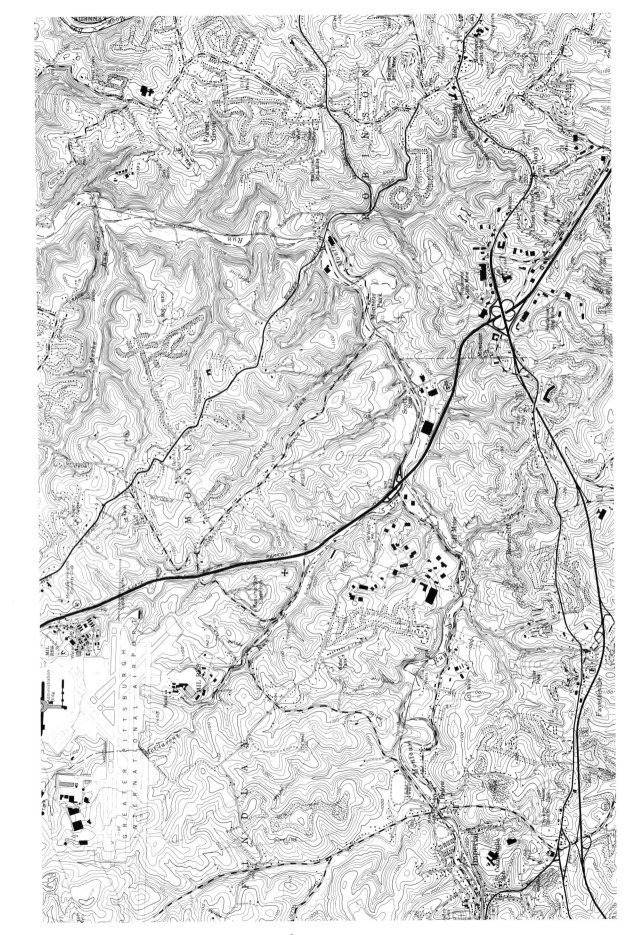

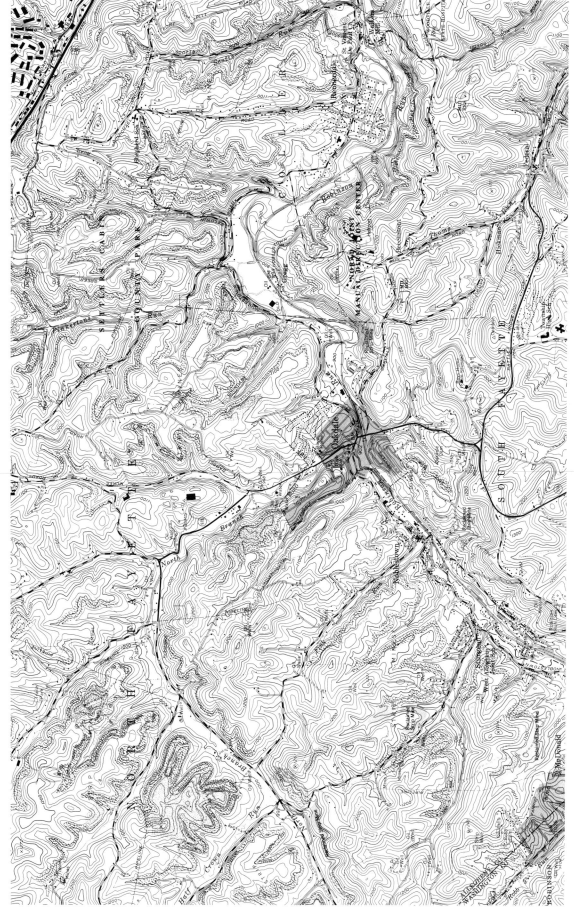

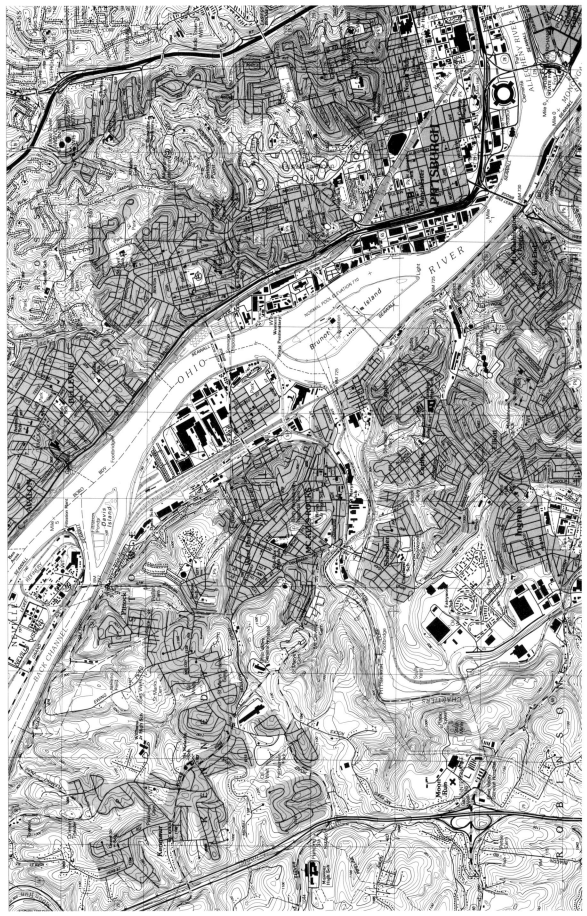

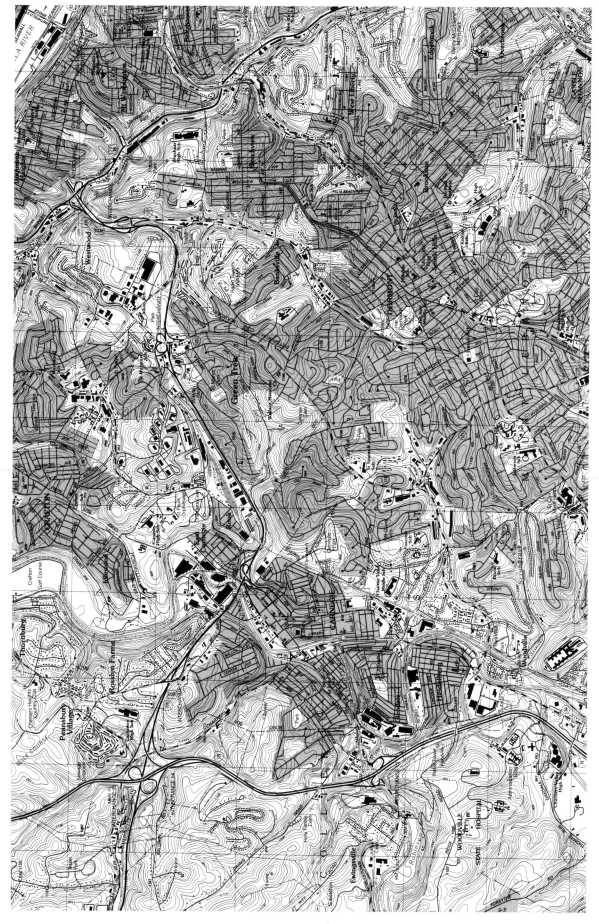

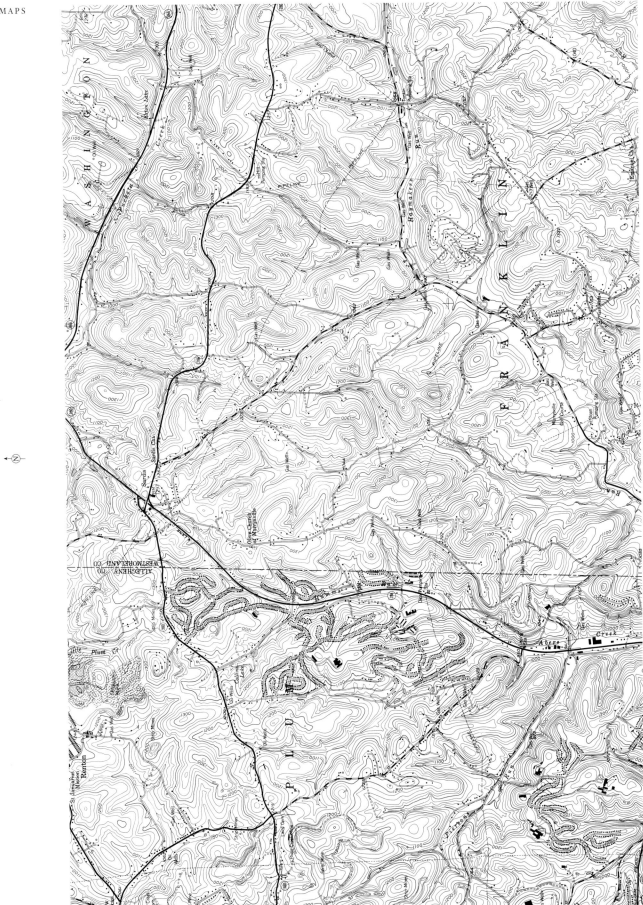

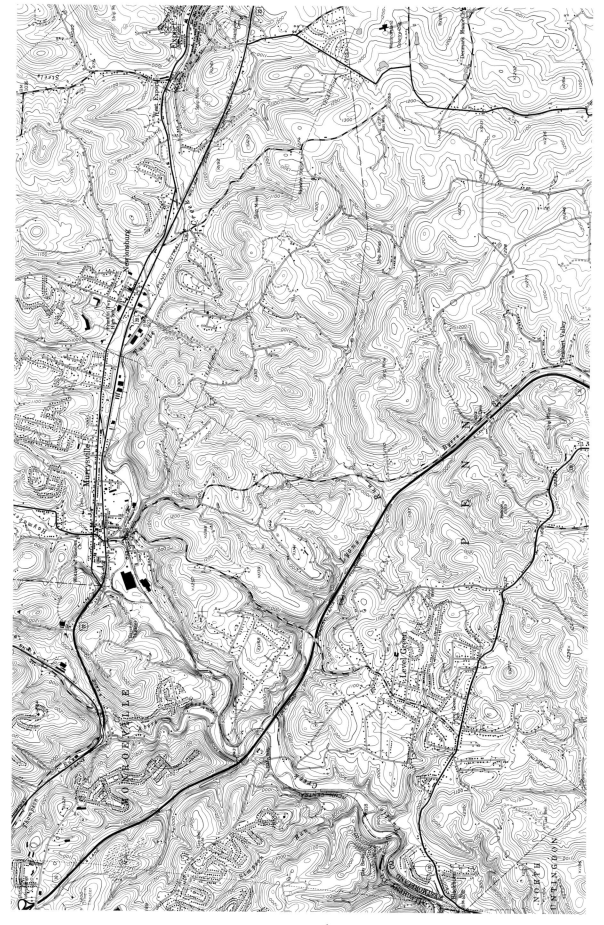

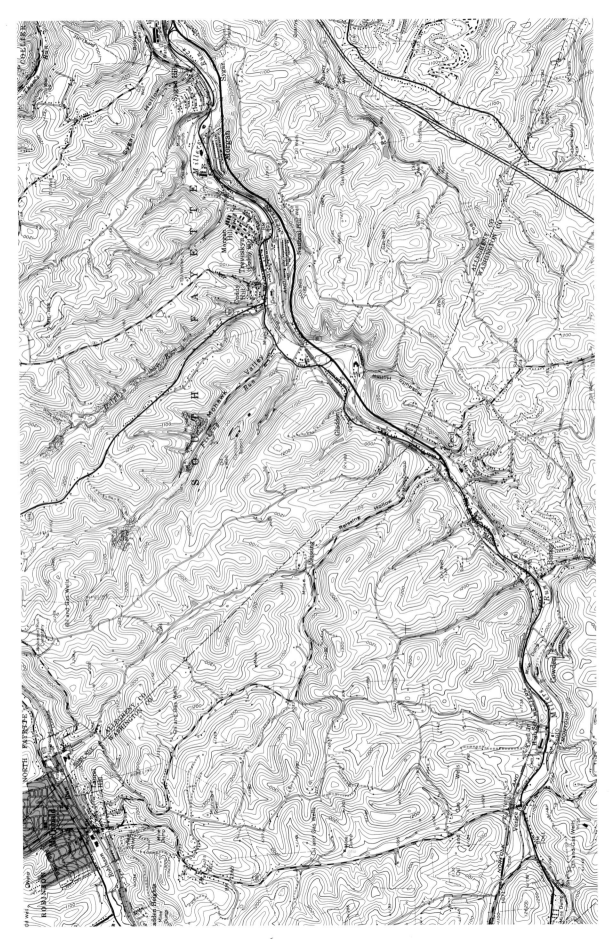

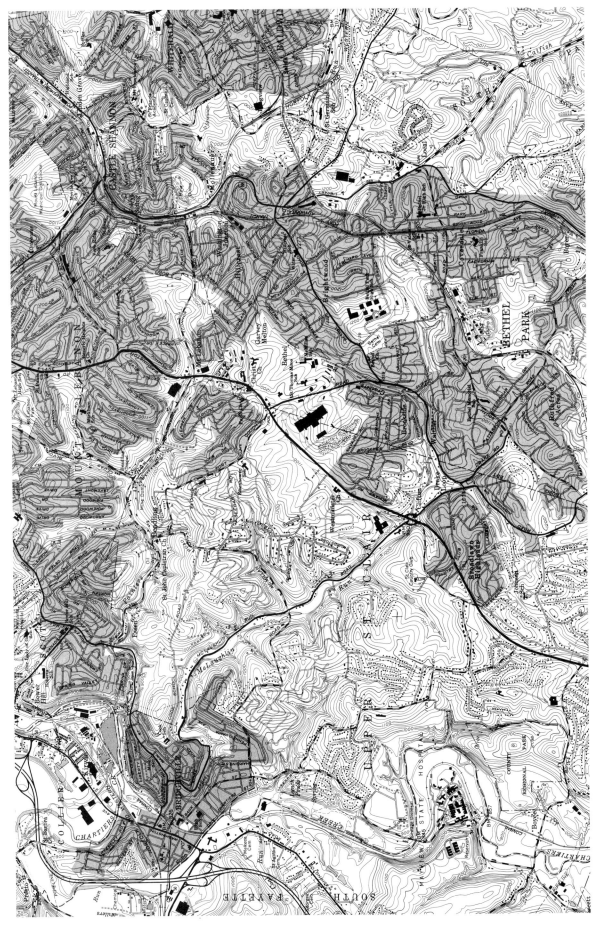

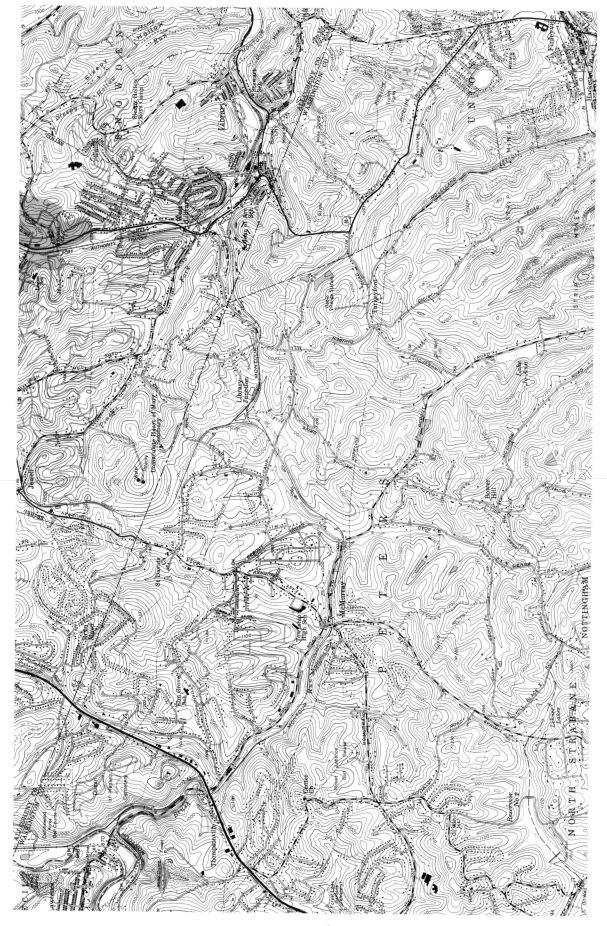

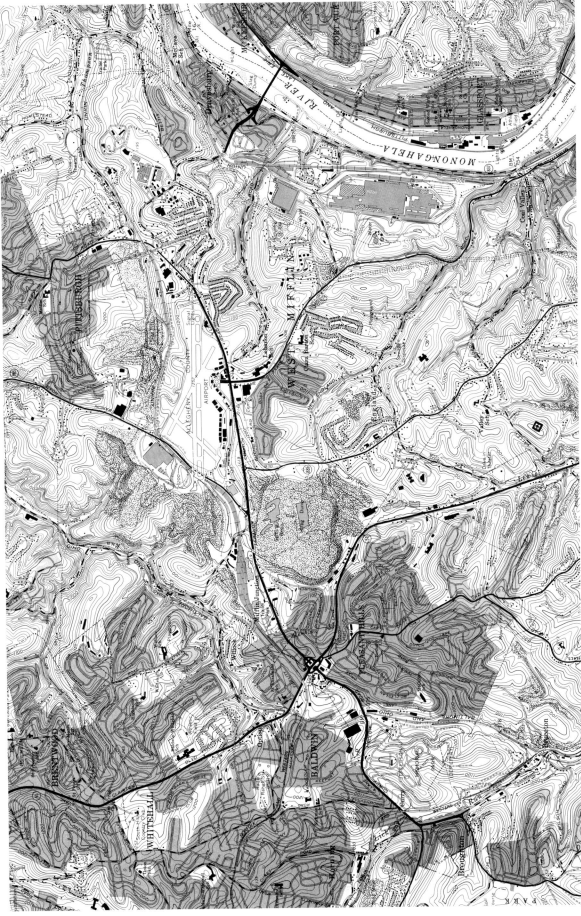

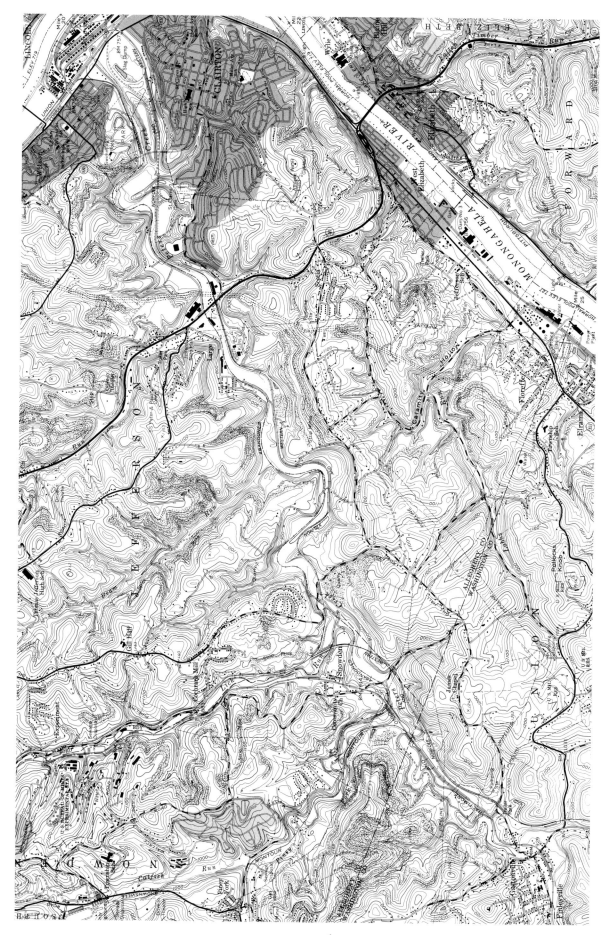

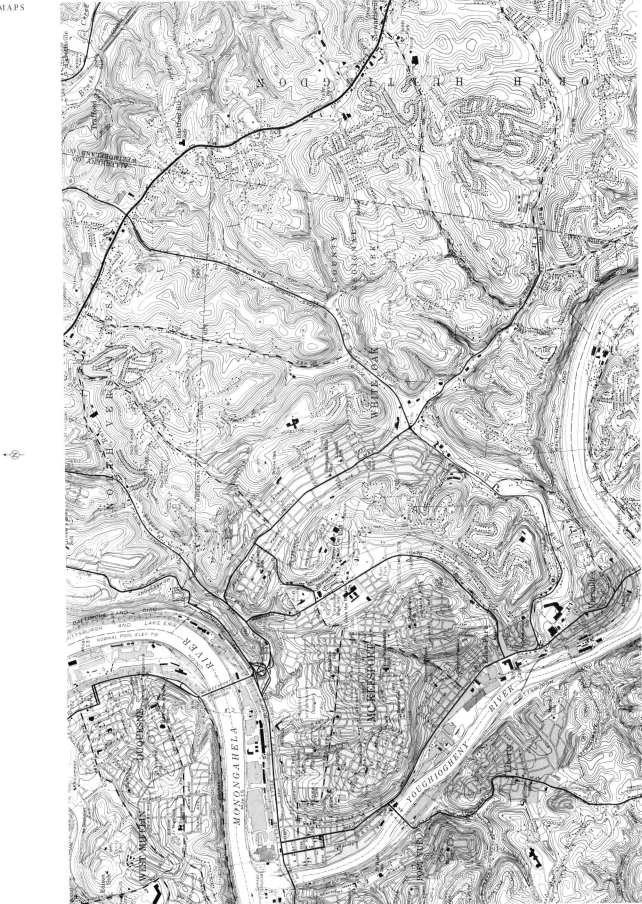

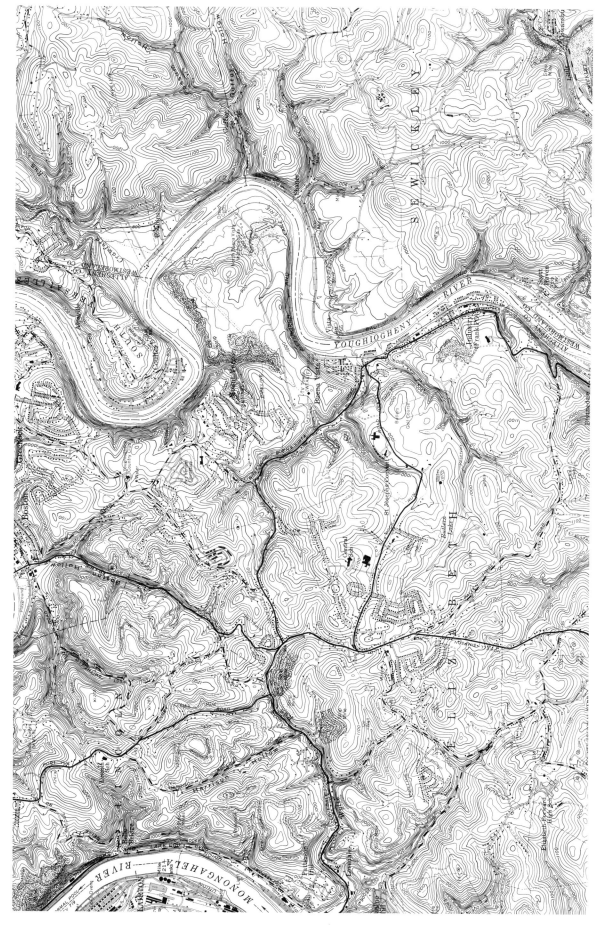

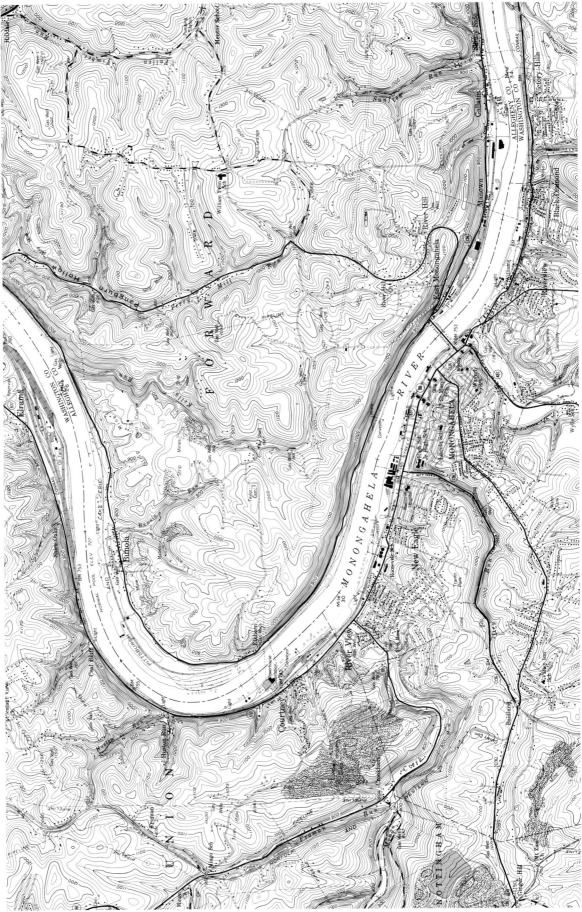

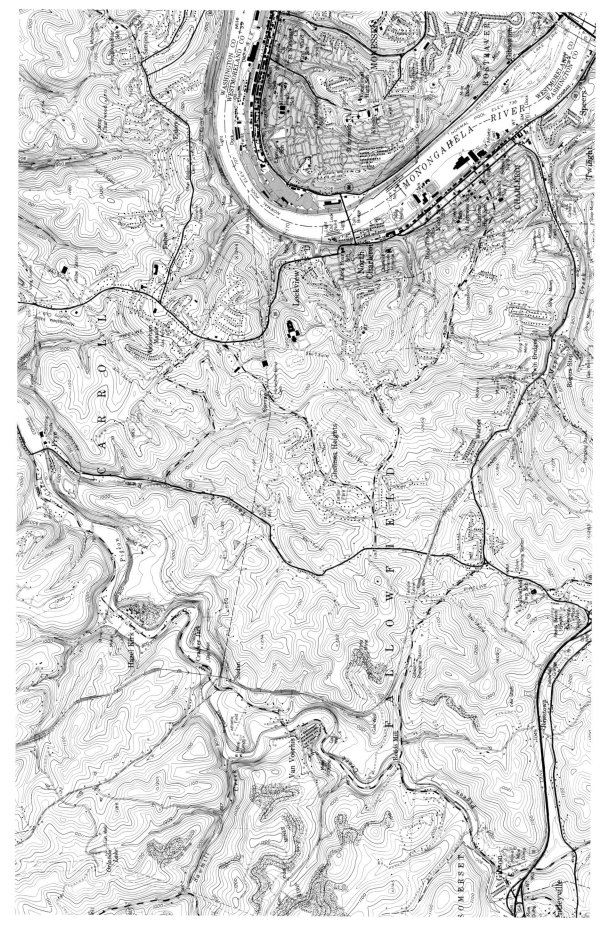

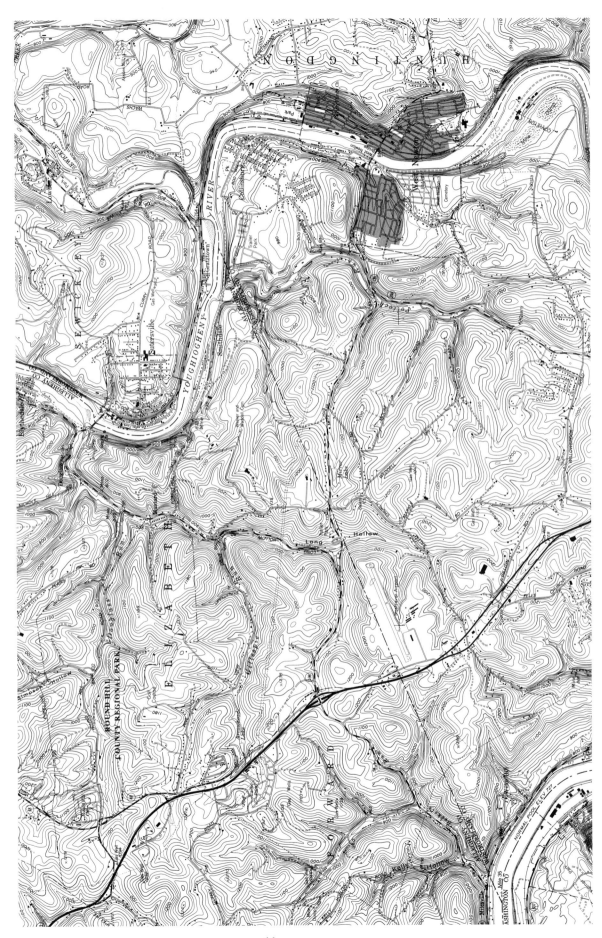

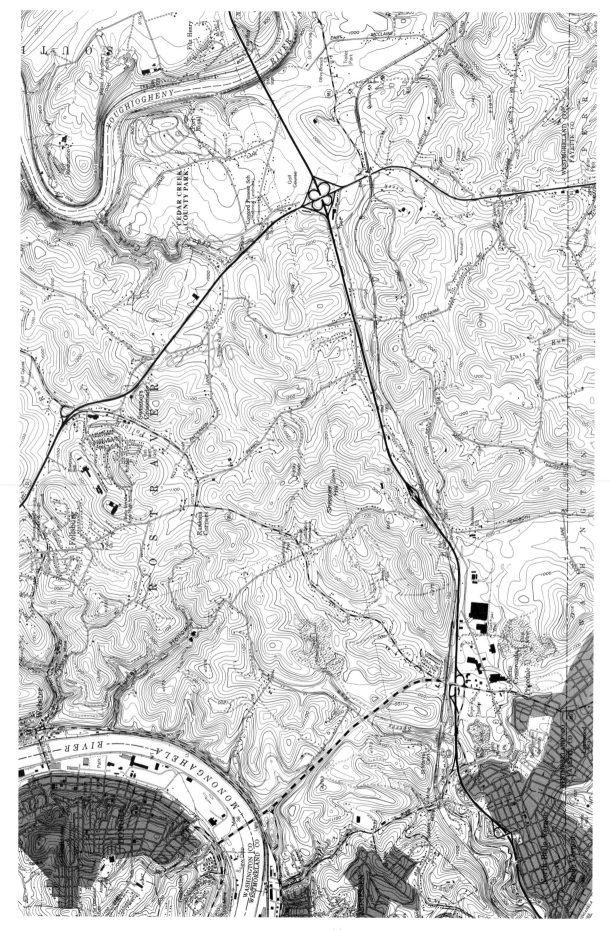

Frank Lloyd Wright's San Francisco Field Office, designed and installed in 319 Grant Avenue in 1951, served as his West Coast headquarters until his death. The office was dismantled in 1988, acquired in 1992 by The Heinz Architectural Center, The Carnegie Museum of Art, and installed there in 1993.

A SELECT BIBLIOGRAPHY OF
LANDMARK ARCHITECTURE
IN PITTSBURGH AND
ALLEGHENY COUNTY

ACKNOWLEDGEMENTS

This bibliography could not have been prepared without the assistance of others.
The first debt to be acknowledged is to the late James D. Van Trump; for over half-
a-century he prodigiously researched the buildings and designs, and the builders
and designers of the Pittsburgh area. His research notecards, preserved in the
James D. Van Trump Library of the Pittsburgh History & Landmarks Foundation,
provided many of the citations. I am particularly grateful to my colleagues at
Landmarks, Walter C. Kidney and Barry Hannegan, and to Martin Aurand,
Architecture Librarian and Archivist, Carnegie Mellon University, for their
many valuable contributions. Charlotte Cohen and Joan Gaul generously shared
information about Phipps Conservatory and Pittsburgh glass, respectively.
My thanks to Michael D. Eversmeyer, A.I.A., Principal Historic Preservation Planner,
Department of City Planning, City of Pittsburgh; Marilyn Holt and Audrey Iacone,
Pennsylvania Department, The Carnegie Library of Pittsburgh; Dennis McFadden,
The Heinz Architectural Center, The Carnegie Museum of Art; John Schulman,
Caliban Books; and Dr. Judith S. Hull who reviewed and commented on the
bibliography. Cheerful and patient assistance was provided by librarians in various
departments of The Carnegie Library of Pittsburgh, in particular Kathryn Logan
and her colleagues in Music and Art, Gregory Priore of Special Collections, and the
Pennsylvania Department reference staff; and by Sharon Mauro and her staff at
the Historical Society of Western Pennsylvania.

A SELECT BIBLIOGRAPHY OF LANDMARK ARCHITECTURE IN PITTSBURGH AND ALLEGHENY COUNTY

This bibliography consists of selected books and articles about historic buildings, landscape design, and city planning within Allegheny County. The bibliography has been limited to structures and places approximately fifty years old or older. Taking the millennium into account, a date of 1950 has been adopted as a convenient demarcation; even then, there are exceptions and these are duly noted.[1]

Dissertations, theses, and other unpublished studies have been omitted. No thorough attempt has been made to unearth articles from regional magazines of a general nature, newspapers, or institutional newsletters, or to include builder's announcements, or photographs of individual structures found in architectural journals with minimal text; these remain to be explored by the diligent researcher.[2]

Until recently, studies of regional architecture appeared most frequently in a few local periodicals, principally the defunct *The Charette* [1920–1971], begun by the Pittsburgh Architectural Club and subsequently supported by the Pittsburgh Chapter of the American Institute of Architects and the Pennsylvania Society of Architects; the Carnegie Institute's *Carnegie Magazine*; *The Western Pennsylvania Historical Magazine* and its successor *Pittsburgh History* published by the Historical Society of Western Pennsylvania; and *PHLF News*, published by the Pittsburgh History & Landmarks Foundation. Between 1956 and 1983, many articles in these and other serial publications were written by James D. Van Trump (1908–1995), Pittsburgh's preeminent architectural historian; in 1983, sixty-four of Van Trump's some 500 writings—both previously published and unpublished—were published as *Life and Architecture in Pittsburgh*. Because of the scope and importance of Van Trump's writings, this bibliography cites *Life and Architecture in Pittsburgh* rather than the publications in which the pieces first appeared; *Life and Architecture in Pittsburgh*, although now out of print, is more readily available and includes original publication data.

It is my hope that readers will use this bibliography as they would an "open" library stack: connections are made and knowledge comes from browsing; from the unexpected discovery.

Albert M. Tannler
Historical Collections Director
Pittsburgh History & Landmarks Foundation

GENERAL[3]

American Institute of Architects, Pittsburgh Chapter. [John T. Comes and Charles T. Ingham]. *A Plan for the Architectural Improvement of Pittsburgh*. Reprint. Sixth Annual Convention of the Architectural League of America, n.p.: 1904.

Arnold, Bion J. *Report on the Pittsburgh Transportation Problem*. Pittsburgh: Republic Bank Note Company, 1910.

Art Work of Pittsburg. Chicago: W. H. Parish Publishing Co., 1893.

Art Work of Pittsburg, Penna. N.p.: George E. White Company, 1899.

Ashworth, Ralph. *Greetings From Pittsburgh: A Picture Postcard History*. Vestal, NY: Vestal Press, 1992.

Aurand, Martin. *Pittsburgh Architecture: A Guide to Research*. Pittsburgh: Carnegie Mellon University Architecture Archives, 1991.

Aurand, Martin. "Prairie School Architecture in Pittsburgh," *Pittsburgh History* 78:1 (Spring 1995): 5–20.

Bigger, Frederick. "The Limitations of City Planning." *The Charette* 15:8 (April 1935): 1–6.

Bigger, Frederick. "The Pittsburgh Plan." *The Charette* [Part One] 5:10 (October 1925): 1–3; [Part Two] 5:11 (November 1925): 6–8.

Bigger, Frederick. "Pittsburgh's New Zoning Ordinance Accentuates the Positive." *The Charette* [30:10] (October, 1950): 19, 33.

Bolden, Frank E., Laurence A. Glasco, and Eliza Smith Brown. *A Legacy in Bricks and Mortar: African-American Landmarks in Allegheny County*. Pittsburgh: Pittsburgh History & Landmarks Foundation, 1995.

Brown, Eliza Smith, et al. *African American Historic Sites Survey of Allegheny County*. Harrisburg: Pennsylvania Historical and Museum Commission, 1994.

Brown, Mark M., Lu Donnelly, and David G. Wilkins. *The History of the Duquesne Club*. Pittsburgh: The Duquesne Club, 1989.

Buckingham, James S. "Pittsburgh." *The Eastern and Western States of America*. London: Fisher, Son & Co., [1837?]. Vol. 2: 170–204.

Cámara de Comercio de Pittsburgh. *Notas Interesantes Acerca de Pittsburg 1889*. Pittsburgh: Otto Krebs, 1889.

Chalfant, W. B. "The Pittsburgh Architectural Club." *The Charette* 5:8 (August 1925): 1.

Church, Samuel Harden, et al. "Pittsburgh as an Art Center." *Art and Archaeology* 14:5/6 (November/December 1922), 267–356.

Collins, John Fulton Stuart. *"Stringtown on the Pike": Tales and History of East Liberty and the East Liberty Valley of Pennsylvania*. Pittsburgh: East Liberty Chamber of Commerce; printed by Edwards Brothers, c. 1966.

"Competition for the Pittsburgh Court House-City Hall, Pittsburgh, Pa." *The Architectural Review* (Old Series 20) III:3 (March 1914): 36–40, plates 21–28.

"Concerning the Pittsburgh Architectural Club." *The Charette* 14:5 (March 1934): [6–7].

Dickson, Harold E. *A Hundred Pennsylvania Buildings*. State College, PA: Bald Eagle Press, 1954: 50, 57, 80, 81, 83, 84, 85, 86, 89, 99, 100.

Embury, Aymar, II. "Impressions of Three Cities, III, Pittsburgh." *Architecture* 31:4 (April 1915): 105–109.

Evans, George E. "Is Low Cost Housing Possible in Pittsburgh?" *The Charette* 17:3 (March 1937): 1–3.

Evert, Marilyn. "Sculpture in Schenley Park." 53:6 *Carnegie Magazine* (June 1979): 29–35.

Fifield, Barringer. *Seeing Pittsburgh*. Pittsburgh: University of Pittsburgh Press, 1996.

Fleming, George T. *Fleming's Views of Old Pittsburgh*. 1905. rev. ed., ed. Henry Russell Miller. Pittsburgh: The Crescent Press, 1932.

Fleming, George T. *Pittsburgh: How to See It*. Pittsburgh: Wm. G. Johnston, 1916.

Gall, George H. *Homes and Country Estates of Pittsburgh Men*. Pittsburgh: Privately printed by Eichbaum Co., 1905.

Gangewere, R. Jay. "Schenley Park." *Carnegie Magazine* 53:6 (June 1979): 20–28.

Gangewere, R. Jay, Marilyn Evert, and James D. Van Trump. "Highland Park." *Carnegie Magazine* 54: 6 (June 1980): 7–17.

Gay, Vernon, and Marilyn Evert. *Discovering Pittsburgh's Sculpture*. Pittsburgh: University of Pittsburgh Press, 1983.

Griswold, Ralph. "The Western Pennsylvania Architectural Survey." *The Charette* 13:2 (February 1933): 1–3.

Greater Pittsburg[h]. Portland, ME: L. H. Nelson Co., rev. ed. 1908.

Hannegan, Barry. "Pittsburgh's Emerald Necklace." *PHLF News* 143 (August 1996): 8–13.

Hannegan, Barry. "Pittsburgh's Landscape Tradition." *PHLF News* 138 (May 1995): 8–9.

Hannegan, Barry. "Schenley Plaza—Place of Dreams." *PHLF News* 144 (November 1996): 10–15.

Heineman, Kenneth J. "The Changing Face of Schenley Park." *Pittsburgh History* 72:3 (Fall 1989): 112–127.

Joseph Horne Co. *Small Homes for Better Living in Greater Pittsburgh: Prize Winning Plans Designed by Local Architects for the Architectural Competition Sponsored by Joseph Horne Co*. Pittsburgh: Joseph Horne Co., 1946.

Hull, Judith S. *A Century of Women Landscape Architects and Gardeners in Pittsburgh*. Pittsburgh: The Heinz Architectural Center, 1996.

In and About Allegheny. Portland, ME: L. H. Nelson Co., 1904.

"Interesting Brick Architecture in Pittsburg, Pa.: Domestic." *The Brickbuilder* 11:11 (November 1902): 228–232, plates 81, 82, 87, 88; 2 unnumbered plates.

"Interesting Brick Architecture in Pittsburg, Pa.: Public and Commercial." *The Brickbuilder* 11:12 (December 1902): 253–257, 267, plates 89, 96.

C. C. Johnston Co. *Illustrated 1898–99 Guide to the Leading Hotels and Boarding Houses, Amusements and Resorts of the Twin Cities*. Pittsburgh: Nicolson Press, 1898.

Jordon, John W., compiler. "Edward Manning Bigelow." *A Century and a Half of Pittsburg and Her People*, Vol. 3. N.p.: Lewis Publishing Company, 1908: 142.

Jordon, John W., compiler. "James Graham Chalfant." *A Century and a Half of Pittsburg and Her People*, Vol. 3. N.p.: Lewis Publishing Company, 1908: 234–35.

Judd, Barbara. "Edward M. Bigelow: Creator of Pittsburgh's Arcadian Parks." *Western Pennsylvania Historical Magazine* 58:1 (January 1975): 53–67.

Kelly, William M. *Edgeworth Club 1893–1993*. Edgeworth: Privately printed by the Hoechstetter Printing Company, 1992.

Kidney, Walter C. "Getting Across and Coming Across. Part I: Sick Bridges; How Allegheny County's Bridges Got in Trouble." *Pittsburgher Magazine* 2:3 (August 1978): 56–59.

Kidney, Walter C. "Getting Across and Coming Across. Part II: Money to Cure the Bridges; Where We Might Get It." *Pittsburgher Magazine* 2:4 (September 1978): 48–54.

Kidney, Walter C. "Grand Introductions: A Business-hours Tour of the Triangle's Interiors." *Pittsburgher Magazine* 2:2 (July 1978): 50–58.

Kidney, Walter C. *A History of the Pittsburgh Builders Exchange 1886–1986*. Pittsburgh: Pittsburgh Builders Exchange, 1986.

Kidney, Walter C. *Landmark Architecture: Pittsburgh and Allegheny County*. Pittsburgh: Pittsburgh History & Landmarks Foundation, 1985.

Kidney, Walter C. "Locks and Dams." *Executive Report* 1:3 (August/September 1981): 10–12, 30–33.

Kidney, Walter C. "The Mellon Bank Buildings: Spanning Eras of Architectural History." *Executive Report* 3:10 (April 1985): 28–37.

Kidney, Walter C. "Modern Architecture in Pittsburgh." *Pittsburgher Magazine* 2:5 (October 1978): 54–62.

Kidney, Walter C. "New Life for a Dead Letter Office." *Progressive Architecture* 53:11 (November 1972): 100–105.

Kidney, Walter C. *A Past Still Alive: The Pittsburgh History & Landmarks Foundation Celebrates Twenty-Five Years*. Pittsburgh: Pittsburgh History & Landmarks Foundation, 1989.

Kidney, Walter C. "Pittsburgh: An Introduction." *PHLF News* 122 (February 1992): 10–11.

Kidney, Walter C. "Pittsburgh: A Study in Urban Identity." *Progressive Architecture* 49:3 (March 1968): 117–127.

Kidney, Walter C. "Pittsburgh Architecture." A series of articles on little-known aspects of Pittsburgh's built environment. *PHLF News* 117 (Spring 1991): 10–11, and issues thereafter.

Kidney, Walter C. "Pittsburgh Architecture: the Good, the Bad, and the Ugly." *Pittsburgher Magazine* 3:10 (March 1980): 40–45.

Kidney, Walter C. "Pittsburgh Architecture: What Boston Has Done for Us." *PHLF News* 131 (September 1993): 9–11.

Kidney, Walter C. "Pittsburgh Houses." *Pittsburgher Magazine* 3:4 (September 1979): 59–61.

Kidney, Walter C. *Pittsburgh in Your Pocket: A Guide to Pittsburgh-area Architecture*. rev. ed. Pittsburgh: Pittsburgh History & Landmarks Foundation, 1994.

Kidney, Walter C. "Pittsburgh's Rivers, Part I: By the Rivers." *The Pittsburgher Magazine* 3:2 (July 1979): 65–69.

Kidney, Walter C. "Pittsburgh's Rivers, Part II: On the Rivers." *The Pittsburgher Magazine* 3:3 (August 1979): 35, 37–39.

"Alexander Hayes King." *History of Pittsburgh and Environs: Encyclopedia of Biography*. [Clugston to Ressa]. New York and Chicago: American Historical Society, 1922: 204–05.

Kropff, Henry M. "Recollections of Some of the Old Timers." *The Charette* 12:3 (March 1932): 1–2.

Lacey, Adin Benedict. "Soldier's Memorial, Allegheny County, Penna." *American Competitions Published by the T Square Club 1907*. Philadelphia: T Square Club, 1907: 1–3, plates 1–24.

Lacey, Adin Benedict. "Western University of Pennsylvania, Pittsburg, Pa." *American Competitions Published by the T Square Club 1908*. Philadelphia: T Square Club, 1909. Vol. 2: plates 40–55.

Lacey, Adin Benedict. "Young Women's Christian Association Building, Pittsburg, Pennsylvania." *American Competitions Published by the T Square Club 1908*. Philadelphia: T Square Club, 1909. Vol. 2: plates 23–29.

Leonard, J. W. *Pittsburgh and Allegheny Illustrated Review: Historical, Biographical and Commercial*. Pittsburgh: J. M. Elstner & Co., 1889.

Lewis, Virginia E. "Some Aspects of Stained Glass in Pittsburgh—Past and Present." *Stained Glass* 56:1 (Spring 1961): 13–27.

Lewis, Virginia E. "Stained Glass in Pittsburgh." *Stained Glass* 43:11 (Summer 1948): 35–46.

Lloyd, Anne. "Pittsburgh's 1923 Zoning Ordinance." *Western Pennsylvania Historical Magazine* 57:3 (July 1974): 289–305.

Lorant, Stefan, et al. *Pittsburgh: The Story of An American City*. Garden City: Doubleday & Company, 1964.

Lowry, Patricia. "Pittsburgh's Public Plazas Make the Grade (From 'A' for Animated to 'D' for Dismal)." *Pittsburgh Press*, Sunday Magazine (October 7, 1990): 22.

Lubove, Roy. "City Beautiful, City Banal: Design Advocacy and Historic Preservation in Pittsburgh." *Pittsburgh History* 75:1 (Spring 1992): 26–36.

Lubove, Roy. *Twentieth Century Pittsburgh: Volume 1, Government, Business, and Environmental Change*. 1969. Reprint. *Volume 2, The Post-Steel Era*. Pittsburgh: University of Pittsburgh Press, 1996.

McMullen, Leo A. "Architecture in the Diocese." *Catholic Pittsburgh's One Hundred Years* by the Catholic Historical Society of Western Pennsylvania. Chicago: Loyola University Press, 1943: 186–200.

Miller, Annie Clark. *Chronicles of Families, Houses and Estates of Pittsburgh and Its Environs*. Pittsburgh: Privately printed, 1927.

Monkhouse, Christopher. "The ABC's of an Architectural Library in Pittsburgh: Anderson, Bernd and Carnegie." *Carnegie Magazine* 63:2 (March/April 1996): 20–26.

Monkhouse, Christopher. "A Century of Architectural Exhibitions at The Carnegie: 1893–1993." *Carnegie Magazine* 61:12 (November/December 1993): 28–32, 37–43.

Muller, G. F. "The City of Pittsburgh." *Harper's New Monthly Magazine* 62:367 (December 1880): 49–68.

Palmer's Views of Pittsburgh. Pittsburgh: R. M. Palmer, 1903.

Phelps, Hartley M. *Palmer's Pictorial Pittsburgh and Prominent Pittsburghers Past and Present 1758–1905*. Pittsburgh: R. M. Palmer, 1905.

Pittsburgh. Art Commission of the City of Pittsburgh. *An Account of the Work of the Art Commission of the City of Pittsburgh from Its Creation in 1911 to January 1st, 1915*. Pittsburgh: Pittsburgh Printing Company, 1915.

Pittsburgh. Citizens Committee on City Plan of Pittsburgh. *The Pittsburgh Plan*: No. 1, "Pittsburgh Playgrounds" (June 1920); No. 2, A Major Street Plan for Pittsburgh" (September 1921); No. 3, "Transit" (September 1923); No. 4, "Pittsburgh Parks" (September 1923); No. 5, "Railroads of the Pittsburgh District" (October 1923); No. 6, "Waterways" (October 1923). Pittsburgh: Citizens Committee on City Plan of Pittsburgh, 1924.

Pittsburgh, Illustrated. New York: Illustrated Postal Cards Co., n.d.

Pittsburgh, Pennsylvania, U.S.A. [Pittsburgh]: Eichbaum Press, 1898.

Pittsburg and Allegheny. Illustrated. Pittsburgh: Myers, Shinkle & Co., 1892.

Pittsburg & Allegheny. Columbus: Ward Bros., 1894.

Pittsburgh and Allegheny Picturesque [for J. R. Weldin & Co.] Pittsburgh: J. C. Bragdon, 1905.

Pittsburgh Board of Trade. *Up-Town, Greater Pittsburg's Classic Section; East End, The World's Most Beautiful Suburb*. Pittsburgh: Pittsburgh Board of Trade, printed by Stewart Bros., 1907.

Pittsburgh Illustrated, Published in Twelve Parts. Pittsburgh: H. R. Page & Co., 1889.

Pittsburgh Leader. *Pittsburgh at the Dawn of the 20th Century: The Busiest City in the World*. Allegheny: Jos. T. Colvin & Co. Printers, c. 1902.

Retail Lumber Dealers' Association of Western Pennsylvania. *Pennsylvania Homes: A Select Collection of Practical Designs for Moderately Priced Homes*. 6th ed. Pittsburgh: James McMillin Printing Co., 1929.

Richman, Irwin. *Pennsylvania's Architecture*. University Park, PA: Pennsylvania Historical Association, 1969: 29, 30, 42, 43, 45, 47, 49, 50, 52, 53, 54, 56, 57, 60.

Richman, John H. "James D. Van Trump: Studies in the Architecture of Pittsburgh," with an introduction by Franklin Toker. *Western Pennsylvania Historical Magazine* 63:1 (January 1980): 63–75.

Roper, Matthew. "Stained Glass in Pittsburgh: Styles, Techniques, Innovators." *Carnegie Magazine* 52:10 (December 1978): 9–16.

Samson, Harry G. *Pittsburgh's Civic Center*. Pittsburgh: Edward M. Power Co., 1927.

Schenley Farms Company. *Letters from Schenley Farms Dwellers*. Pittsburgh: Privately printed, 1915.

Schumacher, Carolyn. "The Schoolhouse Beautiful: Public School Architecture in Pittsburgh." *Carnegie Magazine* 57:3 (May/June 1984): 13–18; 33.

Schuyler, Montgomery. "The Building of Pittsburgh": "Part One: The Terrain and the Rivers"; "Part Two: The Business Quarter and the Commercial Buildings"; "Part Three: A Real Civic Center"; "Part Four: The Modern Auditorium Church"; "Part Five: The Homes of Pittsburgh." *Architectural Record* 30:3 (September 1911): 204–282.

Smith, Arthur G. *Pittsburgh Then and Now*. Pittsburgh: University of Pittsburgh Press, 1990.

Souvenir of Pittsburg. Portland, ME: Lyman H. Nelson Co., n.d.

Souvenir of Pittsburgh [for R. S. Davis & Co.]. Brooklyn, NY: Albertype Company, n.d.

Stevenson, W. H., et al. *The Story of the Sesqui-Centennial Celebration of Pittsburgh*. Pittsburgh: R. W. Johnston Studios, Inc., 1910.

Stotz, Charles Morse. *The Early Architecture of Western Pennsylvania*. 1936. Reprint, with a new introduction by Dell Upton. Pittsburgh: University of Pittsburgh Press, 1995.

Stryker, Roy, and Mel Seidenberg. *A Pittsburgh Album 1758-1958*. Pittsburgh: Pittsburgh Post-Gazette, 1959.

Tannler, Albert M. *Pittsburgh's Landmark Architecture 1785–1950: A Concise Bibliography*. Pittsburgh: Pittsburgh History & Landmarks Foundation, 1994.

Thompson, Eleanor. "Picturesque Old Homes." 25 (Special Holiday Issue). *The Index* (December 1911): 34–36.

"To Beautify Pittsburgh." *Construction* 1:16 (April 22, 1905): 3–4.

Toker, Franklin. "Oakland: The Second Founding of Pittsburgh." *Urban Design International* 5:1 (Spring 1984): 34–35, 40.

Toker, Franklin. *Pittsburgh: An Urban Portrait*. 1986. Reprint. Pittsburgh: University of Pittsburgh Press, 1994.

Toker, Franklin, ed. *Planning the Pitt Campus: Dreams and Schemes Never Realized*. Pittsburgh: University of Pittsburgh, 1993.

Toker, Franklin. "Reversing an Urban Image: New Architecture in Pittsburgh, 1890–1980." *Sister Cities: Pittsburgh and Sheffield*, ed. by Joel A. Tarr. Praxis/Poetics Series 3. Pittsburgh: Carnegie Mellon University, 1986: 1–11.

Toker, Franklin, and Helen Wilson. *The Roots of Architecture in Pittsburgh and Allegheny County: A Guide to Research Sources*. Pittsburgh: Historical Society of Western Pennsylvania, 1979.

Union Trust Company. *Industrial Pittsburgh*. Pittsburgh: Chasmar-Winchell Press, 1908.

Van Trump, James D. *An Architectural Tour of Pittsburgh*. Pittsburgh: Pittsburgh Chapter of the American Institute of Architects, 1960.

Van Trump, James D. "A Century of Worker Housing in Natrona." *Tribune-Review Focus Magazine* 10:22 (April 17, 1983): 6.

Van Trump, James D. "From Log Cabin to Cathedral: The Pittsburgh Church Building, 1787–1940; a Changing Image." *The Charette* 41:9 (September 1961): 2–8, 11–13.

Van Trump, James D. *The Gothic Revived in Pittsburgh: a Medievalistic Excursion.* The Stones of Pittsburgh, No. 10. Pittsburgh: Pittsburgh History & Landmarks Foundation, 1975.

Van Trump, James D. "A Heritage of Dreams: Some Aspects of the History of the Architecture and Planning of the University of Pittsburgh, 1787–1969." *Western Pennsylvania Historical Magazine* 52:2 (April 1969): 105–116.

Van Trump, James D. *A History of the Bridges at the Point of Pittsburgh and the Brady Street Bridge.* Washington: U. S. Department of the Interior, Historic Conservation and Recreation Service, 1973.

Van Trump, James D. "The Lamp of Demos: Some Pittsburgh Public School Buildings of the Past." *The Charette* 42:3 (March 1962): 17–20.

Van Trump, James D. *Life and Architecture in Pittsburgh.* Pittsburgh: Pittsburgh History & Landmarks Foundation, 1983.

Van Trump, James D. *Majesty of the Law: The Court Houses of Allegheny County.* Pittsburgh: Pittsburgh History & Landmarks Foundation, 1988.

Van Trump, James D. *"Our Eastern Domes, Fantastic, Bright. . . ." Some Orthodox and Byzantine Rite Churches in Allegheny County.* The Stones of Pittsburgh, No. 12. Pittsburgh: Pittsburgh History & Landmarks Foundation, [1982].

Van Trump, James D. "The Palace, the Loft and the Tower: Some Notes on the Development of the Urban Hotel in Pittsburgh." *The Charette* 42:11 (November 1962): 12–17, 20.

Van Trump, James D. "Pittsburgh Chapter, A.I.A.: the First 75 Years." *The Charette* 45:8 (August 1965): 4–5.

Van Trump, James D. "The Romanesque Revival in Pittsburgh." *Journal of the Society of Architectural Historians* 16:3 (October 1957): 22–29.

Van Trump, James D., and Arthur P. Ziegler, Jr. *Landmark Architecture of Allegheny County Pennsylvania.* Pittsburgh: Pittsburgh History & Landmarks Foundation, 1967.

Van Trump, James D., et al. "Pittsburgh." *Landscape Architecture* 53:3 (April 1963): 190–217.

Views of Pittsburg. Pittsburgh: J. C. Bragdon, 1903.

Wadlow, Frank T. "Early Pittsburgh." *The Charette* 17:5 (May 1937): 1–3.

White, Edward, ed. *Pittsburgh the Powerful.* Pittsburgh: Pittsburgh Chamber of Commerce, printed by Industry Publishing Company, 1907.

White, Joseph, and M. W. von Bernewitz. *The Bridges of Pittsburgh.* Pittsburgh: Cramer Printing & Publishing Company, 1928.

Wilbert, Katherine. "Stained Glass in Pittsburgh." *Carnegie Magazine* 42:10 (December 1968): 333–337.

ARCHITECTS AND DESIGNERS

Franklin Abbott, see **Benno Janssen**

Alden & Harlow, see **Longfellow, Alden & Harlow**

Charles M. Bartberger

"Charles Mathias Bartberger." *History of Pittsburgh and Environs: Encyclopedia of Biography* [Clugston to Ressa]. New York and Chicago: American Historical Society, 1922: 4–5.

Lowry, Patricia. "Old World Meets Modern Realities." *Pittsburgh Post-Gazette,* Sunday Magazine (January 31, 1993): 14–15.

Peter Berndtson and Cornelia Brierly Berndtson[4]

Besinger, Curtis. *Working with Mr. Wright.* Cambridge: Cambridge University Press, 1995: 15, 28, 41, 74, 118.

Guggenheimer, Tobias S. *A Taliesin Legacy: The Architecture of Frank Lloyd Wright's Apprentices.* New York: Van Nostrand Reinhold, 1995: 27, 30, 37, 71, 98–101.

Henning, Randolph C., ed. *At Taliesin: Newspaper Columns by Frank Lloyd Wright and the Taliesin Fellowship 1934–1937*. Carbondale, IL: Southern Illinois University Press, 1992: 58, 82, 85–87, 92, 94–95, 103, 110–112, 125–127, 129, 130, 139, 144, 151–155, 159–60, 170, 310.

"House in the Round: A Residence for Dr. and Mrs. Abraam Steinberg, Peter Berndtson, Architect." *The Charette* 31:3 (March 1951): 18–19.

Miller, Donald, and Aaron Sheon. *Organic Vision: The Architecture of Peter Berndtson*. Pittsburgh: The Hexagon Press, 1980.

"Recipe for a House." *The Charette* 37:3 (March 1957): 20–21.

Sheon, Aaron. *The Architecture of Peter Berndtson*. Exhibition Catalogue. [An Exhibition of Contemporary Architectural Drawings, Photographs and Color Slides, The University Art Gallery, March 28th through April 18th, 1971]. Pittsburgh: University of Pittsburgh, 1971.

"Squirrel Hill House on a Slope." *The Charette* 29:9 (September 1949): 32–33.

Ungar, Anne Jean. "Three Contemporary Houses." *The Charette* 33:5 (May 1953): 9–17.

Van Trump, James D. "Peter Berndtson, Pittsburgh Architect." *Carnegie Magazine* 55:9 (November 1981): 27–29.

Van Trump, *Life and Architecture in Pittsburgh*, 64–68.

William Boyd, Sr., see **Ingham & Boyd**

Marcel Breuer, see **Walter Gropius**

Lawrence Buck

"Concrete Residence Construction in the West: Concrete Residence in Pittsburg." *Cement Age* 9:4 (October 1909): 238–240.

D. H. Burnham & Company

Graham, Anderson, Probst and White. *The Architectural Work of Graham, Anderson, Probst and White, Chicago, and Their Predecessors, D. H. Burnham & Co. and Graham Burnham & Co.* London: Privately printed by B. T. Batsford, Ltd., 1933. Vol. 1: 56, 170. Vol. 2: 289, 299.

Hines, Thomas S. *Burnham of Chicago: Architect and Planner*. New York: Oxford University Press, 1974: 288, 291, 292–293, 298–300.

Kidney, Walter C. "The Frick Building." *Executive Report* 1:2 (June/July 1981): 16–19.

Kidney, Walter C. "The Oliver Building." *Executive Report* 1:11 (May 1983): 24–27.

Moore, Charles. *Daniel H. Burnham: Architect Planner of Cities*. Boston: Houghton Mifflin Company, 1921. Vol. 2: 213–214.

[Shaw, John E.?] *The Frick Building, Pittsburgh*. Pittsburgh: n.p., 1905.

Van Trump, James D. *Pittsburgh's Neglected Gateway: The Rotunda of the Pennsylvania Railroad Station*. The Stones of Pittsburgh, No. 6. Pittsburgh: Pittsburgh History & Landmarks Foundation, 1968.

Van Trump, *Life and Architecture in Pittsburgh*, 62, 71, 229, 245–247.

Lamont H. Button

Button, Lamont H. "Post-War Planning." *The Charette* 23:4 (April 1943): 9, 11.

Harper, Frank C. "Lamont H. Button." *Pittsburgh of Today: Its Resources and People*. Vol. 3. New York: American Historical Society, 1931: 249.

[A House on Bennington Avenue in Pittsburgh and Houses in Mission Hills, Mt. Lebanon], and "A Candy Shop and Tea Room for Reymer Bros. Co." *The Charette* 8:12 (December 1928): 15–18.

[McKee, Tally?] "Charette Vignette: Lamont Hartung Button." *The Charette* 28:9 (September 1948): 8–9.

Theophilus Parsons Chandler

Van Trump, *The Gothic Revived*, 8–10.

Van Trump, *Life and Architecture in Pittsburgh*, 34, 202.

John Chislett

Buckingham, *Eastern and Western States of America*, Vol. 2: 179.

Stotz, *Early Architecture*, 20, 30, 43, 253, 267, 268.

Van Trump, *Life and Architecture in Pittsburgh*, 55–56, 183–185.

Van Trump, *Majesty of the Law*, 16–30.

William Y. Cocken, see Benno Janssen

John T. Comes

Comes, John T. *Catholic Art and Architecture*. rev. ed. Pittsburgh: n.p., 1920.

Maginnis, Charles D. "The Work of John T. Comes." *Architectural Record* 55:1 (January 1924): 93–101.

See also **Ralph Adams Cram; William Richard Perry General: American Institute of Architects**

Charles J. Connick

Connick, Charles J. *Adventures in Light and Color: An Introduction to the Stained Glass Craft*. New York: Random House, 1937.

Lowry, Patricia. "Glassmates: The Sacred Meets the Secular in Heinz Chapel's 23 Windows." *The Pittsburgh Press*, Sunday Magazine (April 19, 1992): 8.

See also **Charles Z. Klauder; J. Horace Rudy**

Ralph Adams Cram

Comes, John T. "Calvary Church, Pittsburg, Pa." *Architectural Review* 15:1 (January 1908): 1–9.

Comes, John T., et al. *Calvary Church, Pittsburgh, Pennsylvania*. Boston: Richard G. Badger, Gorham Press, 1908.

Cram and Ferguson. *The Work of Cram and Ferguson, Architects, Including Work by Cram, Goodhue, and Ferguson*; with an introduction by Charles D. Maginnis. New York: Pencil Points Press, 1929: 29–36, 215.

Cram, Ralph Adams. *My Life in Architecture*. Boston: Little, Brown, and Company, 1936: 132, 237, 241, 253–256.

The East Liberty Presbyterian Church. Pittsburgh: East Liberty Presbyterian Church, 1935.

Robshaw, Charles P. *The Art and Architecture of the East Liberty Presbyterian Church*. 1977. Pittsburgh: East Liberty Presbyterian Church, 1983.

Van Trump, *The Gothic Revived*, 10–13.

Van Trump, *Life and Architecture in Pittsburgh*, 203–205.

Titus de Bobula

Aurand, *Progressive Architecture of Frederick G. Scheibler, Jr.*, 7-8, 22, 55.[5]

Samuel Diescher

Bothwell, Margaret Pearson. "Incline Planes and People—Some Past and Present Ones." *Western Pennsylvania Historical Magazine* 46:4 (October 1963): 323.

"Samuel Diescher" *History of Pittsburgh and Environs: Encyclopedia of Biography* [Werntz to Righi]. New York and Chicago: American Historical Society, 1922: 93–94.

George Grant Elmslie

Aurand, "Prairie School Architecture in Pittsburgh," 7–8.

William Falconer

Hannegan, Barry. "William Falconer and the Landscaping of Schenley Park." *Carnegie Magazine* 63:3 (May/June 1996): 28–32, 39, 43.

Leland, Ernest Stevens, and Donald W. Smith. "William Falconer: Horticulturalist, Editor, Park and Cemetery Executive," *The Pioneers of Cemetery Administration in America*. New York: Privately printed by The Stirling Press for the Association of American Cemetery Superintendents, 1941: n.p.

See also **Historic Sites: Allegheny Cemetery**

Frank Furness

Tannler, Albert M. "A Little Building Designed by an Architectural Giant." *Tribune-Review Focus Magazine* 21:27 (May 19, 1996): 6–7.

Thomas, George E., et al. *Frank Furness: The Complete Work*. Princeton: Princeton University Press, 1991: 251, 287, 336.

Thomas, George E., and Hyman Myers. "Checklist of the Architecture and Projects of Frank Furness," *The Architecture of Frank Furness* by James F. O'Gorman. Philadelphia: Philadelphia Museum of Art, 1973: 203, 207, 208.

Van Trump, *Life and Architecture in Pittsburgh*, 33, 201–202, 221–222.

Thomas B. Garman

Harper, Frank C. "Thomas Brenner Garman." *Pittsburgh of Today: Its Resources and People*. Vol. 4. New York: American Historical Society, 1931: 451.

Bertram Grosvenor Goodhue

"The Goodhue House." *The Charette* 2:4 (April 1921), 1–5.

Kidney, Walter C. "Two Granules on the Mountain of Knowledge." *PHLF News* 135 (July 1994): 9.

[Lincoln, William Ensign?] *The First Baptist Church*. Boston: Privately printed by D. B. Updike, Merrymount Press, 1925.

Oliver, Richard. *Bertram Grosvenor Goodhue*. Cambridge, MA: MIT Press, 1983: 79–83.

Van Trump, *The Gothic Revived*, 11.

Van Trump, *Life and Architecture in Pittsburgh*, 122, 204.

Graham, Anderson, Probst & White

Chappell, Sally. *Architecture and Planning of Graham, Anderson, Probst and White, 1912–1936: Transforming Tradition*. Chicago: University of Chicago Press, 1992: 208–209.

Graham, Anderson, Probst and White, *The Architectural Work of Graham, Anderson, Probst and White*, Vol. 2: 259–260, 317–321.

Tannler, Albert M. "Three Distinguished Offspring of a Not-So-Famous Family." *Tribune-Review Focus Magazine* 20:26 (March 5, 1995): 6, 11.

Van Trump, *Life and Architecture in Pittsburgh*, 71–76.

Walter Gropius and Marcel Breuer[6]

Berdini, Paolo. *Walter Gropius: Works and Projects*. Barcelona: Editorial Gustavo Gili, S.A., 1994: 176–177.

Blake, Peter. *Marcel Breuer: Architect and Designer*. New York: Museum of Modern Art, 1949: 74–75.

Giedion, Sigfried. *Walter Gropius*. 1952. Reprint. New York: Dover, 1992: 187.

"House in Pittsburgh, Pa.: Walter Gropius and Marcel Breuer, Architects." *Architectural Forum* 74 (March 1941): 160–170.

Wolfe, Lawrence C., Jr. "Breuer Comes to Town." *The Charette* 28:6 (June 1948): 12.

Isaac H. Hobbs

Hobbs, Isaac H. *Hobbs's Architecture: Containing Designs and Ground Plans for Villas, Cottages, and Other Edifices Both Suburban and Rural, Adapted to the United States, with Rules For Criticism, and Introduction by Isaac H. Hobbs & Sons, Architects*. Philadelphia: J. B. Lippincott & Co., 1873: 64–65, 70–71, 96–97, 98–99, 106–107, 108–109, 114–115, 156–157, 166–167, 172–173.

Van Trump, *Life and Architecture in Pittsburgh*, 57, 101.

Henry Hornbostel

The Bellefield Company. *Schenley Apartments: A Description*. Pittsburgh: The Bellefield Company, 1922.

[Grant Building] *Metalcraft* (July 1929): 18.

Harper, Frank C. "Henry Hornbostel." *Pittsburgh of Today: Its Resources and People*. Vol. 3. New York: American Historical Society, 1931: 145–46.

Hornbostel, Henry. "Architecture." *Allegheny County: a Sesqui-centennial Review*, ed. by George E. Kelly. Pittsburgh: Allegheny County, 1938: 237–256.

Hornbostel, Henry. "History of Architecture in Pittsburgh and Allegheny County." *The Charette* 18:9 (September 1938): 1–4.

Kidney, Walter C. "Getting Acquainted with Hornbostel." *PHLF News* 128 (March 1993): 12.

Kidney, Walter C. "Less Hornbostel at Pitt." *PHLF News* 131 (September 1993): 5.

Lacey, "Soldier's Memorial," *American Competitions* 1907, plates 1–5.

Lacey, "Western University of Pennsylvania," *American Competitions 1908*, plates 40–44.

Lowry, Patricia. "Remnants of Pitt's 'Campus Beautiful' May Face Demolition." *Pittsburgh Post-Gazette*, Sunday Magazine (November 7, 1993): 12.

"A Night Course in Architecture." *Construction* 2:17 (October 28, 1905): 407.

"Professor of Architecture: Henry Hornbostel, Ph.B., of New York, to be Instructor at Carnegie Technical Schools." *Construction* 2:13 (September 30, 1905): 307.

"Schenley Apartments, Pittsburgh." *Architectural Forum* 41:5 (November 1924): 241–242.

[Strassburger, W. J.] *Grant Building*. Pittsburgh: Grant Building Incorporated, 1928.

Swales, Francis S. "Master Draftsmen/XVII Henry Hornbostel." *Pencil Points* 7:2 (February 1926): 73–92.

Van Trump, James D. "An Architectural History of the University Club." *University Club News* (September 1966): 11–19.

Van Trump, *Life and Architecture in Pittsburgh*, 131–148.

See also **Edward B. Lee** (City-County Building)

Hunting-Davis Company

Hunting-Davis Company. *Selections from the Work Designed By and Erected Under the Supervision of the Hunting-Davis Company, Architects and Engineers, Pittsburgh, Pa.* New York: Architectural Catalogue, 1924.

Ingham & Boyd

[Charles T. Ingham] *The Charette* 23:7 (August/September 1943): 2–3.

Harper, Frank C. "Charles Tattersall Ingham." *Pittsburgh of Today: Its Resources and People*. Vol. 3. New York: American Historical Society, 1931: 95.

Pastorius, Mary Beth. "Architect William Boyd." *Sewickley Herald* (May 14, 1986): 6, 26.

See also **General: American Institute of Architects Historic Sites: Chatham Village**

Benno Janssen

Bettos, Benjamin F. "Public Votes on Architecture in Pittsburgh." *American Architect* 137 (June 1930): 34–35, 104.

Brown, Mark, et al., *Duquesne Club*, 73–82, 173.

"Competition for the Pittsburgh Court House-City Hall," 39, plates 26, 28.

"Four Views of Recent Work in Pittsburgh." *The Charette* 8:6 (June 1928): 13–16.

Janssen, Benno. "What Architecture Has Meant to Me." *The Charette* 27:6 (August/September 1947): 3–4.

Lacey, "Western University of Pennsylvania," *American Competitions 1908*, plates 45–47.

"La Torelle [*sic*]: The Residence of E. J. Kaufmann, Esq., near Pittsburg, Pa." *Country Life* 65:3 (July 1928): 30, 57–60.

Lacey, "Young Women's Christian Association Building," *American Competitions 1908*, plates 23–27.

Lee, Marianne. "A Grande Dame Named William Penn." *Pennsylvania Heritage* 17:2 (Spring 1991): 30–37.

Mellon Institute. *Behind These Columns: Mellon Institute*. Pittsburgh: Mellon Institute, 1937.

Mellon Institute. *Symbolism in Mellon Institute*. Pittsburgh: Mellon Institute, 1937.

"Mellon Institute of Industrial Research." *The Charette* 17:4 (April 1937): 1–4.

"The Norse Room, Fort Pitt Hotel, Pittsburg." *The Brickbuilder* 19:4 (April 1910): 103–105.

"A Rookwood Room—the Norse Buffet of the Fort Pitt Hotel at Pittsburgh." *Architectural Record* 29:4 (April 1911): 345–355.

Schuyler, Montgomery. "Country House Design in the Middle West: Recent Work by Janssen & Abbott of Pittsburgh, Pa." *Architectural Record* 32:4 (October 1912): 336–348.

Van Trump, James D. "The Stones of Venice in Pittsburgh: the Pittsburgh Athletic Association Club House." *The Charette* 39:4 (April 1959): 24–27.

Van Trump, *Life and Architecture in Pittsburgh*, 111–118.

van Urk, J. Blan. *The Story of Rolling Rock*. New York: Charles Scribner's Sons, 1950: 252.

"William Penn Hotel." *The Brickbuilder* 25 (July 1916): 187; plates 102–105.

"William Penn Hotel." *The Builder* 32:11 (March 1916): 37–39; 8 unnumbered plates.

Wilson, Cathy A. "Building a Temple of Science: Pittsburgh's Mellon Institute." *Pittsburgh History* 77:4 (Winter 1994/95): 150–158.

See also **Joseph Urban**

Joseph W. Kerr

Leeds, Lewis W., "The Ventilation and Warming of the Municipal Hall, Pittsburgh, Pa." *The Architectural Review and American Builders' Journal*, ed. Samuel Sloan. Philadelphia: Claxton, Remson & Haffelfinger, 1869. Vol. 1 (March 1869): 564–569.

"The New City Hall, Pittsburgh, Pennsylvania." *The Architectural Review and American Builders' Journal*, ed. Samuel Sloan. Philadelphia: Claxton, Remson & Haffelfinger, 1869. Vol. 1 (March 1869): 554–557.

Pittsburgh City Hall Commission. *The City Hall, Pittsburgh*. Pittsburgh: Stevenson & Foster, 1874.

Van Trump, *Life and Architecture in Pittsburgh*, 41–44.

See also **Historic Sites: Evergreen Hamlet**

Kiehnel & Elliott

Aurand, "Prairie School Architecture in Pittsburgh," 8–16.

"Competition for the Pittsburgh Court House-City Hall," 38, plates 25, 28.

Tannler, Albert M. "Richard Kiehnel: Architect of International Modernism and Tropical Splendor." *Tribune-Review Focus Magazine* 21:30 (June 9, 1996): 6–7.

Charles Z. Klauder

Bowman, John G. *Unofficial Notes*. Pittsburgh: Privately printed by Davis and Warde, 1963: 49, 70–84, 113–120.

Brown, Mark M. *The Cathedral of Learning: Concept, Design, Construction* Exhibition Catalogue. [University Art Gallery, March 19–May 17, 1987]. Pittsburgh: University of Pittsburgh, 1987.

Gaul, Joan. *The Heinz Memorial Chapel.* Pittsburgh: University of Pittsburgh, 1994.

Klauder, Charles Z., and Herbert C. Wise. *College Architecture in America.* New York: Charles Scribner's Sons, 1929: 19, 21, 292–293.

Van Trump, *Life and Architecture in Pittsburgh*, 205–209.

Watts, Harvey M. "The Challenge of the Klauder Tower." *Arts & Decoration* 23:1 (May 1925): 41, 74.

Benjamin Henry Latrobe

Cohn, Jeffrey A., and Charles E. Brownell. *The Architectural Drawings of Benjamin Henry Latrobe* (The Papers of Benjamin Henry Latrobe, Series II: The Architectural and Engineering Drawings, Vol. 2). New Haven: Yale University Press, 1994: 560–577.

Edward B. Lee

" 'Briar Cliff,' Pittsburgh's Most Picturesque Estate." *The Builder* (October 19, 1918): 9.

"City-County Building." *The Builder* 33:3 (October, 1916), 14, 43; 9 unnumbered plates.

Harper, Frank C. "Edward Brown Lee." *Pittsburgh of Today: Its Resources and People.* Vol. 3. New York: American Historical Society, 1931: 222.

Lacey, "Soldier's Memorial," *American Competitions 1907*, plates 19–20.

Lacey, "Western University of Pennsylvania," *American Competitions 1908*, plates 54–55.

Lacey, "Young Women's Christian Association Building," *American Competitions 1908*, plates 31–33.

Lee, Edward Brown, and Edward Brown Lee, Jr. *A Pencil in Penn: Sketches of Pittsburgh and Surrounding Areas.* Pittsburgh: Privately printed by Meriden Gravure Company, 1970.

[McKee, Tally?]. "Charette Vignette: Edward Brown Lee." *The Charette* 38:12 (December 1948): 13–15.

Schmertz, Robert W. "About Sketching and Sketchers, One in Particular." *The Charette* 10:1 (January 1930): 1–4.

The Work of Edward B. Lee Architect, Pittsburgh. New York: Architectural Catalog Company, n.d.

See also **Stanley L. Roush**

Pierre A. Liesch

Harper, Frank C. "Pierre A. Liesch." *Pittsburgh of Today: Its Resources and People.* Vol. 3. New York: American Historical Society, 1931: 27.

See also **Frederick J. Osterling**

Albert F. Link

"Albert Francis Link." *History of Pittsburgh and Environs: Encyclopedia of Biography* [Clugston to Ressa]. New York and Chicago: American Historical Society, 1922: 351.

See also **Edward J. Weber**

Longfellow, Alden & Harlow, and Alden & Harlow

Brown, Mark M., et al., *Duquesne Club*, 5, 19, 25–30, 33-39, 44, 46–48, fig. 11.

Floyd, Margaret Henderson. "Longfellow, Alden & Harlow's First Carnegie Library and Institute (1891–1895)." *Carnegie Magazine* 61:7 (January/February 1993): 23–30.

Floyd, Margaret Henderson. *Architecture after Richardson: Regionalism before Modernism—Longfellow, Alden, and Harlow in Boston and Pittsburgh.* Chicago: University of Chicago Press in association with the Pittsburgh History & Landmarks Foundation, 1994.

Harlow, Alfred B. "Architectural Reveries." *The Charette* 6:5 (May 1926): 1–3.

Lacey, "Soldier's Memorial," *American Competitions 1907*, plates 13–14.

Leonard, "Longfellow, Alden & Harlow," *Pittsburgh and Allegheny Illustrated Review*, 79.

Pittsburgh Leader, "Alden & Harlow," *Pittsburgh at the Dawn of the 20th Century*, n.p.

Toker, Franklin. "Carnegie Institute: A National Historic Site." *Carnegie Magazine* 53:10 (December 1979): 4–6.

Van Trump, James D. *An American Palace of Culture: The Carnegie Institute and Carnegie Library of Pittsburgh.* Pittsburgh: Pittsburgh History & Landmarks Foundation, 1970.

Van Trump, James D. "The Past as Prelude: A Consideration of the Early Building History of the Carnegie Institute Complex." *Carnegie Magazine* 49:8/9 (October/November 1974): 346–360.

Van Trump, "Romanesque Revival in Pittsburgh," 25–26, 27.

Zelleke, Ghenete. "Two Classic Pittsburgh Rooms: The Founder's Room." *Carnegie Magazine* 59:2 (March/April 1988): 30–33.

See also **Historic Sites: "Sunnyledge"**

MacClure & Spahr

"Competition for the Pittsburgh Court House-City Hall," 36, plates 21, 22.

Kidney, Walter C. "What Boston Has Done for Us," 9–10.

Lacey, "Soldier's Memorial," *American Competitions 1907*, plates 15–16.

Lacey, "Young Women's Christian Association Building," *American Competitions 1908*, plates 37–39.

Samuel Thornburg McClarren

Phelps, H. M. "A Hillside House." *House Beautiful* (April 1911): 150.

See also **Historic Sites: Thornburg Historic District**

John Notman

Greiff, Constance M. *John Notman, Architect, 1810–1865.* Exhibition Catalogue. Philadelphia: The Athenaeum of Philadelphia, 1979: 30, 175–176.

[James, Earl D.] "St. Peter's: The City's Loss." *PHLF News* 113 (Spring 1990): 1, 3.

Stanton, Phoebe B. *The Gothic Revival & American Church Architecture: An Episode in Taste, 1840–1856.* Baltimore: Johns Hopkins Press, 1968: 116, 284.

Van Trump, James D. "St. Peter's, Pittsburgh, by John Notman." *Journal of the Society of Architectural Historians* 15:2 (May 1956): 19–23.

Olmsted Brothers[7]

Olmsted, Frederick Law [Jr.]. *Pittsburgh: Main Thoroughfares and the Down Town District; Improvements Necessary to Meet the City's Present and Future Needs.* Pittsburgh: Pittsburgh Civic Commission, 1911.

Bauman, John F., and Edward K. Muller. "The Olmsteds in Pittsburgh: (Part I) Landscaping the Private City." *Pittsburgh History* 76:3 (Fall 1993): 122–40.

Bauman, John F., and Edward K. Muller. "The Olmsteds in Pittsburgh: (Part II) Shaping the Progressive City." *Pittsburgh History* 76:4 (Winter 1993/1994): 191–205.

Frederick J. Osterling

Aurand, Martin. "Frederick J. Osterling and a Tale of Two Buildings." *Pennsylvania Heritage* 15 (Spring 1989): 16–21.

"Frederick John Osterling." *History of Pittsburgh and Environs: Encyclopedia of Biography* [Clugston to Ressa]. New York and Chicago: American Historical Society, 1922: 60–61.

Kidney, Walter C. "The Union Trust Building." *Executive Report* 1:4 (October 1981): 10–11, 22–23.

The Magee Building. N.p., n.d.

Nelson, J. Franklin, compiler. *Works of F. J. Osterling, Architect, Pittsburg.* Pittsburgh: Murdoch-Kerr Press, 1904.

Pittsburgh Leader, "F. J. Osterling," *Pittsburgh at the Dawn of the 20th Century,* n.p.

Van Trump, James D. *Legend in Modern Gothic: The Union Trust Building, Pittsburgh.* The Stones of Pittsburgh, No. 3. Pittsburgh: Pittsburgh History & Landmarks Foundation, 1966.

See also **Historic Sites: "Clayton"**

Peabody & Stearns

Kidney, "What Boston Has Done for Us," 9–10.

[Kidney, Walter C.] "Motor Square Garden and Our Market House Tradition." *PHLF News* 106 (Summer 1988): 6.

Lacey, "Soldier's Memorial," *American Competitions 1907,* plate 23.

William Richard Perry

Wilson, Fr. Thomas R. *St. Bernard Church, Mount Lebanon, Pennsylvania.* Mt. Lebanon: St. Bernard Church, 1995.

Henry Hobson Richardson

• **Emmanuel Episcopal Church** (1885–1886)

Floyd, *Architecture after Richardson,* 129–131.

Hitchcock, Henry-Russell. *The Architecture of H. H. Richardson and His Times.* 1936. rev. ed. Hamden, CT: Archon Press, 1961: 255, 278.

Klukas, Arnold. "H. H. Richardson's Designs for the Emmanuel Episcopal Church, Pittsburgh." *American Art Review* 2:4 (July/August 1975): 64–76.

Ochsner, Jeffrey Karl. *H. H. Richardson: Complete Architectural Works.* Cambridge, MA: MIT Press, 1982, 310–311.

Van Trump, *Life and Architecture in Pittsburgh,* 159–165.

Van Trump, "Romanesque Revival in Pittsburgh," 24–25.

• **Allegheny County Courthouse and Jail** (1884–1888)

Arensberg, Charles C. "Restoring Courtroom No. 321." *PHLF News* 106 (Summer 1988): 2.

Floyd, *Architecture after Richardson,* 7–9, 13–19, 63–64, 129–131, 195–196, 241–242.

Hitchcock, *Richardson and His Times,* 145, 178, 247, 264, 267, 273, 275, 276, 277, 281, 282, 283, 299.

Huff, William S. "Richardson's Jail." *Western Pennsylvania Historical Magazine* 41:1 (Spring 1958): 41–59.

[Kidney, Walter C.] *H. H. Richardson's Allegheny County Courthouse and Jail.* Pittsburgh: Allegheny County Bureau of Cultural Programs, 1981.

Kidney, Walter C. "Two Classic Pittsburgh Rooms: Room 321: The Court of Common Pleas of Allegheny County." *Carnegie Magazine* 59:2 (March/April 1988): 35–37.

[Kidney, Walter C.] "Richardson's Jail: Adaptive Use." *PHLF News* 140 (October 1995): 4–5.

Ochsner, *Architectural Work,* 325–336.

O'Gorman, James F. *H. H. Richardson: Architectural Forms for an American Society.* Chicago: University of Chicago Press, 1987: 50–51.

O'Gorman, James F. *Three American Architects: Richardson, Sullivan, and Wright, 1865–1915.* Chicago: University of Chicago Press, 1991: 26–32.

[Simo, Melanie, and Franklin Toker]. *Henry Hobson Richardson: The Allegheny County Courthouse and Jail, Part I: An Exhibition of Selected Drawings from the Collection of Allegheny County;* with a preface by James D. Van Trump. Exhibition catalogue. Pittsburgh: Allegheny County, 1977.

Toker, Franklin. "Richardson *en concours*: the Pittsburgh Courthouse," *Carnegie Magazine* 51:9 (November 1979): 13–29.

Van Rensselaer, Mariana G. *Henry Hobson Richardson and His Works*. 1888. Reprint. New York: Dover: 1969: 89–93.

Van Trump, *Majesty of the Law*, 31–172.

Van Trump, "Romanesque Revival in Pittsburgh," 22–24.

Stanley L. Roush

Roush, Stanley L. "A Study of Domestic Architecture in Pittsburgh." *The Charette* 6:2 (February 1926): 1–4.

Roush, Stanley L. "The Sixth, Seventh and Ninth Street Bridges, Pittsburgh, Pa." *American Architect* 133:2538 (February 5, 1928): 191–196.

[Roush, Stanley L., and Edward B. Lee]. "The City of Bridges—Pittsburgh." *The Charette* 5:3 (March 1925): 1–3.

J. Horace Rudy

Connick, Charles J. *Adventures in Light and Color*, 116–119, 134.

Connick, Charles J. "My Friend, J. Horace Rudy." *Stained Glass* 35:1 (Spring 1940): 4–13.

Gaul, Joan. "J. Horace Rudy and the Rudy Brothers Company Stained and Leaded Glass." *Stained Glass* 91:4 (Winter 1996): 277–282.

Lowry, Patricia, "Glassmates," 8.

Pittsburgh Board of Trade, "Rudy Bros. Co.," *Up-Town, Greater Pittsburg's Classic Section*, n.p.

Saint, Lawrence. "J. Horace Rudy, An Appreciation." *Stained Glass* 35:1 (Spring 1940): 33–34.

Sotter, George. "J. Horace Rudy, Master of Friendship." *Stained Glass* 35:1 (Spring 1940): 32–33.

Tannler, Albert M. "Horace Rudy: Pittsburgh's Master of Glass." *Tribune-Review Focus Magazine* 21:21 (April 7, 1996): 8–10.

Rutan & Russell

"Competition for the Pittsburgh Court House-City Hall," 37, plates 23–24.

Ferree, Barr. "The Work of Rutan & Russell, of Pittsburgh." *Architectural Record* 16:2 (August 1904): 83–114.

Kelly, *Edgeworth Club*, 47–53.

Lacey, "Soldier's Memorial," *American Competitions 1907*, plates 21–22.

Lacey, "Young Women's Christian Association Building," *American Competitions 1908*, plates 28–30.

Pastorius, Mary Beth. "Rutan and Russell Help Weave Sewickley's Architectural Fabric." *Sewickley Herald* (November 1, 1989): 4–5.

Pastorius, Mary Beth. "Russell Puts His Stamp Here." *Sewickley Herald* (October 23, 1985): 5, 33.

Pastorius, Mary Beth. "Rutan Designs: A Local Legacy." *Sewickley Herald* (November 1, 1985): 5, 21.

Frederick C. Sauer

Kidney, Walter C. "Pittsburgh Architecture: St. Mary Magdalene." *PHLF News* 130 (July 1993): 8.

Van Trump, *Life and Architecture in Pittsburgh*, 25–29.

Frederick G. Scheibler, Jr.

Aurand, Martin. *The Progressive Architecture of Frederick G. Scheibler, Jr.* Pittsburgh: University of Pittsburgh Press, 1994.

Aurand, "Prairie School Architecture in Pittsburgh," 16–18.

Jordon, John W., compiler. "Frederick Gustavus Scheibler, Jr." *A Century and a Half of Pittsburg and Her People*. Vol. 4. N.p.: Lewis Publishing Company, 1908: 16.

Shear, John Knox. "Pittsburgh Rediscovers an Architect Pioneer, Frederick Scheibler." *Architectural Record* 106 (July 1949): 98–100.

Shear, John Knox, and Robert W. Schmertz. "A Pittsburgh Original." *The Charette* 28:9 (September 1948): 4–5.

Van Trump, James D. *The Architecture of Frederick G. Scheibler, Jr., 1872–1958*. Exhibition Catalogue. [An exhibition organized by James D. Van Trump and James H. Cook, 11 October–18 November 1962, Department of Fine Arts, Carnegie Institute]. Pittsburgh: Carnegie Institute, 1962.

Van Trump, *Life and Architecture in Pittsburgh*, 282–290.

Wilkins, David G., et al. *Art Nouveau: Works by Tiffany, Mucha, Toulouse-Lautrec, Gallé, Beardsley, Scheibler, and Others*. Exhibition Catalogue. [University Art Gallery, January 13–February 12, 1978]. Pittsburgh: University of Pittsburgh, 1978: 15–16.

Robert W. Schmertz

Lowry, Patricia. "Troubadour of the 2-by-4." *Pittsburgh Post-Gazette*, Sunday Magazine (July 18, 1993): 5.

McKee, Tally. "Charette Vignette: Robert Watson Schmertz." *The Charette* 29:1 (January 1949): 14, 24, 29.

Schmertz, Robert W. "Architecture in Pittsburgh." *The Charette* 30:1 (January 1950): 10–11, 20–23.

Schmertz, Robert W. "Architecture in Pittsburgh up to 1900." *The Charette* 29:11 (November 1949): 12–13, 20–21.

See also **Edward B. Lee; Frederick G. Scheibler, Jr.**

Shepley, Rutan & Coolidge

Schuyler, Montgomery. "The Romanesque Revival in America." 1891. *American Architecture and Other Writings*, ed. William H. Jordy and Ralph Coe. Cambridge, MA: Harvard University Press, 1961. Vol. 1: 203–204, 218–219.

Van Trump, James D. "The Mountain and the City: the History of Shadyside Presbyterian Church, Pittsburgh, as Seen Through Its Architecture." *The Western Pennsylvania Historical Magazine* 44:1 (March 1961): 21–34.

Van Trump, "Romanesque Revival in Pittsburgh," 26.

Simonds & Simonds

Van Trump, James D. "Figures in a Landscape: Simonds and Simonds of Pittsburgh." *Landscape Architecture* 54:2 (January 1964): 127–130.

Brandon Smith

"Five Drawings by Brandon Smith, R.A." *The Charette* 8:7 (July 1928): 15–18.

Kelly, *Edgeworth Club*, 96–108.

Smith, Brandon. "Some Thoughts on Architectural Education." *The Charette* 21:11 (November 1941): 3–4.

Starrett & Van Vleck

"Department Store for the Kaufmann & Baer Company, Pittsburgh, Pa." *Architecture and Building* 46:7 (July 1914): 258–267.

Edward Stotz, Edward Stotz, Jr., and Charles Morse Stotz

Harper, Frank C. "Edward Stotz." *Pittsburgh of Today: Its Resources and People*, Vol. 3. New York: American Historical Society, 1931: 308–09.

MacLachlan, Cornelius & Filoni. *In Detail: The Celebration of a Century in Architecture*. Pittsburgh: MacLachlan, Cornelius & Filoni, 1989: 3–25.

McKee, Tally. "Charette Vignette: Charles Morse Stotz." *The Charette* 38:11 (November 1948): 11–13.

McKee, Tally. "Modern Banking . . . Before and After." *The Charette* (May 1950): 10–11.

Stotz, Edward. "Notes on the Thirty-third Annual Convention of the American Institute of Architects held in Pittsburgh, November, 1899." *The Charette* 16:4 (April 1936): 1–4.

Stotz, Edward. "Ramblings in Retirement." *The Charette* 25:3 (March 1945): 7–8.

Stotz, Edward. "What Architecture Has Meant to Me." *The Charette* 27:8 (December 1947): 3.

Upton, Dell. "The Story of the Book," *The Early Architecture of Western Pennsylvania* by Charles Morse Stotz, xi–xii, xxii–xxiv.

See also **General: Stotz**
Historic Sites: Forks of the Ohio

Carlton Strong

"The Bellefield Dwellings." *The Pittsburgh Bulletin* 10:3 (January 31, 1903): 18.

Reid, Alfred D., Jr., and Michael W. Stuhldreher. "History of the Firm." *Reid & Stuhldreher, PC. A Hundred-Year Retrospective: The Architect's Drawing as a Communicating Medium.* Exhibition Catalogue. [University Art Gallery, March 20–April 17, 1988]. Pittsburgh: University of Pittsburgh, 1988: 7–12.

Hisrich, Sr. Maria Thecla, and Fr. John M. Unger. *A Sermon in Sculptured Stone and Jeweled Glass: Sacred Heart Church.* Pittsburgh: Sacred Heart Church, printed by Pickwick-Morcraft, 1976.

"How the Modern Family Lives: The Luxury of Real Apartment Life Has Many Advantages Over the Private Dwelling." *The Index* 10:23 (June 4, 1904): 20–22, 33.

Saylor, Henry H. "The Bungalow of Mr. S. P. Austin, Aspinwall, Pa." *Bungalows.* New York: McBride, Nast & Company, 1913: 96, 123.

"Carlton Strong." *History of Pittsburgh and Environs: Encyclopedia of Biography* [Clugston to Ressa]. New York and Chicago: American Historical Society, 1922: 280–81.

Strong, Carlton. "When Nighthood is in Flour." *The Charette* 6:4 (April 1926): 9–12.

Tannler, Albert M. "Victorian Estate Lives an Extraordinary Double Life." *Tribune-Review Focus Magazine* 20:26 (May 14, 1995): 6–7.

Robert Maurice Trimble

Harper, Frank C. "Robert Maurice Trimble." *Pittsburgh of Today: Its Resources and People.* Vol. 3. New York: American Historical Society, 1931: 147–48.

Trimble, Robert Maurice. "Rambling Reminiscences." *The Charette* 14:2 (February 1936): 1–4.

Trimble, Robert Maurice. "More Rambling Reminiscences." *The Charette* 14:12 (December 1936): 1–4.

Trimble, Robert Maurice. "Final Rambling Reminiscences." *The Charette* 18:5 (May 1938): 1–4.

Trimble, Robert Maurice. "The Unknown Profession, Part I." *The Charette* 19:12 (December 1939): 1–3.

Trimble, Robert Maurice. "The Unknown Profession, Part II." *The Charette* 20:1 (January 1940): 1–2.

Trimble, Robert Maurice. "The Unknown Profession, Part III." *The Charette* 20:3 (March 1940): 1–3.

Trowbridge & Livingston

Kidney, Walter C. "The Gulf Building: The Company is Gone—its Monument Endures." *Executive Report* 4:3 (September 1985): 62–63.

Van Trump, *Life and Architecture in Pittsburgh*, 75–76.

Joseph Urban[8]

Tannler, Albert M. "Hidden Mysteries of Pittsburgh Dot the Urban Landscape." *Tribune-Review Focus Magazine* 21:41 (August 25, 1996): 6–7.

Teegen, Otto. "Joseph Urban." *Architecture* 69:5 (May 1934): 255.

Van Trump, James D. "A Palace Up to Date."
Pittsburgher Magazine 3:12 (May 1980): 25–27.

Van Trump, *Life and Architecture in Pittsburgh*, 78.

Frank Vittor

Gay, Vernon, and Marilyn Evert, *Discovering Pittsburgh's Sculpture*, 24–25, 28, 69, 84, 93, 94, 95, 100, 149, 151, 172, 182, 198, 213, 278, 282, 293, 295, 300, 339, 346, 354, 357, 434–35.

Harper, Frank C. "Frank Vittor." *Pittsburgh of Today: Its Resources and People*. Vol. 4. New York: American Historical Society, 1931: 387.

Edward J. Weber

Kidney, Walter C. "Pittsburgh Architecture: Out of the Ordinary." *PHLF News* 142 (April 1996): 20.

Lowry, Patricia. "An Architect Out of Time." *Pittsburgh Post-Gazette*, Sunday Magazine (February 9, 1997): G1, G10–11.

Weber, Edward J. "The Architecture of the Universe." *The Charette* 22:1 (January 1942): 2–5.

Weber, Edward Joseph. *Catholic Church Buildings: Their Planning and Furnishing*. New York: Joseph F. Wagner, 1927.

Weber, Edward Joseph. *Catholic Ecclesiology*. Pittsburgh: Herbick & Held Printing Company, 1927.

Weber, Edward J. "When Knighthood Was in Flower" [series title]. *The Charette* 6:1 (January 1926) [Part 1] "What Ecclesiastical Art Should Be in This Country Today": 1–2; 6:2 (February 1926) [Part 2] "French for the Church Architect": 12; 6:3 (March 1926) [Part 3] "Concerning Stained Glass": 20–21; 6:6 (June 1926) [Part 4] "Essentials in the Catholic Church Plan": 6–8; 6:8 (August 1926); [Part 5] 1–7.

William Halsey Wood

Floyd, *Architecture after Richardson*, 193–194.

Van Trump, *Life and Architecture in Pittsburgh*, 171–176.

[Wood, Florence]. *Memories of William Halsey Wood*; with an introduction by Ralph Adams Cram. Philadelphia: Privately printed, [1938]: 36.

Frank Lloyd Wright[9]

Cleary, Richard. "Edgar J. Kaufmann, Frank Lloyd Wright and the 'Pittsburgh Point Park Coney Island in Automobile Scale'." *Journal of the Society of Architectural Historians* 52:2 (June 1993): 139–158.

Cleary, Richard. "Frank Lloyd Wright's San Francisco Field Office." *Carnegie Magazine* 61:12 (November/December 1993): 25–26.

"Mr. Wright Comes to Town." *The Charette* 30:6 (July 1950): 14, 24–25.

Wilk, Christopher. *Frank Lloyd Wright: The Kaufmann Office*. London: Victoria & Albert Museum, 1993.

"Wright Visits Tech." *The Charette* 29:6 (June 1949): 8–9.

HISTORIC SITES

1. General

Pittsburgh Department of City Planning, Historic Review Commission. *Pittsburgh Register of Historic Places*, 1994.

Pittsburgh Department of City Planning, Historic Review Commission. Brochures:
• *Allegheny West*
• *Fourth Avenue*
• *Grant Street*
• *Historic Interiors of Downtown Pittsburgh*
• *Manchester*
• *Market Square*
• *Mellon Square*
• *Mexican War Streets*
• *Monongahela Wharf*
• *Penn-Liberty*
• *Pittsburgh's Downtown Churches*
• *Schenley Farms*

2. Buildings and Places (listed chronologically)

Forks of the Ohio (c. 1750 and after)

Alberts, Robert C. *The Shaping of the Point: Pittsburgh's Renaissance Park.* Pittsburgh: University of Pittsburgh Press, 1980.

Griswold, Ralph E. "From Fort Pitt to Point Park: A Turning Point in the Physical Planning of Pittsburgh." *Landscape Architecture* 46:4 (July 1956): 192–202.

Stotz, Charles Morse. *Outposts of the War for Empire: The French and English in Western Pennsylvania: Their Armies, Their Forts, Their People 1749–1764.* Pittsburgh: Historical Society of Western Pennsylvania, 1985; distributed by University of Pittsburgh Press: 81, 127.

Stotz, Charles M. "Point State Park: Birth Place of Pittsburgh." *Carnegie Magazine* 38:1 (January 1964): 15–20.

Woods, C. Ronal. "A Point of Interest to All." *The Charette* 17:1 (January 1937): 1–2.

"Woodville," the Neville House (c. 1785)

[Kidney, Walter C.] "More Luck at the Neville House." *PHLF News* 120 (October 1991): 12.

Stotz, *Early Architecture,* 7, 43, 45, 46, 57–59, 145, 167.

Tannler, Albert M. "Revisiting 'Woodville'." *PHLF News* 131 (September 1993): 3.

"Newington" (1816–23; gardens, 1823 and after)

Griswold, Mac, and Eleanor Weller. *The Golden Age of American Gardens.* New York: Harry N. Abrams, 1991: 137.

Lockwood, Alice F. B., ed. "Newington." *Gardens of Colony and State: Gardens and Gardeners of the American Colonies and of the Republic Before 1840.* The Garden Club of America. New York: Charles Scribner's Sons, 1931: 379–380.

Stotz, *Early Architecture,* 27, 30, 151, 267.

Van Trump, James D. "Living with Antiques: Newington, the Pennsylvania House of Mr. and Mrs. J. Judson Brooks." *Antiques* 95:5 (May 1968): 656–659.

Croghan-Schenley oval room/ballroom from "Picnic House" (1835)

Cooper, Wendy A. *Classical Taste in America 1800–1840.* New York: Abbeville, 1993: 140–141.

Kennedy, Roger G. *Greek Revival America.* New York: Stewart, Tabori and Chang, 1989: 12, 13, 251, 314–315.

"*Life* Visits a Haunted House." *Life* 18 (June 11, 1945): 122–125.

Lowry, Patricia. "It Was All Greek Revival to Them." *Pittsburgh Post-Gazette,* Sunday Magazine (August 15, 1993): 15.

Stotz, *Early Architecture,* 7, 20, 25, 28, 108, 110, 126–131, 145.

Van Trump, *Life and Architecture in Pittsburgh,* 255–256.

Allegheny Cemetery (established 1844)

Allegheny Cemetery. *The Allegheny Cemetery, Pittsburgh, Pa.: Its Origin and Early History; also a Report of Its Condition, Progress and Business During the Last Ten Years, June 1, 1900–May 31, 1910;* with an introduction by William Falconer. Pittsburgh: Pittsburg Photo Engraving Company, 1910.

Kidney, Walter C. *Allegheny Cemetery: A Romantic Landscape in Pittsburgh.* Pittsburgh: Pittsburgh History & Landmarks Foundation, 1990.

Van Trump, James D. "A Pittsburgh Pantheon: Allegheny Cemetery." *Carnegie Magazine* 33:8 (October 1959): 271–273.

Evergreen Hamlet (1851–1852)

Arensberg, Charles C. "Evergreen Hamlet." *Western Pennsylvania Historical Magazine* 38:3/4 (Fall/Winter 1955): 117–131.

Huxtable, Ada Louise. "It's Hard to Despise Victorian Houses Anymore." *The New York Times,* Section 8 (Sunday, May 3, 1970): 1, 6.

Lowry, Patricia. "Hamlet Out of Hiding." *Pittsburgh Press,* Sunday Magazine (January 13, 1991): 4.

In Greek Revival America *(1989), Roger G. Kennedy writes: "Only the Croghan-Schenley rooms, removed to the University of Pittsburgh's Cathedral of Learning, remain to remind us of scores of lost, high style Northern, big city Greek Revival interiors."*

Van Trump, James D. *Evergreen Hamlet. The Stones of Pittsburgh*, No. 4. Pittsburgh: Pittsburgh History & Landmarks Foundation, c. 1967.

Van Trump, *Life and Architecture in Pittsburgh*, 187–189.

Sewickley Area [1850–1915]

Dennis, Stephen Neal. *Historic Houses of the Sewickley Valley*. Edgeworth, PA: Edgeworth Preservation, 1996.

Floyd, "Sewickley and the Country House," *Architecture after Richardson*, 305–343.

Hannegan, Barry. "Mrs. Curry, Mrs. Shipman, Mrs. Cobb: The Garden of 'Elm Cottage' in Sewickley Heights." *PHLF News* 142 (April 1996): 6–9.

Sewickley Borough Council, Historic Review Commission. *Preserving the Historic Architecture of a Classic American Village: Sewickley, Pennsylvania*. Sewickley: Sewickley Borough Council, 1995.

Van Trump, *Life and Architecture in Pittsburgh*, 345–348.

See also **Architects and Designers: Ingham & Boyd; Rutan & Russell**

John F. Singer house (1863–69)

Massey, James, and Shirley Maxwell. *Gothic Revival*. New York: Abbeville, 1994: 48–49.

Van Trump, *Life and Architecture in Pittsburgh*, 190–191; 257–261.

The Homewood Cemetery (established 1878)

Lowry, Patricia. "City of the Dead." *Pittsburgh Press*, Sunday Magazine (February 2, 1992): 4.

Smithfield Street Bridge (1883; later alterations)

Condit, Carl. *American Building Art: the Nineteenth Century*. New York: Oxford University Press, 1960: 127, figure 58.

[Kidney, Walter C.] "Smithfield Street Bridge: the Paint Job." *PHLF News* 141 (January 1996): 11.

Petroski, Henry. *Engineers of Dreams: Great Bridge Builders and the Spanning of America*. New York: Alfred A. Knopf, 1995: 126–129, 141.

Plowden, David. *Bridges: the Spans of North America*. New York: Viking Press, 1974: 66, 74, 167, 168.

Van Trump, James D. *A Trinity of Bridges: the Smithfield Street Bridge over the Monongahela River at Pittsburgh*. Washington: U.S. Department of the Interior, Historic Conservation and Recreation Service, 1973.

Van Trump, James D. "*A Trinity of Bridges: the Smithfield Street Bridge over the Monongahela River at Pittsburgh*." Western Pennsylvania Historical Magazine 58:4 (October 1975): 439–70.

Ziegler, Arthur P., Jr., and Walter C. Kidney. "The Smithfield Street Bridge: a Grand Restoration, Finally." *PHLF News* 139 (July 1995): 4–5.

"Sunnyledge" (1886)

Floyd, *Architecture after Richardson*, 177–180.

Tannler, Albert M. "Historic Review Commission Recommends City Historic Structure Designation for Sunnyledge." *PHLF News* 137 (March 1995): 3.

Tannler, Albert M. "The Mystery of the Balustrade: Spindles on a Staircase in Boston, Chicago, and Pittsburgh." *Tribune-Review Focus Magazine* 19:39 (August 14, 1994): 4–5.

"Clayton" (c. 1870; 1891–1892)

Brignano, Mary. *The Frick Art & Historical Center: The Art and Life of a Pittsburgh Family*. Pittsburgh: The Frick Art & Historical Center, 1993.

Helen Clay Frick Foundation. *Clayton: The Pittsburgh Home of Henry Clay Frick; Art and Furnishings*. Pittsburgh: University of Pittsburgh Press, 1988.

Lowry, Patricia. "A Piece of Pittsburgh Past: Clayton, the Point Breeze Home of Henry Clay Frick, Is Reborn as a House Museum." *Pittsburgh Press*, Sunday Magazine (September 23, 1990): 10.

Phipps Conservatory (1893)

Guttenberg, Gustave. *Botanical Guide Through the Phipps Conservatories in Pittsburg and Allegheny.* Pittsburgh: Foster, Dick & Co., 1894.

Hannegan, Barry. "Pittsburgh's Oldest Surviving Designed Landscapes? Gardens Under Glass: Phipps Conservatory and Its Tradition." *PHLF News* 142 (April 1996): 10–13.

Schenley Park Officers. *Souvenir of Phipps Conservatory, Schenley Park: 27 Triennial Conclave Knights Templar.* Pittsburgh: Murdoch-Kerr Press, 1898.

Van Trump, James D. "Henry Phipps and the Phipps Conservatory," *Carnegie Magazine* 50:1 (January 1976): 26–35.

Station Square (1897–1918; remodeled 1976 and after)

Breen, Ann, and Dick Rigby. *The New Waterfront: A Worldwide Urban Success Story.* London: Thames and Hudson Ltd., 1996: 193.

Gratz, Roberta Brandes. *The Living City: How America's Cities are Being Revitalized by Thinking Small in a Big Way.* rev. ed. Washington: Preservation Press, 1994: ix–xi, 286–288.

Kidney, Walter C. "The Freight House, Station Square." *Pittsburgher Magazine* 3:5 (October 1979): 29–32.

Toker, Franklin. "In the Grand Manner: The P&LE Station in Pittsburgh." *Carnegie Magazine* 53:3 (March 1979): 4–21.

Van Trump, James D. *Station Square: A Golden Age Revived.* The Stones of Pittsburgh, No. 11. Pittsburgh: Pittsburgh History & Landmarks Foundation, 1978.

Kennywood (1898 and after)

Rodriguez, Alicia. "Kudos: Economic Revival and Community Rebirth Through Historic Preservation are Epitomized by the 1994 National Trust Honor Award Winners and the Crowninshield Honoree: Kennywood Park, West Mifflin, Pennsylvania." *Historic Preservation,* 46:6 (November/December 1994): 65.

Jacques, Charles J., Jr. *Kennywood.* Vestal, NY: Vestal Press, 1982.

Thornburg Historic District [1900–1909]

Christner, Alice Crist. *Here's to Thornburg.* Thornburg: Thornburg Community Club, 1966.

Tannler, Albert M. "Historic Thornburg: Variations on a Theme." *PHLF News* 125 (September 1992): 4–5.

Roslyn Place (1915)

Jacobs, Allan B. *Great Streets.* Cambridge, MA: MIT Press, 1993: 16–19, 280, 283, 295, 297, 304, 306, 307, 310.

Chatham Village (1931–35)

"Chatham Village, Pittsburgh." *The Town Planning Review* 20 (October 1949): 252–258, 281, figs. 57–62.

"Chatham Village, second unit, Pittsburgh, Pennsylvania" *American Architect and Architecture* 150:2654 (February 1937): 63–66.

Jacobs, Jane. *The Death and Life of Great American Cities.* New York: Random House, 1961: 64–65, 73, 80, 84.

Lewis, Charles F. "A Moderate Rental Housing Project in Pittsburgh." *Architectural Record* 70:4 (October 1931): 3–18.

Lubove, *Twentieth Century Pittsburgh,* Vol. 1: 70–82.

Mumford, Lewis. *The City in History.* New York: Harcourt, Brace & World, 1961: Plate and caption 43: "Conquest of Suburbia."

Newton, Norman T. *Design on the Land: The Development of Landscape Architecture.* Cambridge, MA: Harvard University Press, 1971: 496–500.

Roth, Leland M. *A Concise History of Architecture in America.* New York: Harper & Row, 1979: 268.

Stern, Robert A. M., ed. *The Anglo-American Suburb* (AD Profile). London: Architectural Design, 1981: 47.

Van Trump, James D. "Incomparable Chatham Village." *Tribune-Review Focus Magazine* 10:14 (February 20, 1983): 6.

Swan Acres (established 1936)

"'Homes All to Be Modern' is the Startling but Financially Sound Restriction in a Pittsburgh Subdivision." *Architectural Forum* 67:5 (November 1937): 442–443.

"Ewan [sic] Acres." *The Bulletin Index* 112:12 (March 31, 1938): 28–29.

"Swan Acres, A Planned Community in the Country, Opening Today." *Pittsburgh Press* 53:61 Sunday (August 23, 1936): 15.

FOOTNOTES

[1]Some books about buildings designed after 1950 will be found in Albert M. Tannler, *A List of Pittsburgh and Allegheny County Buildings and Architects, 1950–1996*, Pittsburgh, Pittsburgh History & Landmarks Foundation, 1995. Photographs documenting Pittsburgh's life and architecture during the second half of the twentieth-century are found in *Clyde Hare's Pittsburgh: Four Decades of Pittsburgh, Frozen in Light*, Pittsburgh, Pittsburgh History & Landmarks Foundation, 1994.

[2]Martin Aurand, *Pittsburgh Architecture: A Guide to Research* (1991) lists dissertations and theses, and provides complete bibliographic information about regional architectural journals and serial publications (some of which are not cited in this bibliography). This indispensable booklet, which superseded Toker and Wilson (1979), contains detailed descriptions of key regional architectural resources to 1991 and their location in public and private repositories. Several architectural studies in preparation are listed in Albert M. Tannler, *Pittsburgh's Landmark Architecture 1785–1950: A Concise Bibliography* (1994).

[3]Readers should also be aware of audiovisual tape recordings produced by public television station WQED-13 which provide visual documentation of historic buildings and sites in Western Pennsylvania.

[4]The Berndtsons' partnership extended from 1946 to 1957, although each continued to practice independently thereafter. In 1989, seventeen years after Peter Berndtson's death, the Historic Landmark Plaque Designation Committee of the Pittsburgh History & Landmarks Foundation waived the fifty-year requirement and awarded special recognition plaques to ten Berndtson houses designed between 1949 and 1965; an eleventh house was designated in 1995.

[5]The complete bibliographic citation is found under Frederick G. Scheibler, Jr.

[6]During the last year of their partnership (1937–41), Gropius and Breuer designed a housing project near Pittsburgh, Aluminum City Terrace, in New Kensington, Westmoreland County. Marcel Breuer designed a house near Ligonier, Westmoreland County, 1946–50, for Mrs. A. W. Thompson.

[7]Regional work by Frederick Law Olmsted, Sr. appears to be limited to Vandergrift, Westmoreland County, designed in 1895; the degree of Olmsted, Sr.'s involvement in the project is in dispute.

[8]Randolph Carter and Robert Reed Cole, *Joseph Urban*, New York, Abbeville Press, 1992, discuss and illustrate Urban's 1926 unexecuted remodeling project for Kaufmann's Department Store (184, 185, 188) but omit any mention of the ballroom Joseph Urban designed in 1929 as part of the 1927–29 expansion of the William Penn Hotel.

[9]Frank Lloyd Wright's San Francisco Field Office was designed and erected in 1951 and has been reassembled in The Heinz Architectural Center, The Carnegie Museum of Art. The Kaufmann Office, Wright's only executed Pittsburgh design (1937), is now in the Victoria & Albert Museum. Frank Lloyd Wright's major Western Pennsylvania structure is "Fallingwater" (1935–39) in Fayette County. Wright also designed "Kentuck Knob" at Chalk Hill, Fayette County, for I. N. Hagan in 1954.

INDEX

Looking toward the Triangle across the South Side flats and the domes of St. John the Baptist Ukrainian Catholic Church.

The title of each entry in "A Guide to the Landmark Architecture of Allegheny County" is given in bold face. Pittsburgh neighborhoods outside the Golden Triangle are specified.

The slender strength of the Allegheny County Courthouse tower.